W9-AKB-549

More praise for

THE HEMINGSES
of MONTICELLO

Winner of the Society for Historians of the
Early American Republic Book Award

Winner of the New Jersey Council of the
Humanities Book Award

Finalist for the 2009 Mark Lynton History Prize

"[A] commanding and important book."　　—Jill Lepore, *The New Yorker*

"[A] very important and powerfully argued history of the Hemings family.
. . . [Gordon-Reed] has the imagination and talent of an expert historian."
　　　　　　　　　　　　　　　　　　—Gordon Wood, *The New Republic*

"*The Hemingses of Monticello* is a brilliant book. It marks the author as one
of the most astute, insightful, and forthright historians of this generation.
Not least of Annette Gordon-Reed's achievements is her ability to bring
fresh perspectives to the life of a man whose personality and character
have been scrutinized, explained, and justified by a host of historians and
biographers."
　　　　—Edmund S. Morgan, Marie Morgan, *New York Review of Books*

"[A] deeply researched, often gripping story. . . . Gordon-Reed has given us
an important story that is ultimately about the timeless quest for justice
and human dignity."　　　　—Sanford D. Horwitt, *San Francisco Chronicle*

"Hunting down every tiny thread of evidence about the family, Gordon-Reed has created a powerful alternative vision of the past . . . [and] has created a monument to lives lived under the shadow of a vicious institution. For the first time, Jefferson is one part of the Hemingses' story, rather than vice versa."   —Scott McLemee, *Seattle Times*

"Not since Fawn Brodie's masterwork biography has there been a better depiction of Thomas Jefferson's life at Monticello than Gordon-Reed's story of the Hemings family. This is American history at its best." —*Tennessean*

"*The Hemingses of Monticello* makes a powerful argument for the historical significance of the Hemings family not only for its engagement with a principal architect of the early Republic, but also for the ways the family embodies the complexities and contradictions of slavery in the United States."   —James Smethurst, *Boston Globe*

"Thomas Jefferson often described his slaves at Monticello as 'my family.' Annette Gordon-Reed has taken that description seriously. Surely more seriously than Jefferson ever intended! The result, the story of the Hemings family, is the most comprehensive account of one slave family ever written. It is not a pretty story, but it is poignant beyond belief. And it demonstrates conclusively that we must put aside *Gone With the Wind* forever and begin to study Faulkner's *Absalom, Absalom!*"
                            —Joseph J. Ellis, author of *American Sphinx*

"From years of painstaking research and deep personal engagement with all the Jefferson controversies, Annette Gordon-Reed has crafted a brave, compelling, and moving family saga about slavery and freedom. . . . This work is a beautifully written, textured story about race, tragedy, and some-times hope—America's story. If this country has a modern Shakespeare looking for material, Gordon-Reed has provided it."
    —David W. Blight, Yale University, author of *A Slave No More: Two Men Who Escaped to Freedom, Including Their Narratives of Emancipation*

"Annette Gordon-Reed's splendid achievement will have the last word on Thomas Jefferson and Sally Hemings, for one cannot imagine another

historian matching her exhaustive research and interpretive balance."
—David Levering Lewis, author of *W. E. B. Du Bois*

"With astonishingly meticulous research, working with documents notoriously slim on personal details of the lives of slaves, she has created a beautifully rendered story of a family: Elizabeth Hemings; her children, most notably Sally; and, in turn, Sally's children from her long relationship with Thomas Jefferson."   —William S. McFeely, author of *Grant: A Biography*

"A powerful composite portrait of the African American family whose labors helped make Jefferson's Virginia residence a fountainhead of American culture.... A must-have acquisition for every American history collection."
—Bryce Christensen, *Booklist*, starred review

"[Her] early, firsthand experience with the interplay of race and history informs much of Gordon-Reed's work, including her compulsively readable new book, in which she traces the family history of Sally Hemings."
—Jennie Yabroff, *Newsweek*

"This is an important book."   —*Richmond Times-Dispatch*

"Fascinating, wise, and of the utmost importance.... Gordon-Reed's genius for reading nearly silent records makes this an extraordinary work."
—*Publishers Weekly*, starred review

"There is no clue in the life of this intertwined family that Gordon-Reed does not minutely examine for its most subtle significance.... Sagacious and ultimately rewarding."   —*Kirkus Reviews*

"Annette Gordon-Reed convincingly argues in this monumental and original book ... [that Thomas Jefferson] cohabited for more than 30 years with an African American woman with whom he conceived seven children. ... [She] shines an uncompromisingly fresh but not unsympathetic light on the most elusive of the Founding Fathers.... Her deconstruction of this occluded relationship is a masterpiece of detective work."
—Fergus M. Bordewich, *Washington Post*

"A remarkable new book. . . . Gordon-Reed has pulled off an astonishing feat of historical re-creation, involving equal measures of painstaking archival detective work, creative historical imagination, and balanced judgment. . . . [She] doesn't use the Hemings family as a metaphor for the 'black experience,' or Sally Hemings to humanize 'slave women.' She focuses instead on the individuals who struggled messily to survive despite these categories and, every once in a while, broke through them."

—François Furstenberg, *Slate*

"A sobering moral lesson of almost Shakespearean dimensions . . . a riveting and compassionate family portrait that deserves to endure as a model of historical inquiry. . . . [It] stands dramatically apart for its searching intelligence and breadth of humane vision. . . . We owe Annette Gordon-Reed tremendous thanks."   —Kirk Davis Swinehart, *Chicago Tribune*

"A sweeping, prodigiously researched biography."

—Motoko Rich, *New York Times*

"Gordon-Reed brings meticulous research, lustrous prose, and admirable objectivity to be the combustible subject in a massive yet magisterial work."

—Jonathan E. Lazarus, *New Jersey Star Ledger*

"[A] towering work of historical investigation and human empathy."

—Elinor Langer, *The Oregonian*

"As the title suggests, *The Hemingses of Monticello: An American Family* brings an entire family out of the historic shadows that have been cast across Jefferson's famous Virginia home. The book succeeds on this score by showing how generations of Hemingses labored at Monticello. A stunning illustration of the tragedy that slavery could wreak."

—Michael A. Elliott, *Atlanta Journal Constitution*

"A detailed and intimate chronicle of the slave family whose history is inextricably intertwined with the life and times of Thomas Jefferson."

—Frank Wilson, *Philadelphia Inquirer*

"Annette Gordon-Reed is a prodigiously gifted historian, and *The Hemingses of Monticello* is her masterpiece. Bringing the Hemings family out of the shadows and into vibrant life, Gordon-Reed restores them to their proper role at Thomas Jefferson's mountaintop home. . . . Jefferson's Virginia—and Jefferson himself—will never look the same."

—Peter Onuf, author of *Jefferson's Empire:*
The Language of American Nationhood

"Perhaps the greatest success of Gordon-Reed's work is that she is able to portray the Hemings family as dynamic and vivid characters, giving an intimate look into a fascinating historical family."

—Casey Hynes, *Roll Call*

"Gordon-Reed reconstructs not simply the private life and estate of an American demigod but reveals much of the characteristic structure and style of early Virginia society. . . . This is a masterpiece brimming with decades of dedicated research and dexterous writing."

—Thomas J. Davis, ASU, reviewed in *Library Journal*

"Gordon-Reed not only reminds readers of the elements that fostered the slave system, she also gives a perspective, through her captivating narrative, of one family's struggle for independence and recognition."

—Clarence V. Reynolds, *The Network Journal*

"This is not only a riveting history of a slave family on a grand scale, it is also a rarely seen portrait of the family in the Big House, with a remarkable account of the relationship of white and black families. This work catapults Gordon-Reed into the very first rank of historians of slavery."

—John Hope Franklin, author of *From Slavery to Freedom*

"Annette Gordon-Reed has broken a path into territory that has hitherto eluded historians: what happens to intimate human relations, those between lover and loved, parent and child, brother and sister, when one among them is enslaved to another. The result is not simply a fascinating story in itself, but a new perspective on how the humanity of slaves and a slave owner

could adjust and survive in circumstances designed to obliterate it."
—Edmund S. Morgan, author of *American Slavery*

"These freshly discovered papers not only enrich our knowledge of the world of Monticello, but also of the development of slavery in Virginia during the eighteenth century. Gordon-Reed's work is a milestone in historiography."
—Barbara Meade, *Politics & Prose Holiday Newsletter* 2008

"A behemoth of a book that offers more information about the relationship than anyone might have envisioned, it represents seven years of research and spells out links, connections, bloodlines, and familial ties so completely that it shreds any question of authenticity. . . . [It] explores a thorny but important chapter in American history with distinction and clarity, offering a poignant, if also often ugly, chronicle of slavery, secrecy, and family tension."
—Ron Wynn, *Bookpage*

"Gordon-Reed presents an equally powerful and rich picture. She achieves it not in the manner of a 'faction,' mingling the made-up with the verifiable, or by resorting to theory-driven psychosexual speculation, but rather by putting her sources together, taking all of her characters seriously, and constructing the richest, most explanatory account of them that the evidence permits her to make."
—Edward Countryman, review in *William and Mary Quarterly*

THE
HEMINGSES
of MONTICELLO

ALSO BY ANNETTE GORDON-REED

*"Most Blessed of the Patriarchs": Thomas Jefferson
and the Empire of the Imagination* (with Peter S. Onuf)

Thomas Jefferson and Sally Hemings: An American Controversy

Vernon Can Read!: A Memoir (with Vernon E. Jordan, Jr.)

Race on Trial: Law and Justice in American History (editor)

THE
HEMINGSES
of MONTICELLO

AN AMERICAN FAMILY

ANNETTE GORDON-REED

W. W. NORTON & COMPANY

NEW YORK LONDON

Frontispiece: Watercolor of Monticello. (Courtesy of Massachusetts Historical Society)

Copyright © 2008 by Annette Gordon-Reed

All rights reserved
Printed in the United States of America
First published as a Norton paperback 2009

For information about permission to reproduce selections from this book, write to
Permissions, W. W. Norton & Company, Inc., 500 Fifth Avenue, New York, NY 10110

For information about special discounts for bulk purchases, please contact W. W. Norton
Special Sales at specialsales@wwnorton.com or 800-233-4830

Manufacturing by LSC Harrisonburg
Book design by Chris Welch
Production manager: Andrew Marasia

Library of Congress Cataloging-in-Publication Data
Gordon-Reed, Annette.
The Hemingses of Monticello : an American family / Annette Gordon-Reed. — 1st ed.
p. cm.
Includes bibliographical references and index.
ISBN 978-0-393-06477-3 (hardcover)
1. Hemings family. 2. Hemings, Sally—Family. 3. Jefferson, Thomas,
—1743–1826—Family. 4. Monticello (Va.)—Biography. 5. Albemarle County (Va.)—
Biography. 6. Slaves—Virginia—Albemarle County—Biography. 7. African American
families—Virginia—Albemarle County. 8. African American families. 9. African
Americans—Biography. 10. Racially mixed people—United States—Biography. I. Ttile.
E332.74.G67 2008
973.4'60922—dc22
[B]
2008014642

ISBN 978-0-393-33776-1 pbk.

W. W. Norton & Company, Inc., 500 Fifth Avenue, New York, NY 10110
www.wwnorton.com

W. W. Norton & Company Ltd., 15 Carlisle Street, London W1D 3BS

To my husband, Robert Reed, and our daughter, Susan Jean Gordon Reed, and our son, Gordon Penn Reed

CONTENTS

PART III
ON THE MOUNTAIN

Chronology of the Hemings Family

1735   Elizabeth Hemings (EH) is born.

1746   The marriage of John Wayles (JW) and Martha Eppes brings EH to the Forest.

1748   Martha Wayles is born. Martha Eppes dies and leaves EH as JW's property.

1753–61 EH gives birth to Mary and Martin Hemings, Betty Brown, and Nancy Hemings.

1762–70 EH gives birth to five children by JW: Robert, James (JH), Thenia, Critta, and Peter.

1772   Martha Wayles Skelton (MWJ) marries Thomas Jefferson (TJ), and Betty Brown comes to Monticello as MWJ's maid.

1773   John Wayles dies at the Forest. The Hemingses come under the ownership of TJ and (MWJ). Sarah (Sally) Hemings (SH), the last child of EH and JW, is born.

1774   The Hemings family moves to Monticello

1776–77 TJ in Philadelphia drafts the Declaration of Independence; fourteen-year-old Robert Hemings (RH) lives with him as a manservant. John Hemings, last son of EH, is born at Monticello; in 1777 her last child, Lucy, is born.

1780   Joseph Fossett, son of Mary Hemings, is born.

1781   Wormley Hughes, son of Betty Brown, is born.

1782   Martin Hemings is left in charge of Monticello when TJ escapes from Tarleton's troops.

1782   MWJ dies at Monticello.

1783   SH goes to Eppington with TJ's daughters. Burwell Colbert, son of Betty Brown, is born.

1784   RH trains as a barber. JH goes to France with TJ.

1787   SH travels to London and lives with Abigail Adams, then joins her brother JH in Paris. Mary Hemings is leased to Thomas Bell.

1789   When SH balks at returning to America, TJ promises her a good life and the freedom of their children when they become adults. JH and SH return to Monticello in December.

1790   JH and RH go to New York with TJ. SH gives birth to her first child, who dies.

1791   JH goes to Philadelphia to serve as chef de cuisine in TJ's home.

1792   Mary Hemings asks to be sold to Thomas Bell. Martin Hemings asks to be sold to anyone.

1793   TJ puts his agreement to free JH in writing.

1794   TJ draws up a deed emancipating RH.

1795   TJ files the RH deed, and RH becomes legally free. Harriet Hemings I, daughter of SH and TJ, is born at Monticello.

1796   TJ draws up a deed emancipating JH. JH goes to Philadelphia, TJ files the deed, and JH becomes legally free.

1797   Harriet Hemings I dies.

1798   William Beverley Hemings, son of SH and TJ, is born.

1799   The first published allusions to TJ and SH appear in the press.

1800–01 Mary Hemings and her children Robert Washington Bell and Sarah Jefferson Bell inherit Thomas Bell's property upon his death. Harriet Hemings II is born at Monticello. JH turns down TJ's request that he become chef in the President's House. JH commits suicide in Baltimore.

1802   James Callender exposes the relationship between SH and TJ.

1805   James Madison Hemings, second son of SH and TJ, is born. Beverley Hemings is identified as the eldest son of TJ and SH.

1807   EH dies at Monticello. Joseph Fossett takes charge of the blacksmith shop at Monticello.

1808   Thomas Eston Hemings, the last child SH and TJ, is born at Monticello.

1809   TJ retires from public life. Burwell Colbert becomes his principal manservant and butler. John Hemings takes charge of the Monticello joinery.

1810–26   Beverley and Madison and, then, Madison and Eston Hemings serve as apprentices to their uncle John Hemings, at Monticello and Poplar Forest. Harriet Hemings learns to weave.

1822   Beverley and Harriet leave Monticello to live as white people.

1826   TJ drafts a will formally freeing Burwell Colbert, Joseph Fossett, John Hemings, and Madison and Eston Hemings. TJ dies. SH, Madison, and Eston Hemings move to Charlottesville.

1827   The auction at Monticello disposes of TJ's personal property; the Hemings family is dispersed.

1831   Monticello is sold.

So the beginning of this was a woman . . .

—Zora Neale Hurston,

Their Eyes Were Watching God

PREFACE

A NUMBER OF YEARS back, while at the Massachusetts Historical Society for a speaking engagement, I had the chance to read through the original version of Thomas Jefferson's Farm Book, an extremely valuable part of the society's collection, a pivotal document within the vast array of the written material that Jefferson produced over the course of his very long lifetime. In it he recorded the names, births, family configurations, rations, and work assignments of all the people enslaved on his plantations. Waiting for books in research libraries was nothing new to me, but this time the anticipation was almost exponentially heightened because I was finally going to get to see and touch an item that I had been reading in facsimile form since high school. The librarian brought the Farm Book out to me, and I was slightly startled by its size. It was much smaller than I had imagined it would be and much more well-preserved, and I knew the society was taking great pains to keep it that way. The librarian left me alone. When I opened the pages to see that very familiar hand and the neatly written entries, many of which I knew by heart, I was completely overwhelmed. For a time I simply could not continue.

There had been other moments before then when I was brought up short while reading through the Farm Book and thinking of the people described in it and of the man who wrote it: *Just who do you think you are!?* He determined who got fish, and how many; who got cloth, and how much; and the number of blankets that were given out—the course of the lives of grown men, women, and their children set by this one man. I knew everything that was in the book, and understood what it meant long before I sat down to look at it again that day. Still, it was wrenching to hold the original and to know that Jefferson's actual hand had dipped into the inkwell and touched these pages to create what was to me a record of human oppression. It took my breath away.

Of course, Jefferson did not see the Farm Book as I did. Had he thought it merely a record of oppression (greatly as he craved posterity's favorable judgment), he would never have kept it. Certainly members of his legal white family would not have preserved it. They, too, were anxious to safeguard and cultivate his legacy because they loved him deeply and because their own sense of self was so firmly tied to that legacy. It is, in fact, highly unlikely that it ever occurred to Jefferson that his record of the lives of his slaves would become the subject of scholarly interest, even a passion among some—that his slaves' lives would be chronicled and followed in minute detail, the interest in them often unmoored from any interest in him. No, this was a workaday document to tell him what he had to buy from year to year, to keep some sense of what would be needed to continue operations. In Jefferson's monumentally patriarchal and self-absorbed view, one shared by his fellow slave-owning planters, this was *Oh, the responsibilities I have! Here is what I have done and have yet to do for all "my family."*

The word "family" brings us to the subject of this book: the Hemingses of Monticello. No one can know what they, who were his family both biologically and in the figurative sense in which Jefferson meant it, thought about the Farm Book. They are listed there too—his wife's sisters and brothers, their children, their mother, and his own children. Members of the family almost certainly knew it existed, and if they knew, their other relatives knew as well. Martin, Robert, James, and Sally Hemings—their nephew Burwell Colbert—among others, were close enough to Jefferson to see his books, to come upon him working, to know the important and not so important things, emotional and physical, that were in his life.

However familiar they were with its contents, one thing that all of the enslaved people at Monticello would have known about the Farm Book, not just the Hemingses, is that it described some parts of their lives, but definitely not all, reproducing only a tiny fraction of a snapshot of life at Monticello that provides a very useful baseline for inquiry. What is in the book must be added to information from other sources, including the statements and actions of the Hemings family, Jefferson's family letters, even some writings from Hemingses that reveal the family's complicated relationship to the master of Monticello, and the wealth of information about the institution of slavery as it was lived during the Hemingses' time.

That the names of the children of Sally Hemings and Thomas Jefferson appear in a book detailing the lives of slaves conveniently and poignantly encapsulates the tortured history of slavery and race in America. But Monticello was a world unto itself for four generations of Hemingses whose lives cannot be reduced to the saga of one nuclear family within its bloodline, important as that subset was. We must, and will, pay attention to them, but they were only part of a much larger family story. Opening the world of the other members of this family—to see how those particular African Americans made their way through slavery in America—is the purpose of this book. Theirs was a world that is (mercifully) gone, but must never be forgotten.

THE

HEMINGSES

of MONTICELLO

INTRODUCTION

I n September of 1998, the Omohundro Institute of Early American History and Culture and the College of William and Mary, in Williamsburg, Virginia, hosted a conference designed to give scholars of slavery a preview of a newly compiled database of transatlantic slave voyages. For the first time in history, records of every known voyage of slave-trading vessels operating between Africa and the Americas would be available in a CD-ROM format. The implications for scholarly research were staggering. Information about an activity central to the development of the modern Western world would be available at the touch of a finger.

Though the conference unveiling this new research tool was designed primarily for scholars, with a heavy tilt toward those interested in economic history, scores of laypeople—mainly blacks—came too, hoping to find some word, some trace, of their ancestors. Not all were looking for "ancestors" in the general sense in which many blacks refer to those enslaved in America from the seventeenth century through most of the nineteenth. It was clear that many hoped the database might help them find *their specific progenitors*—what their names were and where they came from. Others not interested in their own genealogy apparently had come hoping to hear more of the lives of individuals who endured the Middle Passage.

Their hopes were largely dashed. There were no passenger manifests for slave voyages. Slavers were not interested in the names of the Africans bound for bondage in the New World. Notations about the voyages served strictly business purposes and included the names of the vessel, the captain, and, perhaps, a first mate, the number of the human cargo, where they came from, and where they were going, along with any onboard events that might inform future voyages. Was there a revolt, a problem with rations? It was left to the enslaved Africans to keep the memory of their identities and origins alive—no small task, particularly in the land that would become the United States, as generations passed and Africans became Americans.

While the conference was just about what I had expected, it frustrated many of those who had come to Williamsburg hoping to make a personal connection to the African captives. Each day when we broke for lunch or refreshments, I could hear murmurs of concern about the way things were proceeding. By the end of the conference, one participant, angered by what he perceived as the coldness of historians talking about slavery in terms of "the numbers of people sent here" and "the numbers of people sent there," erupted. The conference, he charged, was devoid of feeling and emotion. Where was the scope of the human loss? Where was the sense of the bottomless tragedy of it all?

Of course, the evidence of human loss and tragedy was right there. The numbers told a story, but in the detached and steely way that numbers tend to do. Slavery had many aspects, and getting a handle on the logistics and economics of the institution (how many people were moved, how many ships were used, how many miles over the ocean were covered, how much money was made) is as vital as telling personal stories—as vital but, perhaps, not as immediately compelling. It is a safe bet that most people respond more forcefully and intensely to other *people* than to numbers. So the lament about the conference's alleged focus on numbers compiled to suit the aims of businessmen, if not a little unfair, was understandable. Statistical data about a cargo of human beings, deplorable and heartrending as that is, is depersonalized. One yearns to know the individuals behind the statistics. What were their names? There is great power in a name. What were their lives like before the horror that engulfed them? How did they cope in the New World? What were their stories?

While it is true that the lives of the vast majority of people who lived during the time of American slavery are lost to history, the anonymity of American slaves is even more pronounced. The business of shipping slaves required no gathering and recording of information about the captives as individuals, and the business of keeping slaves was similarly minimalist. And few slaves had the chance to supplement the record by setting down their "stories" in either diaries, letters to family, or official records—marriage banns, birth announcements, wills proved—the kinds of documents that allow many white Americans to reconstruct at least some part of their family stories, or the story as they would like to tell it. The medium of biography, so effective in conveying information about times gone by, and perhaps the most accessible and popular form of historical writing, is problematic in the context of slavery.

Remaining for those who seek to "know" American slaves (and the institution of slavery) are the memories of those enslaved, the records of white owners who in taking care of business kept track of their human property, and information about the larger historical context in which all these individuals operated. Getting at this last source, the historical context, is by necessity a huge interdisciplinary enterprise—a matter of law, anthropology, psychology, archaeology, and economics—all the universe of influences that shaped lives under slavery. In gathering information, we must cast the net as widely as possible if we want to see slavery through the eyes of the enslaved.

The Hemings family of Monticello escaped the enforced anonymity of slavery for a number of reasons: first, because multiple generations of this large clan were owned by one of history's most well-known figures, Thomas Jefferson, an inveterate record keeper and writer of letters. Jefferson's papers have been grist for the scholarly mill for many years, and members of the Hemings family have long figured in Jefferson scholarship, but only as side characters in the saga of Jefferson and his white family. Only recently have the Hemingses and other members of Monticello's enslaved community become the focus of scholarly attention. It is a sad paradox, in a story overrun with paradox and irony, that their being the "property" of a famous man ensured that, as the Jefferson scholar James A. Bear has pointed out, more would be known about this family of slaves than is known about the vast majority of freeborn white Virginians of the time.

And then there is the place itself. Monticello, one of the best-known residences in the United States during Jefferson's time and today, is rich with the history of the Hemings family. Hemingses helped build and maintain the house, crafted furniture for it, and laid its floors. They worked as servants within the household, tended the gardens, and performed other essential tasks throughout the plantation. They lived there as husbands and wives, raising their children in slavery as best they could. Some died and were buried there. It is, quite simply, impossible to tell an adequate history of the mountain without including Hemingses.

Of course, the main reason that people all over the world have known about this particular enslaved family, during and after the era of slavery, is Jefferson's relationship with Sarah Hemings, known most famously by her nickname Sally. Hemings and Jefferson were talked about in their immediate community during the 1790s, and their story, or a version of it, burst upon the national scene in the early 1800s when Jefferson's enemies sought to use their relationship as a weapon to destroy his presidency and to prevent his election to a second term. The tactic did not work. Jefferson won in a landslide, bringing to office with him a large Republican majority in Congress. "The people," whose wisdom Jefferson trusted (sometimes almost too implicitly), either did not believe the Hemings story or thought it trivial when compared with what they felt Jefferson and his administration had to offer them.

These events were not just about the life and fortunes of Thomas Jefferson. Other people were involved. Sally Hemings, her children, her mother, and other members of her family were dragged into the national spotlight in a way unprecedented for individual American slaves. During the early part of the nineteenth century, Sally Hemings appeared in newspapers as "Dusky Sally," "Yellow Sally," and even "Mrs. Sarah Jefferson." She was depicted in cartoons and lampooned in bawdy ballads—all alongside Thomas Jefferson. The story crossed the Atlantic, with foreign commentators weighing in with their own perspectives.

Sally Hemings is often treated as a figure of no historical significance— a mere object of malicious personal gossip. That shouldn't surprise. Aside from forays into "history from the bottom up"—a perspective that has been given increased emphasis over the past forty years—historical writing tends to favor the lives of individuals who spoke, acted, and had a direct hand in shaping whatever particular "moment" they lived in. Hemings does not fit the bill on any of these accounts. She neither spoke publicly about her life nor engaged in any public acts that have been recorded. Others—journalists, Jefferson's enemies—determined how she entered the spotlight; and they put her there with no real interest in her as a person.

Even though she was not in control of her life, Hemings must be seen as a figure of historical importance for a multiplicity of reasons, not the least of which is that her name and her life entered the public record during the run-up to a presidential election. Much has been written about Jefferson's daughters and grandchildren, and they are treated as historically important simply because of their legal relationship to him, even though none of them ever figured in the politics and public life of his day. On the other hand, politically ambitious men with power used Hemings and her children as weapons against Jefferson while he was alive and in the decades immediately following his death. Her connection to him inspired the first novel published by an African American. It had resonance within black communities as ministers and black journalists in the early American Republic preached on and referred to Hemings's family situation, one that would have seemed quite familiar to their predominately mixed-race audiences, most of whom were free precisely because their fathers or immediate forefathers had been white men. Finally, Hemings's story affected members of Jefferson's white family, notably his grandchildren who, for the benefit of the historians who they knew would one day come calling, fashioned an image of life at Monticello designed in part to obscure her relevance. Even without direct agency in these matters, Sally Hemings has had an impact on the shaping of history.

More important for our purposes, we must also see the public spectacle surrounding Hemings and Jefferson as a defining episode in the lives of all the Hemingses. No contemporaneous evidence of what members of the family were thinking as the talk of the pair made its way through the country's newspapers and communities has come to light. They surely knew that people were talking because others at Monticello—members of Jefferson's white family, his friends, and at least one white Jefferson employee—are on record stating that the relationship was much talked about in Jefferson's neighborhood. In every community, throughout history, slaves and servants have been privy to the innermost secrets, anxieties, strengths, weaknesses, successes, and failures of the people they served. The Hemingses were no different.

There is much evidence that the Hemings-Jefferson connection meant a great deal to some members of her family. Madison Hemings, who at age sixty-eight spoke of his life as the second son of Sally Hemings and Thomas Jefferson, told part of his family's story to an interviewer in 1873, setting down valuable information about the family's origins, life at Monticello, and the lives of one branch of the family after emancipation. The historians Lucia Stanton and Dianne Swann-Wright have noted the other ways in which the Hemings-Jefferson liaison helped keep the Hemingses' story at Monticello alive for successive generations of the family. Apparently, the relationship and its notoriety were critical reference points, not only for the descendants of Sally Hemings and Thomas Jefferson but for collateral branches of the family as well, serving as a guidepost that helped them remember who they were and where their family had been. Even the descendants of slaves at Monticello who were not members of the Hemings family carried the story of Hemings and Jefferson as an important truth about life on the mountain. When other things were forgotten, that understanding remained.

Sally Hemings and her children have overshadowed the lives of other members of her family. How could they not, given their relationship to Thomas Jefferson, who himself looms like a colossus over the lives of all those who will be discussed in these pages. In recognition of the importance of the topic, chapters 14 through 17 veer slightly from the narrative to provide an in-depth analysis of the pair's beginnings in Paris. There is, however, far more to the Hemingses than "Sally and Tom," and although that pair must be a critical part of our consideration, this book is not designed to tell just their story. There are many others who complete the picture of the family's time in slavery and whose lives deserve to be woven into the tapestry of American history.

No look at Monticello and slavery would be complete without a portrait of Sally Hemings's brother James Hemings, who lived in France with Jefferson for five years along with his sister Sally. These two members of the Hemings family traveled the farthest distance from slavery at Monticello, experiencing life in what was, at the time, perhaps the most cultivated city on earth and even witnessing the start of the French Revolution. Their time in France forever altered the course of their lives. For Sally Hemings it marked the beginning of her time with Jefferson. For James Hemings it marked the beginning of the end. In his life we see the tragedy of talent thwarted by the limitations of slavery and white supremacy.

Then there is the story of John Hemings, the extremely talented carpenter and joiner whose work is still on display at Monticello. In John Hemings's life we see the blend of slavery as a work system and as a system of personal relationships. Hemings, who helped Jefferson realize his vision for the look of Monticello, was also a surrogate father to Jefferson's sons Beverley, Madison, and Eston.

It was not just the males in the family who were prime movers, as much as enslaved people could be. Mary Hemings, the eldest of the first generation of Hemings siblings, exerted a remarkable influence upon the family. She was the first to maneuver her way out of slavery on the mountain. She was able to be a source of refuge, stability, and monetary support for her relatives who remained in bondage at Monticello—up to and beyond the time of the family's dispersal in 1827, when Jefferson's human property was sold after his death to pay his enormous debts.

Every story has a beginning, and we will start there. One could argue strenuously that the central (and most compelling) figure in the family's history was not Sally Hemings but her mother, Elizabeth, whose experiences in life helped project her influence down the family line. Elizabeth Hemings, known as Betty, was the matriarch of a family that over four generations numbered in the dozens. She was well suited to that role for many reasons, not the least of which is that she lived a very long time—seventy-two years, well beyond the average life span of Virginians of her day, black or white. Also, she had many children—by one count, fourteen of them, although only twelve have been positively identified as hers. Half of her children had a black father, half had a white father. Her grandchildren, some of whom were born while she was still bearing children, had black fathers and white fathers. The mixing continued into succeeding generations until some of her descendants decided to move totally away from their African origins, while others resolutely clung to it.

Behind all of this stands Elizabeth Hemings, the person of origin for the family and their story. The unnamed African woman who was her mother, John Wayles (who fathered six of her children, including Sally Hemings), Martha Wayles Jefferson (Wayles's eldest daughter, Jefferson's wife, and Sally's half sister), Thomas Jefferson, and Sally Hemings—all of them lived for a time under her knowing gaze. If one person could be brought forward to help tell this story of slavery, intertwined families, pain, loss, silence, denial, and endurance, hers would be the most valuable voice.

Like all enslaved parents, Elizabeth Hemings lived with the possibility that her family would be broken up by sale or gift. In fact, two of her adult children were sold—one to be united with her enslaved husband, who lived on a nearby plantation, the other to cohabit with a white merchant in Charlottesville. Jefferson freed two of her sons during her lifetime, and they left Monticello to live on their own. Another daughter was given as a wedding present to one of Jefferson's sisters. For the most part, however, the Hemings family remained intact, or within close proximity to one another, for their entire lives. As a result each member had, in the person of Elizabeth Hemings, a mother/grandmother to be the repository of family lore and center of family attention.

The women of the family were house servants who worked alongside one another for years. Their brothers, sons, and nephews were butlers or valets to Jefferson. The Hemings men who were not in the house were artisans who worked just outside of it on Mulberry Row, which abuts and runs parallel to the main house at Monticello. One of Hemings's many grandchildren set the scene recalling a childhood spent running errands in and out of the big house surrounded entirely by (and this to him was extraordinary and important) members of his family. In this compact area, the Hemingses would have seen and interacted with one another every single day.

In sum, this family was at least as much "together" as many other families who lived on farms during the eighteenth and nineteenth centuries. Moreover, in the Hemingses' confined world on the mountain, the entire enslaved community in which they lived was basically stable over the years. With few exceptions—births, deaths, temporary moves from one household to another—the rolls of Jefferson's Monticello slaves do not change much over the decades. That the Hemingses were enslaved thus did not automatically render them incapable of knowing who they were, of knowing their mothers, fathers, sisters, and brothers. Slavery did not destroy their ability to observe, remember, and reason. It did not prevent them from forming enduring and meaningful attachments. It did not make them untrustworthy—certainly not when compared with the people who held them in bondage. In short, nothing about their enslaved status makes them undeserving of our considered and unprejudiced attention.

We do not have, in the Hemingses, an enslaved family with loose ties, little knowledge of family history, and no family cohesion. That Virginia law did not protect their family does not end the inquiry, for legal regimes are not omnipotent. Powerful as they may be, they never have (and never will, because they cannot) control all human feelings and arrangements. While it is certainly important to be aware of what *could have* happened to this enslaved family because its members were not ultimately in control of their destiny, that knowledge should not overshadow what can be gleaned by considering what *actually* happened to them. Under the circumstances of their lives, the Hemingses were able to achieve and maintain a coherent family identity that existed within slavery and survived it.

Central to the Hemingses' identity was their being of mixed race. Basing American slavery on race created a world where, put simply, it was better to be white than black. Being "in between" was meaningful as well, and the

Hemingses' interracial origins helped determine the course of the family's history. The conventional wisdom that white slave owners sometimes valued more highly those slaves who most resembled white people was very much a part of life at Monticello, and the Hemingses benefited from it. Although, as we will see, at least one other enslaved family, the Grangers, who appear to have been of completely African origin, rivaled, if not exceeded, the Hemingses in the amount of trust Jefferson reposed in them.

Thomas Jefferson Randolph, Jefferson's eldest grandson, extolled the virtues of the Hemingses specifically. He said that while slaves on the plantation had their own theories for why the Hemingses were favored, the true reasons were their "superior intelligence, capacity and fidelity to trust." There is no cause to doubt that the Hemingses were indeed intelligent, but we should also consider what role their appearance and the knowledge of their genetic makeup may have played in his assessment of them. Randolph was likely influenced by the common view among whites that intermixture with white people eugenically improved black people, making the children from these unions smarter and more attractive than those of full African heritage. Under the circumstances, Randolph, and his grandfather, would have been inclined to see, credit, and encourage the talent they saw in men and women who looked more like themselves. That is one way prejudice works.

Like architecture, which can convey meaning as eloquently through the spaces left empty as the areas built over, Randolph's statement about the Hemingses is illuminating for what it says (he gives a view of the family's overall talent) and intriguing for what it does not say. Just what were those other unnamed reasons the slaves gave for the Hemings family's ascendancy? Was it just that they were fair-skinned? Or was there something else? Although Randolph chose not to elaborate on this point, it is not too hard to figure out what he had in mind. The Hemingses were not only part white; their white "parts" came from the master's family. Naturally, the other slaves at Monticello might have assumed that this counted for something, influencing the way they and others saw the Hemingses, and the way the family saw itself. It would be hard to look at a household filled with members of the same family and not come to the conclusion that their shared blood was why they were all there.

How did others enslaved at Monticello see the Hemingses? Thomas Jefferson Randolph provided one perspective. Among "the other slaves," he said, the Hemingses' role at Monticello was "a source of bitter jealousy." The enslaved people down the mountain were watching and, evidently, weighing the Hemingses. Jeff Randolph may well have been right that the source of friction between Hemingses and non-Hemingses was jealousy. But couldn't the "other slaves" have had concerns that Randolph would not likely have perceived? What about the fact that some Hemingses clearly identified with Jefferson and his family, sometimes displaying extreme loyalty to them? Did the other slaves find that grating? The Jefferson-Randolphs, after all, were keeping all members of the enslaved community—Hemingses and non-Hemingses alike—in bondage. Their "superior intelligence, capacity, and fidelity to trusts" were not saving the overwhelming majority of them from that fate. At least some of those enslaved at Monticello might view the Hemingses' way of accommodating to their circumstances as problematic.

Or perhaps the friction was merely the result of the much discussed tension between slaves who worked in the fields and those who worked in the master's house? Scholars have rightly cautioned against calling house slaves "privileged," mainly because the term does not take into account the views of the enslaved. It just assumes that they would have thought spending their days around white people a desirable thing, that being "chosen" to be in proximity to white masters was a sign of good fortune. White slave owners may have thought so, but that was only their view.

It also assumes that the relative "easiness" of housework when compared with fieldwork dramatically outweighed all other considerations. While house slaves like the Hemingses may have generally been exempted from more physically challenging fieldwork, there were some advantages to being outside the constant eye view of white masters and mistresses. Enslaved people who worked away from the master's house had greater personal autonomy and the chance to commune with one another in the manner they chose—they could more easily say what they wanted, the way they wanted. Every moment spent away from white masters and mistresses gave them the chance to fashion and maintain their own sense of identity in matters of family, religion, and other social practices. The things most real and important about slaves' lives were the things most hidden from the white world. In the field, even with an overseer making rounds, slaves were largely free from too intimate involvement with the whims and personalities of their oppressors. For some, this could well have been a psychological relief more precious than the extra calories burned and effort expended in tending crops.

We must remember that, in the society in which the Hemingses existed, family was all. This was as true for blacks as for whites. Importantly, during the Hemingses' time at Monticello, family at its most elemental level was about blood ties. The Hemingses' situation vis-à-vis other slaves in their community was especially complicated because they were slaves in a household where they were genetically related both to one another and to those who held them in bondage. Because of that connection, the master of that household chose to treat them in a way that separated them from the rest of the enslaved population—for example, letting some of its members hire themselves out and keep their wages, exempting the women of the family from any hard labor, freeing only people from that family, giving certain of its males virtual free movement, and selecting them for special training as artisans. The master then chose a woman from the Hemings family, had children with her, and arranged for the freedom of that nuclear family. Any enslaved member of that community who knew the history of Monticello would have known that the only route to freedom (one traveled only infrequently) was the possession of Wayles, Jefferson, or Hemings blood. No one else had a chance. It is doubtful that other members of the community could have avoided seeing the Hemingses as different from themselves. It is also unlikely that members of the Hemings family could have avoided seeing themselves in something of a special light, even if the harsh reality of slavery might have served to check the tendency to see themselves as completely separate from other enslaved people. These and many other issues must be considered as we examine the Hemings family's progress through the eighteenth and nineteenth centuries.

History is to a great degree an imaginative enterprise; when writing it or reading it, we try to see the subjects in their time and space. Imagining requires some starting point of connection. Even though we acknowledge that the connections will not be perfect—we cannot really know exactly what it meant to be a Hemings at Monticello, or a Jefferson, for that matter— we have to reference what we know of human beings as we try to reconstruct and establish a context for their lives. Historians often warn against the danger of "essentializing" when making statements about people of the past—positing an elemental human nature that can be discerned and relied upon at all times and in all places. Warnings notwithstanding, there are, in fact, some elements of the human condition that have existed forever, transcending time and place. If there were none, and if historians did not try to connect to those elements (consciously or unconsciously), historical writing would be simply incomprehensible. Think of attempting to read a foreign language in a script you had never seen before. You could stare at the pages for an eternity, but without some point of commonality between the unknown script and something you already know—a connection—no matter how long you stared, you could never crack the code.

Therefore, we should not be afraid to call upon what we know in general about mothers, fathers, families, male-female relationships, power relationships, the contours of life in small closely knit communities, as we try to see the Hemingses in the context of their own time and place. This will require thinking of the family members in a way they were not thought of during their lives and, it must be said, during most of the period that Monticello has been the object of scholarly attention—as fully formed persons with innate worth and equal humanity that links them directly to us all, no matter what our race. I asked in an earlier work, "In what universe could the humanity, family integrity, and honor of slave owners count for more than the humanity, family integrity, and honor of slaves?" My answer was that we Americans have lived in that universe since the founding of the country, and have only recently begun the process of moving beyond its boundaries. I hope this work adds to the momentum of that journey.

The lives of the various members of the Hemings family, which must include the white men who had children with Hemings women, provide important windows through which to view the development of slavery and the concept of race in the Virginia of the eighteenth and nineteenth centuries. While there was much about the Hemingses that made them unique—Jefferson and Monticello—like other enslaved people, they were subject to all the insecurities and deprivations associated with that condition. It seems especially appropriate to tell one part of the story of slavery through life at a place that holds such symbolic importance for many Americans—Monticello. For it is there that we can find the absolute best, and the absolute worst, that we have been as Americans. We should not get too far into the twenty-first century without looking back at the Hemingses and their time to remember and to learn.

PART I

ORIGINS

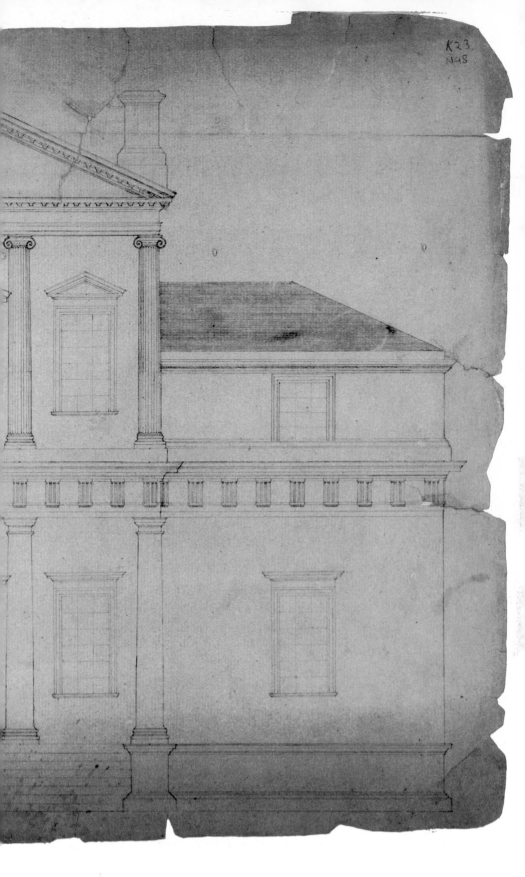

(OVERLEAF)

JEFFERSON'S ELEVATION OF THE FIRST MONTICELLO.

(Courtesy of Massachusetts Historical Society)

I

❦

YOUNG ELIZABETH'S WORLD

LIZABETH HEMINGS BEGAN life when America was still a colonial possession. She lived through the Revolution in the home of one of the men who helped make it and died during the formative years of the American Republic, an unknown person in the midst of pivotal events in national and world history. Hemings lived at a time when chattel slavery existed in every American colony, but was dramatically expanding and thriving in the Virginia that was her home. She was, by law, an item of property—a nonwhite, female slave, whose life was bounded by eighteenth-century attitudes about how such persons fit into society. Those attitudes, years in the making by the time Hemings was born, fascinate because they are at once utterly familiar and totally alien.

Most Americans today admit the existence of racism and sexism, even as we often disagree about examples of them. When we encounter these practices while studying the eighteenth century, we react knowingly. "These are the things," at least some of us say, "that we're still working to overcome." We also know that hierarchies, based on any number of factors, exist in every society, enriching the lives of some and blighting the lives of others.

Yet, slavery is a different matter altogether. There are workers all over the world who live desperate lives with little hope of advancement for themselves or their children. There are women who are held in bondage and forced to work as prostitutes or to clean others' homes and care for others' families while their own families go unattended. None of these conditions approach the systematic degradation and violence of American slavery sanctioned by state and church. People were bought and sold against their will. They were defined in statutes as chattel or real estate. With the law's protection they could be beaten to death as part of legitimate "correction." They were denied legal marriage. Slave women were unprotected against rape. Forcing a slave woman to have sex against her will was considered a trespass against her owner. If her owner raped her, it was no crime at all. What the violation meant to the woman was irrelevant. The law prevented slaves from giving testimony in courts against white people. It was a world where one could pick up the daily newspaper and see advertisements touting "Negroes for sale" and descriptions of "runaway slaves" complete with stock caricatures that made them instantly recognizable to all readers. These and all the other depredations of the slave system present a world that seems far removed from daily life in the United States in the twenty-first century. Though we hear echoes of that world and understand that its effects are still present, much about this time feels otherworldly.

Understanding the path of Elizabeth Hemings's life requires some consideration of the contours of the community into which she was born, an elastic place with boundaries that expanded, contracted, shifted, and evolved over time. At the broadest level, Hemings was part of a large Atlantic world, comprising Europeans and Africans on both sides of that ocean whose lives were shaped by the demands of slavery. While the characteristics of that world must inform our view, a thorough investigation of all parts of it is beyond the scope of this book. Instead, we will draw the circle around Hemings more closely to look at the world she would have known most intimately—the world of an enslaved woman in eighteenth-century Virginia.

To say to an American that Elizabeth Hemings was "born a slave" is to call forth a particular image of who she was, how she lived her life, and even how she spoke and carried herself. That is because slavery lives in the minds of most Americans as a series of iconic images: a slave ship packed tight with human cargo, a whip, the auction block, slaves speaking one universal and timeless dialect, black figures toiling in cotton fields. That last image—the cotton field—has most strongly influenced our view, freezing the institution in its antebellum period when cotton was "king" and when slavery had, in the view of one influential historian, been thoroughly domesticated.[1] By the time "King Cotton" arrived in the nineteenth century, enslaved Virginians of African origin, and those of English extraction whose ancestors introduced slavery into the Old Dominion, had long since become Americans, and the institution that defined their existence together had adapted itself, it seemed, for the long haul.

What had gone before, the process that brought those two groups into their "Americanness," is largely the province of scholars of the seventeenth and early eighteenth centuries. There are many reasons for this, but several immediately come to mind. First, American slavery at its beginnings—obscure, distant, and tragic—is probably for most people a less attractive point of focus than the story of the discovery and political founding of the American nation. If you like your history heroic—and many people seem to—the story of slavery in the early American period is simply not the place to go looking for heroes, at least not among the people most commonly written about.

Second, with the exception of periodic bouts of "founders chic,"[2] in which the men credited with drawing up the blueprint for the United States are pitted against one another—*Hamilton was really better than Jefferson, Madison was better than Adams, and Franklin was better than all of them*—the colonial and Revolutionary period in America has so far failed to capture the cultural imagination the way the Civil War era has. There is no *Gone with the Wind* for the seventeenth and eighteenth centuries, no literature wallowing in the romance of defeat, no passionate attachments to divisive symbols that live on to poison contemporary race relations and threaten the American future. The Civil War is over, but the politics that fueled it and helped design its aftermath are still very much with us, playing out in various racially charged and seemingly intractable disputes about desegregation, affirmative action, even the continued use in the public sphere of a Confederate battle flag that once flew against the United States of America. The years running up to, during, and after the Civil War mark the beginning of the America we know today—a modern country, powered by the market and free labor, multiracial in its composition (if somewhat uneasily), and at its most fundamental core, united.

It is not as if no heroism or romance were to be found in the colonial period. Schoolchildren are told an uplifting story about English men and women escaping religious persecution to build their own cities upon the hill in what would become New England. Who could not identify with the urge to live one's life in peace and freedom, and not admire people willing to cross an ocean to do it? That some of the later immigrants to New England were Puritans, who almost immediately went about the business of persecuting those who did not toe their particular version of "the line," does not diminish the attractiveness of those early aspirations. It was the *idea* that counts. We can (and do) without embarrassment draw a direct line from the dreams of those Americans in the making to our dreams today.

Elizabeth Hemings's Virginia, however, presents a real problem. It is hard to associate the earliest Virginians who controlled society with any aspiration loftier than that of making a killing. The colony was, after all, founded by the *Virginia Company*. It was from the very beginning a money-making enterprise, a place for men seeking their fortunes with limited reference to spirituality, with no nod to sentimentality and, apparently, very few limits on how the moneymaking could proceed. In one historian's words, the people who settled the colony were all adventurers "in the fullest sense of the term," men "seeking the main chance for [themselves] in that part of the new world which . . . seemed to offer [them] the best chances." The term "adventurer" doesn't really do justice to the men who helped usher in this world, for we must instead think of what those high-stakes gambles actually entailed. Voracious land grabbing and land speculation, aided and abetted by the manipulation of public offices, made a relative handful of people wealthy.[3]

Those who had to rely chiefly on their physical labor to amass property were at a distinct disadvantage. By the end of the seventeenth century, the white indentured servants who came to the colony hoped that, in a not too distant future, they too could own enough land to do more than subsist. Their dreams, however, were very seldom realized. That this economic and social system eventually came most fully into its own on the backs of enslaved Africans adds depravity to the overall picture of venality. Unless one is willing and able to overlook extremely important details about the fundamental nature of this society, the story of Virginia's origins does not lend itself to romanticizing. This is probably why for most Americans the national narrative begins at Plymouth Rock instead of Jamestown, even though the Virginia fortune seekers arrived more than a decade before the Pilgrims.

All this seems worlds away from where we are now, but despite its comparative remoteness, the colonial period in America, as experienced in both the North and the South, in very critical ways helped define who we are today. For one thing, it was during that period that the basic meanings of "whiteness" and "blackness" were in the process of being defined for the

American population. However it has been expressed over the years, the association of whiteness with power and privilege, blackness with relative powerlessness and second-class status, began to take shape in this time and has been a persistent feature of life in America ever since. It has survived Revolution, Civil War, massive immigration, two world wars, the Cold War, and the tremendous social upheaval during the latter part of the twentieth century. Because we are still living with this, it is worthwhile for us to consider the world that greeted the matriarch of the Hemings family in the mid-1700s.

The Africans and the English

By the 1730s, the decade in which Elizabeth Hemings was born to an African mother and an English father, the institution that would define her life and those of her descendants for years to come was firmly in place. Virginia was a full-fledged slave society 116 years after a small number of Africans ("negars") arrived at Jamestown, the English colony on the James River. It was during those years that white Virginians transformed their laws, culture, and economy to make slavery based upon race the very foundation of their way of life.[4]

The transformation was hardly instantaneous. Slavery in Virginia did not spring up overnight. It took time—spanning the last seven decades of the 1600s—for the English colonists, or the leading lights of the colony, to define the terms of engagement between Africans and the English in that corner of the New World. What they settled upon foretold a life of pain and struggle for the Africans and their progeny over many generations, and prosperity (or at least the hope of it) for the English and their descendants. Scholars have long debated the reason for this turn of events, why the Virginia colonists turned away from the labor of white indentured servants and decided to enslave Africans. Some have cited race and religion as the deciding factors, allowing men who jealously guarded their liberty to obliterate the liberty of others who were of a different color and different faiths. Other scholars suggest it was a straightforward economic calculation. Still others assert that it was some combination of these and other influences.[5]

In the beginning, when the numbers of Africans were few, there was some ambiguity about their status in Virginia. The scant evidence that exists on this question suggests several alternative scenarios. While most

Africans may have been treated as slaves for life from the very start, others became free in the years immediately following the arrival of the first group. Were these freed slaves treated as indentured servants, or had they been seen as slaves but emancipated for some reason by their owners—as happened occasionally all throughout the time of slavery in America? We may never know for certain. As the number of Africans increased—slowly at first—their labor was mixed with the indentured labor of Englishmen, and a smaller number of Englishwomen. For a good part of the seventeenth century, these two groups (along with a smaller number of Native Americans) worked side by side. In the words of the historian Philip D. Morgan, "they ate, smoked, ran away, stole, and made love together." But Morgan also wisely cautions against seeing their situations as the same. Enslaved Africans were distinguished from their white counterparts by the "sheer nakedness of the exploitation to which they were subject."[6]

Although the peoples of Africa and Europe were not unknown to one another, it is safe to say that the majority of seventeenth-century Africans and English people would not have been in extensive contact. There had been an African presence in Great Britain since ancient times, but not a substantial one until the beginning of the slave trade. Englishmen and their predecessors in the trade from other parts of Europe created outposts along the African coast in order to conduct the traffic in human beings, forming alliances with the leaders of those societies and having children with African women, who often became involved in the trade themselves.[7] It was in the New World that the lives of these people with different skin colors became most closely entwined. They greeted one another in this land as strangers across a divide that was both physical and cultural, and each had views about the other that centered on notions of difference and inferiority.

Negative views about the color black existed within English culture long before Englishmen actually encountered people with "black" skin. Black was evil. Black was dirty. Although other evidence suggests that people of African origin were not universally reviled in England, the tendency to see black negatively was definitely a part of English culture. Naturally, its view of whiteness carried all the opposite meanings. Color, then, became an expression of a person's essence.[8]

This was a two-way street, with the Africans thinking along the same lines about their white counterparts, but in the process reversing the conclusions. They saw themselves as different from whites and often imbued whiteness with negative characteristics. Whites were physically ugly—one "African ruler thought 'all Europeans looked like ugly sea monsters'"— cannibalistic, and disfavored by God. A seventeenth-century European traveler reported that some "local blacks" he had met said that "'while God created Blacks as well as White Men,' the Lord preferred the blacks." Others referred to a Danish man as being "'as white as the devil.'"[9] Once blacks and whites were together in the new world of Virginia, where Anglo-American colonists controlled society, only the whites' perception of the meaning of differences between the races counted. They could, and did, codify their understanding of what it meant to be black and what it meant to be white, with devastating consequences for people of African origin.

Matters were complicated further because the "Africans" were anything but monolithic in their cultures. "Black men and women were transported to America as members of specific tribes—as Ibos, Yorubas, or Ashantis but not simply as Africans."[10] Africa is the most linguistically, culturally, and genetically diverse of the continents, and though no one at that time could have dreamed it, the enslaved Africans, under the skin, at the genetic level, were more "different" from one another than the English were from their fellow Europeans.

White Virginians, particularly members of the slave-owning class, did recognize that Africans were not all alike. Over the course of time in the early days of slavery, some planters even came to prefer workers who were brought from one region over those from others.[11] But respecting and preserving the culture of these very diverse people was never the point for the white colonists. Developing and maintaining a work force were the real issues, and as these goals were realized, all the various African ethnic groups were gradually subsumed under the category of enslaved black people. In that more literally minded age, surface appearances were what counted, and the various shades of black told Anglo-Virginians everything they thought they needed to know about who could be a slave and who could not.

In the end the physical differences—skin color, facial features, and hair type—between Africans and English people in Virginia helped create and maintain a critical dividing line. What the Africans "did" became less important than what they "were" as signaled by their physical appearance. Even if Africans chose to adopt the mores of the English, they could never overcome the powerful view that the differences between the groups were elemental and largely insurmountable. As a result, the lowliest indentured white servants could be, and were, encouraged to identify with their white masters while distancing themselves from the blacks with whom they worked.

Some historians have seen early examples of cooperation between Africans and white indentured servants in the seventeenth century as evidence that racial prejudice was a creature of slavery and argue that the institution taught white colonists to look down upon black people. They also suggest that the colonists' willingness to allow some of the early Africans to be freemen while others were enslaved for life reveals a degree of flexibility in race relations, and that flexibility suggests racial attitudes had not been firmly set.[12] Highlighting the variable experiences of the earliest blacks in Virginia is much less useful than keying in on the one constant in the lives of whites from Jamestown to Appomattox: they were *never* to be designated as chattel who passed their condition down to their children, and their children's children, in perpetuity. Significantly, this distinction between black and white was drawn well before Virginia became bound to slavery as the economic foundation of its society.

And why wouldn't it have been? The Virginia colonists did not exist in a vacuum. They were travelers in the Atlantic world of which slavery was so much a part. Who Africans were, and how they had been used in that world for centuries, was well known to them. Long before the English got involved, the Portuguese had enslaved Africans, as had the Spanish. Englishmen certainly heard tales of the Arabs' enslavement of Africans that began centuries before Europeans even thought of the notion. The ease and swiftness with which blacks were written out of the social compact indicates that notions of essential difference and inferiority took hold very early on in the Virginia experiment. As more Africans arrived and the commitment to the economic system of slavery grew deeper, the perceived differences between whites and blacks provided a workable excuse for widening the social gap between indentured white servants and blacks, until that gap became a yawning chasm.

Religion played a role in the process as well. The English colonists, of course, were Christians. Some Africans had converted to Christianity even before their arrival in the New World, but the overwhelming majority of them had not. They had their own religious traditions, and whether those traditions were animist or Islamic, those who adhered to them were, in the eyes of the English, "heathens." At first, this difference was offered to explain why Africans alone were eligible for chattel slavery. Christianity is an evangelical religion of faith, not blood, and carries in its very heart the expectation that multitudes will become Christian through the ritual of baptism. The question arose, "What happens when an African heathen becomes a Christian?" Shouldn't that wipe away the stain of slavery? Some masters who wanted to free their slaves thought so, and for a time their actions appeared to threaten—albeit in a minor way—the stability of the institution. The Church of England shut down that avenue of emancipation when it confirmed that baptism of a slave into the Christian faith did not require the emancipation of that slave, an understanding that Virginia codified in law. Christians could, in good conscience, hold other Christians in bondage.[13]

In the end, the Anglo-Virginians introduced a form of chattel slavery unknown in their home country—a system of bondage based upon race. This was indeed a brave new world. Proceeding on an ad hoc basis, the colonists put together rules and customs to accommodate the new society taking shape. There was no direct precedent from their home country for doing what they did; in fact, it required them to break rather quickly with one important long-held tradition and understanding that they had carried with them across the Atlantic Ocean. That fateful deviation from English tradition—one that would set the course of Elizabeth Hemings's life and the lives of her descendants—was the Virginia colonists' decision to abandon the English tradition that determined a person's status by the status of the father. In England you "were" what your father "was." A person could be born free or as a member of a group of "unfree" people who existed during various points in English history—for example, a villein (serf) attached to the land of a lord or to the lord himself. Inventing the rules of slavery, in 1662, Virginians decided to adopt the Roman rule *partus sequitur ventrem*, which says that you were what your mother was.[14] This important departure from tradition had enormous consequences for the progress of slavery and the mapping of Virginia's racial landscape. Why take this route? Although the preamble to the legislation states the impetus for the law—"doubts have arisen whether children got by an Englishman upon a Negro woman should be slave or ffree"—there is no language explaining exactly why, in the context of Virginian colonial society, the ways of ancient Rome should emerge as superior to the more readily available and familiar English tradition. There are some reasonable speculations.

One way to think about it is to imagine what might have been the course of slavery in Virginia had the colonists followed their English tradition. White men, particularly the ones who made up the House of Burgesses, the legislature in colonial Virginia, were the masters of growing numbers of African women, owning not only their labor but their very bodies. That these women sometimes would be used for sex as well as work must have occurred to the burgesses. Inevitably offspring would arise from some of these unions. Even white males who owned no slaves could contribute to the problem by producing, with enslaved black women, children who would be born free, thus destroying a critical component of the master's property right: the ability to capture the value of the "increase" when female slaves gave birth.

That exact situation was at issue in 1655, when a mulatto woman, Elizabeth Key, who later married her lawyer, successfully sued for her freedom on the basis of the fact that her father was English. This case, and probably others that never made it to court but would have been part of the social knowledge of the community, caught the burgesses' attention, and they acted to close this possible escape route out of slavery for one potentially large category of people of African origin: the children of white fathers and enslaved mothers. The law passed in the wake of Key's case actually had two components—the new rule determining status through the mother and a provision for doubling the fine for mixed-race couples who engaged in sex over those levied against unmarried same-race couples. The historian Warren M. Billings, who was the first to do extensive work on the case, saw the law as a strong anti-race-mixing measure. "Writing a seldom used civil law doctrine, *partus sequitur ventrem*, into the statute indicates the depth of the lawmakers' desire to prevent miscegenation." While the double fine reflects a wish to discourage mixed-race sex, the same cannot be said for *partus sequitur ventrem*. The doctrine assured that white men—particularly the privileged ones who passed the law, who would not likely have been haled into court for fornication even with white women—could have sex with enslaved women, produce children who were items of capital, and never have to worry about losing their property rights in them.[15]

Partus sequitur ventrem, then, was an important first principle in this nascent slave-owning society based upon race. Like all efficient legal rules, it achieved its aim—here, the maximum protection of property rights—with little or no intervention by the state or other third parties. The private conduct of men would have no serious impact on the emerging slave society as a whole. White men could engage in sex with black women without creating a class of freeborn mixed-race people to complicate matters. Men, who can produce many more children than women, and who throughout history have been less subject to social stricture for their sexuality, constituted the greater potential threat for bringing this class into being. Following the dictates of their English heritage would have required some white men to tell other white men what women they could and could not have sex with, knowing full well the day might come when others would have the opportunity to return the favor. Under the rules of the game the burgesses constructed, there was no need to interfere with other men's conduct, even as the efforts to control white women's sexual activity grew ever more strenuous. Whatever the social tensions and confusion created by the presence of people who were neither black nor white, Virginia's law on inheriting status through the mother effectively ended threats to slave masters' property rights when interracial sex produced children who confounded the supposedly fixed categories of race.

The "Full-blooded African" Woman and the "Englishman"

As the daughter of an enslaved African woman and an Englishman, Elizabeth Hemings physically embodied the strange and devastating encounter between black and white in colonial Virginia. As we will see, Hemings's father indeed cared that his daughter might be in perpetual bondage. There was nothing he could do. His whiteness and free status could not save her from the fate ordained by seventeenth-century legislators. What loomed before her, at Bermuda Hundred, the Forest, Guinea, Elk Hill, and, finally, Monticello grew out of their very particular construction of slavery, status, and race.

The law did not solve everything. The colonists could not simply ignore the fact that people like Hemings were neither "purely" African nor "purely" English—their physical appearance showed the melding of two different "types." This could never have been totally ignored in a world that put great stock in surface appearances. When Isaac Jefferson, who would meet Hemings many years later at Monticello, described her as a "bright mulatto woman," he was using a term adopted early on in America to categorize racially mixed people. Calling such people "mulattoes," from the

Spanish word meaning "mule," insinuated that blacks and whites, though related, were close to being separate species, as a mule is the offspring of a horse and a donkey. Using this term in letters, legislative enactments, court opinions, and other documents seems to have been more wishful thinking than anything remotely descriptive. The English colonists, and their predecessors, knew that the analogy did not work. Mules, evidently as a consequence of their mixed parentage, are sterile. Children born to one black parent and one white parent are not, barring some personal physical impairment. This was not the first, nor would it be the last, time that pseudo-biological notions would be employed to degrade people possessing any degree of African heritage.[16]

Naturally, mixed-race people could and did reproduce themselves, though there is no way to know how many people like Elizabeth Hemings existed at the time of her birth. We do know that sensitivities about the differences between blacks and whites were particularly heightened during her early childhood as large numbers of Africans were arriving daily into the colony. In contrast to previous generations who had undergone "seasoning" in various West Indian ports before arriving in Virginia, this new generation of enslaved Africans came directly from the continent with their languages, religions, and cultural practices intact. Language was a barrier to cooperation in some cases. But very often slave ships brought cargoes of people from the same region who disembarked together and were sold as a group. In addition, there was always the possibility of making contact with earlier captives from one's region.

The shock, misery, and anxiety of being forcibly brought to a strange world by people who seemed equally strange, and who by their actions showed their willingness to impose their will through violence, was enormous. After the terror and uncertainty of the Middle Passage, many of the new arrivals clung to one another determined to face together whatever they were going to confront. From the Anglo-Virginians' perspective, these new arrivals seemed more "outlandish" and threatening, their greater numbers literally changing the face of Virginia. A child like Elizabeth Hemings, a mixture of the familiar and the increasingly frightening unknown, excited a whole host of reactions, from fascination to confusion and repulsion.

Although mixed-race people like Hemings were a recognized category in early Anglo-American statutes, they enjoyed no advantages at law. The statutory listings of "negroes" and "mulattoes" were really a way to emphasize that mixed-race people had the same status as blacks. The defining fissure lay between those born slaves and those born free. Law in the books, of course, often operates very differently (and sometimes hardly at all) out in society at large. While being mixed race did not stop people from being slaves, it could affect the course of an individual slave's life, helping determine the type of work one performed and the likelihood that one might someday go free. During most of the time of slavery in Virginia, emancipated slaves tended to be of mixed race. That should not surprise. Some fathers wanted to free their children. It also makes perfect sense in a world fueled by white supremacy. Whites could reject equality for those who were not all white, but distinguish people who were partly white from the masses of blacks. There was a marked tendency to cast mixed-race people as superior to their black fellows, for no partly white person could be all bad. In the end, although the overwhelming majority of mixed-race slaves endured lives every bit as harsh as those of slaves who were not mixed, being mixed race mattered, and Hemings and others like her complicated in ways large and small whites' determination to create a slave society based upon race.

Madison Hemings, one of Elizabeth's many grandsons, said one such complication arose early on in young Elizabeth's life. Hemings, speaking about his grandmother's origins, said that the disjuncture between having an enslaved black mother and a free white father was the source of conflict in Elizabeth's early childhood. Her father, "the captain of an English trading vessel," met Elizabeth's mother, described as a "full-blooded African, and possibly a native of that country," at or near Williamsburg. Captain Hemings wanted to buy his daughter, whom he had acknowledged as his "own flesh." Even though he offered "an extraordinarily large price for her," Hemings's owner, identified as "John Wales," refused to sell the child. When this happened, Captain Hemings plotted to "take the child by force or stealth." His plans were thwarted when "leaky fellow servants" of Elizabeth's mother alerted "Mr. Wales," who then brought mother and child into the "great house," where he could keep an eye on them. Hemings explained that his grandfather refused to sell his grandmother because he was interested in how this mixed-race child would turn out. After a while Captain Hemings gave up and left Virginia and his child.[17]

Exactly where in Africa Elizabeth Hemings's mother was supposed to have come from is unknown. That she was African fits extremely well with

the demographic profile of Virginia at the time of her daughter's birth. The
1730s marked the high tide for importation of Africans into the colony.
More were brought into the Old Dominion during this period than in any
other decade in which the slave trade was legal. Newly imported Africans
made up 34 to 44 percent of the colony's total slave population. The largest numbers were from Angola, followed by the Bight of Biafra (off the
coast of Nigeria) and the region of Senegambia (Senegal and Gambia). The
Williamsburg area had particularly high concentrations of people who had
been born in Africa, making it a place full of Africans of diverse ethnic origins, native-born blacks, Anglo-American colonists, and English seamen—
a multicultural, multilingual province, where an English ship captain would
likely encounter a "full-blooded African" woman.[18]

Under law Elizabeth Hemings's father had no right to her, and if he
wanted his child, unless her owner in the spirit of generosity wanted to give
her away, he would have had to buy her. If the owner refused, there was
no recourse. But just who owned Elizabeth when she was born? Although
John Wayles did live near Williamsburg, in Charles City County, he apparently did not own Elizabeth Hemings at her birth. Rather, he came into
ownership of her when she was about eleven years old upon his marriage to
Martha Eppes in 1746. The couple's marriage settlement (essentially a contract that, among other things, allowed the wife to retain control over property brought to the marriage, which in slaveholding areas very often meant
slaves) included Elizabeth Hemings and, presumably, her mother because
whoever owned the mother owned the child.[19] This confusion over ownership, and the tangle that emerges in sorting it out, reveals with great clarity
what happened when human beings were treated as "things."

Martha Eppes Wayles's father, Francis Eppes IV, died in 1734. In a 1794
listing, Jefferson's Farm Book recorded Elizabeth Hemings's year of birth
as "abt" 1735, but dropped the equivocation in other listings. So it cannot
be said with certainty whether she was born just before Eppes died or just
after. By his will drafted in 1733, Eppes set out with great specificity what
property he wanted to leave to each of his children. When speaking of his
daughter Martha, he wrote that he gave "unto my my daughter Martha
Eppes Several negroes following, the negro woman Jenny, my negro girl
Agge, my negro girl Judy, my negro girl Sarah, my negro girl Dinah. . . ." At
the end of the section devoted to Martha, Eppes also gave her a share with
her sister Anne in two male slaves, Argulas and Will, and a female slave

named Parthena, stating, "[M]y will and desire is that the increase if any from ye said Parthena may be equally divided between them when they, or either of them shall come of age or mary [*sic*]."[20] Was one of these six the "full-blooded African" woman?

Not one of those names is African, but we would not expect them to be, since most slave owners called their African captives by the names they wanted when they arrived in the New World, instead of what their names actually were. Two names in that group, however, are very closely associated with later generations of the Hemings family. "Sarah" was the name of Elizabeth's youngest daughter, more famously known by her nickname, Sally. In turn Sally Hemings would have nieces and a granddaughter named Sarah, and the name would continue in the family. As we will see, however, Sally Hemings more likely got her name from her father's family. "Parthena" was an alternate spelling of the name Parthenia, which stands out among the usual run of Marthas, Marys, Elizabeths, and Annes. Elizabeth Hemings would have a daughter and several granddaughters called Thenia in Jefferson's records, a diminutive of Parthenia. In the marriage settlement between John Wayles and Martha Eppes, the five female slaves given to Martha by her father are mentioned in the same order in which they appeared in Francis Eppes's will—Jenny, Aggie (now spelled with an *ie*), Sarah, and Dinah. The slave Judy, whose name appears between Aggie and Sarah, is rendered as Judah. Several other names were added in the next line of the will, "Kate, Parthenia [now spelled with an *i*], Betty and Ben, a boy."[21]

Just which of these women was Elizabeth's mother? When preparing his will giving Elizabeth Hemings to his own daughter Martha, John Wayles makes clear that Elizabeth was the "Betty" referred to in the property settlement when he married Martha Eppes. Elizabeth must have been the daughter of one of the Eppes slaves given to Martha, as she had evidently not been born yet when the will was written. That the Eppes-Wayles marriage settlement lists these new names along with the five enslaved women given to Martha in her father's will suggests that in the years between 1733, when Francis Eppes willed the slave women to his daughter, and 1746, when the settlement was drawn, these women had given birth. Some, if not all, of the added names may represent their children who by law would automatically have belonged to Martha as well.

Given the uniqueness of the name, and the prevalence of its diminutive in Elizabeth Hemings's family, it seems very likely that Parthenia, whose

"increase" Francis Eppes said should be divided between his two daughters, was related to Elizabeth. She may, in fact, have been her mother. The
provisions of his will indicate that Francis Eppes IV was a hard man. He
clearly had no compunction about separating mothers from children to
achieve some sort of parity between his own offspring, as sections of his
will make clear. He wanted to be fair to each child (but with a tilt toward his
sons), down to the number of "silver spoons" and "feather beds."[22] Indeed,
that was apparently the reason for having Martha and Anne Eppes share
Parthenia and two other male slaves. They appear at the end of the section
of the will as if Eppes had been rounding up a sum of money. He knew that
to give Parthenia to one daughter would be giving that daughter a bonus.
Parthenia would have children who would always belong to her owner, while
Will's and Argulas's children might not, if the males were to have children
with a woman owned by another. Eppes's resolution—sharing Parthenia
and her increase—contained a built-in cruelty, for while Parthenia could
not be in two places at one time, she could have children who could be
divided between two sisters, thus separating mother from children and siblings from one another. This outcome was avoided by means of partition,
with Parthenia going to Martha, and the other two slaves to her sister Anne.
Whatever her mother's name, any tussle over young Elizabeth Hemings
occurred between Captain Hemings and some member of the Eppes family, not John Wayles. The Eppeses resided at Bermuda Hundred, in the
immediate vicinity of Williamsburg. It was there that Elizabeth Hemings
was most likely born.

The Eppeses

Elizabeth's owners, the Eppeses, were among the earliest arrivals to Virginia
from their native England. The founding settler, Francis, served on the Council
of Virginia in the 1630s. The family took up residence along the James and
Appomattox Rivers in Henrico County, which would later be divided in two,
creating a new county called Chesterfield. Like other arriving families of the
day, the Eppeses achieved large landholdings through the headright system, a
scheme designed to stimulate immigration to Virginia.[23]

   In the beginning years of the colony, when the experiment seemed in
danger of failure—with immigrant indentured servants dying of disease at
alarming rates, starving, or being killed by Native Americans who resented

the encroachment on their land—the owners of the Virginia Company decided to take drastic measures to get bodies into the colony to do productive work. Throughout the seventeenth century and into the beginning of the eighteenth, anyone who paid his way or for passage of other immigrants to Virginia received fifty acres of land for each person, hence the term "headright." For a time, people received headrights for bringing in African slaves.[24]

Francis Eppes obtained seventeen hundred acres of land under this system, giving his family a valuable head start in the emerging colony.[25] As the years passed, members of the clan followed the standard practice of elites the world over, marrying into other families of similar "rank," or sometimes even their own cousins. These unions further concentrated landownership within the small planter elite, although by the middle of the eighteenth century the Eppeses were no longer at the forefront of Virginia power and society. With the greater amount of land came the greater need for hands to work the fields of tobacco that quickly emerged as the colony's lifeblood. Until a population bust and improved economic prospects in England dried up immigration, white indentured servants provided the bulk of the work. The expansion of the slave trade provided a new labor source. In this way those who would later be called the first families of Virginia became enthusiastic promoters and beneficiaries of African slavery.

Because there was no grant of land at the end of the indentured servant's tenure, the Virginia system led to huge inequities between families like the Eppeses and the average Englishmen and Englishwomen who came to the colony. By the beginning of the eighteenth century, the Virginia elites had taken the best land for themselves, leaving the former indentured servants land poor and resentful. Inequalities of class proved the source of great tension in the colony, fostering instances of rebellion great and small. These tensions were buried when race entered the picture as the prime dividing line for status within the colony. There would be no alliance between blacks and lower-class whites, who each in their own way had legitimate grievances against their overlords. Instead, poor whites, encouraged by the policies of the elites, took refuge in their whiteness and the dream that one day they, too, could become slave owners, though only a relative handful could ever hope to amass the land, wealth, and social position of the most prominent members of the Virginia gentry, who gained their place early on and would keep it for decades to come.

By the time Elizabeth's owner, Francis Eppes IV, took his place at the family seat in Bermuda Hundred, this group had firmly established an identity and way of life. Determined to smooth out the rough edges of their origins, they aspired to gentility. They built fashionably large houses, spent their leisure time visiting other members of their social set, and attended hunting parties and horse races. Members of the Eppes family, in particular, were known for their fondness for horse racing. In sum, the Eppeses and their cohort sought to reproduce the accoutrements of upper-class life in England—to the extent that could be done in the still feral wilderness of Virgina.[26]

But Virginia was not England. It was a frontier society, complete with an inhospitable terrain and an often hostile native population that the colonists felt had to be conquered or removed. Upper-class Englishmen could dominate ordinary people who at least looked like them, who spoke the same language, and who, for the most part, had religious traditions they could understand. Imagine the scene. Virginia's soi-disant elite imported thousands of people who looked nothing like them, spoke foreign languages, and had cultures and religions that white Virginians could never have truly comprehended. The colonists knew exactly what it took to bring these people to their shores, into their fields, and into their homes. Theirs was a society built on and sustained by violence, actual and threatened. The Eppeses and their kind thus led a fragile existence among people they had to subdue, uncertain whether that job could ever really be done.

This was the hostile world into which Elizabeth Hemings was born. Besides the story of a tug-of-war between her father and her owner, no other details of Elizabeth's earliest years at Bermuda Hundred survive. That story and what we know of her subsequent history suggest that her life as a slave who worked primarily in the house began during childhood, establishing a pattern for her family that would extend well into the nineteenth century.

The house where Elizabeth worked as a child no longer stands. The Eppes family seat became Eppington, a structure built by Francis Eppes VI in 1766. That residence would play a recurring role in the lives of Elizabeth and her children as they lived there off and on even after the family was moved permanently to Monticello. We do not have physical evidence of what young Elizabeth's immediate surroundings were like, but given her owners' wealth and prominence, in that very status-conscious environment, they would have built a home suitable to persons of their station.

Before they were sent "into the ground" to cultivate tobacco or whatever crop their owners chose, or before they took their places as servants in the house, young slave girls were often used to serve as companions or play-mates to the master's children, to run errands, or to watch over other slave children while their mothers worked in the fields. Their experiences and duties varied according to the material circumstances and needs of their owners, their mothers and fathers having no capacity to override the own-ers' control over their children's lives. Elizabeth, after being taken into the "great house," apparently never made the transition to fieldwork. Instead, she began a life that would require daily interactions with and the immedi-ate service of whites. She would come to know, indeed have to know, white people in ways that slaves more isolated from them would not.

We can only wonder what this might have meant to the development of Hemings's attitudes about herself and her place in life, understanding that it must have meant something. There is some evidence from the actions of her children and grandchildren that the Hemingses saw themselves as a caste apart. Whether this was an idea born in their individual generations or whether the seeds were planted when Elizabeth, because of her mixed-race status, began to live a life different from that of other slaves cannot be known. We do know that at every stage of her existence Elizabeth Hemings ended up being singled out for special consideration.

One obvious aspect of Elizabeth Hemings's story often gets lost in deal-ing with the gravely serious issues of slavery and race, and that is the issue of how she looked. Superficial as it is, appearance matters; and it matters even more for women—it probably mattered as much in the eighteenth century as it does today. The only physical description we have of Elizabeth Hemings is that she was a "bright mulatto" woman. But descriptions of several of her daughters and granddaughter refer to them as having been extremely attractive women. White men said this as well as black men. Elizabeth herself was able to attract males of both colors well into her for-ties, when by the standards of that day she would have been considered relatively old. Saying that whites reacted to Elizabeth Hemings in a particu-lar way because she was mixed race, and thus physically more familiar to them, may not do justice to all that was going on with her. Not all mixed-race women would have been considered attractive. If Hemings, as a child and later as an adult, was seen as pretty, that might also account for the way people reacted to her, and not only in a sexual sense. Being pretty, of course, would not have made her free, nor would it have made those who dominated her life see her as an equal human being. Those truths, however, are not the only criteria for considering the important influences in her life.

While work shaped the daily routines of slaves, and a few like Elizabeth were "favored" in some sense by their masters, being considered property made all slaves' lives inherently unstable. Designating an item (of whatever form) as property gives the owner the right to use, sell, and prevent others from having access to that item. Whim, caprice, careless indifference, cruelty, grim determination, self-centered passionate attachment—every emotion or thought that owners can have about their property ranged over the lives of Elizabeth and other enslaved African Virginians. They, this inappropriate property, responded as best they could within the small spaces their circumstances allowed, but the regime of private property set the tone, pace, and progress of their lives. When a master died, when one of his children got married, when a creditor had to be paid, a slave's life could be transformed in an instant. Husbands were separated from wives when they were given as wedding presents. Slave families, assets in the hands of executors, were often scattered to the four winds to pay off a decedent's debts. All of these things would touch the lives of various members of the Hemings family for more than a century. But one, the marriage of John Wayles to Martha Eppes, would turn out to be the signal event in the young life of the African and English woman who was to become the family's matriarch.

2

✿

JOHN WAYLES: THE IMMIGRANT

ELIZABETH HEMINGS LEFT her childhood home at Bermuda
Hundred in 1746, when Martha Eppes married a prosperous English
immigrant named John Wayles. As a woman of the eighteenth century, Eppes became a feme covert when she married Wayles—a wife under
the cover of her husband, who gained the right to control her property,
among other things, in return for his protection.[1] Wealthy families very
often had great concerns about losing property that could have been in
the family for generations simply because one of its female members got
married. Marriage settlements, essentially prenuptial agreements usually
entered into before the couple wed, provided a way out of the bride's and
her family's predicament. The couple, or typically their fathers, negotiated
a contract that allowed the wife to maintain control over specified property
that she held before she married. The prospective bride, in turn, often gave
up the right to the dower interest that would have given her a life interest in
one-third of her husband's freehold estate upon his death.

That was the way Elizabeth Hemings came into John Wayles's household,
as part of the property that Martha Eppes wanted to keep in her family line
even after she married. Some men found these premarital arrangements
vaguely insulting—a hint that they as prospective husbands would not necessarily have their wife's best interest at heart or were incapable of managing
their affairs. One wonders whether Wayles's lower-class origins played any
role in the decision to have a premarital agreement keeping certain Eppes
property in the Eppses' hands. Although he was already wealthy by the time
of his marriage, and had strong connections to an extremely well-regarded

patron, he had no family ties in the colony, a definite drawback in a society run on family linkages and influence. If ever there was a case for a rich and powerful family's reticence about a future in-law, this might seem to be one. Given their relative positions in society, Wayles had more to gain through his alliance with an old Virginia family than he lost by giving up what would be, in the absence of a contract, his property rights as a husband.

As it turned out, Elizabeth's move away from the Eppes family was not permanent. Over the next five decades, she, her children, and even some of her grandchildren returned to them periodically as items of property passing between and among the extended families of the Eppeses, Randolphs, and Jeffersons. Actually, Elizabeth did not have far to go. Her new home, "the Forest," John Wayles's plantation, was in Charles City County, across the James River from Bermuda Hundred.[2] Wayles chose to build his home among the hardwood trees just inland from the banks of the James.

Most prominent planters in Wayles's region built their homes as close to the river as they could, for very good reasons. The James, with its numerous tributaries, meanders before emptying into the Chesapeake Bay, which gives it a direct link to the Atlantic Ocean and the world beyond. The very first settlement in the colony, Jamestown, lay forty miles upriver. The people who lived in the area and knew the river before the white settlers arrived named it after Powhatan, the leader of the powerful Powhatan tribe and the father of Pocahontas, whose name has lived on in history and myth. As the years passed, and the Native Americans were displaced, other settlements and Tidewater plantations stretched out along the river to take advantage of its connection to the bay and Atlantic markets. A similar process unfolded along the Potomac, York, and Rappahannock, three of the other major waterways in Virginia. The waters of all these rivers carried indentured servants, African slaves, and consumer goods into the colony and transported its life-defining staple crop, tobacco, out to foreign markets. Wayles was intimately familiar with all aspects of life on the James. He lived and worked as a lawyer in the area, and it was from Bermuda Hundred that he sometimes carried out one of the most important parts of his life as a businessman—selling slaves.

Elizabeth's move from one home to another in 1746 was symbolic. We would consider the nearly twelve-year-old a child. By the standards of Elizabeth's day, twelve marked the beginning of the end of childhood for most females, but particularly for female slaves whose status as property made the designation "child" short-lived. At the Forest the life Elizabeth would lead as an adult started to take shape. There she continued to serve as a house slave, became a mother to children by a black man, and a mother to children by John Wayles, thus forming blood and family ties that ensured that her father's name would echo across the years. We know nothing of the man, or men, who fathered her first four children. We do, however, know some things about the man who fathered her next six.

Jefferson noted in a family Bible that John Wayles was born in Lancaster, England, on January 31, 1715,[3] but gave no additional information about Wayles's parents or family. Little is known of his early life in England or Virginia. The loss of the official records of Charles City County, along with the loss of Wayles's papers, which were taken to Eppington with his daughter Elizabeth, helps explain the dearth of personal details about him. History books define Wayles solely by what he accomplished in America, as if he had had no life before he arrived, no family, and no parents. If the boy is father to the man, nothing of the boy's life has appeared in print to shed much light on what sort of man he really was. The people who would have known what Wayles's early life in England was like—his daughters Martha, Elizabeth, Tabitha, and Anne—apparently did not write of their father's early beginnings, or, if they did, those writings are not extant or have not been included in historians' writings about the Wayles and Jefferson families. When the issue was addressed at all, the assumption was that Wayles had been trained as a lawyer before he arrived in America. That bit of information, which would tend to point toward an upper- or at least middle-class birth, appears not to have been correct.[4]

On August 14, 1715, "John, son of Edward Wales of Lancaster," was christened in St. Mary's parish. As no other child named John Wales (or John Wayles, as he became known) was baptized between 1712 and 1724 in Lancaster, this record of baptism almost certainly referred to John Wayles of Virginia and confirms Jefferson's notation about his father-in-law's date of birth. Following the pattern common in those days, the record listed only the father's name. In the year before Wayles's baptism, however, the parish records noted the November 11 marriage of "Edward Wales of Lancaster and Ellen Ashburner of Bulk," a small town north of Lancaster. The young couple settled into their married life in the small village, and left no apparent traces of what life was like for them. That they married in the church and had their son baptized there points toward a very conventional

existence for the pair. If Ellen was born in Lancaster, there is no record of
her baptism. Ellen Wales would be memorialized in the names of two of
her son John's great-granddaughters through his white family line, and one
great-granddaughter through his black family line. Edward and Ellen Wales
apparently had only one other child in Lancaster, a daughter, Mary, whose
baptism took place in November of 1718. No other records of children born
to Edward are noted in the parish records.[5]

Whatever the town may be like today, one gets the sense that Lancaster
was a place to be from rather than to run to during John Wayles's early life.
The noted author Daniel Defoe was there in 1726, when Wayles was eleven
years old. He characterized it as a

> country town . . . situated near the River Lone or Lune. The town is
> ancient; it lies, as it were, in its own ruins and has little to recom-
> mend it but a decayed castle, and a more decayed port (for no ships of
> any considerable burthen); the bridge is handsome and strong, but, as
> before, there is little or no trade and few people.[6]

A town with "little or no trade and few people" held no real prospects
for a person as ambitious as John Wayles. This is especially so given that
Liverpool, which Defoe also visited and accurately described as having "an
opulent, flourishing, and increasing trade to Virginia and English colonies in America," lay just to the south. Liverpool, a thriving entrepôt at the
beginning of the eighteenth century, was booming because of the trade
that would help Wayles make his fortune: the transport and sale of African
slaves. Even farther south, London beckoned young people from all over
the country. Slavery, and the staple crops tended by enslaved people, had
created a truly global economy, tying together European, North American,
and African villages in the traffic in human beings. Although Lancaster
may not have been an economic powerhouse during John Wayles's boyhood, it did have a long-standing connection to Virginia, through its
tobacco trade with the colony, which started in the late seventeenth century. Tobacco did not bring prosperity to Lancaster. It was, instead, the
trade in Africans that transformed the place from the somewhat sleepy
village that Defoe described in 1726 into a smaller version of neighboring Liverpool, though Lancastrians came somewhat late to the game. It
was not until 1736, when Wayles was twenty-one, that Lancaster began

its involvement in the slave trade. The *Prince Frederick* sailed to the coast of Guinea, thus beginning a trade that lasted until the first decade of the nineteenth century, during which period Lancaster became the fourth-most-prosperous slave-trading port in England.[7] Although Wayles was in Virginia by the time the Lancaster slave trade was at its peak, he probably knew before he came to America about its ability to make rich merchants out of men who otherwise would likely have been small farmers or artisans. As one observer of Lancaster's society, writing about the men who had participated in the trade, put it, "Here lived the wealthy merchants who flourished, so it is said on the slave trade, and grew rich on their importations of mahogany and rum."[8] Away from his native Lancaster, John Wayles grew rich himself off of Africans. He used them as items of trade, held them in bondage, and mixed his blood with theirs.

Nothing in the record suggests that the Wayleses were prosperous people. The name, spelled with or without a *y*, was not common, and it is very likely that people who shared that last name in tiny Lancaster were related in some fashion. The Wayleses who appear in the public records around the time of John Wayles's early life were definitely what we would call working class, and in some instances they were struggling mightily. In 1719 an Elizabeth Wayles of Lancaster, described as a widow with several unnamed children, was sent to debtor's prison for about two years. John Wayles's father's profession is unknown, but his probable grandfather, also named Edward Wayles, was a butcher who died in 1686. His wife, Elizabeth, handled the letter of administration concerning his property on behalf of their four children: John, Thomas, Edward, and Anne. Neither Edward nor Elizabeth could write, and both signed the testamentary documents with their marks as signatures. Edward Wayles clearly wanted more for his children. In a rare move for his area, he left a bond with instructions to his wife to make sure that his children received as much education as the money would provide.[9]

That John Wayles's life was a version of a rags-to-riches story is further supported by a note appended to an 1839 copy of a Lee family memoir transcribed from a document that William Lee wrote in 1771. Lee, who died in 1795, chronicled the family history, discussing individual members' lives, fortunes, and contributions to society. The note states that Wayles came to Virginia as a "Servant Boy" brought over by a Lee family ancestor, Philip Ludwell, a name renowned in early Virginia history.

More on the back of the paper lent me by Mrs. Lee was written—on
what authority I know not—"The Daughter of a Servant Boy brought
back from England by Philip Ludwell, grandfather of Portia Hodgson,
now living in Alexandria who finding him so Promising that he educated him, gave him a handsome set out in Life, and finally left him
executor to his will, was the Wife of Mr. Jefferson["]

Jefferson married 1772 Martha Skelton, a young beautiful childless widow, daughter & heiress of John Wayles a leading lawyer of
VA-wealthy Veno. Anc.[10]

There were three Philip Ludwells of note in Virginia's colonial period: father,
son, and grandson. The Philip Ludwell referred to in the Lee papers was Philip
Ludwell III, who was born in 1716 and died in England in 1767. Like his father
and grandfather before him, Ludwell III ranked high in Virginia's political
and social hierarchy. The family's connection to William and Mary was close
because his father had been the rector of the college. Ludwell III, who attended
the college and was also on the board of visitors, was in the perfect position
to have furthered Wayles's education. In later years, one of Jefferson's slaves,
Isaac Jefferson, mentioned Wayles in connection with Archibald Cary, a graduate of William and Mary, in a way that suggested that the two men had gone
to school together—"he went to school to old Mr. Wayles." This is a somewhat
cryptic comment, but there was evidently talk within Isaac Jefferson's earshot
of a William and Mary connection for Wayles.[11]

Each generation of Ludwells held a seat on the Council of Virginia.
The first Philip Ludwell had married Governor Berkeley's widow, Frances
Culpepper, thus bringing the well-known plantation Green Spring, about
five miles from Williamsburg, into the family line. It was, evidently, to
Green Spring that Philip Ludwell III brought John Wayles, probably in
the late 1730s after one of Ludwell's trips to England. The *Virginia Gazette*
noted that he had traveled there in 1738, and Wayles once referred to one of
his earliest memories in the colony as having taken place in 1740. Ludwell
was the last of the male line of his family. In the convoluted and circular
world of early Virginia's family life, the Ludwell connection continued into
the next generation when Ludwell's daughter Lucy and her husband, John
Paradise, became friends with Thomas Jefferson (Lucy perhaps too friendly
for Jefferson's tastes) while he was in Paris, France, with Wayles's children
James and Sally Hemings.[12]

The notations to the Lee family memoir are in two separate hands, the last paragraph added at a later date by someone who evidently wanted to give further details about just who the "Wife of Mr. Jefferson" was. The "authority" providing this information was most likely William Lee or one of his children, who were in good positions to know of Wayles's origins. Lee, the father of Portia Hodgson mentioned in the note, married his first cousin Hannah, the daughter of Philip Ludwell III. William Lee's mother, also named Hannah, and Philip Ludwell III were siblings. William Lee lived with his uncle Philip in London during the early 1760s. He was so devoted to him that he urged his own son, William Ludwell Lee, to drop the Lee name to preserve Ludwell for future generations. After Ludwell died, William married Ludwell's daughter, and took charge of handling his father-in-law/uncle's business affairs from London. He knew all the executors of Ludwell's will—Wayles, Robert Carter Nicholas, Richard Corbin (related to the Lees by marriage), and Benjamin Waller. Indeed, Lee corresponded with Nicholas about various aspects of Ludwell's business affairs in the years immediately following his death. It was, most likely, William Lee who arranged to have Ludwell's will probated in England in 1767. After years in London, he returned to America in 1783 and became the master of Green Spring, living there with his son and daughters until his death. It would have been entirely natural for him to have mentioned to his children the link between Jefferson, by then a national figure, and their family.[13]

The references to Wayles appear in papers that were in the possession of the Lee family, with whom Jefferson had both bad and good relations. But they were really not about him. The information was included in the story of the Lees in order to memorialize one of their ancestor's very decent and worthy contributions to an important aspect of "Mr. Jefferson's" life in a way that put both Ludwell and Wayles in a good light. Though just a "servant boy," Wayles deserved to be elevated: he had shown great promise and was extremely intelligent. Moreover, the Lee ancestor was astute and good-hearted enough to discern and want to cultivate that promise. The clear message is that, had it not been for Philip Ludwell III, there perhaps would not have been a John Wayles in America who was able to develop his talent and become prosperous enough to overcome his origins and produce a daughter for "Mr. Jefferson" to marry.

There was, quite simply, no more influential a man whom Wayles could have had as a benefactor than Philip Ludwell. Who but one from the highest ranks of society could have lifted him from the position of servant to a place where he could be the executor of Ludwell's will, sharing that role with men who held extremely important positions in their society: Corbin, "his Majesty's Receiver General," Nicholas, "Treasurer of Virginia," and Waller, who had represented James City County in the House of Burgesses and became the clerk of the General Court. Wayles must have been impressive, indeed, to have been given the chance to join men like that, although it has to be noted that, unlike those other men, he never held a position of public trust in his community. Instead, he worked with them to take care of Ludwell's interests in Virginia after Ludwell decided to return to England permanently following his wife's death, at the end of the 1750s. He and the other executors were to be the guardians of the Ludwell girls if they decided to return to America before they came of age.[14]

Several letters between Ludwell and Richard Corbin describe his partnership with "Mr. Wayles" on Ludwell's behalf, usually overseeing the sale of tobacco. Corbin told Ludwell when he would be meeting "Mr. Wayles at Green Spring" to discuss business matters, and at one point he felt obliged to apologize after he "and Mr. Wayles" had made an "unlucky mistake" when handling a shipment of tobacco that had caused Ludwell to lose money. He assured Ludwell on behalf of both men that "an error of this kind [would] not happen again." After Ludwell's death, seven years before the outbreak of the Revolutionary War, Corbin wrote to one of his daughters to tell her, "Mr. Nicholas, Mr. Wayles & myself proved your father's will," noting that "Mr. Waller" had not participated. There had been some disagreement about timing and process, and Waller wanted to take more time.[15]

When Wayles ceased to be connected to Ludwell's household and started his career is unknown, but he made reference in a letter to traveling to other homes in the Williamsburg area in 1740.[16] By this time Williamsburg had been the seat of colonial government for forty-two years. About five miles from Jamestown, situated between the James and York Rivers, Williamsburg was originally called Middle Plantation. In the earliest days it served mainly as an outpost that the settlers retreated to whenever they were attacked by the Native Americans upon whose land they were encroaching. As early as 1677, the year after participants in Bacon's Rebellion had laid waste to "the state house and all other buildings at Jamestown," Middle Plantation was proposed as an alternative to Jamestown as the seat of government. Another twenty-one years passed before that happened. In the intervening years work began on the establishment of the "free school and college" that became the College of William and Mary.[17]

When the statehouse at Jamestown burned again in 1698, Governor Francis Nicholson suggested, and the assembly approved, the transfer of the capital from Jamestown to Middle Plantation with the new name Williamsburg. One additional impetus for the move was "Middle Plantation's exemption from mosquitoes," which had plagued the settlers in Jamestown, an almost sea level swamp whose miasma took the lives of scores of immigrants before they figured out that it was not the healthiest place to settle. Unlike other parts of "Eastern Virginia," Williamsburg with its higher elevation and different climate was said to be "wholly free from the pests."[18]

The Williamsburg that Wayles encountered in the 1740s would certainly have been primitive by the standards of London. Even when Jefferson arrived there in the 1760s, the dirt roads tended toward dustiness or muddiness, depending upon the season. Most of the housing stock in the town was made of wood and painted white, although numerous buildings—the courthouse, prison, and some churches, as well as the residences of a few prominent people—were made of brick. All in all, the town was said to have made a "handsome appearance" and was considered by some a good place to live. It boasted a thriving merchant class and a vibrant commercial district, and a number of upper-class families made their homes there.[19]

William Gooch, already thirteen years into his twenty-two-year tenure as the governor of the colony, was well liked and respected by the inhabitants. The functions of government worked well for that period with the General Assembly, a legislature consisting of the House of Burgesses, comprising representatives elected from each county, and the Virginia council—twelve men from prominent families appointed by the king. True to its role as the seat of government, Williamsburg thrived on the presence of government officials and lawyers. Though the resident population of the town was around two thousand, it could rise to twice that whenever members of the assembly arrived to do business and when the courts were in session during the spring and the fall. Court days, especially, were times of great activity and importance, settling the affairs of individuals and reinforcing within the community at large a particular conception of the rule of law and order in that emerging society.[20]

Except for the symbols of royalty that were part of the day-to-day scene in Virginia—having a royal governor and references to a "king"—much about this world would seem familiar. The town had a college, the symbol of the will to and respect for education, a courthouse at which lawyers and litigants gathered before magistrates to provide for the orderly settlement of disputes, a governmental structure made up of an executive, a legislature, and courts—these are things that exist in the modern world. In fact, we pride ourselves on our present-day connection to these institutions and ideas, suggesting that they have helped create the best that we are today. There were, however, other features of the Williamsburg of John Wayles's day that seem to belong to a different world.

The most striking aspect of Williamsburg that a traveler from modern times would note is that it was home to large numbers of enslaved people of African origin. Though the laws of Anglo-Virginians dominated, the face of Africa was as prevalent as the face of Europe. Afro-Virginians made up fully half of the town's population, along with a small handful of free, often mixed-race men, women, and their families. These people, enslaved and free, performed a variety of tasks that put them on display as integral parts of the community. Walking through the streets of Williamsburg, Wayles encountered black people who were coopers, carpenters, blacksmiths, agricultural workers, and household slaves going to the market. Some of those blacks were born in America and spoke English as their native tongue. A good number of others had come from Africa, bearing the facial markings of their particular ethnic group, still speaking their native language to their fellows who knew it, while at the same time learning to speak the language of their Euro-American captors.

On court days, as an observer and participant, Wayles saw Afro-Virginians as the subjects of contract disputes between businessmen, as items of property fought over in contests over wills, on rare occasions as petitioners for their freedom, and as defendants in criminal actions that for whatever reason could not be handled by the plantation justice of an individual master. He knew that these people were the objects of law, but also outside of it in every way that counted.

Wayles could stand in Market Square and observe, or even participate in, public auctions of enslaved black people—some newly arrived from Africa or the West Indies, others who would be sold as "Virginia-born." Perhaps he walked past homes where sales of blacks were carried out. In March of 1744 "at Mr. Vope's door in Williamsburg," a "young Negro wench perfectly well qualified for all sorts of House-work" was to go on sale. At the same event a "young Negro Fellow who under[stood] driving a chariot, and [was] most careful handling horses," was to be offered for sale along with the horses for him to handle. In 1745 "a Parcel of Negroes, being about 16 Men, Women and Children," were to be sold by John Brodie "at John Taylor's house in Williamsburg." These scenes played themselves out on a daily basis.[21]

In short, John Wayles had come to a world that held out the promise of enormous wealth and prestige for a few whites and was for blacks something of a living hell. No man in his position could have been more fortunate. He lived in the midst of, participated in, and benefited from what would become the largest forced migration in history—one that created a slave society that lasted another century and a quarter and a racial hierarchy that has yet to be fully undone.

John Wayles was thirty-one when he married Martha Eppes, the same age as Peter Jefferson when he married Thomas's mother. Both men evidently wanted to establish themselves before they took on the important role of husband. Wayles was already a member of the establishment by the time he married, for he had been admitted to practice in the county courts in April of 1741, just a few years after his arrival in the colony.[22] This fits very much with his son-in-law Thomas Jefferson's description of him as an amiable man who flourished in his law practice, not because of his intellectual command of the law, but because of his hard work and appealing personality. Having Philip Ludwell in his corner was actually the main thing. We see some of Wayles's disposition and the way in which he gained acceptance in his surrounding community in the letters of Maria Byrd to William Byrd III in which she refers to Wayles's efforts to find suitable speakers for their church. In a 1760 letter Byrd wrote, "Mr. Wayles is extremely kind in doing what he can in that respect, he has engaged Parson Masson already and designs likewise to get Parson Duglish, he says to make us laugh."[23] Byrd also noted that attendance at church had been falling off and that Wayles and "Co. Harrison" and "Will Randolph" were making efforts to get "Parson Kenney" to come to preach. Wayles's and Byrd's interactions at church were apparently commonplace. In the preceding year she reported that during the "very last Sermon Sunday Wayles comes to our pew before Church began & says Madam I give you joy of Mr. Byrd's being made Governor of Pittsburgh."[24]

Though Wayles's supreme act of reinvention has become the quintessential American story, he effected this transformation long before Americans started glorifying such feats. The preference for leaders born in log cabins, or from otherwise humble origins, came into vogue during the age of Andrew Jackson, who ushered in the era of the common man. With the support of a prominent mentor and the sheer force of his personal will, Wayles made a place for himself in Virginian society that he could never have made in Lancaster.

Will alone is not enough. One must have the opportunity to exercise it. Virginia's burgeoning commitment to slavery, driven by the tobacco economy, created the environment that gave Wayles the chance to make his fortune. He was very much involved in all parts of the institution, from its most public aspects to its more hidden and private ones. Regarding the public face of slavery, not only did Wayles own slaves himself to work on his farms, but he also served as a broker who helped others buy slaves. He acted as a plaintiff's attorney in a case that divided slaves among several members of a slave-owning family. He served as executor for a number of estates in which slaves were sold to pay debts. Numerous ads in the *Virginia Gazette* of the 1760s track his activities along these lines. His name appears most often for domestic sales of slaves in which he and other lawyers represented clients who wanted to sell their human property.[25]

Advertisements for sales of newly arriving Africans list two names— Wayles and Richard Randolph—and near the end of Wayles's life, the two were agents for John Powell & Co., an outfit that regularly imported slaves directly from Africa. Even though Virginia was dependent upon slaves, slave traders were generally looked down upon in society. Although southern slave owners went into the market to buy slaves, they wanted to draw a firm distinction between acquiring slaves in that manner and taking them by force from the shores of Africa. Obviously, if there had been no slave trade from Africa, there could have been no sales of Africans in Virginia. Despite that reality, the trade was portrayed as a singularly awful business. Whatever stigma may have attached to slave trading, the commissions that agents could earn on these types of transactions were large enough to overcome any sense of shame, if that was ever really an issue.

Being the agent on consignment arrangements also carried a built-in hazard that was not merely psychological. "Selling agents" like Wayles and Randolph "were expected to guarantee payment from the buyers of slaves consigned."[26] They would be on the hook should anything go wrong and were therefore exposed to potentially catastrophic liability. That very thing happened in the years just before Wayles's death. He and Richard Randolph secured a loan from Farrell & Jones, a British merchant house with which they had dealings that enabled them to play their designated role in one of these transactions, bringing slaves over on a ship called the *Prince of Wales*. Indeed, the firm had suggested the two men as agents on the deal. When Wayles died in 1773, in the midst of a deep depression in Virginia, none of the money for the slave sales—almost seven thousand pounds sterling— had been sent to John Powell & Co.

Most of the buyers that Wayles and Randolph had lined up had bought the enslaved people—who numbered 400 when the ship set sail, but only 280 by the time it arrived—on credit during a period when economic times were flush. They expected to be able to pay Powell in tobacco. When that market collapsed in the early 1770s, their tobacco became nearly worthless as payment for the slaves, and many farmers did not want to ship their crop when the price was so low. At that point Farrell & Jones stepped in to pay the amount and then sought repayment from Randolph, as the surviving "partner" of Wayles. Randolph's inability to meet the obligation set in motion a lawsuit that continued long after his death. Farrell & Jones came after both men's estates for indemnification, eventually obtaining a smaller judgment from Randolph's. But these contretemps all took place after Wayles's death. In life Wayles benefited enormously from every aspect of the institution of slavery.[27]

Wayles's appointment as Farrell & Jones' agent in February of 1763 further cemented his place in his adopted society.[28] To say that he was an agent does not adequately convey a sense of the role he played in the Virginia society of his time for it suggests an individual arranging deals between eager planters and willing British houses. That was part of it, but an agent had another role, one that may be more suggestive of Wayles's capacities and personality: he was a debt collector. That was no small task, for debt was a way of life in Virginia. Over the course of Wayles's career in the colony, planter indebtedness to British merchants grew to such enormous heights that some scholars have suggested it as a chief catalyst for the Virginia colonists' decision to break away from the British Empire. Whether it was the chief reason or not, the terms of repayment of debts incurred during the pre-Revolutionary period were without question a sore point for the colonists and remained so well after the birth of the United States.

John Wayles was at the center of this commercial maelstrom. It was his job to make sure that planters paid their creditors. How did he do this?

Wayles did not just sit at the Forest and issue dunning letters. He went out to meet the planters at their homes and at other venues—catching up with them during court day—to ask them face-to-face, "When are you going to pay Farrell & Jones?" We get a glimpse of Wayles at work in a letter to the firm in which he describes his efforts on their behalf.[29] The document is worth considering in some detail for the insight it provides about the character of the man who fathered Elizabeth Hemings's children and about the world in which he moved.

In this letter Wayles ticks off the names of debtors, one by one, offering sometimes acerbic assessments of their personalities, along with evidence of his implacability in the face of their evasions. Thomas Mann Randolph, whose son would one day marry one of Wayles's white granddaughters, had "gone to some Springs on the Frontiers to spend the Summer," thus escaping a Wayles collection visit. Wayles was not letting the matter rest. He went on, "But as he [Randolph] has altered his Port I shall endevor to make Lidderdale pay the Debt." Of Carter Harrison, "Next month I shall go up Country and make it my business to settle Carter Harrisons Affair as you desire. You are not to be Surprized at his selling his tobacco this Year & disapointing the Ships, because the Man is Acting in Character."[30]

The estate of Benjamin Harrison owed money. When a family member was addressed about the debt and promised to "discharge it soon," Wayles showed benevolence, promising, "I shall Apply to him Differently." How did he originally plan to apply to him? Another member of the Harrison family proved more problematic: "As to Nat. Harrison, I have wrote more Letters & made more Personal Applications for so small a Sum, then I ever did to any other Gentleman. This family is somehow or other so connected with your other Friends, that, where the debt is not in danger, indulgences are unavoidable, They require more then other People, & therefore on that Score are less desirable correspondents."[31]

Wayles goes on and on in this vein. He suggests that one planter, Robert Ruffin, acting as a surety for Archibald Cary's debt to Farrell & Jones, tricked him into taking some bonds as his payment for the obligation. Wayles took the bonds "without having time in the Hurry of Court to examine the Obligors, the Securitys, & c." It turned out that the obligors on the bonds were "people . . . [who] lived on the Borders of Carolina." He estimated that "it would take 7 years to Collect" on them and then at a reduced rate. The attempt to return the bonds, Wayles complained, "Occationed me much Vexation, besides two Rides up to his House before I could meet with him to Re-deliver the Bonds." Wayles persisted so tenaciously that Ruffin agreed to take them back only when Wayles promised "not to distress him" further until he had heard something directly from Farrell & Jones. "So much for gratitude," Wayles said. Later when he tried to get Ruffin to buy some tobacco, he (Ruffin) "had not Spirit to Risque a shilling." Wayles final assessment of the planter?—"a skin flint in every sence of the word."[32]

This was hardly a job for just any man. Imagine his son-in-law Jefferson in that role! Wayles must have been incredibly aggressive and assertive to endure in his position, hounding and no doubt provoking the enmity of some members of a planter class, many of whom were mired deeply in debt. Some of these men were from the oldest and most powerful families in the colony and, as Wayles suggested, were all connected to one another by blood or friendship. They were inclined to help one another out against their common antagonists, Wayles and people like him. They would not have seen Wayles as their kind.

Take the example of Richard Hanson as a comparison. After the American Revolution, Hanson acted as a Farrell & Jones postwar "John Wayles," with responsibility for collecting Virginia's prewar debts to the firm. Hanson, an old business partner of Wayles's, was a much reviled figure. Granted, the new Americans may have seen Hanson as a symbol of the country from which they had just won independence. And here he came reminding them that that was not the end of the story. Fair or not, debt collectors, in any era, seldom engender warm feelings. Jefferson said that Hanson's form "haunted [him] nightly."[33] Wayles must have haunted a few planters' dreams in his time, too.

Wayles's letter hinted at one point that he knew that others looked down on the way he spent his time. He wrote of the arrival of "Mr. John Morton Jerdon [Jordan] & his very Pretty wife" into the colony. Jordan was a partner in Jordan and Maxwell, a tobacco house in England. After noting that Jordan's "retinue is little inferior to any Lord's," Wayles suggested that Jordan was above haranguing individuals to pay their debts. "I believe that he will not Medle with Baker [a local banker] as he had said he should not dirty his fingers with trade. However *that will not throw me off my Guard.* Baker is a Capital Object with me & takes up much of my Attention" (emphasis added).[34] Strictly speaking, Jordan was involved in trade, too, but in his mind (at least as presented by Wayles) at a different, "higher," "cleaner" level. Wayles himself was heavily involved in trade—the tobacco trade and the African slave trade, as dirty a one as ever existed. And he proudly differentiates himself from Jordan as a man without a "retinue," let alone a "Lord's" retinue, saying in effect, "Unlike Jordan, I will ride up to the man's house myself and get the job done. Whatever it takes, I will do."

The record shows that this was the way Wayles approached his business operations. He would do whatever it took. Philip Ludwell must have spotted this capacity in the young man from Lancaster. This is not to say that he would have done anything illegal, but legality aside, one has to have great fortitude to build wealth, as opposed to inheriting it or marrying into it. It helps to be given a stake by a patron, but maintaining one's position and building on it takes effort and commitment. And John Wayles knew how to spot opportunities for building wealth, and he seems never to have hesitated. We see this in another of Wayles's business ventures. Above all else, land was a valued commodity in the colony. The chance to own property was what had impelled thousands of immigrants across the Atlantic to face death and all sorts of hardships. Wayles pursued land as tenaciously and cleverly as he did Farrell & Jones's debtors. The Virginia Land Patent Books from the 1740s and 1750s show how Wayles operated in this arena. He worked Virginia's land patent system to great advantage, amassing thousands of acres over the course of about ten years.

To promote the economic progress of the colony, the crown allowed settlers to purchase land in fifty-acre segments, upon payment of quitrents and with a requirement that the land be cultivated. If the purchaser failed to fulfill these obligations, others who were interested in the land could file suit and take the property. That is how John Wayles acquired much of his land. In the first such transaction Wayles obtained "500 acs" (acres) in Cumberland on "Angola Cr." (Creek) after the named patent holders "failed to pay quitrents and cultivate" the property. "John Wayles hath made humble suit and hath obtained a G. [grant] of the same." That process was repeated for 1,000 acres, again in Cumberland, along "Great Guinea & Angola" Creeks, another 245 acres in the same area, and 400 acres on the "N.side of the Appomattox" River. In one transaction Wayles consolidated several holdings from patent challenges for a total of 3,713 acres.[35] In another he and seven others were given right to "sixty-four thousand acres on the waters of the New River in Augusta below the mouth of the Bearskin

Fork" if they had it surveyed and paid a set amount within three years. In sum, Wayles possessed sufficient ambition and energy to have had his hand in almost every major form of wealth building available in Virginia.

For all of his wealth and participation in economic activities in the Williamsburg area, Wayles seems not to have made a lasting mark on the place. He was there, but not there, in some very telling ways. Informal sketches of life in Williamsburg during his time that discuss the leading lights of the town fail to mention him. Except in connection to his very famous son-in-law, his name seldom appears in scholarly histories of that time either. Granted, he shared the stage with some very impressive people: George Wythe, mentor to Thomas Jefferson, future signer of the Declaration of Independence and holder of the first professorship of law at the College of William and Mary; Patrick Henry, the famous orator and revolutionary; as well as others whose "great family" connections ensured that they would get talked about whether they were truly worth talking about or not. Still, Wayles's few appearances in the historical record of his day suggest that, despite his financial success and his connections to wealthy patrons, he was not considered a full-fledged member of the leadership class.

There are other probable reasons for Wayles's absence from the collective memories of his home territory. First, he had no legitimate sons to carry on his name and business operations. His money, land, slaves, and, most disastrously, his debts would be taken over by the men who married his daughters. Wayles effectively disappeared into a Skipwith, an Eppes, and a Jefferson, although for a time his black and white descendants kept his name alive in the names of their children. In addition to his service as a debt collector, the way he conducted himself as a lawyer may account for his absence from the record. In the eighteenth century, as always, there was some ambiguity about lawyers' place in society. People called upon and admired lawyers when they needed them, but feared and slightly loathed them when they did not. Rightly or wrongly, some practitioners were seen as more inherently respectable than others. There is a hint of this in Jefferson's description of Wayles: he was successful not because of his intellectual abilities and approach to law but because he was an energetic, in today's parlance, "rainmaker." Of all the codas to place on one's father-in-law's career, why that one? It is possible that Wayles was the victim of snobbery because of his lower-class origins and because he was too obviously a striver, more concerned with making money than with seeing law as just another eighteenth-century gentleman's field of scholarly knowledge supplemented by payments.

Wayles did briefly receive a degree of attention in his community, although it was probably not the kind he wanted. For a few astounding weeks in 1766, Wayles's name appeared in Virginia's leading newspaper in connection with a sensational murder case. Wayles represented John Chiswell, who was accused in 1766 of killing Robert Routledge during a quarrel in a Williamsburg tavern. Chiswell was let out on bail, causing a firestorm of controversy among the citizenry who believed he had received special treatment because he was well connected. The case split people along class lines. As the lawyer for the accused, John Wayles, the former "servant boy" turned lawyer, merchant, and trader, was on the side of the grandees.[36]

This already sensational case gained further attention when the president of the Virginia council, John Blair, a man who had twice served as acting governor of Virginia, took to the pages of the *Virginia Gazette* to accuse John Wayles of lying in his deposition recounting the facts of Chiswell's encounter with Routledge. Wayles denied the charge, but Blair and other correspondents who joined in the fray did not back down. Several more items appeared on the subject, with Wayles being parodied in two awful, and largely incomprehensible (for modern-day readers), poems printed in the *Gazette*. Both attack his veracity, one beginning,

> When Judas lavish'd laud on honest Wayles
> Men, laughing, thought they heard Vermillio's tales;
> To him should grateful W——— like praise return,
> Mankind would swear all language forsworn—[37]

A stanza in the other poem is notable for its reference to Wayles's background:

> See Manners beam, from ill-bred Wayles;
> See Manners fraught with fairy-tales—
> The bastard of St. Judas!
> God send that Manners, praising Manners
> (And all who follow Folly's banners)
> Were banish'd to Bermudas[38]

The snide reference to him as "the ill-bred Wayles" suggests that people considered him of lowly birth and were willing to play that card when necessary.

Indeed, the tone of some of the criticism was so contemptuous that one wonders if Wayles's background did not make his critics think they had extra license when attacking him. In one long letter addressed "To Mr. Wayles" and printed in the *Virginia Gazette*, the correspondent, signed "R.M.," ridiculed Wayles's complaint that his reputation was being damaged by Blair's accusation and those of his supporters.

> You are pleased to intimate that your veracity has been called in question, and your reputation like to suffer, by the President's indiscretion.
>
> Pray sir, was your veracity never questioned before? And as to your reputation, would you not be obliged to those who would take away or annihilate it, provided they furnish you with another, as it is not at all probable that you could be a loser by the exchange.
>
> I think it will not be unreasonable to suppose that you will throw abundance of scurrility and abuse (of which you always have plenty at command) about on this occasion considering with what ill manners and disrespect you have treated a Gentleman who I believe deserves the regard and esteem of every honest man in the country, and that is beloved and respected by all that have the pleasure of knowing him, yourself excepted; but men do not expect to 'gather grapes of thorns, nor figs "of thistles."[39]

Wayles's response to the charge that he had lied in his deposition appears in the same edition:

> Out of tender regard to the President, I have long both patiently and silently born the blame of his indiscretion; but for reasons obvious enough, I must beg to be excused from doing it longer, and put the saddle on the right horse.

He also included a letter from Thomas Randolph and Richard Randolph supporting his version of events. He went on to say that he had "endeavoured to express [himself] in the most decent terms" to Blair, showed him what he was going to say about the deposition before he published it in the press, and asked Blair to tell him if anything was wrong with it.[40]

Neither side would relent. Reacting to critical comments about the handling of the Chiswell matter, Wayles, on behalf of the justices who had given Chiswell his freedom, sued William Rind, the editor of the fledgling newspaper who printed some of the negative comments. Wayles lost the suit.[41] Rind's paper had been created to counter what was thought by some in the colony to be the too pro-Royalist tendencies of the Purdie & Dixon *Virginia Gazette*. Ironically, one of the men who urged Rind to start the newspaper (an action he would repeat controversially in a completely different context many years later) was none other than Thomas Jefferson. Six years after this episode, he would marry Wayles's daughter Martha. The whole business ground to a halt when Chiswell committed suicide while awaiting trial.[42] Very soon all references to this matter disappeared from public discussion, at least in the *Gazette*. After all, the Anglo-Virginia colonists had more important things on their minds during the last half of the 1760s, as their relationship with England grew ever more fraught.

3

🌣

THE CHILDREN OF NO ONE

NGLING LAWYERS, INDEBTED planters straining to meet their obligations to British merchants, enslaved Africans struggling to survive the cruel realities of their new home, and Anglo-Virginian colonists beginning to chafe at colonial authority were elements in the world outside as Elizabeth Hemings grew to adulthood in the home of John Wayles. Neither her first home at Bermuda Hundred nor the main house at the Forest still stands. We are left to imagine the kind of shelter Wayles chose to create, keeping in mind that he had every reason to build a home that reflected his much-strived-for station in life. Hemings worked in that house, doing household chores other than cooking, as she was too young for that task when she came to the Forest. By the time she had become an adult, another woman held the position of the Wayles family cook.[1]

Hemings's precise duties are unknown, although it has been suggested—given what happened later in her life—that she served as a nurse or "minder" of Wayles's daughter Martha. Martha was born two years after her parents' marriage, a year after her mother had given birth to twins who did not survive. As it has been for most of human history, childbirth was a dangerous event for women. In 1748, several weeks after bearing her daughter, Martha Eppes Wayles died.[2] A young enslaved girl who was used to working in the house would have been considered suitable for the task of looking after a young child, or at the very least for helping an older woman do it.

Whatever her early duties at the Forest, Hemings took on another role five years later, in 1753: motherhood. She gave birth to her first child, a daughter named Mary, when she was eighteen years old. After Mary came Martin in

1755, Betty in 1759, and Nancy in 1761. There is reason to believe that she had a daughter Dolly in 1757, who never resided at Monticello. The father of her first children, one described in later years as a "darker" mulatto was apparently a black man, though no record of his name or status has been found. Family tradition from one of Mary Hemings's descendants suggests that she may have been the daughter of a white man.[3] Hemings's pattern of childbearing resembled that of other slave women in Virginia. Eighteen was the average age at which enslaved women gave birth for the first time. Whether because of better diet or the lesser demands of cultivating tobacco compared with sugarcane or other crops, Hemings and other enslaved women in North America achieved fertility rates that allowed for the natural increase of the slave population—unlike their West Indian and South American counterparts. In the critical years that Hemings bore her first set of children, Virginia slave owners became able to keep up with the demand for slave labor without importing large numbers of slaves from Africa.[4]

With the decline in new imports from the continent, the multilingual, multicultural world of Elizabeth's African mother began to give way to the culture created by American-born children of slavery. This transformation had lasting consequences for the development of the black community in what would become the United States. The memories of Africa faded more rapidly among blacks born in North America than among blacks carried to other parts of the New World, where the new cargoes of slaves that continued to arrive long after the legal slave trade in the United States ceased in 1808 constantly replenished connections to the African continent.

Hemings's children, who would eventually total fourteen, were one generation removed from their African ancestry. They were in a sense symbolic in that their individual family lines followed nearly all the various trajectories of black life during the eighteenth and nineteenth centuries. Some in those lines would become free well before the end of slavery in America (Hemings would live to see this), whereas others would not. Some, facing the enormity of white supremacy, would reject their African ancestry; others would continue to embrace it. These various pathways were forged out of the circumstances of Elizabeth Hemings's early life.

During the years between 1746 and 1760, Hemings's place at the Forest became firmly established. John Wayles himself gave a small indication that, at least in his eyes and those of his family, her status was in some way different. By the time he wrote his will in 1760, Wayles possessed many slaves, among them Elizabeth Hemings and a woman named Jenney, who came under his control in the marriage settlement between him and his wife. He singled these two women out for special mention in the document, calling Elizabeth Hemings "Betty" and identifying "Jenney" as the cook. Wayles directed that they, along with twenty-three others not named in the will itself, were to become the property of his new wife, Elizabeth Lomax, whom he married that same year, should he predecease her. Upon her death, they were to become the property of his oldest daughter, Martha, who was twelve at the time.[5] That Wayles gave his wife a life interest in Hemings reveals that, while he clearly thought Hemings should ultimately belong to Martha, he was thinking primarily about Hemings's—and the cook, Jenney's—usefulness to his wife, not her present value to his daughter. As far as anyone knew then, Elizabeth Lomax Wayles could have lived for several more decades. In that time Martha would surely have grown up, gotten married, and had her own household, and Hemings would still belong to her stepmother. This indicates that, as of 1760, Wayles did not think there was, or did not care if there was, a close association between his daughter and Hemings. He wanted to provide his present wife with a good housekeeper and cook. His daughter, however, may have had different priorities.

Another item to note about Wayles's will is that he listed Elizabeth with her last name. One of the many ways that slave societies sought to drive home slaves' inferior status was to be careless about the use of slave surnames, signaling that bondpeople had no families that white society had to respect. Like the old practice among some southern whites of taking the liberty of calling every African American woman "Auntie" or every man "Uncle," the carelessness about names, both first and last, telegraphed white privilege. Throughout slavery, whatever whites may have thought, many, if not nearly all, slaves adopted last names that their owners either did not know about or acted as if they did not know or care about. To be sure, there were instances where masters and others did recognize slave surnames, which can be found on planters' slave rolls and in other documents. The origins of these names varied—some came from present or former owners, some were simply self-selected, and others grew out of family relationships.

In European culture surnames signal the paternity of those born in wedlock and those born out of wedlock whose fathers acknowledge them.

Children of unmarried women typically carry their mother's name, which in most instances would have been the woman's father's last name. Enslaved women had no legal marriages, and fathers had no rights to their children, so it seems unlikely that Hemings's African mother had a last name that her white owner felt compelled to recognize and pass down to her daughter.

Given the family's explanation for why it was named Hemings, there is no reason to believe that Elizabeth herself simply plucked the name Hemings out of thin air and John Wayles abided by her decision so surely that he used it in a legal document. The only other slave mentioned in the will, the cook, Jenney, appears without a surname. This is additional evidence that a man named Hemings did acknowledge his daughter and communicated that fact to Elizabeth's original owner. Even though the law did not protect slave families, patriarchal views about family construction evidently influenced the way some masters saw them. If a man acknowledged a child, why not let the child carry his last name, even if it meant nothing legally? Law aside, having a recognized last name evidently meant a great deal to Elizabeth Hemings's family. Sixty-six years after her death, her grandson Madison Hemings would begin his family story by talking not about his African great-grandmother but about the uniqueness of the family's name, taking care to explain how they came to own it.

WITHIN THE DOZEN years following Martha Eppes's death, Elizabeth Hemings saw John Wayles marry and bury two more wives. His second marriage, to Tabitha Cocke, produced three daughters: Elizabeth, who would play a prominent and fateful role in the life of Hemings's daughter Sally; Tabitha; and Anne. After his second wife died, Wayles married Elizabeth Lomax, to whom he was married when he wrote his will, although she died the following year. It was sometime after her death that Wayles took Elizabeth as a "concubine." Over the course of roughly eleven years, they had six children together; Robert, born in 1762, James in 1765, Thenia in 1767, Critta in 1769, Peter in 1770, and Sally in 1773.[6] This set of children represented a further blurring of racial lines, moving branches of the Hemings family tree farther away from the African woman who was by law the reason for their enslavement, toward the Englishman who was the source of their last name. With three white grandparents and one black grandparent, these children were by the racial classification of the day "mulattoes," Virginia laws making no distinction between various gradations of racial mixture. But by a term that gained wider currency and greater meaning in the nineteenth century, these children would be called "quadroons." Their racial classification (legal or biological), however, made no difference to their legal status. Like their "darker mulatto" older siblings, these "bright mulatto" children were born of a slave woman. So they were slaves, too.

It would be very hard to find two people who occupied more vastly different positions than Wayles and Hemings—the prosperous white slave-trading lawyer and the Anglo-African female house slave. Given what we know about their world, the idea that these two would have children together seems utterly banal. Their society was set up for such things to happen, with a much touted, but essentially weak, barrier to prevent it. The pervasive doctrine of white supremacy supposedly inoculated whites against the will to interracial mixing, but that doctrine proved to be unreliable when matched against the force of human sexuality. People are prone to having sex, especially when they are in daily contact with potential objects of sexual attraction. That inclination has permeated every slave society, every frontier society, and every colonial society that has ever existed. Virginia was no exception.

Giving a group of males total dominion over the bodies of a group of females and relying on externally imposed notions of race ("I'm superior to her") and manners ("I'm a gentleman) to prevent them from having sex with those females was always a doomed proposition. That the mixing could be done entirely on the terms of the males, beyond the eyes and the scrutiny of the outside world, only increased the odds that it would happen—either through rape, using outright or implied force, or, in some cases, when the men and women were genuinely attracted to each other.

In all the ways that counted, the Virginia of the eighteenth century was designed to further the interests and positions of men like John Wayles. The opportunity to apply whatever talents he possessed allowed him to make a place for himself that he could never have made in his native England, where neither thousands of acres of land to be parceled out to men of lower or no rank nor a place to exploit the labor of an imported "alien" race existed. Abundant land and African chattel slavery, the engines of Wayles's success, gave him enormous power not only in economic terms but also culturally and socially. One cannot divorce the power to sell a shipload of slaves at Bermuda Hundred from the power to decide what to do with the slaves who are in one's home.

Elizabeth Hemings's place was exactly the opposite of Wayles's. Slavery, white supremacy, and male dominance—indeed, practically every feature of Virginian society—combined to keep her down. Law formed the foundation of this system, and its role in fashioning Hemings's oppression and Wayles's privilege can hardly be overstated. It determined their relative positions during their lives, and, as is often the point of legal rules, its influence has continued down the generations, helping to shape the way Hemings and Wayles are seen to this very day. Specifically, the laws of slavery, of what was called "bastardy," and of marriage set ironclad limits on Hemings's capacity to determine her fate and that of her children. These laws had everything to do with how Wayles and Hemings came to have children together, how the society of their time would protect Wayles in his activities as a slave owner, and how that protective instinct would thrive well beyond his life as a sort of patrimony bequeathed to his legal family and descendants, to be used as they saw fit.

Under cover of the laws of slavery, Wayles could sell slaves, punish them, and make them work for no pay without interference from outsiders. He could have sex with Hemings because she was his property. He could produce children with her who would never be recognized unless he chose to do so. She had no power to challenge this situation formally. Because of slavery and the dominant society's adherence to white supremacy, no one would have believed her had she named Wayles as the father of her children; or, one should say more properly, few if any white people would have admitted belief in her words, especially if Wayles had chosen to contradict them. Doing so would have run counter to one of the chief tenets of Virginia's culture—that the words of blacks could not legally be used against a white person.[7] Thus, blacks were never to be allowed to shape the "official" reality of a white person's life.

The laws and culture of slavery aside, that Hemings was not, and indeed could not, have been John Wayles's wife is also crucial to the way their relationship would be viewed by most people during their time and by many in our own. Under law any child born out of wedlock was considered *filius nullius*, "the child of no one." It was as if the child had dropped from the sky. At the same time, the children of a marriage were presumed to be the offspring of the husband. These were legal fictions and presumptions that deliberately ignored certain unassailable realities: everyone who has ever lived was the child of a mother and a father, a marriage license is no guarantee of biological paternity, and the fathers of children born out of wedlock can actually be known.

The fictions and presumptions about bastardy and marriage served definite purposes in a legal system seeking easy ways to determine who was eligible to inherit property, who had the right to a child's labor, and who could be held liable for support of a child. Efficient as they may have been, these fictions yielded answers that were not always truthful and certainly not always moral. Although they were tailor-made for the needs of the law, and not so perfect a fit for historical or biological conclusions, there is little doubt that they have come to represent what people take to be actual reality. They hover in the consciousness even when outside indicators suggest they should not be relied upon. If by law Hemings's children had no father, as even extralegal convention would have it, John Wayles could not be their father unless he was willing to say he was.

There is a twist. This way of thinking does not apply to the black men who fathered children with enslaved women to whom they could not have been legally married because the absurdity of the fiction as a statement of actual reality would then be too patently clear. Applying the precepts of *filius nullius* to enslaved families would require pretending that from the late 1600s to 1865 no American slave ever knew who his or her father was, an idea that is nonsense on stilts. Why would slaves have known who their fathers were when those men were black, but not know when the man was white? Indeed, if the black man who fathered Elizabeth Hemings's older children had been named, it is a safe bet that no question about his paternity would ever be raised. But when demonstrably mixed-race people speak of their white father or forefather, at most the white man is portrayed as the "alleged" father or the "said to be father," as if there had been some white "Mr. Nobody" ("Mr. *Nullius*"?) out there impregnating all the enslaved women in America. Presenting the life of mixed-race individuals in slavery poses a great challenge precisely because there is such hesitancy about accepting their competence when they explain how they came to be mixed race. The reluctance to accept the prevalence of interracial sex, other than as a generalization, avoids the perceived "cost" or "hazard" of naming a specific white man.

What accounts for this hesitancy? It cannot be the difference in the assessment of the ability to know black fathers versus white ones. That makes no sense. Race is certainly a factor. In a world where even today saying that a white man has black children is the ultimate put-down in some quarters, it is not surprising that some might pause over the claim that a white man in history had done so.[8] One is saying something negative about the man, and there is always a higher standard for saying something "bad" about a person than for saying something "good." Whole black family lines have been erased on that principle. Law, a powerful force, helps along the tendency to protect white slave owners against claims of paternity because it shapes our understanding of reality and what we are willing to accept as reality. People in history who, like John Wayles, were under the law's protection during life tend to remain under the law's protection—statutes, rules, presumptions, privileges, legal fictions, and all. People outside of the law's protection, like Elizabeth Hemings, generally remain outside, particularly when aspects of their lives do not comport with the law's strictures and fictions.

What we have in considerations of white male slave owner's paternity of slave children is a version of Anglo-American law without its usual complement of Anglo-American equity. The doctrines of equity exist alongside law to help mitigate the harsh and unjust results that come from too strict adherence to legal rules. For example, when no formal documents exist to prove that individuals entered into a contract, but the circumstances strongly indicate that an agreement was made and that one party will be severely damaged if the contract is not recognized, equity allows stepping outside formalities to consider other evidence and, when possible, to do justice.[9]

Law, not equity, lay at the heart of the American slave system. Under this regime of law with no equity, John Wayles's power as a slave owner remains as potent as the power he held as a legal husband and father. Slave owners like Wayles, who could force others to see the world through their eyes, virtually guaranteed that their lives and interests would be seen as of paramount importance in the writing of history. And because Wayles was a legally married man—three times—no one would ever think to suggest that the children born of his legal marriages could have been the children of someone else, though that was certainly possible. Even to open that inquiry, other than in the most extreme circumstances, would provoke outrage. Historians might pause at suggesting that a white man might have fathered a child of his own race outside of marriage, a so-called bastard, whom he did not acknowledge. That, too, would be considered a "bad" thing, although one wonders what stake a historian could have in protecting a subject's legal family against what could be legitimate, that is to say, historically and biologically accurate claims established through means other than a marriage license. One can understand a legal family's interest: they want to keep "Daddy" or "Grand Daddy" and his legacy all to themselves. Deeply felt as that desire may be, it simply cannot be taken seriously as a matter of history.

What do we make of this in the context of Hemings's life under eighteenth-century Virginia's system of slavery? We know she lived in a slave society with rules of law specifically fashioned to make possible, and then to obscure whenever necessary, the nature of one group's oppression of another. In ways that should be clear to modern observers, even if it was not to the people of the time, the law in that setting functioned essentially as a racket designed for the protection of whites. How does one begin to get at what was "real" or "true" in such a context? Playing along with the racket is an all too easy, wholly unworthy enterprise because it ratifies the view that "extralegal" blacks, like Elizabeth Hemings, deserve no protection and that "legal" whites, like John Wayles, are to be protected at all costs—even at the cost of all reason. This simply reenacts the world of master and slave in the pages of history. It is only through piercing the veil of southern society's laws, including its fictions about family, that we can take the first step toward getting at the reality of black and white lives under slavery.

The law's protection of John Wayles in his absolute ownership of Elizabeth Hemings rendered his connection to the children she had with him invisible for all official purposes. Nevertheless, law, despite its power, is not the only word on the subject. The children of white men like Wayles who grew up in cohesive family units, often within the household of their fathers, knew who their fathers were in the same way that most people throughout the ages have known, even without the benefit of Anglo-American law. In addition, although white families could hide behind the protections that law and legal fictions afforded, there was still such a thing as the social knowledge of parenthood.

From time immemorial, people have "known" who others' parents were through a variety of extralegal ways, including reliance on a mother's word, observations of physical resemblances that indicate a family connection, interpreting a man's actions toward a set of children and their mother, overall reputation in the community for parenthood—in other words, through indicators that people pulled together to help them make sense of who was who in their world. The day-to-day experiences of life in a community, particularly small ones, give its members information about the nature of relationships among their neighbors. At times even the law (when seeking equity) has looked to these sources in the absence of a legal relationship between a man and a child to make judgments about the likelihood of a family connection.[10]

As Joshua Rothman, a scholar of the operation of social life in Virginia during the eighteenth century, has noted, "interracial sex was ubiquitous in urban, town, and plantation communities throughout the state. Moreover . . . knowledge of precisely who participated in it was widely shared."[11] While some may quarrel with the term "ubiquitous," there is no doubt that sex across the color line was a common part of life in Virginia. What is more, people were inclined to gossip about it. Why is easy to understand. People have always been interested in the lives of others, particularly in matters involving sex. And though some Virginians sought to replicate the lifestyles of the English gentry, they faced special circumstances in one area. Any illegitimate children fathered by an Englishman with a servant girl or other lower-status woman in England would be white. Unless the child looked like the man, his or her existence signaled nothing beyond that fact that they were alive. The presence of a mixed-race child signaled something more; the child all but announced that some white person and some black person had broken the taboo against interracial sex.

Rothman goes on to note, "Virginians, like white southerners elsewhere, tolerated and accommodated a wide array of sexual activity across the color line, ranging from viable and supportive interracial families that bound extended networks of free and enslaved blacks and whites across space and time to family-shattering rapes that exposed the routine abuse, violence, and ruthless power of racial slavery. . . ."[12]

That is not the story most often told about interracial sex in the South. If views about slavery have been frozen in a particular image of immediate pre–Civil War southern society, beliefs about interracial sex during slavery have been heavily influenced by the sexual panic and hysteria of white southerners in the post–Civil War era and well into the twentieth century.

That sex across the color line inspired legal and social opprobrium very early on in Virginia does not mean that there was one, continuing response to it among the citizenry over the course of slavery's existence.

It is often said that though the South lost the Civil War, it won the peace. As many scholars have noted, David Blight with particular force, as a gesture to promote national reconciliation southerners were given almost unfettered power to define their prewar identities and, most devastatingly of all for black people, their prewar identities as well. White southerners declared war on the black people in their midst—ushering in the era of Jim Crow and the terrorism of lynching, as well as other measures that grew out of a determination to reassert control through whatever means available over the people they had once held as items of property. Rewriting the story of slavery in the South was a necessary part of the process.[13]

Southern racial laws and legal opinions, like those in Virginia which had determined whiteness by a formula of fractions—persons who were one-eighth black were legally white—and such evidentiary rules as "white by reputation in the community" fell by the wayside. The "one-drop rule" replaced them. The laws against interracial marriages became more uniform, while interracial sex itself was not outlawed. The historian Charles Robinson cites two reasons for the attention to interracial marriages and cohabitation as opposed to interracial sex. "First, Southern white patriarchs had long enjoyed interracial liaisons. By the time of the Redemption period informal interracial sex constituted a white male privilege. . . . Second, Southern whites focused their attention on formal interracial relationships because of their growing concerns about the effects of black freedom on white supremacy." Sex itself was no threat. Legal marriages, and perhaps common law marriages, might give black partners property and some degree of power.[14] John Wayles's great-grandson Thomas Jefferson Randolph shed light on the differing sexual mores during slavery, insisting in his unpublished memoirs, written after the Civil War, that any married white man who took up with a black woman "lost caste" with his cohort. He made this claim despite the fact that married men in his own family (he purported to identify them) had children with black women and remained respected members of the community.[15]

Randolph's postwar statement dovetails with the prewar assessment of his grandfather Thomas Jefferson's close friend John Hartwell Cocke, who spoke frankly of the ways and preferences of white men in the Old South.

Commenting upon Jefferson's relationship with Sally Hemings in a private diary, Cocke said that Jefferson's situation was common in Virginia: "bachelor and widowed slave owners" often took a slave woman as a "substitute for a wife."[16] There was no suggestion that *unmarried* men lost caste for doing this. His was simply a resigned statement about the way men lived in Virginia's slave society, as they have in every one that has ever existed. John Wayles had done exactly what Cocke described.

This is not to minimize white Virginians' announced hostility toward sex across the color line. It was there. The legal response to it shows that very clearly. But it would be unwise to read late post–Civil War and twentieth-century responses to interracial sex back into the days of John Wayles and Elizabeth Hemings. Theirs was a different time. The forces driving the post-slavery and pre–civil rights response to black people in the South simply did not exist in their age. And there are important reasons why. To expose Wayles, or a man like him, would have required blasting through deeply held beliefs and customs about the sanctity of the right to private property. Who could come to the Forest and inquire about the paternity of the obviously mixed-race children living there? On what basis would they complain? As long as Wayles did not try to elevate Elizabeth Hemings and their children to the status of white people—by going through a marriage ceremony, drawing attention to the children by publicly claiming them as his heirs, or making other public attempts to insinuate them into white society or bestow attributes of white privilege onto them—he would be left alone to do with his property as he pleased. With blacks firmly under the control of slavery, there was no need to interfere with the way planters conducted their lives with the slaves on the plantation. As the historian Philip Schwarz has shown, except in the most extreme circumstances, such as murder or a slave's intrusion upon the interests of a white person other than the master, slave owners in Virginia were the law in their realm.[17]

It is instructive that white Virginians' expressed disdain for interracial sex did not lead them to outlaw it more specifically in the context of the master-slave relationships that so obviously posed the greatest danger for the crossing of racial lines. Had the will of legislators been strong enough, they certainly could have taken such an action. They did not. The difficulty of enforcement does not explain their failure. Laws are sometimes put on the books not for purposes of strict enforcement but as statements about the community's values. Nor does the value Virginians placed on the sanctity of private property provide an adequate explanation. Throughout history even societies deeply committed to the right to property have enacted limitations on its uses when some other important competing interest was at stake. If its members really considered interracial sex so vile and destructive of public morals, the Virginia legislature could have passed laws specifically designed to outlaw interracial sex in the places it most easily thrived—the homes and plantations where Afro-Virginians lived in daily contact with whites.

It seems, then, that hostility toward racial mixing did not constitute an important enough interest to justify meddling with the notion that slave owners had absolute property rights to their slaves. As a result of this determination, the people who ran afoul of the state's laws regulating sexual activity—which pulled in whites who engaged in sex across the color line—were almost invariably members of the lower classes. Lower-class people's overrepresentation in prosecutions involving interracial fornication fueled the shibboleth that only "low status" people engaged in sex across the color line. So might a not very insightful observer conclude. In much the same way, a historian from the twenty-second century who looked back at American society at the end of the twentieth and twenty-first centuries and concluded that middle- and upper-class whites did not take illegal drugs, because the overwhelming majority of people in prison for drug offenses were people of color and lower-class whites, would have missed a central reality of those times. Without understanding that deference to middle- and upper-class whites kept them out of the legal system, and without a commonsense understanding that poor people of color alone could not possibly have supported a multibillion-dollar drug industry in the United States, the truth would have been lost. The response to sex across the color line during John Wayles's time offered Virginia society an extremely useful narrative. Because there was no chance that a slave owner like Wayles could be penalized legally for producing children with his slave Elizabeth Hemings, his activities would never see the "official" light of day. Linking interracial sex with low-class criminality (through legislative choices and in the stories white slave owners told about their world) helped hide the behavior of the "best" of white society.

It is impossible to say exactly when the social knowledge of Wayles's relationship to Elizabeth Hemings and her children entered their community. By the time of the Chiswell affair, Wayles was fifty years old, and

Hemings had given birth to his two oldest sons, Robert and James, who were both under five years old. Public references to Wayles as the father of Hemings's children appeared in a newspaper in 1805, long after his death, and in the reminiscences of Isaac Jefferson, in 1847, and in those of Madison Hemings, a Wayles grandchild, in 1873. In addition, historians have accepted the Hemings-Wayles connection for a variety of reasons that appeared after the time the two were together at the Forest. Specifically, observations of the way Hemings and her children were treated after they came under the ownership of Thomas Jefferson lent support to that conclusion.[18] From the very start, in ways that will become clear in large parts of the rest of this work, Jefferson viewed Elizabeth Hemings and all those connected to her in a light different from the one in which he viewed other enslaved people. Her children by Wayles did not drop from the sky; they were not the children of no one in Jefferson's eyes. His response to them, and the way it set the family's course in life, shows slavery as the immensely tragic and complicated institution that it was.

4

※

THOMAS JEFFERSON

WHEN THOMAS JEFFERSON began visiting the Forest at the beginning of the 1770s, he could scarcely have imagined that the names Jefferson and Hemings would be forever linked in the pages of history. Elizabeth Hemings herself would have found such a possibility unimaginable. Although she knew the role that slaves played in the lives of whites, she would have had no reason to believe that the world might someday pay attention to that. And even if the young man who came courting John Wayles's daughter had any inkling that succeeding generations might know his name, the idea that the names of enslaved people would live on as well ran counter to every tenet of the world he knew. Lower-status people (and slaves were at the bottom of the social strata) were not seen as wielding the kind of influence that would make their lives worthy of notice. Certainly few white slave owners would have acknowledged that those whom they enslaved shaped their lives. Society gave Elizabeth Hemings and her children no power to direct the course of John Wayles's life or that of his white wives and children. Yet their very presence influenced the lives of those around them, and a household that included the master's mixed-race children had issues that were not present in households without them.

Consider Martha Wayles Jefferson's life. She, like her father, remains something of a cipher, a person whose face can exist only in the imagination for, unlike many other women of her class, she did not sit for a formal portrait that remains extant. There is not even a family story (that has been shared with historians) about when and how she and Jefferson met. That they did meet was no surprise. Theirs was a circumscribed world, small enough for the local post office to run a notice in the *Virginia Gazette* like the one in 1767 announcing that "Patty Wayles" (Patty was Martha's nickname from girlhood) had a letter awaiting pickup.[1]

Only one letter from Martha Jefferson's hand survives, along with a set of household accounts that she made as the young mistress of Monticello.[2] We know her chiefly from Jefferson's few references, some brief comments of people who met her as his wife, and the family stories told mainly by a great-granddaughter born decades after she died. Even if there were more written material by or about her, there is virtually no chance that any of it would have ever referred to her mixed-race half brothers and sisters and their mother. Nor is there anything to tell us, for that matter, what she thought of her father, who had brought them into her life. We are left to infer her feelings about her early family life from what we know of the choices she did and did not make, as well as the actions of the man who became her husband. By every indication, Elizabeth Hemings and her children remained close to Martha until her death. She chose to have them around when she could have chosen not to, installing in her own household her father's slave mistress and the children they had together. Jefferson, taking a cue from his wife's responses, kept faith with his wife's choice and continued the connection with the Hemingses until his death.

Martha's soon-to-be husband was no stranger to the ways of life in slave-owning Virginia. Thomas Jefferson was born at his father's plantation, Shadwell, on April 13, 1743, under the Old Style calendar, April 2.[3] His father, Peter, a wealthy man who made a name for himself as a land surveyor and planter, rose to positions of leadership within his community. He was among the first of the group of Virginians who pushed the frontier west, away from the Tidewater plantations near the Chesapeake into the interior. Peter Jefferson, much loved and admired by his first son, died around age fifty when Thomas was fourteen years old.[4] Because of the times he lived in, his discipline, and his business acumen, Peter Jefferson had been able to provide a very privileged life for his family without going into debt, in contrast to many other members of Virginia's gentry. He died leaving assets and no liabilities to his children.[5]

On the other side, Jefferson's mother, Jane, was a Randolph, a family more numerous and socially prominent than the Jeffersons. She lived another nineteen years after her husband and saw her son begin his life

as a public man. Because he did not write about her with the same feeling as he wrote about his father, and because as a teenage boy he reproduced excerpts from poems and other literature that can be interpreted as
hostile to women, it has been suggested that Jefferson did not care very
much for his mother. Fire destroyed his boyhood home at Shadwell, engulf-
ing letters or diaries that may have given a clue about what they meant to
each other. His failure to write about her in any detail in the years after her
death has led one Jefferson biographer to suggest, rather extremely, that
Jane Jefferson was a "zero quantity" in young Thomas's life.[6] He placed the
misogynistic excerpts in his commonplace book at a time when he had not
been out in the world long enough to have gained any creditable knowledge
of the opposite sex.[7] What women did he really know besides his mother
and sisters? He adored his older sister Jane and seems to have gotten on
well enough with his other sisters, leading some scholars to conclude that
the more likely target for his adolescent resentment was his mother.

What the youthful Jefferson chose to put in his commonplace book
probably distorts the view of his feelings about his mother. His relationship with her could indeed have been complicated. But while he was
almost surely angry with her at times (completely natural in any event, but
certainly for a boy trying to carve out a separate masculine identity for himself), that does not mean he did not love his mother deeply. Peter Jefferson
died while Thomas was too young to have begun the process of separation and could more easily stay an idealized figure in his son's eyes. Jane
Jefferson, the parent who remained, may have for a time borne the brunt
of her eldest son's grief at the death of his father. While Jefferson's true
feelings about his mother cannot be recovered through his extant writings
about her, failure to write more, and the snippets of literature he copied
down, his actions are more telling. He lived with her past the age of majority, when he did not have to. When she died, he was physically ill for weeks
with one of his stress-induced migraines.[8] Whatever Jefferson felt about
his mother, there is little doubt that her family name gave him a tremendous advantage in Virginia's pre-Revolutionary society and created connections that would last a lifetime.

To say that Jefferson began life on the frontier of Virginia perhaps creates
a mental image of him in a plainly furnished residence, wearing homespun
clothes, surrounded by enslaved people whose circumstances were only
marginally worse than his own. As Susan Kern has shown, archaeological

work done at Shadwell, combined with her careful look at the family's inventories, and new insights from the work of social historians who have studied the ways of the gentry during Jefferson's early years, indicate that the young Thomas lived a very comfortable existence as one of the wealthier members of his society.[9] Jefferson's tendency toward extravagant living has long been noted, and criticized, by some of his contemporaries and, later, by historians. He clearly wanted, and expected to be able, to live in a beautiful environment, filled with beautiful objects and rarefied things. That habit of a lifetime began early.

Though the main house at Shadwell was not very large and in no way rivaled the house his son would build and call Monticello, or some other Tidewater plantation houses, in terms of size, it was "fashionable" in that Peter Jefferson designed it for the kind of entertaining and presentation that socially prominent families of the period thought necessary. He could accomplish this because the Jeffersons, though located on a frontier, really did not live in isolation. Their home on the Rivanna River gave them direct access to overseas markets, both for shipping tobacco and for acquiring consumer goods, and they took full advantage of their position. Indeed, Peter and Jane Jefferson filled their home with fine linens, silverware, and furniture ordered from well-known merchants. The couple bought cloth imported from "England, India, and Ireland" and shoes from England for their children, and had their clothes handmade by tailors, thereby developing in their son an aesthetic sense that he carried with him all his life—how things looked mattered a great deal to him.[10]

Not only did the Jeffersons consume like wealthy people; their attitude about work mirrored that of the wealthier class. While Jefferson's mother and sisters had spinning wheels and sewed, they did not, as did some other plantation mistresses, take primary responsibility for sewing clothing for the family's slaves or even knitting their own family's stockings. They paid other women in the community to do this work, apparently reserving their womanly skills with the needle and wheel for largely recreational purposes.[11] As an elderly man, Jefferson recalled that his first memory was of being handed up on a pillow to be carried by a slave on horseback.[12] Early in their lives, each of the Jefferson children received an enslaved child to serve as a personal attendant, establishing Thomas's lifelong habit of associating with blacks in the most intimate circumstances. In a letter to a boyhood friend, Thomas, after noting that it was late and that his candle was about to go out, mentioned casually that his "boy" had gone to sleep and that he was about to do the same himself.[13] He could well have been referring to Jupiter Evans, born the same year as he. Susan Kern has suggested that an enslaved woman probably served as a wet nurse to the infant Thomas. Evans's mother is a likely candidate. Isaac Jefferson referred to this as being "one year's child" with another infant.[14] Jupiter played the role of boyhood companion to Thomas until the inevitable time that Thomas began serious preparation for the role he would play in life and Jupiter fell into the role destined for him. An enslaved black woman would have been responsible for the daily care of the Jefferson siblings. From his earliest days Thomas was used to having a black person nurture him, follow him around, give him things, smooth the way, and make sure that the mundane things in life were taken care of so that he could concentrate on doing only those things he cared to do. It turned out that he had a lot of things he cared to do, and his ability to do them derived from his astral talent and tenacity and the enormous reservoir of help (slaves) at his disposal.

Unlike some other sons of the planter class, Jefferson was not sent to study in England, but received the best education that Virginia could offer, and he made the most of it. Ambitious, brilliant, and hardworking a young man as he was, he could not have foreseen the heights to which he would rise, because those "heights" did not exist. Although it was clear by the time he fixed his eye on Martha Wayles Skelton that trouble between Virginia and the mother country loomed on the horizon, he could not have imagined how the struggle would turn out and the role that he would play in it. Even without knowing that, he had every reason to believe in the brightness of his future.

Uncommonly tall, a little over six feet two inches, Jefferson remained slender all his life—one of the overseers at Monticello likened him to a racehorse with "no surplus flesh." His hair was red, but from the descriptions of his sister Martha Carr, James Madison, and Isaac Jefferson, he was "a light red head" with hazel eyes.[15] He had remarkably good teeth for that era, but seldom showed them when smiling, a mark of his reserve in public venues. Though his overall countenance was "pleasant," views differed about whether he was handsome—some people found him very much so, and others, not. The most attractive things about him, and what Martha Wayles Skelton would have seen, were his obvious intelligence, extreme good manners, and capacity to talk with people in ways that set them at ease. As Thomas Worthington, a Jeffersonian Republican who went on to be the first senator from Ohio, put it, there was no requirement for his company other than being polite.[16] His capacity for friendship bound people to him, male and female, but he was especially good at gaining the sympathy of women, perhaps from having grown up chiefly among sisters.

Jefferson possessed a curious and, in the end, enormously creative and effective combination of stereotypically masculine and feminine traits. He was an architect and builder who loved, he said, nothing so much as "putting up and pulling down" and being among, in his son Madison's words, "his mechanics," the people who transformed wood and metal into usable forms and objects.[17] Men of his class often disdained anything that suggested physical labor. But he actually loved the sensation of working with his hands—on his own terms, of course—much like his mother and sisters, who sewed for their own recreation, but were not serious providers of services to their nuclear family or slaves. He made keys, kept his own set of carpenter tools, and occasionally tried his hand at making furniture. His sons Beverley, Madison, and Eston were placed under the tutelage of their uncle John Hemings to become carpenters, the type of "mechanic" with which he most closely identified.[18] A lifelong lover and collector of gadgets and measurer of things, he kept in his pockets a compass and memo pad, which he could take out at a moment's notice and record some observation. A physical man, he loved horseback riding and tests of strength, so long as they did not involve hurting anyone. Like his father, he was inordinately strong for a slender person. And though he never seemed to figure out its exact application to economics, he loved mathematics in his youth and returned to that discipline for amusement as an older man.[19]

At the same time Jefferson was very verbal, a stereotypically feminine attribute. People noticed his facility with language very early in his career, and that talent formed a central core of how people perceived him. He adored words—reading them, exploring their meaning, writing them, and saying them. Although public speaking was not at all his strong suit, his face-to-face conversation impressed with the clarity of his presentation when it did not oppress, for once he became comfortable with people in social settings, he verged, at least in some situations, on chattiness. John Quincy Adams, who dined with him at the President's House during the early 1800s, showed evidence of being worn down by Jefferson's unbidden lectures on wine or on whatever the topic of the evening.

Architecture was Jefferson's "delight," but "music," he said, was "the favorite passion of [his] soul." He eagerly listened to it, played it, and sang. Those in daily contact with him at Monticello said that he sang very well, and did so as a matter of course, without embarrassment—loudly enough for others to hear him as he worked in his bedroom/study or rode his horse, or for the specific amusement of others. One of his overseers remembered that when he was not "talking" he was singing aloud or humming to himself. He played the violin and cello, but he especially liked the violin, practicing for hours at a time as a young man. Though very competent, he was not a natural; he could not play by ear like Patrick Henry, whom he seemed to envy for that ability. The love of music bound him to his future bride, described as accomplished on the pianoforte. Like his love and admiration for woodworking, this other deep passion he passed along to his sons, all of whom played the violin. The youngest, Eston, who also played the piano, was apparently the most talented, for he eventually made a very good living as a professional musician.[20]

When he began to seriously court Martha Wayles Skelton, Jefferson was in his late twenties and just beginning the practice of law. On entering the House of Burgesses in 1769, he became an official member of Virginia's leadership class, though he was already well known in Williamsburg, having attended the College of William and Mary, studied law with one of the town's most illustrious figures, George Wythe, and endeared himself to the town's leading figures. The overlapping network among lawyers at Virginia's General Court and men associated with William and Mary was his likely route to Martha's door, for business blended into social life in myriad ways, pulling members of Virginia's elite into a near-seamless web of relationships. Jefferson began practicing in Virginia's General Court in 1767 and very likely came into contact with John Wayles then, if not before. He certainly had heard of him. The Wayles-Blair-Chiswell contretemps had been fodder for the *Virginia Gazette* for weeks during 1766, and Jefferson avidly read that paper. Perhaps the earliest written connection between the two men was the deed settling property among the daughters of Wayles's benefactor, Philip Ludwell—Hannah (married to William Lee, who also received property in the transaction) and Lucy Ludwell Paradise and her husband, John. John Wayles, as one of the original executors of the Ludwell estate, and designated guardian of the sisters, helped prepare this later deed, dated November 6, 1770. The witness was none other than Thomas Jefferson.[21]

We are unlikely ever to learn precisely how Jefferson came to be in that group of men dealing with Ludwell's interests, but one can play connect the dots. One of John Wayles's coexecutors of the original Ludwell will, Benjamin Waller, formed a bridge between Jefferson's pre- and post-Wayles lives. Waller, who along with John Wayles helped look after Ludwell's interests, had a busy practice before the court and acted as a lawyer with John Wayles selling land and slaves. Most important of all for the Jefferson connection, he also had taught law to George Wythe, Jefferson's own law professor and mentor. Wythe and Waller remained extremely close friends until Waller's death in the 1780s. It is inconceivable that Wythe did not introduce his own beloved teacher to his beloved pupil, and extol the virtues of the one to the other. Jefferson's records show that he knew of Waller from his earliest days as an attorney. Wayles and Jefferson had another Ludwell family interest in common: both men were visiting Ludwell's Green Spring in the late 1760s. Wayles, of course, went there to look after Ludwell's business before and after his death in 1767. Jefferson visited there in 1768, recording the tip he gave to a servant in the household. Green Spring's landscape evidently impressed him, for in the early 1770s he used plants received from the orchards and gardens there for his own grounds at Monticello.[22]

The young man who witnessed the actions of the Ludwell executors in 1770 had waited a long time (for his day) to get married, but he was still ahead of his father, who married at thirty-one his nineteen-year-old bride. False starts had brought him much frustration, and he was beyond ready to make a match. Although he had just suffered the devastating blow of losing his home at Shadwell,[23] he had many reasons to think he had much to offer John Wayles's oldest daughter, including the prospect of a new home that he had already started building for himself on a mountain not far from his birthplace. Martha, the daughter of a very wealthy man, had much to offer him. Contemporaries described her as an attractive and personable woman, and Jefferson seems to have loved her deeply. One must be careful, however, because in those days marriage, particularly among the upper classes, had as much to do with property and social position as with being in love. Or, one might say that being upper class, having property, and social position were attributes that made a person lovable. Had Thomas encountered Martha as the beautiful and charming daughter of the blacksmith who shod his horses or, for that matter, as "the daughter of a servant boy" who had remained a servant, he might have loved her, but it is unlikely

that he would have married her. It was not uncommon, or at all problematic, for ambitious men to seek advancement by "marrying up." Both Peter
Jefferson and John Wayles had done it. Peter Jefferson, however, had never
been a servant and—as far as we know—had never been referred to in a
public forum as "ill bred," so he did not have as far "up" to go.

Thomas was not the first young man to have fallen in love with Martha.
She was a widow when she met him, having married Bathurst Skelton in
1766, when she was eighteen years old. The couple had one son, John, the
following year, and Skelton died in 1768. Martha, a young widow, returned to
her father's house with her young son. More sorrow followed. Jack Skelton
died in 1771.[24] Almost unthinkable to modern observers, these types of tragedies happened frequently in her time. Children of all classes and races
often died, young people perished of diseases that in our time could easily
be cured, and women died in childbirth. Martha Wayles Skelton, however,
seems to have suffered more than her share of losses—her mother, two
stepmothers, her husband, and her child had all died by the time she was
twenty-three years old. Against this backdrop of pain and loss, her acceptance of her father's mistress and their children seems understandable. Life
was simply too hard and unpredictable, connections to loved ones were too
fragile, for her to burn bridges carrying any supply of comfort, familiarity,
and stability.

Between the years of Martha's husband's death and her marriage to
Thomas Jefferson, Wayles and Elizabeth Hemings had three more children,
bringing the total number to five. Their last son, Peter, arrived during the
year that Jefferson began courting Martha. One would love to know his initial reaction to her "bright"-skinned young brothers and sisters. As a resident in a slave society—and an intelligent and observant man—Jefferson
knew that race mixing between planters and their enslaved women
occurred. He followed his society's preferred method of responding to it:
look the other way and take great care not to incorporate this activity into
the tacitly agreed-upon narrative of Virginia life. He would never have publicly acknowledged, or left for posterity, any suspicions about his father-in-
law—not even to refute them. Such matters were never to become part of a
family's written legacy.[25]

During the very year Martha Skelton came into his life, Jefferson served
pro bono as a lawyer for a mixed-race man, Samuel Howell, who brought
suit to be freed from indentured servitude. Jefferson appeared against his

mentor and law teacher George Wythe. As punishment for having a child out of wedlock by a black man, Howell's white grandmother had been fined and her child (Howell's mother) was supposed to be bound out for service for thirty-one years. Howell was born during the time of his mother's decreed service; this was an event that legislators knew would be common because the odds were very great that a woman in that era would have children before she reached the age of thirty-one. Because of *partus sequitur ventrem*, a form of servitude that tracked slavery could continue indefinitely in one family line so long as daughters were born who had children before they reached the end of their terms.

Howell sued his master to gain his freedom. Jefferson's brief in *Howell v. Netherland* shows that he worked with extreme diligence on the matter, searching for any legal precedents or theories that might aid what was from the start a very weak case. This document is more interesting, however, because it contained his first known public comment on the natural rights of man. Jefferson wrote in his argument for Howell's freedom, five years before he drafted the Declaration of Independence, "all men are born free [and] everyone comes into the world with a right to his own person and using it at his own will. This is what is called personal liberty, and is given him by the author of nature, because it is necessary for his own sustenance." Jefferson was able to use this idea to much greater effect in 1776, since he had no chance to present it to the Virginia court to obtain Howell's freedom. The judge cut him off almost in midsentence before he could begin and rendered the decision against Howell. Jefferson lost the case and, as a consolation, gave Howell money—a rare circumstance indeed, a lawyer giving the client money. Howell sought another solution to his problem: he ran away, no doubt aided by the money given to him by his defeated lawyer.[26]

Jefferson's brief in the case contained intriguing language in light of circumstances at the Forest and as they would be at Monticello. When analyzing the purpose of laws penalizing white women for engaging in sex across the color line, Jefferson explained that these strictures were to "deter women from the confusion of species which the legislature seems to have considered an evil."[27] The legislature *seems to have considered an evil?* This is very curious language for a man who took great care with words, because it suggests that he was making light of the legislative judgment that sex across the color line was inherently evil or even that it was ever an evil at all. Jefferson's wording, while acting as a lawyer and trying to put his client in as sympathetic a light as possible, was a bit risky. His hint of equivocation on the substance of the legislative judgment on this point might have offended the justices as much as making them inclined to grant his client's application. Certainly once he became a famous public man with great responsibilities, he would make other comments about racial mixing that were more in line with those of the legislature that he ever so slightly mocked as a young man. To pause here for a detailed examination of all of Thomas Jefferson's very human contradictions over his long life would take us far afield. It is worth keeping in mind, however, that the young man who questioned whether "confusion of species" was as dire a threat as lawmakers thought was about to join his life and fortunes to a family that he knew had more than its share of confusion.

Martha Wayles Skelton married Thomas Jefferson on January 1, 1772, at the Forest. Jefferson's memorandum book entries for the period reveal the festive nature of the event—money paid to the minister, for the marriage license, and to a fiddler. It also marks the first appearance of Elizabeth Hemings in Jefferson's records—listed as "Betty Hemmins." Jefferson tipped the household slaves or the servants of his hosts. Hemings received a gratuity that day, most likely for services rendered in connection with the wedding ceremony. There was also a payment to Hemings's seventeen-year-old son, Martin, the second such reference to him in the memorandum books. In the year before the wedding, Martin received a gratuity during Jefferson's visit to the Forest to court Martha. This first mention of the Hemings family in Jefferson's records foreshadows the ties that bound him to them for decades to come.[28]

Elizabeth Hemings was thirty-seven years old the day Martha married. Her older children—Mary, Martin, Betty, and Nancy—were nineteen, seventeen, thirteen, and eleven years old, respectively. Her children with the father of the bride—Robert, James, Thenia, Critta, and Peter—were ten, seven, five, three, and two. Over the course of the next five years, three more children arrived—her last child with John Wayles, a daughter Sarah, called Sally, and the two children she bore after age forty, John and Lucy. Of these final three, only Sally and John lived to adulthood, and they, of all members of the family, became most closely associated with the man Martha married on that winter day. The laws of marriage united the Wayleses and Jeffersons. The laws of property and slavery brought Elizabeth Hemings and all of her children, present and future, into that union.

The Dawn of Revolution

At the dawn of the 1770s Elizabeth Hemings was one of half a million people of African descent in what was still British North America. Although they represented 20 percent of the entire population of the thirteen colonies, the vast majority of black people were enslaved in the South—most of them concentrated in Hemings's Virginia and in South Carolina. In the preceding decade, tensions between London and the American colonists had risen to the surface as colonial authorities began to alter the nature of their relationship to the American colonies, issuing proclamations that limited westward expansion in deference to Native American tribes, instituting various tax provisions designed to pay for the French and Indian War and the administrative costs of maintaining the colonies, and enacting and enforcing trade policies that benefited British merchants at the expense of American producers.[29]

As that conflict unfolded and many white colonists in the North and the South sought ways to express their unhappiness with England, they began to fashion themselves ever more urgently as a people under the threat of enslavement by the mother country's colonial authorities. Although they had extensive, firsthand knowledge of what slavery actually meant, and knew that they were not experiencing its full force, they defined their freedom in relation to the nonfreedom of the Africans whom they were enslaving. The irony of their posture, when real-life slavery was legal in all the American colonies, was noted during the time and has been analyzed almost endlessly ever since, although for its brevity and absolute dead-on insight Samuel Johnson's justly famous query in *Taxation No Tyranny* remains unmatched: "How is it that we hear the loudest yelps for liberty from the drivers of Negroes?"[30]

The "Negroes" in the North and the South, driven and otherwise, immediately saw a connection between their situation and the metaphorical "enslavement" that white colonists said they were trying to escape. Some sensed that the looming colonial conflict might benefit them, and hoped that all the talk about liberty would be a contagion spreading to all parts of the society. How could men who understood the worth of liberty, and were willing to fight and kill for it, keep men and women in bondage? Most blacks, particularly in the South, adopted the view that "the enemy of my enemy is my friend." People of their color were actually, not symbolically, bought, sold, and owned. Even free northern blacks were not totally safe in this world, and they well understood the precariousness of their positions. Slavery based upon race greatly circumscribed their lives, since they were part of a group deemed most eligible for enslavement because of their supposed innate inferiority. These men and women looked to the conflicts stirred by the Revolution with hopes for a new future.[31]

Very early on, enslaved blacks in Hemings's Virginia saw their struggle as linked to what was going on between their white Virginia masters and the English, and they looked for ways to use the simmering dispute to their advantage. Although held in legal bondage, blacks made up nearly half of Virginia's population and were always a potential threat to their masters. They knew it, and so did white slave owners. White Virginians were quite nervous about the prospect that the English might encourage an uprising among blacks and, perhaps, Native Americans, who could still seriously threaten from Virginia's western frontier.

Even before Lord Dunmore, the last royal governor of Virginia, issued his proclamation in November 1775 promising freedom to blacks belonging to rebels who joined the Royalist cause, some enslaved Virginians expressed their willingness to take up arms against their masters. They approached British officials and directly offered to help. If antebellum slave owners and their post–Civil War neo-Confederate descendants constructed an idyllic, fairy-tale version of slavery depicting benevolent patriarchs ruling over loyal and completely contented slaves, pre-Revolutionary white Virginians harbored no such fantasies about their relationship with their work force. Rebellions and rumors of rebellion during the 1750s and 1760s shaped their attitudes about the enslaved work force within their colony. Enslaved Afro-Virginians were an alien group that had to be subdued and from whom labor had to be coerced.[32]

Against this backdrop, Lord Dunmore, who had lived long enough in Virginia to understand the dynamic between black and white very well, hinted that he might simply declare the slaves of rebels free and perhaps even arm them. This was a nightmare scenario for white Virginians; suddenly they had to contemplate that their move for freedom from the British might result in the freedom of those whom they were enslaving. If they struck at the king and did not succeed, they would remain yoked to England, while being surrounded by their black former slaves. This was never likely to happen. Neither Dunmore nor his masters would have seriously embarked upon a course that might have resulted in the extermination of large numbers of whites in favor of blacks. They wanted to bring the colony back under control, not to destroy it. Human emotions are seldom bound solely by what is realistic, particularly when the most informed view of the possible is from the position of hindsight. In the midst of the turmoil, white Virginians' fears of what could happen, and how bad it would be if it did, helped shape their attitudes about breaking free from the mother country.

On the night in 1775 when violence actually broke out in Virginia, it was a black seaman who enthusiastically helped to ferry the royal governor to safety. Slaves, male and female, many trailing children, and some from Jefferson's plantations, ran away to join the British forces. These "black banditti," as they were called, escaped into the unknown, seeking what they hoped would be a better future. As one scholar of blacks in the Revolutionary period put it, anyone who chose to become involved in the conflict between the colonists and the mother country was likely to "join the side that made him the quickest and best offer in terms of the 'unalienable rights' of which Mr. Jefferson had spoken."[33]

"Mr. Jefferson" had not yet spoken those words in the years that Elizabeth Hemings first encountered him, but he was certainly preparing to do so. Although he devoted himself during the first two years of his marriage to "personal and professional" matters, Jefferson had "identified himself with the most aggressive group of the local patriots," working "behind the scenes" to further the cause of the American colonists.[34] Jefferson's involvement in the American Revolution transformed him, his career, and the world at large. It also transformed the personal worlds of Elizabeth Hemings and her family. As they became bound to one of the most well-known Revolutionary figures, they too were caught up in the fallout from the move toward independence.

Elizabeth Hemings was neither a political actor nor a potential soldier, although she had thoughts about the events breaking around her. The enslaved community was generally nonliterate, but nonliterate does not equal nonobservant and nonknowledgeable. Because they could not easily send each other letters, slaves developed a much remarked-upon ability to pass information from community to community while running errands for their masters, visiting spouses on other plantations, or on trips with masters as they visited their friends and family. The Virginia colonists talked of revolution in their homes, committee meetings, and other venues, but there was not much that whites knew that the blacks around them did not know as well.[35]

Whatever Hemings perceived of these events, more directly personal concerns would have overwhelmed any consideration of the white colonists' complaints about their circumstances. The really pivotal year in Hemings's personal life during the decade came before the Revolution started in earnest. Seventeen seventy-three was the year she gave birth to her last child with John Wayles, a daughter Sarah, called Sally, and it was also the year that he died.[36] Up until then, the year and a half between the Wayles-Jefferson marriage and John Wayles's death had been much the same as the years before. She remained a house servant at the Forest. All that had changed was that she was older, with one set of children poised to begin their own lives and another set still young enough to cling to her.

Wayles's death put Hemings, her children, and other Wayles slaves on an uncertain path. The death of a master was often a calamitous event for enslaved people, but not chiefly for the reason given by apologists for slavery—the slaves' extreme love for and sorrow at the death of Ole Massa. Enslaved people had a completely practical, eminently personal reason for sorrow. When the master died, the chances of being sold and separated from family members increased enormously. In fact, slaves were most often separated when executors had to settle decedents' estates. Creditors had to be paid and property divided among the legally recognized children of the owner. Under either scenario slave families frequently ended up separated forever. If any weeping and wailing occurred when slave owners died, the most serious reason for tears was the fear of what might lie ahead.

As things turned out, Elizabeth Hemings and her children were not separated from one another forever, although there was no way for her to have known with certainty what would happen. We are left to ponder the strangeness of her situation. What did Hemings feel after having borne six children by Wayles? There is every indication that she loved her children and that they loved her. The closeness of the family over the years supports this. But what did she think of him? Hemings had lived in Wayles's household from the time she was eleven years old, and she had a marriage with another man that produced several of her first four children. Wayles seems to have turned to her only after his third wife's death. He was forty-five at the time, with three wives behind him, and four daughters. He lived for twelve years after his last wife's death and evidently did not think it necessary to marry a fourth time.

Slave owners only rarely acknowledged their sexual activity with slave women, and the women themselves effectively had no voice. So getting at the nature of the relationships between masters and their slave families is a delicate business. First and foremost is the issue of whether one can call sexual activity between a slave master and a slave—even over a long stretch of years—a "relationship" in the sense we know it. Enslaved women practically and legally could not refuse consent. Certainly the testimony from former slaves and the memory of slavery among black American women makes clear the prevalence of rape during slavery.

While the true-life experience of large numbers of African American women settles the matter for the overwhelming majority of cases, it cannot realistically settle it for every single one. There can be no denying that law and the cultural attitudes that at once inform and arise out of it exert immense control over the lives of individuals. It is also true enough that people do not always see themselves according to what the law and their neighbors say they are. At various points slaves were considered real estate for purposes of property law. At other times they were likened to personal property, like furniture and jewelry—things that could be bought and sold more easily than real estate. It is doubtful that many slaves thought of themselves as anything other than people—people who were oppressed and enslaved, but people nonetheless. Slaves, male and female, constantly tested the boundaries of their existences and had their own personal sense of themselves as individuals within the context of slavery. Without getting too far ahead in our story, the experiences of Elizabeth Hemings's daughters Mary and Sally offer examples of enslaved women who were amenable to unions with white men who were their legal masters—relationships that worked very much to their advantages and to the advantages of their children and later descendants.

Madison Hemings described his grandfather as having taken his grandmother "as a concubine." Later he described his mother as having become "Mr. Jefferson's concubine." Can we learn anything from his description? To modern readers the term "concubine" conjures up images of the exotic and decadent—oversexed males with multiple females, usually kept in harems, to satisfy their merely carnal urges. In America, before the usage became archaic sometime in the twentieth century, the law defined a concubine as a woman who lived with a man without being married to him. That straightforward definition carried no implication of unbridled sexual license. Nor did it automatically signal how a man and a woman felt about each other, except insofar as people believed that if a man truly loved a woman he would marry her and that not marrying her proved a lack of love. In Virginia, of course, any black woman who lived with a white man could only have been his concubine. It was legally impossible to be anything else.

Examples of case law from Madison Hemings's Virginia give a good sense of the term's usage. In an 1857 suit involving a dispute over property in a white family, the judge referred to the decedent as having left part of his estate "to his six acknowledged illegitimate children, and to his concubine one tenth." In another, a judge observed that "a man was allowed to do for his concubine what he could not do had she been his lawful wife." In that case, the woman and man had lived together without marriage for a time, and then married, and the dispute involved what this meant for the couple's creditors. The opinion referred to the woman in question as the man's "concubine" before marriage and then his "wife" afterwards.[37]

In other words, "concubine" was a part of the language and terminology of Madison Hemings's nineteenth-century world. To have called his grandmother a "common law wife" would have been inapposite, because Hemings knew his grandmother was a slave, and thus not "in law." The phrase "common law" is used to distinguish male-female unions made outside the statutory law of a state or jurisdiction, and defines the range of legal obligations and privileges a state might choose to confer upon a couple living under that arrangement. John Wayles and Elizabeth Hemings could never have had a statutory marriage, nor could any legal obligations have arisen between them on the basis of their having lived together. "Mistress" would not have seemed appropriate either, because that term was often associated with women who were "kept" by married men. Hemings's reference to his grandmother's situation fits exactly with John Hartwell Cocke's statement about Jefferson and other widowed Virginia planters and bachelors. They often took slave women as a "substitute for a wife," the classic definition of the term "concubine" and the one that was used in both Hemings's and Cocke's time.

We cannot know, given the present state of information, exactly what went on between Hemings and Wayles beyond the facts that he was her master, she was his slave, and they had six children. Unlike her daughters Mary and Sally, Elizabeth Hemings took no known actions that telegraph what she thought about John Wayles, what she told her children about him, and what he thought of her. It may be instructive that at least two of Hemings's grandchildren gave some version of John Wayles's name to their own children, keeping the Wayles connection alive beyond whatever was the story of Elizabeth and John. Not every mixed-race family followed that practice. Many wanted absolutely nothing to do with the white males who were their biological fathers or grandfathers, feeling no desire to memorialize these men by naming their children after them. These men, and the connection to whiteness, were to be buried along with the institution of slavery. At least some of the Hemingses chose a different path.

One admittedly imperfect way to approach the possible nature of a slave owner's relationship to his enslaved biological family is to look at how the men treated the children from these unions. Their actions must be viewed along a continuum. At one end were men, a rare few, who acknowledged their children, freed them and their mothers, and made provisions for their futures. The vast majority of white men who had children with enslaved women did not do any of these things. They neither freed nor acknowledged their children, and by their actions—or inaction—showed that they could not have cared less about the mother or their offspring. One thing about the Wayles children is of note in this regard. We know definitely that two of his children with Hemings, if not all of them, knew how to read and write. Robert Hemings's letters to Jefferson are no longer extant, but James Hemings's writings show great proficiency. One wonders who taught them.

It is not impossible, but would seem improbable, that Jefferson had any direct hand in this, that he taught them to read and write once they came into his life. Although they were certainly able to serve him better because of their literacy, there is no indication that Jefferson felt this skill was so important to him that he would take the time to teach them. It seems more likely that Hemings' children learned to read when they were still in their father's household. Either John Wayles himself or their sister, Martha Wayles Jefferson, was the possible source of their literacy. John Wayles had been able to rise in the world because his illiterate grandfather had made sure that his sons and daughter received at least a basic education. He was also an apparently religious man, or at least he took the trappings of religion seriously, attending services regularly and involving himself in the affairs of the congregation. A number of slave owners, under the influence of religious beliefs, taught "favored" slaves to read so that they could study the Bible. This might explain why Wayles remained an important figure to the family, even though he did not free his children. His grandson Eston Hemings named his first son John Wayles Hemings.

It is impossible to know Wayles's thoughts about freeing his children. On the one hand, he may have had no consideration of freeing Elizabeth Hemings and his children at all. There is little reason to believe that a man who could involve himself so directly in the African slave trade, knowing the deaths he was purchasing in the process, would necessarily feel sentimental about his enslaved children or their mother. Pleasant as he may have been to his white neighbors, Wayles was a hard man. On the other hand, Wayles died before Virginia's post–Revolutionary War liberalization of its emancipation laws. The statute of 1723 was still in effect when he died: "no negro, mullatto or indian slaves shall be set free upon any pretence whatsoever, except for some meritorious services, to be adjudged and allowed by the governor and council." The statute went on to say that if a master tried to free a slave, "the churchwardens of the parish" could "take up, and sell the said, negro, mulatto, or indians, as slaves" and keep the proceeds for the benefit of the parish.[38]

To free Hemings and their children, Wayles would have had to convince the governor of Virginia and the Virginia council that they had performed some "meritorious services" to him. That would have been a tough sell, and the man who apparently started in the colony as a servant and had been raised to a point where he could marry the daughters of the upper classes may not have wanted to press his luck much further. Moreover, what Elizabeth Hemings had "done"—save Wayles from a lonely existence as a widower—was more his doing than hers, and it probably was not what the burgesses had in mind when they required "meritorious services." Wayles's small children could not have fit the bill either. Instead of being emancipated, all the Hemingses ended up as the property of Wayles's son-in-law Thomas Jefferson, and it was through him that the Wayles-Hemings children reaped the benefits of their paternity.

It took until January of 1774 to settle John Wayles's estate, dividing property among his legitimate heirs. The Forest was now occupied by Wayles's

daughter Elizabeth and her husband, Francis Eppes. As the division pro-
ceeded, and the Wayles heirs sorted out what was theirs, human and non-
human, Elizabeth Hemings and her children—Nancy, James, Thenia,
Critta, Peter, and Sally—and her grandchild, Daniel Farley, the son of
Mary Hemings, were sent to live at "Guinea," a Wayles farm in Amelia
County. They stayed there until Jefferson moved them to another farm, Elk
Hill, in Goochland County. He took several of her older children to live
at Monticello. Mary, the eldest, served as a seamstress and pastry cook for
Jefferson's family. Martin became Jefferson's butler and would remain in
that position for twenty, somewhat tempestuous years. Betty (whose last
name was Brown) became a house maid—she was actually the first to go.
Two of Elizabeth's Wayles children came along, too: Robert and James. Not
long after this period of transition, the entire Hemings family was reunited
when Elizabeth and the rest of her children were brought to Monticello,
which became their principal home for the next five decades.[39]

5

❧

THE FIRST MONTICELLO

W HEN THE HEMINGSES assembled at Monticello, they entered the somewhat quixotic dream world[1] of their new owner. Jefferson was already five years into his determined effort to build and constantly improve his home in the sky, an effort that would continue almost unabated for the next five decades. In the early years, Jefferson referred to his emerging homestead as the "Hermitage," but soon settled on the name Monticello, "little mountain," to describe the place where he would make his home.[2] Living there was a reverie of long standing for him. But the space on the mountain and the structures he built there (two different versions of the main house at Monticello would emerge) represented much more than a mere residence. In ways both intended and unintended, Monticello became an almost perfect projection of Jefferson's personality—his vaulting ambition, his respect for and adherence to aspects of a classical past, his faith in innovation and optimism about the future, his extreme self-indulgence, and his genius.

There was something else. The historian Rhys Isaac has written eloquently about the "possible meanings" of Jefferson's choice to build his home where he did, atop a mountain separated "from the corn and tobacco culture that paid for its buildings." He also set himself apart from "the African-American communities" that populated his estates, from the "women who nurtured him in his infancy, and whose youngsters had been his companions."[3] Monticello, the "home" plantation, towered above Jefferson's immediately surrounding quarter farms, Shadwell, Lego, and Tufton. Isaac astutely raised the core predicament of Jefferson's existence.

His love of his country, Virginia, and his ambivalence about the institution central to the life of that colony, and then state, emerged as a constant theme throughout his life. This man who wanted desperately to be seen by his contemporaries and posterity as a progressive had a way of life that depended upon what ultimately was—and he took to be—a retrogressive labor system. Certainly Jefferson's years in Paris were among the happiest in his life in part because he could live there as an enlightened aristocratic gentleman without depending upon the labor of enslaved people. In Dumas Malone's words, in Paris, Jefferson "was able to be the sort of man he wanted to be."[4]

Having absolutely no will to divest himself of his human property, Jefferson was in a bind. There were, however, examples of very prosperous Virginian slave owners of his class who did relinquish their property rights in human beings and freed their slaves. But religion strongly influenced these men, and Jefferson, a creature of ethics, was not like them. Throughout history, religion has been the source of many an "irrational" act, for both good and evil. The ethical sense has never been so good at exciting passionate, caution-thrown-to-the-wind actions. And certainly by the standard of any age, the act of voluntarily giving up the entire basis of one's wealth that could be passed on to one's children would be considered irrational. That slaves were human property is an issue that naturally concerns us in the twenty-first century very much. It did not, to any great degree, concern members of Jefferson's generation in Virginia, or else they would not have held slaves.

Operating under the constraints of his personality, Jefferson opted for a different course: one that allowed him to continue to espouse the progressive belief in emancipation, thus holding on to his very deep need to be seen as an intelligent man of the future, while maintaining the lifestyle to which he had become accustomed. Though he understood viscerally that slavery was wrong, he resigned himself to the institution and rationalized that the project of emancipation was best left to future generations, his revolutionary generation having done its part by creating the United States of America. The debate about the best course of action regarding slavery would remain for him largely a political abstraction, carried on in the republic of letters. But what was to be done about the problem on a day-to-day basis? With the help of architecture and landscaping, Jefferson arranged his personal life to minimize the reminders of his entanglement with African slavery. He took to the mountain with his wife, surrounded himself with enslaved people—some of whom, his wife's blood relatives, he could treat as something other than slaves—and set about creating his own world with them.

For most people the word Monticello invokes an image of the second house that Jefferson built atop his 867-foot "little mountain." It is, perhaps, the most well-known private residence in the United States—the only one to appear on a piece of U.S. currency. Less often thought about is what it took to build the place and to provide an adequate lifestyle there. Other planters built homes with fine views that required a great amount of work to construct and maintain. Situating a house at Monticello presented not only unique problems but also familiar ones on a far greater order of magnitude than was typical.

First, building the house required shaving the top off the mountain, a huge earth-moving enterprise in an era that had neither earth movers nor bulldozers, at least not mechanical ones. Human beings, slaves Jefferson hired from a nearby planter, engaged in this massive effort, digging with shovels in Virginia's hard red clay to level the ground and then digging a foundation and cellars for the house. This was backbreaking work carried out over twelve-hour days. On one occasion Jefferson observed as "a team of four men, a boy, and two sixteen-year-old girls" worked. It was winter. There was snow on the ground, it was extremely cold, and the laborers periodically stopped their digging to warm their hands over a fire before they returned to their arduous task.[5]

There was no ready water supply on top of the mountain. A well had to be dug, an especially difficult undertaking, because the workers were required to dig deeper to find water than they would have had to if they been digging on level ground. It took them forty-six days to excavate sixty-five feet of mountain rock before they hit water, almost twice the depth of a normal well in Virginia. Even with that, at times when not enough rain fell to provide a constant and ready supply, water had to be hauled up the mountain.[6] Jefferson did not consider these issues a serious problem. From his perspective, as from that of any man of his class, his tasks were to imagine the design for his life on the mountain, engineer ways to execute the design, and then find people—slaves and hired workmen—to complete his projects. As long as labor was available, the job would be done.

The first Hemingses who came to Monticello with Martha Wayles Jefferson in 1772 saw a dwelling that was still in a very rudimentary state.

Martha and Thomas Jefferson began their married life in the South Pavilion at Monticello, the one-room building—the first at the site—that Jefferson built while still a bachelor. They ate and slept in the room that housed his books, the furniture, and their clothing.[7] Fifteen-year-old Betty Brown, who served as Martha's maid, was apparently the very first Hemings to arrive; as fate would have it, she would be the last one to leave the mountain.[8] Indeed, she likely accompanied the couple on their much written-about winter journey to the mountain, though no mention is ever made of her. Members of Jefferson's class did not generally travel by themselves, and certainly a bride going to her new home would not have left her personal maid behind, for there was much to do to create a new household. We have no indication where young Betty or the other later-arriving Hemingses stayed. Nor do we know where the rest of the family members lived when they were all brought together in 1775. It would not have been a difficult task to build cabins to house them, although one wonders how a couple living in such small quarters could have made use of a butler, two maids, and two other personal attendants. The only plausible explanation is that the Jeffersons set out right from the start of their life together to live as if they were in normal circumstances—entertaining family and friends in their small quarters—since it was a given that it would be some time before their family home was finished.

This marked a dramatic change for the Hemingses. Elizabeth Hemings had grown up serving in two well-established households, the Eppes home at Bermuda Hundred and the Forest. Her children's experiences had been the same. They probably did not know it, but they were now beginning a way of life that would feature constant physical upheaval and change—living and working in what was to become a perpetual construction site. While this may have been exciting to Jefferson, who as the owner and conceiver of the projects would have had a strong incentive to put up with any of the adverse consequences of his choices, those who had to live and work amid the chaos may have felt differently.

Elizabeth Hemings was no stranger to Jefferson's personality and quirks, and one yearns to know what she thought of this bookish and eccentric young man with the gadgets in his pockets and a tendency to sing as he went about his business. Even before Wayles died and Jefferson came into formal ownership of her family, there were signs that her children's destinies would be shaped by his demands and desires. We can trace the beginnings of this process in Jefferson's memorandum books in the early 1770s. In those years Hemings's eldest son, Martin, then a teenager, appears several times receiving gratuities and payments for catching and selling to Jefferson his beloved mockingbirds.[9] From those early days Hemings's sons began to learn to do things Jefferson wanted to have done. Once he took ownership of them, the process of shaping all the Hemingses to suit his aims only intensified.

Almost as soon as he became their owner, Jefferson singled out the older generation of Hemings males—Martin, Robert, and, as he matured, James—for special treatment. Each man had some degree of freedom within his enslaved status. All were allowed to travel around by themselves, to learn trades, to hire themselves out to employers of their own choice, and to keep all their wages. Despite their status on the law books, Jefferson treated them, to a degree, as if they were lower-class white males. That Robert and James Hemings were his new wife's half brothers was reason enough to make him see them as different from other slaves. They would have been his in-laws, had slaves been "in law."

Not all slave owners who shared family ties with enslaved people responded this way, but it should not come as a surprise that some of them might have felt sentimental about blood relationships. Blood mattered a great deal in Virginia society. Race and caste complicated this further, but there are enough instances of fathers who emancipated their children to show that race and status did not always obliterate attentions to family connections. Although Martin Hemings, Elizabeth's eldest son, had no blood tie to Martha Jefferson, Jefferson's response to him evidently derived from the fact that he shared a mother with the Hemings-Wayles children. As things turned out, Jefferson freed two of these men—Robert and James— the only slaves he legally emancipated during his lifetime. They, along with Jefferson's children Beverley, Harriet, Madison, and Eston Hemings, were set free as young people when they had their lives ahead of them. The other slaves Jefferson emancipated, all Hemingses—John Hemings, Joseph Fossett, and Burwell Colbert—were, by the standards of the time, old men who had given their lives to Jefferson; they were the "trusted," "worthy" slaves, freed on the basis of "merit." Put another way, Robert, James, Beverley, Harriet, Madison, and Eston Hemings gained freedom because of who they were—Wayles's sons, Martha's brothers, and Jefferson's children, respectively—while the other men were freed because of what they had done.

In keeping with gender roles of the day, Elizabeth Hemings's sons had more opportunities than their sisters to broaden their lives by going outside of the home. Enslaved males were generally employed at a much greater variety of jobs than female slaves. If they were not agricultural workers, they were carpenters, blacksmiths, coopers, or barbers, engaged in the types of jobs deemed unsuitable for women. Sex segregation became even more pronounced when Virginia's economy diversified after the Revolutionary War. The shift from tobacco to wheat as a cash crop opened up a host of subsidiary jobs for slaves to fill. More and more enslaved men were taken out of the fields to perform tasks associated with the processing of this new crop, working in mills and granaries, turning wheat into flour. As men were shifted into these and other types of jobs—working in mines, iron works, and other industries—fieldwork became even more the province of women and children.[10] The Hemings men were not agricultural workers. They spent their time in the house or traveling with and attending to Jefferson, and were transformed by the kind of work they did and experiences they had, whether it was being trained to become a barber or chef, traveling alone to places near and far from their home, or living by themselves in various Virginia towns.

The Hemings women were not eligible for the transformative experiences that shaped the lives of their male relatives, but they were not treated like other enslaved women at Monticello. Although they, like the male Hemingses, were attached by blood and affinity to Jefferson's wife, he viewed them differently because they were females. His response to Elizabeth Hemings and her daughters over the years was a gender-appropriate—that is, by eighteenth-century standards—mirror image of his response to the male Hemingses. He constructed the Hemings women along more traditional European feminine lines. The women were exempted from work in the fields, even when everyone else had to go there at harvest time; they instead performed chores not unlike those that many white women were doing—sewing, mending clothes, looking after children, and baking cakes.[11]

Jefferson took the Hemings women out of the pattern that had been well established in his home territory. From the very beginning, Virginia's slave society situated black women outside the scope of European notions of femininity. If Virginians wanted to make the most of slavery as an economic and racial institution, they could have no qualms about the treatment of African women. A notion grew up very early that black women were an "exception to the gender division of labor" and could be sent into the fields to work, while wealthy white women were seen as too delicate for that. White Virginians codified this idea in 1643 when free black women were made "tithables." This meant that a tax could be placed on their labor, just like that of free white men and enslaved men and women. White women were not tithables, because they worked in the home. In other words, black women who were out of slavery were treated like white *men* instead of like white women. As the years passed, the connection between black women and hard physical labor became so firmly entrenched in the minds of white masters that the women "were as one with their farming tools and called, simply, 'hoes.'"[12]

In truth, lower-status white women worked in the fields during the period of indentured servitude and alongside their farmer husbands thereafter. People knew that. The nature of life on an ordinary farm is such that, at some point, everyone has to pitch in and help. But the ethos of a society is often most tellingly expressed in its mythology, emphasizing what people want to believe about themselves, and what they want to tell others about who they are, rather than what one can observe about their nature by simply opening one's eyes. Ignoring reality is a part of the game. Very often in these mythologies, people of higher rank become the standard of measurement for people in the community. The everyday reality of the lives of lower-class white women in Virginia disappeared under the weight of the need to defeminize black women. Women (some might say "ladies") became defined by the actions, demeanor, and attitudes of high-status females.

True to his time, Jefferson saw fieldwork as unfeminine, and he criticized Native American men for sending their women into the fields and assumed that the intensity of the experience accounted for the low birthrate among the group. While discussing their example, Jefferson posited that, whenever the men in a given society are "at ease," the first thing they do is take women out of hard labor and put them in the home. He had been brought to this observation as he noted with disdain the presence of peasant women in the fields during his time in Europe. While traveling through Holland in the spring of 1788, Jefferson made clear what he thought of women engaging in agricultural pursuits.

> The women here, as in Germany do all sorts of work. While one considers them as useful and rational companions, one cannot forget that

they are also objects of our pleasures. Nor can they ever forget it. While employed in the dirt and drudgery some tag of ribbon, some ring or bit of bracelet, earbob or necklace, or something of that kind will shew that the desire of pleasing is never suspended in them. How valuable is that state of society which allots to them internal emploiments only, and external to the men. They are formed by nature for attentions and not for hard labour. A woman never forgets one of the numerous train of little offices which belong to her; a man forgets often.[13]

He could well have been describing a scene in the fields at Monticello or another of his farms. Enslaved women attended to their "little offices" just as diligently as the laboring women of Holland. They wore bracelets, ribbons, and earrings, too, and that behavior had the same object as that of their European counterparts. Having lived among them, Jefferson knew that enslaved women wanted to make themselves attractive to their male companions. Yet, when talking of this matter of women and fitness for hard labor, he resorted to the Native American example, ignoring the more logical comparison—the laboring women in his own fields. Jefferson, however, really did know that fieldwork was inappropriate for black women. He daydreamed while in France about planting fig, mulberry, and olive trees in "countries where there are slaves." In those places, he noted, "women and children are often employed in labours disproportioned to their sex and age. By presenting to the master objects of culture, easier and equally beneficial, all temptation to misemploy them would be removed, and the lot of this tender part our species be much softened."[14]

Jefferson's characterization of enslaved women as "this tender part of our species" engaged in labor "disproportioned to their sex" demonstrates that he knew the obvious: black women did not have physical strength equal to that of black men. In addition, black women, not black men, were the ones having babies and breast-feeding them, thus interfering with their capacity to work efficiently. Everything he wrote about women suggests that for Jefferson biology was destiny. Their defined roles vis-à-vis males and children were the reasons that the home was the most suitable place for them. Where did that leave the enslaved women at Monticello who were not members of the Hemings family?

The issue, as in so many other areas of Jefferson's views on race, was that certain truths had to be overridden (or rationalized) when they bumped up against an extreme self-interest that did not rest comfortably with the implications of those truths. Jefferson could place black women among the "tender part" of the human species, along with the peasant women in the fields of Europe and the Native American women in his own country, see them as ill equipped relative to men for fieldwork, and still send them there because it suited his needs and the needs of his society. White supremacy does not demand deep conviction. Ruthless self-interest, not sincere belief, is the signature feature of the doctrine. It finds its greatest expression, and most devastating effect, in the determination to state, live by, and act on the basis of ideas one knows are untrue when doing so will yield important benefits and privileges that one does not care to relinquish.

Jefferson's special treatment of the Hemings women allowed him to think of himself as a "good" and "kind" master. By exempting them from labor in the fields, he set them apart from the other black women who tended and harvested his tobacco and wheat, putting them in a social and, no doubt, psychological limbo—for the women themselves and the white males around them. The great irony is that, in doing this, he also cut the women off from the traditions of their African foremothers. Wherever she was from, the chances were great that Elizabeth Hemings's mother would have grown up to work in the fields, as would her daughters and their daughters. In the vast majority of the West African communities from which most slaves in North America were brought, agricultural work was women's work to a substantial degree. To the African mind, there was nothing unfeminine about this.[15]

Not having an African mind, Jefferson defined the Hemings women, just one generation separated from Africa, along European lines. He saw them as the kind of women who were formed for the "attentions" of men, not for "hard labor." Accordingly, he dressed them differently from other enslaved women on the plantation. When he was away from Monticello during his political life, he bought the Hemings sisters Irish linen, muslin, and calico, making sure they were not all in the same pattern to avoid monotony in their dress. He purchased fitted cotton stockings for them, taking note of the sizes. Other enslaved women at Monticello "received a uniform allotment of osnaburg, the coarse brownish linen issued to slaves all over the south . . . and baggy stockings of woven cloth."[16] At one point, when she was ill, Elizabeth Hemings's daughter Critta was sent to "the Springs" to take the cure, her room and board paid for by Jefferson.[17] The Hemings women were not free white women, but they were not hard-laboring black women either. They were something else. Just what that "else" was is difficult for us with our well-developed sense of racial identities and meanings to gauge precisely. That the Hemings women's existence in this "middle category" did not lead to their immediate freedom did not make their life in that state meaningless to them. Even though enslaved, these women had inner lives that were shaped by what did and did not happen to them on a daily basis—and by what they saw happening to others.

Jefferson's attitude toward the male Hemingses has long been commented upon and, generally, portrayed in a positive light, as an example of his innate humanity breaking through a slave owner's persona that many find troubling today. In this view, Jefferson's seeing male Hemingses through a different lens allowed him to connect with them almost as if a form of male bonding occurred between these men that transcended the day-to-day reality of slavery. As we will see in the coming chapters, Jefferson acknowledged their masculinity (particularly that of Robert and James Hemings) and refused to take all of it—letting them do some of the things that men of the day would be expected to do, allowing them to have a measure of control over the course of their lives. All this raises an obvious question avoided for many years: If Jefferson responded to the masculinity of certain Hemings males, how did he respond to the femininity of their sisters?

By all accounts of them, in contemporary writings and the family histories of Jeffersons and Hemingses, the Hemings women were seen as beautiful and desirable. Thomas Jefferson Randolph commented on this himself. The white males on the mountain, Jefferson family members and his employees, responded to them in that way. The duc de La Rochefoucauld-Liancourt, upon visiting Monticello, noted the prevalence of interracial relationships between the white men who worked there and "mulatto" slave women, reinforcing the idea that lower-status white males alone were responsible for the white-looking slave children. But there were other indications that the practice was not strictly divided along class lines. Practically every adult Jefferson male associated with Monticello was said, either by his own family members, the families of those enslaved, or nonfamily members (white and black), to have had sexual relations with Hemings women: Jefferson, Peter Carr, Samuel Carr, and John Wayles Eppes. In a way that seems at once astounding and unsurprising, Monticello seems to have resembled a mini-version of the stereotypical view of New Orleans—a place where white males pursued and attached themselves to light-skinned black women.[18]

Throughout their time at Monticello, none of the Hemings women married men from "down the mountain" who worked in the fields. They were either in long-term liaisons with high-status white males or white workers at the plantation, or they married household servants from other plantations who were also mixed race or, in the case of Critta Hemings, a free black man.[19] One could say that these women had no choice regarding the white men, even the men who did not own them. It is also possible, of course, that given a choice they would have preferred white mates. That might be a disturbing thought from a modern perspective, with our knowledge of slavery and views about the value of solidarity in the face of oppression. This possibility, however, must not be discounted outright, especially in light of the behavior of some of the Hemings children and grandchildren.

Tempting and romantic as it may be to construct a monolithic population of slaves who acted cohesively across color and genetic lines because of their common enslaved status, it is more realistic to accept that different individuals and families had different understandings about where they stood in relation to other slaves, within the slave system and, indeed, within America's racial hierarchy. People's individual experiences shaped their way of seeing the world. The Hemingses did not, any more than other human beings, always live with reference to the "big picture" of their society. They lived, instead, in the day-to-day interactions with the people around them, the values they formed in the context of their surrounding society, and their sense of the best way to make the most of their lives before they died.

We cannot simply assume that the Hemingses, living in a world that valued whiteness—whites' culture, hair, skin color, and facial features—regarded their status as slaves as vastly more meaningful than the reality that they were also part white. To be a slave was hard, but being black was not easy either. Even emancipated blacks lived under the harsh regime of white supremacy, denied the right to full citizenship, the quality of their lives determined by the whims of the dominant white community. This world expressed open contempt for the tightly curled hair, broad noses, and full lips of African people. White society could change the Hemingses' legal status with the stroke of a pen, or the Hemingses could change it themselves, as some of them did, by walking away from Monticello and blending in with the rest of free white society—leaving the stigmas of slavery and blackness behind. The only way to destroy their proximity to whiteness would be for the Hemingses to marry and have children with a person who was not as "bright" skinned or light bronzed as they were. That, for generations, many of the Hemingses refused to do. When one considers the harshness of life in the eighteenth and nineteenth centuries for people of African origin, it is not surprising that some black people who could leave life under slavery and white supremacy behind might have wished to do that.

For the women in the Hemings family, being treated as a caste apart and having their femininity reinforced rather than forcefully denied—circumstances that may seem trivial to present-day observers viewing the enormity of slavery—may have had deep meaning. Elizabeth Hemings, her daughters, and granddaughters knew that their enslavement limited their horizons. But their everyday existence encouraged them to think of themselves as different from others who shared the same legal status. They could, as women of all races and classes have often done, use their femininity to seek better lives through their association with men who had some degree of status—white males, mixed-race house servants, or free black men. Jefferson would not take any Hemings woman completely out of slavery until 1822, when he freed his daughter Harriet to go live as a white woman and escape *partus sequitur ventrem*. Instead, the Hemings women served as seamstresses, maids, and, in Sally Hemings's case, Jefferson's "substitute for a wife." But these events, which will be discussed more fully in later chapters, unfolded over decades. It took years to build the Hemingses' story at Monticello.

MARTIN HEMINGS WAS between seventeen and eighteen years old when he became the butler at Monticello. In any of the cultures that contributed to his identity—African, English, and, finally, American—he would, as the eldest son, have had special status within his family. This may have shaped his personality. Of all of Elizabeth Hemings's children, he had the reputation for being the most difficult (from the perspective of a slave owner) and aggressive. Jefferson family tradition cast him as the prototypical surly manservant, whose saving grace (in the eyes of whites) was his extreme loyalty to Jefferson. Hemings presented himself as one who did not want others to perform tasks for the master of Monticello—he wanted to do them himself. On the other hand, he complied with others' orders and requests only grudgingly, indeed "with scarcely concealed anger."[20] Whether this attitude grew out of his genuine attachment to Jefferson, or whether it was a strategy designed to achieve some other goal, cannot be known definitely. It is understandable that the Jeffersons would have looked at Hemings's behavior and seen and, perhaps hoped, that it grew out of some foundational loyalty to the master. Given that Jefferson and Hemings often quarreled and actually ended on bad terms, it may be that Hemings fashioned himself in this way for a different purpose. The young man seems to have found a way to carve a space out in life while he accommodated himself to his circumstances.

Consider the practical results of Hemings's posture. If he was Jefferson's "man," the only one who could attend to his needs, then he had to be free from others' demands in order to fulfill this important role. This appears to have been about more than just shirking work. The descriptions of Martin Hemings betray no hint of that as the reason for his behavior. It was a matter of pride, in the Jefferson family's view—pride at being able to serve Jefferson so well and to please his master. From Hemings's viewpoint it could well have been about achieving pride for himself. Insofar as he could, Martin Hemings attempted to minimize his exposure to the vagaries of the life of a slave, answering willingly only to one person, while signaling to others that he was off-limits. Note that there are two separate parts of his persona: the man who wanted to be Jefferson's only servant and the man who did not want to serve anyone else. The two do not necessarily go together. By combining these two attributes, Hemings constructed himself along the lines of a contract employee of one person, rather than an enslaved black man who, like all other slaves, had to answer to any white person who addressed him. This was almost certainly more about Hemings's self-image than any undying love for the man who legally owned him. As later events made clear, he did not build his world around Jefferson.

If he performed the typical role of a butler, Hemings was in charge of making sure that the Jefferson household ran smoothly. He supervised the work of the household staff as well as of the cooks, although his position was somewhat distinctive because the staff he managed consisted mainly of his mother, sisters, and brothers. Early on in his tenure Jefferson devised a very petty (though probably not unheard of) way of testing Hemings's loyalty. He kept a tally on some bottles of liquor to which the young man had access to see if Hemings's "fidelity" would remain intact.[21] Martin Hemings passed the test.

One outsider to the group was under Martin Hemings's supervision. Jefferson had purchased a woman named Ursula in 1772. He paid 210 pounds for her and her two sons, George and Bagwell. Soon thereafter, he bought Ursula's husband, George Granger, and their experiences on the mountain all but destroy the long-held conventional wisdom that Jefferson favored only light-skinned slaves.[22] The Grangers' time at Monticello also reveals the great problem with taking Jefferson's writings on race in *Notes on the State of Virginia* as a blueprint for how he actually lived at Monticello. In his famous Query 14, he stated that blacks had no ability to reason above telling a simple narrative and insisted that white blood improved blacks.[23] Yet members of this family, who by the appearance of their son Isaac Jefferson, in his near iconic photograph, had no trace of European ancestry, were at least as trusted and "privileged" as many members of the mixed-race Hemings family. George Granger Sr. was a paid overseer at Monticello, the only black person ever to hold that position on any of Jefferson's farms. Indeed, Jefferson may have freed him informally before he died. His son George Jr. was the foreman at the nail factory, an operation that Jefferson viewed as critical to his family's finances in the late 1790s and early 1800s.[24] Neither man would have been in his important position had Jefferson truly believed that no blacks could reason above telling a simple story, or that they had to have an infusion of white blood to be basically intelligent. Ursula Granger became a cook, "house woman," and laundress for the family, and she and her husband were given the nicknames "Queen" and "King." When Jefferson was away in Paris, he explicitly exempted them, along with Elizabeth Hemings, from being hired out, while the man administering Jefferson's estates in his absence hired out both Thenia and Critta Hemings.[25]

If Martin Hemings enjoyed any special status as the eldest of Elizabeth Hemings's sons, Robert Hemings also had status as John Wayles's firstborn son; and that became apparent very early during his time at Monticello. From his days at William and Mary, and even before, Jefferson had been attended by his boyhood enslaved companion, Jupiter Evans. The two men went everywhere together. After his marriage, however, Jefferson transferred Evans's duties to Robert Hemings, despite Robert's youth. Evans took charge of Jefferson's stables and was sometimes his coachman.[26] A twelve-year-old assumed the duties of a thirty-one-year-old. When he replaced the same-age companion of his childhood with his wife's half brother, Jefferson not only made a statement about the merger of two families—one side enslaved, the other side legally free—he also signaled that he had come of age as an adult family man. His wife's brother would now be the closest to him physically, the keeper of secrets and the possessor of intimate knowledge of him, just by virtue of their being in daily proximity to one another. Robert's siblings and his mother would keep Jefferson's household running, building a cocoon for him spun out of family relations on the mountain in which some of his most elemental needs, physical and emotional, would be satisfied by members of this one family bound to him by the laws of slavery and blood.

Though Jefferson never stated why he put Robert in Evans's place, Thomas Jefferson Randolph explained that his grandfather favored the Hemingses because of their talent and intelligence.[27] We do not know about Jupiter Evans, but Robert Hemings was literate. Though it is not known how he learned to read and write, there is no reason to suppose that he did not learn early on. Indeed, his literacy may have been part of the reason why Jefferson made the switch. It would have compensated for whatever he lacked in experience and maturity, making him more useful to Jefferson. Robert's abilities aside, family doubtless played a role in this scenario. A valet is privy to the most intimate details of his employer's or, in this case, his master's life. The position requires extreme trust and discretion. Jefferson, who preferred manipulation (he would say incentive) to outright coercion, would easily have known how to build the trust of his wife's young brother, particularly since the foundation, a shared father, had already been laid. In the context of their slave society, who would be better suited to fulfill this role? Throughout the early days at Monticello, Robert Hemings traveled extensively with Jefferson in Virginia, and in 1776 the fourteen-year-old lived with Jefferson in Philadelphia when he was a member of the Continental Congress and wrote the Declaration of Independence.[28]

We know something of Elizabeth Hemings's daughters' occupations at Monticello, but her precise role there is perhaps lost to history. There is some indication that later in life, long after the days of Martha and Thomas's marriage, she spent her time looking after her ever-growing number of grandchildren. But in the years immediately after moving to Monticello, she was probably responsible for looking after Martha's children. At the same time, she still had her own small children to care for, including her final two off-spring, John and Lucy, born in 1776 and 1777, respectively. They were the only ones of her children to be born at Monticello. Her grandson Madison Hemings named a white man, Jefferson's chief carpenter Joseph Neilson (Nelson, by another spelling), as John Hemings's father. He did not discuss Lucy, most probably because she died in 1786, nineteen years before he was born. But her proximity in age to her brother John—they were just one year apart—suggests that Neilson was likely her father as well.[29]

Neilson's apprentice, William Fossett, most probably fathered Elizabeth's daughter Mary Hemings's son Joseph, who also became a talented artisan on the mountain.[30] Neilson and Fossett participated in a phenomenon described by one of Jefferson's white grandchildren over half a century later. They were white Monticello workingmen who lived openly with or had more casual encounters with enslaved women on the plantation. Where these two men fit on that continuum is not known. Both Fossett's and Neilson's employment at Monticello ended in 1779. Joseph Fossett was born the following year. Either Mary Hemings was pregnant when he left, or they kept their association after he stopped working on the mountain. John Hemings was three years old when Joseph Neilson stopped working at Monticello. Sometime near the end of the Revolutionary War, Neilson married a local woman named Mary Murphy. By 1784 they were living in downtown Charlottesville.[31]

Although they were not the legal owners of Elizabeth and Mary Hemings, and were certainly of lower status than Jefferson, Neilson's and Fossett's whiteness put them in a position of power over mother and daughter. If either man's attentions had been unwanted, both women would have had to resort to violence or hope these men might take no for an answer—out of either vanity or a sense of personal restraint. No one knows for certain what, if anything, Jefferson would have done if Elizabeth Hemings had complained about Joseph Neilson or if Mary Hemings had complained about William Fossett. The question is whether Jefferson's view of the Hemings women as different from other female slaves on his plantation provided them with any measure of protection against sexual abuse. If Hemings women did not have to go into the fields, or answer to the overseer, did they have to go to bed with Jefferson's white employees?

Rape was an ever-present threat to slave women, so it is understand-able to think of it immediately when faced with any example of interracial sexual relations during slavery. Striking a rare insensitive note, Fawn Brodie referred to Elizabeth Hemings's "cheerful giving of her body" when talking about her many years of childbearing.[32] We do not know whether Hemings was cheerful about it or not. She may have welcomed some of her partners and not others, while loving unequivocally the children those unions produced. Lacking either Hemings's or her daughter Mary's voices on this matter—or any direct statements from her family hinting at how these women felt about Neilson or Fossett—we cannot know what they thought about these two white men (or for that matter, the black men) who fathered their children. While their relations with white men draw more scrutiny because of the natures of slavery and white supremacy, one finds, upon examining their children's behavior, subtle indications that not all sex between blacks and whites was the same, and that enslaved black families recognized that and had different responses to it.

Lucia Stanton, who has studied the enslaved families at Monticello, has noted a difference in Elizabeth and Mary Hemings's sons' responses to their fathers, one that does not give us a definite answer about the quality of the relationships between their parents, but is suggestive. John Hemings did not take Joseph Neilson's last name, but kept his mother's. On the other hand, Mary's son Joseph took the last name Fossett when he became an adult, a name he actually may have been using himself all along. Slaves at Monticello often had their own understandings about their first and last names that Jefferson either did not know about or knew about and did not bother to credit. Whereas he used diminutives when writing about slaves, or seldom mentioned their last names, except for the Hemingses and one or two other families, slaves used their full first names and last names when describing who they were.[33]

There is actually even more evidence of Joseph Fossett's attitude toward William Fossett. He named one of his own sons William. Fossett's willingness to keep a connection to his father's line suggests that he may have had more positive feelings about the man or, at least, not hostile ones. There was nothing wrong with the name Hemings. In fact, that name meant a great deal at Monticello. It was Joseph Fossett's membership in that family, not his relationship to William Fossett, that put him on the road to his eventual freedom. He must have thought there was something honorable in his father's name, and the rest of his family seemed to think so, too. Joseph's sister Betsy had a son whom she named Joseph, and he, in turn, named his first son Fossett Hemings.[34] It would be more than a little unfair to Joseph Fossett to simply assume that he would willingly wear the surname of, and name his own son after, a man whom he regarded as his mother's rapist. That assumption seems highly improbable.

As for John Hemings, less can be made of his decision not to use his father's last name. It could have been the result of hostility toward Joseph Neilson because of the way he had treated Elizabeth Hemings, or maybe it simply did not matter enough to him. As a second-generation Hemings, he could well have felt the meaning of the name more strongly than members of the younger generation. His nephews Joseph Fossett and Burwell Colbert were one more step removed from Elizabeth Hemings and were willing to forge a different identity for themselves and their families.

While Elizabeth Hemings's two oldest sons began their lives in service primarily to Jefferson, she and her daughters were tied to the home, needs, and demands of his wife, Martha. As the daughter of a much married Virginia planter, and a woman who had been married before, Martha Jefferson was well acquainted with what was expected of her as a planter's wife. We have no records of her life at the Forest, so we do not know with any certainty just how she grew up. Her short first marriage produced no record of her life that has been preserved either. Martha Jefferson has benefited from the tendency to fill in the empty spaces in the lives of whites in the planter class with the most positive speculations that can be ventured. Usually, in the absence of information about blacks, the spaces are filled in with the most negative speculations about their capabilities and personae. Her great-granddaughter described Martha Jefferson as having been "well educated for her day,"[35] which still leaves us somewhat in the dark about her. The norm for young women in Martha's day seems to have been to educate females to read, play music, be pleasant companions to their husbands, and attend to the efficient running of the house. By the accounts of some contemporaries, Martha was said to have excelled in all these functions, although we have only one short, somewhat formulaic letter, to judge her literary capabilities.[36] Her mother, Martha Eppes, was from a prominent family, but we are still left to ponder what, if any, influence her father's origins had on her conception of herself and her capacities.

Historians have long speculated about a possible inner tension in Jefferson because his father's and mother's families were not evenly matched in terms of social prominence. Much has been made of his mildly sarcastic comment in his unfinished autobiography about his maternal rel-atives' ability to trace their origins "far back in England and Scotland," say-ing that everyone could make of that what he wanted—implying that there was really nothing worthwhile to be made of it. Jefferson's words have been interpreted as a defensive gesture in favor of his father, the self-made man who married into a large and well-connected family.[37] They may also betray a recognition of the fact that his much loved wife was the daughter of a person who had started life at an even much lower level than his own father. His children with Martha were just one generation away from a for-mer servant.

Jefferson listed in a family Bible the vital statistics of the closest mem-bers of his family. Indeed, that is how we know the place and year of John Wayles's birth. Other than those stark listings, there was no tracing of John Wayles's family back in England, not even to record his mother's or father's names. One would not have expected Jefferson to have reproduced a detailed genealogy of the Wayles family. But the failure even to mention for future generations the names of his father-in-law's parents, which he certainly knew, is curious. As far as Jefferson was concerned, Wayles's life mattered only in terms of what he accomplished after he came to Virginia.

Jefferson knew that both Peter Jefferson and John Wayles had raised themselves through their talent, hard work, and good luck. Their examples fit perfectly with his idea about what could be achieved in an America that was open to the advancement of common people, that is to say, common white male people. If Jefferson had any degree of self-consciousness about his father's position relative to his mother's, think of what Martha, "the daughter of a servant boy," might have felt in a society concerned with rank and family position. Both she and Jefferson, no doubt, had seen the paro-dies and insults leveled at her father in the pages of the *Virginia Gazette* a mere two years before their courtship. Members of Virginia society knew who her father was before he became prosperous. It is unlikely that so socially conscious a group of people would ever have forgotten where he had come from, or ever let her forget.

Martha barely had time to become a wife to Jefferson before she became a mother. In September of 1772, exactly nine months after her marriage, she gave birth to the couple's first daughter, whom they named Martha. Over the course of the next ten years, Martha Jefferson would conceive five more times, and her physical condition grew more precarious with each pregnancy and birth. The first birth was something of a portent as Martha had difficulty nursing her newborn daughter. As they did for so much in their lives, the Jeffersons turned to a slave for help. Ursula Granger had given birth to her son Archy around the same time, so the Jefferson's baby daughter was given over to her to nurse along with her own newborn son. Martha thrived, but Archy lived only one year.[38]

When upper-class plantation wives like Martha Jefferson spoke of keeping house—making soap, brewing beer, and the like—what they were really saying is that they supervised the slave women who actually performed the physical labor these tasks entailed. It is a safe bet that Martha Jefferson did not stir boiling pots of lye to make soap, or empty hops into containers to make beer. She may have tried her hand at a few domestic tasks as a lark, but certainly one of the points of having slaves was to relieve oneself of the drudgery of actually having to make a cake or cook the family meal under conditions far removed from modern standards. Cooking in the eighteenth century was a hazardous operation, involving much heavy lifting and open-fire ovens. This arduous task would not have been Martha Jefferson's responsibility, although her household accounts during her marriage record how much soap she made, how much beer she brewed.[39] Isaac Jefferson remembered her standing with a cookbook reading instructions to his mother, who actually baked the cakes.[40] It is also likely that Martha stood giving instructions to the Hemings women, some her half sisters, who performed the tasks that helped her provide a comfortable existence for her husband and children.

6

♣

IN THE HOME OF A
REVOLUTIONARY

HE AMERICAN REVOLUTION came most meaningfully into
the lives of the Hemings family in 1779. By that time the armed
conflict had been going on for four years, and the family's only
connection to the escalating crisis was Robert's time with Jefferson
in Philadelphia when he was a delegate from Virginia to the Second
Continental Congress. The whole family, however, was involved by proxy
because its owner had entered the revolutionary fray with the publication in 1773 of his essay *A Summary View of the Rights of British North
America.*[1] To the extent that his life and fortune were in jeopardy, the lives
of his slaves were precarious as well. The *Summary View* was Jefferson's
very public debut as a full-fledged opponent of British colonial policy.
The document impressed readers in the northern and southern colonies and, in part, led to the invitation in 1776 for Jefferson to draft the
American Declaration of Independence, which would ensure his fame
throughout the ages.[2]

Jefferson's memorandum book entries for the days immediately
before and after he wrote the declaration give no hint of the important
step the colonists were about to take and, then, had taken. There are,
instead, various quotidian notations, including references to purchases
for "Bob" (Robert Hemings), his fourteen-year-old manservant.[3] There
was no occasion for Hemings to take part in the drama in Philadelphia
in any serious way, although everyone in the vicinity knew they were living in momentous times. It was, however, during Jefferson's term as the

Revolutionary War governor of Virginia, from 1779 to 1781, that members of the Hemings family became intimately involved with the outcome of the Revolution.

Jefferson had not actively sought the position of governor. He had, in fact, thought about retiring from public life altogether, a step that would have kept him and members of the Hemings family at Monticello. As early as 1776, after serving in the Continental Congress, he had declined a commission to go to Paris, along with Benjamin Franklin and Silas Deane, stunning several of his colleagues into issuing stinging rebukes in letters that hinted that Jefferson was acting selfishly when selflessness was the order of the day.[4] None of them realized, because he never said it, that Jefferson's ambivalence about remaining a public man centered very much on his concerns about his wife's health. After the birth of her first child, Martha, she had given birth to a daughter and a son. The boy died in infancy. Her health was at risk both times.

Although Jefferson was not enthusiastic about it, the governorship, to which he was elected in June of 1779, at least allowed him to remain in Virginia. Having been nominated for the position and won a narrow victory over two of his closest friends, John Page and Thomas Nelson, Jefferson evidently felt he could not refuse the honor. He came into an office for which he might have been well qualified in times of peace, but for which he was ill suited in a time of war. He seemed to know this from the very start, expressing a degree of pessimism at the outset of his term that foreshadowed the difficulties, most not of his own making, that would later engulf him. "The appointment," Jefferson wrote, "would not likely . . . add to my happiness." In fact, it did not. On one occasion he pronounced himself "mortified" whenever people expected things of him that he could not deliver, such as turning an often reluctant group of Virginia militiamen into an effective fighting force against the British.[5]

His wife could not at first be persuaded to join him in Williamsburg,[6] and Martin Hemings was given money to take care of the household expenses. Although not specifically mentioned in any of his documents, it is likely, given the roles they played in his life, that Robert or James Hemings also had responsibilities. By September, Martha Jefferson, who had been staying at the Forest with her sister, had decided that she would come to Williamsburg with the two Jefferson daughters, Martha and Mary, called Patsy and Polly. The gathering of the whole Jefferson family in the capital thus meant bringing along a larger contingent of Hemingses to carry out the requisite duties of daily life in the household.

Seventeen-year-old Robert Hemings drove the phaeton that brought Jefferson and the family to the capital in Williamsburg in 1779. His brothers Martin and James rode alongside on horseback. All three men were there to perform the same services they performed at Monticello—Martin, to be the butler for the governor's household, and Robert and James to be Jefferson's personal servants. Their half sisters Mary Hemings and Betty Brown were brought along as well. Mary was twenty-six and by then the mother of Elizabeth Hemings's first two grandchildren, Daniel Farley, who was seven, and Molly, who was two. The Hemingses were joined by at least six other slaves: Jupiter and his wife, Suckey, the cook John, and George and Ursula Granger and their son Isaac, who went by the name Jefferson. Isaac's recollections along with other Jeffersonian documents form the basis of our knowledge about the origins and activities of some members of the Hemings family. He was seven years old at the time, and his memories were probably reinforced by many family retellings of this momentous event in their lives. He recalled that his family, the Hemings brothers, their sisters, a niece, and a nephew, along with the other slaves, lived in a section of the House of the Assembly.[7]

The Jeffersons, and the Hemingses who accompanied them, were not in Williamsburg for long. Concerned about the rapid advance of British troops, the Virginia General Assembly and Jefferson decided it would be prudent to move the capital farther inland, to Richmond, for the duration of the conflict. Jefferson, with his wife and daughters, Patsy and Polly, in tow, packed up his household and moved to what was then thought to be the temporary capital, where they set up household in a home owned by one of his relatives.

As to the enslaved members of the Jefferson household, one gets a sense from Isaac Jefferson's recollections that being away from their normal home in the midst of all the turmoil was something of an adventure, which expanded their horizons beyond what they, particularly the women, would have encountered had they been living exclusively at Monticello. There was the spectacle of war itself, a frightening yet energizing force, the troops in uniform, the urgent meetings of the governor and his advisers, a heightened sense of danger, and the prospect that however the conflict turned out, a way of life might be altered forever.

And then there were new faces. Two men in particular stood out in Isaac's memories: a white man named Bob Anderson and a black man named Mat Anderson. Isaac's description of the two men does not make clear the nature of their relationship beyond the fact that they worked together. Both men were part of the regiment that came to the governor's residence several times a week to "salute the Governor." Bob played the fife and Mat the drum. They were, apparently, quite a sight—"marching about there drumming and fifing." Although Isaac does not mention it, both Andersons may well have been in some type of uniform if traditional military protocol was followed. At least one member of the Hemings family was duly impressed, and her feelings were reciprocated.

During the course of their visits, the black Anderson, Mat—in Isaac's phrase—"was sort-a making love to Mary Hemings." While his white counterpart, Bob, went into the governor's residence for drinks, Mat Anderson kept company with Mary Hemings in the kitchen. We can probably never know whether Anderson's courtship of Hemings was more than platonic. "Sort-a making love to"[8] could be a euphemism for flirting with, attempting to court, or something more serious. We also do not know the precise months that Isaac was speaking of when he described the Jefferson household's interactions with both Andersons.

As all of these personal matters unfolded, a larger drama was, of course, being played out in the enslaved community of which Isaac makes no mention. There is no word about what, if anything, Lord Dunmore's proclamation offering freedom to any of the slaves of rebellious colonials who joined the British cause meant to the black people who attended the Jefferson family.[9] They certainly were aware of it as news traveled fast throughout enslaved communities, and whole families prepared themselves to link up with the British forces on the march. Hundreds of slaves, in fact, joined Dunmore's Ethiopian Regiment, and there would have been more had they not been felled by smallpox and other camp-related diseases.

Isaac Jefferson, still a child, perhaps had no personal thoughts about the matter. Yet his recollections reveal that he was surely paying attention to life among the adults at both Williamsburg and Richmond. Did they have anything to say that he remembered, or was he being discreet in front of Charles Campbell, the white Virginian newspaperman to whom he gave his recollections in 1847? At that point in history, with the South and North in the throes of a deepening sectional crisis, Isaac may have thought it unwise to suggest, or Campbell may have thought it unwise to repeat, that any among Thomas Jefferson's slaves had been anything other than completely loyal to him. In the coming battle between North and South, Unionists and Confederates alike would use Jefferson as a symbol for their respective causes. That process had already started when Isaac Jefferson talked to Campbell. The truth is that some of Jefferson's slaves—at least twenty-three men, women, and children—had a different conception of loyalty and did run away from him. Jefferson noted their departure in his Farm Book. These slaves, he wrote without any apparent trace of irony, ran away and "joined the enemy."[10]

What led some slaves to decide to take advantage of Dunmore's promise, while others did not? Individual personality surely counted: the runaways would have had to have considerable faith in their abilities to evade capture, along with a certain level of trust that the British would honor their word, or that whatever fate awaited them was better than life as a slave in Virginia. The ones who stayed may have been uncertain about their chances for escape or thought that the devil they knew was better than the devil they did not know. And some, like the Hemingses and other slaves living with Jefferson in Richmond, may have had reason to believe that their current positions were about the best that they could hope for in life at that moment. The slaves who ran away from Jefferson were from his outlying plantations and did not have the kind of relationship with him and his family that could have made them cling to any hope of freedom in the future or moderate treatment under slavery, not that freedom necessarily constituted a realistic hope for *any* of Jefferson's slaves at that point. Of the Hemingses, Martin, Robert, and James were the only ones who had virtually free movement. They could have run to the British had they wanted to. Perhaps they believed that any opportunity for unfettered emancipation in the future would be jeopardized by running away at that time, or perhaps they never seriously considered it.

War being the live chess match that it is, capturing the "king" (Governor Jefferson) was a principal object for British troops. Hence, it was no surprise when they came for him in Richmond in January of 1781. Under the command of Benedict Arnold, who had gone over to the Loyalists the year before, the British had executed a daring attack on Virginia by way of the James River as part of a campaign to establish a presence at Portsmouth and cut off supplies to the Continental army. With Arnold proceeding up the James River, Jefferson directed Robert and James Hemings to take Martha Jefferson and their daughters to Tuckahoe, the plantation of his mother's kinsman and his father's friend, Thomas Mann Randolph.[11] Jefferson had spent part of his boyhood there and in the years to come would be reunited with the place when his daughter Martha married Thomas Mann Randolph Jr.

Arnold's forces met only token resistance when they reached Richmond. Apparently Jefferson did not know the number of troops that were advancing toward the capital and delayed calling out the militia from Petersburg, Richmond, Albemarle County, and the Shenandoah Valley. Even had he acted more quickly, there was little chance the capital could have been defended against the British forces. During these days fraught with tension, the people of Richmond, black and white, waited anxiously. And then soldiers arrived. Isaac Jefferson remembered the confusion about whether the advancing troops were hostile or friendly. Some people, taking them to be militiamen "from Petersburg" who had come to "join them," started out to greet them. The British cleared up the confusion by firing cannons, which touched off a chaotic scramble among the women and children at Jefferson's home and, no doubt, throughout the town. Isaac was playing in the yard when his mother ran out from the kitchen to take him to safety. Mary Hemings gathered up her daughter, Molly. As soon as the fighting started, Thomas Jefferson rode off into the mountains on horseback to evade capture. He spent the night at Tuckahoe and then sent his family, most probably along with Robert and James Hemings, off to Fine Creek, a farm inherited from his father that was deeper into the Virginia countryside.[12]

With Robert and James gone, the other Hemingses remained in Richmond along with the rest of the household staff. The British came to the governor's residence looking for Jefferson, telling the slaves who remained there that they "didn't want to hurt him; only wanted to put a pair of silver handcuffs on him" and that they "had brought them along with them on purpose." They apparently did no physical damage to the governor's residence, but used his corn to feed their horses, made liberal use of Jefferson's always well-stocked wine cellar, and filled each soldier's "knapsack" with meat taken from the "meat-house."[13]

Unable to take Jefferson into custody, the British did take along some of the enslaved people from the governor's residence, including Mary Hemings and her children, as well as George and Ursula and their son Isaac. The adults were forced to walk—the children were allowed to ride—as the British continued their advance through the Virginia countryside, taking slaves (or being voluntarily joined by them) from plantations as they moved toward Yorktown. It is not clear how long the Hemingses and other slaves taken from Jefferson's plantations remained with British forces. But they and many others endured the harshness of life in the encampments, where rampant smallpox and camp fever led to many slaves' deaths. Jefferson returned to Richmond shortly after the British quit the town and resumed something of a life there. In the middle of all this tumult, Jefferson noted that he had paid a "Midwife for Bet." The Hemings family added a new member when Betty Brown gave birth to her son Wormley Hughes, in March of 1781.[14]

Martin Hemings and other members of the Hemings family had apparently traveled to Fine Creek to join the rest of the Jeffersons, for references to them show up in his account book entries during weeks following the siege at Richmond.[15] Over the next weeks Jefferson went back and forth between Fine Creek, Westham, Manchester, and other towns, carrying on official business, most likely with Robert and James Hemings. A combination of bad luck—the French troops that were expected to arrive and supplement the paltry Virginia militia were engaged in a battle and came too late to stop Arnold—and poor military strategizing on Jefferson's part— he failed to see the urgency of the situation and therefore could not alert General Washington in a timely fashion to dispatch some of his own forces to help—left Governor Jefferson vulnerable to charges that he had failed to protect the people of Virginia.[16]

Jefferson's reputation as war governor sustained a further blow after Virginia's government moved to Charlottesville to avoid another confrontation at Richmond. Now, back on his home turf at Monticello with his family, he dealt with the war and his own personal tragedies. His baby daughter, Lucy Elizabeth, had died in mid-April, a death that hurt her father so deeply that he once again contemplated leaving public life to attend to his family.[17] His term as governor was supposed to end on June 2, and he eagerly looked forward to that day, although there is some indication that other members of the government were unwilling to let him go. The death of children in those days was tragic, but not unexpected. Even if Jefferson had spoken freely about his family difficulties and how they were affecting him, he would not have received the sympathy that a grieving parent would receive today. In fact, he was roundly criticized whenever he suggested that his family duties took precedence over his life as a public man; correspondents hinted that it was the simple "pleasures" of family life that called him. It was actually more often life's fears that gripped Jefferson; the thought that his wife might die in his absence kept him tethered to the mountain.

Although he was at his core a man of the eighteenth century, much about Jefferson's attitude toward his wife and family would be familiar to twenty-first-century observers, especially his belief that he should not readily sacrifice family life for his public career and his direct involvement in the care of his ill wife and children. Hard as it was for him, Lucy Jefferson's death, quite understandably, hit Martha Jefferson especially hard. Her fragile health could only have added to the anxiety that was now a part of Jefferson's existence on public and private fronts alike.

There was simply no respite from the tensions and instabilities of war. Around the time Jefferson was slated, at least in his own mind, to leave office, Lord Cornwallis, recently arrived in Virginia, ordered Banastre Tarleton to go to Charlottesville to take into custody Jefferson and any other government officials he could find. Once again Jefferson sent Martha and his daughters away, probably with Robert and James Hemings. Jefferson's term as governor ended on a Saturday, but the assembly postponed the decision to elect a new governor until the following Monday. That decision left Jefferson in office for the coup de grâce: being forced to flee his own home at the approach of Tarleton's advancing troops. With enemy troops on the march, Jefferson had stayed at Monticello, following their movements through a telescope. At the very last moment, when they reached the base of Monticello and started up, Jefferson escaped, as he had done six months before, on horseback, toward Carter's Mountain, leaving Martin Hemings in charge of the household. Although Tarleton's approach scattered many other government officials, Jefferson, as the governor, symbolically embodied Virginia, and he became the special target of opprobrium that lasted for decades. It is hard to know what Jefferson's critics at the time and later expected him to have done in that situation—engage Tarleton's troops in a single-handed, meaningless fight to the death (probably just his own) or allow himself (the governor) to be captured and held for ransom? Flight was the only prudent decision.

This event made enough of an impression upon the Hemingses and the Jeffersons that the story about what happened on those days passed down through both family lines. Jeffersons and Hemingses told a version of the "slave/servant hides the silver from the marauding invaders" story so common in Revolutionary War as well as Civil War memories. In this instance, Martin Hemings took it upon himself to hide the Jefferson family silver under the planks covering the floor of one of Monticello's front porticos. Just as he finished his task, the British appeared on Monticello's lawn. Hemings "slammed down the planks," leaving an enslaved man named Caesar under the floorboard.

The British tried to get Martin Hemings to tell where Jefferson had gone, threatening to shoot him if he did not answer. He was said to have remained defiant. To Thomas Jefferson's white family, who saw slaves as mere instruments and extensions of their master's will and interests, Hemings's actions appeared as a selfless and comforting display of a slave's intense loyalty to his master. The early Jefferson biographer Henry Randall, who wrote the Jefferson family tradition into history books, was also remarkably willing to give Hemings attributes of aggressive manhood in this situation. "'Fire away, then,' retorted the black, fiercely answering glance for glance, and not receding a hair's breadth from the muzzle of the cocked pistol."[18] In Randall's depiction, the depth of Hemings's devotion to Jefferson sparked his defiant response, which would have been inappropriate for any other reason. Former slaves at Monticello and their descendants also kept the story of what happened that day on the mountain, although it is very likely that their stories of defiance had a different end in mind: to highlight a moment when enslaved people took the initiative in a dangerous and unpredictable situation.[19]

Whatever hopes contemporaries or latter-day observers grafted onto Hemings's actions, the record that we have of his personality suggests that he tended at all times to be a very contentious man. If he did risk death rather than respond to threats, there is a good chance that it was his own natural aggression and flintiness, infused with adrenaline, and not mere sentimentality that fueled his stubborn resistance in the face of British demands. His actions were in keeping with a character that apparently existed well before the crisis with the British at Monticello, perhaps even well before he met Thomas Jefferson. With Jefferson in flight and great uncertainty about what was going to happen, Martin Hemings was as much his own man at that moment as he could ever have been in his life to that date. During Hemings's confrontation with the British, and for eighteen hours more, while the troops occupied Monticello and then decided that neither the house nor its environs should be disturbed, Caesar remained trapped under the floorboard. The British left the mountain. Jefferson later expressed gratitude for Tarleton's uncharacteristically benign treatment of his home plantation.[20]

Perhaps the unique beauty of the place stayed the hand of the British at Monticello, because they were not so careful at Jefferson's other plantations. Elk Hill, where Elizabeth Hemings and her younger children had lived for a brief period after John Wayles's death, became Cornwallis's headquarters for a time. In contrast to what happened at the governor's residence and Monticello, he allowed his troops to do substantial physical damage to the place, burning barns and fences and destroying crops in the fields. They did the same at Jefferson's plantation Willis Creek, just across the James River.[21] The bulk of the slaves who ran away from Jefferson's plantations ran from Elk Hill and Willis Creek; some were whole families. These individuals joined members of the Hemings family at Yorktown, which had turned into a death trap for many slaves so desperate to escape the oppression of slavery that they risked severe hardship in order to gain freedom. In the end, their experiences in the British encampments affected all enslaved people who escaped from Jefferson's plantations. Fifteen died of either smallpox or other illnesses contracted during their time with the British.[22] When Jefferson made arrangements to have his human property returned to Elk Hill and Monticello (he even dispatched Martin Hemings to bring a runaway slave back from Williamsburg with the aid of George Wythe, the otherwise staunch champion of black emancipation), other slaves died from their contact with the returnees, whom they had attempted to nurse back to health.[23]

By the fall of 1781 all of the Hemingses were back at Monticello with Jefferson, who remained firm in his desire to leave public life. An inquiry into his actions as governor deeply wounded him for the rest of his days. Of all the brickbats hurled at him over the course of a very long and contentious public career, the official probe into his conduct as governor hurt the most. Though he was exonerated in the end, he never forgot that some of his fellow Virginians, most notably Patrick Henry, had encouraged others to undertake the inquiry and had been eager to have him censured. Jefferson closed the door on this low period of his life and joined his family at his retreat at Poplar Forest, a hundred miles from Monticello. There he turned to writing what would become his only published book, *Notes on the State* of *Virginia*, in which, among many other musings, he disparaged slavery, but offered as "a suspicion only" (one that he seemed more certain about than he was willing to say) that black people were inferior to whites. On one point he did not equivocate: the mixture with whites improved black people. There is little doubt that he had most in mind the young men who traveled with him and ran his household staff and the young women and girls who attended his wife every day—the people who were his wife's blood family were the mixed-race people he knew the best.

The End of an Era

Within a year after Jefferson's disastrous turn as governor of Virginia, a profound and catastrophic event at Monticello would change his life and ultimately alter the course of life for Elizabeth Hemings, her children, and grandchildren. Martha Jefferson, who had endured at least six pregnancies while married to Jefferson, and one when she was married to her first husband, gave birth to a daughter in May of 1782. It appears that the difficulties she had throughout the pregnancy did not abate following the birth of her daughter, whom she named Lucy Elizabeth after the Lucy Elizabeth who had died the year before.[24] Martha Jefferson was a small and delicate woman who lacked the robust constitution of her husband. Even with that one wonders exactly why her pregnancies took such a toll. Her family provided no real details about her illnesses, and in truth they may not have known what was going on themselves. This was an era of primitive medical knowledge. Another sixty years would pass before people came to understand the importance of the simple act of washing hands before and after any type of medical procedure, including the delivery of babies. While there is no definitive answer to the question why Martha Jefferson had persistent problems with pregnancy and childbirth, it is certain that bearing children put her life in jeopardy. The fear that she might die must have surfaced with each pregnancy. That was certainly the case in 1782 when Jefferson wrote to James Monroe announcing the birth of his daughter and describing Martha's condition as dangerous.[25]

Many years later, when recalling her mother's last illness, Martha Jefferson Randolph remembered that in those final months it was her father, her mother's sisters, and sisters-in-law who nursed and cared for Martha Jefferson.[26] Her memory, however, rendered invisible the enslaved women who had actually performed many of the tasks that helped her mother play the multiple roles of plantation mistress, wife, and mother. This happened even though these women played an even greater role in Martha Jefferson's day-to-day life precisely because her physical makeup impaired her ability to live up to the demands of those roles. In an era without reliable birth control, and with likely hostility to the concept even if it had been generally available, Martha had been pregnant every other year of her marriage. The events surrounding childbearing were largely the province of women. Although none of the Hemings women were midwives, they were certainly involved in caring for Martha during her confinement, and assisted at her births and during the lying-in times after the births.

While Martha Randolph undoubtedly told the truth from her perspective of her mother's last days, there are good reasons to believe that she drew an incomplete picture. Her father talked and wrote about the wheat or corn or peach trees he had "planted" when we know that he did not actually plow or sow his fields. When he made his famous trip to upstate New York and New England, ostensibly to study the Hessian fly but really for political reasons, only fleeting references reveal that James Hemings was along with him. So when Martha Jefferson Randolph spoke of her immediate white family as having been the sole actors in the day-to-day drama of her mother's lingering illness and death, one must keep in mind slave owners' predisposition to make slaves disappear from the central dramas of their lives—unless talk of their presence served the owners' need in some fashion.

Taking care of a seriously ill and bedridden person is an emotionally and physically difficult task. On the emotional side, the nurse must remain steady while attending to the needs of a perhaps melancholy, depressed individual who may lash out from frustration at the circumstances. If the sick person is a relative or friend, the caretaker feels frightened at the prospect of losing a loved one. Jefferson, Martha's white sisters, and her sisters-in-law no doubt experienced these aspects of caretaking to the fullest degree. They worked, and they surely grieved. But it is unlikely that they were primarily responsible for carrying out the more physical aspects of tending to the sick. The bedding had to be changed, the patient bathed, or at least wiped clean, and the remnants of sickness, from whatever source, had to be washed away. It is hard to believe that Jefferson and the white women in his household were doing all these unpleasant tasks for five months while Elizabeth Hemings and her daughters simply stood by and watched from afar, with nothing else to do. Socializing had ceased, and there was no steady stream of visitors that had to be attended to. Those days focused everyone's attention on the bedridden young woman fighting a valiant but losing battle for her life.

One Jefferson biographer, probably taking a cue from Martha Randolph's recollections, described the Hemings women as being "allowed to file in" on the day of Martha's death—implying that these women had been deliberately kept from her sick room during the entire period of her sickness, while Jefferson and the female members of his family did all the nursing.[27] This construction of events becomes even more problematic when one considers that none of this would have been new to Elizabeth Hemings. She had been looking after Martha in one way or another from the time she was a small girl, no doubt acting as something of a surrogate mother after Martha's mother and then her two stepmothers died by the time Martha was twelve. Elizabeth Hemings was the one adult female fixture in Martha Jefferson's life from the day she was born until the day she died. Even after Martha's death, the connection continued, as Hemings's daughter Sally was sent along with Martha's two youngest daughters to live with Martha and Sally's sister Elizabeth Eppes, while Jefferson took charge of his eldest daughter.

Contemplating Martha Jefferson's ordeal with childbearing, the historian Jack McLaughlin wrote that "it is a tribute to her strength of will and dedication to what she perceived as her mission in life" that she persevered in the face of all her difficulties.[28] That may be true, but it also must be seen as a tribute to the enslaved women—Elizabeth Hemings, her daughters, and Ursula—whose labor sustained Martha through all her trials and allowed her to make a home for her family. Without that support she would not have made it as far as she did. These women were there at the end of Martha Jefferson's life, precisely because they had been there all along.

It has been the lot of women throughout the ages to bear children with heads too large for the birth canals of human beings, whose ancestors inexplicably began to walk upright, changing the shape of their pelvises and making childbirth a more deadly proposition for humans than for any other species. Women have suffered pregnancy-induced high blood pressure and diabetes, postpartum depression and infections that sapped their strength and took their lives. The vast majority of them endured these problems while looking after other children, tending houses, and crops and performing whatever other tasks required of them as wives—and while being slaves. Tragic as her story was, at least Martha Jefferson had the advantages of a household of women—her white sisters and in-laws, her enslaved half sisters, and other enslaved women.

The deathbed scene that the Hemings women described to people at Monticello is both poignant and intriguing in light of what was to come in the lives of some of the people in the room. Just as the Jefferson family tradition memorialized the events surrounding Martha's death, the Hemingses also passed down stories about that day and relayed their memories to others. According to family tradition, during her final hours Martha Jefferson gave her youngest half sister, Sally Hemings, then nine years old, a handbell as a memento. The young girl, perhaps called by that very bell, had run errands for her older sister.[29] The story of this rather ambiguous keepsake highlights with great clarity the strangeness of this world. One sister makes a gesture to another sister that reinforces their family connection, even as it reminds us that one sister was the slave of the other. It is also possible that the story held a different meaning for the Hemingses. Lucia Stanton and Dianne Swann Wright's studies of the oral histories of Monticello's enslaved families note how stories passed down contain information that can be literal and/or symbolic—the story becomes a mechanism for conveying some important truth that the family wants known about itself beyond just the bare assertion of a discrete fact.[30] On the surface the story of the handbell is about Martha giving over something concrete to her sister Sally, singling her out above all the other Hemings sisters in the room that day as someone to whom she had a special link, even though Martha had known Sally, the youngest of the female slaves in the room, the shortest time. Sally Hemings grew up to have something far more important that had once belonged to Martha: her stricken husband, with whom she shared the deathbed watch that day, a moment that undoubtedly helped permanently define her view of him. Sally, in time, would have children by him and live with him for the rest of his life on the mountain, where he had dreamed of living with her sister.

Edmund Bacon, an overseer at Monticello, recounted a more extensive version of the Hemingses' memories of Martha Jefferson's death, focusing largely on Martha and Thomas. Bacon arrived long after the event, but knew the Hemings women very well. He remembered their saying that when Mrs. Jefferson lay dying, Elizabeth Hemings, her daughters Betty,

Nancy, Critta, and Sally, along with Ursula "stood around the bed." Her distraught husband, who had scarcely left her side for months on end, "sat by her" while she told him "about a good many things that she wanted done," for it was apparently clear to all involved that she would not recover.

> When she came to the children, she wept and could not speak for some time. Finally she held up her hand, and spreading out her four fingers, she told him she could not die happy, if she thought her four children were ever to have a stepmother brought over them. Holding her hand, Mr. Jefferson promised her solemnly that he would never marry again. And he never did.[31]

The story of Jefferson's promise clearly impressed Bacon, who went on to note that Jefferson was "quite a young man and very handsome," and Bacon "supposed he could have married well; but he always kept that promise."[32] Years after Bacon's account, Israel Gillette, another enslaved man from Monticello, said that the older servants there, people of the generation of Elizabeth Hemings's daughters, referred to the promise—a thing that no doubt shaped the everyday understanding about an unusual aspect of life at Monticello: Jefferson had no wife, so the place had no formal "Mistress."[33] Men lost wives and remarried fairly quickly. John Wayles responded more typically to the deaths of his wives—he got married again. That Jefferson at age thirty-nine promised not to do so was extraordinary.

It was also an extraordinary request. Why would Martha Jefferson ask such a thing of her husband? The historian Fawn Brodie suggested that Martha "may have been as possessive of him in death as she seems to have been possessive of him in life, as jealous of any future wife as she had been jealous of his 'passion' for politics," or "she was simply revealing her terrible sadness in relinquishing him altogether with life."[34] On the other hand, the story suggests that Martha herself stated rather plainly the root of her concerns about Jefferson's remarrying. Her reported words do not appear to have been motivated by a desire to die knowing that her husband would in some perverse way always belong just to her. This was not about him. It was about her children. She was concerned about the prospect of her daughters' growing up under the control of a woman who was not their mother.

We should consider Martha's reported request against the backdrop of her childhood. She had never known her own mother, who died when she

was just two years old. There followed a number of years with her first stepmother, who gave birth to Martha's sisters. After her death, there came a
second stepmother, who lived for only one year of her marriage to John
Wayles, dying when Martha was twelve. Her sisters were surely close to her
and played very important parts in her life. They helped care for her, and
one, Elizabeth Eppes, loved and looked after Martha's motherless children
as if they were her own. Without any Wayles family letters or reminiscences
to speak of, we have no idea what Martha's relationships with her two stepmothers were like. We can perhaps infer at the very least that if her experiences with her stepmothers had been good, she would not have been so
keen to make sure her own children did not have one. In fact, a positive
experience with a stepmother might have encouraged Martha to *insist* that
her husband find a good woman to help him raise her daughters. Instead,
she apparently felt it better that he raise the girls alone, or with the help of
the numerous women in both their families, whom she must have thought
she could count on. On that last point, she was right.

Jefferson was inconsolable. His widowed sister, Martha Carr, who sometimes lived at Monticello with her sons, had to help him from the room before
Martha died. They took him to a room, where he was said to have actually
passed out for a time.[35] Although his wife's death could not have been unexpected, Jefferson was not prepared for the finality of their separation. She had
struggled in some manner with each pregnancy, and he no doubt harbored
the hope—even this last time—that she would rally once again. When this
did not happen, he gave himself over to a grief that was so enormous that
it frightened those around him. He stayed in his room for weeks, walking
"incessantly night and day only lying down occasionally when nature was
completely exhausted." He emerged from this self-imposed exile, taking out
into the open air the solace that repetitive motion seems to have brought him.
Where once he had walked in his room "incessantly," he now rode his horse
with the same intensity, often in the company of his oldest daughter.[36]

Guilt almost certainly played a role in Jefferson's extreme reaction to his
wife's death. It was quite clear, well before his time, that some women were
simply not equipped to bear children safely. Doctors warned couples about
this, after a wife had repeated near-death experiences in childbirth. Even if
he never received a specific warning, Jefferson was as intelligent and well
versed in medical knowledge as most doctors of that era. He knew that he
was, in part, responsible for what had happened to Martha. In writing about

Jefferson's relationship with Sally Hemings, the historian Andrew Burstein has argued that Jefferson believed that sex was a necessary component to maintaining a healthy life, a not uncommon view then and now.[37] The true intensity of Jefferson's sexual nature, and his implacable belief in his right to have a rich sexual life is displayed most clearly, however, not in his relationship with Sally Hemings but in the way he conducted his sexual life with his wife. Martha Jefferson's fragile health made the stakes extremely high for the couple. His relationship with Sally Hemings always threatened embarrassment to his family, but his sex life with his wife was a matter of life and death—for her.

The terrible predicament the Jeffersons, and other couples, faced—marriage with no birth control—pitted Jefferson's own sexual desires against Martha Jefferson's health, and Martha lost. Jefferson, it must be said, acted in accordance with the mores and expectations of the time.[38] Martha Jefferson probably did as well, for she and Thomas were raised in a society where husbands were expected to have unfettered access to their wives' bodies, and girls were raised to submit. This is not at all to suggest that Martha did not benefit in her sexual life with her husband, that she was not a sexual being herself. The reality was, however, that she and other women had to think about sex in a different way than their husbands. As an elderly man, Jefferson remembered his marriage as "ten years of unchequered happiness."[39] But he had survived his marriage, and we cannot simply assume that Martha Jefferson, who did not survive, felt the same about it—that she was unequivocally happy to have to endure nine months of pregnancy, six times within ten years, and to be brought to death's door nearly every time. For practically her entire marriage she was either pregnant or lactating. Her body was not her own. Women of the eighteenth and nineteenth centuries, and even, as we will see, Jefferson's daughter Martha, expressed exasperation with constant childbearing. In fact, women have rather dramatically shown the world, and everyone inclined to romanticize perpetual pregnancy, how they really feel about the matter. In every society where they have had the choice, they have dropped the birthrate down to at or below the replacement level. After all her struggles with childbearing, Martha Jefferson died at age thirty-four, when she did not have to. Jefferson understood this, and it fueled his agony.

Martha's brothers Robert and James Hemings, while acting as personal valets, carriage drivers, and traveling companions to Jefferson, had shared experiences with him all around Virginia and other states, setting the stage for their eventual freedom from slavery. Despite their differences in status, they had gotten to know each other's basic personalities very well and knew things about each other that others in their lives would never have had the occasion to know. But during the ordeal at Monticello in the fall of 1782, it was the women in the Hemings family who witnessed and participated in a transformative family drama, sharing with Jefferson some of the most intimate details and probably the hardest moment of his life—the excruciating end to his marriage brought by his wife's death. Just as Elizabeth Hemings and her daughters had seen Martha in her weakest and most vulnerable moments, they had seen her husband at his lowest point as well, and they shared memories of this defining time at Monticello.

Seeing the "Master of Monticello" break down helplessly in abject misery gave the Hemings women a different picture of him, one that only a handful of people, the several white female relatives who were there, ever got to see. It was an indelible image. This was another piece of information about Jefferson that informed the Hemingses' understanding of who he was and how they should (and could) deal with him in the future. Enslaved people—actually any group under the control of oppressors—had, for their own welfare, to become adept at discerning the character and temperament of those who directed the course of their lives. It was an essential way to bring some semblance of personal order and self-mastery to their world within a system of oppression.

For Jefferson, who guarded his inner life so closely, to know that Elizabeth Hemings and her daughters had seen him in such a parlous state could only have underscored the notion that members of this family were different from other enslaved people at Monticello, who would never witness so stark and open a display of his vulnerability. He was not the master of everything. Although the Jefferson family did not think it important to note the Hemingses' participation in the tragedy that had unfolded in the midst of what had been a hard year all around, the Hemingses did not forget this pivotal moment in their history. The person who had brought them to this place was now dead, and they were left to deal with her husband, who now seemed nearly out of his mind with grief. Though Martha's death did not raise the terrible specter of family disruption by sale, the Hemingses knew that life on the mountain would change. The only question was how.

PART II

THE VAUNTED SCENE
OF EUROPE

5659.

Élévation sur le jardin.

Elévation

iarden

(OVERLEAF)

THE ELEVATION OF THE HÔTEL DE LANGEAC.

(Bibliothèque Nationale de France)

7

❦

"A PARTICULAR PURPOSE"

ARTHA JEFFERSON'S DEATH did indeed mark the beginning
of a new life for the Hemingses because it marked a new beginning for the man who owned them. On September 6, 1782,
death closed one path to the future, obliterating Thomas Jefferson's dreams
of a particular life in a particular place with "the objects of [his] affection."[1]
At the same time it cleared a path that he used to escape from the memories
of loss at Monticello. In those agonizing months when thoughts of suicide
crossed his mind, he did not know which direction that path would take
him or that his soon to be even deeper engagement with the new nation he
had helped create would set his inner compass.[2] For the next twelve years
he would be away on the country's business, seeing his farm only intermittently, living for periods in American cities large and small, away from the
provincial plantation society that had formed him. He would spend five of
those years living even farther removed from that society as a resident of a
foreign capital, on a belated version of the grand tour.

Elizabeth Hemings and her children moved with the flow of Jefferson's
suddenly altered course of life, and they had to adjust their own expectations and hopes for the future accordingly. During his years of quasi-exile,
the family experienced the beginnings of its dispersal—physical and psychological—as some members left Monticello to do work in other venues.
Some traveled with Jefferson to cities within the country and abroad, one
was sent with his children to live with relatives, some worked in the homes
of others, and a few pursued their own interests.

Within two months of Martha Jefferson's death, James Madison urged the

Continental Congress to ask Jefferson to go Paris to participate in negotiations for peace with Great Britain. The request was actually a renewed one, for he had been appointed the year before to serve with, among others, Benjamin Franklin and John Adams. Jefferson had declined the original appointment, citing family considerations. He had done the same after a previous request in 1776 that he represent America overseas. Martha's precarious health had prevented him from going both times.[3] Now, with no reason to decline and with a very good one to accept—the need for a change of scenery and a new project to lose himself in—Jefferson decided to go to Paris.

The commission came through in November of 1782, and Jefferson immediately set about planning for his trip. His journey, however, was delayed for almost a year and a half, which he spent traveling between Monticello, Richmond, Philadelphia, Baltimore, and Annapolis before he was finally able to set sail. The first and perhaps most important family decision he made about his trip, one that could be called fateful for both him and the Hemingses, was to take his oldest daughter, Patsy, to Paris and to send his two youngest daughters, Polly and the infant Lucy, to live with Elizabeth Eppes, the younger sister of his deceased wife. Mary and Lucy, however, did not go alone to their aunt's home, for Elizabeth Hemings's youngest daughter, Sally, nine years old at the time, went along as well. The tangled nature of the Wayles, Hemings, and Jefferson families appeared once again in sharp relief in this setting. Elizabeth Wayles Eppes was married to Francis Eppes VI, the namesake and descendant of the man who had originally owned Elizabeth Hemings when she was a child, and the move brought together two half sisters, Betsy Eppes and Sally Hemings.[4]

Twenty-one-year-old Robert Hemings accompanied Jefferson on his journeys. By 1782 he had traveled so extensively with Jefferson and alone that James Bear wrote of him that "of all the third generation Hemingses . . . Robert's life was the least onerous as a bondsman and the most productive as a freedman."[5] Bear was, no doubt, highlighting the fact that Hemings, unlike the vast majority of enslaved people, moved about the country with almost "unrestricted" movement. One says "almost" because Hemings was still at Jefferson's beck and call. When Jefferson summoned "Bob," he arrived.

Robert Hemings, his older brother, Martin, to a lesser extent, and his younger brother, James, lived their lives as slaves essentially bound to Jefferson, and when they were not serving him, Jefferson sometimes did not know where these men were. When he was away and planned to return home for a visit, he might write to family members and direct them to find out where Martin was and tell him to be at Monticello by the time he got there. Once, referring to Robert Hemings, Jefferson wrote, "If you know any thing of Bob, I should be glad of the same notice to him, tho' I suppose him to be in the neighborhood of Fredericksbg. and in that case I will have him notified thro' Mr. Fitzhugh." These men had developed lives of their own outside of Monticello and the immediate Charlottesville area. Richmond recurred as a frequent site of their activities. Jefferson wrote to a resident of the town in search of the Hemings brothers: "If you should know any thing of my servants Martin and Bob, and could give them notice to be at Monticello by the 20th. I should be obliged to you."[6]

Robert and James Hemings seemed to alternate duties to Jefferson. When one was not available, the other stepped in. After Jefferson was elected to Congress in June of 1783, James rather than Robert accompanied him and Patsy Jefferson through the Shenandoah Valley up to Philadelphia.[7] This relatively loose arrangement, and the experiences the Hemings males gained while on their own, seems to have heightened their expectations about what they were entitled to do in life. Theirs was a more open existence that taught them how to function—and that they could function—in the world outside of slavery at Monticello.

Jefferson's memorandum books during the months he was waiting to go to France record numerous payments to "Bob" for, among other things, household expenses, clothing, shoes, and trips to Wilmington, Eppington, Richmond, and Baltimore. Several entries are particularly significant. On February 1, 1784, while Hemings and Jefferson were in Annapolis, there is a reference—"Pd. Barber for 1.month20/"—and then another—"Bob begins with barber @ 15/per month." Nine days later—"Pd for barber's apparatus for Bob/30"—and then a final entry the following day fleshes out the story—"shavg. box for Bob 7/6." Robert Hemings was in training to become a barber. He had a two-month apprenticeship with a man named Le Bas and was the first member of his family to learn a trade.[8]

Whether becoming a barber was Hemings's idea or Jefferson's is unknown. Being a barber, however, was considered a high-status occupation for men of African descent, during and even after slavery. It was to Hemings's decided advantage to have a defined skill in a trade that could bring him income. If it was solely Jefferson's idea, there is no indication how he thought Hemings would use his training, and nothing in the years to come sheds any additional light on the original plan. Whatever the purpose, Hemings gained a new skill that he could use during those times when he was not required to be with Jefferson, which may have been the impetus for the apprenticeship. As things turned out, he would need something else to do for a long time, because Jefferson made another important decision (we do not know exactly when) that affected the Hemings family: whenever the final word came that he was to start for France, it would be James, rather than Robert, Hemings who would accompany him.

From the New World to the Old

James Hemings was nineteen years old when he received word that he was going to France. Why Jefferson chose him instead of his brother Robert, who was older and had been the most closely associated with him, is an interesting question. Robert Hemings's new skills as a barber would have been useful to Jefferson beyond what he knew about being a manservant. Taking him along for what Jefferson expected to be a two-year stint would seem to have been the most natural thing to do. On the other hand, Robert was very likely already a married man, and Jefferson could have been acceding to his desire to be with his wife, something he would do in the years to come. The decision could also simply have been based on Jefferson's assessment of the younger man's temperament and potential talent for the profession he wanted to bring him to Paris to learn: James Hemings was going to France to study cooking and to become a French chef in Jefferson's household there and, when they returned, at Monticello.

We get the first hint of Jefferson's plan for Hemings in a letter dated May 7, 1784, that he wrote to his soon to be secretary in France, William Short.

> I propose for a particular purpose to carry my servant Jame with me. . . . If you conclude to join me I would wish you to order Jame to join and attend you without a moment's delay. If you decline the trip, be so good as to direct that he shall immediately come on to me at Philadelphia.[9]

Short, who was in Richmond, replied, noting the small amount of time he had "to get Jame down here and to reach Philadelphia."

The Moment I recieved your Letter, I looked out for an Express to send to Albemarle. Whilst in this Search I was informed Jame was in Town with a Mr. Martin whom he accompanied as a riding Valet. I sent immediately to his Lodgings and was told he had set out that Morning to some Place and would return probably in a Day or two. To-day he returned. To-morrow Jame goes off on his way to Albemarle.[10]

That was not the end of the matter. Short wrote again the same day and addressed the issue of how to get Hemings to Jefferson in time to make the preparations for France.

Jame sets out to Albemarle this Morning. My Intention was, as it was impossible for me to set out immediately that he should go on from Monticello to the Northward. But a Gentleman who is going from hence immediately to Philadelphia wishes very much that he should accompany him. As it will be much more secure for him to travel under his Wing than alone, I have agreed, if the Gentleman, Capt. Bohannon, can await his Return from Albemarle, that he may come this Way. As the Gentleman can furnish him an Horse I wished Jame to go straight from hence to Philadelphia, but he insisted on seeing Albemarle first. Jame has gone now to get the decisive Answer of the Gentleman, whether he could await his Return from Monticello and this is to determine his Route.[11]

Before Short could finish the letter James returned with an answer.

Jame has this Moment come here and says Capt. Bohannon cannot set out as soon as he had intended by 10 or 12 Days. He will therefore go on from Albemarle. He has been Yesterday Evening and this Morning in Search of an Horse to hire. I understood from him last Night that he had procured one, but this Morning he tells me the Man of whom he was to have the Horse has disappointed him.[12]

This exchange reveals important aspects of Hemings's way of life, his personality, his knowledge of Jefferson, and his relationship with his own family. The young man was living in Richmond, having gotten a place to stay on his own and found work that paid enough for him to support himself—not only to get housing but also to rent a horse for travel. He, like his brothers, knew how to ride and did so routinely. Horses were symbols of power and prestige in Virginia. Most enslaved people, and poor whites, walked to their destinations, sometimes for miles. Hemings, atop a horse, actually saw the world from a different perspective, and was seen in a particular way by the people whom he passed on the road. He had known contacts in Richmond because, as Short looked for a way to relay Jefferson's message to him, the people he spoke to about Hemings knew who he was, that he was already in town, and where he was staying.

One part of Short's letter—his statement that it would be "much more secure" for Hemings to travel "under the Wing" of Captain Bohannon—reminds us of the problem with taking too rosy a view of Hemings's situation. Travel with companions always provides additional security for travelers, but even adjusting for the differences in Bohannon's and Hemings's statuses, Short's notion of Hemings being "under the Wing" of Bohannon for the sake of his security hints at something else: Hemings was in potential danger when he traveled about alone. His youth was probably not the issue. A nineteen-year-old male during that time would not have been seen as requiring another man's protection to travel.

Hemings, however, was not just any nineteen-year-old male. He was a male slave. The institution of racially based slavery was so entrenched in Virginia that any person of African ancestry was presumed to be enslaved. On that point, Short's expression of concern perhaps gives us another bit of important information about Hemings. This young "bright mulatto" was exactly that—a very light-skinned person who was also recognizably of African origin. That alone was reason to fear for his safety from the people whom he might meet on the road, particularly as he moved beyond his normal haunts in the environs of Charlottesville and Richmond. Slave patrols sometimes met blacks traveling alone in Virginia and assaulted them physically and verbally. For African Americans like Hemings, meeting random white people on the road, even if not in organized patrols, carried a potential hazard.

The Hemings brothers' relatively free movement on the roads of Virginia was never totally free, because it took place in a slave society under a regime of white supremacy. Slavery was more than just the relationship between an individual master and an individual slave. The entire white community was involved in maintaining the institution and the racial rules that grew up around it, rules that often required interfering with an individual master's decisions about how he wanted to handle his slaves. As far as Jefferson was concerned, the Hemings brothers could come and go as they pleased, so long as they showed up when he needed them. The community at large, however, had an interest in the unsupervised travel of enslaved people. As early as 1680, Virginia statutes mandated that slaves who traveled without supervision of a master had to carry a pass. If they were caught without one, they could receive up to "twenty lashes."[13] Virginia passed a law in 1782 providing that slaves who were "permitted to go at large as free or to hire themselves out would be seized and sold."[14] Given these restrictions, the Hemings males may have carried a pass from Jefferson stating who they were and that they had permission to be on the road.

Short's role as an intermediary between Hemings and Jefferson reveals another crucial feature of the Virginian slave society in which they lived: it was a place of densely packed social and family connections, even between masters and slaves. Short was the nephew of Robert and Henry Skipwith, through his mother, Elizabeth Skipwith. The Skipwith brothers were married to John Wayles's daughters Tabitha and Anne Wayles, respectively. These women were James Hemings's half sisters. Short was twelve when his uncle Robert married Tabitha Wayles, and fourteen when Henry married Anne.[15] He had a connection to the Hemings family by these marriages that predated his connection to Jefferson, who came into his life prominently when he was an older teenager.

One might think that, having heard the directive "he shall immediately come on to me at Philadelphia," Hemings would be on the first available transport out of Richmond going north. He decided instead to go immediately to Monticello. Short clearly wanted Hemings to follow Jefferson's direction, but he told his mentor that Hemings "insisted on seeing Albemarle first."[16] Hemings knew Jefferson well enough to know that he had some leeway to interpret "immediately," and he did that in a way that allowed him to attend to his own personal concerns. Going to France was, after all, a momentous event. Anyone not used to sea travel might be humbled by the prospect of crossing the Atlantic Ocean. Short, who expected to join Jefferson, probably knew and mentioned to Hemings that Jefferson was supposed to be away for about two years. So the young man had at least some idea of what he was facing, and it was to be nothing like his accustomed jaunts between Virginia and other towns along the eastern seaboard, where he was always within easy striking distance of home. His mother and siblings were at Monticello, and he wanted to see them before he left the country.

Hemings need not have hurried. He made it to Jefferson and Patsy in Philadelphia in enough time before they went east to catch the vessel that would take them to Europe. Robert Hemings traveled with them. Even after they arrived in Boston, following stops in New York and other parts of New England, there were additional delays as Jefferson found "on his arrival that there [was] no vessel going for France from any Eastern port."[17] During this waiting period Jefferson repaid money he had borrowed from Robert Hemings and bought him shoes and clothes. He then made arrangements for Hemings to travel through New York with "30 dollars to carry him home" to Virginia, a valediction that would cover the next five years. The next day he wrote to Nicholas Lewis, who was overseeing his plantations in his absence, to tell him that Robert Hemings should be allowed to hire himself out.[18] After two weeks of waiting, James Hemings and Thomas and Patsy Jefferson left Boston Harbor on the *Ceres*, at four in the morning on July 5, 1784, with six other passengers on the ship.[19] This young man, of English, African, and Welsh extraction, was the first of his family to reverse the route over the ocean his ancestors had crossed on their very different journeys to Virginia.

The voyage was uneventful, the weather fair, and the *Ceres*, a brand-new vessel, made the crossing in a mere three weeks. The party "landed at West Cowes," on the Isle of Wight, on July 26.[20] Patsy had become ill at some point and required the services of a doctor while they were in port. This delayed their departure to Portsmouth, on the mainland of England, from where they were to take a ferry across the English Channel to Le Havre, a port at the mouth of the Seine River. Unlike the smooth Atlantic voyage, the Channel crossing was an extremely choppy trek, through a terrible storm in very rude quarters. Patsy Jefferson's cabin was so small that she had to crawl into it.[21] James Hemings's quarters would not have been any better, as he was almost certainly given an inferior berth for the trip.

Hemings and the Jeffersons arrived at Le Havre on July 31. The next day Jefferson wrote that he "gave James to bear expenses to Rouen 72f."[22] As far as we know, the young man spoke no French at the time, though he likely knew enough words or phrases to get along in a rudimentary fashion. Patsy Jefferson had received some instruction in the language before departure, and Jefferson had studied French from the time of his school years. Both had an interest in at least telling Hemings how to address the people he might meet on the journey. He went alone, through what Jefferson later described as the "fertile" and "elegantly improved" countryside of Normandy, to make arrangements for their lodgings at Rouen.[23]

Hemings's destination was the ancient capital of Normandy, famous as the site where Joan of Arc was burned at the stake. He accomplished his mission apparently without a problem and with great efficiency because Jefferson noted that on August 3 he had "Recd. Back from James of the money given him 36f."[24] From Rouen, Hemings and the Jeffersons made their way to Paris, on a route that took them through even more beautiful French countryside along the Seine River during harvest time. Hemings had been to the largest cities in North America and had probably seen beggars on the streets. He may not have seen so many and so aggressive a group as the ones who gathered around the Jefferson carriage at every stop. James Hemings had his first look at Paris on August 6, 1784.[25]

While Patsy settled into life as a student at the prestigious Abbaye de Panthemont soon after their arrival, Hemings and Jefferson lived in what would turn out to be temporary residences until October of 1785, when they moved to the Hôtel de Langeac, their permanent residence until they left the country near the end of 1789. At the very beginning, there was the Hôtel d'Orléans in the rue de Richelieu for six days and then the Hôtel d'Orléans "in the rue des Petits-Augustins" for several more weeks. From there Jefferson moved into an actual house at "No 5 cul de sac Taitbout," which he immediately set about remodeling, although he had only a one-year lease.[26]

In that very peripatetic first year or so in Paris, Hemings had new faces to get used to and old faces to meet in a new environment. One of Jefferson's first orders of business after he was, to some degree, settled was to assemble a household staff. A man of his station, the diplomatic representative of a country, needed a suitable coterie of servants. Hemings could not join that group in his usual role as Jefferson's personal attendant, because his days would be taken up training for his new profession. His replacement for a time was a man named Marc, whom Jefferson hired in late August as his "Valet de Chambre." Marc eventually went on to become Jefferson's maître d'hôtel until he was fired, in 1786, and replaced by Adrien Petit, who had worked for John and Abigail Adams. There were other servants,

Legrand and Vendome, and a *frotteur* named Saget, whose job it was to wax the floors by sliding along on them "on foot-brushes," which must have been as interesting a sight for Hemings to see for the first time as it is to imagine it now.[27]

Then there were the arrivals from America whom Hemings already knew, men who stayed with Jefferson at various points during his time in France. David Humphreys, the secretary to the American commission, came early on. Humphreys, who had been an "aide decamp to George Washington," said that Jefferson's "politeness and generosity" had led him to suggest that Humphreys stay with him while they were in "residence in Europe." He did that for a while, but left France and returned to the United States in 1786.[28] Jefferson's protégé William Short joined the household as Jefferson's private secretary. He lived off and on at the Hôtel de Langeac for the rest of Jefferson's stay.[29] While in Boston, Jefferson had met a man named Charles Williamos, who was also traveling to France, and, as a friendly gesture, offered him a place to stay while he was in Paris. He should not have been so trusting. Williamos, who died sometime in 1785, was possibly a British spy, which may explain why he worked so hard during their time together in Boston to become "a very great intimate" of Jefferson's.[30] Over the coming years many more visitors floated in and out, using Jefferson's residence as a hospitable place of rest and refuge where they could enjoy meals that James Hemings prepared.

Exciting as this adventure undoubtedly was to him, Hemings actually got off to a difficult start in Paris. He fell ill sometime in October of 1784. The nature of his illness is unknown, but it was serious enough to require the attentions of a doctor. Dr. I. MacMahon, a "physician and instructor at the Ecole Militaire" and the Jeffersons' personal physician, treated him. He was evidently bedridden, for Jefferson also hired a nurse to take care of him until he recovered.[31] He probably suffered from a more extreme version of the kind of traveler's malaise that often afflicts people when they go abroad and are exposed to different kinds of food and a new water supply. Jefferson, sick himself around the same time, explained his own illness in those terms, saying that he had been through the "seasoning . . . that is the lot of most strangers" when coming to the city for the first time. We get a sense of what that first winter was like for the newly arrived Virginians from Jefferson's complaint about the "extremely damp air" and the "very unwholesome water."[32] Jefferson's health problems continued into the spring, but Hemings was back on his feet by December and ready to begin his training as a chef.[33]

Something else happened during Hemings's and Jefferson's first months in France that contributed to Jefferson's acute discomfort that winter and set in motion a chain of events that changed his life and the lives of the Hemings family as well. He received word in January that, not long after he had left the country, his two-year-old daughter, Lucy, had died of whooping cough at Eppington. This very common and serious childhood disease had also carried off Elizabeth Eppes's own daughter, Lucy, who was about the same age as Jefferson's little girl. Lucy's older sister, Polly, had been sick, too, but had recovered.[34] Jefferson was distraught. The thought of bringing Polly over had been on his mind even before he received news of Lucy's death. That drastic course seemed unnecessary then, because he did not expect to be in France much longer. But in May of 1785, nine months after his arrival, when he was appointed to succeed Benjamin Franklin as the American minister to France, he was adamant about having Polly with him.[35]

Jefferson had outlived a wife and four of his six children. He had never had the chance to get to know his youngest daughter, Lucy. After giving her over to her aunt's care, he had been away for most of her infancy. Now, facing this new tragedy, he apparently could not bear the thought that something might happen to Polly, that she, too, could die a stranger. He wrote to the Eppes family, asking them to send his daughter, stating his preferences for how that might be done. Instead of immediately complying with his request, both Elizabeth and Francis Eppes, who had grown to love Polly as parents, and she them, embarked upon a plan of avoidance, hoping that Jefferson might change his mind about wanting his daughter to join him and her sister. In the end, it would be almost two years before Polly and the young girl who was sent along with her—James Hemings's sister Sally—arrived in France.[36]

James Hemings was certainly aware of this family tragedy and was told, or able to discern, that there was some problem with getting Polly to her father, as the date for her impending arrival never seemed to materialize. The fascinating, and unanswerable, question is exactly how Hemings reacted to the news of Lucy Jefferson's death. He was certainly close enough to Jefferson to have sympathized with him and understood his grief at the passing of his child, the one whose birth had hastened the death of his wife. This sad event could only have dredged up for both men memories of Martha Jefferson's final struggle.

Let us consider Hemings's situation. A man is born into a society that allows his half sister and her husband to hold him as a slave. The child of the couple—the enslaved man's niece—dies. Does the enslaved uncle grieve for the child? Did Hemings grieve for his half sister Martha years earlier? Would Jefferson think the deaths of his wife and daughter meant anything at all to their enslaved brother and uncle? Hemings had no legal relationship to either Martha or Lucy Jefferson. While he grew up around his sister, and had thoughts and feelings about her, he certainly cannot have known his niece very well; she was a baby, and he was traveling with Jefferson while the little girl was at Eppington. Whatever emotions Lucy's death did or did not call forth, it provided yet another opportunity for Hemings to ponder his relationship to the man who owned him. The connections between these two men are so divorced from anything resembling what could be recognized today as "normal" human relations that they can be recovered only in the imagination and, even then, only with great difficulty.

White families had the unparalleled capacity to control the flow of written information during slavery with their near-monopoly on literacy and record keeping. They were committed to, and adept at, hiding information about race mixing within their ranks and about their family relationships with black people. As a result, we lack ready prompts to help us visualize what people linked as Hemings and Jefferson were said to one another in times like these. Of course, that is what white slave owners intended—to make these matters literally unthinkable to posterity, to try to erase the identities of their black relatives in order to protect the reputations of their white families. In this way they hoped to maintain ownership over black people's identities in perpetuity, in the manner of holding a fee simple absolute in real property—a thing that could be given up only at the owner's choice.

Becoming a Chef

In the weeks before learning of Lucy Jefferson's death, Hemings had started his apprenticeship with his first teacher, Combeaux, whom Jefferson paid 150 francs to begin the training. Combeaux was Jefferson's *traiteur* (caterer), and he was also a "restaurant keeper" in the city.[37] Although Jefferson gave no address for his establishment, it must have been relatively close to the Hôtel de Langeac. Hemings continued with Combeaux until February of 1786, mastering the technique of French cooking that would form the basis of his career during the rest of his time in slavery and after he became a free man.[38] While Combeaux and the French people Hemings worked with may have spoken some English, he was probably largely immersed in French and forced to communicate as best he could. He apparently did not do so well early on. During that same February, Jefferson sent the following humorous message to Elizabeth Hemings through Antonio Giannini, his gardener at Monticello: "James is well. He has forgot how to speak English, and has not learnt to speak French."[39]

Jefferson, who was obviously exaggerating the situation for comic effect, may well have secretly sympathized with Hemings's plight. Although he could read French well, he never became as comfortable with the language as his daughters. One understands why. They were young girls, and he was in his early forties when he went to France, and it was simply more diffi-cult for him to pick up the language. Martha revealed that her father did not know how to speak to people when they arrived in France. Again, that is no surprise because the only way to learn to speak a language is through practice. However many years he studied with his tutor, Jefferson cannot have had much opportunity to practice speaking French. He himself admit-ted that he could not write the language, but his biographer Dumas Malone would not take him at his word on this.[40] Jefferson evidently meant that writing French was not as easy for him as reading it, that it did not come as quickly to him as other mental tasks.

Though not as young as Patsy Jefferson, Hemings was younger than Jefferson and better suited to achieving some level of proficiency in conver-sational French. Jefferson made the comment about Hemings's struggles with the language just eighteen months into his time in France, very early to expect fluency in a new language. He had over three more years after Jefferson's report to achieve the kind of breakthrough that can occur almost overnight when the basic system of a language is suddenly and inexplica-bly revealed. Unlike Jefferson, who had some familiarity with the structure and vocabulary of French, Hemings likely had next to nothing to start with, other than what the Jeffersons may have taught him so that he could at least greet people and make his basic desires known. Though he began with the disadvantage of no previous introduction to the language, he had the advantage of youth and energy. Unlike Jefferson, who frequented English-speaking salons and had relations with other English-speakers, Hemings was thrust, during his apprenticeships and when he was at the Hôtel de Langeac, into a world where English was not spoken.

There was a sad coda to Jefferson's communications with Giannini about Hemings. When the gardener wrote back, he passed along Elizabeth Hemings's "compliments" to her son and word that his sister Lucy, nine years old, had died.[41] The cause of her death is not known. This was likely a terrible blow to Hemings. His mother had been unusually lucky for a woman of her status, indeed for any woman of that time. Losing family members was an almost unheard-of thing for the Hemingses. Lucy is the only one among Elizabeth Hemings's many children who is known to have died as a child. Jefferson was more used to this, if such a death was ever really gotten "used to." He had lost several siblings by the time he was a young man.[42] Now Hemings's youngest sister was the thirteen-year-old Sally. He had no idea that Lucy's death would be the catalyst for bringing her to join him on what was surely the time of his life.

Despite all the bad news from home, both Hemings and Jefferson continued on: Hemings learning his trade and Jefferson his. When his apprenticeship with Combeaux ended, Hemings graduated to more specialized training: learning the art of French pastry making. He had several teachers, but by far the most impressive was one of the prince de Condé's cooks. The prince, Louis-Joseph de Bourbon, was a member of the royal family and lived on a very extravagant country estate several hours outside of Paris called Chantilly, which made Monticello (even in all its later incarnations) appear decidedly déclassé. Its architecture, grounds, and art collection were impeccable. The stables, considered "the grandest in the world," could house 240 horses. Chantilly had been known since the days of Louis XIV, who dined there, for the sumptuous meals the prince's cooks prepared.[43] Hemings was indeed learning with a master, with results that extended beyond his lifetime and live on in recipes that survive at Monticello today.

Hemings first worked with the prince's cook "one day in town, five days in the country, and four after their return to town."[44] The lessons were particularly expensive and got him into a bit of trouble with Philip Mazzei, a Jefferson friend who had arranged for them. Mazzei described the problem to Jefferson in a letter in April of 1787. According to Mazzei, Hemings said he did not know until he arrived at the country estate that the lessons would cost "12 francs a day," with his "maintenance" included in the price. The cook claimed that he had told Hemings the price before they left, but Mazzei was annoyed at Hemings. He reasoned that even if the young man had not known how much it would cost until he got to the country, he should not have taken the four additional lessons when they returned to town. He was evidently concerned that Hemings's "improvident or unwary" decision would cost Jefferson too much money.[45] The prince's cook offered to continue with Hemings whenever the prince was in residence in Paris, and to "take [James] to Burgundy during the session of Parliament there." Another cook, evidently associated with the prince's household, offered to work with Hemings for "100 francs a month if the arrangement [was] by the year at 200 francs by the month."[46] Jefferson, on a trip through the south of France, wrote back to Mazzei as concerned about the price of the lessons as his friend was.[47]

Though Mazzei presented this as a problem of Hemings's making, even a cursory consideration of what happened reveals that he, not James Hemings, made the most "improvident" decision. Mazzei, through his "good offices,"[48] had arranged to have a man in the employ of an important member of the French royal family, a cook in what was surely one of the most celebrated kitchens in the country, take on his friend's servant as a pupil. He was not dealing with Combeaux the *traiteur*. Mazzei surely knew that such an arrangement would not come cheap. Yet, he did not bother to determine in advance how many lessons would be involved and how much each would cost—in other words, to proceed carefully—and then tell Jefferson so that he could decide whether the price was bearable to him. If he did not have time to reach his friend, he could have made the decision on Jefferson's behalf. That would have been the most sensible course of action, especially since Mazzei was making a deal with Jefferson's money, not his own. Instead, he left it to James Hemings to decide that twelve francs a day was too much and that he should not get as many lessons from the prince's cook as he could, and then Mazzei chastised Hemings when he made the "wrong" decision.

Was it so clearly a bad decision? Consider the terms of the new cook's offer to train Hemings, which can be taken as a measure of what at least he thought was the market for his services. Even if Mazzei and Jefferson thought the cook's offer—100 francs per month if there was a contract for a year, and 200 if it was month to month—was too high, it still reflected the

very reasonable practice, then and now, of charging more for short-term contracts for high-end services than for long-term contracts. The price of a day-
to-day contract is not merely a year-to-year contract divided by 365 days.

Why would Hemings know how much the celebrated prince de Condé's
cook was going to mark up his charges for training him on a day-to-day
contract and whether that markup was definitely too much for Jefferson?
Hemings had seen enough of Jefferson to know how extravagant he could be.
They were, after all, living in a resplendent mansion that had a complement
of servants and was being filled with the expensive furniture Jefferson was
purchasing. High-priced cooking lessons could well have been just another
of his extravagances. Had Mazzei inquired about the cost ahead of time, the
matter could have been resolved before there were any hard feelings. But he
professed ignorance of all of the arrangements, though by any measure it
was exactly his job, as one acting as Jefferson's agent, to be informed about
them. And when it looked as if his plan was going to cost his friend a lot of
money, a fact that no doubt embarrassed him, he shifted the blame for his
own negligence onto James Hemings.

Hemings was in no position to turn around and chastise Mazzei for the
lack of forethought that had led to this debacle, certainly not in a fashion
that would have made its way into history books as a comment on Mazzei's
capabilities and character. It was Mazzei and Jefferson who had the power
through their letters to characterize for posterity the nature of this problem
and in doing so define James Hemings and his role in this matter in their
own way, one that preserved a sense of Mazzei's basic competence while
diminishing Hemings's. These men were of the same class and race, and
whatever he may have thought about it in his own mind, Jefferson could
not, in the letter responding to Mazzei about all of this, acknowledge his
friend's error by asking the obvious question: *Mr. Mazzei, why didn't you
find out how much it was going to cost me before you sent James out to work with
the prince's cook?*

8

♦

JAMES HEMINGS:
THE PROVINCIAL ABROAD

THE IDEA OF Paris as a liberating force in the lives of Americans is
a cliché of long standing, and it is often said that the city liberated
Thomas Jefferson. In Henry Adams's formulation, he was able "to
breathe with perfect satisfaction nowhere except in the liberal, literary, and
scientific air of Paris in 1789."[1] For the first and last time in his life, he lived
in a society with a large social cohort whose intelligence, erudition, and
accomplishments matched or exceeded his own. No place could have provided a more perfect respite from the wreckage of his personal life. Here
this ever forward-thinking man began to overcome, as much as he could,
the pain of his wife's death and to open himself to the possibilities of making a new future with the family and the acquaintances still left to him.
Never again would he know such a complete marriage of his interests—
social, personal, political, aesthetic, and cultural—as he experienced during
his five years in France.

James Hemings was a particular kind of American in Paris, an enslaved
one. Talk of his "liberation" in that place must encompass more than just
the abstract or psychological. Certainly Hemings had an individual personality that was ripe for development in a place with very different morals and
mores, a language he had to learn, and a great cuisine that he was to study
and to master. In all his previous travels with Jefferson, Hemings had never
encountered the opulence of the architecture on display in the churches,
cathedrals, and some of the private residences where he trained as a chef
and that he passed on a daily basis. He was from a frontier society, and he
had come to the very opposite of that—a visibly old country, whose battles,

successes, and values were on display in the buildings, statues, streets, and public areas he would come to know well. Young men of rank took the grand tour though the great cities of Europe, with Paris as an obligatory stop, as a way of finishing their educations and preparing themselves for their lives as gentlemen. Hemings, of course, was not considered a man "of rank" and would never lead a gentleman's existence. But his journey from the Virginia wilderness to what passed for cities in the United States and to the sophistication of Paris was perhaps even more personally transformative for him than it would have been for most gentleman travelers. The distance between the life he had led and the one he would experience in Paris was far greater than it was for members of the upper classes seeing the city for the first time. There was much more for Hemings to learn, about himself, the society he had come from, and the man who owned him.

The knowledge, for example, that Jefferson and his daughter—among the elite of Virginia society—were considered poorly dressed by Parisian standards, and quickly had to have clothes made so that they could appear in polite society, was a revelation.[2] He had come of age in a world that told him, and other enslaved black people, that their white masters were at the very pinnacle of human existence, achievement, and refinement. Yet, here was a society in which his master, though greatly respected and admired by those who knew him, took on the aspect of a hick.

Moreover, Hemings, and later his sister, encountered Paris at a singular moment in its history. Much has been written about France on the eve of revolution—the extremes of wealth and poverty, the confused and deteriorating economic situation, its ultimately doomed political culture. During this same time, the society was heavily influenced by the intellectual and cultural ferment of the Enlightenment, a force that was in play in other parts of the world, but found its apotheosis in France. The country was still very hierarchical, and the labor force "corporate"[3] in organization, but the hierarchies were fraying at the edges as progressive thinking about the rights of man, the benefits of science, progress, and reason, and the need for challenging orthodoxy filtered down to the masses. In ways impossible in previous generations, ordinary people found opportunities in Paris that heightened their expectations about what was possible in life.

The vast majority of the city's residents had come from outlying towns and provinces in search of new lives and new futures, as people have done throughout the ages. Paris in the 1780s, however, offered its pilgrims even

more chances to forge new identities and to reject the notion that the circumstances of one's birth determined what one deserved in life. There
was "a democratization and modification of elite culture" as ordinary people began to feel comfortable participating in activities that had long been
the province of the upper classes. Poor people partook of high culture.
Observers were "astonished, amused, or irritated at the number and variety
of people who descended upon the Louvre, after the bienniel art salons were
instituted there in 1737. Not only the educated and discerning came, but a
'swarm of would-be connoisseurs,' 'people of every sort,' 'countless young
clerks, merchants, and shop assistants.'" It was a place where servant girls
and workingmen hired carriages, where public events and theater commin-
gled the masses with the elite, and where even a seamstress hosted a literary salon that met on Sundays, the one day that she and her working-class
guests had off and could get together.[4] At all levels of French society there
were people who were, as one historian put it, "living the Enlightenment."[5]
While Jefferson consorted with the elites who were doing that, Hemings
worked daily alongside their working-class counterparts who were doing
the same thing in their own ways.

Hemings had free movement, as he did in Virginia, and was able to take
part in Paris' many public spectacles. Even before he began to receive a
regular wage, Jefferson gave him money that allowed him to go about the
city with some level of assurance. With Jefferson paying for necessities—
clothes, a watch, shoes, and food—Hemings could use his money for his
own purposes, but entertainment did not always require money.[6] A host of
"street performers, automatons, marionettes and shadow puppets, animal
displays, scientific exhibits, acrobats, and—observed one English visitor,
Arthur Young—'filles' without end," were on display on Parisian streets.[7]
On a "fine day" Hemings and countless other residents of Paris could enjoy
"the spectacle of the crowds themselves, the parade of jostling, laughing,
humanity" that can be a form of entertainment itself. A number of theaters
opened up in the 1780s, charging such low prices for admission that all but
the completely destitute could attend.[8] For people like Hemings, those at or
near the bottom of the social scale, there was much more to do, many more
ways for him to assert himself than existed back in Virginia.

As liberating as Paris could be to Hemings's inner life, his enslavement
was an important external reality, not the stuff of metaphor or psychology.
This was a matter of American law and culture that he had lived since birth.

But he was no longer in America. The country that Hemings was now in adhered to what has been called the "Freedom Principle," which held that every slave who stepped onto French soil was free. There were, the saying went, "no slaves in France."[9] Although this idea was deeply embedded in the country's collective psyche, the matter was more complicated than the aphorism suggested.

Slavery was not unknown to the French. It was, however, largely confined to the French colonies in the New World, Senegal, and on the Indian Ocean. Many features of American slavery that were familiar to Hemings—gangs of slaves in the fields, public auction blocks—did not exist in Paris. Slavery "came" to France proper whenever French colonial masters returned to the country and brought slaves as personal servants. Throughout the eighteenth century periodic crises arose as more masters arrived in France with their slaves, and some of those slaves, invoking the Freedom Principle, did not want to return home with their masters.[10] What mechanism, if any, could make them go back if presence on French soil made the enslaved free?

French kings and the parlements (the supreme courts in all the provinces of France, not to be confused with legislative bodies) and the admiralty courts, which had primary jurisdiction over transactions involving the seas, were often at odds about the correct answer to that question. The kings—Louis XIV, Louis XV, and Louis XVI—periodically issued edicts and declarations about the status of slaves brought into the country. These rulings most often gave a safe harbor to visiting colonial masters, who were allowed to keep their slaves so long as they followed certain specified procedures. In the earlier regulations, masters were to register incoming slaves and assert that they had a plan to have them taught a trade or undergo religious instruction—not particularly onerous burdens. After the colonial masters began bringing in their slaves and letting them stay long past the time they would be receiving any kind of training, regulations were promulgated that put a three-year limit on slave apprenticeships, after which time all slaves were to be returned to the colonies.[11]

These deviations from the Freedom Principle, which in regulating slavery implicitly recognized its existence, were prompted, in part, by concerns that an influx of people of African origin into the country would lead to the "tainting" of French blood. When the actual numbers are considered, the charge—carried forward most energetically by Guillaume Poncet de la Grave, attorney general to the Admiralty Court—that a "deluge" of black people was inundating France was mere hyperbole. Perhaps for Poncet de la Grave even a handful of black persons might have constituted a deluge, but, then, the entirety of his career suggests that he was something of a crank.[12] For example, there never were as many blacks in France during the eighteenth century as there were in England. In the latter half of the century, France had a population of over 20 million people. Historians put the number of blacks in the country at any one time between 4,000 and 5,000, with the largest concentration of them—hovering around 1,000—in Paris. At the same time England had a population of around 9 million people. Estimates of the number of blacks living there range from a minimum of 10,000 to as high as 30,000.[13]

Poncet de la Grave and other officials were determined to make sure that the black population in France did not grow, and their agitation led to the appointment of a commission (with Poncet de la Grave as an adviser), charged with solving what they perceived to be a great problem.[14] At least two great interests were at play: Poncet de le Grave's and others' racist hysteria over the prospect of mixed blood and the concerns of powerful French colonials upset by the effect that the liberalizing influence of France and the Freedom Principle had upon black people who came to the country. The drafters of the declaration that would be called the *Police des Noirs* took special note of *"l'esprit d'indépendance et d'indocilité"* that blacks in France displayed, and they attributed it to their residence in the country.[15] This phrase, written into the law's preamble, addressed what was thought to be a serious problem: life in France changed black slaves, not only while they lived there; it made them a threat upon their return home, where they would be more likely to press for changes in the social structure of colonial societies. Whether they went home to become agitators or not, just hearing that there were slaves who had been emancipated in France would have influenced enslaved people back in the colonies.

While Ponce de la Grave fixated on racial intermixture, French colonists considered interracial mixing a fact of human life and not a galvanizing problem—they had found ways to deal with that. Indeed, by the time the Hemingses were in Paris, many free, property-owning, and tax-paying French colonists were products of liaisons between white males and black females. Dangerous political ideas that threatened their way of life in the colonies were another matter. As the commission members contemplated its parade of horribles, they even expressed the fear that blacks in their own colonies would be further radicalized by the words and actions of the thirteen colonies on the nearby North American continent, which threw off their colonial masters in 1776.[16]

There was, however, a conflict. Residing in France altered a slave's sense of self and threatened the foundations of slavery in the colonies, but colonial property owners generally had the right to use their property as they saw fit—including to bring their black servants to France if they wanted to. As in Virginia, successfully maintaining a slave society often required interfering with slave owners' absolute property rights, and for the commission members and their white colonial supporters, slaveholders' personal whims meant little when measured against the overall well-being of France's enormously profitable slave colonies. The solution was clear: to close the loopholes in earlier declarations that had allowed the supposed excess of blacks to come and then remain in the country, the *Police des Noirs*, declared in 1777, forbade the entry of blacks, mulattoes, or any "people of color" into France altogether—not just slaves, any black people. Those who were there before the date when the law took effect were supposed to register themselves, or be registered by their masters if they were slaves, with local authorities. They were allowed to stay. Those who arrived after that date were to be taken into custody, registered, and held in a *dépôt des noirs* set up in France's port cities for that purpose. They were then to be put on the first ship back to the French colonies.[17]

Although the law was designed with French colonials in mind, its first article said that its provisions applied "meme à tous étrangers." Jefferson was not supposed to bring Hemings into France. His status as a foreign diplomat gave him no immunity from this, as one of the principal shapers of the declaration made clear. The law was supposed to be the definitive word on the subject, its last article stating emphatically that its provisions replaced all previous declarations and superseded any law that contradicted its provisions.[18] If things had proceeded according to the *Police des Noirs*, Hemings would have been detained at Le Havre, placed in the *dépôt* there, and then sent back to Virginia. Jefferson, like all other masters, was also supposed to register Hemings's name with local authorities so that they could keep track of which blacks were in the country, where they were, and, if they came into the country after 1777, when they had been deported. Noncompliance with the law brought a fine of 3,000 livres or more. One section provided that masters holding slaves at the time of the law's declaration would lose their right to keep their slaves in bondage if they did not register them within one month after the law took effect, a serious penalty designed to encourage the simple act of registration.[19]

Jefferson never registered James Hemings. Nor did he register Sally Hemings when she arrived in France a little over two years after her brother.[20] That neither sibling was arrested and held in custody is not surprising. The system of policing blacks had broken down considerably by the time the two arrived. The captains of ships who were supposed to keep track of people of color often did not bother to do that. Many masters did not register their slaves and generally suffered no penalty for it. Blacks sometimes defied the registration requirements and were not sent out of the country. Compliance with the law was especially lax in Paris.[21]

During every incarnation of the laws designed to control the black population in the country, the Parisian courts, as opposed to their counterparts in other jurisdictions, zealously upheld the Freedom Principle. By tradition, the parlements in France had the duty to review each law the king proposed to see whether it accorded with legal tradition. One of the ways they could signal their displeasure with a law was to refuse to register it, which is exactly what the Parlement of Paris, the oldest parlement and the one with the largest jurisdiction in the country, did with respect to most of the edicts and declarations that weakened the Freedom Principle. The king could override the effect of a parlement's nonregistration by holding a *lit de justice*, at which the king could force a registration, though the powerful Parlement of Paris sometimes refused to recognize forced registrations.[22] No French kings took this route in defense of their edicts designed to help French colonial slave masters. There was a question whether the Parlement of Paris would register the king's declaration of 1777, given its position on slavery. In a way that anticipated the early American states' struggles with how to portray slavery in its Constitution, the commission that drafted the *Police des Noirs* found a way to get around the Parlement of Paris' likely refusal to register the new rules: it took out the word *esclave*. After "slaves" were turned into "servants," the parlement agreed to register the declaration.[23] Although registering it, the parlement had no intention of seriously implementing it. The Parisian Admiralty Court, under the Parlement of Paris' jurisdiction, simply ignored its provisions, in keeping with what had been both bodies' long-standing commitment to the Freedom Principle. Slaves in the city who wanted their freedom could make the request to their master, and the master would grant it if so inclined. If the master refused, the slave could go to the Admiralty Court and file a petition for freedom, and many did, sometimes asking for back wages. Over the entire course of the eighteenth century, the Parisian Admiralty Court granted every such petition filed, almost two hundred, and it continued to do so even after the *Police des Noirs* had been declared and registered.[24]

The Admiralty Court's position was well known among slave owners and slaves, and the tribunal's view of the law affected the balance of power between them, giving slaves greater leverage in their dealings with their masters. During the decade before the French Revolution, the Admiralty Court, for the first time, received more filings from slave owners to voluntarily manumit their slaves than petitions from enslaved people to obtain their freedom.[25] These records do not show, of course, how many masters simply freed their slaves without following the formalities. The historian Sue Peabody has suggested that slave owners often thought it better to come to their own private arrangements with their slaves, freeing them and turning them into their paid servants if they were willing.[26]

The history of the *Police des Noirs* presents a clear example of just how dangerous it is to look at laws on the books of a society and assume they precisely reflect its day-to-day life. Some laws gain widespread acceptance and become part of the bedrock basis of a community's view of itself. Others fall by the wayside. Laws can be passed and declared, but it is up to the people at every level below the lawgivers—bureaucrats, judges, police, and the ordinary members of the community—to decide when and how they will abide by them unless whatever government in power is willing to use force to make them fall into line. Apparently the French government did not think the *Police des Noirs* worth that effort. It was willing to have the law declared, as a statement of principle, but not to expend too much effort to enforce it. There were many other, more important things to worry about during the 1780s than chasing down the few blacks in their midst. With few aggrieved parties to bring claims against violators of the rules, the draconian law remained on the books until the Revolution, invoked on a number of occasions, but widely flouted in James Hemings's Paris, the most populous and powerful jurisdiction in the country.

We do not know when or how Hemings learned about the Freedom Principle, but there were many ways for him to have found out, and by the end of his five-year stay in the country he knew that he could become

a free man. The most likely sources were members of the black community in Paris who made and kept contact with one another. They were well
situated to do this. Although prosperous *gens de couleur* from the colonies
visited and lived in France, many of the one thousand or so blacks in Paris
were the servants (the majority of them free) of whites and were generally
concentrated in the city's wealthiest neighborhoods.[27] The progress of freedom suits during the eighteenth century shows that some form of a network existed among them. Newly arrived blacks from the colonies learned
from black veterans of Parisian society what French law had to say about the
rules governing their lives. Their white masters certainly had no interest
in telling them about the law, unless they were prepared to set them free.
The neighborhoods where Hemings first lived with Jefferson in Paris had
among the highest concentrations of blacks. It was not the "deluge" that
Poncet de la Grave spoke of, but their visibility—their physical difference—
heightened the power of their presence in the predominately white environment. Fewer blacks were living in the relatively new neighborhood of the
Hôtel de Langeac, where Hemings and Jefferson eventually settled, but it
still bordered neighborhoods with larger numbers of blacks.[28] By the time
they moved to the Hôtel de Langeac, Hemings had undoubtedly encountered other people of color in his first neighborhood, and in adjacent ones,
as he went about his business. In time his increasing familiarity with the
French language made it easier for him to speak with them.

Slaves in America effectively communicated information between and
among slave communities as they moved about doing the work of their masters. People of color in Paris saw one another on the streets or while attending their masters and mistresses as they visited the homes of their friends,
and they conversed with and supported one another. Indeed, the historians
Pierre Boulle and Sue Peabody have both suggested that it was the concentration of blacks in the more affluent areas that led Poncet de la Grave and other
French officials to form a distorted view of the number of people of color in
Paris.[29] They saw black servants walking along the streets of their own fashionable neighborhoods, saw them in the homes of their friends, and wrongly
assumed that these numbers could be extrapolated out to the whole of the
city. That they suspected (with good reason) widespread noncompliance with
the registration requirements only fueled their paranoia.

It made perfect sense for black people to be in the best neighborhoods.
Most were in France primarily because wealthy French colonials had brought

them there. It would have done upper-class French men and women no good to have their slaves or servants living in some other distant part of the city. It might seem intuitively obvious that not many impoverished or even middle-class French people, struggling to stay afloat themselves, could really have been buying and keeping large numbers of slaves in the less fashionable parts of Paris. But then, when one is in the grips of a deep irrationality as the commission members were—in their case, racism— one is by definition unable to think straight and see and accept things as they are. In fairness, the commission members did have an additional concern that seems more in touch with reality: fear of the mobility of the rising merchant class. Servants were status symbols. The elites within French society saw "ordinary" people who possessed them as challenging aristocratic privilege. This is especially true when they had black and mixed-race servants, who in late eighteenth-century France were more highly prized than white servants. They, as the highest type of status symbol, were to be reserved for aristocrats and courtiers. James Hemings and, later, his sister Sally would have been much sought after in upper-class households, had they decided to leave Jefferson and seek employment in Paris or some other part of France.[30]

The servants at the Hôtel de Langeac were also important sources of information about French law and customs, as they exchanged with Hemings stories about their respective societies and lives. One cannot assume that because Jefferson's French servants were, as far as we know, white like him, they would have taken his "side" on the questions of slavery and of blacks. As the coming Revolution would make clear, Parisian workers took the notions of liberty, equality, and fraternity seriously. Hemings worked alongside them, drawing wages just as they did, and dealing with the trials of life in service. His was no longer the world of Virginia slavery. There was also life outside of the Hôtel de Langeac. Within the last two years of his stay in Paris, Hemings hired a tutor, Perrault, to help him learn more formal French.[31] Before their falling out, these two men had ample opportunity to discuss the differences between Hemings's life in Virginia and his life in Paris.

We can compare Hemings's situation with that of Abby, a girl whom John Jay enslaved. During his early diplomatic career, Jay, the future chief justice of the Supreme Court and one of the shapers of *The Federalist Papers*, brought Abby to France. While he was in London in 1783, and she was still in Paris, evidently under the watch of William Temple Franklin, Abby ran away. Jay expressed surprise that she had done so, given that he had promised to free her upon their return to the United States. He blamed her escape on too much "Indulgence & improper company," which had led her into bad ways. Jay, with the aid of Franklin, sought help from the authorities to apprehend Abby. It is not known what the authorities were told about her, or whether she had taken any property that belonged to the Jays when she left, but she was apparently held in custody for a time. Benjamin Franklin suggested that she be left in jail for about twenty days, and John Jay agreed, both men saying this would teach her a lesson. What happened instead was that as a result of the terrible conditions in prison, Abby grew ill and died just three weeks after the authorities let her go home to the Jays.[32]

This story also reminds us that enslaved people in Paris like Abby and James and Sally Hemings made contacts in the world outside of their one-on-one relationship with their masters. In Jay's view, these contacts had been bad for Abby because they encouraged her to think she had a right to freedom on her own terms. It appears, however, that Abby was willing to go only so far or did not fully apprehend how firmly the law was on her side. Had she filed a freedom petition, she would almost certainly have prevailed. But, then as now, personality and circumstances—as much as knowledge—influence whether an individual decides to engage the legal system. We do not know what Jay meant by "indulgence," but it is unlikely that Abby was receiving a monthly salary like James Hemings or even Sally Hemings—certainly not at the rate these two were being paid. She may not have had the confidence, if she had no family members with her, to stand against Jay, particularly if he renewed his promise of emancipation when she returned to America.

There were still more ways for the enslaved to find out about French law and custom. A small, but vibrant, legal practice had grown up around freedom suits, which helped ensure that word would spread about the possibility of filing petitions, the availability of help, and the processes to be followed. By Hemings's time in Paris there was a long tradition of success among members of the bar in the city who developed an expertise in bringing such suits, including men like Henrion de Pansey, a critic of royal despotism who voiced his challenges to the monarchy through the metaphor of slavery. While Pansey and other lawyers were motivated to take on freedom suits pro bono, there are indications that some lawyers represented slaves primarily for financial reasons.[33]

Apparently, some of these freedom suits were brought under a system that allowed fee shifting: the losing side had to pay the costs of the action.[34] This made sense for slaves filing petitions for freedom and explains, in part, why some lawyers were willing to take on clients who could not pay. Fee shifting is designed to prevent litigants from wasting the court's time by bringing or defending suits where the outcome is virtually predictable. Certainly slave owners in Paris who chose to fight their slaves' freedom petitions were essentially wasting the Admiralty Court's time, because the conclusion was foregone. Even with that, very few slaves had sufficient funds to pay a lawyer's fee. Unless the lawyer had some deep philosophical purpose for getting involved, it made no sense to spend time working on cases for which he would have received no compensation, and end up losing money for time and effort spent, although one wonders how much "work" had to be done, given the court's track record for freeing everyone who filed a petition. The possibility for fee shifting might also explain the reverse in the ratio of masters' declarations of freedom and slaves' petitions for freedom, mentioned previously. If certain victory by the slaves meant paying lawyer's fees, it might have seemed better to forgo that by just emancipating the slave and, perhaps, keeping him or her on as an employee if the former slave was so inclined.

James Hemings could have afforded the cost of hiring a lawyer on the salary Jefferson paid him once he became the chef of the household. Unlike enslaved petitioners who had no money, he was drawing a decent salary by Parisian standards. The range of yearly pay for live-in domestic male servants in the city was between 100 to 150 livres per year. The range of pay for a cook in an upper-class household, considered a high-level servant in the 1780s, was between 200 and 250 livres. Jefferson paid Hemings 288 livres per year. When his sister Sally arrived and began to receive a regular wage, she was paid at the rate of 144 livres per year, again, a good deal more than the average of 100 livres for female domestic servants.[35]

Jefferson paid all of his servants in France at a very high rate. He also paid them in a manner atypical for the country. French household servants were usually paid on a yearly basis. That they received wages at all was a mid-eighteenth-century concession. In earlier times French servants signed on with an employer with the expectation of getting a room, food, and clothing from their masters. That was their payment—that plus the "benefit" of being in the company of their social betters, from whom they could learn

manners and styles of presentation, and have the protection of being associated with a good household. The advent of wages brought the contract with
wages to be paid at the end of the term—a year or six months, for example.
Of course, money at the end of a given term is, at best, hypothetical money,
and on some occasions the employer did not pay. The servant was left either
to sign on for another term, with the hope of receiving the last year's wages,
or to leave the master's service and then fight over the separation payment.
James and Sally Hemings, by contrast, had money in hand every month.
They could save some or all of it because they did not have to pay for housing and food. Their pooled resources gave them enough money to afford
lawyers who did not work pro bono. Indeed, some of the lawyers who did
work pro bono on freedom suits might actually have welcomed any level of
contribution they could get from a client.[36]

Finding a lawyer would not have been terribly difficult either. By the late
1780s, officials at the Admiralty Court itself provided referrals to lawyers
who they knew worked on freedom suits.[37] It enraged French colonials, and
others who favored restrictions upon blacks in France, that the results of the
invariably successful petitions in Paris were widely disseminated in the city,
alerting other blacks to the possibility of taking the same route. There were
people in Paris, most likely blacks and their most ardent supporters, who
wanted to strike a blow against slavery on French soil and sought to spread
the word about the Admiralty Court as an avenue to freedom. One French
official complained that the "posters and *mémoires*" (case reports) put up
around the city talking about the freedom suits encouraged blacks to think
they were equal to the "superior beings they were destined to serve."[38]

The status of blacks, or *gens de couleurs*, was part of a larger conversation. Along with the Enlightenment talk of natural liberty in general, the
abolition of slavery became a particular focus of attention for a number of
prominent Frenchmen during the very time that Hemings was in Paris.
The Société des Amis des Noirs, the Society of the Friends of the Blacks,
was founded in 1788, although some of its members had been meeting
to discuss the issue and promote abolition as early as 1786. The Société
approached Jefferson about joining their effort. He declined, explaining
that he thought it would be inappropriate for a government official to join
such an organization, since it might be taken as the American government's endorsement of their aims.[39]

The Société was extremely elitist, highly theoretical, and largely ineffectual in its aim to influence the French government, primarily because there was no legislative body for it to appeal to. It pressed its claims through newspaper articles and pamphlets that put its members' views into wider circulation than they would have been had they simply confined themselves to meeting in one another's homes. They helped inject abolitionist sentiments into public life as part of the discourse about the rights of man that paved the way toward revolution.[40] Hemings did not know French at first and probably could not enter that discourse at a high level until near the end of his five-year stay in Paris. But it would not take much to have a sense of the issues being discussed, not only in his own home by the Anglophone residents who lived there but also in the outside world in which he moved.

Even fifteen-year-old Patsy Jefferson got caught up in the spirit of the times. In 1787, not long before her sister arrived with Sally Hemings, she issued a literal cri de coeur when she wrote to her father, "I wish with all my soul that the poor negroes were all freed. It grieves my heart when I think that these our fellow creatures should be treated so teribly as they are by many of our country men."[41] Patsy wrote this when there was only one enslaved black person in her immediate world: her uncle. She cannot have written those words, had those thoughts, without considering how her wish, if carried out, would have affected him. This was, for all the transplanted Americans at the Hôtel de Langeac, a time and place to think about the world in a different way.

Slave or Free? Black or White?

One wonders just how James Hemings described himself and how Jefferson described him to the people they encountered. Did the French men and women in their circle understand that he was enslaved and not simply Jefferson's servant? Even in Virginia, Jefferson, like others of his cohort when they wrote of enslaved people, preferred to call them by that less morally charged term "servants." If he continued to avoid the use of the word "slave" in France, it is possible that his French acquaintances did not know the status of the young man who sometimes attended him and who eventually had charge of his kitchen.

There are good reasons to believe that Jefferson was not always forthcoming about having a slave in his home. Two years after Hemings and he arrived in the country, Jefferson engaged in some altogether extraordinary correspondence with a man named Paul Bentalou, whom he had met in Williamsburg. Bentalou had been in the town as the commander of a "troop of dragoons" and was an aide-de-camp of the famed Count Casimir Pulaski during the American Revolutionary War. He settled in Maryland during the 1780s.[42] While in France in 1786, he sought Jefferson's advice about how his wife might "keep her Little Negro-Boy" as a slave while she resided in the country for about eighteen months. Bentalou, citing Jefferson's well-known benevolence, wanted the minister to intercede on his behalf with the French ministry to make the argument that the Bentalous should be allowed to keep the child, who was "between Eight or Nine years old."[43] Jefferson, in full self-protective mode, wrote back to Bentalou,

> I have made enquiries on the subject of the negro boy you have brought, and find that the laws of France give him freedom if he claims it, and that it will be difficult, if not impossible, to interrupt the course of the law. Nevertheless I have known an instance where a person bringing in a slave, and saying nothing about it, has not been disturbed in his possession. I think it will be easier in your case to pursue the same plan, as the boy is so young that it is not probable he will think of claiming freedom.[44]

Jefferson was the "person" he was describing. That was probably not obvious to his correspondent, and Jefferson was unwilling to make it clear to him. Surely his anecdote about "a person bringing in a slave" would have been more meaningful to Bentalou had he known that the American minister to France was the unnamed individual. That, however, would have required Jefferson to admit in writing that he was breaking the law. He did not go into detail about his reasoning, or whom he consulted, but the letter indicates that he was, just as he said, basically conversant in the law on slavery in France.

Jefferson was disinclined to make a formal declaration of his ownership interest in Hemings and in his sister, when she arrived later. He believed (correctly) that the Admiralty Court, following the lead of the Parlement of Paris, under whose jurisdiction he lived, would not uphold his property interest in the enslaved brother and sister if they decided to challenge him. His statement that "it [would] be easier," in Bentalou's case, to say nothing because the boy was so young highlights his more precarious situation with twenty-one-year-old James Hemings. He had a young man in his household, not a little boy; a young man who had a far greater range of movement and freedom than the enslaved child in Bentalou's home would have had, far more ways to learn about his status in France, and more confidence that he could assert his rights.

Despite his knowledge of French law on slavery, Jefferson seemed not to make, or know, perhaps, the distinction between what was going on in Paris and what was going on in other parts of the country that were less zealous in upholding the Freedom Principle. He spoke of "the laws of France" as if there were no differing interpretations of the law elsewhere in the country—as in fact there were. Over the years, jurisdictions outside of Paris had dutifully registered and attempted to enforce all the edicts and declarations that curtailed the Freedom Principle. Indeed, Bentalou, who wrote to Jefferson from Bayonne, was in just such a jurisdiction—Bordeaux, which was heavily invested in the French slave trade. The admiralty court there was likely more inclined to act on the provisions of the *Police des Noirs* than its Parisian counterpart.[45]

Most tellingly of all, Bentalou was French. He had "adopted" the United States as his home. Registration had been at the heart of every eighteenth-century declaration on the status of slaves in France.[46] French officials always wanted information about how many blacks were in the country and where they were. Just as people in the United States have long understood the peculiarities of differing regions in the country about certain social matters, Bentalou was familiar with that very basic rule about registration and knew that he was in a part of his native land that was likely to take it seriously. That is why he knew he had to ask for a "dispensation" from the law and understood that, if he did not get it, the boy could be sent home. While Jefferson was aware that Bentalou (and he) had a duty to let French officials know that they had brought slaves into the country, he thought that alerting the authorities to the boy's presence would provoke the youngster to claim freedom and that, if he did, he would be set free with no conditions. Bentalou's letter indicates that he was writing not long after the boy had arrived in France. If he had registered him quickly, there would have been no question of his actually losing a property interest in his slave. He would simply have had to pay to send him home.

Although Jefferson had far more cause than Bentalou to think that his slave would be unconditionally freed, he ended up being right for the wrong reason. His counsel—silence—was not legal, but it was perhaps the best practical course for Bentalou's interests as a slave owner. Enforcement of the law was lax in many parts of the country because of difficulties of administration and outright hostility to it, but to have directly approached the authorities in a jurisdiction like Bordeaux would have been to dare officials there to uphold the law and force Bentalou into doing what he did not want to do: send the enslaved boy back to Maryland. Given the boy's age, and the Bentalous' concerns, the local officials might not have been inclined to send him home alone, especially since Mrs. Bentalou did not plan to stay in France very long. But the couple could not be sure of that. If they followed the law, the decision would be out of their hands.

Nothing in Jefferson's circumstances in France encouraged him to be forthcoming about having an enslaved person in his household, and much militated against it. Unlike Bentalou, Jefferson came to Paris with a self-image as the revolutionary author of the Declaration of Independence and valued his connection to some of the philosophes of French society who shared his views on the natural liberty of all mankind and took seriously his denunciations of slavery. Registering James and Sally Hemings with French authorities, and perhaps attempting to argue for some dispensation to keep them there during his tenure, would have put his status as a slave owner front and center for no good reason. A confrontation with an admiralty court had only disadvantages.

Even in the extremely unlikely event that a French court would have been inclined to favor the American minister to France (and there is no reason to think that a body that had challenged French kings on this very point would have buckled before Mr. Jefferson of Albemarle County), to be seen arguing for keeping his slaves would surely have damaged Jefferson's image. The same can be said for his helping Paul Bentalou. Jefferson had nothing to gain, and a good deal to lose, if he approached the French ministry on Bentalou's behalf. His French admirers and friends knew he had slaves back in Virginia. But their invisibility made it easy to avoid confronting his direct and continuing involvement in slavery, despite his eloquent and trenchant pronouncements against the institution. James Hemings, appearing before a court as a breathing person whom Jefferson wanted to keep away from the benefits of freedom, was not an abstract concept.

Hiding, or failing to mention, Hemings's status would not have taken up too much psychic energy on either man's part. In many ways Jefferson's course of dealing with Hemings in Virginia fit more perfectly their new environment in France. Here Jefferson's use of the term "servant" could appear as more than just an avoidance technique. Like all people of color in pre-Revolutionary France, Hemings was supposed to carry *cartouches*, identity papers.[47] Given the low level of compliance with other rules governing blacks in the city, and Jefferson's failure to register him in the first place, he may have gotten away with not carrying papers. Even though French society remained highly stratified along class lines—William Short, who was soon to join Jefferson in Paris, wrote to him in near-despair that he had been warned that, no matter how personally close he was to Jefferson, he would still be considered by the French as one of Jefferson's "higher order domestics"[48]—the racial atmosphere was not as highly charged as it was in Virginia.

Hemings's background and experiences left him perfectly suited to use the different circumstances in Paris to make the most of his time abroad. His appearance alone would have affected the way people perceived him in this new land. It is quite possible that some people would not have been aware of his African origins, because France's Mediterranean connections brought a wide range of phenotypical characteristics to Parisians. Moreover, determinations of race are very much contextual. A person who might be instantly recognized as "black" in one setting could be considered something else in another. When he went around by himself, and was not attached to the very American Jefferson, or identified as his servant, there would be no reason to wonder about his racial origins or status. In the United States, African Americans who "passed" for white have often claimed to be, among other things, part or all Native American, Jewish, Italian, Spanish, or Portuguese. In the years to come, some members of Hemings's own family would take this route out of blackness as they sought to find a safe haven for themselves in America.

Unlike residents of France, eighteenth-century white Virginians were used to looking at and living among large numbers of black people of differing shades, hair textures, and facial features. In court cases, judges and overseers, who were sometimes brought in to serve as expert witnesses as to racial identity, inspected the facial features of African Americans in legal proceedings involving questions of race. Having more reasons to pay attention to who was "white" and who was "black," white Virginians who encountered Hemings were probably much more adept at spotting his African origin than the French, who encountered such people only rarely, if at all. Once he got past Le Havre, where customs officials may have seen every person of color who came into the country through that port, and were likely more savvy about these matters than their countrymen, the perception of Hemings's identity could well have been quite fluid. He was not so black that the French would have considered him an African and, in their view, at the very bottom of the racial hierarchy. As in his native Virginia, in French society there was a preference for mixed-race people over those who were "purely" black, whose non-European features—broad noses, tightly curled hair, and full lips—were openly disparaged. This was the era of much speculation about and assertions of racial differences that were supposedly based upon or proven by science.[49]

Of course, many Europeans came to this belief in African inferiority well before proponents of these ideas put pen to paper, and whites who had never read these materials believed the same things fervently. This form of racialized thinking became more pronounced in societies whose economies were becoming ever more dependent upon the enslavement of Africans. Eighteenth-century France found itself in the grips of a contradiction: the country "becoming thoroughly entangled in the Atlantic slave system" that had become an essential part of its economy at the same time as it was "developing a radical new political discourse based on notions of freedom, equality, and citizenship."[50] Racism helped resolve the tension between these seemingly incompatible considerations by positing that Africans, because of their racial inferiority, were a species of people who were exceptions to the rule about the natural right to liberty of all mankind. They could be slaves.

Much as the ideology of white supremacy progressed in France during the eighteenth century, and burned even more brightly during the Napoleonic era, it was nothing like Hemings's Virginia, probably because there were not enough blacks in the country to stoke a thoroughgoing racial animus. It appears that a well-placed band of racial zealots and anxious colonials were responsible for the antiblack legislation during that century, while most French subjects, though not necessarily welcoming of blacks, did not feel as strongly threatened. A ban on interracial marriages enacted in 1778 was seldom enforced. When the local authorities of one village attempted to deport a black man who had married a white woman, the couple's community rose up and so strenuously opposed the move that the authorities backed down.[51] The small number of blacks seemed to be able to make decent lives for themselves in largely white communities.

Class distinctions in France were almost as powerful as race distinctions. A number of French men and women did not accept the idea that all black people were in the same category. They held blacks who were servants in low regard in much the same way that they looked down on white servants.[52] African kings sent their sons to France, where they were received by French nobility.[53] Had these same people shown up in Virginia, they might well have been captured and taken to the fields. Some French people considered the often quite prosperous, usually mixed-race blacks in the colonies who were related by blood to prominent white families to be above ordinary servants. They deserved something better—not to be treated exactly as whites, but better than their "all" black brethren. Their idea grew, in part, out of self-interest. If whites did nothing to "shock" the "self-respect"[54] of upper-class blacks, French colonial society, with its large number of black people, could create a class midway between whites and black slaves to serve as an important buffer between the two races. This "buffer" would ultimately safeguard the interests of white people. As long as white supremacy reigned, whiter would always be better, and members of this midway class, understanding that, would have a great incentive to distance themselves from their less favored and ill-treated black cousins. Under those circumstances there would be little chance that "nonwhite" people, of whatever degree would band together to destroy privileges based upon whiteness.

The mixed-race children of a number of French white colonial fathers were sent to France to be educated, and in later years, when the sons of Toussaint Louverture came to Paris, they visited and dined with Empress Josephine.[55] James Hemings undoubtedly saw such people as he went about the city. Virginia could never have produced a figure like Joseph de Boulogne, the so-called Chevalier de Saint-Georges. Boulogne was the son of George de Boulogne de Saint-Georges, whose very wealthy family had been on Guadeloupe since the mid-1600s. The elder Boulogne, a married man, fell in love with a seventeen-year-old enslaved girl on his plantation named Anne, but nicknamed Nanon, Senegalese by birth. Nanon was described by one who knew her in Paris as "the most beautiful gift that Africa ever offered" and by others as "the most beautiful woman on the island of Guadeloupe."[56]

George had Joseph educated in France and later lived in Paris with Anne in Saint-Germain—along with his wife! The younger Boulogne became a notable fencer, violinist, and composer, who influenced Mozart. He served as an officer of the guard in the king's army and was a celebrated figure in France. His well-received and much publicized series of concerts in 1787 in Paris brought out the wealthy and aristocratic in Parisian society, including Marie-Antoinette. Perhaps Boulogne's greatest fans were the wives of various French nobles who found his dark good looks irresistible and became his lovers.[57]

Then there is also the family story of Alexandre Dumas, the famous French novelist and author of *The Three Musketeers* and *The Count of Monte Cristo*. Dumas's father, Thomas-Alexandre, was also the son of a French colonial, Alexandre-Antoine Davy, the marquis de la Pailleterie, and an enslaved woman named Marie-Cessette Dumas. After her death the marquis moved to Paris and, by one account, in deep depression allowed all his property, including his children, to be sold. He soon regretted his action and then repurchased Thomas-Alexandre and brought him to Paris for his schooling. As a result of his father's change of heart, Thomas-Alexandre Dumas, who was just three years older than James Hemings, was able to have a rich and very colorful life himself and to produce a son who became one of the foremost novelists in France during the nineteenth century, achieving a worldwide renown that lives to this day.[58]

It would be wrong to minimize the racism of the French during the time Hemings lived among them. Celebrated though he was in French society, Joseph de Boulogne could never have had a true place in it other than as a celebrated phenomenon—a spectacle. He could attend the dinner parties and dances of the upper class. He could carry on discreet affairs with the French society women who flocked to hear his concerts and watch his fencing exhibitions. But he could never have married into that society, settled down, and become a real part of it. Certainly, the French colonies were extremely cruel and hard places for black slaves in ways that would have been quite familiar to Hemings. The most critical difference for him specifically was that some French slaves who had blood ties to wealthy white families had opportunities that they would never have had under Anglo-American slavery. These men and women and their descendants constituted a significant portion of the free people of color in French society. Boulogne could go only so far, but his range was far more extensive than that of any of the Hemings males. James Hemings did achieve much in his life, but had he been the mixed-race son of a prominent Frenchman, he would have stood a better chance of being trained to become a gentleman planter himself, or having a son who might become a prominent author. Committed to white supremacy as many French men and women definitely were, one does not get the impression that they were as determined as white Virginians to strike at every single particle of black people's humanity. Despite some very real and substantial obstacles, James Hemings's soul had a much greater chance to flourish in Paris than in his native country.

9

"Isabel or Sally Will Come"

I F JAMES HEMINGS came to France by deliberate design, his sister Sally made it to the country only after the collapse of a series of best-laid plans. The first and most serious plan to go awry was Jefferson's idea of leaving his two youngest daughters, Polly and Lucy, with their aunt in Virginia. It had been a reasonable thought. The girls were very young, and it was natural for a man of his time to think they needed to have something closer to a mother's touch. Lucy's death awakened an implacable desire in Jefferson to have his other surviving daughter with him. He wrote to his brother-in-law, Francis Eppes, in August of 1785, stating his firm conviction that Polly should be sent to him.

> With respect to the person to whose care she should be trusted, I must leave it to yourself and Mrs. Eppes altogether. Some good lady passing from America to France, or even England would be most eligible. But a careful gentleman who would be so kind as to superintend her would do. In this case some woman who has had the small pox must attend her. A careful negro woman, as Isabel for instance if she has had the small pox, would suffice under the patronage of a gentleman. The woman need not come further than Havre, l'Orient, Nantes or whatever other port she should land at, because I would go there for the child myself, and the person could return to Virginia directly.[1]

That plan did not work out the way Jefferson intended. Over the course of the next twenty-four months, the Eppeses and Jefferson traded letters, with one of Jefferson's sisters contributing to the round robin about when and how Polly would get to France.[2] From the Eppeses' side, and that of Polly, who was not happy about the prospect of leaving her aunt and uncle, there was always a reason Polly could not start out. Bad weather and missed letters complicated matters. There was an initial problem with Isabel, whose married name was Hern. She had not had smallpox and had to be inoculated, which was another occasion for delay. More months passed, and Hern got pregnant and had her baby around the same time that the Eppeses realized that they could delay no longer.[3] Finally, on June 26, 1787, Jefferson saw the words he had been waiting for in a letter that had been sent the preceding April. Francis Eppes wrote, "Polly will certainly sale on 1st of May in a Ship call'd the Robert commanded by Capt. Ramsay bound for London. . . . The Ship in every respect answers to your discription. Isabel or Sally will come with her either of whome will answer under the direction of Mr. Am[onit]."[4]

Jefferson knew who "Sally" was and probably had a good idea about how old she was—how young, might be more apt under the circumstances. Eppes's missive made clear that Jefferson's first idea of having his daughter travel under the protection of a woman on her way to Europe had not materialized. He adopted Jefferson's second suggestion, having Polly travel under the supervision of a gentleman with a female to attend her. But the female was not exactly what Jefferson had specified. Isabel Hern was twenty-seven years old when he suggested her as a traveling companion for his daughter, twenty-nine when he heard the final word that either she "or Sally" would be making the trip.[5]

Sally Hemings, at around fourteen years old, was almost half Hern's age and not the kind of "careful negro woman" Jefferson had envisioned as Polly's travel companion.[6] Indeed, he knew that Hemings was already with his daughter, yet he did not suggest to the Eppeses that she be sent along with Polly. There is no indication of what he thought about the prospect of the young girl's undertaking such a mission. The letter announcing Polly's travel date, and a later one describing the day of her departure, reached him long after the girls had set sail. If Jefferson had any concerns, he had little time to fret, for within a few days of hearing that his daughter was on the way, he received word from Abigail Adams that she had arrived in London safely.[7]

Unlike her older brothers, Sally Hemings probably had no extensive traveling experience. While James Hemings had seen Philadelphia, Boston, and New York, along with a smattering of smaller towns, his little sister had spent, as far as the records reveal, the entirety of her life in Virginia, going back and forth between Jefferson's plantations and the Eppes family home at Eppington. She was too young to have had any memories of her father's seat at the Forest; nor would she remember her times at Guinea and Elk Hill, her mother's homes for brief periods while John Wayles's estate was being settled. Monticello, where she had arrived as a two-year-old, was the site of Hemings's first memories, the place where her principal identity was formed—an insular community atop a mountain.[8]

The trip to England and then to France was a life-defining event for Hemings, one that she seems never to have gotten over. Edmund Bacon, Jefferson's overseer at Monticello from 1806 until the early 1820s, remembered Hemings as "often" talking about her "trip across the ocean" with Jefferson's daughter—her stories coming long after 1787.[9] The voyage was a salient part of Hemings's identity that she could take out and share with others at whatever she thought was the right moment, keeping the experience alive within herself and forcing others to discover and acknowledge something she thought was very important for them to know about her.

This memory of an adventure repeatedly, and perhaps tiresomely, described to others is especially poignant when one remembers that the person holding on so fast to it was an enslaved woman. Had she been born a free white woman of the status of her sister Martha Wayles Jefferson or her niece Polly Jefferson, her expectations would have been very different. Under those circumstances, Hemings, described as beautiful, could have looked forward to life as a young woman whose appearance alone would have made her much sought after as a wife. Married life would have brought her the recognition, respect, and support of her surrounding community. None of these were available to Hemings, and she, like other enslaved people, had to build a structure to contain the meaning of her life out of whatever raw material was available. Her trip to France was a reminder of her journey to a place where she learned that another type of life was possible, even if that possibility was never realized.

Hemings arrived in London on June 26, 1787, after five weeks at sea, her journey with Polly having begun with something of a cruel trick. The Eppeses devised a way to get the still reluctant Polly to stay on board the *Robert*. They brought their children and Hemings onto the vessel to stay "a day or two." At one point when Polly fell asleep, the Eppeses left, the

Robert pulled anchor and went out to sea, bound for London.[10] By the time Polly awoke, everyone she knew was gone except Hemings. Sadly, there is no record of the voyage. The letter that Polly wrote describing what happened on the trip is not extant, so we may never know the details of the girls' lives aboard the ship.[11] Abigail Adams, in London with her husband, John, America's first ambassador to the Court of St. James, met the girls. She wrote to Jefferson the day they arrived, assuring him that his daughter was safe and telling him how attached she had become to Andrew Ramsey, the captain of the ship. Adams then brought up Sally Hemings, though not by name:

> The old Nurse whom you expected to have attended her [Polly], was was sick and unable to come. She has a Girl about 15 or 16 with her, the Sister of the Servant you have with you.[12]

Adams sent another letter the next day with more information about Polly, along with other comments about Sally Hemings:

> The Girl who is with her is quite a child, and Captain Ramsey is of opinion will be of so little Service that he had better carry her back with him. But of this you will be a judge. She seems fond of the child and appears good naturd.[13]

July 6 brought yet another letter from Adams to Jefferson about his daughter, this time especially extolling her virtues, with more disparaging comments about Hemings, and a reference to buying clothes for both girls.

> The Girl she has with her, wants more care than the child, and is wholy incapable of looking properly after her, without some superiour to direct her.
>   As both Miss Jefferson and the maid had cloaths only proper for the sea, I have purchased and made up for them, such things as I should have done had they been my own. . . .[14]

Adams was wrong about Hemings's age. We do not know the month of her birth, but she was probably fourteen when she met Abigail Adams.[15] Although a difference of two years may not seem to matter generally, in the

lives of teenage girls the period in question—between fourteen and sixteen—
can work a real change in appearance. They can go from having the bodies of prepubescent girls to being as physically developed as they will be
as women. That Adams thought Hemings was as old as sixteen, may say
something about Hemings's appearance and, more important, also account
for Adams's repeated comments about her immaturity.

That young Hemings was not qualified to be Polly's sole nurse may well
have been true. But it is a long way from that to the charge that a putative
sixteen-year-old was less mature than a nine-year-old, particularly in light
of Adams's later very revealing comments about Polly's extremely childlike behavior in London. Francis and Elizabeth Eppes had observed Sally
Hemings in their home for over two years. One of Jefferson's children had
died while in their care. They would not have sent his other child on an
ocean voyage with a person who was less mature than she, a person who
could have hurt her more than helped her. Adams, confronted with the reality of Hemings's youth compared with what she had been expecting, was
simply confounded by the surprising young girl in her midst. Under the circumstances, there was probably little Hemings could have done to change
Adams's opinion of her.

Over the course of the next decades, several generations of the Adams
family would comment directly and indirectly on Hemings. Thinking seriously about Abigail Adams's reaction to her in London in the summer of
1787 requires keeping in mind that this was an encounter between a free
adult white woman and an African American slave girl. Class, wealth, status, and race divided these two people. Without a doubt, the first three differences affected the way the two saw each other, but contemplating how
the racial divide shaped their interactions is perhaps the most crucial to
consider. The Adams family is well known for some of its members' strong
and, even heroic, stances against slavery, particularly that of Abigail's son
John Quincy. Yet it has long been apparent that being antislavery is not the
same as being nonracist, and the example of the Adams family reinforces
that observation.

We get a very telling glimpse of Abigail Adams's own views about one
aspect of race relations in a letter she wrote upon seeing the play *Othello*
in 1786, just one year before she met Sally Hemings. By her own admission, Adams was simply undone by the play's depiction of the marriage
between a Moor, portrayed by a white man done up in black face, and a

white woman. Adams wrote of her "horror and disgust" every time the "sooty" actor touched the "gentle" actress who played Desdemona, even though she knew they were just actors on a stage.[16] She was not sure why she felt that way and seemed discomfited by her response, but her reaction against racial intermixture was visceral and extremely powerful. Her son John Quincy, who would later write a number of satirical poems about Sally Hemings, saw *Othello* thirty years after his mother. He offered more detailed responses to the play in two essays in which he was able to put into words, in a way that his mother could not in 1786, exactly what was troubling about the play. Adams wrote,

> Who can sympathize with the love of *Desdemona*? The great moral lesson of the tragedy of *Othello* is, that the black and white blood cannot be intermingled in marriage without a gross outrage upon the law of Nature; and that, in such violations, Nature will vindicate her laws. . . . The character takes from us so much of the sympathetic interest in her sufferings, that when *Othello* smothers her in bed, the terror and the pity subside immediately into the sentiment that she has her just deserts.[17]

The only reasonable reading of this passage is that Adams was saying that Desdemona deserved death for race mixing with Othello. As it happens, he made exactly that point very graphically to the renowned actress Fanny Kemble at a dinner party in Boston in 1839. Kemble described Adams's face as displaying "the most serious expression of disgust" as he told her that Desdemona should have died for marrying, in Adams's words, "a nigger." Kemble was offended by Adams's use of what she called "that opprobrious title."[18] Her journal entry on the conversation reads as a biting *esprit d'escalier* moment, with Kemble noting sarcastically that some might think Adams's characterization superior to Shakespeare's. At the right moment on stage, she wrote, Iago could adopt Adams's language and say in a soliloquy, "I hate the nigger" instead of "I hate the Moor."[19] If in the play Desdemona had escaped the wrath of her jealous husband, and lived long enough to have had a daughter, that child should have been portrayed by someone who looked much like the young girl who was in the Adams's home in London, the obvious product of the race mixing she and her son so abhorred.

Even though the references to Hemings in Adams's letters are brief, they reveal other important truths about the world in which she lived. First, Hemings was a "girl," in terms not just of her gender or age but of the amount of respect that whites, upper class and not, could be expected to give her. Her personhood was ignored. In the Adams correspondence she literally had no name. After almost two weeks in the Adams household, and three letters from Abigail Adams to Jefferson specifically referring to her, Hemings was still "The Girl," even though it is inconceivable that Adams did not know her name was Sally.

Adams was not doing anything unusual. That was the way most whites dealt with black slaves and, if they had them, white servants; that manner of dealing communicated to them their subordinate status in the world. Think, however, of a life lived daily under the power of that kind of profound social dismissal. Even if Hemings did not know what Adams had written to Jefferson about her, it is unlikely that an attitude revealed so freely on paper was not discernible in face-to-face interactions, especially since it probably never occurred to Adams that she was expressing any attitude that had to be hidden.

Hemings surely knew the social realities of her time—that there were people who felt she was unworthy of being called by her name—yet could still feel the sting of being dismissed or discounted as a person. She, and other slaves and black people, knew from their intimate family relations what it felt like to be a person who mattered—to be someone's mother, someone's daughter, sister, or friend. Those experiences as valued members of a family or a community provided a critical counterpoint to the world they lived in with the whites with whom they were forced to interact. It is a safe assumption that a person who has a name would prefer to be called by it. Enslaved people could not force whites to give them the dignity of using their names, and they often had to appear as if all the slights and dismissals did not matter when, often, they mattered very much. It was a rare enslaved person who got to record her observations of the whites who controlled her life, so we do not know what Sally Hemings thought of Abigail Adams's character.

An even more telling detail is Adams's recounting of Captain Ramsey's "opinion" that Hemings would be of "so little Service that he had better carry her back with him." Although willing to offer Jefferson a wealth of advice about other things, Adams had no preferences about this issue that she was willing to express openly. Her nonchalance about Hemings's welfare is striking and highlights the distance between the enslaved girl and her charge. Jefferson was unwilling, because he would have thought it neither wise nor proper, to send his daughter on a five-week voyage with a ship full of men with no woman attached to her. He understood, as people have throughout the ages, that young females need to be protected from the sexual attention of males and, when they are of a certain age, from the effects of their own emergent sexuality. These concerns are expressed through the concept of the "appropriate" and the "inappropriate" in male-female relations. Without requiring openness about the delicate topic of sexuality, this shorthand saves members of the community from having to cast aspersions on the character of a man who may never do the thing feared—flirt inappropriately with a young girl, make a sexual advance or comment. Designating a male-female situation inappropriate also acknowledges that some young females do in fact want male attention, even when it is not what is best for them. The age of consent in eighteenth-century Virginia was ten.[20] There prevailed then an understanding about girls and sex very different from that of our day. Rather than let people drift into a circumstance where the character of an individual male had to be tested, or where the preferences of a young female were left unchecked, steps were taken to ensure that the people were never in questionable circumstances.

There is no evidence that any of these considerations entered into Abigail Adams's or Captain Ramsey's mind about Sally Hemings. It apparently did not occur to them that, whether she would actually have been harmed or not, it would have been simply inappropriate for her to go, without female support, on a multiweek ocean voyage with Ramsey and his crew. Had Hemings been a free white girl, Ramsey would have consulted her father before making so momentous a determination about her life, and turned to her mother in her father's absence. Even if he had considered it in passing, he probably would have kept it to himself, not wanting to appear unmannerly before the genteel Adams, who would have seen that he was overstepping a boundary. She would have wondered about him if he had offered to take a sixteen-year-old unchaperoned white girl off in that way.

Hemings had no parents to consult, or to be a force that Ramsey and Adams had to reckon with even if they were not present. John Wayles was dead; had he been living, the circumstances of Hemings's birth would likely have precluded an outsider from approaching him as a father on her behalf.

Elizabeth Hemings was certainly in no position to demand anything for her daughter. She may not have wanted her to make the trip at all. Without a "legal father" and with a mother who was not in law, the most logical person to have consulted was the man who owned Hemings: Jefferson.

Captain Ramsey had communicated with the Eppeses before the trip.[21] Perhaps they relayed Jefferson's instructions about the slave woman going back after delivering Polly to France, and this may have prompted his suggestion. That is not the import of Adams's letter, which highlighted Ramsey's belief that Hemings was too immature to be of service—presumably to Polly—and that was why she should go back to Virginia with him. Whatever Jefferson had written two years before, the circumstances had changed dramatically. The Eppeses knew they had not sent the mature woman Jefferson requested. As an enslaved woman, the almost thirty-year-old Isabel Hern might well have been vulnerable on the voyage, too—but not so vulnerable as fourteen-year-old Sally Hemings.

Recall Jefferson's correspondence with Paul Bentalou, who sought his help in trying to get the French ministry to allow him to keep his nine-year-old slave in France. Bentalou expressed his great fear that his family would have to send the boy home alone. He said his wife's "feelings would be very much hurt," at the thought that on the trip he might be "Ill used by a Captain" or "spoiled . . . by the bad example of sailors" because of his tender age.[22] The Bentalous were thinking enough about the realities of life to know that the young slave boy traveling for weeks by himself would be at the mercy of whoever was on the ship. His devalued status made him fair game for insults or anything else so long as he suffered no serious physical damage.

A teenage enslaved girl voyaging across the Atlantic alone would have been in at least as much peril as the nine-year-old boy whom Bentalou was talking about; and her London hosts should have known this. Captain Ramsey might well have appointed himself responsible, but for all Hemings or Adams knew, once Polly Jefferson was not attached to the teenage enslaved girl, he could have become the "ill-us[ing]" captain of the Bentalous' very perceptive formulation, with no inclination to rein in or closely monitor his crew. Abigail Adams had not known Ramsey long enough to make a real judgment about this.

The unwillingness to see Hemings as a person of value and the complete inattention to her vulnerability as an adolescent—and her even greater vulnerability as a female slave—were the kinds of things that have gotten enslaved and servant girls into trouble throughout history. It is impossible to write the story of the lives of these girls without always being aware of the ways in which sexual exploitation—either the potential for it or the actual experience of it—was a constant threat in their lives. Because they were left uncloaked by the support and protections given to higher-status females, the dynamics of their interactions with higher-status males were very different from those of the interactions between males and females of equal rank, and they must be analyzed differently.

Hemings's predicament as an "uncloaked" female, then, requires a hard look at the attitude of Captain Ramsey, whose reported comments about her are the earliest male responses to Hemings that exist in the historical record. Although he may actually have had absolutely nothing untoward on his mind, Ramsey's very quick, and extremely presumptuous, suggestion, on the very day he arrived in port, even before he had any word from Jefferson about what he wanted to have done—that he "better carry her [Hemings] back with him"—is worth pausing over. Ramsey appears just a bit too eager. What was it to him that Hemings would be of "little service" to Polly, especially now that she would be safely under her father's care? This seems a strange call for him to have made about another man's servant—indeed, a higher-status man's servant—especially since he and Adams believed at the time that Jefferson would be coming to London straightaway and be able to see Hemings for himself.

Just days after he left Hemings and Polly with Abigail Adams in London, Ramsey wrote to Jefferson. After praising Polly's virtues and noting their mutual attachment to one another, he offered to bring her to Paris himself, if no arrangement had been made for her trip. He did not mention to Jefferson the idea of carrying Sally Hemings back to Virginia with him.[23] By that time, he evidently thought better of it or more seriously about how the suggestion might sound to Jefferson, for it really was quite a thing for him to act as if the configuration of Jefferson's household was his concern.

Adams's statement that Jefferson "should be the judge" of whether Hemings stayed in Europe or went home shows that she immediately apprehended the problem with Ramsey's suggestion. Unlike the captain, however, Adams thought this was an important enough issue that she could not let the matter drop. In three of the four letters she wrote to Jefferson during a two-week period, she felt compelled, in tones from veiled to very frank, to disparage Hemings's capacity to take care of Polly on her own. That she should take this tack is especially intriguing because she knew all along that Hemings would not be Polly's main caregiver in Paris anyway and that Jefferson could never have been counting on her, or anyone else, to play that role. Polly, as Adams specifically noted somewhat ruefully to Jefferson in one of the letters that referred to Hemings, would soon join Patsy at the "convent" and would be under the everyday care of nuns. She dreaded the prospect, but she could not reasonably have thought that Jefferson would have sent his older daughter to school and not his younger one.[24] Adams knew that, even if the "old nurse" had made the trip with Polly, she would have been similarly eclipsed as the sole caretaker of Jefferson's daughter. The issue was not the relative skill of Polly's companion from Virginia; it was that Polly's circumstances in Paris would make any full-time nurse superfluous. Adams's warnings about Sally Hemings's specific unsuitability were really meaningless in this context.

Oddly enough, this passive effort to convince Jefferson of Hemings's uselessness was really insensitive to Polly's needs, though both Ramsey and Adams professed to care so much about them. The Eppeses sent Hemings when Hern could not make the trip precisely because she had been with Polly all her life. There were other enslaved women from Monticello who could have gone, but they did not turn to them. Hemings's mother, Elizabeth, had no very small children to care for at that point. Her older children could have looked after their younger siblings during the several months or so that it would have taken to travel to England and return immediately to Virginia as Jefferson had originally planned.

Despite Adams's extreme praise of Polly's preternatural maturity, some of her other comments sound a discordant note. Her description of the way Polly clung, almost desperately, to each adult who came into her life for any length of time is inconsistent with the picture of her being a well-adjusted and wise-beyond-her-years child. At first Polly did not want to leave Captain Ramsey. Then she did not want to part with Abigail Adams, whom she had known for only six days. Adams wrote that she had been "so often deceived" that she did not want to leave whoever was the last person who had charge of her.[25] Polly was evidently traumatized by the events leading up to her arrival in Europe, and given the circumstances of her life to that time, one understands why. Hemings was, no doubt, a comforting presence to the little girl. Taking her away from Polly would seem to have been the last thing for anyone to think of doing.

In the end Captain Ramsey's and Adams's expressions of doubt about Hemings were couched as their mere observations that she would be of no use to Polly, when what they really were trying to convey to Jefferson was that Sally Hemings would be of no use to him in his household. And because of that, neither of them seemed to think she should go to Paris. One wonders why they cared so much. Fawn Brodie's explanation for Ramsey's and Adams's responses to Hemings very reasonably centered on her appearance. The very course of females' lives may turn on whether people find them attractive. The eighteenth century was no different on this point. Even as standards of beauty have varied from culture to culture, and epoch to epoch, the concept of attractive versus unattractive has always operated in human affairs. Hemings was a very attractive young female, an attribute that could awaken one response in Ramsey (sexual desire or just a more platonic wish to be around such a person) and quite another in Abigail Adams, who would be greatly attuned to how others—namely men—would view her.

Brodie suggested that the quite astute Adams took one look at Hemings, saw a beautiful young girl, and made the silent determination that it was not a very good idea to send her to live on a long-term basis with an unmarried man who was, for all she knew, lonely.[26] No matter how opinionated and blunt Adams may have been throughout her life, if that was truly the root of her concern, she could never have conveyed that sentiment to Jefferson. On the other hand, if we take seriously Adams's statement that Hemings was still young enough to require supervision herself, she may have thought that the last thing her friend the minister needed to take on, in addition to his already long list of duties, was the responsibility for a teenage girl with time on her hands. That was something Adams could have said outright. But she did not, and instead repeatedly voiced concerns about a problem she knew did not exist.

With no apparent qualms about having Hemings continue on to Paris with his daughter, Jefferson took immediate steps to make that possible. He did not, however, in the coming weeks or ever, register her with French authorities. For all the years the Hemingses were in Paris, Jefferson was subject to a fine of 3,000 livres—the going rate for a slave in France—for each one of them.[27] To put this in perspective, Jefferson's yearly rent for the spectacular Hôtel de Langeac was 7,500 livres, until he bargained it down to 6,000 the last year he was there. He paid around 5,400 livres a year for his daughters' combined tuition at the Abbaye de Panthemont.[28] A fine of at least 6,000 livres would have been no small thing to the cash-strapped Jefferson. A penalty of that magnitude, coupled with the loss of the value of his slaves if they filed a freedom petition, would have been tremendous.

Jefferson's decision not to register the Hemings siblings was essentially a gamble that weighed the uncertain chance that they might find out about their status against the virtual certainty that they would discover it if he were to get into a confrontation with French officials. His failure to register the siblings provided the court with an additional ground, besides the Freedom Principle, for granting any petition they filed.[29] As we will see, not too surprisingly, he lost the gamble that the brother and sister would never find out about the law, but he hit upon another way to deal with the situation, a very Jeffersonian solution—one-on-one persuasion—when the conflict arose.

Jefferson did, however, attend to his own official administrative requirements related to Hemings's and his daughter's arrival in France. He kept a ledger in his own hand of the passports he issued during his time as minister to France. In his entry for July 1, the day after he received Adams's first letter announcing his daughter's arrival along with Hemings's, Jefferson wrote, "Petit, Polly J. & Sally Hemings 2.m," indicating that he had issued passports for each that would be effective for two months from the date of issuance. On that same day he wrote to Abigail Adams that he would be sending his servant, Adrien Petit, to get his daughter. He did not mention Hemings at all.[30]

Although Adams's letters to Jefferson warning him about Hemings arrived after Petit had already left, there was still time, had he thought Adams's worries at all important, to arrange to have Hemings return to Virginia. When the clearly perturbed Adams wrote to him on July 6 upon hearing that Petit, instead of he, was coming for Polly, she told Jefferson that she had promised the little girl that she would not have to leave London with Petit until they had gotten another letter from him. Jefferson received Adams's letter on July 10 and responded the same day. His missive shows that he was well aware of the situation in the Adams household—Polly's tendency to cling to adults, her specific attachment to Abigail Adams, but he made no mention at all of Adams's view of Hemings and whether she should come to Paris or go home.[31] As far as he was concerned, the matter was settled. He had abandoned his idea of having Polly's companion return immediately to Virginia.

Hemings's journey to Paris was really assured when Jefferson sent Petit to London with passports and enough money to pay for his passage to England and to buy return tickets to Paris for both her and Polly Jefferson.[32] Jefferson's action raises at least two questions, the first more puzzling than the second: Why did he not go himself to pick up his daughter, and why did he not send Hemings back to Virginia? Jefferson offered an answer to the first question, but never addressed the second one. He explained to the Adamses that he had recently returned from a trip through southern Europe just two weeks before he received the letter announcing Polly's arrival, and was detained by the press of catching up on the business of the ministry. His principal biographer, Dumas Malone, accepted this explanation.[33] Jefferson could well have been sincere about handling ministry business, but his choice is still odd, given how fervently he had wished to see Polly and that he understood what his daughter had gone through from the time she had been put on the *Robert* and sent on an Atlantic voyage.

One of the recurring criticisms of Jefferson over his career was that he was too much attached to his family, to the detriment of whatever office he held. Why he abandoned that inclination at so critical and singular a moment in his family's life is hard to understand. It was a few days' journey at most to pick his daughter up and return home. If he did not want a Channel crossing, he could have at least met her at Le Havre for a symbolic welcoming to France. In addition, he did have a secretary, William Short, to help with the business of the ministry.

In Fawn Brodie's view, Maria Cosway's (Jefferson's paramour of sorts) impending arrival in Paris kept Jefferson in the city instead of venturing to London.[34] He certainly could never have given that as an excuse to the Adamses or anyone else. Cosway had written to him that she would soon be there, but did not give a firm date. Brodie believed he did not want to miss her, and opted for the chance to be with her over welcoming his daughter to Europe. This might seem a natural choice for a man in the throes of an attraction to a woman whom he seldom saw. He was now sure he was going to see Polly, not so sure that he might ever get to see Maria Cosway again. But Cosway was set to be in Paris for more than the few days it took to get Polly and return. He could have retrieved Polly in London and socialized with Cosway when he returned.

Conor Cruise O'Brien, an infinitely more hostile commentator on Jefferson's behavior than either Malone or Brodie, who both loved him, offered that there must have been a serious and deeply personal reason for Jefferson's failure to fetch his little girl, one that matched the seriousness of his breach of fatherly duty, and it centered on Sally Hemings and slavery. He did not, O'Brien surmised, want to be so visibly and recognizably a slave owner in the home of Abigail and John Adams. He wanted to avoid having to interact with Hemings under their eyes.[35] This was before Jefferson and the Adamses became estranged and even longer before the men achieved a rapprochement during their retirements from public office. In the late 1780s, before the bruising political battles to come, these three were really at the highest point of their mutual affection, and each wanted the esteem of the other. O'Brien's view is quite plausible.

The Adamses knew that Jefferson owned slaves. John may actually have seen Robert Hemings in Philadelphia in the 1770s, and the couple either saw James Hemings or knew of his existence when they were all in Paris together for a brief period before John Adams became the minister to the Court of St. James in London. The situation with Sally Hemings was different and more problematic. It would have been one thing to see Jefferson with an enslaved manservant before the couple actually knew him very well, or to hear a story of how he had brought a servant to be trained to a trade, quite another to personally observe a much respected friend acting the role of a slave owner before his own child with the most vulnerable type of person in the system: a young enslaved girl.

Jefferson's New England friends would have observed the most critical means through which slavery perpetuated itself—from parent to child. This feature of the institution prompted one of Jefferson's most perceptive and famous criticisms of slavery: parents passed on the habits of mastery to their own children.[36] That male slave owners exercised this mastery over females like Hemings was a particularly delicate issue. By the time she was in London with the Adamses, the stories of what slavery meant for men like her brothers and what it meant for females like her was already well known, with the differences centering on embattled motherhood, the sexual exploitation of women, and the stigma of interracial sex. The Adamses, both enormously intelligent people, knew what slavery involved. They could not have looked at Jefferson, Polly, and what they took to be the sixteen-year-old Hemings in the same room, and not have had at least a fleeting thought of what Hemings's life as an enslaved woman might turn out to be.

All the factors Malone, Brodie, and O'Brien identified—business, a

prospective rendezvous with a lover, and embarrassment about his position as a slave owner—may have contributed to Jefferson's surprising iner-
tia. Whatever his reason for not going to get his daughter, even Malone
acknowledged that it was a great mistake on his part.[37] Jefferson knew that
Polly was expecting to see him, and it jars to note that so normally sensitive
a man as he did not perceive how his daughter and others would take his
failure to meet her entirely reasonable and foreseeable expectations. John
and Abigail Adams were extremely unhappy with Jefferson; and their letters
to him contain only thinly veiled rebukes of what they took to be a form of
parental negligence. Polly was devastated to learn that her father was not
coming for her, and it took a while to persuade her to leave with Petit, and
when she left, she left reluctantly.[38]

As to the second question, we will probably never know why Jefferson
did not send Hemings back home, because neither he nor any anyone else
left an explanation to be analyzed. This seems a less mysterious decision
than his choice not to meet Polly in London. Sending Hemings home by
herself would have made no sense to anyone who had any feeling at all
about her as a person. Just as the Bentalous fretted over sending a nine-
year-old enslaved boy alone on an Atlantic voyage, Jefferson's closer relations with Hemings's family would certainly have led him to think more
about her potential vulnerability as a young female than either Abigail
Adams or Captain Ramsey did. Jefferson knew he would be sending his
late wife's and James Hemings's sister home under extremely questionable
circumstances. She was someone he actually knew, and he understood how
her brother might feel about this. The stakes for Jefferson were quite different. There is, of course, great irony in this; but that could not have been
known at the time.

There was also a great advantage to Jefferson and his family if Hemings
stayed in Europe. As Polly's father, he probably discerned a fact that Adams
and Ramsey either had not noticed or had suppressed in favor of their own
preferences: the comfort of Hemings's familiar face might help ease his
daughter's transition into her new life. That was no small matter to him,
because he knew from his sister-in-law's correspondence that Polly did not
really know him or her sister, and they did not know her.

As the mere "Girl" in this Adams-dominated tableau, Sally Hemings did
not have her responses to these extremely stressful, but also exciting, days

recorded. London in 1787 was a huge, teeming city with buildings and sights the likes of which she had never seen. One is reminded of the reaction of Harriet Jacobs, another enslaved woman whose life has reached iconic status, upon seeing Philadelphia for the first time. Writing of her escape from the rural south, Jacobs remembered being staggered by the sights, sounds, and the crowded masses of people in the city. Her first morning there, she woke early to sit at the window and gaze at "that unknown tide of life" filling the streets below her. Her next destination, New York, drew a similar response within her.[39] Hemings was no doubt at once awed, a little confused (Jacobs's term for her response to her new urban environment), and perhaps even afraid of the city and the people who had charge of her. Again, one does not get the impression of great warmth emanating from Adams to Hemings during the time they were together. The New England matron did buy her new clothes, saying that she had done so as if she and Polly were "her own," but that was more about Jefferson's and Polly's requirements than Hemings's.[40] Adams was very much aware, as she told Jefferson, of how important it was to keep up appearances in France, with one's home, clothing, and servants. Hemings simply could not go around without proper clothing, since badly dressed servants reflected poorly on their employers.

For Sally Hemings there was no one in London to welcome her to this strange land with the same heartfelt enthusiasm with which Polly was welcomed—and no one to be as patient and understanding in calming whatever were her entirely natural fears as the Adamses were with Jefferson's daughter. Just because those things were not forthcoming does not mean they were less needed and desired by this young girl. Like Polly, she had suffered the loss of a sister the preceding year, nine-year-old Lucy. The reality of death was in her view. She was separated from her mother and other siblings and sent across the Atlantic Ocean for no reason that had anything to do with her, but solely to suit the aims of her white owners. It had been a time as difficult for her as for Polly, and she, too, could have been traumatized by the hasty and forced nature of her travel. While the adults who had charge of her on her trip to and during her stay in London found time and space to record their reproaches of Hemings, there was no time or space to express any sympathy for her equally difficult circumstances.

And then another stranger came to take her somewhere else, Adrien Petit, who spoke a language Hemings could not yet understand. Over the next years they would become friends, but during these first days she was likely as perplexed by him as Polly Jefferson professed to be.[41] Although Sally Hemings was older than Polly, and although we can never know whether she was happier about being sent on this journey than her young charge, or what she made of her time in London and the Adamses, we do know that she was as much in the dark about what awaited her in Paris as the frightened little girl whom she accompanied to Europe.

10

❦

DR. SUTTON

WHEN SALLY HEMINGS arrived in Paris on July 15, 1787, at least one person was there to welcome her with the enthusiasm and warmth of family: her brother.[1] He had last seen his youngest sister when she was eleven years old, and she had probably changed greatly in appearance during that time. While he had gone from age nineteen to twenty-two, the changes in the elder Hemings were likely more psychological and emotional than physical, but nevertheless profound. Sally Hemings met in her older brother a man who had traveled throughout France, lived and worked among people from a completely different culture, and been responsible for himself in this foreign environment. He knew firsthand, as his sister would come to know, that there were different and more varied ways for them to go through the world than existed in Virginia. She also met a man who was about to come into his own as a highly skilled professional. James Hemings was nearing the end of his various apprenticeships, and in the months immediately after his sister's arrival he became the official chef de cuisine at the Hôtel de Langeac in charge of the kitchen and, thus, a supervisor in his own right.[2]

With the new title came a larger steady monthly wage for Hemings, instead of the spending money that Jefferson had doled out to him over the years and the smaller salary he had been receiving in the months just before he took on the role of chef.[3] He also had available to him now one of the traditional perquisites of the chef in great houses, one that could bring him substantial side income, given the number of people who dined at the Hôtel de Langeac: the right to sell the renderings from the chickens, pork, beef, and any other animals prepared in the kitchen. Nothing was wasted in that era, and there existed a lucrative market in grease and animal skins that might be cast off today. Though he was used to working for wages for other employers, Hemings's new job marked an evolution in his self-image and in his relationship with Jefferson. He now had a true trade that he could ply for others, though it seems clear that Jefferson expected Hemings's services, if not for a lifetime, for the foreseeable future. Things did not work out as Jefferson expected, and they ended up working to James Hemings's advantage, but that was all to come. In that summer of 1787, Sally Hemings brought a new dimension to James's life. He now had someone to share this adventure, for the present and the future, should they decide to take their freedom in France. For the immediate moment, she could fill him in on the state of things in Virginia, while he could speak to her frankly about all that had happened to him since he had come to France and what it meant to him. And, best of all, probably to his great relief, he could do that in his native language.

For Jefferson's part, it was not Sally Hemings's arrival but the reunion with his daughter that ranked uppermost in his mind. He noted with great emotion that neither he nor her sister would have recognized Polly had they encountered her on the street, she had grown so much. With only a dim memory of her father, Polly did not remember her sister at all.[4] Making matters even more delicate, Patsy had spent almost three years living in a completely different and more complicated world than her younger sister. The two girls clearly had much ground to cover in getting to know each other again, and their father was eager to see them do that.

What Jefferson initially thought of his daughter's young companion is unknown. He remembered Hemings as the little girl who was present at his wife's, her sister's, deathbed. These were at best bittersweet associations that called forth memories both of loss and of Virginia. Indeed, when Hemings had last seen Jefferson, he was still in the emotional fog brought on by Martha's loss. Not much time had passed between the day they had gathered together as Martha lay dying and the day he left his daughters at Eppington to begin the journey that would take him to France. What did Hemings make of Jefferson's now rejuvenated and resplendent self, hair powdered and dressed—when he could sit still for it—outfitted in the French style? However he had thought of Hemings previously, he had to think about her differently now for several reasons, not the least of which was how to fit her into his present household. There was no reason for Hemings to play the role that had brought her to France, at least not in the same way, for Polly almost immediately joined Patsy Jefferson at the abbey, where she would now have the companionship of her sister and the opportunity to make new friends at school while she pursued her studies.[5]

It has been suggested that Hemings could have gone to live with Patsy and Polly at their school, for some of the girls at the abbey might have brought their servants. Although it is possible she spent time there, Jefferson's records place her at the Hôtel de Langeac with her brother. No known records—account entries or references in letters to paying for her food and board, which Jefferson would have to have done—link her to Panthemont.[6] His very quick placement of Polly in school indicates he felt it important for the young girl to bond with a sister whom she did not remember, make more rapid progress in learning a new language, and find new friends. Having Hemings continue her relationship with Polly might have impeded each one of these desired developments.

Whatever it meant for the Jefferson girls, it might have been much better for Hemings if she had lived at the abbey, even if that meant seeing her brother only on the days when Jefferson's daughters came home to visit their father. Being at the school, with its religious atmosphere and rituals, would have provided a powerful and educational experience for Hemings. Many people have been moved by the beauty of the rituals of the Catholic Church, even when they did not understand the words of the Latin Mass or adhere to the faith at all. Living at the abbey full-time would also have offered Hemings the chance to be with, and get to know, girls her own age. No one would have expected her to develop true friendships at a school attended by France's elite. But "true" friendship is not always required. There can be great comfort in the superficial, particularly when one is in a foreign country and simple curiosity about a person from a different culture can often substitute for true affinity.

Just observing the girls and listening to their conversation would have broadened Hemings's world, exposing her to different ideas and ways of doing things, even though she would not have taken part in the formal lessons. Despite the social and cultural distance that existed between her and elite girls, there were some very important points of commonality—first and foremost, getting used to their changing bodies and coming into womanhood. This was one of the main reasons for having an all-girls school and, no doubt, one of the unstated reasons the widower Jefferson found the abbey attractive. He almost certainly thought it better to have these transformations involving what he referred to as "certain periodical indispositions to which nature has subjected" women (and any awkward conversations about them) take place among females without his involvement.[7] Instead, at the Hôtel de Langeac, Hemings was a young girl in a predominantly male environment. Her brother and Jefferson, the people with whom she was most familiar, were very busy with their own tasks and not likely attuned to the preoccupations, tendencies, and needs of girls her age. Jefferson's letters to his own much loved young daughters show that he sometimes had a poor understanding of these matters, though he was much better by the time he had grandchildren.

Despite the potential benefits to Hemings of living at the abbey, there were significant disadvantages to Jefferson and his daughters beyond the fact that she might slow Polly's acculturation into French society and her bonding with her sister. The most important benefit of all to Hemings posed the most direct threat to the Jeffersons. If she lived at the abbey, she would make contact with people outside of their circle, who might influence her. She, in turn, might charm them and inspire their sympathy. There is no reason to think he knew anything of this prior incident, but decades before Jefferson and Hemings were in Paris, the sisters in a convent in Nantes refused to turn over an enslaved girl who had been left in their care when her owner came to retrieve her. The case, pivotal to the development of French laws regarding slavery, was decided in favor of the young girl and the nuns.[8] That was well before the very public rights of man/anti-slavery rhetoric became a part of the conversation in Paris as it was during Hemings's time there. Even with no knowledge of that situation, Jefferson was astute enough to see that giving Hemings a life away from the Hôtel de Langeac, under the direction of other adults on a long-term basis, posed significant risks.

There was also the issue of Hemings's status under French law. That she was African American would have alerted the curious among the residents of the abbey to the fact that she was something other than just a servant to the Jefferson girls. The French believed there were no slaves in France, but they knew there were slaves in America. If asked who Hemings was to them, Patsy and Polly could lie, or tell the truth and perhaps provoke the kind of embarrassment their father tried so hard to avoid. What of the officials at the school? Sending Hemings to live at the abbey would needlessly have involved them in his decision to skirt the law, having them house his unregistered slave in their midst. It is hard to say precisely how law figured into the way Jefferson dealt with Sally Hemings, because when he addressed the issue of slavery in France, he wrote in a manner that was at once clear and cryptic. He lived a good part of his life in letters and understood what tactics and maneuvers to use to protect himself as he moved in that very specialized and enduring world.

As was noted in chapter 8, many people took their chances with the laws regulating the black presence in Paris and managed to get away with it. One does not get the impression that there was great efficiency in carrying out the law's provisions. Jefferson, however, was not just any person. He was a minister from a new nation trying to establish its bona fides on the world stage. The Americans had thrown off a government by revolution and instituted a new one that claimed its legitimacy through its origins in and adherence to law. There was great skepticism about this new, unprecedented, untried, and still fragile enterprise. Those who represented the country abroad could ill afford to be seen picking and choosing which laws to comply with, because taking laws seriously—whether one thinks them merely irritating or outright inane—shows respect for the concept of the rule of law, the sine qua non of a civilized society. Jefferson "was" the United States in France. Any potential embarrassment he suffered would reflect on the country. For reasons personal and legal, whatever it meant for her, it was better all around for the Jeffersons not to have Hemings living away from the residence full-time.

Forty Days

More important for Jefferson than figuring out what role Sally Hemings would play in France was the pressing issue of her health. In addition to her youth, there was another important way that Hemings did not fit his specifications for the female attendant who was to come to France. He expressly asked that a person who had had smallpox make the journey. The Eppeses complied only partially with this request by having Isabel Hern inoculated.[9] They did not have Hemings inoculated, and no extant letters reveal whether the issue was ever raised with Jefferson. This suggests that the decision to send Hemings was made at the very last minute. Inoculating her would have involved several more weeks of waiting, and they opted, one might say, negligently, given Jefferson's stated concern, to send her anyway. Jefferson had arranged for Hemings's older brothers to be inoculated—Robert in Philadelphia in 1775 and Martin and James in 1778—but he knew he had no hand in inoculating their little sister.[10] This was a quite pressing matter, and he must have asked Hemings as soon as she arrived at the Hôtel de Langeac whether she had, in fact, been inoculated. She had not. Jefferson needed to deal with this issue as quickly as possible, and his concerns about her contracting the disease militated against allowing her to move too freely in her new environs. In those very first months of her time in Paris, Hemings's life very likely centered on her new residence and immediate neighborhood.

As it had been since ancient times, smallpox was a periodic scourge during the eighteenth century. Seemingly out of nowhere, epidemics swooped down and carried off large numbers of people to excruciating deaths. Thirteen years before Hemings arrived in France, an epidemic at Versailles took the life of many, including King Louis XV, famous for his apocryphal last words, *après moi, le déluge*. Jaded French society reeled upon hearing the horrifying details of Louis's agonizing death. Voltaire himself was moved to write a pamphlet on the subject, citing the king's terrible end. Up until that time, France had been slow, compared with England, to adopt the procedure of inoculation. After King Louis's ordeal the French nobility in particular enthusiastically embraced it.[11]

There is no cure for smallpox, and throughout the ages populations across the globe have had to find ways of preventing its spread. Inoculation, also called variolation, after the name of the smallpox virus *Variola major*, was practiced in Africa, the Middle East, and the Far East.[12] White Americans first became aware of the procedure from African slaves who described it to them. Cotton Mather brought it to the widespread attention of the American public after an African-born slave, Onesimus, told him that he had undergone the procedure while still in his native land and was thus immune to smallpox. In the mid-1700s, after much debate, the American colonies initiated the procedure with great trepidation. The technique involved taking from an infected person a small amount of the secretions from the pustules (the inoculum) and transferring it to a healthy individual with the aim of creating a milder version of the disease and permanent immunity to it. This was done by creating an incision and placing the inoculum into it.

Naturally, this very crude version of the procedure often failed—the healthy person contracted full-blown smallpox and died or lived, but was seriously disfigured by the scarring.[13]

Jefferson was an early believer in inoculation. In 1766, during his first trip to the northern part of what would become the United States, he went to Philadelphia for the specific purpose of being inoculated. In the months after his wife's death, he took Patsy and Polly to undergo the procedure, personally caring for them at the Ampthill home of his friend Archibald Cary.[14] While many religious people had deep reservations about the practice—thinking it somehow interfered with the will of God—forward-thinking people like Jefferson regarded inoculation as a milestone in the march of progress and reason. One scholar has written that the procedure was "regarded by the age itself as the greatest medical discovery since Hippocratic days" and "shared with Newtonianism a prominent position in enlightened scientific thought." Newton was very famously among Jefferson's trinity of personal gods, along with Francis Bacon and John Locke.[15]

When Jefferson wanted to have Sally Hemings inoculated in Paris, he had available to him, and Hemings got to meet, a member of the foremost family of inoculators in the world: the Suttons. In the mid-eighteenth century, Robert Sutton Sr., an English doctor, developed a more sophisticated method of inoculation. Building upon the work of earlier physicians, Dr. Sutton discovered that he could bring on a mild case of smallpox by eschewing "deep incisions that thrust the virus directly and dangerously in the bloodstream and that increased the chances of secondary infections."[16] Sutton also took the inoculum from patients who had been inoculated rather than from individuals suffering from a full-blown case of smallpox. Dr. Sutton and, later, his six sons "reduced variolation [inoculation] to a slight pricking of the skin" that was so gentle that the patient might not even feel when it had happened.[17] The "Suttonian method" or "Suttonian system" was very well known in the American colonies, and Jefferson certainly had heard of the Suttons before he came to Europe and had to deal with getting Hemings inoculated.[18]

The mortality rate for the Suttons' inoculations was remarkably low for what was, after all, a very dangerous undertaking because the men were especially adept at carrying out their own procedures. They personally inoculated thousands of people and lost only about one percent of their patients, which meant that the chances Hemings might die were extremely low. An

additional advantage for Hemings was that Sutton's method almost invariably reduced the amount of scarring down to the site of the pricking on the
arm, leaving the kind of scar that would be familiar to millions of twentieth-
century Americans who received smallpox vaccinations before entering
kindergarten. Other inoculators were not as successful in reducing complications from the procedure, and their patients were sometimes grossly disfigured, even blinded.[19] This, too, would have been of great importance to
the vanity of a young girl in a world where the appearance of females (at all
strata of society) was more important than that of males: a man with pock-
marks on his face suffered fewer social consequences than a woman with
even just a few. Voltaire appealed to Frenchwomen's vanity in the cause of
persuading the French to inoculate, reminding them how a full-blown case
of the disease could ruin "their beauty."[20]

After inoculating entire communities in England, for it was thought safer
to inoculate on a mass basis rather than run the risk that one inoculated
person would imperil a village, the Suttons eventually branched out to other
parts of Europe and were invited by members of the nobility and heads of
states on the Continent to perform inoculations. Although they emphasized
their services to the poor in England, their reputation for beneficence was
exaggerated. They certainly came to the Continent to make money, and the
patients of the brothers who practiced there tended to be rich and aristocratic. The family operated very much as a business, keeping aspects of its
method secret, sharing it only with designated inoculators in the manner of
a franchise operation.[21] Jefferson wrote that he paid "Dr. Sutton for inoculating Sally" about three months after she arrived in Paris, and he paid an
enormous sum indeed—about forty dollars, the equivalent of roughly one
thousand dollars today.[22] That was very much in keeping with the Suttons'
practice of charging wealthy patients, in this case the owner of the patient,
very high fees. One nineteenth-century detractor noted that the Suttons
had been especially "popular" with the "nobility who paid them immense
sums for their services," and suggested that an air of celebrity surrounded
the Suttons that outstripped their true medical skill. The Suttons, he pronounced dismissively, had merely discovered the importance of hygiene to
the process of inoculation, referring to their "device of cleanliness" as if it
were some devious and underhanded strategy.[23]

Modern observers know that the discovery of the role that hygiene plays
in *all* medicine transformed the field. Certainly, the attention to hygiene

contributed to the Suttons' ability to prevent scarring on their patients. Then, as now, it was hard to argue with success. Jefferson and others were willing to pay the high price because the Suttons' demonstrated skill and success rate were so great and the disease they were fighting so nightmarish. And while the brothers' reputation tumbled greatly after the advent of Jenner's vaccine, inoculation was the only pre-Jenner alternative for those who did not want to risk developing the disease in uncontrolled circumstances.[24] Hard businessmen that they were, the Suttons insisted upon payment before services were rendered. So unless Jefferson was able to persuade Dr. Sutton otherwise, Hemings must have been inoculated on the day of or sometime just after his November 7 notation that he had made the payment.

Jefferson did not say which Sutton inoculated Hemings. Robert Sutton Sr. had died by 1787. The most famous of his sons was Daniel, who fashioned himself grandly as "Professor of Inoculation in the Kingdom of Great Britain and in all the dominions of his Britannic Majesty."[25] All of the sons were in the inoculation business, each setting up his own practice in various parts of England and on the Continent when that market opened up, with Robert Jr. having the greatest presence in France. Robert Jr., whose bad experience with inoculation when he was a boy had prompted his father's interest in the subject, was in charge of the Suttons' inoculation house outside of Paris. In 1774 he, and perhaps at least one of his brothers, Joseph, was brought in to try to help King Louis XV. Given the patient's prominence, the Bourbons would have brought in all six Sutton brothers if that had been necessary to save him, although there is evidence that at least some of the French physicians resented having the Suttons in the role of last-resort rescuers.[26] A French biographer of the king when describing Louis's final days wrote of the arrival of "*les* Sutton, *les* célèbres inoculateurs anglais," and "*leur* remède" as if there were more than one Sutton present at the king's bedside during those days working together to save this famous and powerful patient. But the efforts of whatever number of Suttons were to no avail. King Louis was beyond anyone's help.[27]

Inoculation carried with it the great risk of touching off an epidemic because the patient was, for a time, contagious—another important reason beside religious zealotry for skepticism about the practice. To guard against that problem, patients were quarantined for a period of weeks. When Robert Hemings was inoculated, Jefferson noted that he had paid

"Ambo for lodging & nursing Bob four weeks." When he mentioned paying to board "Martin & Jame," he did not say how long they remained in isolation, but there is no reason to suppose that their situation was drastically different from their brother's.[28] As one might expect, things were a bit more rigorous in metropolitan France. There the quarantine was to last at least forty days after the day of inoculation, and it was illegal to inoculate anyone within the city limits of Paris.[29] Sally Hemings was sent to an inoculation house outside of town to have the procedure performed.

But where did she go? The exorbitant fees the Suttons charged paying clients like Jefferson included the housing and feeding of the patients, though tea and wine were extra.[30] Hemings's inoculation was handled the same way the Suttons handled other patients in their two-tiered system of treatment. Poor patients back in England, usually treated in mass or group inoculations for nothing or next to nothing, stayed in their villages, which were then kept strictly quarantined. The Suttons made the rounds on a schedule to take care of them. Paying clients were sent away to comfortable inoculation houses that the Suttons set up in areas far from towns, and the brothers made the rounds there to look after them. Like these patients, Sally Hemings underwent the procedure "in private, quarantined from the community at large."[31] Indeed, by the time she arrived in Paris, the Suttons had long had their own inoculation house on the outskirts of the city.

In keeping with the brothers' insular franchise mentality, which favored their relatives, the family impresario Daniel Sutton sent his father-in-law, Dr. Worlock, to set up the Suttons' inoculation house in France. It was "an isolated house outside of Paris with fresh air, near Mont Louis, called P. Lachaise." By 1804 the Sutton's inoculation house was closed, and Père-Lachaise became the site of "the most famous cemetery in Paris," which still exists today, although now within the city's limits.[32]

If it ever existed, no correspondence between Jefferson and Sutton survives, and none of his extant letters to anyone else mention the doctor. The record of all of Jefferson's incoming and outgoing letters, the SJL (Summary Journal of Letters), can yield no clue. The pages covering the end of 1787, through October 1789, after he and the Hemingses had left Paris, are missing—the only part of this record that is not extant.[33] Yet, the men must have communicated. How else would Jefferson have found Sutton and made arrangements for him to care for Hemings and receive payment for it? He probably dealt with Sutton face-to-face. The amount of money was too great, and Jefferson's interest in the topic too long-standing and deep, to imagine that he passed up the chance to meet with a member of a family so esteemed in such an important field of medicine, an area that always fascinated him.[34]

While one could see Jefferson viewing Hemings's inoculation from both his personal and his scientific perspective, the matter was probably almost all personal for her. Even with today's greater knowledge of medicine and disease prevention, vaccination, a much less dangerous technique than inoculation, frightens many parents whose children undergo the process and some individuals who must be vaccinated as adults. The idea of being given a dread disease to prevent the dread disease quite naturally raises conflicting emotions: gratitude at the prospect of being spared a terrible sickness and, at the same time, fear of being among the tiny percentage of people who suffer as a result of the procedure.

James Hemings, Jefferson, and his daughters were living testaments to the benefits of inoculation when everything went well. But Sally Hemings knew what contracting smallpox meant. It was a disease of her time in a way that it is emphatically not in our own, and it affected all classes. While in Paris, Jefferson noted the death of a prominent society woman from smallpox. George Washington had had it as a young man and carried the scars of the disease. Hemings was old enough to have known of the turmoil and horrific suffering of the slaves who returned to Jefferson's plantations after the war. Several of her close relatives had been at Yorktown, where the disease was notoriously rampant.

Jefferson knew the extent of the Suttons' good reputation and that he could not have put Hemings in better hands. Hemings, however, probably had little reason to know about the Suttons, and even if Jefferson chose to act as the good patriarch and explain to her just who Sutton was and the significance of his involvement in treating her (and try to allay any fears), it could not have erased all doubt. Anyone with ordinary intelligence would have understood that a required quarantine of forty days indicated that one was about to undergo a very serious medical procedure and that there was always a chance that things could go wrong. After the trip over the ocean, the sojourn in London with Abigail Adams, and the stressful introduction to city living, new food, new faces, and new surroundings, Hemings faced yet another trial.

The Suttons religiously followed a strict regime that they believed was the key to their success. The method was all. After years of attempting to keep the exact nature of that method secret, Daniel Sutton published a book in 1796 revealing their protocol, complete with a handy chart of the daily routine that patients like Hemings were put through.[35] Those who followed the Suttonian method, and those who did not, commonly prescribed a before-inoculation program for prospective patients. According to Sutton's prescription, at the beginning of her confinement Hemings was to be put on a diet that restricted the amount and type of food. She was not supposed to eat any animal protein. She could not drink any alcohol, which was probably not yet a part of her routine anyway. The Suttons had turned away from the extensive use of the harsh purgatives, fasting, and induced vomiting in the pre-inoculation phase that other inoculators relied upon. Their approach was more moderate, although there were elixirs she had to take on a precise schedule.[36]

After the inoculation was performed, usually by making a small incision on the upper arm and placing a piece of thread that had been exposed to smallpox pustules into the wound, those attending Hemings at the inoculation house followed her condition. Her "duly restricted" diet continued with a set menu that had a very limited range of choices. After a "Breakfast" of "tea with dry toast" and "milk porridge" or "honey and bread" or "bread with the addition of sugar and currants," Hemings could look forward to a "Dinner" featuring various types of pudding—"bread," "rice," or "plum or plain pudding"—and "the production of the kitchen garden," presumably vegetables. For "Supper" she could be given any of the items from previous meals, along with "roasted apples or potatoes." She could not have "fish, flesh, butter, cheese, eggs or spiced food." The Suttons did not want their patients to eat foods that they believed created a "heating quality." So, in addition to watching the foods she ate, whatever fluid Hemings took in would have to be "perfectly cooling" to her body. After a few days "purging syrup" was administered periodically. To control the symptoms of the mild case of smallpox—chief among them, a high fever and, sometimes, very intense aches and pains—Hemings was given a dose of a serum that included, controversially even at that time, a tiny amount of "calomel," a form of mercury. In earlier days, inoculators had used mercury more liberally, often weakening their patients to an alarming degree.[37] John Adam's description of the "Mercurial Preparations" that seemed an almost daily part of his regime under inoculation, mentions symptoms easily recognizable as mercury poisoning. By the time his wife, Abigail, was inoculated twelve years later, the Suttons had appeared on the scene and most of the extreme aspects of the process had been mitigated, including the heavy doses of mercury.[38]

Along with their attention to hygiene, the Suttons had a great belief, approaching mania apparently, in the benefits of fresh air. They emphasized rest, to prepare the body to take and control the mild case of smallpox. At the same time, they believed that it was important for the patient to move around. In the days after the procedure, Hemings was thus supposed to engage in moderate exercise, defined as walking around the grounds of the quarantine area for a set period of time each day. That is why the Suttons wanted their patients out in the country away from everyone else. A daily walk through a community might bring them into potentially fatal contact with others. Once Hemings developed a fever, it was to be "treated with cold water, warm tea and thin gruel by mouth." After her "eruption appeared," she would be directed once again to get up and walk around—and take in more fresh air. Then she would return for more rest.[39]

Although, or perhaps because, he had a generally low opinion of doctors, Jefferson often played the role of physician in his own life—personally nursing his daughters when they were ill, as he had his wife, giving doses of medicine to slaves, watching the schedule for that, setting their bones, and stitching up wounds.[40] With Hemings's inoculation program, there was medicine to be given and a regimen to follow that had been prepared by a celebrated physician notorious for guarding the secrets of his success. The whole business spoke to virtually every aspect of Jefferson's personality: his boundless curiosity, his addiction to routine, his interest in progressive scientific methods, and his self-fashioning as a dutiful patriarch and competent quasi-health professional. Hemings probably had to answer many questions from him about everything that had taken place while she was under Sutton's care in his very secretive world.

Just months into her stay in France, Hemings was living amid strangers, apart from her brother, and others familiar to her, on the opposite side of Paris from the Hôtel de Langeac. Her mother was an ocean away. She had come from a family of numerous siblings and spent most of her childhood living in a place where there were always lots of people her age and older around her. What she faced living on the outskirts of Paris was about as far from the life she had known as one could imagine. Being ill, even under controlled circumstances, is difficult. Being ill and alone in a strange country where people speak a language one cannot understand is on another order of magnitude of difficulty.

Dr. Sutton, of course, spoke English, and Hemings could communicate with him when he made his round of visits. The attendants at the house may have been bilingual or not, as the house was specifically designed to serve French-speaking patients. The Suttons' long presence in France gave them ample opportunity, and a great financial incentive, to speak to their prospective customers—and any local attendants who worked for them—in their native language. If Sutton thought he could take over the care of Louis XV and deal with his doctors, he probably had at least some knowledge of French. This was very likely Hemings's first really intensive experience with language immersion, when she was surrounded by people for whom English was a second language. If they talked to her in her native tongue, they would have spoken to one another in their own, sharpening her ear for French even as she wondered what they were talking about.

Hemings was at the right age to quickly achieve proficiency in French. Her son Madison recalled that, by the end of her time in Paris, she had learned to speak the language "well," which makes sense given her age at the time she came to the country and the length of her stay there.[41] When he first arrived in France, a very impressed William Short noted how much faster the teenage children of Jefferson and John and Abigail Adams picked up the language as compared with their elders. This was not a matter of formal study or educational level. The elder Americans had studied French, Jefferson for many years, themselves. Human beings are primed to learn languages, and can do that very well without studying them formally. Hemings was one year younger than Patsy Jefferson and six and eight years younger than the Adams children Short was referring to, John Quincy and Nabby, and thus well within the time period when acquiring language is easier.[42]

What did Sutton and his attendants make of the young African American girl who had been put into their care by the American minister to France? Did they know she was a slave? It is probably impossible to recover just how many blacks were being inoculated in the city at that time. There cannot have been very many, for there were not that many blacks in the country. Their overall small numbers in Paris as compared with Hemings's Virginia, or the French colonies, for that matter, made blacks a less immediate threat to Parisian whites. She probably faced a different, less forbidding racial dynamic than the one that existed back in Virginia. The people at the Suttons' inoculation house (who would have had no reason to go around thinking of themselves as "white" and attaching daily significance to that) were most likely very different from the whites she had encountered for most of her life. Still, Hemings was undoubtedly something of a curiosity at the place. Here Abigail Adams's observation about her good nature and others' testimony that she was very pleasant to look at may have given her an advantage as a patient. From Hemings's standpoint, this may have been the first time she had ever been attended to by white people. In her life to date whites were the centers of attention—that of other whites and of blacks as well. Even at her young age, she had been raised to care for white children who were not much younger than she. "The Girl," for an extended time, was now the focus of attention, being looked after by others who were there to serve and care for her.

Hard as it must have been, perhaps because it was hard, the entirety of this experience—the isolation, the facing down of an inherently frightening situation, and the process of recovery from the ordeal—helped shape Hemings's personality just as surely as her transatlantic crossing. Those forty days alone with no tasks to perform, save relying on her own inner strength to get well, left her with no one's interests to look after but her own. Perhaps for the first time since she was a small girl, Hemings had the perfect occasion to think intensely about herself, what her life had been to date, and what she would like to have happen in the future, and to daydream a great deal about all of that.

II

🌿

THE RHYTHMS OF THE CITY

T HE HOME THAT Sally Hemings returned to after the end of her
time at the inoculation house was just inside the city limits of Paris.
Indeed, the Hôtel de Langeac was right next to the Grille de Chaillot,
one of the many gated entry points into what was still at the time a walled
city. The house, abutting the Champs-Elysées and along the rue Neuve de
Berri, was more expensive than Jefferson could afford. He thought, however, that his position demanded a suitable residence for all the entertaining
that he expected to do. Whatever its merits as a standard-bearer for the representative of the newly formed United States of America, the house also
suited Jefferson personally.[1]

This residence was truly worthy of a French aristocrat. The expansive
grounds entered by a way of an impressive courtyard, contained "green
houses," an extensive kitchen garden, and another "graceful" one that
Jefferson pronounced "clever," admiring its English style. Just off the entry-
way into the courtyard from the rue de Berri were the porter's lodge and
servants' quarters. The house itself, torn down in 1842, seems to have been
a gem. It "had a basement, ground floor, a mezzanine," and a top floor.
Howard C. Rice, who wrote extensively about Jefferson's time in Paris, provides a description of the sumptuous home that James and Sally Hemings
came to know that is well worth reproducing.

> To the right upon entering, were steps going to the front-door, beyond
> which was a large antechamber or reception hall. On the left-hand side
> of this hall a stairway led to the upper stories. Passing through the

reception-hall one entered a circular room with a sky-light. Adjoining this circular room was an oval drawing-room from which steps led into the garden. . . . Next to the oval drawing room, looking out over the Champs-Elysées, were a smaller drawing room and the dining room. Along the rue de Berri side were a bath-room and a series of passage-ways including a stair-case leading down to the kitchens in the basement. Although no plan of the *entresol* or mezzanine floor has been preserved, it may be supposed that this contained a series of bed-rooms and informal apartments. The first floor . . . included spacious bedrooms [three], each of which had a convenient dressing-room adjoining it. The house was equipped with the latest inventions in modern plumbing, in the form of water closets, "lieux à l'anglaise."[2]

Living at such a place gave both Hemingses ample opportunity to compare their surroundings in Paris with those they had seen in Virginia, and they could only have found Virginian residences wanting. The amenity of having indoor bathrooms was remarkable for both them and the Jeffersons. Along with the *lieux à l'anglaise* on the upper floors, the ground floor had a room designed for taking baths. The very complexity of the house, with its multiple stairways (one large formal one and two smaller private ones) and its numerous passageways leading into different areas of the mansion, no doubt piqued their interest as well. If Jefferson's English-style garden was "clever," so was the house designed by Jean Chalgrin, one of France's premier architects, who later created the Arc de Triomphe. It was, in Jack McLaughlin's words, "the most splendid house Jefferson had ever lived in."[3] Rice's supposition that the mezzanine floor consisted of "bedrooms" and "informal apartments" is sound. All the other rooms that go into making a house a home—kitchen, dining room, parlor, master bedrooms—were accounted for in the plans for the other floors. Having a floor of available bedrooms explains why Jefferson so confidently invited guests to stay with him while in Paris: he had enough space to put them up comfortably, and he was able to play the gracious host, a role he liked very much.

Jefferson's own living area was quite opulent. His personal quarters consisted of an oval-shaped combination library and study that looked out over the garden in which he planted traditional southern fare like sweet potatoes and Indian corn. His library-study led into his bedroom and dressing room, a setup he reproduced at Monticello years later. One of these rooms had a ceiling "richly ornamented with a painting of the rising sun," a bit of extravagance that one does not immediately associate with republican virtues. But it was, at its core, a very practical configuration of a personal world where the maximum amount of privacy could facilitate the maximum amount of work. Even this sequestered realm was not enough for him, for there were always household matters to deal with, so long as he was at home. He solved that problem by taking an apartment at a nearby monastery, Mont Calvaire, which he called his "hermitage." There he retreated when he felt a need to close himself off completely from the world.[4]

It is not known whether James and Sally Hemings lived in the adjacent servants' quarters or whether the mezzanine floor, the entresol in architectural terms, contained rooms for servants as well. Those half-story sections within great houses, with their lower ceilings, were often designated for the use of servants or as bedrooms for people other than the master or mistress of the house. Sally Hemings's closeness to the girls may not have made much of a difference for most of the time they were in Paris. Until their father took them out of school, they came home only on the weekend, usually on Sunday.

Whether brother and sister would have been happier with a room in the house or one in the separate, but nearby, servants' quarters is unclear. Maids' and cooks' rooms within great houses were usually just simple affairs, so there may have been little difference in the relative comfort of their accommodations wherever they lived at the Hôtel de Langeac. On the other hand, James and Sally Hemings would have derived very real benefits from having some distance from Jefferson, Patsy, and Polly. Abundant evidence suggests that enslaved people benefited emotionally and culturally when they had a space apart from their owners. Greater autonomy allowed them to create their own worlds and to be their true selves within them. Complaints, grievances, and disappointments could be more openly aired, hopes and plans for the future hatched outside the earshot and eyesight of masters.[5]

By the time Sally Hemings arrived, her brother was well used to the splendors of the Hôtel de Langeac. What was new about his time there was his elevation in early October of 1788 to chef de cuisine, which drastically changed the level of his responsibilities and probably of his stress. No longer an apprentice, he was in charge of the kitchen and his assistants. His position made him responsible for every success and failure regarding a critical component in that diplomatic household. Jefferson entertained on a large scale, as he did throughout his life. Hemings's talents were on constant display at meals that could be for a few people or for up to thirty, as at one dinner celebrating the Fourth of July. The hectic pace and pressure for perfection drove many chefs to drink, and as the years went by, Hemings himself would fall prey to that professional hazard. He had to please not only Jefferson's exacting palate but that of the people whom Jefferson wanted to impress. He and Patsy's early experiences having to meet Parisian fashion standards taught him a valuable lesson about the kinds of things that mattered in the city. The French were as serious about their cuisine as about fashionable attire. In fact, the two were closely related, since the presentation of food—the look—took its place alongside taste as a mark of true distinction. Every dish Hemings prepared invited a judgment by a man who was a perfectionist.

While James Hemings was busy plying his trade in 1788 and 1789, his younger sister had little to do but absorb the routine of the household. This meant getting used to the other servants, who spoke another language and had their own cultural manners. Having no apparent role in the operations of the residence for long stretches of time, she was essentially cast as an observer, watching what other people did to make things run smoothly at the place. At the beginning, Hemings really was a fifth wheel at the Hôtel de Langeac, as Abigail Adams had implied she would be. From her perspective that may not have been at all a bad thing, rather a source of immense joy as her nonessential status left her free to experience her new surroundings in more of her own way.

As she noted all that was going on around her, Hemings had to adopt a new way of looking at herself, because the role she had played in life had changed rather dramatically. She was no longer a part of pair, and there was no person for whom she was in any way responsible. With Polly away at school, those days were gone—which could be at once liberating and lonely. Because Jefferson's almost six-year absence from Monticello had disrupted the course of life there, Hemings's switch from doing a job that was closely associated with young slave children to playing a more adult role came late for her. And that switch took place in a completely foreign environment.

Enslaved children at Monticello above the age of ten left their roles as messengers, playmates, and minders of other younger slave children and quickly moved into the roles they would play as adults. They were designated to work as artisans or went to the fields, or "into the ground," to use a phrase of that time. Hemings, not destined for any of those roles, was supposed to take her place as a servant with adult responsibilities in the house when she came of age. By that reckoning, when she arrived in Europe, she was a few years behind schedule and may have continued in that dream state that one of her great-nephews, the grandson of her sister Mary, described many years later when speaking of his early life at Monticello. Peter Fossett said that as a young boy he never thought of himself as a slave, because his life was so unlike that of the boys down the mountain whose situations more clearly telegraphed their status. He was dressed differently from them. He spent all of his time in or near the house without much to do and identified greatly with the people there—his own family—who focused closely on the affairs and interests of their own genetically connected world.[6]

Fossett's recollections are really not surprising when one recalls that enslaved children were, in fact, children and by definition lacked the maturity and foresight of their parents. When they are allowed to, children can have priorities very different from those of adults. They tend not to be so focused on the outside world and determining their exact place in it, unless some event—the death of a close relative or, for enslaved children, the sale or mistreatment of relatives—forces them to pay attention to those things. While even extreme poverty is not on a par with slavery, it is nevertheless interesting that Fossett sounds very much like people who grew up poor who say that they did not define themselves as poverty stricken when they were small children. It was only as they grew older that they realized all they did not have.

When a child like Fossett sees others in the immediate community whose lives are more severely constricted than his, and when that child has a stable and nurturing family, as he did, one can see why he would not as a small boy have recognized or dwelled on the realities of his legal and social standing. Peter Fossett's self-characterized childhood idyll ended at age eleven when Jefferson died and he learned in the hardest way possible that his status as a member of the Hemings family did not protect him from the vagaries of life as a slave. When all was said and done, the first-generation Hemings/Wayles slaves fared much better after Jefferson's death than other members of the clan. Fossett's father, Joseph, was freed, but neither his mother nor he nor any of his siblings were freed along with him. In the end, they were not so different from the people down the mountain, after all.[7]

Peter Fossett's statements about his early life naturally raise a question about Sally Hemings's state of mind during her childhood and the way she carried herself as a young girl. If Fossett, a fourth-generation Hemings, who was not a Wayles descendant, could pass through the early part of his boyhood without seeing the magnitude of his enslavement, there is little reason to think that Sally Hemings was not similarly disposed. Everything that had happened in her life pointed toward that. A blood relation to Jefferson's wife and daughters, she had been chosen because of those relationships to be constantly in the presence of the Jefferson family and knew she was not destined for arduous physical duties in adulthood. She had older brothers who were allowed to go off on their own, work for themselves, and keep their money—money they could give to their mother and siblings or use to buy presents and clothes for their little sister. Hemings, as a child, may have dwelled even less upon her legal and social status than Peter Fossett.

Perhaps it was in part an unknowing manner in the young Sally Hemings that so disconcerted Abigail Adams, a manner exacerbated by her tangled family relations. She was both the aunt of the little girl whom she was serving and the half sister of the woman in whose house they had lived for four years before coming to Europe. Adams almost certainly had no idea of any of this when she met Hemings in London, but it was not just her knowledge that counted. It was what Hemings knew about who she was in relation to the Jeffersons that fixed her inner life and the way she presented herself to Adams and others.

In Adams's eyes, Hemings just was not "grown up" in the way a servant girl should have been grown up—maybe with harder edges, and a more resigned or deferential demeanor. Adams was not a slaveholder, but she was familiar with the trajectory of servants' lives. The sixteen-year-old enslaved girl she mistakenly thought Hemings to have been was supposed to be well into that defined role, and she evidently was not. Adams's petulant comment that Hemings needed "more care" than Polly is suggestive. Hemings may have acted more like Polly's friend than her servant, and expected some attention from Adams, as if she were still in the pre-adult stage of her life as a slave dealing with her half siblings and their spouses back in Virginia who out of a mix of guilt and paternalistic benevolence acted out more literally an old saying about servants, "She's just like a member of the family." Support for this appears in a reference to Hemings from one of Patsy's French friends, Marie de Botidoux. After Patsy returned to America, Botidoux wrote to her and asked her to say hello to "Mlle [Mademoiselle] Sale [Sally]" for her.[8] In rigidly hierarchical ancien régime France, the honorifics monsieur, madame, and mademoiselle were strictly reserved for those of high standing, and they were guarded jealously. One cannot say it "never" happened, but members of the French upper class did not refer to *serviteurs* by any of those titles; "Sally" should have sufficed. Patsy Jefferson was a "mademoiselle" in that world. Botidoux, for purposes of the letter, put Hemings on a par with her. The young Frenchwoman was evidently making a bow to her American friend's sensibilities, which indicates that Patsy Jefferson's behavior toward Hemings signaled to outsiders that she was something more than just a normal servant in the Jefferson household.

Indeed, one wonders what the Jefferson daughters told people about who Hemings was. Their father had hidden James Hemings's status in his letter to Paul Bentalou and was, in effect, hiding both Hemingses by not registering them. All three girls had an incentive to play down the relationship they bore to one another under American law. Patsy's impassioned outburst before Hemings arrived, about wishing that all the "negroes" were free, shows that she had taken to heart some of her father's pronouncements and was emboldened by having lived comfortably and well—in better surroundings than she had ever been in before—without chattel slavery. Treating Hemings more as a companion, one who her friends would think to mention in their letters, may have been a way to minimize guilt. Polly followed the same course. She passed along Hemings's message of regards in a letter she wrote to Angelica Church's daughter, Catharine (Kitty), in a way that emphasized casual closeness rather than distance. Sometimes when Jefferson went to pick Polly up from school on the weekends, Kitty came along to stay at the Hôtel de Langeac. Hemings knew her well enough to think that a greeting might be in order and welcomed, and Polly agreed with her and carried out Hemings's wishes.[9]

The family connections at play make the girls' situation even more intriguing. Patsy was the image of her father, while Polly was said to have looked liker her mother, Hemings's half sister. It is entirely possible that Polly and Sally (and perhaps even James) resembled each other, which would have provoked all kinds of questions in the minds of those who saw the Hemingses and Jeffersons together. Sex between masters and servants/slaves was not unknown in France, and the presence of mixed-race servants and slaves from the colonies was clear evidence of across-the-color-line sex in French society. In addition, it was not unheard of in eighteenth-century French society for poorer relations to be servants (*femmes de chambre, valets de chambre*) in the homes of their wealthier cousins. The French would have understood the configuration of the Jefferson/Wayles household very well.[10]

The City

While the Hôtel de Langeac was certainly the center of James and Sally Hemings's universes in Paris, neither sibling's life was bound solely by the interior of the place. They were not galley slaves chained to a bench within the hold of a ship. Nor will it do to think of them as being in the same circumstances as slaves, in the field or house, embedded in the isolated and deeply rural environment of their home at Monticello. Indeed, during their time in Paris, they were able to move through an expansive world as if they were free persons of color. Brother and sister were now city dwellers, in the largest city in Europe, home to over 700,000 people.[11] Though they did not live in the heart of the city—their neighborhood was a relatively new one pushing toward the city's boundary—they were part of it and were touched by attributes of the metropolis that radiated out from its center. A much reproduced engraving depicting the Hôtel de Langeac, and the scene just outside of it, a mere eight years before the Hemingses lived there, tells part of the story of what their new status as urbanites meant.[12]

The engraving displays a spectacular view of the Champs-Elysées stretching out toward the heart of Paris. In the rue de Berri, which led into the residence, there are no fewer than twenty people and two carriages. Across the street is a government building housing officials in the customs service, and on either side of the Champs-Elysées are households with no connection to the residents of the Hôtel de Langeac, save their mutual presence in the neighborhood. This mix of intimacy and impersonality is a mark of urban life, where people can live and work in close proximity to one another and be as friendly or as distant as they choose, producing a very different set of expectations about social life than exists in the country. In our times, technology brings the values and mores of urban life into the villages and homes of people living in the most remote parts of the globe, giving them some inkling of what life is like in the big city. As eighteenth-century pro-vincials abroad, James and Sally Hemings had no similar template. There was much they had to learn and get used to.

One of the first things to get used to was the pace of this new setting. Although there are predictable and definite patterns of city life, there are also daily surprises—faces that one has never seen or transactions among strangers that break up the monotony of the day in a way that makes life seem more hurried and transitory. With more people to encounter, more situations to figure out quickly (and more things to be wary of), city dwell-ers become "sharp," a word that has both positive and negative connota-tions. Those who are "wised up" about the world may be less subject to being fooled, but if they are not careful they can also become jaded.

We see some of this in Patsy Jefferson's lament about how her father was cheated when they first arrived in France, being grossly overcharged for having luggage transported from the port at Le Havre to their lodg-ings.[13] She was shocked. It is very likely, though, that the Jeffersons and the Hemingses were more attuned to the possibility of being hoodwinked dur-ing transactions with strangers. This loss of innocence, at the same time, brought increased awareness and sophistication. This ever-changing, quick-moving aspect of city living was very much a feature of life in the place where James and Sally Hemings lived. The Grille de Chaillot brought in visitors or immigrants from the villages and towns of France on a steady basis, people moving with all their possessions, dressed in different types of clothing, creating a show that was at once a spectacle and a routine. Just by being at the Hôtel de Langeac, the Hemingses encountered the outside world in various ways every day.

James Hemings's five-year sojourn in Paris and his sister's of a little more than two years gave them ample time to get to know what one historian of Paris in the eighteenth century calls the "regular rhythms and meanings that structured the lives of most of the city's inhabitants."[14] Monticello moved solely to rhythms set by the needs of Jefferson and his family. He did not con-trol Paris; nor could he even control what went on in the area immediately sur-rounding his house. Life was more contingent for everyone—circumstances and situations were more up for grabs—sometimes literally.

Near the end of their stay, when the government office that operated across the street closed and moved its employees elsewhere, taking the secu-rity detail with them, the Hôtel de Langeac was periodically burglarized.

Jefferson eventually had to ask for special police protection for the residence, making the appeal on behalf of the "inhabitants of this quarter." His was just one of a number of "other houses in the neighborhood,"[15] which one could never say about Monticello. Cities have a way of cutting people down to size, as was, no doubt, obvious to the young African Americans in his household. Jefferson could only appear a much smaller person in this much larger place.

The Hemingses did not live apart from the culture that surrounded them. They were in a city that lived on rituals that they learned about from their own observation and from the servants with whom they worked. Secular and religious festivals abounded within the Catholic country, celebrating the lives of numerous saints and observing various holy days, which noticeably took the Hemings's fellow servants out of the workplace on some days or formed the basis of their conversation on the days leading up to or following the events. Some of those holidays had their own special features that involved both private and public gestures—one bought a turkey for Mardi Gras or one participated in parades on other special days.[16]

Parisians celebrated Carnival with "feasting, dancing, and ribaldry" to mark "both the end of winter and the beginning of Lent, usually in February."[17] Brother and sister did not have to go very far to witness some of the spectacles of Parisian life, because they sometimes took place right outside their home. The Promenade à Longchamps brought all classes of French society together to parade up the Champs-Elysées to attend a concert at the nearby Abbey of Longchamps. The spectacle could go on for three days.[18] One of the balconies of the Hôtel de Langeac provided a perfect site from which to view the proceedings, and on at least one occasion Jefferson invited his friends to do that. Although neither Hemings ever went to school, taking in the rules and rituals of this vibrant city and complicated culture was an education for both of them. These two young people saw more of the world and experienced more of what was in it than did the vast majority of their countrymen, white or black, who during that time lived and died without venturing far beyond the confines of the isolated farms where they were born.

James Hemings attempted a more formal approach to his education in French culture, for he was very serious about improving his French. Just before his sister Sally came to Paris, he hired a local man to teach him French grammar. Sally may have been included when she arrived. There

is no indication how he found Perrault, and it is perhaps significant that
Hemings did not turn to any of Jefferson's French servants to help him with
the language. He may have had good reason not to. Little is known about
the French servants at the Hôtel de Langeac, but it is well known that a large
majority of the servants in Paris came to the city from villages speaking the
languages and dialects of their home region. There was no national French
identity in the 1780s. By some estimates, that would not arise until the latter
half of the nineteenth century. Eugen Weber, the great historian of France,
has offered that the abbé Grégoire, who conducted a survey in 1790 to determine the prevalence of French speaking in the country, was being overly
optimistic when he found that "3 million [out of a population of about 20
million] could speak French,"[19] the language of the elites in the country, predominantly those in Paris. Those new arrivals to the city worked hard to
make themselves understood as they gained proficiency in what was a foreign tongue, but it was often a struggle for them. Even the servants who
spoke French natively spoke the language "of the streets and market," which
often disregarded the grammar and pronunciation of "proper French."

At the other end of the scale stood a smaller group of servants who mas-
tered several languages with the aim of getting better positions and making
themselves useful to masters who traveled the Continent. When advertising
their services, they carefully noted their language skills.[20] It seems unlikely
that any of the servants at the Hôtel de Langeac were in this last category.
If they had been, barring other difficulties, such as a lack of time or a clash
of personalities with Hemings, at least one of them should have been willing to give basic lessons for a price. Adrien Petit spoke French, though his
letters reveal a man with only a basic education.[21] As maître d'hôtel, he may
have been far too busy to undertake the job or simply was not, in Hemings's
view, the right person. His association with Perrault is the first indication
that Hemings thought he might have a future in France. Speaking French
as best he could, while being a native English-speaker, made him attractive
as an employee in a culture that was, in the 1780s, enamored both of servants of African descent and of English culture.[22]

Perrault, who emerges as a somewhat sad character from his description of his relations with Hemings, wrote to Jefferson at the beginning of
1789, complaining that Hemings owed him money for some of the twenty-
one months' worth of tutoring he had provided. Perrault sought redress
from Jefferson after having approached Hemings about the unpaid fees

with outstandingly bad results. The letter makes clear that Hemings had quite a temper and was not a man to be trifled with. The report of the event comes from Perrault alone, so no one knows what he said to Hemings or how he said it, but in his version Hemings insulted him and overwhelmed him physically, kicking him and hitting him with his fists. Perrault apparently did not fight back, and he suggested that he had been seriously hurt during the assault.[23]

Assuming Perrault was white, one wonders how his skirmish with Hemings would have played out in Virginia. Slaves did attack whites, and those altercations sometimes ended up in court or were more often punished by plantation justice. There also must have been times when slaves and whites fought with no serious consequences for the slave, either because the white person involved chose not to press the issue or because the slave's master had some reason to side with the slave. It would thus not be right to say that we know for sure that Hemings would never have hit a white man in Virginia. Perhaps his years in France, four by the time of this encounter, had emboldened him to think that he had the right to take this action if he felt that Perrault deserved a good beating. We do not know how Jefferson reacted to this. There is no record that he ever paid Perrault; it was not his debt. But if he had any suspicions before, he certainly knew for a fact after Perrault's letter that he had in James Hemings a very volatile and forceful personality.

While Sally Hemings did not have much of a formal occupation during her first year in Paris, there were many things for her to see and learn; and she did not have to go far to do that, with all that was going on in her immediate neighborhood. This was important because, as a female, she probably did not have as much freedom to wander around Paris as her brother. But James was there to squire her about, and he was likely eager to do that because she was family and because he had been the lone African American in the household for so long. Even with a more restricted range of motion, the Champs-Elysées was right outside her home. She could venture a short way down from the Hôtel de Langeac and see a statue of King Louis XV or continue on that route to view the Château des Tuileries. A trip down the rue de Berri would bring her to the very fashionable, then as now, rue du Fauborg-Saint-Honoré and the relatively new site of the church built in the style "of a Roman basilica."[24]

None of this required great effort on the young girl's part, and there was ample opportunity for "people watching" on a scene that changed each day.

Carriage rides with Jefferson and his daughters, or even on her journey to and from the Suttons' inoculation house outside Paris, brought a new world to her. Most important of all, none of these rich and enlightening visual experiences required having any money or special social status; enslaved and free, black and white, could look upon the products of French civilization and be impressed, disquieted, stunned, or simply moved. And while her brother had been in the city long enough to take his experience somewhat for granted, Sally Hemings probably had not. She was there just long enough to get comfortable and to remain excited about all that she was seeing and learning.

One of the things Hemings learned fairly early on was how it felt to receive pay for one's work. In January of 1788 she received her first recorded wages—twenty-four livres, plus an additional twelve as a New Year's tip.[25] She was paid the same amount as James Hemings, in his very important role as chef de cuisine. One can only surmise that Jefferson had not thought things through, for this was a little unfair to James. There is a probable answer to the anomaly. She received no recorded pay in February, either because she did no work or because Jefferson made an adjustment for the seemingly inappropriate January payment, thus spreading the twenty-four livres over two months. He then left on a seven-week tour of northern Europe at the very beginning of March. Hemings did not receive pay again until November of the same year; when she did, the wage was half that of her brother, Jefferson having concluded that this was the appropriate rate for her. Working women of that time in France typically received half the pay of men, even when they did the same job. Twelve livres was also the amount Jefferson gave to his daughter Patsy as an allowance for most of her time in France. Despite the cut, Hemings's salary of twelve livres per month was actually well above that of the average female live-in servant in Paris.[26]

It has been suggested that Sally Hemings was apprenticed during the months when she received no salary and that this accounts for the absence of payments to her during certain periods of her stay in Paris.[27] There is, however, no evidence for that, and there almost certainly would have been, had this actually happened. Jefferson's memorandum books show no record of payment for Hemings to be apprenticed to anyone for the fifteen months that she received no wages. No artisan would have trained her for that amount of time for no pay, and may not have been able to in a Paris dominated by trade guilds. And though he did from time to time fail to record purchases or expenses, Jefferson would have at some point recorded so extensive an ongoing obligation.

Having an informal status did not mean that Hemings was not expected to help out around the house. There surely were many times when she could run errands for her brother or assist him when he had to prepare meals for larger than normal dinner parties. She also had a skill—sewing—that could be put to immediate use without Jefferson's thinking to put her on a fixed salary for doing it. He viewed sewing as one of the foundations of a woman's domestic life and advised his daughters that resort to "the needle" would be necessary for the smooth running of their households once they became married women, providing vital services to their families even as it relieved their own ennui.[28] In fact, Jefferson believed that sewing was even better for women than reading. In a circumstance where other essential jobs at the residence were already taken care of, it would be natural for him to turn to that most basic task performed by plantation women and girls, upper and lower class, white and black, alike.

Sewing and mending clothing were skills that were in perpetual use during Hemings's time. Jefferson certainly had someone to perform those tasks before she arrived, but it would have been a simple matter to turn any extra mending that needed to be done over to Hemings without thinking to make this into a formal daily job for which she would be paid regularly. The times when Hemings had no set job in Paris foreshadow what was to come at Monticello. When Jefferson was away for long stretches during his public life, and his daughters were married and moved away, the Hemings women had nothing to do, and that did not bother Jefferson. When he was president, he declined to purchase a female slave for Monticello because, he said, he already had too many house servants in "idleness," but he made no move to employ them. He told his overseer not to give them anything to do, and he leased out other slaves, but not Sally Hemings and her female relatives.[29]

Still, Hemings's return to regularly paid status during the latter part of 1788 is intriguing. Petit was in charge of the household servants, paying them wages with the money Jefferson gave him for that purpose. There are no indications from either him or Jefferson what her job was. As is so often true with Jefferson, in the absence of a direct statement of why he did something, information from other sources (sometimes documents he created for other reasons) clarify an opaque situation. The pay scale of French servants in this period, where Hemings's salary fit on that scale, and her later role at Monticello provide a good answer to the question of what her job was in Paris. Jefferson paid all of his servants the going rate, actually a little above it, for their designated jobs. He evidently consulted people about what a maître d' hôtel or a valet de chambre, for example, should receive in the way of wages. When he began to pay Sally Hemings, he paid her at the rate of the highest-level female *serviteur* within a French household, which would be a cook or a *femme de chambre*.[30] Her brother was the chef, so there was no other role for her, beside *femme de chambre*, that merited so high a rate of pay—but, whose chamber?

Hemings did not get paid twelve livres per month simply to be the *femme de chambre* to Patsy and Polly when they came home on Sundays, which they had been doing ever since she and Polly had arrived in Paris and for which Hemings had not been paid. The evidence indicates that it was at the Hôtel de Langeac that Hemings began to act in what would be her roles as an adult at Monticello: chambermaid to Jefferson, a seamstress doing "light sewing"[31] for the household, and helping out Patsy and Polly as they needed. Jefferson never had a designated housekeeper at the Hôtel de Langeac. One of his servants, presumably the porter, was responsible for the upkeep of the place, doing the heavy lifting and cleaning. The luxury of having Hemings arrive as an extra servant—a female servant at that—lay in her ability to efficiently manage his personal belongings. Who better to take care of his wardrobe and linens than a person who knew how to mend clothing and other items if required? The even greater efficiency was that she could, as he apparently thought she would, continue in this capacity once they returned home. Just as Jefferson intended it to be for her brother, the Hôtel de Langeac was a training ground for Sally Hemings's life at Monticello.

Knowing Hemings's most likely job, however, does not explain why her formal employment suddenly returned in November. Given their later lives, one immediately wonders whether the resumption of her regular employment marks the time when Jefferson became more seriously interested in her or, if not, when their relationship actually began. Did she become his permanent *femme de chambre* because she was already his mistress and this role provided an excuse for her to be in his rooms, was he merely thinking of having her as a mistress and set up circumstances that would put them in close contact, or did he become seriously interested in her only after having encountered her daily in the intimate setting of his living quarters? Liaisons between masters and chambermaids, enslaved and not, have been prevalent enough in all ages to be the stuff of cliché. In the eighteenth-century France of Hemings and Jefferson, some men refused to marry women who had been *femmes de chambre* to males, knowing what could happen when unrelated men and women come into contact with one another in the man's private chamber.[32] The woman, under the power of the master, could be sexually violated or abused, or the man and woman, interacting with each other in this very intimate and suggestive setting, could develop a mutual attraction. While an evolving relationship growing out of the cumulative effect of daily interactions would not explain what led Jefferson to give Hemings a regular job that November, it is more likely what happened. She had been paid wages once before without any reason to think that it was the result of any sexual interaction between them, and her wages ceased for eight months.

The feeling of being paid for her work, in a place where she considered herself to be a free person, could only have been empowering to Sally Hemings. For the first time in her life, she had something that belonged to her that she had worked for. Work, and payment for it, tends to foster a sense of independence and encourages thoughts about the future. Writing of Harriet Jacobs, Virginia Cope has noted that Jacobs's "initial act of freedom consist[ed] of walking into a Philadelphia shop and making a purchase,"[33] a moment of supreme importance to one who had lived as an item of property and could now confound her status by purchasing her own. The moment riveted Jacobs. Even though she had not worked for the money, which she used to buy gloves and veils to help shield her from the prying eyes of slave catchers, Jacobs's participation in the market transformed her sense of self.

Hemings, working for a set salary, was in an even greater position than Jacobs to feel the effects of having money and the ability to transact business. There were now new things to consider about the way she lived. She could decide to save or to spend—thinking of what to spend her money on or what she might be saving for—all this in a society that offered a dizzying array of choices about how, when, and whether to become a consumer. Any money she did not save she could spend on clothing or use to go with her brother to museums, or to the many low-cost theaters that were cropping up to serve lower-class patrons—there was no Jim Crow in eighteenth-century Paris. She could give charity to those who had no money, or buy gifts for people back home. Paris, unlike Virginia, provided a world outside her own thoughts that was right at hand to strengthen her powers of imagination. The people who saw her would have had no reason to doubt that she was anything other than a free person of color, confirming the very different and expanded options open to her in this new place. With no suffocating community ethos upholding her enslavement, Sally Hemings, like Jefferson, was able to breathe the air of liberal eighteenth-century Paris with "perfect satisfaction."

Having a thing in hand almost naturally raises expectations about getting other things. Perhaps Hemings might receive a raise, or if she did work for others, she might be paid more, and someday she might even be able to work for herself. People dream, despite whatever supposed realties may be before them, and dreamers were all around both Hemingses, their new cohort in Paris—their fellow French servants. The experience of managing their own money caused many among their number in ancien régime France to think of their jobs as a launching pad to better things. They wanted their own businesses or situations that would take them from under the immediate thumb of a master, and their aspirations ranged from the grandiose, and nearly unachievable, to mundane wishes that were actually within their grasp. For the grandiose, the West Indies held a special allure as a place to go to make fortunes. A number of servants, spurred by stories about the incredible turns of luck of a minuscule number of people, saved their money with the idea of going to the French colonies and becoming wealthy planters. Cooks with far less impressive training than James Hemings placed advertisements in newspapers offering their services to families traveling to the islands, hoping to break away at some point and buy their own plantations. That this actually happened on occasion no doubt fueled these aspirations, even though the rarity of the occasions suggested how unlikely an outcome this really was.[34]

At the other end of the spectrum were the more easily achievable dreams—dreams of being an innkeeper, of having a modest market stall to sell fruits and vegetables. A number of freed slaves took this route. Although the majority of them remained in service, male former slaves in Paris were in many occupations. The historian Pierre Boulle has found that they tended more than their female counterparts to work in the homes of aristocrats, becoming maîtres d'hôtel and valets de chambre. But they also worked as carpenters, hairdressers, and tailors, among other things. James Hemings with his exquisite training in France, and his years of service to Jefferson, was well positioned to take his place as a chef in an upper-class household. Young female former slaves tended to work in the clothing industry, as seamstresses, though some of them did become attached to upper-class households as *femmes de chambre*. One suspects that the brother and sister would have been quite attractive as a pair to prospective employers. *Femmes de chambre* and seamstresses, young women in Sally Hemings's occupations, longed to become the proprietors of their own dress shops. A two-year apprenticeship in dressmaking that would prepare young women for that could be had for 200 livres, a sum that neither James nor Sally Hemings, the former being paid 288 livres per year, the latter 144, would have thought out of their reach if they worked hard enough, pooled their resources, and saved their money.[35] These dreams of life out of service were not specific to any culture, race, or country. When their older brother, Robert, was emancipated in the 1790s, he left behind his life as a servant, as soon as he was able, to open his own fruit and vegetable stand and hauling business in Richmond. He struggled, but his labor was his own.[36]

Sally Hemings: Female and Obscure

Although Jefferson's records of his financial dealings seem almost maniacally detailed, they were not exhaustive. His correspondence and other sources refer to expenses that he did not record in his memorandum books, so we know that he did not keep a record of every single one of his financial transactions over the course of his long life. It should be noted, however, that Jefferson's records indicate that he apparently did not, while he was in France, give Sally Hemings spending money as he gave her brother James and his daughters. Of all the Virginia members of the household, only she was, ostensibly, left out of this show of Jefferson's largesse. While James Hemings was a man and Jefferson believed that men had broader lives that required having money on hand—to spend in taverns, to go to the theater, on clothes, on women—he also gave money to his daughters, who were living in a convent six days a week. The decision whether to provide spending money could not have been a matter of gender alone. Notions of gender *and* propriety likely shaped Jefferson's actions. Hemings was a slave like her brother, a female like Patsy and Polly, but she was different from all of them. It is one thing to dole out spending money to a male servant for no particular purpose or to one's daughters. It is quite another to do the same for a female nonrelative. When a presumptively heterosexual man makes gratuitous transfers of money to a woman who is not his wife or daughter, it raises, fairly or not, questions about the man's motivation.

Imagine going through Jefferson's memorandum books and substituting the name Sally for James every time there is an entry noting the payment of money. Even if there were no back story about Sally Hemings and Thomas Jefferson, readers might pause over those entries and wonder about the nature of the relationship between the male and the female engaged in those transactions. This is not to say that Jefferson was attempting to hide anything during those early years in France. There was, at that point, no reason for him to act as if anyone were looking over his shoulder at any of this. Who would ever go that carefully through his memorandum books? It is to suggest how gender influenced Jefferson's thinking about the way to deal with male slaves versus female ones. They were not all the same in his eyes, and he was conscious of the fact that he had to behave, or at least be seen to behave, very differently toward them. Getting into the habit of giving and recording payments of pin money to a female slave put the master-slave relationship too obviously close to the terrain of typical husband-to-wife, lover-to-mistress transactions. This does not mean, of course, that Jefferson never gave Hemings any spending money that he simply did not record. He may well have. It is also likely that he knew her brother would share with her, as families, black and white, were expected to do. He gave James Hemings money over and above his salary, some of which he could have expected to go to his little sister.

Sally Hemings's position as a slave who was an important, but somewhat mysterious, figure in the Jefferson household began in Paris as soon as Polly went to join her sister at the abbey. When trying to reconstruct her life in Paris, and afterward, one has to look to Hemings's own family and people outside of Jefferson's immediate family to find personal information or comments about her. One might say that the lack of information about her was a function of American slavery, an institution that forced most enslaved people into anonymity. Even with that there is something strange about her near-invisibility in Jefferson family exchanges. Given the length of time she spent with Polly and Patsy, and the intimate and unique circumstances in which they interacted, one might expect to see some substantive references to her in the letters written over the course of her life by those two women. Yet there is nearly total silence. The letter Polly Jefferson wrote to her aunt describing her trip to France, which held the greatest promise of a reference to Hemings, is no longer extant. Except for Polly's letter to Kitty Church while they were still in Paris in May of 1789, and in another letter written to her brother-in-law in the fall of 1790, Polly said nothing about Hemings.[37] Near the end of her life, Patsy mentioned giving Hemings "her time," freeing her without a formal document and a request to the legislature or county court that she be allowed to remain in Virginia.[38] Other than that, neither Jefferson daughter talked about Sally Hemings at any length in any of their correspondence that has come to light—from the time either before or after they returned from France—although they did talk about other Hemingses and other enslaved people.

We can know something of James Hemings in France through Jefferson's correspondence and memorandum books, yet his sister lives pretty much only in the memorandum books. There is no way to tell for sure, but Fawn Brodie raised the possibility that some culling of Jefferson's correspondence had gone on over the years to erase any possible reconstruction of what went on between Hemings and Jefferson—removing letters that contained even innocent references that might give information about her place in the Monticello household.[39] Jefferson's family was in charge of his correspondence for years after his death. While preparing the documents for publication to raise money to help retire the massive debts he left behind, his daughter Martha and some of her daughters combed meticulously through the letters to transcribe them for Thomas Jefferson Randolph, the named editor of the volumes. What was in the documents and how they would be received by posterity was very clearly important to them. Randolph actually held back letters that he thought might reflect poorly on his grandfather, including correspondence relating to James Callender, who first wrote openly about Jefferson and Hemings.[40]

Randolph, his sister Ellen Coolidge, and to a lesser degree, their mother, played prominent roles in the white Jefferson family's attempt to cover up Jefferson's relationship with Hemings, and Randolph and Coolidge pressed their efforts on paper.[41] There is no reason to think that members of the family who were willing to create documents to hide the truth about Hemings and Jefferson would have paused for a second over destroying documents that dealt with her in any substantive way. While one cannot rule out the possibility that letters were removed or destroyed, removing letters after the fact was probably not necessary. Given the state of things between the pair once they returned to Monticello, no members of the family would have been very keen to write about Hemings at all. They simply did not create the kind of letters that had to be destroyed at some later point.

Consider two events in Hemings's life in France: first, her inoculation. The Suttons were to the world of inoculation what Edward Jenner was to the world of vaccination. Imagine Jenner showing up at Monticello, and Jefferson never writing a word about it. How odd that he, who was so curious about the subject of smallpox and enthusiastic about efforts to eradicate it that he was moved to write a fan letter to Jenner, should have written nothing to one of Jenner's precursors before or after he treated a member of his household.

Then there is the matter of Hemings's absence from the Hôtel de Langeac for five weeks.[42] Because none of Jefferson's letters or other accounts state explicitly why Hemings lived with Dupré, the Jeffersons' launderer, there have emerged alternative explanations for what she was doing there and even for when she was there. In one view, Jefferson sent her to Dupré's during his seven-week trip through eastern France, Germany, and Holland in the spring of 1788 to protect her in his absence.[43] The most obvious problem with linking Hemings's time at Dupré's with Jefferson's concerns about leaving her unattended at the residence is that he was gone for seven weeks, and she was with Dupré for only five. Why would he not care about the two-week gap? Moreover, the payment to Dupré was made in April of 1789, a year after this trip, though Jefferson frequently paid his bills late. But his records are really fatal to the "Dupré as protector" scenario because they indicate that Dupré did not become his launderer until eight months after he took this trip.[44]

It has also been suggested that Jefferson sent Hemings to Dupré for instructions in how to improve her sewing and to learn how to care for fine fabrics, skills that she would need if she were to be a truly useful lady's maid to Patsy and Polly. That idea is certainly more reasonable than the suggestion that Jefferson sent her there to be protected while he went on his tour through northern Europe. This is particularly so since Dupré first appears in Jefferson's records just when he began buying more expensive clothing for Patsy, who started to venture out into society in 1788.[45] There are launderers for different occasions and types of clothing, and when one has made a substantial investment in precious items of apparel, one chooses the right professional to care for them. Patsy was going to take these clothes back to Monticello, and someone had to care for them.

Jefferson, however, speaks only of paying for "board of Sally" and says nothing about having her trained. His account entries recording payments for her brothers' apprenticeships do not require speculation about what is going on. He specifically states the purpose, or one can discern it from other correspondence or immediately adjacent memorandum book entries. If Hemings was sent to Dupré's for more than just boarding, Jefferson would have just said that. While she may have received some instruction while living there, his matter-of-fact notation suggests that boarding Hemings was the real issue. An extremely important event in the lives of the residents of the Hôtel de Langeac—indeed, a nearly, catastrophic family crisis—points to why Hemings was away from her home for five weeks.

At the beginning of December of 1788, both Patsy and Polly Jefferson contracted typhus. When they failed to improve, they were sent home from school to recover under the care of Dr. Richard Gem, whom Jefferson many years later credited with helping them through the ordeal.[46] The disease waxed and waned in both girls at first, and Patsy, always heartier than her younger sister, recovered more quickly. Polly remained critically ill from the final weeks of December until sometime near the end of January, and one can sense from her normally upbeat father's letters that he feared for her life at points. After giving general reports of the girls' sickness to correspondents, he confided to William Short on January 22 that Polly "had been in considerable danger" and that even though she was better, she was still "very low and her fever continu[ed]."[47] That was as close as he came to unburdening himself on paper, but, in fact, Polly's illness led to a problem that remained buried in the Jefferson family history, or at least in its correspondence, for many years. Long after her sister's death and a year after her father died, Patsy Jefferson, by then known as Martha Randolph, wrote of the "horrors of typhus" that she knew well from her personal bout with it, revealing in a letter to her sister-in-law that as result of the disease her sister Polly "was for many weeks Deaf and stupid." She went on to say that she believed that Polly's "mind" never "entirely recovered from" the effects of typhus and that she retained "a torpor of the intellect" that she did not think "natural for her."[48] Typhus, she believed, had damaged her sister's brain.

This was serious business indeed. Deafness and mental impairment are side effects of very serious cases of typhus, and though usually temporary, both can persist to varying degrees after the disease has run its course.[49] One can imagine Polly's terror—as well as that of her father, sister, and the Hemings siblings, particularly Sally, who had known her and been close to her for many years by this time—upon learning that Polly had lost the ability to hear without knowing whether her deafness would continue. Her mental confusion during her illness may have alarmed them less at first. That could have been attributed to the high fever, with the expectation that her faculties would return to normal once the fever broke. But Martha Randolph's description of Polly as "stupid" during her illness, and linking that to her impaired mental capacity for the rest of her life, suggests that Polly's confusion while sick may have been different from the delirium brought on by a high fever. They lacked a full understanding of the risks posed by typhus-induced encephalitis (brain swelling); indeed, they were probably unaware of the phenomenon at all.

Typhus was known to be extremely contagious, but it was not understood until the early twentieth century how it was transmitted. The disease is carried by arthropods like body lice and fleas, infecting those who live in the kind of close quarters that allow the organisms to go from one person to the next, as was evidently the case at the abbey. Before this discovery, it was thought to be spread simply upon contact with ill persons, sharing their air or touching them. Even if he did not know how the disease was transmitted, or call it typhus, Dr. Gem was almost certainly familiar with the basic nature of the illness and the dangers it posed, including, perhaps the permanent loss of hearing.[50] Under that state of knowledge about transmission, and with the frightening prospect of deafness, even if the person recovered from the disease, it would have made perfect sense to get Hemings, who had the most intimate contact with Polly and Patsy, away from the household so that she would not get sick, and perhaps go deaf, too. In the gender construction of the day, as the only young female in the Virginia coterie at the Hôtel de Langeac who had not become ill, the men in the house would have thought her particularly vulnerable. Whether her chief value at this time was to Jefferson, because she had already become or he wanted her to become his mistress, or to Polly, to have Hemings—and Polly—deaf would have been a disaster all around. The length of Hemings's stay at Dupré's coincides almost precisely with the length of time that Polly was most seriously ill.

That Jefferson did not want to put down on paper the nature and extent of Polly's illness may explain why there is no written reason why Hemings had gone to Dupré's. What is most important about the notation about her time away from the Hôtel de Langeac is that it reemphasizes the veiled nature of her existence, which in the final analysis is the most important theme in her life. Even years before stories about their relationship appeared in newspapers, and Jefferson had more obvious reason to be careful about his references to Hemings, a mystery always surrounds her (a person who was at the very heart of his nuclear family circle from her and his daughters' earliest lives) that seems wholly unnecessary, while references to her relatives, male and female, are much more straightforward. *I sent James to Rouen to make our hotel arrangements, and I got this amount of money back from him. Martin and I have quarreled. Have Bet knit some stockings for me, if she knows how. I need Critta to help with my child. Burwell is only one who is able to keep the house clean and in order.* With Sally Hemings, one is constantly forced to try to decipher what is happening with her.

There was in Jefferson's white family, understandable reticence about saying outright just what role Hemings played in the Jefferson household. Clarity sometimes peeked through the clouds. While making her ill-fated claim that one of her relatives, Samuel Carr, had fathered all of Sally Hemings's children, Ellen Coolidge, a Jefferson granddaughter, gave indirect confirmation that Hemings was Jefferson's chambermaid. In a letter written to her husband in the 1850s, Coolidge claimed, "No female domestic ever entered his chambers except at hours when he was known not to be there and none could have entered without being exposed to the public gaze."[51] What she wanted to assert, but could not do so explicitly, was, *The woman everyone is talking about, Sally Hemings, was my grandfather's chambermaid, but she never went into his room when he was there, and if she did everyone would have seen her.* She could not have said that without giving too much away about the daily routine at Monticello and risk letting people know just how intimate Hemings's association with Jefferson was. Instead, she spoke in generalities about what unnamed female domestics never did. Coolidge focused on an enslaved woman going into Jefferson's rooms precisely because that was what Hemings, the "female domestic" in question, actually did every day Jefferson was in residence at Monticello until the day he died.

In lieu of being frank about Hemings's role at Monticello, Coolidge, describing Hemings for posterity in this same letter, reached all the way back to France to give Hemings an identity. Even though Coolidge was born in 1796, had known Hemings all her life, and actually lived at Monticello with her for over fifteen years, when she ventured to say who Hemings was, she chose to identify her as the slave girl who accompanied Jefferson's daughter to Europe and served as both daughters' lady's maid while there, as if Hemings had been in suspended animation between 1790 and 1826.[52]

Being generally absent from Jefferson family records is not the same thing as being unimportant. In truth, Hemings's situation presents a clear case where a person was not talked about because she was indeed so important. It is quite telling that the major narratives of life at Monticello, written by people not in the Jefferson family, talk about her, seemingly out of nowhere. Although little discussed in Jefferson family letters and the subject of relatively few statements of other people who knew her directly, the young woman feeling her way through a new life on foreign, but more hospitable, soil was not destined for anonymity. Her life in Paris, where she took on a role that would last through the next four decades, set the stage for the national and, no doubt, completely unwanted attention that she would receive twelve years after she left the city that changed her life.

The Eve of Revolution

As James and Sally Hemings went about their business, enjoyed each other's company, learned French language and culture, and moved about Paris, the ancien régime was crumbling around them. Historians can point to various signs along the way that foreshadowed things to come, and even fix upon different pivotal moments that marked the time when the country was put firmly on the road to revolution, past the point of any return. To those living in France at the time, however, the happenings of the day—noteworthy and serious as they often were—did not foretell any particular momentous destination for their society. They were merely events punctuating their own progress through life, certainly not harbingers of a cataclysmic reordering of the whole world. No one could have seen in the crises of the 1780s the fall of the aristocracy, the beheading of the king and queen, the Reign of Terror, and the rise of Napoleon.

There was no question that France was in trouble, and that its troubles were a long time in the making. Years of borrowing money to finance costly wars and lavish spending at home had taken its toll on a country already weakened by feckless political leadership and structural changes in society. By the early 1780s it was clear that the practice of attempting to put out a fire by pouring oil over it—borrowing heavily, rather than raising taxes or forgoing costly military adventures and profligate domestic spending—had bankrupted the treasury.[1] The Americans at the Hôtel de Langeac had a connection to all of this that perhaps only Jefferson fully understood.

In lieu of raising taxes, Jacques Necker, France's once and future comptroller-general, took out a large number of loans at the end of the

1770s, with extremely favorable rates for lenders, in order to finance France's struggles against its perennial rival, Great Britain.[2] When a government borrows, it has to repay, lest its investors, foreign and domestic, lose confidence and withdraw their capital. Necker's loans came due near the end of the 1780s, and there was no money to repay them. It fell to his successor, Charles-Alexandre de Calonne (Necker had fallen out of favor for other reasons), to inform King Louis XVI that France was essentially bankrupt. They were in this situation, in part, because many of the loans had been taken out to allow France to help the American colonists in their own efforts against England. The successful American Revolution laid part of the groundwork for the destruction of the monarchy and the transformation of French society.[3]

Jefferson followed the events leading up to the French Revolution with considerable interest, and even advised Lafayette and other French liberals who favored change in the French political system. Initially skeptical of the prospects for real reform, he became, very famously, a great supporter of the Revolution when it arrived. Although his position allowed him to know far more about the inner workings of French politics than either James or Sally Hemings, the looming crisis was such that all but the smallest children knew that something very serious was going on in Paris between 1786 and 1789.[4]

The country had known crises before. The grave problems that now beset France had far greater effect because the country was very different from what it was when it faced earlier economic and social upheavals. The public was more literate than it had ever been before, and there existed, really for the first time, such a thing as public opinion to which French participants in the political battles of this era appealed in new ways and to an unprecedented degree. These very public battles attracted attention at all levels of society.[5]

Jefferson, somewhat lightly—he was talking to Anne Bingham—described Paris in 1788 as a "furnace of politics" where "[m]en, women, children talk[ed] nothing else."[6] And servants talked as well. Ordinary people felt that they had a stake in, and a right to make pronouncements about, all matters that concerned them. The creeping despotism in French society emerged as a particular concern. Rule by arbitrary edict, whether in public or private settings, surfaced as an intolerable insult to people who were now familiar with Enlightenment concepts about the rights of man.

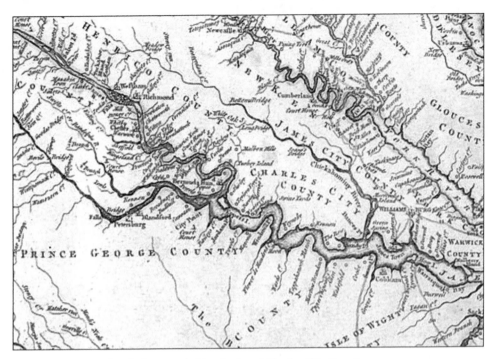

Fry-Jefferson map, detail of Bermuda Hundred and Charles City County, Elizabeth Hemings's early world. *(Courtesy of Monticello / Thomas Jefferson Foundation, Inc.)*

Daguerreotype of Isaac Jefferson. Isaac Jefferson's true family name was Granger. He provided valuable information about the Hemings family in his recollections taken in 1847. *(Courtesy of Tracy W. McGregor Library of American History, Special Collections, University of Virginia Library)*

VIII. Sales of Slaves Imported in
The Prince of Wales

[Sep.-Dec.1772]

Purchasers Names	Men	Wom.	Boys	Girls	Numr.		
Thomas Mann Randolph	9	1			10	437	
Richard Daves Hines	1				1	43	
Richard Baugh	1				1	43	
John Harmer Esqr	10				10	442	
Henry Anderson	2				2	86	
Daniel Price	2				2	86	
Thomas Harris	2	1			3	131	
William Byram	1	1			2	88	
John Radford Junr.		1		1	2	83.14.6	
Richard Stith		1			1	43	1482.14.6
Daniel Lawrence Hylton	2				2	86	
Samuel Phelps		1		1	2	84	
[Jo]hn Green			1		1	41	
Richard Allen	1	1			2	86	
James Wilkins				1	1	37.162 3/4	
Robert Walker	4	3			7	301	
Isham Smith	2	1			3	129	
Arch Austin	2				2	86	
Richd Radford	1	1			2	86	936.162.2 3/4
Bartho. Dandridge	4	8			12	200.9	
John Loftin	1				1	43	
Thomas Johns	1	1			2	86	
Haley Blaton		1			1	43	
Caleb Davis	1				1	45	
Arch Mitchell	1	1			2	86	
Edward Hatcher	1	1			2	88	
Thomas Evans				1	1	42	633.9
John Hawkins	29	18			47	1565.2	
Wilson Miles Cary	3				3	131.2.6 3/4	
Jeremiah Ellington	2				2	87.8.4 1/4	
Walter King Esqr.	6	4			10	430	
Daniel Weisiger & Co.	4	3	1		8	293.14	

DEBT TO FARELL AND JONES

Purchasers Names	Men	Wom.	Boys	Girls	Numr.		
William Robinson	1				1	43	
William Henderson	1				1	43	
James De'Sear	1				1	41.19.2	2635.6
William Aylett	12	8			20	700.	
William Murray	5	5			10	367.2.6	
William Fleming	1	1			2	83.18.4	
John Jas. Woodfin				1	1	34.19.3 3/4	
John Rowland & Co.	5	5			10	350	
William West				1	1	31.9.4	1567.9.5 3/4
Hugh Montgomery	22	10			32	972	
John Marr				3	3	110. 8 1/4	
Duncan Rose & Co.	10	23			33	807.13.6	
James Johnson		1			1	45.9.1	
John Harris		2			2	88.2.3	2023.5.
	151	103	3	9	266	£	9279. 9 3/4

Commissions on £9279. 9 3/4 at 8 ⅌ Ct.   742.6.4

Nett proceeds   £8536.14.5 3/4

Virginia 30th. Decr. 1772.   Exam'd

Errors Excepted ⅌

J Wayles

Richard Randolph

MS (Vi: USCC); at head of text: "Sales of 266 Slaves Imported in the Ship Prince of Wales James Bivins Commander on Accot. of Messrs. John Powell & Co. Merchants in Bristol 28th Decr. 1772"; docketed. The MS occupies two pages, and the two lines for "Carried Forward" and "Brot Forwd" are here omitted.

Listing of purchasers of Africans brought in on the *Prince of Wales*. *(Courtesy of the Papers of Thomas Jefferson)*

Jefferson's first Farm Book listing of the Hemings family at Monticello and Elk Hill. *(Courtesy of Massachusetts Historical Society)*

1774.   **Location of Slaves.**   for 1774.   15

Monticello.

+ Martin. 1755.
  Bob.. 1762
  Jamey 1765
+ Mary. 1753.
+ Bett 1759.
  Scilla. 1762.
+ Old Jenny.
+ Ned. 1760.
+ George
+ Ursula
  George. 1759.
  Bagwell. 1768.
  Archy. 1773. died July 1774.
− Juno
− Luna
+ Dinah.
+ Jupiter
+ Suck
+ Frank
+ Barna
+ Sanco.
+ Abra̅m
+ Billy/Lewis
+ Jame
+ York
+ Peter
+ King

* Goliah.
* Hercules.
* Gill.   died 1774.
* Fanny
  Suckey. 1765.
  Frankey. 1767.
  Gill. 1769.
* Quash.
* Nell.
* Prella. 1757.
* Charles. 1760.
  Jenny. 1768.
* Betty.
* Toby. jun̅r. 1753.

1774. Elk hill. cont?   Elk hill cont? 1774.

* Tomo
* Prove.
* Turpin.
* Jack
* Patt Kennon.
  Tom. 1767.
  Jeffery. 1769.
* Branford.
* Jenny
− Sam.
* Polydore.
* Suckey.
* Mary. 1773. died Feb. 1774.
  Jack.
* Ambrose.
* Hanah.
  Harry. 1770.
  Nanny. 1772.
* Cate.
* Cuffey
* Stephen.
  Sall. 1764.
  Phill. 1766.
  Daniel. 1772.
* Sam
* Nancy.

+ Betty Hemings.
  Nancy. 1761.
  Thenia. 1767.
  Critta. 1769.
  Peter. Aug. 1770
  Sally. 1773.
  Daniel. 1772.
+ Aggy.
  Jenny. 1764.
  Dick. 1767.
* Sall
  Billy, Harry. 1763.
  Aggy. 1769.
  Jemmy. 1771.
* Will.
* Betty
* Tom.
* Isabel.
* Peter.
* Hanah.
  Betty 1772.
* Mingo.

187. in all.

Bell given to Sally Hemings by Martha Jefferson. *(Courtesy of Moorland-Spingarn Collection, Howard University)*

Composite of items Jefferson carried in his pockets. *(Courtesy of Monticello / Thomas Jefferson Foundation, Inc.)*

Thomas Jefferson's ivory notebooks. *(Courtesy of Monticello / Thomas Jefferson Foundation, Inc.)*

Grille de Chaillot, view of the Hôtel de Langeac and the Champs-Elysées, James and Sally Hemings's world in Paris. *(Courtesy of Bibliothéque Nationale de France)*

John Trumbull's miniature of Jefferson in Paris. *(Courtesy of Monticello / Thomas Jefferson Foundation, Inc.)*

Sarah Delivering Hagar to Abraham. The painting that inspired Jefferson's longing to be the patriarch Abraham. *(Courtesy of Arthotek Peissenberg / Collection Alte Pinakothek, Munich)*

William Birch, High Street, from Ninth Street, Philadelphia, 1799. A period view of the street where James Hemings lived in the 1790s with Jefferson. *(Courtesy of Monticello / Thomas Jefferson Foundation, Inc.)*

Ointment pot from Paris. Item found on Mulberry Row during recent archaeological digs at Monticello. *(Courtesy of Monticello / Thomas Jefferson Foundation, Inc.).*

James Hemings's inventory of kitchen utensils. *(Library of Congress)*

This indenture witnesseth that I Thomas Jefferson of the county of Albemarle have manumitted and made free Robert Hemings, son of Betty Hemings: so that in futu[re] he shall be free & of free condition, with all his goods & cha[ttels] and shall be discharged of all obligation of bondage or servitu[de] whatsoever: and that neither myself, my heirs executors or [admini]-trators shall have any right to exact from him hereafter services or duties whatsoever. in witness whereof I have pu[t my] seal to this present deed of manumission. Given in Albe[marle] this twenty fourth day of December one thousan[d seven hundred] and ninety four.

Signed sealed and
delivered in presence of
D. Carr.

Th. Jefferson

Robert Hemings's
deed of
manumission, 1794.
*(Courtesy of Special
Collections, University of
Virginia Library)*

James Hemings's
deed of
manumission,
1796. *(Courtesy of
Special Collections,
University of Virginia
Library)*

This indenture made at Monticello in the county of Albemarle commonwealth of Virginia on the fifth day of February one thousand seven hundred and ninety six witnesseth that I Thomas Jefferson of Monticello aforesaid do emancipate manumit & make free James Hemings, son of Betty Hemings, which said James is now of the age of thirty years so that in future he shall be free and of free condition, & discharged of all duties & claims of servitude whatsoever, & shall have all the rights and privileges of a freedman. In witness whereof I have hereto set my hand & seal on the day & year above written, and have made these presents double of the same date, tenor & indenture one whereof is lodged in the court of Albemarle aforesaid to be recorded, & the other is delivered by me to the said James Hemings to be produced when & where it may be necessary.

Signed, sealed & delivered
in presence of

John Carr

Francis Anderson

Th. Jefferson

The individual, his or her thoughts and feelings, mattered. Talk of liberty and justice filled the air. An uneven grain harvest and problematic economic reforms drove up the price of bread and emboldened people to act. They rioted in Paris and participated in large demonstrations protesting the actions of a government that seemed to flail about as it tried to avert catastrophe.[7]

None of the public aspects of this struggle remained hidden from either Hemings sibling, who moved about the city and had contact with their fellow servants, black and white, in their residence and in other households. Black Parisians had legitimate reasons to see that the logical conclusion of all the talk about liberty and progress might bring changes in their circumstances, even if they could not predict what those changes might be. Enslaved people, or anyone at the bottom of the social hierarchy, had little reason automatically to fear chaos among the ruling class. Social disorder presented them with an opportunity to wrest a better deal for themselves, and some of African origin took an active role in the political agitation of the day for that very reason.[8]

James and Sally Hemings also had opinions about the upheavals that brought the notion of liberty and equality to the lips of those French men and women who took to the street in support of those ideals, sometimes in noisy demonstrations in the neighborhood of the Hôtel de Langeac. During their last year in the country, the Société des Amis des Noirs engaged in a very public, contentious, and unsuccessful struggle to include free, tax-paying blacks in the deliberations of the newly constituted National Assembly. The issue arose when white colonists demanded representation in the body. One delegate, Count Mirabeau, one of the famous architects of the Tennis Court Oath, in which the Third Estate pronounced itself France's National Assembly, chided the colonists with words that echoed the debate among the delegates to the American Constitution:

> You claim representation proportionate to the number of inhabitants. The free blacks are proprietors and taxpayers, and yet they have not been allowed to vote. And as for the slaves, either they are men or they are not; if the colonists consider them to be men, let them free them and make them electors and eligible for seats, if the contrary is the case, have we, in apportioning deputies according to the population of France, taken into consideration the number of our horses and our mules.[9]

Jefferson attended the proceedings of that body daily and was there for the opening of the debate about representation begun in May of 1789. He was, therefore, very likely aware of this battle and familiar with Mirabeau's statement, offered in June. He did not, however, comment upon it, at least not in any writing that is extant. Had he stayed in France just a few months more, he would have seen something unimaginable in his own Virginia legislature: wealthy mixed-race taxpayers and white supporters confronting the National Assembly, arguing for admission to that body.[10]

Within four years after the Hemingses left Paris, a *gen de couleur* sat in the revolutionary National Convention, and the country abolished slavery in its colonies in 1794. The *Police des Noirs* and all the royal declarations were wiped away. These events were not simply the results of what had taken place in France; blacks in the French colonies had a major hand in directing the course of change. In the early 1790s they revolted against their French masters in Saint Domingue, fusing ideas from the French Revolution with their own already long-simmering critique of the way they were treated in their homeland. At least some of the groundwork for these changes was laid during the final years that James and Sally Hemings spent in the country. As these two enslaved people served the Jeffersons, an old order was being challenged, and the challenge was both bold and open for all to see.

New Identities

With the world outside poised to be turned upside down, the Americans gathered at the Hôtel de Langeac between 1784 and 1789 were experiencing their own forms of personal revolution. Each of them was doing things—significant things—that they would not have been doing had they been in their native Virginia. Because they were living abroad, from the oldest to the youngest, the most powerful to the least powerful, black and white alike had their normal patterns, places, and expectations in life disrupted significantly. Foreign countries are well-known venues for trying on new identities and discovering things about oneself that one may never have known. The residents in Jefferson's household seemed to have been doing a bit of both.

For his part, the forty-three-year-old Jefferson embarked in 1786 on a dalliance with a married woman, the twenty-seven-year-old Maria Cosway, a beautiful and talented artist married to a more famous and somewhat unstable man, Richard. Though of English extraction, Cosway had lived a very cosmopolitan existence in Europe, growing up in Italy and traveling much on the Continent. It was to her that Jefferson wrote his famous "Head and Heart" letter that has been analyzed almost endlessly since it came into the hands of scholars, who debate whether the Head or Heart comes out on top in the dialogue.[11]

Historians have also debated whether the Jefferson-Cosway relationship was sexual or merely flirtatious in nature. Neither he nor she ever said that they had sex. If they did, and just did not write about it, no children were produced. We have no word from anyone who would know with any degree of certainty. On the other hand, to go looking for documentary evidence on the question, given the mores of the time and Jefferson's extremely private nature, would seem an obvious fool's errand. Whether or not the relationship was sexually consummated, Jefferson actually fell in love with Cosway, an act that marks his recovery from the body blow of his wife's death. His reaction upon meeting her—he seems to have come completely undone—is the clearest evidence of his emotional reawakening in those days in Paris. The two spent time alone together and wrote each other the kind of letters that affirm that the attraction was mutual. Jefferson could not so easily have accomplished that in Virginia. Writing transparent love letters to the wife of another Virginia gentleman (even if he added polite salutations to her husband) would carry the serious risk of being "called out" and shot, as Jefferson learned firsthand in the years to come when a youthful indiscretion came back to haunt him during his first term as president.[12]

A Virginian version of "Jefferson and Cosway" would have come complete with an extended and overlapping kinship network that would not have taken kindly to the pair's insouciant treatment of Cosway's marriage. Paris was just the place for this sort of thing. Deeply unhappy with her circumstances when she met Jefferson, Cosway was eager to find a way out, a reason that probably impelled her to become involved with him in the first place. She eventually found her way out in the person of Luigi Marchesi, the Italian opera singer with whom she ran off in 1790, leaving her husband and the child she bore that year. Marchesi, a castrati, had the status of a present-day rock star. Women threw themselves at him wherever he went. Castrati were not always impotent, but they were all sterile. Indeed, some upper-class women, notoriously in Italy, favored them for sexual affairs precisely for those attributes: they could have sex with the men and avoid pregnancy. Cosway traveled the Continent with Marchesi, apparently becoming, for a time, a late eighteenth-century equivalent of a groupie.[13]

Unless it remains extremely quiet, desperation is fairly easy to spot; and Cosway's dissatisfaction with her marriage was likely evident (perhaps even frightening) to the highly intuitive Jefferson—as well it should have been. For most of 1788 and 1789, she was by far the more insistent partner, reduced to writing him reproachful letters for having failed to write to her. Jefferson apparently realized, at some point, that he was dealing with a woman who was actually willing to pull the trigger and destroy her marriage, with his reputation in the line of fire. Much as he may have cared for her, he was never going to become involved with anything like that on her behalf. He got the message about Cosway fairly early on, for his famous "Head and Heart" letter, written in 1786, is by its very terms (*"I'm in love with you, but I'm thinking hard about that"*) far from an unalloyed declaration of devotion. The letter confused Cosway, and his hot and cold attitude after writing it shows a man saying politely, firmly, and very carefully, "Thanks, but no thanks."

Jefferson's young protégé William Short was also taking advantage of being in a foreign venue. Short's affair with Rosalie, the very young wife of the duc le la Rochefoucauld, is well noted in major biographies of Jefferson.[14] What has received no attention in these biographies, or other writings about Short himself, is a prior affair that he engaged in from roughly 1786 to 1790, before he became involved with Rosalie, one whose origin closely parallels the situation between Jefferson and Hemings. Short, newly arrived in France, wanted to achieve better fluency in French and was greatly disappointed that Jefferson was not proficient enough in speaking the language to give him the practice he desired. The only solution, he thought, was to separate himself from other English-speaking people. He moved to a town fifteen miles outside of Paris, Saint-Germain-en-Laye, and lodged with a local family there, hoping that if he buried "himself among French people . . . he would hear no word of his native tongue and have no opportunity to speak it." He settled with the Royers, "a genteel family of modest means." While living there, the twenty-six-year-old Short fell desperately in love with the family's fifteen-year-old daughter.[15]

Over the next few years Short wrote excitedly of his secret love to friends in Virginia, one of whom became worried that the more Short "persisted in his infatuation," the harder it would be to say 'the *adieu à jamais* which you must sooner or later bid—to Paris.'"[16] Short explained that the "monotony" of his life in Paris had been relieved by his newfound association. The Royers' daughter, who had a string of Christian names but was known familiarly as Lilite, was never specifically identified in these letters. Instead, Short and his correspondents, referred to her as the "Belle of St. Germain" or "the fair Pomona of the village" or "his secret love." Short was more open about her in his journal of expenses, and his entries track the progress of his growing affection for Lilite, with numerous references to the cost of trips to the park and other places he took her and of buying her what seems like an almost unhealthy amount of candy and other sweets. Short's infatuation took a different turn when Lilite got married at age sixteen. Despite her new status, he continued to visit her and her husband, writing to friends of his consuming love for the young girl until the end of the 1780s.[17]

Why Lilite's parents and, more particularly her husband, tolerated Short's presence over the years is a mystery. If his feelings for her were obvious to others, they were obvious to the people who actually saw them together. Whether Short and Lilite had sex before her marriage, and whether her husband, Henri Denis, was cuckolded will likely remain unknown, but neither possibility can be dismissed out of hand. Though unsavory, it is not unheard of for families, or even husbands, to look the other way when a more prosperous and well-connected man—particularly one who they know will not be around forever—takes an interest in a woman of the family. Short did, in fact, become a benefactor to Lilite's sons for many years.[18]

No word of the situation with Lilite appears in the correspondence between Jefferson and Short. It may have been the kind of thing that Short felt more comfortable sharing with his contemporaries in Virginia than with a man who was his father figure. Certainly if he chose to share this with Jefferson, it would have made sense for him not put his mentor in the position of writing about his love for the teenage girl in letters, especially after she got married. They lived in the same house and could handle matters requiring circumspection in a delicate and tactful way. Short's predicament with Lilite—and, as we shall see, Jefferson's with Sally Hemings at the Hôtel de Langeac—supports an observation that may not have the force of a law of physics but is strong enough to be taken seriously: one has to be very careful about mixing teenage girls and heterosexual adult males in intimate circumstances.

While their father and his protégé explored all that life in France had to offer, Patsy and Polly Jefferson were in a place where they would not have been in America: a Catholic boarding school. It may be difficult in today's more inclusive times to appreciate what a departure from the norm this was for that era. Jefferson decided to enroll them there because he had learned that it was one of the most, if not the most, well-regarded schools in the city. There was to be no religious proselytizing, as he took care to note to one of his friends who had expressed concern, and he was satisfied that all would be well.[19]

Less is known about Polly Jefferson's experiences in Paris than about Patsy's, for Jefferson's second daughter was much more in the background in the life of her first nuclear family. Patsy's time in Paris profoundly affected her. Not long into her stay in the city, Patsy thought she might convert to Catholicism and may have even contemplated becoming a nun. Being in an atmosphere suffused with Catholic culture, rituals, and ceremonies changed the way this young woman thought about herself for a time—that, and in her daughter Ellen's words, "a spirit of proselytism which prevailed among the nuns and which operated on the daughters of protestant parents to withdraw them from the faith of their fathers."[20]

Patsy's decision mortified Jefferson, and he proceeded to handle his daughter through his preferred method—emotional suasion (he would say "incentive") rather than outright coercion. This man who hated confrontation and discord did not lay down the law to his daughter. Nor did he, as has been suggested, immediately take both girls out of school. He first heard of Patsy's inclination well before the girls left the abbey. He asked her to reconsider, and then proceeded to raise her allowance fivefold, started to spend even more money on her wardrobe, and allowed her to go out to society events and to balls. He wanted her to see the world she would lose if she followed her plan.[21]

Jefferson's effort killed off one problem—after receiving a taste of social life, Patsy decided that being a nun was not for her—even as it created another: she enjoyed herself so much that she did not want to go home, and even talked about renting rooms at the convent while Jefferson went on his leave of absence back to Virginia.[22] Patsy knew her father very well. One of her own children said many years later that Jefferson simply never talked about anything that he did not want to talk about. After France, father and daughter apparently never again discussed her youthful flirtation with the veil.

As has already been shown, the new environment of James and Sally Hemings gave them enormous opportunities for self-fashioning. The historian Daniel Roche's observations about Parisian servants during the years the Hemingses lived in the city are useful for considering their situation. To the ruling classes of France, Roche observed, "servants were obviously social and cultural cross breeds." They were hardly the same as the elite, but their association with them provided access to information unavailable to the masses, who never even glimpsed the way their social "betters" lived. "Through servants, the objects and actions of the upper classes were filtered through to the lower social categories." Certainly elements of that phenomenon could be found in the plantation system of the South, with the cross-cultural and racial pollination going both ways.[23]

A life lived in between two cultures at odds with each other often required special adaptations to one's personality. This was even more the case for the Hemingses, who were not just "social and cultural crossbreeds"; they were, to follow Roche's terminology, racial "crossbreeds." Whether it affected their legal status or not, they could identify with what the dominant society took to be their racial "betters"—that is, white people—because they were part white and were being directly rewarded for that. Roche's question—"who is more caught up in a web of appearances than a servant?"[24]—is also very useful for thinking about the ways in which eighteenth-century attitudes about race and status (along with Jefferson's attitude and actions toward them) helped shape the Hemings siblings' existences and self-images. The background of one visitor to the Hôtel de Langeac helps clarify the complicated and tragic positions of these two young people.

Lucy Paradise, a native Virginian who lived in London with her husband, John, socialized with Jefferson when he visited the city in 1786, and she also appeared on the scene in Paris and made something of a nuisance of herself. She seems to have been more than a bit in love with Jefferson and sought to keep contact with him by insisting that he help solve her personal problems with her husband along with their joint disastrous financial affairs, all the while adopting a bizarre and discordant posture as a married "damsel" in distress. In some of her letters she asked Jefferson, who she knew corresponded with and was friendly with her husband, to keep things she said to him secret from her husband, carving out an inappropriate private world for the two of them that could only have made Jefferson uncomfortable. Yet he was almost infinitely patient with her and responsive, to the extent he could be, to her many entreaties.[25]

Paradise was, of course, the daughter of Philip Ludwell III, John Wayles's former benefactor and mentor. It made perfect sense for her to have latched onto Jefferson as a financial and personal adviser because, as noted in chapter 4, his father-in-law had been one of her designated guardians and was intimately involved in dividing up the Ludwell estate between Lucy and her sister, Hannah. Jefferson himself had witnessed the signing of that document and had at least some knowledge of her circumstances.[26] When Lucy Paradise came calling in Paris, she entered a household that contained people who owed her father a great deal. James and Sally Hemings owed him their existences; Jefferson, almost that much. If Ludwell had not raised John Wayles to a level that enabled him to marry Martha Eppes, there would not have been a Martha Wayles, a Patsy or Polly Jefferson, a Hemings family, or a Wayles fortune for Jefferson to inherit. It is no wonder that he so graciously put up with Ludwell's importuning and annoying daughter.

John Wayles was not born a gentleman. He most likely learned to act and sound like a gentleman in his service to people like Philip Ludwell, although some in his community in Virginia never totally accepted his new persona. He evidently waited on people, just as James Hemings waited on Jefferson, having the opportunity, as Roche described it, to learn the ways and mores of upper-class life so well that he could play the role when his time came—a time that could never come for his son James or any other of the Wayles-Hemings children. James Hemings was ineligible to have happen to him what happened to his father, to be chosen by a white man and raised above his station to become something other than what his birth had foretold: a wealthy landed gentleman of Virginia.

In the days before his ascent, Wayles was intelligent and impressive enough to have caught the eye of a man at the highest level of Virginia society, who saw through the shroud of class to the talented person beneath. Because Wayles's children were part black and enslaved rather than white servants, there would be no looking past the shroud for either James or Sally Hemings, even though both may have been at least as natively intelligent as their father. Doing that would have struck at the very heart of the racially based, deliberately closed system that was American slavery. Even outside the context of slavery, allowing talented people of color to rise would have threatened the doctrine of white supremacy. The Hemings siblings' self-fashioning within the confines of their circumstances, impressive as it was to Jefferson and his family, could get them only so far. James Hemings was intelligent enough to have been a lawyer. But Jefferson could never have thought to play Philip Ludwell and turn him into one, no matter how brilliant, energetic, or talented Hemings was. That was well beyond what American society would have accepted then and for many decades afterwards. He could, however, raise Hemings to the status of enslaved highly trained French chef. Sally Hemings, no matter how beautiful, feminine, intelligent, or talented she was, could never be a "lady" in the sense that white Virginians meant that term, or a legal wife to a wealthy white man. She could, however, be a wealthy white man's substitute for a wife.

Sally Hemings in the Beau Monde

In the midst of the impending collapse of French society, Jefferson decided to go back to Virginia to leave his daughters with their relatives, settle his financial affairs, and then return to France briefly to finish out his mission. He had been thinking of doing this for a while, but did not make his formal request for a leave of absence until the early fall of 1788.[27] His plans were not secret, and James and Sally Hemings, along with the rest of the Jefferson household, knew their time in the country was not long. Jefferson's plan actually had very different implications for the brother and the sister. If James Hemings did not want to take his freedom at that point, he could expect to return to France with Jefferson and resume his old role as chef de cuisine. Sally Hemings was more likely destined to remain in Virginia with Patsy and Polly. Going home would be the end of what had been an extraordinary experience, particularly given what had happened during her last year in Paris. She was receiving a steady monthly wage, and Jefferson spent a good amount of money on her clothing—nowhere near as lavishly as he spent on his daughter Patsy over her years in Paris, but enough to make a definite change in Hemings's self-image and her day-to-day existence. In a relatively short period in the spring of 1789, Jefferson spent about thirty-two dollars on clothes for her—in today's terms, a little under a thousand dollars.[28]

Neither Jefferson nor anyone else gave a reason for the sudden rise in his spending on Hemings, although Fawn Brodie portrayed this as signaling the beginning of the Hemings-Jefferson affair.[29] Jefferson, in time-honored fashion, was rewarding and seeking to impress a young woman who was, or whom he hoped to make, his mistress. Lucia Stanton has noted, however, that the expenditures were made at the same time that Patsy Jefferson began to appear more frequently at society functions in Paris, and Jefferson started to spend even more money on her clothing after he removed his daughters from school, anticipating their return to America.[30] Patsy had been going out before April 1789, but with no school in her life, she was now free to do so more frequently. According to Jefferson's white family's tradition, she was strictly "limited . . . to three balls a week" and participated in other social occasions that took her into the homes of others.[31] The daughter of a diplomat had to appear dressed in a style suitable to her station, and Hemings, who went along to the balls and dinner parties as her lady's maid, had to be properly dressed as well.

Polly Jefferson, too young to be presented into society, received no similar attention to her wardrobe. The uniform and clothing of a school-girl remained suitable attire for her. Jefferson's spending on Polly never approached the amount he spent on Patsy. Even for the years before Patsy began her time in the Parisian social whirl, one finds more entries in Jefferson's memorandum books for clothes, hats, and shoes for Patsy than he ever recorded for Polly. Patsy's allowances were always larger than her younger sister's, which one might expect, given that the older girl may have had greater need for money. Even when she was Polly's age, Patsy received more money from her father. Jefferson denied it in later years, when Polly very delicately suggested it, but the evidence indicates that though he adored both Patsy and Polly, he favored the older sister over the younger.[32]

The two explanations for Jefferson's sudden burst of spending on Hemings's clothing are not mutually exclusive. Jefferson had the final say about whether Hemings went along to attend Patsy at parties and balls, and he knew these occasions would have meant a great deal to her. Dressing Hemings in nice clothes and allowing her to go to social functions with Patsy fits as easily with the notion that he was attempting during this period to make her feel good about him, as would buying her nice clothes just so she could wear them as she walked around the Hôtel de Langeac.

The reasons for the clothes aside, one would love to have some account of Sally Hemings, the slave girl from country Virginia, being outfitted for clothes in Paris. One day after recording one of the expenditures for cloth-ing made "for Sally," Jefferson noted his payment for tickets to attend "a benefit concert for [a] nine-year-old mulatto violinist" held at his daughters' school.[33] The violinist whom Jefferson went to see and support was young George Bridgetower, who made his Paris debut that year, performing three times at the renowned Concert Spirituel. Jefferson was fortunate indeed to have caught him at the beginning of what turned out to be a very long and distinguished career. Bridgetower was born in Poland to a Polish mother and a black father from Barbados, the personal servant to an English noble-man. His Paris turn was of more than merely artistic significance, as one review of his performance makes clear.

> A curious debut, and what is extremely interesting is that he (Mr. Bridgetower), the young black from the colonies, who played various violin concertos with a clarity, a facility, and execution and sensibility, that is very rare to encounter at so young an age (he is not yet ten). His talent that is really precocious, is one of the best answers that can be made to the Philosophers who want to deprive those of his Nation and his color the opportunity to distinguish themselves in the Arts.[34]

By the end of the eighteenth century, the image of blacks had rapidly deteriorated in the face of Europe's increasingly urgent need to justify its dependence on African slavery.[35] At least some Enlightenment thinkers, however, were unwilling to abandon so easily the idea of a truly universal conception of the rights of man, and looked for any evidence they could to rebut charges of blacks' natural inferiority and inability to advance. No less than the reputation of the entire black race was placed on Bridgetower's young shoulders. He carried that impossible burden admirably for many years. By the age of twelve he was performing in orchestras all over England. In the 1790s, he drew the attention of the Prince of Wales, who provided him with tutors and masters of music to help him perfect his technique. Bridgetower eventually took a degree in music from Cambridge, and he later befriended Beethoven and became well known for his deft perfor-mances of his works.[36]

Over the years, supporters of black equality would call to Jefferson's attention other "Bridgetowers" with the hope that he, a well-known adher-ent to the Enlightenment, might be impressed. Their efforts met with varying degrees of success, as Jefferson was reluctant to accept that the individuals presented to him were true measures of African capabili-ties, especially since most of them tended to be of mixed race. Was the individual's genius African or European inspired? We do not know the spirit in which Jefferson went to the benefit concert for Bridgetower, how he responded to the performance, and what, if anything, he said to the young prodigy. The man who called music the passion of his soul and was

especially enamored of the violin, practicing for hours at a time, could certainly be expected to want to attend a concert at his daughters' school, no
matter what the race of the performer. Still, it is unlikely that he failed to
notice the great interest that this young musician's appearance aroused and
the social implications that were very publicly grafted onto it. Jefferson's
going to see Bridgetower fit well with his own interest in assessing the
capabilities of people of African descent.

At the abbey Jefferson sat among an audience whose members came
out to support and watch as a young child, not so different from James and
Sally Hemings, began to make his way in the world, fulfilling his talent to
the best of his abilities and earning the admiration of his fellow human
beings. Jefferson's own sons would all become violinists, one of whom
(Eston) was a "master" of the instrument who, though never so famous
as George Bridgetower, was celebrated for many years in his home community in Ohio, using as his signature tune one of the few popular songs
whose melody his father bothered to copy out in his own hand and keep
among his papers.[37] One hopes that Bridgetower's concert was among the
social events that Hemings used her new wardrobe to attend, or at least
that she and her brother heard from the Jeffersons about the young mixed-
race boy who had a future that he could never have had in her own country
despite his demonstrated genius.

Acting as lady's maid to Patsy Jefferson as she explored the Parisian
social circuit, Hemings was an observer, waiting while others danced, had
dinner, or conversed. Though not an active participant, she was there, on
the periphery with the other servants, to be sure. In these environments,
however, Hemings saw things—opulent architecture, artwork, food presentation, clothing, and makeup—and heard things—music that Jefferson said
was played at a far superior level in Europe than in the United States—that
she would never have seen or heard back in Virginia. Hemings knew that
the overwhelming majority of the people in her native Virginia, particularly the white people with all their dangerous pretensions, would never
have access to the kind of civilized world that manifested itself in Paris. She
shared this distinction with her brother James, and the Jeffersons, making
them a special band privy to something quite distinctive. She could always
compare those who considered themselves "grand" back in Virginia with the
people and the places she had seen in some of the finest homes in France.
While moving in this world, Hemings, treated as an item of property in her

native Virginia, gained knowledge and experience that she owned and could never be taken away, like her trip-across-the-ocean stories repeated to others many years later.

Just as those evenings in the beau monde had a deep meaning for Patsy Jefferson that she carried with her throughout her life, and helped to make her the woman she became, they had a deep meaning for Sally Hemings and shaped the woman she became. They were both young females, around one year apart, who probably looked forward to and enjoyed very much dressing up and making themselves look attractive, thinking of how they compared to other females in the room (and, no doubt, silently comparing themselves to each other) and of what effect they were having on the males. Not one of the feelings, thoughts, and yearnings of a young person was foreclosed to Sally Hemings; not a hair on her head or wish in her heart was less important than Patsy Jefferson's. She had the misfortune to be born into a society where the people in power chose not to recognize that reality.

While the social events Hemings attended were not called for her benefit, they were calculated to awaken feelings in all young people, and their allure could not have been lost on her. These gatherings and dances were very obviously set up as opportunities for young males and females to engage with one another in a supervised setting. Patsy Jefferson, however, was not on this scene to find a husband—at least her father did not want her to be—though these occasions served that function. Dances and balls were a form of mating ritual, which is why young women had to be of a certain age to attend them. According to French custom, of which Jefferson strongly approved, ladies did not dance after they were married.[38] Going to a ball was about the life and future prospects of a young unmarried woman, and Patsy Jefferson and Sally Hemings learned some important things about the basics of male-female interactions attending these events. No young female, enslaved or free, black or white, could be in this setting and watch others of her age and sex being asked to dance and not think about herself, the time and place where that might happen to her, and what her prospects in life would be.

13

❦

"DURING THAT TIME"

A T SOME POINT, it is impossible to say when, a major shift occurred in the nature of the relationship between the Hemingses and the Jeffersons. It may be that no one but Sally Hemings and Thomas Jefferson knew that the change had taken place until after, perhaps even well after, it had happened. When speaking of the beginning of his parents' relationship in France, their son Madison Hemings simply said, "[D]uring that time my mother became Mr. Jefferson's concubine," with no elaboration on how that happened or exactly when. The only marker of the onset of sexual activity for Hemings is that she gave birth to a child in 1790 in the months after she returned from France. The conception of that child took place during her final months, if not actual last month, in Paris.[1]

The timing of Hemings's pregnancy suggests that what happened between them evolved over time, but did not get serious until near the end of their stay, setting up a confrontation about her future as a woman and a mother. If we cannot say when Hemings became "Mr. Jefferson's concubine," a mere glance at the setup of life at the Hôtel de Langeac reveals circumstances highly conducive to its happening.

A teenage girl had been sent to live with a heterosexual middle-aged man who was not her blood relative. There was no female counterpart to the man in the household—no wife, no sister, no maiden aunt—no age and socially equivalent female whose very presence would have influenced the way all parties interacted with one another. Indeed, there was no steady adult female presence at all. The dangers inherent to this situation are apparent, and would be so apparent at any point in history that we can be sure that neither Patsy nor Polly Jefferson would ever have faced them. Jefferson's daughters would never have been sent to live with a man under those circumstances. Reliance on the character or restraint of the man would not have been enough. For it would have been thought foolish to place a male and female in a situation where anyone's character or willpower had to be tested—to put social and, in this case, racial strictures in dubious battle with biology.

The situation at Jefferson's residence presented, if you will, a more extreme version of the Captain Ramsey problem, "more extreme" because more than two years were available for something to go wrong at the Hôtel de Langeac, instead of just several weeks on Ramsey's ship. It was an inappropriate circumstance that was not made acceptable because Hemings was "just" an African American slave girl. To remove the designation "inappropriate" from Jefferson and Hemings's living arrangement in Paris because slaveholders ignored such considerations is to accept and promote their version of a status quo in which the embedded hazards of that arrangement did not exist; it banishes the reality of young female slaves' physical and emotional vulnerability in odd deference to the southern planter elite's preferred image of who they were in relation to their slaves. Topsy-turvy, slave owners' self-reports are allowed to define the boundaries and character of the institution at the expense of the real-life experiences of those whom they enslaved.

As Abigail Adams seemed not to think (did not care enough to think) there was anything wrong in sending Hemings unaccompanied on a six-week cruise with a group of sailors, it probably never occurred to Jefferson that there was any problem with having Hemings in his household for an extended period of time. On the day he decided to bring her from London to Paris, Polly Jefferson, not Sally Hemings, was likely foremost in his mind. Over the preceding months that had turned into years after he had determined that Polly had to make the trip to France, he had been sick with worry about her Atlantic voyage, and the news that all had gone well naturally overshadowed any incidental details about her traveling partner.

Although it would have been entirely natural for Jefferson to be curious to see his beloved wife's half sister almost grown up, his most probable thoughts about Hemings centered on her connection to Polly. Hemings was her longtime companion, and he wanted to make sure that his daughter was as comfortable in her new surroundings as she could be. Hemings could play her designated role in that process—a continuation of the role that Jefferson himself had chosen for her by sending her to Eppington with his daughter—only if she was at his residence, even though that meant she would be living there without the presence of an adult female. In the almost unthinkable event that a pretty, free, white, sweet-natured, and intelligent teenage girl had been sent to live with Jefferson under the same circumstances, no one would have been surprised if the end result had been that he became infatuated with her and, perhaps, wanted to marry her. One suspects that only a family seeking the title "Mrs. Thomas Jefferson" for its daughter would have tolerated that type of living arrangement for her.

Infatuation can exist without the will or ability to marry, and, of course, marriage was precluded for Hemings and Jefferson. The elemental problem with the way they lived in France, however, still remained. The "protections" offered to enslaved women as substitutes for the concept of inappropriateness were the supposedly ironclad dictates of racism—"all women of color were so degraded that only a tiny category of white men, the totally depraved or hopelessly immoral, would be attracted to them, so those women generally had nothing to worry about during slavery"—and class superiority—"southern gentlemen did not get intimately involved with their female social inferiors." Those notions would be worth merely laughing at if they had not totally trivialized the lives of a great many African American enslaved families.

What of his daughters? Patsy Jefferson was the most important person in her father's life until the day he died. Yet she was not a counterpart to him in the way that a wife would have been, even though there has been a tendency to treat the father and daughter as if they were, at least symbolically, a married couple. Patsy was not Jefferson's wife. As a daughter, she had a separate role that could not as effectively check the development of her father's response to Hemings or, for that matter, Hemings's response to him. The kind of unspoken day-to-day shorthand that passes between husbands and wives would not have required so blatant a statement as "Thomas, stop gazing at Sally." A husband's memory of many admonitions, spoken or unspoken, about what he is or is not supposed to do, often shapes his behavior, especially when the wife is physically present. As a purely logistical matter, Patsy was away from the Hôtel de Langeac during the week. Whole days went by when neither she nor her younger sister would have been in a position to observe Hemings and their father at the residence.

Jefferson did not go out to an office every day: he worked where he lived. Just as his daughters had their own world among their classmates at the abbey that their father knew of only at second hand, or not at all, the Hemingses and Jefferson lived in their own private universe at the Hôtel de Langeac. That world on the rue de Berri contained the kinds of rituals, chance encounters, tensions, domestic mishaps, and humorous incidents that make up daily life. For better or worse, the intimacy of a house where one steps away from the world outside and performs the most private functions in life creates a knowingness among fellow residents, a unique culture that excludes others who do not have the same experience in the daily life of that culture.

Even had Hemings lived with Jefferson's daughters at school for all her time there and been at the residence only when they came home, her presence in the close circle of the household would still have been problematic. As things turned out, it was when the four actually did live together full-time for over half a year, after Jefferson took his daughters out of school in preparation for their return to Virginia, that Hemings and Jefferson became more fatefully involved. She was a young, unattached female, at the very least, a natural object of attention, platonic or otherwise, for a heterosexual male—no matter how many other people were at the residence.

"There is not a sprig of grass that shoots uninteresting to me, nor anything that moves,"[2] Jefferson wrote to his daughter Patsy in 1790. With that extremely self-aware declaration, confirmed by virtually every aspect of his life, he could not fail to be interested in the progress of a girl whom he had known since childhood, who had been suddenly taken out of her environment, one he knew very well was vastly different from the milieu she was now in. That she was a person of color thrown into this circumstance was the kind of thing that interested him.

Jefferson observed black people (sometimes one wishes he had not) and fancied himself an expert on the subject. Of all the white southern members of the founding generation, he devoted the most time to thinking about blacks as a group—what they did, what they were like, and how they responded in certain situations. He searched out albinos among slaves to try to figure out the mystery of their coloring. He wrote out algebraic formulations showing what percentage of "white" blood a black person had to have before he or she became white. And then, of course, there are the well-known and unfortunate passages in *Notes on the State of Virginia*, where he commented on what he took to be the greater attractiveness, talent, and intelligence of mixed-race blacks compared with those who were not.[3] What better, more readily available object of observation: a mixed-race African American girl taken out of her context and forced to make adjustments to her new life under his very eyes.

Most important of all for the dynamic between Hemings, Jefferson, and his daughters in Paris, the traditional conception of marriage made the marriage bed the wellspring of the rights and obligations flowing between husbands and wives. Patsy and Polly Jefferson were certainly not in that arena with their father, and thus had no wifely claim on his sexual life. In Western culture, wives have (at least) the right to expect and demand sexual fidelity from their husbands. *Do not have sex with anyone but me!* Daughters do not have the right to demand that their fathers abstain from sex on their behalf. For unlike wives, they have nothing to give in return for such a requirement, since they are not supposed to provide an outlet for their father's sexuality.

That Jefferson was a widower helped concretely shape the course of his relationship to Hemings while they were in France. It was not just that he did not have a wife who could provide a psychological affirmative check on his emotions and behavior. It was that his lack of a wife ensured that Hemings was in his view and thoughts in ways that she would not have been had he been married. A year after Hemings's arrival, Jefferson complained in a letter to his friend James Madison about the complications of his domestic life in Paris that "called for an almost womanly attention to the details of the household." He found being in that position "perplexing, disgusting and inconsistent with business."[4] He felt emasculated. So perilous was his financial state that he had to attend to every facet of running the residence, no matter how small, to make sure there was no waste. Jefferson's language conveys his indignation: here was the minister to France, forced to act like a housewife looking for ways to scrimp and save. If Hemings had come to Paris with Martha Jefferson at the helm of domestic life at the Hôtel de Langeac, Martha would have had the primary responsibility for thinking of something for her to do and noticing whether she was fitting in with the plan for the household.

Instead, as soon as Hemings arrived at the residence, she, by necessity, became the object of Jefferson's attention. First, there was the matter of her inoculation. Thinking that it had to be done drew Jefferson's and probably everyone else's attention to her. Hemings could not have been in top form when she returned to the Hôtel de Langeac after having endured both an inoculation-induced mild case of smallpox and the restrictive diet that she was put on while under Dr. Sutton's care. It was the woman of the house's job to attend to the sickness of house servants—if not to nurse them, at least to watch their condition to see when and if they were well enough to return to their duties. Jefferson had to be involved in this in some way, observing Hemings when she was in a particularly vulnerable state. Playing this role drew upon individual affect and emotion, making use of the kind of intimate sympathy that women of the day were supposed to have in greater abundance than males. This required something more than just paying the bill. It required exactly the kind of "womanly attention" to household duties that Jefferson referred to in his letter to Madison.[5]

At the most primary level, the practical result of being unmarried was that Jefferson had to talk directly to Hemings more than he would have had to if she had been under the charge of his wife. And we can think of how the greater number of interactions in the daily life of their household shaped the way they came to view each other. Jefferson's overall easiness of manner with people familiar to him and his long history with Hemings's family to that date suggest that his encounters with her would have been similarly "smooth and even," as Madison Hemings described his temperament. The preferred social atmosphere for Jefferson was an amiable one, and he had a great ability, as genuinely smart and sensitive people do, to speak to others at whatever level he found them and make them feel at ease. As one observer has noted, "Jefferson valued above all else amiability—'good humor,' as he called it—in a friend rating it above integrity, industry, and science." Jefferson said that if he had to choose, he and most people would prefer to associate "with a good-humoured, light principled man, than with an ill-tempered rigorist in morality."[6] Abundant evidence shows that he had similar preference for amiable women, and the young Hemings was described as that.

Because both of them were out of their places, Hemings and Jefferson had more good reason to *want* to talk to each other than they would have had in Virginia in a household with many layers of her older relatives between the two of them. When one is abroad, and past the initial thrill of burying oneself in a foreign culture, familiar faces, accents, and manners can be quite comforting, even if found in a person whom one might have virtually ignored at home. The teenage Hemings might not have had very much to say to Jefferson at Monticello. In France, however, he and her brother were her most familiar links to Virginia. Just by being together in a foreign land, all three had more to say to one another, certainly more interesting things, than if they had been at home. The quality and substance of their conversations had to have been different since they could not have centered on issues that grew out of their surrounding slave society, because they were not in one.

The accounts of many who knew him, enslaved and free, confirm that Jefferson was a veritable font of information, which he conveyed at a moment's notice to any and all who asked for it—or did not. This impressed many. Isaac Jefferson, who portrayed him as the man to go to for answers, admired Jefferson's "mighty head" tremendously. Not all were charmed. The supremely educated and cosmopolitan John Quincy Adams often found Jefferson's disquisitions tiresome. There were altruistic reasons for Jefferson's behavior. His desire to spread knowledge to others was a part of his unshakable belief in the benefits of progress; the more people knew, the better the world would eventually become. He took no proprietary interests in his ideas and thoughts, and did not believe others should either.[7]

At the same time, there must also have been something personally gratifying (ego-enhancing) to Jefferson to be the person in the room who knew things, the one to whom others looked for answers, and whose intellect impressed people at all stations of life. His dealings with Isaac Jefferson show that he wanted to be that person, even for those who were not considered his social equals. It could not have been very hard for him to have impressed a fifteen- or sixteen-year-old girl, and there is no reason to suppose that he would not have been quite happy to do that. Sally Hemings, more like Isaac Jefferson than John Quincy Adams in her relationship to him, would have felt entirely comfortable looking to Jefferson on occasion to help sort out the new territory that she had to negotiate in Paris.

For his part, Jefferson enthusiastically welcomed contact with Americans, and his letters to family and friends and his attempt to re-create a Virginia garden at the Hôtel de Langeac betray hints of his homesickness.[8] In Hemings he had a late envoy from Virginia, his "country," as he called it, who could talk to him about people and places he knew and had not seen for years. She also brought valuable information about his daughters' lives at Eppington—both that of Polly, whom he had to get to know, and that of

Lucy, whom he would never get to know. She was also another person who spoke English, a critical thing for a man who wrote and read French well, but was never at home speaking the language.

Then there is the simple matter that Jefferson very much liked attractive females, and Hemings was attractive. All of the women associated with him—his wife, Maria Cosway, and Sally Hemings—were thought exceptionally good-looking in their day, a criterion that evidently meant a lot to him. He loved beautiful things. An agreeable personality in a woman was important, but not quite enough for Jefferson. There is no portrait of her, but men of both races noted Hemings's beauty, as well as that of her sisters and daughter.[9]

For the world and time in which she lived, the African American Hemings had attributes associated with white standards of beauty. In addition to pronouncing her "very handsome," a term used in those days to denote feminine beauty as well as masculine attractiveness, Isaac Jefferson described her as "mighty near white" with "straight hair down her back."[10] Her son Madison had light gray eyes. A man well acquainted with her youngest son, Eston, who like all her children was genetically "whiter" than she, described him as "light bronze colored" with "a visible admixture of negro blood."[11] His brother Madison had a similar appearance. The Hemings brothers did not get those traits from their extremely fair-skinned, European-looking father, whose skin did not tan in the sun, but burned and peeled when he did not wear a hat. Eston Hemings's wife, Julia, was said to have looked more like a white person than he. This suggests that Sally Hemings was a light-skinned, very obviously black woman—someone whose racial makeup could be immediately discerned upon looking at her—a "bright mulatto," just as Isaac Jefferson described her.

In his *Notes on the State of Virginia* Jefferson pronounced white skin more aesthetically attractive than black skin because it enabled whites to blush and thus to display sincere emotions, "the expression of every passion," which included the exchange of sentiment between males and females, as the blushing female is a staple representation in stories of courtship and love. He also offered "flowing hair" as a particularly important attribute of whites' beauty. Jefferson knew that not every white person, and he was speaking really about females, had flowing hair and that people who were not "all" white could have it. Jefferson lived his entire life among black people, and was familiar enough with them to know that many African

Americans, of varying degrees of skin color, from yellow to light bronzed, can blush. These were the effects of the racial intermixture that Jefferson said brought on the "improvement[s] in body and mind" of black people "in [their] first mixture with whites," improvements that he said had been "observed by every one."[12]

Sally Hemings and her siblings were the products not of the "first mixture" of blacks and whites but of the second. This almost certainly accounted for the Jefferson family's view that they were of "superior intellect" compared with their fellow slaves, who could have been just as intelligent or creative as the Hemingses but, lacking "white" blood, would never have been given as much credit for it. That was also why the African American Sally Hemings was light-skinned enough to blush and have long flowing hair.

There is more. In the passages in the *Notes* in which he casts doubt on blacks' equal intellectual capacity, Jefferson expressed his greatest confidence in blacks, besides his opinion that they had better rhythm than whites, in matters of the heart stating with great certainty that nature had done them "justice" in that department. These formulations about people of African origin—skepticism of their equal intellectual capacity and certainty about the quality of their hearts—were ideas from which he apparently never wavered. According to one visitor to Monticello late in Jefferson's life, he echoed these sentiments, saying that he had not yet found a true "genius" among blacks, but believed that they had the "best hearts of any people in the world."[13] Sally Hemings, then, combined what Jefferson regarded as the best in white people with what he regarded as the best in black people, an evidently appealing blend of the head and the heart.

The men testifying to Hemings's attractiveness saw her when she was older. The teenager at the Hôtel de Langeac had not yet given birth to seven children, or experienced the inevitable results of gravity, and may well have been absolutely stunning to look at. Talking to her would have been more of a pleasure for Jefferson than a chore, whether there was any immediate sexual frisson or not. Males and females, even of different rank and race, engage in light banter that acknowledges the other's gender. That is one of the ways that relationships—licit and illicit—are formed. Sometimes male-female small talk rises to the level of flirting, especially when no one else is around. Male-female banter and flirting are usually totally meaningless and innocent—empty, stylized—perhaps even biologically influenced, faux mating rituals. They can, however, take on a wholly different import when external constraints are loosened, that is, when people ignore the concept of inappropriateness.

Though Patsy and Polly were away at school, Hemings and Jefferson did not have the Hôtel de Langeac to themselves. Their household included her brother, the other servants, and the many people who enjoyed Jefferson's hospitality there on a periodic basis. He had come to Paris very willing to share quarters with others who needed a place to stay, though of the people who had started out living with him in those early days, only William Short remained by the time Sally Hemings arrived.[14] Though Hemings and Jefferson shared space with others, the pair need not have conducted themselves in ways that drew attention, and the spacious house, with its "ingenious arrangement of passageways," was specifically designed to protect the privacy of its residents. Jefferson's easy and sociable personality was undoubtedly trained on everyone in the household, Hemings included. Noticing that he reacted to her in a positive way—and she to him, for that matter—would not have given immediate cause to think that they were, or were going to be, having a sexual relationship.

If anyone in the household *did* suspect something, it would not have occasioned writing down what they suspected or even what they knew. It is hard to imagine a French servant, particularly the one most closely associated with Jefferson, Adrien Petit, being shocked at the idea that a man—an unmarried man at that—had taken a mistress. Having no woman in his life might have seemed more bizarre. The adage is true: "No man is a hero to his valet." A valet's job, if he is doing it the right way, is *not* to be shocked. As for the rest of the servants—gardener, coachman, *garçon de cuisine*— it is unlikely that they would have regarded it as unusual or have acted as impediments. If Jefferson paid their salary on time, which he always did, making him an anomaly in that society, and was good and decent otherwise, his affair with a chambermaid would have been just one more example of the kinds of things that members of the servant class knew about their masters—an occasion for gossip, but not one for judgment or memorializing. It is also unclear how many of Jefferson's servants were twenty-four-hour presences at his residence. While the higher-level servants almost certainly lived there, the "lower"-level ones, like the gardener and *frotteur*, probably did not.

Other people lived at the Hôtel de Langeac for varying lengths of time— for example, the American painter John Trumbull, famous for his rendition of the signing of the Declaration of Independence. Based in London in the 1780s, Trumbull met Jefferson when he came to the city in 1785. Trumbull first stayed at the Hôtel de Langeac in 1786, before Sally Hemings arrived. He made a return visit in December of 1787 and remained there until February 1788. Near the end of the Hemingses's stay in France, he came back to Paris and was able to see his friend Jefferson off on what everyone thought would be a temporary visit home. Trumbull met both James and Sally Hemings.[15]

Of course, William Short had used the Hôtel de Langeac as his primary residence throughout all of Jefferson's time there. He was well familiar with Hemings and her family even before he came to Paris. He did not, however, have a presence at the mansion that would have inhibited a liaison between Hemings and Jefferson, assuming anyone's presence would have mattered. As was noted in chapter 12, Short effectively divided his time between Paris and Saint-Germain—a town then fifteen miles outside of Paris. Between 1785 and 1788, he made almost monthly visits there, staying for extended stretches of time with the Royers. In September 1788 he left Paris for an eight-month tour through Europe, returning to the city in the second week of May 1789. Just a week later he headed straight for Saint-Germain to visit his beloved Lilite. Throughout all the time that Sally Hemings was in Paris, there were many, quite long periods of time (months), when Short was not at the Hôtel de Langeac with her and Jefferson at all.[16]

Both Trumbull and Short venerated Jefferson. If they suspected or knew about Hemings, they had no incentive to make a written record of whatever they knew. Men often keep the secrets of their male friends, especially where women are involved, hoping the favor will be returned, if needed. Short knew very well from his own experiences how valuable it was to have others be sympathetic about one's socially unacceptable liaisons. If he knew about Hemings and Jefferson, his infatuation with Lilite Royer, taking place at the same time, left him little room to make judgments about his mentor. All the while Short was visiting the married Lilite, he wrote and spoke to his friends of his deep love for her. It is unclear what he ultimately hoped to gain by carrying on in this way, but the besotted American evidently could not help himself. What could he, doggedly acting the role of the "extra man" in Lilite's marriage just to remain close to her, reasonably have said about Jefferson and his teenager? Even after giving up on Lilite after 1789, Short moved on to Rosalie, the young wife of the duc de La Rochefoucauld with whom he lived without marriage for a number of years. Nothing about

Short's life suggests he was a moralizer on sexual matters. Jefferson's "protégé" was not at all put off by the unconventional.

We know of Lilite Royer only because Short *himself* could not resist writing
to a few friends about her, always hiding her identity, but writing about her
nevertheless. One correspondent, a Virginian, Preeson Bowdoin, who was
also in France at the time, promised Short, "Every thing you have said, or may
say, respecting the Belle of St. Germain, you may rest assured, shall remain
a profound secret. Yes, I have been too often a Lover myself not to know the
value of such a confidance."[17] Howard Rice has suggested that Jefferson knew
about Short and Lilite, and it made him uneasy. Jefferson knew where and
with whom Short was living. If the sensitive mentor was at all perceptive
about the demeanor and attitudes of his "adoptive son,"[18] he figured out that
something more than the prospect of learning and keeping up his French
kept drawing the young man back to the countryside even after he had made
it clear to him that he wanted him to spend more time in Paris.[19] Yet Jefferson
apparently never wrote to his friends about anything that he suspected or
knew about the reason for Short's intense attraction to Saint-Germain.

Unlike Short, Jefferson could never and would never write to anyone
about Hemings in a way that revealed their connection. Already a man of
note, he knew what his white countrymen would make of this. When it
came to the care and deployment of his image, which if managed properly would leave him with the positive legacy of "great man," Jefferson
was supremely disciplined and controlled. At the same time, his status as
Hemings's master actually made it easier for him to carry on a relationship
with her in relative secrecy and security than it would have been for William
Short to have had an extended affair with Lilite Royer. All he had to do was
be hard minded enough *never* to write anyone about it. It is unlikely that we
will ever learn how much Jefferson knew about Short and his "secret love"
in Saint-Germain, and how much Short knew about Jefferson and Sally
Hemings at the Hôtel de Langeac. It was, however, an interesting, though
not surprising, confluence of circumstances.

Amazons and Angels

Until very recently, the focus on Jefferson's relationships with women in
Paris centered largely upon his dealings with Maria Cosway, with side references to his correspondence with Abigail Adams, several French society

ladies, and well-born American visitors to the Continent like Angelica Church. Because it is fairly plain that his interest in Cosway was more than merely platonic, their letters have been used as a guide for his views about love and romance. Jefferson did not have an extensive or, one should say a very varied, career in this regard insofar as we know, and so every scrap of information on that subject counts.

One could get the impression from some depictions of the Jefferson-Cosway affair that it was steady and long-standing, stretching from the time he arrived in Paris until the time he left. They wrote to each other over a long period, but the actual time they spent together was quite short. And by the start of 1788 Jefferson seemed to lose interest in actively pursuing the affair or very practically saw the complete hopelessness of it. The most telling sign of this is that he, the inveterate correspondent, sometimes let long periods go by before answering Cosway's often very impassioned letters.[20] When he did answer her, he followed a course he often took with correspondents, one that makes it difficult to gauge his true feelings from merely considering what he said in letters. He responded to her as the man he knew she very much wanted him to be, saying what he perceived she wanted to hear. He wrote as if they were still quasi-lovers with a relationship that was ongoing, with some definite and fixed place to go. His actions, or inaction (not writing to her during periods when he wrote many letters to other people, sometimes multiple letters to certain individuals, and sent out missives dealing with absolutely mundane things), tell a different story.

Because we do not know precisely when Jefferson took an interest in Sally Hemings, we cannot know how, or even whether, his feelings about her accelerated or influenced the marked cooling of his ardor for Cosway. It is possible for a man to maintain an attraction to more than one woman at a time, and for attraction to wax and wane. In fact, at points in 1788, if one were to read Jefferson's letters to Angelica Church, whom he met in Paris in 1787, and Maria Cosway together, one would be hard-pressed to know which woman he liked better. This gives a good indication of the depth of his feelings about these two women, as the equally flirtatious tone taken with both tends to cancel out the idea that either one was the object of a serious pursuit. Or to put it another way, Jefferson's pursuit may have been serious in that he would not have minded having sex with these women, but not serious in the sense that he ever thought of making a life with either of them. Just as men can be interested in more than one woman simultaneously, they can also have women for different purposes—short-term dalliances or long-term alliances.

Though Jefferson continued to flirt harmlessly and intermittently in his letters to Church after he returned to the United States, it is not likely that he contemplated a deep involvement with her. Not only was she married, she had four children. An affair would have threatened her marriage and her family. It is almost inconceivable that Jefferson would have been serious about, or even comfortable with, a woman who would have sacrificed her relationship with her children for him. Of Cosway, Church, and Hemings, Hemings was the only one he had any reasonable prospect of being involved with on a serious and long-term basis. Except in the occasional letters that passed between him, Cosway, and Church over the years, once Jefferson returned to America with Hemings, he never again developed with any other woman the kind of relationship he had with Cosway and Church or engaged in the same type of playful quasi-sexual epistolary banter.[21]

Although we can never really know what Hemings was like with Jefferson when they were alone, her status and, even more particularly, her age may well have made her the very embodiment of the domestic and submissive woman that he so clearly favored. The thirty-year gap in their ages meant that at every stage of their existences he would appear drastically older and wiser—she would never outgrow him personally. The few comments about her personality and her role at Monticello—taking care of his rooms and his clothing, that is, taking personal care of him—suggests this. It is hard to imagine the extravagant and worldly Maria Cosway being content to live on Jefferson's farm mending his stockings and shirts, bottling the cider he liked so much, and chatting about the goings-on among the denizens of Monticello.

The women Jefferson met in France alternately fascinated and repelled him. He enjoyed mixing with the attractive and intelligent among them, so long as the conversations did not veer into politics or get too serious. At the same time, they frightened him. The very things he found delightful about these women—their openness, their ability to move in the world freely—also hinted that they might be just a bit too much, not feminine in the way that was most satisfying to him in the long term. These were sophisticated "city girls," wonderful and reliable for the casual amusement of witty repartee, but not the type of woman he wanted a serious life with in the intimacy of his domestic realm. What a contrast Sally Hemings must have presented! When he came home to the Hôtel de Langeac after spending time with the Cosways, Churches, and Madame de Tessés of that world, there he would find his wife's half sister, the extremely attractive, sweet-natured, sewing, Virginia farm girl. She was the very opposite of frightening.

At the end of the 1780s in Paris, when Jefferson was ready to go home, Hemings represented the place and way of life he expected to return to, with no inkling at the time that he would ever leave it again for any sustained period. He knew that when they got back to Monticello they could resume life in a shared universe of which he would be the unquestioned center. Aside from all the other reasons a male might want to attach himself to a particular female—her looks, personality, their personal chemistry—it made sense for Jefferson to have fixated on a young woman who knew and understood that universe, his place there, and how she could best fit into it. Near the end of his stay in France, Jefferson contrasted American "Angels" with European "Amazons."[22] Who was an angel in his eyes?—a domestically oriented woman who believed that her place was in the home, attending to the needs of the man in her life and her children, not out engaging in adulterous intrigues with foreign diplomats or other such persons. An angel let the man in her life take the lead and make the important decisions affecting their lives. She accepted his well-tempered dominance as a show of his love and desire to protect her and their family. The dreaded Amazons, on the other hand, were politically and socially assertive women who sought self-fulfillment outside of the home, challenging men in what was supposed to be an exclusively male domain. Women in France were out of synch with the natural order of things. Their determined self-assertion emasculated the men in their lives.

Amazons also posed a grave sexual threat. While counseling a parent about the best place to send her son to learn French, Jefferson picked Canada because "in France a young man's morals, health, and fortune are more irresistibly endangered than in any other country in the universe."[23] What imperiled young men did he have in mind? Jefferson had a way of silently exempting himself from many of the admonitions and platitudes he passed along to others, and probably did not count himself as a young man in Paris, though his affair with Maria Cosway and his construction of the liaison with Sally Hemings had the air of a man anxious to start a new life as if he were operating, as a young man would be, on a clean slate. The two young men Jefferson observed most closely in France were the ones who lived in his house: James Hemings and William Short. We know nothing of James Hemings's dealings with women, although it is highly probable that a young man between the ages of nineteen and twenty-four who had money and free movement had the chance to meet them. The women of his family were described as beautiful, and one might assume that he, too, was attractive. Short's amorous adventures have already been noted. He surely counted as a young man who took advantage of the easier relations between males and females in France.

Jefferson knew that men's greater role out in the world necessarily led to an imbalance in power, because it gave them greater access to and control over the wealth and resources of the community. He did not believe that men should take advantage of this and mistreat women who relied upon them for protection. In fact, he wrote that men showed their highest level of civilization when they refused to use their superior physical power to hurt women. The onus, however, was on women to find a way to live under this system so that they would never directly challenge male authority. When one of his sisters had trouble with her alcoholic and abusive husband, Jefferson—in a mildly scolding tone that suggested she was being an Amazon—put the burden on her to adjust in response to her husband's aggression. Sixteen-year-old Sally Hemings could never have been his idea of an Amazon.

Jefferson made his views on women's proper roles in life very clear to his daughters. While both Patsy and Polly received what would be considered first-class educations for girls while in France, meaning they studied languages and took art, music, and dance lessons, he disparaged that somewhat when he told his sister-in-law that what the girls had learned there would not make them particularly "useful in [their] own country." He characterized women's traditional domestic duties "as being of more solid value than anything else." He wanted to know how well his daughters sewed, what type of dishes they knew how to cook, the kinds of things one would expect a farmer's wife to be doing instead of being a Madame de Staël *manquée*, trading bons mots about various literary works or debating philosophy or politics.[24]

Jefferson well understood that marriage is both a social institution and an intensely personal one. His daughters would not spend all their married life sewing, setting hens, and making puddings. There was a social aspect of marriage that addressed itself to the place of the couple in the world outside the home. For an upper-class man, that required an acceptable woman to play the role of wife, to bear legitimate heirs, to be presented to the world at large as the extension of her husband, and to move with her mate throughout their social set. This is, in part, the reason Martha Jefferson is often treated as a known quantity when surprisingly little about her is actually known. As "Mrs. Thomas Jefferson," she was he. His talents and accomplishments are imputed to her, as are his values, tastes, and feelings. Having picked her for a wife, he told us who she was, and we trust that she must have been a certain kind of person, even though we know far less about Martha Jefferson than we know about Sally Hemings. That kind of trust based upon our assumptions about the meaning of legal marriage, and the putatively "universal" qualities of upper-class white women, is unavailable to Hemings. Her attributes and personality are likely to be defined solely by assumptions about the legal status of being a slave and assumptions (usually negative ones) about being African American.

The personal aspect of marriage directs itself to the intimate domestic relations between husband and wife and addresses issues of compatibility (emotional and sexual), affection, and trust between partners. The deepest and most telling expressions of these aspects of marriage take place totally out of public view. One could, of course, have all the attributes of a social marriage with none of the personal ones. A couple perfectly matched in terms of their social qualifications may not really connect on the personal level, because there is no real compatibility, affection, or trust between them. The social function of the marriage is the lifeblood of that type of union. None but the closest, or most cynical, observers of the couple will be able to discern the absence of the personal connection, particularly if the couple is good at acting and has significant reasons for keeping up the front.

Though admittedly sparse, the available evidence indicates that Jefferson and his wife were matched socially and personally. By 1789, however, Martha Jefferson had been gone almost as many years as Jefferson had been married to her. He had already had, in Rhys Isaac's phrase, his "parlor and dining-room wife,"[25] who had given him legitimate heirs and who, when she was not too ill to do so, entertained his guests and was an appropriate ornament at social functions. Either because of her request or his own determination, Jefferson was not going to replace her. His socially acceptable white female relatives could carry out those duties as needed. This says nothing at all about Jefferson's desire for the more personal aspects of a union with a woman. A question arises: If it is possible to have a union based solely on the social attributes of marriage without the personal ones, can one have a relationship based solely on the personal aspects of a union without the social attributes? Is social legitimacy the sine qua non of an authentic connection between two people? That Hemings and Jefferson were not merely an unmarried couple but were, under American law, in a specific kind of legal relationship—master and slave—complicates the equation further and raises other questions. Do people always see themselves as the law says they are? Could a man and a woman, in their situation, have an "outlawed" personal human bond that was worthy of any degree of respect or understanding?

Jefferson knew that the young girl living in his house in Paris would never be able to perform the social duties of a legal wife. She was, however, well suited to perform the personal ones that were evidently more important to him—being a familiar presence, telling him what he needed to hear about what was happening on the farm, having sex, attending to his needs, being the person of his private world who listened to him complain or voice fears about matters that he might not want to reveal to others, sharing talk of his very grandiose plans for restructuring Monticello—a project that was dear to his heart for decades and that directly involved members of her family. In the years after their return from France, Jefferson fixed Hemings's life at Monticello so that she was able to do all these things with a minimum amount of friction in his household.

Hagar's Children in Paris

One item in Jefferson's correspondence with Maria Cosway stands out for reasons that have little to do with what he thought of her. The letter, written in April of 1788, is remarkable for the insight it gives into Jefferson's thoughts and for a hint of his frame of mind in the spring of that year. He wrote it just after he returned from his tour through northern Europe, a trip that he thoroughly enjoyed, perhaps so much so that he was a very poor correspondent. He did not write a single letter to Cosway during that time, and she was deeply hurt by that, as he learned upon returning to the Hôtel de Langeac and finding a very angry letter from her. Jefferson attempted to mollify Cosway by telling her of his journey, revealing that at various points he deeply yearned for her company. He also made a recondite sexual reference (a joke about a man's penis size) from the novel *Tristram Shandy* that clearly went over Cosway's head, as many other things he said to her seemed to. At another point in the letter, Jefferson included one passage, startling in ways that Cosway probably did not grasp. When describing his trip to an art museum in Düsseldorf, Jefferson wrote,

> I surely never saw so precious a collection of paintings. Above all things those of Van der Werff affected me the most. His picture of Sarah delivering Agar to Abraham is delicious. I would have agreed to have been Abraham though the consequence would have been that I should have been dead five or six thousand years.[26]

Fawn Brodie, who famously relied on Freud to analyze Jefferson, was the first to highlight this passage, but the implications of Jefferson's wish are not far enough below the surface to even be considered Freudian. The painting referenced the Old Testament story of Abraham and his wife, Sarah. When Sarah became too old to give Abraham a child, she brought him one of her own servants, Hagar, to become his concubine with the idea that should Hagar conceive and bear a child, Sarah would take the child and raise it as her own. Significantly for how the story played out, Hagar was not of Sarah's and Abraham's people. She was an Egyptian. The biblical story is not so much about sex as about the desperate need to provide an heir for the husband's line at any cost—giving up, at the wife's insistence, her right to sexual fidelity and accepting an heir who would be of mixed blood. Jefferson did not want to be Abraham so that he could have more children. It was the erotic nature of the story—the "delicious" depiction of the event—that so struck him that he expressed the depth of his feeling with resort to exaggeration: the chance to have Hagar in his bed would have been worth dying for.

Jefferson used the term "delicious" to denote things that were delightful or pleasing to him, not necessarily in a sexual way, though in this context the word seems to have carried that meaning. Van der Werff painted a scene in which an older man sitting in his bed is being given a beautiful young woman to sleep with. For those who knew the story, as Jefferson did, any notion of guilt about what is taking place is diminished because the person giving the young woman to the man is his own wife. After he had kept faith with her through their many childless years and refused to cast her aside for another wife, Sarah does this for her husband Abraham. Depicting her with her hand over her heart and a determined expression on her face, Van der Werff conveys the years of their struggle culminating with Sarah's solution to their problem. She is saying to her husband, "This is what should happen, and it is all right."

What makes his wish so telling is that Jefferson knew it was not an impossible, or even an improbable, one to fulfill. We might think about this differently if, say, John Adams or some other non-slaveholding northerner had made such a comment, filing it away as just another meaningless male fantasy. One commentator has posited that Jefferson was actually thinking of Maria Cosway as the metaphorical slave girl Hagar, bypassing the reference's infinitely more obvious parallel to Hemings. Even if he had been thinking of Cosway, it does not move us far from Sally Hemings to suggest that of all the reveries available to him, Jefferson would so rapturously fantasize the determinedly free and very white Cosway into the role of a young enslaved woman of a different race.[27]

It is simply impossible to write slavery out of the life, personality, and even the very existence of Thomas Jefferson. Whatever he said about slaves, in any context, requires attention. When he explicitly fantasizes about being given a slave girl to go to bed with, one cannot ignore the fact that his relationship to slave girls was anything but metaphorical. Jefferson lived in a world where having a young slave woman of another race to sleep with was always a real possibility. The products of those types of situations, Hagar's children, were all around him. For that reason it is doubtful that he would ever have written to a fellow Virginian—especially a female—that he at any point dreamed of having someone give him a slave girl to sleep with, because he knew their minds would immediately turn to the Abrahams and Hagars in their own communities. Every Virginian knew that Jefferson could be given a slave girl, and he could keep her. As he wrote those words to Cosway, there was such a girl who had been sent to live with him sitting, sleeping (perhaps already in his own bed), or sewing in his house. That enslaved girl, the somewhat ironically named Sarah, was in his life solely because she had been brought there by his wife.

The situation at the Hôtel de Langeac was incendiary precisely because Sally Hemings was not just a young slave girl: she was his deceased wife's half sister. Neither Hemings's status as a slave nor shifting ideas about race

could have trumped genetics. Half sisters can resemble each other physically, or in the tone and timbre of voice, and mannerisms. Moreover, even
before they were together in Paris, the Hemingses and Jeffersons lived in
close proximity to one another and interacted on a daily basis, creating,
as this did all over the South, a mixed culture of shared language, expressions, sayings, and norms of presentation. Hemings spent her formative
years with Jefferson's daughters, and her manner of speaking was probably
not markedly different from either of theirs. We get a telling clue about the
way Jefferson's daughters sounded, at least as young people, from Patsy
Jefferson's phonetic spelling of "windows" as "winders" as she complained
about the windowless cabin on her trip across the English Channel and
then rhapsodically described the beauty of the stained-glass "winders" in
French churches and cathedrals.[28]

There is no gene for black speech, nor do speech patterns depend upon
one's level of education. That is why it is impossible to spot illiterates just by
listening to them talk. The historian Melvin Patrick Ely has shown, through
a brilliant job of historical detective work, that our modern-day perceptions
about the speech patterns of enslaved southern blacks are faulty. By close
reading of the letters and other documents of white and black residents
of Prince Edward County, Virginia, during the late eighteenth and nineteenth centuries, Ely shows just how much alike black and white southerners in the pre–Civil War years sounded. Idioms and speech patterns that are
today seen as distinctively African American were commonly used by black
and white alike.[29] That should not surprise, given that the two races lived
together more closely during slavery than at any other time in American
history. These transplants from other continents created and learned how
to speak southern American speech together. In light of this, the snobbish
observation of a perennial Jefferson critic, Henry Lee, whose family kept
one foot in England well into the nineteenth century, that Jefferson's dic-
tion was far from perfect, perhaps gives some clue as to the way Jefferson
sounded. It is possible that Lee, and other Virginian elites holding on to the
culture and ways of England, including the way of speaking, resisted the
development of what today would be recognized as a southern accent—a
way of speaking born of the interaction between Europeans and Africans.

The determination to render black speech as always vastly—and uni-
formly—different from that of whites grew out of a desire to cast African
Americans as alien beings, in much the same way that Jim Crow was

designed to communicate the message of essential differences between the races. Even Sojourner Truth, whose first language was Dutch, and who would have spoken English with a Dutch accent, is depicted as speaking in the same manner as slaves from Anglophone communities.[30] But just as Jim Crow created a level of physical separation between the races that did not exist, and could never have existed, during slavery, conventional renderings of the speech of enslaved people have created a distorted picture of both black and white conversational styles.

Three of the four children Sally Hemings reared to adulthood lived successfully as white people among other whites. Her two eldest, Beverley and Harriet, left Monticello as white people, with no learning curve for how to present themselves as Caucasians. They married white people who may not have known they were of African origin or had ever been enslaved. They would not have been able to do this had they spoken in the stereotypical dialect attributed to every black person throughout American history up until today. It is not at all uncommon to see in journalism from the twentieth and twenty-first centuries the speech of blacks recorded in a form of dialect that supposedly conveys the person's "authentic" blackness (read differentness) while the speech of whites who speak in ways that could also easily be put into a form of dialect are faithfully reproduced in standard English. None of Hemings's children had any more contact with whites growing up than she did. They probably had even less on a one-on-one daily basis.

That the Hemingses had a different overall presentation from other slaves at Monticello, as members of the Jefferson family asserted, meshed with Jefferson's desire not to be reminded that those who served him most closely were, in fact, black slaves. If Hemings did resemble his wife in any way, physically or through the use of common expressions, as so often happens with people who spend time with each other, one can imagine the emotions that this evoked in Jefferson, bidden and unbidden. Had he been able to accept the first appointment to France, he would have experienced the country he had come to love so much with his wife.

Even without a family resemblance, there was virtually no way that Hemings and Jefferson could talk with each other without the conscious or unconscious memory of Martha Wayles Jefferson hovering between them. She was why they knew each other. She was why they had come to be living together in a strange land away from family and the society that had formed both of them. What would a man be thinking while talking with a young female who was his slave, but also the sister of his much loved and lost wife? What would a young enslaved female be thinking as she talked to a man who was her master, knowing that he had been married to her sister? Had Hemings been free and white, they would not have been thinking of marrying each other, because that would have been against the laws of their time. In Virginia, under the influence of English law, a man who married his deceased wife's sister was engaging in incest.[31]

Hemings and Jefferson lived in a world obsessed with family connections. Kinship ties were enormously important to enslaved people who tried hard to defend them against the depredations of slavery. Blood and family were important to white Virginians as well, but they added the component of racism to the equation, introducing the notion of "black" blood and "white" blood. Hemings embodied the clash between the values of blood and family and racist views about blood and race, so that white supremacy and slavery complicated her connection to her sister Martha. Enslaved families had different responses to their blood connection to whites. Some thought them meaningful and kept the ties alive through their naming practices and dealings with those families after slavery. Others—one could venture, the vast majority of slaves, indifferent or hostile to their blood ties to white families, or deeply ashamed of them—never made anything of biological relationships to whites. It was a part of them that meant nothing. This was a rational response reflecting the fact that their particular ties were most often the result of rape and that their white relatives usually ignored or even strenuously denied the existence of blood ties to them.

Jefferson's relations with Hemings's family show that his own strong feelings about the meaning of blood and family were never totally overridden by his feelings about blood and race. That the Hemingses' relationship to his wife was biological, rather than legal, meant that he had no external guide for dealing with the connection and had to decide on his own how to handle it. He could ignore it altogether, openly recognize it and make something real of the connection, or make gestures that acknowledged it in a more oblique fashion. Jefferson chose the last course. We do not know all that the Hemings siblings' relationship to his wife meant to him, but we have some idea from his overall treatment of them that it meant a great deal. He viewed the family through the prism of his sentimentality about his wife and the life he had hoped to build with her, and this seems to have affected the way some members of the family viewed him in return.

That is part of the problem. It would be easier to understand the lives of the Hemingses if Jefferson had sent the Hemings-Wayles children to one of his outlying plantations, and if they had grown up as the hidden-away enslaved blood relatives. Rather than doing that, he, probably on the example of his wife and out of loyalty to her, fixed the Hemingses' lives so that they always remained very close to him, which had the confusing effect (for him and the family) of further melding and highlighting their incongruous identities as slaves and family members. Jefferson sought to ameliorate the complications of their dual status by giving the Hemingses back as many attributes of free people as he could without totally removing them from the state of slavery—at least until he freed Robert and James Hemings.

Life in Paris then, far more than in Virginia, was much better suited to the way Jefferson conducted his relationships with the family. James Hemings took on even more of the attributes of a free man—becoming a professional, getting wages, hiring a tutor, and striking other men when the occasion warranted. Sally Hemings took on attributes of a free woman in a different way. She was made, for a period, a wage earner, which acknowledged her ownership interest in her labor. But it was labor of a distinctive sort. Keeping Jefferson's and his daughters' living quarters in order and sewing were not deep signifiers of the degraded status of African American enslaved females. The division of labor between males and females in society in general required a typical white farmer's wife to pick up after her husband and family, and women of all races and classes sewed—from royalty to peasantry: Marie Antoinette, Martha Washington, Jefferson's female relatives. One of the few identifiable possessions of Martha Jefferson that remains is her thread case. That Jefferson kept it as a memento suggests its importance as a trigger for memories of her, her femininity, and her role in his domestic life.

What did Sally Hemings make of all of this in a place where she considered herself to be free? Though this new status represented a change in her attitude about herself and about Jefferson, this important knowledge melded with all that Hemings knew about her origins and their way of life back home. By Virginia society's dictates, Jefferson was far above her—not just in terms of his capacity to wield power but in terms of his very being.

He was supposedly a "better" version of human being than she, and she was supposed to believe that was actually true. While she did not know them personally, Hemings knew that her father and grandfathers were white men just like Jefferson and that she shared the same father with the woman to whom Jefferson had been married. Her blood ran in the veins of Jefferson's daughters. What Jefferson or other white people did or did not make of such a situation was never the complete story, and Hemings would not necessarily have accepted the idea that she was some lower order of human being than Thomas Jefferson. Even if Hemings had been 100 percent black, we could not assume that she would have accepted the idea that Jefferson was superior just because he was white.

Oppressed people do not always internalize the stories their oppressors tell about them. They often, in fact, develop their own internal narratives about who they are, ones that can be enormously self-regarding and vaguely, or even vigorously, contemptuous of their overlords. Think of the actions and reasoning of those slaves who, in the late eighteenth and early nineteenth centuries, began to accept Christianity: they appropriated some of the stories of the Christian Bible to their own use, most particularly the story of the Israelites who lived under the thumb of the pharaoh. The pharaoh (white society) was the bad guy who ruled, not because he was "better" than the Israelites (enslaved black people), who were actually the favored of God, but because of his willingness to do evil to the fullest extent. Being powerful and successful on earth through evildoing was not a true mark of superiority. The children of Israel were the chosen ones who in time, if they passed the test and showed sufficient faith in God, would be delivered from the pharaoh's evil ways. The real meaning those narratives held for blacks during slavery had to remain hidden, buried deep within religious songs and rituals, and in seemingly accommodating behavior. That is what Paul Laurence Dunbar meant when he spoke of black Americans throughout history wearing "the Mask" and hiding their true feelings about their circumstances. That tendency clearly unnerved Jefferson, and that was why in the Notes on the State of Virginia he showed such discomfort about "that immovable veil of black which covers the emotions" of African people. One can never know, he was complaining, what those people are really thinking and feeling.[32]

It must also be said, however, that the way Jefferson treated Hemings and her family probably made her more favorably disposed toward him than hostile. That was certainly the response of other family members. We know little about Sally Hemings's attitudes about her life as a slave. What we have to go on, as we try to reconstruct her biography as completely as possible, is what others have said about what Hemings did and how she felt and what we can make of the various known details of her personal history, of which there is actually more to consider than has been generally allowed. To do this we will step away from strict narrative for the following four chapters to analyze closely the world of the enigmatic enslaved woman whose name has gone down in history with Thomas Jefferson's.

14

♣

SARAH HEMINGS:
THE FATHERLESS GIRL IN A
PATRIARCHAL SOCIETY

THERE HAS BEEN a tendency throughout American history, and into the present day, to see black people as symbols or representations rather than as individual human beings. Even when specific details about an individual life are available for interpretation, those details are often ignored or dismissed in favor of falling back on all the supposed verities about black life and black people in general. For African Americans social history almost invariably overwhelms biography, obscuring the contingencies within personal lives that are the very things historians and biographers normally rely upon to create meaningful depictions of events and lives in the past.

When we think of the young Sally Hemings in Paris dealing with Thomas Jefferson, we must acknowledge that she was born into a cohort—eighteenth-century enslaved black women—whose humanity and femininity were constantly assaulted by slavery and white supremacy. While the experiences typical to that cohort are highly relevant as a starting point for looking at Hemings, they can never be an end in themselves. For Hemings lived in her own skin, and cannot simply be defined through the enumerated experiences of the group—enslaved black females.

Taking account of the larger social context in which Hemings lived is essential, so long as that does not involve relying on stereotypes, whose very purpose is to cut off access to, or treat as invisible, truths about an individual's life that do not conform to conventional wisdom. There is, in fact, no one context to consult in regard to Sally Hemings: she lived many and had the multiple identities that are the normal part of the human makeup. The people and places she encountered gave her multiple personal contexts—the circle of her mother and siblings, her extended family, the larger enslaved community at Monticello, her community in Paris, Jefferson, his white family, and, finally, her own children. Those associations, of varying degrees of intimacy, shaped her inner life and outlook, and becoming familiar with them—and taking them as seriously as one would take them in another human being's life—offers the surest way to develop a picture of who Sally Hemings was.

"Unguarded Intimacy"

The first thing that one notes about Hemings the individual is that she did not know her father, who died the year she was born. As was alluded to in chapter 1, there is reason to believe that he may have gotten to see her, though she could have had no memory of him. Sally Hemings carried the same first name as John Wayles's eldest daughter with his second wife, Tabitha Cocke, a little girl who died in infancy or in early childhood. Writing in his family Bible, Jefferson listed her name above her younger sisters with the simple notation that "Sarah Wayles" had died.[1] It was not uncommon in those days of high childhood mortality for parents to name children after their deceased siblings. This suggests that Sarah Hemings was born before her father died, in May of 1773, and that she came to Paris, in July of 1787, some months past her fourteenth birthday.

Even though there was little chance John Wayles could have the kind of relationship to Hemings that fathers in legal marriages had with their daughters, or the kind that even some enslaved fathers had with theirs, not ever having seen one of the people who was responsible for her being alive shaped part of her identity. Brenda Stevenson, writing of slavery in the mid-nineteenth century, has wisely cautioned against painting too rosy a picture of plucky slaves prevailing against all odds. Many enslaved families, simply crushed beneath the weight of slavery's depredations, exhibited all the traits of families in severe distress: child and spousal abuse, alcoholism, and depression. At the same time, as Stevenson and others have made clear, there is no denying that family life was important to enslaved people.[2]

While we will never know the precise inner workings of the families of all Monticello slaves, one thing is clear: it was a place of stable two-parent families who had extended kin networks in the immediate vicinity. Like all families, each had its own unique characteristics: some couples may have loved each other more or less than other couples, they may have had ways of dealing with their children different from those of other parents, or the children in one household may have been better behaved or kinder to one another than children in other families. Whatever their internal characteristics, they were all together, which was not the case in the overall slave society, where families were regularly disrupted by sale, particularly in the post-Revolutionary period during which the Hemingses lived at Monticello. It was not even the case on Jefferson's other plantations, for when he sold slaves for economic purposes (as opposed to disciplinary reasons or to unite families) or gave them to his relatives, they were mainly from his outlying farms. Because of the services they provided to him and his family as house slaves and artisans, building and maintaining Monticello, and because he lived a very long time, the enslaved people atop the mountain formed a familiar and tightly knit community.[3]

In the Monticello that Hemings knew most intimately in her early childhood, the one that had formed her view of the world by the time she was in Paris, most of the enslaved children had mothers and fathers. George and Ursula Granger, who were very closely associated with the Hemingses, lived with their children. Jupiter Evans and his wife, Suckey, had a least one daughter who was a contemporary of Hemings, as did James and Cate Hubbard, the Gillettes and Hern families. Even the children of liaisons between enslaved women and the white men on the mountain, like Joseph Fossett and John Hemings, got the chance at least to see the man who fathered them, whether they had extensive relationships with him or not. And before he left for France, Hemings knew Jefferson as the loving and attentive father of the little girls with whom she spent her time.

Seeing the face and figure of one's father or mother is important for many reasons. It provides information about appearance: which parent one favors, why one is tall rather than short, why one has a particular type or color of hair and eyes. Paying attention to these things is part of the way people create their identities. It mattered, perhaps in ways that were not altogether positive, that Patsy Jefferson was tall like her father and resembled him facially and that Polly was "low" like her mother and had her facial features.[4]

Although the eighteenth-century understanding of genetics was primitive, people did notice that personality traits, not just physical ones, ran in families. Even if a father rejected an offspring, there was enough of a belief system about the meaning of "blood" relations that, no matter what the law said, Sally Hemings knew that aspects of John Wayles were inside of her. Without getting the chance to observe him, she could not have seen for herself just what those aspects were. Something would always be missing. The orphan inventing stories about, or pining for, the lost unknown parent is enough of a cliché of the literature and history of all ages for us to know that Hemings, at the very least, wondered about John Wayles and knew that she missed valuable information about herself because he was not there. This is even more likely if she knew that she shared a name with her father's lost daughter. The Sarah Wayles–Sarah Hemings connection might explain why, despite all of John Wayles's evident faults, at least two of Sally Hemings's offspring chose to give Wayles's name to one of their children, keeping the name alive for future generations.[5] Wayles meant something to their mother.

We can return to the metaphor of the uncloaked female when thinking about Hemings's identity as a fatherless young girl in Paris. Enslaved children who grew up knowing their mothers and fathers had a psychological buffer between them and the people who legally owned them. White masters were the ultimate authorities in their lives when it really counted—their mothers and fathers could not protect them from work assignments or sale, for example, and that was an ever-present reality. It is also clear that enslaved children thought of their parents as authority figures, protectors in certain circumstances, sources of comfort, and people who deserved respect and sympathy.[6]

The recollections of enslaved people, their naming practices, and the overwhelming evidence of their extreme sorrow at separation testify to the meaningfulness of connections between enslaved parents and their children. Those connections were born of the myriad mundane interactions that families engage in on a daily basis and that bind people together. At Monticello there were many issues that children looked to their parents to resolve—disputes with siblings or other children, illnesses that mothers attended to, fears in the night to be calmed, and tasks that one learned from one's mother or father. There was someone beside the master, at Monticello usually two people, that enslaved children looked to to handle the sorts of issues they faced.

In Virginia, Hemings had her mother. In France, she had neither mother nor father to look to for parental counsel and support. Her brother James, though eight years older, would not have had the true authority of a parent, since he was not even close to being her oldest sibling. Of her nine older brothers and sisters, he was sixth on the list in order of age. While he was no doubt a respected and loved older brother, who provided emotional support and guidance, he was probably not equipped to be cast in the role of father figure. Without question Jefferson was the male authority figure at the Hôtel de Langeac, and he occupied that role without the buffer of any other adult Hemings could have looked to.

Whether largely cultivated or simply a natural part of his personality, Jefferson was well suited to the related roles of mentor, adviser, confessor, and patriarch. He offered himself in those capacities, and others sought him out to play those roles, in a wide variety of contexts. Although he could appear diffident upon first meeting, that impression usually melted after a few moments in his company. His overall demeanor made him approachable, and numerous anecdotes and examples from whites and blacks, enslaved and free, testify to that. People would greet a man they took to be a raw-boned farmer or office clerk, he would begin to talk, and it was only then that they realized this was no ordinary man. Jefferson's personal informality, which might fit well in the modern world, surprised, confused, irritated, and sometimes infuriated many of his contemporaries who equated the level of one's dignity with the level of one's formality. They deemed his loose and easy manner a questionable presentation for one who occupied important leadership roles within his society. Others were charmed by an effortless presentation that inspired a sense of instant intimacy and, later, deep loyalty.[7]

The role that primarily fit the realities of Jefferson's life as the owner of Sally Hemings—at least as he would have understood it—was that of the patriarch, with everything that attended that designation. That was, almost certainly, his earliest presentation of himself to her at the Hôtel de Langeac, which likely contributed to what happened between them there. One of the first acts that Jefferson performed when Hemings arrived in Paris was in keeping with his role as the patriarch of the household. He saw to her inoculation at great expense, although there was probably no reason for him to tell her how much it actually cost him. But, if he had let her know how expensive Sutton's services were, it might have awakened a sense of gratitude in her. Later on, Jefferson would use the large amount of money he had spent on James Hemings's apprenticeships in France as a reason to delay his emancipation until he had trained another to take his place as Jefferson's chef. Jefferson believed that the special things he did "for" the Hemingses—and that is how he would have seen it—should have provoked in them a special degree of loyalty to and affection for him. They evidently saw things differently, but that was his expectation.

Hemings understood Jefferson's action as one that had the positive effect of protecting her for life from what she knew was a gruesome disease. This placed him, very early in her stay, into the role of protector, something that would have been very meaningful to any young girl in a new environment operating without parental support in a foreign country. And calling upon Dr. Sutton to care for Hemings, when he knew that the Suttons were the best at what they did and had consulted at the highest levels of royalty and the nobility throughout Europe, was no doubt meaningful to Jefferson, too. It was something that he could, in his own self-regarding, eighteenth-century white male way, internalize as further evidence of his "goodness" and "soundness" as a patriarch. He had paid dearly to have Hemings, a slave girl, taken care of by a doctor to a king. Though he had the sensibility for it, irony was not always Jefferson's strong suit, but here he knew and could always remember and appreciate over the years that he had engineered this very ironic turn in Hemings's life.

Just as Jefferson had no wife to buffer and to filter his gestures toward Hemings and her responses to them, Hemings was equally exposed to him. History and literature are replete with examples of the potential hazards of older male–younger female interactions when the male is in a position of authority. These pairings inspire concern, and not solely because of legitimate fears about overreaching males. There is an understanding, though a much less comfortable one, that young females—and most uncomfortably of all, teenage girls—are emotional and sexual beings, too. The fear is that older males will take advantage of their sexuality to their own ends, not that they will address a sexuality that does not yet exist.

Ideally, an older male–younger female pair may stave off sexual tension by settling into a quasi–father/daughter relationship, despite their ostensible official or legal roles. The problem with that is the term "quasi." If they are heterosexual, males and females who are not too closely related to each other are generally known to be potential sexual partners. It does not help the construction of a safe quasi–father/daughter relationship that the traditional conception of marriage or romantic relationships, and here we speak of the Anglo-American context that shaped Hemings's and Jefferson's lives, put the husband and wife, or husband and wifelike figures, in a position not far from that of a father and daughter.

In the traditional formulation the man assumed authority over the woman and took over from the father the roles of protector, adviser, and rule maker, hence the idea of a father "giving" his daughter away in marriage to the new man in her life. Women were not only supposed to submit to this arrangement; they were taught to actively look for a male who could perform those tasks at the highest level—to be the greatest protector, the wisest adviser, and most thoughtful rule maker. That was the reason they performed the "little offices" that Jefferson referred to when writing about peasant women working in the fields who in the depths of drudgery still attempted to make themselves pleasing to the eye in order to attract mates.

That the traditional order has fashioned husbands and wives—and husband and wife substitutes—along the lines of fathers and daughters poses acute problems for intergenerational males and females thrown into close contact. Throughout history when the male teacher/guardian/coach closely interacts with the female student/ward/athlete, or any situation where there is no incest taboo to check their feelings and behavior, there is always a great danger of their sliding out of the quasi–father/daughter configuration into the role of lovers or potential spouses. Jefferson and Hemings, locked in the patriarch and erstwhile "child" paradigm in Paris, were from the start at great risk of doing just that.

There is no inevitability in all this, and there was nothing inevitable about Hemings and Jefferson. Some males and females will simply never come close to being attracted to one another, while others in these delicate pairings who do feel the tug of emotional connection develop a firm determination to keep to their allotted sides of the barrier no matter what. That is much easier to do when preventive measures are taken. The male and female do not socialize with each other without others present. They keep appropriate physical distance between themselves and confine their conversations, as much as they can, to whatever strictly defined business they are supposed to be doing. This is much harder to do when the male and female are living in a household together for a long time, with no real supervision of their behavior, indeed when the man has no one at all to answer to.

Compare Hemings and Jefferson's situation to that of another notorious couple who lived during their lifetime. In 1817, thirty-year-old Henry Lee of Westmoreland County, Virginia, married Anne McCarty. Along with his new role as husband, Henry became at the same time the legal guardian of his wife's seventeen-year-old sister, Elizabeth, who after the marriage came to live with the couple at the Lees' renowned family seat, Stratford Hall. When the couple lost their young daughter, and Anne became depressed and sexually unavailable to her husband, Henry turned to her younger sister and got her pregnant. In the family's telling of the story, it was only when his wife became unresponsive to him that Henry took an interest in Elizabeth.[8]

It may or may not be true that Henry did not immediately look upon his young ward in a sexual way once she entered his household. Unquestionably, however, that Henry and Elizabeth were in close daily proximity to each other—even with his wife there—made it easier, and likelier, for them to develop a bond that grew into something more than it should have been. Henry suggested this himself in a letter of 1833 when he tried to minimize the magnitude of his actions by noting that while his affair with Elizabeth was "atrocious," "no instinct of blood [was] interposed" between them and that he and "his wife's sister" had been "thrown into a state of the most unguarded intimacy."[9] The intensity of their living arrangement, Henry was saying, tripped them up. He also offered that it should not be surprising that a man who loved one woman might be able to develop an attraction to her sister. Cynthia A. Kierner has pointed out that the three most notorious sex scandals in late eighteenth- and early nineteenth-century Virginia—including Hemings and Jefferson and Lee and Elizabeth McCarty—involved men who were the lovers of their wives' sisters. In each case the men and women in the relationships, owing to family circumstances, were living for extended periods in the same household.[10]

Jefferson was involved in far too many aspects of Hemings's life in France to be as detached from her as a suitable quasi–father figure should have been. Her ill-defined role in the household meant that there was no one thing to focus upon that could set firm boundaries for his attitudes toward her. Life in Paris demanded from him a higher degree of vigilance about Hemings, as well as about the other Virginians in his household, than if they had all been at Monticello. His Virginia domain extended from the top of his mountain, down its sides, and over thousands of acres from its base. One had to travel some distance to leave it and his influence. That was not true in Paris. As soon as Hemings stepped out of Jefferson's courtyard, she was out of territory he controlled. And there were actually places for her to go on foot in the immediate environs of the Hôtel de Langeac. They were at the inner edge of a large and vibrant city that beckoned, and their neighborhood bordered other fashionable ones with interesting places and sights to see. Could Hemings go out into those places? How far could she go? Could she go alone? How long could she stay gone?

Jefferson had solved the problem of being principally responsible for adolescent girls in the city by having his daughters away in boarding school all week long. Hemings, though not his daughter, was still there in the residence and as the youngest person at the Hôtel de Langeac most of the time—and as a female—was the one who other members of the household would have thought needed some form of supervision and protection. And though she was a wage-earning employee during her last year in the city and saw herself as free, even masters of free servants exerted some influence over the comings and goings of their employees. Although the minister to France certainly had much more pressing things to do than to see to Hemings, and her brother and Petit were primarily responsible for this, a man so curious and controlling as Jefferson certainly had at least some interest in what Hemings was doing, where she was going every day, and, some say, in setting the rules to govern the life of a young girl for whom he had ultimate responsibility.

The extremely personal nature of Jefferson's involvement with Hemings comes through clearly when one considers his buying clothes for her, a fraught endeavor for males and females under any circumstances. Here he was not making general orders for his servants' day-to-day clothing in France, or sitting at Monticello ordering so many yards of "negro cloth" for a large number of enslaved females who, if he knew them at all, he knew them by name and not much more. When they got the cutout cloth, those enslaved women were supposed to sew their clothes themselves. Jefferson had clothes made for Hemings, a female who was not at all detached from him and who lived in his close circle. Very importantly, Jefferson bought these clothes for her so that she could go out into a world as far removed from American slavery as one can imagine.

Although Hemings drew enough of a salary to shop for herself, and her brother could buy things for her, too, having Jefferson purchase her clothing was a different experience altogether. This whole process was new to her and could only have been exciting. As most girls her age would be, Hemings was probably thrilled to be outfitted in new clothes, particularly since it did not diminish her own personal store of cash. She had to have fittings and, when the garments were completed, to try on whatever was bought—a sense of anticipation and then fulfillment. Jefferson noted payments for purchases for her on days or weeks when there were no payments for either of his daughters, suggesting that buying clothes for Hemings was carried out separately from buying clothes for them.[11] It is highly unlikely that the sixteen-year-old girl picked which clothing shops in Paris to go to and went to them by herself or, if the tailor came to the Hôtel de Langeac, picked which tailor it would be—at least not when Jefferson was paying the bill. There had to have been some determination other than her own about what was appropriate in terms of style and cost, and what items were needed at all—dresses, lingerie, shoes.

It is an understatement to say that Jefferson was never averse to shopping for *anything* and seemed to look for any excuse to do so.[12] It would have made practical sense for him to accompany Hemings on these excursions, or be present if the tailor came to their home to work, because he had to pay for whatever she bought. Patsy and Polly were still at the abbey, and one wonders whether their father would have taken Patsy out of school just for this. If Hemings shopped with someone besides Jefferson, or alone, she still had to tell him how much she had spent and, as a matter of simple courtesy, show him what she had bought with his money. Jefferson then saw her in the clothes he paid for when she went out socially with Patsy alone or when he accompanied them.

The spate of shopping for Hemings drew attention to her appearance, to Jefferson's interest in that and in her acquisition of items designed to enhance her looks. Both knew that it was he who had made the enhancement in her life, this good thing, possible. Neither the dynamic between master and slave nor the separate spheres of black and white (artificially created conceptions both) could override the meaning this activity carried in the complex dance between male and female. When a male buys clothes for a female who is not his daughter or wife, it almost immediately raises the intimacy level between him and the female recipient of his gifts, in ways that can make it much more difficult for the two to keep a safe emotional distance from each other. It too much resembles what happens between couples who are romantically involved with each other for the participants not to make that connection, even if just for fleeting moments. This was definitely not the way to maintain a "quasi–father/daughter" relationship, particularly in an intense environment where the results of Jefferson's actions and Hemings's responses to them would be far more direct and concentrated than if they had been back in Virginia.

At the Hôtel de Langeac, Jefferson was not playing "great white father" to upwards of two hundred men and women spread out over his plantations who harbored no illusions about the ultimate meaning of his self-identification as a benevolent patriarch—that it masked the fundamental reality that master and slave were in a state of war with one another. That was, in fact, Jefferson's view of what slavery meant, and he believed that it was the slaves' view as well, which is why he predicted that, if blacks were freed en masse, they would initiate a race war to exact revenge for what had been done to them.[13] In Paris he was playing great white father in face-to-face encounters with a young girl who had been raised to believe that the contours of her relationship with him were shaped by more than just her enslaved status. An important blood tie between the natural antagonists changed the dynamic of the conflict. The conflict was still there, though carried out on different, more psychologically complex and somewhat more flexible, terms of engagement.

The small size of their Virginia-born circle simply enlarged the potential problems inherent to their unique circumstances. Had the Hemings clan been transported as a group to Paris, the atmosphere in the household would have been very different. This is not to say that Hemings and Jefferson could never have begun an affair in Virginia. A stint in Paris was not a prerequisite to master-slave liaisons under American slavery. But living there as they did, for as long as they did, made it easier. Significantly for the pair, no one was watching them in the same way. Virginia's slave society, with all its expectations, customs, and mores that moved like a not so invisible hand to hold each person in his or her place for the sake of the system, was on another continent.

The people with whom Jefferson was most closely allied in France were staunch abolitionists, and at least one of them, his great friend Lafayette, was heavily involved in promoting the interests of blacks outside of slavery. Jefferson corresponded with, and admired, the enormously respected marquis de Condorcet, one of France's foremost abolitionists. Though

Condorcet argued for gradual emancipation, because he believed that slaves had to be prepared to become free citizens, he insisted on the equality of black people and was withering in his criticism of the character of the slave-owning class. In Virginia when an exemplar of that class, the far beyond egregious Archibald Cary, came to visit, he regularly beat Isaac Jefferson when he as a young boy was late opening the entry gate on the road leading up to Monticello. We can safely assume that nothing like that was going on at the rue de Berri. With no reason to attend every moment to those types of outside influences, those kinds of people, in very critical ways, the Hemingses and Jeffersons were able to make at least some of their own rules as they went along.[14]

Under these circumstances it is doubtful that Hemings and Jefferson moved through the Hôtel de Langeac like enemy combatants, as one might assume their legal and social relationship demanded. We are used to seeing a universe of difference between enslaved people and other members of society who lived under the power of upper-class free white males. Jefferson, on the other hand, saw points of immediate commonality. His worldview took in "women, children, and slaves" as individuals whose similar attributes required that they be put under the protection (read control) of white men. White men exerted different degrees of control over the individuals in those categories, their power operating along a continuum. Still, each type and level of control complemented the other and reinforced the basic notion of white male supremacy.

Jefferson as a husband could have forced his wife, Martha, to have sex—there was no such thing as marital rape—he took over her legal personhood and had the primary legal right to the labor of her children. He could not sell Martha or her children, as he could Sally Hemings, their children, or any of his other slaves. That difference was crucial; but for Jefferson it was not equally enduring. He actually foresaw a day when white men would lose the more extensive power they held over slaves, and thought that it would be right if they lost it. He probably *did not* foresee a day when men would or should, cease to be the rulers of the women and children in their lives, for Jefferson believed that slavery violated natural law while male dominance, tempered by restraint, was a tenet of natural law.

As her time in France passed, Hemings was at once slave, child, and woman—during the days of the week when Jefferson's daughters were away, a singular figure as the lone Virginia female in his household. There is no reason to suppose that she, the woman/child living under this patriarchal cover, would not have responded to any displays of male protectiveness and any truly positive attention from Jefferson in the same way that most females of her day, in the American context and others, were trained to respond to them—as welcome and positive things. The political, legal, and social meaning of slavery and the distortions of human relations that it worked, though mitigated in the French setting, were present. The very basic human requirement of finding a way to live daily life with the people in one's immediate surroundings—taking in and processing the meaning of the good and bad gestures they sent one's way—was no less so.

Jefferson's construction of his relationship with Sally Hemings naturally had a very different meaning for her brothers. Patriarchy involves more than just males dominating females; it is also about competition between males, a struggle in which some win and some lose, creating a hierarchy based on relative degrees of power. Like those of other enslaved men, the Hemings brothers' statuses signaled to white men that they had lost that struggle and were to be placed on the lowest end of the scale—stuck in perpetual boyhood or animalized as "bucks." Jefferson's acting the role of benevolent patriarch at the Hôtel de Langeac did not speak to James Hemings's masculinity in the way it spoke to his sister's femininity. Instead, Jefferson's actions toward him emphasized Hemings's diminished status within the male hierarchy. Even a legal father who supported his son long after the son reached adulthood would be seen as diminishing his offspring's manhood.

That was certainly true of Jefferson's son-in-law Thomas Mann Randolph, whose dire financial straits and emotional problems required Jefferson to step in and support his family. Martha (Patsy) Randolph received, and receives, no penalty for being cared for by her father. Her husband, however, was, and is still, perceived differently. His inability to provide for his own family, and dependence upon his father-in-law, is a tacit statement about his worth as a man. Even his eldest son seems to have held his weakness against him.[15] In a world that valued male supremacy, and identified superior males as those who were self-sufficient and able to see to the needs of their dependents, in every way, Jefferson's "care" of the adult James Hemings was infantilizing.

Much as Jefferson's gestures tracked the workings of traditional male-female relations, Sally Hemings knew that they could take her only so far.

She was different from white girls her age: marriage and social respectability could never be the end result of whatever developed with Jefferson at
the Hôtel de Langeac. Even armed with this very obvious bit of knowledge,
Hemings was a human being, and that was as important to her response
to Jefferson as her being, by American law, a slave. A full-fledged person
lived underneath that heavy legal status, one who was subject to a wide variety of often conflicting emotions and influences. What might make sense
for her to think or feel about him from an ideological standpoint could be
overcome, or even made irrelevant, by the promptings of her inner life that
grew out of her own experiences. Her age, fatherless state, time in France,
knowledge of her family's relations with Jefferson, and the way he treated
her specifically contributed to the way she viewed him and evidently gave
her ideas about how she thought she might be able to handle him. French
law, a check on his Virginia-based power over her, also helped shape her
view of Jefferson in this setting. What type of man did she see?

Over the years Jefferson's pattern of dealing with the enslaved people
closest to him was very much like his way of dealing with his white family,
friends, political allies, and even some of his adversaries. He appealed to
their emotions as a way of extracting the behavior he wanted, doing things
to make them feel bound and grateful to him, rather than being directly
coercive. While some persons are quite comfortable with open conflict—
in actual war and its simulations in daily life—and may even enjoy spar-
ring and the sensation of making others uncomfortable, Jefferson never
wanted to be the too obvious source of a person's distress—even when he
was. In both his public and his private lives, "peace" was indeed his "passion," though that imposed peace sometimes came at an enormous price
for himself and others around him; it often amounted to postponing or
submerging and hiding conflict rather than truly ending it.

Jefferson's preference for stratagems over direct confrontation led Henry
Adams to label him "feminine"—associating his elliptical style with females
whose subordinate position made it necessary, even endearing, for them to
adopt an indirect way of dealing deemed unworthy of "manly" straightfor-
wardness. Women's indirection acknowledged and flattered male power.
Jefferson used indirection not to flatter power but to obtain it in the way
that was, for whatever reason, most comfortable for him. Machiavelli's
"wise prince" preferred to be feared than loved because men love "according to their own will" and fear "according to that of the prince."[16] In his

private and public lives, Jefferson much preferred to be loved than feared, and he moved in a way ("operated," his detractors would say) designed to achieve that outcome.

"It is charming," he once wrote to his grandchildren, "to be loved by everybody."[17] Charming, perhaps, but exceedingly problematic unless one adopts a very cramped definition of "everybody." Jefferson did not. He assiduously collected people and sought to bind them to himself in any way he could. He often told people what he knew they wanted to hear, instead of being frank, so that he could stay in their favor. He involved himself deeply in sorting out others' personal problems and tolerated, often to his extreme disadvantage, those who imposed themselves upon him—all so that he would be "loved" by "everybody" whom he could personally persuade to do that. Jefferson was simply unable to follow Machiavelli's advice about the wise prince and love and fear, for he had greater confidence in his ability to inspire the one rather than the other, even though he was in his public and private lives a "prince" and longed to be an effective one. In both realms he determined that people would, in fact, love him according to his will; all he had to do was find the right formula. This was the personality that Sally Hemings confronted at the Hôtel de Langeac.

A DELICATE ISSUE remains. There is the fascinating and important, but ultimately unanswerable, question of when Jefferson first began to look at Hemings as something more than just a teenage girl living in his house. What happened to them near the end of their stay, and the length of their relationship, suggests that he was serious about creating a long-term bond with her from the beginning. How did he go about doing that with her? We are not totally in the dark on this question and do not have to resort to generalizations about master and slave relationships, for there are relevant comparisons to look to from their specific lives.

Sally Hemings was the female counterpart to those of her male relatives who were most intimately connected to Jefferson—her brothers Robert and James and her nephew Burwell Colbert, the son of Betty Brown. The way Jefferson treated these three offers some clues about how he approached her. Of the three, his handling of Colbert is, perhaps, the most instructive. Jefferson emancipated Robert and James Hemings in the 1790s. After they were gone, he had no interest in replacing them with a man who would become as close to him as they had been. The age of the austere, plain, and republican Jefferson had arrived, and such an obvious trapping of aristocracy, moving among "the people" with an enslaved body servant from his plantation, was no longer useful. Instead, he leased John Freeman to serve as a footman at the White House and accompany him to and from Monticello during his presidency.[18] Jefferson did, however, want a personal servant to attend him at Monticello.

Colbert spent his early childhood as a house servant, until at age ten he became one of the "nail boys" (teens and preteens most of them) who worked in the nail factory Jefferson built on the mountain during his first retirement in the 1790s. Some of the boys who originally worked there grew up to become his most trusted artisans and workers: Joseph Fossett served as head of the blacksmith shop, Isaac Jefferson went into the "tinning business," and Wormley Hughes became the head gardener at Monticello. Just as he determined early on that the teenage John Hemings would be a carpenter, Jefferson evidently decided, perhaps because of his appearance and personality, that Colbert might eventually take up where Robert and James left off, as his trusted personal manservant, at least while they were at Monticello.

Colbert's version of personal loyalty to and affection for Jefferson, which, as we will see, was reciprocated, is well known in Jefferson scholarship. Most of the descriptions of their relationship come from Jefferson's retirement years, when the men were older, with little attention given to the origins of their connection. Colbert's apparent attachment to Jefferson was not born in those later years. Nor did it necessarily come naturally. Jefferson specifically cultivated it, making efforts to win Colbert over well before he became an adult. While Colbert was still quite young, Jefferson let everyone who mattered to him know that Colbert was especially important. He instructed his overseer to be lenient with all the nail boys and to avoid whipping them, though his overseers did not always follow that rule. Jefferson made it clear—not only to his overseer but to others on the plantation—that Colbert was *never* to be whipped, no matter what.[19] That strict order was probably not a license for the teenager to do as he pleased. It was a show of faith designed to shape Colbert's character. The young man would avoid doing things precisely because Jefferson had singled him out as a favorite. When he grew older, and became a painter and glazer at Monticello during Jefferson's presidency, serving as the butler/attendant when Jefferson was at home, he remained out of the control of the overseer. In fact, Jefferson directed his overseer Edmund Bacon to give Colbert spending money whenever he asked for it.

This was not just about Jefferson's affection for Colbert, though he certainly cared for him—after all, why him and not someone else? This was also in part calculation. Colbert's identity as an enslaved man was not enough to achieve what Jefferson wanted from him. He had to create another level of identity for the young man, one that would make Colbert the kind of person he wanted to have in his intimate circle. Such a person had to have enough affection for him to make him want to be loyal, know to keep his private affairs private, and never make him ill at ease. It was probably easier to arrive at this point more quickly and naturally with Robert and James Hemings because they were his wife's half brothers, and he could use that connection as a basis for bonding. Jefferson could have made any man on his plantation act as his manservant. He could not, with force or induced fear, make that person genuinely like or love him. His protective and indulgent actions told Colbert, while still young and impressionable, that he was special in Jefferson's eyes. He had saved him from the pain and humiliation that other men on the plantation might have to endure, and he even forced a white man to answer to Colbert's whims. Colbert, from boyhood, knew that this was all Jefferson's doing, and that shaped the way he viewed Jefferson all his life. The strategy apparently worked.

To call this "strategy" or "calculation" is not to say it was cold. It was the opposite. Jefferson did not want—could not have endured—having a person in his innermost circle who obviously did not like him. Many men would not have cared one way or the other, so long as the person did as he or she was told. He preferred to idealize his relationship to Colbert, and shielding him from the "normal" vicissitudes of slavery allowed him to do this. The male servant closest to him would not know the "worst" of slavery, and Jefferson would show himself to Colbert at his "best" when he took him away from all that. He styled Colbert as his "friend."[20] As utterly preposterous a notion as that seems, it is nevertheless instructive that Jefferson felt the need to characterize his relationship with Colbert in this way in order to be comfortable around him.

Close as Colbert and Jefferson would become over the years, Jefferson and Sally Hemings were, from the very start, at another level of intimacy: skin-to-skin, sexual and emotional vulnerability–bearing, closeness. If he worked years to cultivate a favored manservant, to gain his loyalty and affection, there is every reason to believe that when he first determined he wanted Sally Hemings in his life in an even more intimate way, he followed the same pattern. The point could never have been for Jefferson to do things to make Hemings hate him, to fix her identity so that she would recoil every time she saw him or cringe at his touch. He wanted a domestic life that was as comfortable as it could be, and having a young mistress who despised him was not the way to do that. What must always be kept in mind when considering Jefferson's actions toward the Hemingses in Paris is that they were in a place where a serious misstep on his part could have prompted these two young people to leave him for good, under circumstances that would have caused him great embarrassment—and he would have had no recourse. The far easier and more pleasing thing for him in the long run was to try to win her over. That may not have been hard to do.

While the defined category of "teenager" did not exist as we know it today, even in the eighteenth century it was understood that young people like Hemings were prone to making irrational decisions in their dealings with members of the opposite sex. That is why there were legislative attempts to ensure that minors obtained parental consent before marriage. Young enslaved people were expected to seek the guidance and permission of their parents (when they were available) as they contemplated marrying. Older people of all races tried to protect their young people from the hazards of acting under the influence of youthful optimism, and naïveté, conditions that were not the province of free young whites alone.

Sixteen-year-old Hemings, in her particular circumstances in Paris, was perfectly positioned to be swept up in a Jeffersonian charm offensive to the detriment of what made any sense. Throughout his life, men and women far more worldly than she were similarly swayed, even when Jefferson did not seem to be trying very hard. No young girl was better prepared by the complex nature of her family configuration and her life to date to take seriously the professed intentions of a man whom, by any system of logic, she should have seen as an enemy, but who undoubtedly believed himself to be—and presented himself to her and her family as if he were—the very opposite of that.

15

❧

THE TEENAGERS AND
THE WOMAN

MANY THINGS ABOUT the world young Sally Hemings confronted seem almost impossible to grasp. She had spent her first fourteen years in a country that defined her as human chattel. In her fifteenth and sixteenth years, she was in a place where a court would eagerly transform her status, turning her into a legally recognized free person. Sometime between 1787 and 1789, this teenager learned the difference between law in Virginia and law in France. The power of the former could reenslave her, while the power of the latter could set her free. So she stood poised between the reality of life in the place of her birth and the moment when she had to decide whether to take the step toward freedom in a new land. She could make her journey alone or with her older brother, leaving not only slavery behind but also a large and intensely connected family in Virginia.

Then Jefferson intruded into that moment in a way that complicated her understanding of what course her life should take. Becoming "Mr. Jefferson's concubine" had worked a transformation of its own, which linked her even more tightly to the lives of her mother and grandmother. Although she was different from both women in the most salient way— neither her African grandmother nor her mother had the power to turn to law to end their enslavement—what had happened between her and Jefferson was an important part of Virginia's slave society. There were certainly things that the mothers and other female relatives of girls who were in this position said to them when this happened—advice and assurances given. Elizabeth Hemings and her daughters would have been especially equipped to talk to Sally, given their dealings with white men. But to talk to them, she had to be in Virginia and thus back under that state's laws. There was much for this young person to consider.

Not all the incomprehensible aspects of Hemings's world had to do with slavery and her family's complicated connections to Jefferson. Relations between the sexes in those days seem equally far away from our modern understanding of what constitutes civilized behavior. Much as it may assault present-day sensibilities, fifteen- and sixteen-year-old girls were in Hemings's time thought eligible to become seriously involved with men, even men who were substantially older. Jefferson's daughter Patsy became a married woman, with her father's enthusiastic approval, just several months after her seventeenth birthday. That attitude made sense in an era when higher education and career, the reasons for postponing marriage and childbearing in modern times, did not compete with what were thought to be a woman's most basic functions in life: to be a wife and a mother. Jefferson's parents were not really age cohorts. Peter Jefferson was thirty-one or thirty-two to Jane Jefferson's nineteen when they married.[1] Even within enslaved communities "slave husbands tended to be older than their wives." Philip Morgan has noted that "in the eighteenth-century Chesapeake, eight of ten husbands were older than their wives by an average of nine years." Morgan cited the "imbalance of the sexes" as a possible reason for this, along with "African customs," for "large age gaps between spouses were commonplace in many African societies."[2] In all Virginia communities a girl of fifteen would be considered very young, but she would not be totally off-limits, as events in the lives of people in Jefferson's social cohort indicate.

In the year before he left for France, Jefferson played matchmaker between thirty-two-year-old James Madison and fifteen-year-old Catherine (Kitty) Floyd. Madison first encountered Floyd in 1779 as the twelve-year-old daughter of William Floyd, a fellow representative to the Continental Congress. Both men, Floyd with his daughter and two other children, had rooms at Eliza House Trist's boardinghouse, on Market Street in Philadelphia. Out of respect for Madison, we will say that we can likely never know what he thought of the young girl when he first met her as a preteen. We do know that by the time Floyd turned fifteen, the very shy Madison's romantic interest in her burned brightly, and he very much wanted to make her his wife. Time together and—as with Lilite Royer and Short, Lee and McCarty, and Hemings and Jefferson—seeing each other on a daily basis in shared living quarters allowed this intergenerational couple to get to know each other in a way they would not have had their circumstances been different.[3]

Madison's dealings with Floyd were so intensely personal that when he and Jefferson corresponded about her, they did so in their agreed-upon code. During that same period, Jefferson took time out in a letter to his great friend to include a gossipy reference, also in code, telling Madison that one of their fellow Virginians, forty-four-year-old Arthur Lee, whom Jefferson disliked, was "courting Miss Sprig a young girl of seventeen and of thirty thousand pounds expectation."[4] In the end, the much older Lee was unable to capture young Miss Sprig.

Jefferson, a sometime resident of Trist's boardinghouse himself, spoke to Floyd on Madison's behalf on several occasions—talking up his friend's virtues and explaining what he had to offer her as a husband.[5] There is no indication he ever talked to Floyd's father about any of this. In speaking with her alone about Madison, Jefferson treated the fifteen-year-old girl as a free agent in matters of male-female courtship. One wonders what the teenage Floyd really thought of the idea that a man who was more than twice her age had a sexual interest in her, and that a man almost three times her age would approach her repeatedly to encourage her to bring the situation to a formal conclusion.

Marriage is certainly about more than sex, but sex is an integral part of the bargain. Floyd, whose great beauty attracted Madison, knew that if she married him she would be, on her wedding night, having sex with a man in his thirties. Madison knew that if he married Floyd, he would be having sex with a fifteen-year-old girl. That did not bother him, nor did it bother Jefferson, whose efforts on his friend's behalf initially met with some success, as Madison informed him. Floyd sounded amenable to the match— she and Madison exchanged gifts—and his hopes were raised. Then Floyd fell in love with a more age-appropriate fellow, a nineteen-year-old, and she ultimately rejected her older suitor. After many decades, the pain of the experience moved the elderly former president to try to mark over all references to Floyd in copies of the letters that had passed between him and Jefferson. Floyd had meant a great deal to him, and although he had

had a happy life and fulfilling marriage in the interim, her loss wounded him deeply.[6]

John Marshall, the nation's chief justice of the Supreme Court, began to pursue his future wife, Polly Ambler, while he was twenty-five and she was fourteen. He wanted to marry her right away, but the courtship took two years, and he married Polly when she was sixteen and he was twenty-seven.[7] Both Madison and Marshall were younger men and closer in age to the teenage girls to whom they were attracted than Jefferson was to Hemings. From our modern perspective, however, both were still very far outside the range of our tolerance for older man–younger woman attraction.

It was not just males in their twenties and thirties who pursued adolescent girls. Besides Arthur Lee, another man in Jefferson's circle sought a teenage companion. In the year after he returned from France, Jefferson's boyhood friend and father-in-law to his daughter Patsy, Thomas Mann Randolph, married, at age fifty, seventeen-year-old Gabriella Harvie. According to family tradition Harvie did not want to marry Randolph. She was in love with someone else, a man to whom her parents objected. They insisted that she marry Randolph, who was, on paper at least, a man of considerable property and wealth, whose land was adjacent to her family's.[8]

The thirty-three-year gap between Randolph and Harvie was a little beyond the thirty-year gap between Jefferson and Hemings, and unlike his friend, Jefferson did not envision Hemings as a potential legal bride. Neither he nor Randolph, however, would have seen the object of his attention as a child disqualified from sexual activity as we would today. Nor does the trajectory of their lives suggest that either man was an ephebophile, an adult who is sexually fixated on teenagers. Both men had previous marriages and children with females close to their own ages, and clearly intended to make lives with these younger females that extended far beyond the girls' teenage years. Hemings's relationship lasted well into her middle age, as Jefferson lived much longer than Randolph. Hemings and Harvie were attractive because in their day they were seen as young women, and youth in females has attracted men in all eras across all cultures even as the definition of "young woman" has shifted along with changing social mores. As for the girls themselves, whether Harvie wanted Randolph or not, she knew that in her time girls her age did get married and have sex. Hemings certainly knew that as well.

Under Slavery and Edicts

The pivotal differences between Catherine Floyd, Mary Ambler Marshall, "Miss Sprig," Gabriella Harvie, and Sally Hemings, of course, is that Hemings was born an enslaved African American, while her white counterparts were born free. Although the social distance between these females should never be understated, it will not do to treat them as if they were separate species living in different universes with no overlapping attributes and points of commonality. Legal marriage made sex between much older males and sometimes unwilling (and by our lights, immature) teenage girls perfectly acceptable in the eyes of society. This was not pedophilia, ephebophilia, or rape. Nor would it be construed that way in the pages of history, because the female in this circumstance received the title "Mrs.," the right to share in her husband's property, and the honor of giving birth to legal heirs—no matter what private horrors or wounds she suffered at the touch of a man whom she did not want. Being "legal" protected all married couples during their time, and long after their deaths as if their reputations were a property right. Sally Hemings—an item of property herself, according to American law—had no opportunity to create such a property right for her family to help shape the way historians would view her life.

Even though she was not under American law, thinking seriously about the beginning of Hemings's relationship with Jefferson in France requires confronting the vexing issue of sex between enslaved women and white men. Enslaved women's vulnerability to rape is well known, and the question naturally arises about this pair. Exploring this issue for these two people requires moving for a time beyond the kind of discussion that, in understandable deference to the suffering of black female victims of sexual abuse, casts every enslaved woman who ever had sex with a white man during slavery in the United States as a rape victim. This view describes the way things were between enslaved women and white men generally, but deserves greater scrutiny when one takes on the responsibility of seeking to understand and present the story of one individual's life.

There are at least two possible routes to the conclusion that what happened between Hemings and Jefferson during their beginnings in Paris was presumptively rape. One idea rests on an understanding about enslaved women and the other one, which works in tandem with it, on an understanding about white male slave owners. As to enslaved women, we may assume that none—because of the obvious state of war that existed between masters and slaves—would ever have wanted to have sex with any white man. Faced with white men who showed interest in them, enslaved women, for completely sound ideological reasons, would be unwilling. Evidence that sex took place between the two—a child, for example—would itself be evidence of rape. Sally Hemings would think that the only mate allowable to her—indeed the only one she should want in her heart—was a man who shared her legal status and, therefore, her race, a man of African origin. In this view, because her part "whiteness" did not prevent her enslavement, Hemings, acting on an instinctive sense of racial solidarity (solidarity with her black ancestors alone), would stay in her racial place when it came to feelings about members of the opposite sex.

If the young Hemings were open to the idea of having Jefferson as a lover, she would be a traitor who denied the reality of her enslavement and provided her enemy—Jefferson—with something that he very much wanted, while keeping her body from the men who shared her oppression and thus had a superior moral claim to it, that is to say, African American males. Under Virginia law, Thomas Jefferson owned her body by positive, legal right, but black men owned her body by natural right. This formulation has its roots in some very long-held beliefs and assumptions that require examination. Traditionally, in times of war, men of opposing camps who have sex with (forcibly and not) the women of the enemy are seen as encroaching upon territory that belongs to their male opponents—dealing them a heavy psychological blow in the conflict at hand. For victors, taking the women of the defeated group is one of the surest signs of conquest. On the other hand, males of the conquered group who have sex with the women of the conquerors are styled as insurgents or rebels, striking their own direct and meaningful blow against the conquerors by taking "their women"—"their" territory. The intergroup sexuality of these men is not deemed traitorous.

This wholly male-centered construction of the rules and meaning of conflict between warring parties—how one is to behave, how one properly calculates one's individual interests—leaves no room for the feelings, obsessions, and strategies of females. Women are merely objects upon whom men, the prime movers and the owners of female bodies, carry out their battles. Women know this and are supposed to adjust their behavior according to men's rules of engagement. When they run afoul of them, they are to be criticized or punished, if possible, severely.

It is doubtful that the black men whom Martha Hodes, as well as other historians, have written of, who were involved with white women before, during, and after Hemings's and Jefferson's time would be so easily deemed traitors as a willing Sally Hemings.[9] She would appear a less sympathetic version of the lead character in the opera *Aida*, who sings an impassioned and heartrending aria about the pain of being in thrall to a man who was her lover *and* also the determined enemy of her own people. We might be more comfortable with that scenario placed in a nineteenth-century Italian opera about ancient Egypt and Nubia. It provokes a completely different response when set down within the context of the still too close and painful American slave system.

For women of every color, rape has long been a notoriously underreported and unpunished crime, as male-dominated societies have liberally construed the notion of consent against women who complained about male behavior. A married woman could not complain about being forced into sex by her husband, because her marriage was seen as consent to sexual relations with him whenever he wanted. The tendency to liberally construe consent has been markedly worse for black women since the days of slavery. Powerful apologists for the institution long claimed that black women could not be raped because they were so promiscuous anyway. From their very first interactions with Africans, Europeans created a picture of black women as inherently licentious beings to justify their mistreatment of them and to degrade the black race. That notion lasted throughout the days of slavery and has continued into modern times. By the mid-nineteenth century the southern legal commentator Thomas R. R. Cobb in his treatise on southern slavery and law claimed that the rape of black women by white men was an almost unknown event precisely because one could never establish the legal trigger for a rape charge, "no consent," because it was well known that black women always consented to sex.[10]

It makes perfect sense when faced with the devastating effects of such patently vicious, yet extremely influential, thinking—no protection for black female rape victims—to adopt a position to rebut such nonsense. There are, however, some problematic conclusions that flow from countering the Cobbses of the world with the idea that no enslaved woman would ever want to consent to sex with a white man, and if there was sex, there was rape. First, rape is determined by the race of the partners without reference to anything we know about the individuals or the circumstances involved.

We will always know little or nothing about the vast majority of enslaved women and the scores of them who suffered rape. One might adopt a presumption about those anonymous women in deference to their unquestionable status as victims of slavery. What we know about the way slave women were treated generally should most inform our thoughts about their lives. We are on different terrain when there is information suggesting another possible understanding about what has gone on between one specific man and one specific woman. In those very rare cases, it would be intellectually unsound to ignore evidence, or skip over reasonable inferences, in order to return to the presumption based upon the experiences of the overall group of enslaved women.

The idea of the presumptive unwillingness on the part of all enslaved women may be added to the idea that there could never have been consent between Hemings and Jefferson to sexual relations because of the unequal power distribution between them. Whether Jefferson used violence or employed his well-known charming manner with women to win Hemings over, his power was such that one could never be sure of her true desires. Therefore, Sally Hemings when she was at the Hôtel de Langeac did not—because she could not—consent to sex with Thomas Jefferson. If power is the only issue, what we may call the bright-line "no-possible-consent rule" must also include all white men, not just the legal owners of women like Hemings. White supremacy, a force strong enough to have survived slavery, gave even white men who were not the legal owners of enslaved women wildly disproportionate amounts of power over them—far more than enough to force sex upon them without real consequence.

Depending upon how many slaves he had, and how the woman fit into his work scheme, a given slave owner might have had no incentive to seek redress for the rape of his slave, if the rape did not physically impair her ability to work. Her psychological pain, though deep, would not have excused her from the fields or whatever work she was doing. If the woman became pregnant and had a child, it added to her master's capital. No enslaved woman had the power to ensure punishment of her rapist, whether he was white, black, free, or enslaved. Differentiating between white slave owners and non–slave owners when considering an enslaved woman's capacity to consent cuts against the centrality of power in the activity and creates space for consensual interracial sex, so long as it was carried out with white men who had no economic interest in the woman.

There are even more problematic results of the no-possible-consent rule. It suggests that the individual personalities, life stories, and dignity of enslaved women are meaningless or, in the case of "dignity," even nonexistent. The rule also imposes a version of eternal childhood on them, no matter what their circumstances in life. Ironically, that choice, though made for different reasons, eerily echoes slave owners' construction of all enslaved people as "children" who lacked the ability and power to make rational decisions and who needed to be kept in slavery to protect them from the vagaries and harsh realities of living as free people in a hostile world.

An issue remains: How is it possible to get at the nature of a relationship between a man and a woman like Jefferson and Hemings when neither party specifically writes or speaks to others about that relationship or their feelings? Even written words can be quite deceptive and seldom tell the whole story, for people sometimes choose, for whatever reason, to tell a story of their lives that is rosier, or grimmer, than it actually was. In the absence of words, actions may be quite telling. An event in the life of Hemings's oldest sister Mary that took place at the same time that Hemings was in Paris dealing with Jefferson offers some insight into the varied nature of the veiled relationships between enslaved women and white men.

Back in Albemarle County

John Wayles's legacy, which had shaped so many of the Hemings family's experiences over the years, altered the course of their lives at the end of the 1780s. Marriage to Wayles's daughter made Jefferson a wealthy man. Unfortunately, his debts were almost equally staggering. What is more, while serving as executors to the Wayles estate, Jefferson and his fellow executors—the husbands of Martha's sisters—made a strategic error. They decided that there was no chance to repay Wayles's creditors with the income his estate generated through the sale of tobacco. That would take too long, and a good amount of the payments would go solely to pay the interest on the running balance of the debt. It was better, they felt, to sell assets and pay the debt off as quickly as possible, to avoid wasteful interest payments and settle their accounts. To effectuate their plan, Jefferson and his coexecutors, as was perfectly legal for them to do, divided the estate and took their share of land and slaves.[11]

What seemed like a good idea at the time actually had disastrous results that hurt Jefferson financially for many years afterward. Having given themselves the Wayles assets before the estate itself paid the creditors, the creditors could now hold each executor personally liable for repayment of the debts. Had they kept the assets within the estate, Wayles's creditors would have had to satisfy themselves out of the estate alone and could not have proceeded against the executors in their individual capacities. Problems with creditors chased Jefferson all the way to France, and in 1788 he received word that he owed more money on the Wayles debt than he had originally thought.[12]

Jefferson's problems with debt directly affected the Hemingses and all of the enslaved people on his plantations, and would for years to come. When he received word in Paris of his deteriorating financial situation, he saw three alternative ways to deal with the emergency: he could sell parts of his land, sell some of his slaves, or lease his slaves out. Landownership made Jefferson feel like a wealthy man, and he was loath to sell any part of his holdings, for he thought they provided the ultimate form of security for his family. He decided not to sell land. He also did not want to sell any slaves, "if the debts [could] be paid without" doing that. He characterized his "unwillingness" to take this route as being "for their [the slaves'] sake" Leasing them, he thought, was the better choice. He wrote to Nicholas Lewis, a neighbor who was overseeing Monticello in his absence, to proceed with arrangements, specifically stating that George and Ursula Granger and Elizabeth Hemings were not to be leased out at all, and that Martin and Robert Hemings could continue with whatever arrangements they had already made.[13]

Mary Hemings, Sally's oldest sibling, was hired out to a prosperous merchant named Thomas Bell, probably just before Jefferson's financial crisis. She moved, along with three of her children—Molly, Joseph, and Betsy—to Bell's home on Main Street. During the course of her time there, she and Bell began a relationship that lasted until his death in 1800 and produced two children, Robert and Sarah. The hiring out of young enslaved women must be viewed as something of a hazard for them. They were in unfamiliar surroundings with no social support, and if the man who hired them had no wife, it is difficult to imagine that the thought of sex did not at least cross his mind, or any of the minds of other men, enslaved or freed, connected to his household. Mary's younger sister Critta conceived her son James while leased to a man named David Wood. James Hemings's father is unknown. He was not listed in the Frm Book, so Jefferson did not own him.[14]

We do not know the circumstances surrounding the origins of the Bell-Hemings connection: Did he notice her and lease her for the purpose of making her his concubine, or was it something that developed after the leasehold? In either event, things moved quickly, for her children were born soon after she was leased. However matters started, in Mary Hemings we get a rare sense, from her own actions, of an enslaved woman's preferences regarding her choice of mate and the course of her life. Not long after Jefferson returned from Paris, Hemings specifically asked to be sold to Bell. Jefferson complied with her request and gave Nicholas Lewis, still overseeing his affairs, "power to dispose of Mary according to her desire, with such of her younger children as she chose."[15] In an ironic twist on his practice of selling or buying slaves to unite them with family members from other plantations, Jefferson sold Mary Hemings to unite her to her white partner and their children. He knew the couple's situation very well, and he acted in deference not just to the wishes of an enslaved woman but also to the desires of the white father of her children.

Within the extremely narrow constraints of what life offered her—ownership by Thomas Jefferson or ownership by Thomas Bell—Mary Hemings took an action that had enormous, lasting, and, in the end, quite favorable consequences for her, her two youngest children, and the Hemings family as a whole. She found in Bell a man willing to live openly with her, and to treat her and their children as if they were bound together as a legal family. She must have seen that capacity in him during the early stages of their time together. Over the years she would be able to compare notes on her life with a white man with her youngest sister, whom she honored by giving her own youngest daughter the name Sarah (also called Sally), known by the time of her marriage, in the early 1800s, as Sarah Jefferson Bell.[16]

As for Sally Hemings, one might understandably want to resist vigorously eighteenth-century notions about the fitness of fifteen- or sixteen-year-olds for sexual relations and hold fast to a present-day view that would see her as a child during all her time in France, no matter what she or the people of her time would have thought of that idea. Hemings's older sister Mary is a different matter. Nothing of what is known of Mary Hemings and the way she lived suggests that she was in any way childlike after her actual childhood ended. Under the no-possible-consent rule, her clear wish, expressed when she was well into her thirties, to live in union with Bell would be ignored, as if acknowledging this one woman's attachment to this one man would serve to minimize the prevalence of rape in America's slave societies. Anomalies existed in slavery as they do in every facet of the universe. By their very nature they do not destroy—but often highlight—the general principles from which they deviate.

Most interestingly of all, the no-possible-consent rule ratifies the historical equation of black women with degraded sex. During their lifetimes, if Sally and Mary Hemings had sex with black men, it was debased in some quarters because the men could not be their legal husbands. If they had sex with a white man, that was debased too. In the end, their sexuality and that of all other enslaved African American women could not (cannot) escape the appellation "degraded" by someone, for some reason—no matter what they thought of their relationships with particular men. The portrayal of black female sexuality as inherently degraded is a product of slavery and white supremacy, and it lives on as one of slavery's chief legacies and as one of white supremacy's continuing projects. Extreme racists spoke of what "all" enslaved women did and felt about sex and what "no" white slave owner ever did or felt. The opponents of racism and critics of slavery, deeply and justifiably concerned about the rape of enslaved women, tend to do the same in response, but from the other direction, and end up meeting their ideological antagonists on common ground: across-the-color-line sex with enslaved black women always equaled degraded sex.

While those sensitive to the plight of black female slaves like Sally and Mary Hemings paint a vastly more realistic picture of slavery than can be found in the ravings of the likes of Thomas R. R. Cobb, analyzing black-white sexuality during slavery strictly through the vehicle of edicts carries the risks inherent in all bright-line rules. These shorthand formulations, beneficial (and especially necessary in law) as easy-to-apply tools for setting uniform standards on important matters, hinder historical inquiry. They make it unnecessary to pay attention to details, discern patterns, and note sometimes even sharp distinctions between given situations, putting one on a more comforting voyage of reiteration rather than one of potentially disconcerting discovery.

To ensure that everyone gets the vital message that the rape of black women was endemic to slavery, the no-possible-consent rule says that whether Jefferson used force or charm on Hemings is of no great moment. Social history trumps individual biography. But one can safely say that for Hemings, who lived her life as a person, not a statistic, the difference between being forced, physically or psychologically, by a man and being charmed by him would have made all the difference in the world to her inner life, a thing that was and is, indeed, always of great moment.

Celia, Sally Hemings, and Mary Hemings

Though we are greatly attuned to the problem of inequalities of power in sexual relationships—teacher-student, employer-employee—those situations pale in comparison with the power differential between a master and a slave. To own another human being, in a legal system that gave great deference to the rights of private property, meant that a master's use of a slave for work, or for sex, was really his business. No case illustrates that more profoundly than that of Celia, another enslaved teenager whose life has achieved nearly iconic status, though not to the extent of Sally Hemings's. Celia, who had no known last name, lived during a different point in the progress of slavery in the United States than Hemings—the 1840s and 1850s—and she lived in a state, Missouri, that was more conflicted about the institution than Hemings's Virginia.[17] Her story is illustrative, however, for what it says about the brutal reality of the lives of enslaved women across the length and breadth of the American South. Celia's life was far more emblematic of the plight of female slaves than Sally Hemings's and considering it for a moment will help illuminate Hemings's situation in Paris and that of her sister Mary unfolding at the same time in Charlottesville.

Celia's master, Robert Newsom, was a widower, like Jefferson. He had two sons and two daughters. Unlike Jefferson, he was a very small-scale slave owner. Before he bought Celia, he had only five slaves, all male. He purchased fourteen-year-old Celia, evidently, for the sole purpose of sexual gratification. He raped her on the road home from the auction at which he had bought her. At some point, he built a house for her just behind his own. There followed five years in which Newsom continued to prey upon Celia until she decided that she could take it no longer.[18]

While at Newsom's farm, Celia became involved with George, one of the enslaved men on the plantation. George greatly resented Newsom, and he demanded that Celia stop allowing Newsom to come to her home for sex, a very strange request because George knew that Celia did not welcome Newsom's attentions and that their master was heedless of Celia's disdain for him. By the very clear terms and conditions of that society,

George's responses and actions made absolutely no sense. He was a slave, Celia was too, and Newsom was their legal master. George, however, was a man despite what the law and society's rules told him about what he was allowed to feel and do. Legal and social rules could never overcome his very human feelings—jealousy over, anger and possessiveness toward, a woman to whom he was attracted.[19]

One day, when Newsom told Celia he was coming later on that evening to the house that he had built for her, she warned him not to. Newsom, not surprisingly, paid no attention to this and said he would do as he pleased. When he came over that night and tried to approach Celia, she struck him with a large stick that she had brought into her home for this occasion. Newsom, she said later, seemed surprised by her attack but recovered and came toward her again. That time she landed a blow to the head that killed him. After thinking about how to dispose of Newsom's body, Celia decided to burn it in her fireplace, and spent the rest of the evening into the next morning doing just that. Later that day, she came upon Newsom's grandson playing in a nearby tree. She offered him some chestnuts if he would help her remove the large amount of ashes that had accumulated in her fireplace. The young boy eagerly agreed, and proceeded to gather up and then dump the ashes of what he did not know was his grandfather in the forest behind their house.[20]

During George's interrogation, Celia was identified as Newsom's murderer, and she confessed. Her court-appointed lawyers tried to do the best they could with a case in which a slave woman had confessed to the murder of her master. As an enslaved black person, Celia could not testify, but her counsel managed to get before the jury as much evidence about Newsom's sexual mistreatment of Celia as possible. Many in the surrounding community followed the case, and a good number of the predominately white citizens sympathized with Celia. They sympathized so much that a group of them broke her out of jail, with the aim of preventing the carrying out of the death sentence that had been imposed after she was found guilty of murder. At the end of the trial, the judge issued instructions for the jury, one of which stated that Newsom owned Celia, and if he came to her house to have sex, or for any other purpose, he had the right to have his demands complied with. Celia, as an enslaved woman, had no honor to protect and could not, therefore, resist his advances as a white woman could. Celia was hanged.[21]

That encapsulates the legal reality under which enslaved women lived across all the years of slavery, and there is no denying that many white slave owners took full advantage of that and raped black women with impunity. The question is whether having a degree of power, even total power, means that all holders of it will exercise it to the same extent or in the same way. Not *all* of anyone ever *always* does anything. We can know and keep in mind the obscene amount of power that slave owners possessed as we talk about that group of individuals who held, and those who lived under, that power. That cannot be the end of a responsible inquiry when thinking about specific people within those respective groups. One of the fascinating parts of Celia's story, for example, was the Newsom family's response. It would have been entirely possible for them, upon hearing Celia's confession, to have exacted some punishment against her before the authorities entered the picture. Missouri, like other states, prohibited the wanton killing of a slave, but if slaves died during the course of legitimate "correction," there was no sanction against the master.

If ever there was a moment when a slave owner was tempted to bring about a slave's death, it was upon hearing how Newsom died and how Celia involved his grandson in the disposal of his body. Some members of other slave-owning families faced with this story would have "corrected" Celia to death right away. The Newsoms did not, and not because they were thoughtful and caring people—the daughters were absolutely of no help to Celia when she complained about Newsom's behavior. They acquiesced in the torture of another human being. The sons, the most likely candidates for exacting the punishment, may just not have been the kind of people who could kill someone with their own hands. They knew Celia would be killed eventually, and they were not prepared to do that when they did not have to.

Killing is more extreme than rape, but the analogy is still instructive because it dramatically raises the issues of individual will and personality. The tremendously disproportionate amount of power that slave owners, and all white men, had over slave women made rape prevalent, but it was not universal. One simply cannot say that being a slave owner made every white man equally prone to wanting to have sex with slave women or to raping them, that every slave owner would rape any slave woman who refused his advances, or that every slave owner actively preferred his sexual encounters with slave women to be violent and unwanted. While these ideas capture something very real and basic about the nature of slavery, they do not account for every situation.

Celia could not have more emphatically demonstrated that she wanted no part of Robert Newsom. The touch of having the grandson unwittingly dispose of his grandfather's ashes was her curse on the generations, exacting a blood punishment for what Newsom had done to her. On the other hand, Mary Hemings took actions that show that she was amenable to being with a man who owned her just as surely as Newsom owned Celia. Sally Hemings's situation was different still from Celia and her own sister Mary's. Neither of those women ever had any personal recourse to law in their dealings with the men in their lives. To see Celia's life as being the same as the lives of Mary and Sally Hemings, solely because they shared a legal status, obscures the true horror of her daily existence and Robert Newsom's monstrous nature. Celia despised the man who owned her, and he wounded her immeasurably with his sadism. Had there been any route away from Newsom (if Missouri had had France's version of free soil) and the hell she endured living on his farm, Celia would have taken it without a moment's hesitation. In fact, she did take a route, one that she must have known would ultimately lead to her death—an act that shows the depth of her pain and her justifiable hatred of Newsom and his family.

It would be cruel, and nonsensical, to demand that every enslaved woman kill the master who was raping her, lest she be seen as consenting to the sex between them. What we have in Mary and Sally Hemings was something more than just a failure to kill or to resist actively (and foolishly) in some fashion. Both women gave strong indications, during the time of their relationships and after the men they lived with died, that their attitude toward the white men in their lives was different from Celia's, and for good reason. Thomas Jefferson and Thomas Bell were not to them what Robert Newsom was to Celia.

Both Hemings sisters had very firm internal understandings about how they might influence the course of their lives so that they could have what many of the women of their day, black and white, wanted—the ability, during their measured time on earth, to associate with a man who would take care of them and provide the best possible lives for their children with some chance of stability in an unstable world. Mary Hemings experienced firsthand what this instability meant. Although she found a place for herself with Bell, unlike her sister Sally, she experienced one of the harshest aspects of enslaved motherhood. As will be discussed in a later chapter, four of her six children were taken from her. The liaison with Bell ensured that any new children she had would be protected. The contingencies of the lives of Sally and Mary Hemings were such that Jefferson and Bell, for whatever reason—their personalities, their feelings about the women involved—supported these sisters' aspirations. As a result both women, in their own way, achieved exactly what they wanted. That their very elemental desires as women were met in the context of slave-master, black-white relationships is troubling because they mix something that seems almost sacred (the human desire for a secure family life) with something deeply profane (slavery).

The profanity of slavery does not define the entirety of the lives of enslaved people so that everything any one of them ever did, felt, or thought— everyone they touched, every situation in which they were involved, every connection they made—was degraded. There is an inherent danger in automatically transforming women like Sally and Mary Hemings into something they themselves may never have thought they were in order to convey a message about the overall character of slavery—to treat these women as vehicles rather than as persons. No individual's life, hopes, struggles, and dreams should be sacrificed to that instrumentalist end.

The title alone of the historian Walter Johnson's Soul by Soul[22] captures the enormity of slavery's inhumanity and suggests at least one way to go about illuminating it in the pages of history. Slavery was not just one, enormous act of oppression against a nameless, interchangeable mass of people. It was millions of separate assassinations and attempted assassinations of individual spirits carried out over centuries. When we encounter some of those spirits responding to their circumstances as human beings respond and using whatever means available to them to maintain or assert their humanity in the face of the onslaught, their individual efforts should not be minimized or ignored, because they could never alone have killed off the institution of slavery. That is far too heavy a load to place on people whose burdens in life were already almost unimaginably heavy.

Perhaps enslaved women like Sally and Mary Hemings who sought transformation of their lives through their associations with men were too few in number to care about, and talking of them gives us an unrealistic perception of the lives of women in bondage. On the other hand, there is both time and reason enough to explore every single part of black life under slavery, because each item contributes to our understanding of exactly how that institution and white supremacy shaped the American consciousness. No piece of the puzzle is too small or unessential to play its vital role in helping to bring that whole picture into view. Sally Hemings's story in France as she began a phase that would cover the next thirty-eight years of her life with one of the most important men in history is just such an item—small and anomalous, but still an instructive window into the workings of a world that no longer exists but whose legacies are still with us.

16

❧

"HIS PROMISES, ON WHICH
SHE IMPLICITLY RELIED"

JAMES AND SALLY Hemings had many months to contemplate their possible return to Virginia. Jefferson had, in fact, been preparing to go home long before he received official word that his request for a leave of absence had been granted; he had packed his bags to be ready to go on a moment's notice.[1] The Hemingses, as well as his daughters, were expected to return with him, and were likely as much on tenterhooks as he, for they, too, had to be ready to leave as soon as word arrived. When it was clear that return to America was imminent, Sally Hemings was pregnant, and her pregnancy created a problem that she and Jefferson had to address and sort out. Madison Hemings described what happened:

> But during that time my mother became Mr. Jefferson's concubine, and when he was called back home she was *enciente* by him. He desired to bring my mother back to Virginia with him, but she demurred. She was just beginning to understand the French language well, and in France she was free, while if she returned to Virginia she would be re-enslaved. So she refused to return with him. To induce her to do so he promised her extraordinary privileges, and made a solemn pledge that her children should be freed at the age of twenty-one years. In consequence of his promises, on which she implicitly relied, she returned with him to Virginia.[2]

There is much to consider about this very simple, yet powerful, explanation of what happened between Sally Hemings and Thomas Jefferson in France. First, it could only have been a shorthand version of all that actually happened, all the words that passed between these two. There is no way to know whether Hemings first thought of staying in France before or after her pregnancy, whether the struggle with Jefferson was a relatively short one or one that took place with varying degrees of intensity over the months that he hung in suspension waiting for permission to return to America. One thing is clear: the events described were not the heedless work of a passing conversation. The stakes were extremely high for both, but highest for Hemings. She knew all too well what slavery meant, and she lived with the hard knowledge that, were she to return to Virginia, every child from her womb would follow her condition. In this moment and place, she was in the best position she would ever be in to walk away from *partus sequitur ventrem* forever. Most important of all, she could do that without having to depend upon the benevolence of any one man—to trust Jefferson, over French law, with her life and the lives of her children.

Another option, of course, was open to Hemings. Abortion was not unknown to women of all colors and statuses in Hemings's time. Jefferson's daughter, Martha, once warned a sister-in-law that if taken in certain quantities, a particular medicine could induce an abortion, and doctors believed that some women, in this case white women, were using the medicine she referred to for that purpose. Masters sometimes suspected that enslaved women were controlling their fertility through contraceptives or abortion, perhaps with the aid of enslaved midwives who understood the dilemma their sisters faced. A moment normally associated with hope for the future (impending motherhood) was firmly embedded in the unhopeful present-day circumstances of their enslavement.[3]

We cannot know what Hemings thought about abortion for herself or whether the thought of not keeping her baby even crossed her mind. She was away from the network of her mother and female siblings who could counsel her and, as far as we know, without a network of women of color to confide in and discuss a matter so personal. Indeed, one wonders how much preparation Hemings had actually had for womanhood. She left Monticello for Eppington in 1783 when she was ten years old. If her mother went with her, she did not stay, for, as was noted earlier, Jefferson's correspondence with his gardener places Elizabeth Hemings at Monticello in February of 1785. At Eppington, Hemings's half sister

Elizabeth Eppes was the only known maternal figure in her life, and the nature of their day-to-day relationship is completely unknown. Between her time at Eppington and in France, Hemings appears to have gone through all the female rites of passage without the aid and comfort of the women who were her most natural allies—her mother, sisters, and other African American females.

Jefferson's comments on fertility rates among Native Americans may provide some insight into his likely thoughts about whether anything could be done about Hemings's pregnancy. While criticizing Native American men for the way they treated women, he posited that as a result of male behavior "they raise fewer children than we [black and white people] do." He went on to be specific about the nature of the "problem":

> The causes of this are to be found, not in a difference of nature, but of circumstance. The women very frequently attending the men in their parties of war and of hunting, child-bearing becomes extremely inconvenient to them. It is said, therefore, that they have learnt the practice of procuring abortion by the use of some vegetable; and that it even extends to prevent conception for a considerable time after.[4]

One gets the sense from that passage, in the context of his overall discussion, that Jefferson viewed abortion and contraception as things that people resorted to in extreme circumstances, measures undertaken to ensure the outright survival of a person or a community. What had happened with Hemings was a not uncommon feature of southern planters' way of life. This is how he had come to know her and her family. Though problematic, Hemings's pregnancy probably did not rise, in Jefferson's view, to the level of being trapped in a cycle of endless war and periodic famine.

Hemings's son described his mother as "implicitly" relying on his father, which goes to the mystery at the heart of Sally Hemings's life: Why would she trust Jefferson, and why would she, under any circumstances, return to Virginia with him? Trading immediate freedom for herself and her progeny for a life at Monticello with him and a *promise* of eventual freedom for her children was not an even exchange. There was something in the gap between those two conditions—some desired prospect on the other side of the ocean—that motivated her.

Femininity and Echoes from the Past

It is all too easy to ignore how being female shaped Hemings's desires and expectations and focus in on the thing that makes her so different from us today: she was born enslaved. By the time they were in France together, Jefferson had already helped set the terms for the development of Hemings's view of herself as a female. As the authority figure at Monticello, he sent a strong message to her when he acted to protect what he considered to be the femininity of Hemings and her female relatives, while failing to show similar concerns for other enslaved women on his plantations. Hemings watched every female go to the fields at harvest time, except her sisters, mother, and whatever white females were at the plantation.[5] She learned from all this that, in Jefferson's eyes, she was a female to be protected from certain things, when most women of her same legal status received no protection at all. It is a cliché that revolutions in societies occur not at the point of maximum misery but during periods of rising expectations. The same can be said of individuals. Those who are taught to expect things often wind up thinking that they deserve whatever they have, and that they have the right to expect more.

Whatever Hemings felt about her status as a female, the dominant society placed enslaved women—actually all black women in her time—outside of eighteenth- and nineteenth-century conceptions of "the feminine." Their identities and prospects were aligned with those of the males alongside whom they worked. As scholars have noted, the "slave" in America has been constructed as male.[6] Discussions of resistance and agency among enslaved people—when individuals defied authority or exploited cracks within the system to alter some terms of the master-slave relationship—emphasize stereotypically male behavior and do not usually include the actions of enslaved women that were outgrowths of their femininity.[7] The femininity (womanhood) of enslaved women is most often portrayed through their status as mothers, victims of rape, or degraded sexual objects. Hemings embraced the first role and sought, with ultimate success, to protect herself in it. She apparently did not see herself in either of the last two roles, which puts her into something of a historical and cultural bind, trapped between both gender- and race-related stereotypes that inhibit nuanced considerations of her life.

Patriarchal societies often separate women into categories of wives, potential wives, and whores. That we have yet to move fully beyond this has implications for the way Hemings and her life with Jefferson are viewed in modern times. With no access to legal marriage, the indispensable ingredient to respectable femininity for sexually active white women, Hemings is almost inevitably marked for degraded womanhood. Her use of Jefferson's attraction to her to seek and receive benefits from him would not, in a traditional formulation, be considered an exercise in respectable will, because it resulted neither in formal freedom nor in marriage. She would be viewed differently had she used her femininity and sexuality to "marry" and have seven children with a black man. Even though her marriage would have had no legal validity, and she would have remained enslaved, our modern notions of humanity would grant her a safe harbor from debased womanhood. Operating with Jefferson—a white man in a world run on white supremacy, and her master in a slave society—Hemings is in problematic territory all around.

Hemings's use of her femininity does not fit the conventional conception of either an act of conquest (in her society, a white man taking an enslaved woman) or an act of rebellion (a black man taking a white woman). For women's sexuality is most often portrayed as an act of submission—forced or acquiesced in, but submission and surrender nevertheless. The sex act is *done* to the woman. Being the object of an action is the very opposite of resistance, defined as aggressive acts or direct confrontation on some varying level that turns the master into the "object" acted upon. The motherhood that often comes with sex—the searing, life-defining (life-threatening) responsibility for carrying, bearing, and nurturing the next generation—is often sentimentalized. It is seldom, if ever, given the weight of, or glorified in the manner of, brutal conquest or even feckless rebellion usually associated with males.

Throughout history, women of all cultures, races, and statuses have been expected (and forced) to deploy their motherhood and sacrifice their children, in service of whatever male project, conquest or rebellion, is on the table at any given moment. That many women, because of their unique experiences and responsibilities—their vulnerability to their children, their senses of family—may have had other priorities or a completely different understanding about how best to conduct themselves in a time of social or cultural crisis has seldom been deemed important. Women's work has never been taken so seriously as men's work—unless, of course, it resembles men's work.

Because she is ineligible for the mantles of respectable womanhood, conqueror, or rebel, there is no ready vocabulary to describe the young Hemings in Paris who decided to return to America with Jefferson beyond that of presumptive rape victim—so traumatized beyond the power of reason that she did not know better than to negotiate with and trust her rapist—or collaborating whore. One suspects that even an enslaved woman who decided to kill her children rather than have them be slaves (again violence, destruction, or direct conflict as the essence of resistance) might receive more grudging respect than a woman who saved her children, and the rest of her line, from slavery by agreeing to be the partner of the man who held her in bondage. This is likely so even if, in her eyes, she was making the kind of rational calculation that women, at all levels of society, have very often made when considering the pros and cons of a life with a particular male. However dramatic (and perhaps quasi-romantic, at least from afar), infanticide was contrary to what most enslaved women saw as their duties to their children.[8] A far more telling view of their sense of responsibility is that when women ran away from slavery, they almost always ran with children in tow and, therefore, were far less successful at escaping than male slaves, who tended to run by themselves.[9]

One knows infanticide occurred, but one can scarcely fathom the pain of a mother who felt compelled to kill her child rather than give him or her up to the slave system. There can be no more graphic statement about slavery's evil nature, and the hopelessness it could engender, than having the giver of a life end the life given. The mother "saves" the child at enormous cost to herself and is redeemed from the sin of killing by her own deep suffering. Hemings, described by her son as having been well treated by Jefferson, and by one contemporary commentator in the 1800s as "pampered," is ineligible for such self-immolating redemption. She did not lose her children in a show of resistance born of utter hopelessness. Instead, she wanted to be (and got to be) in the position to experience their childhoods and prepare them for their lives as adults in which she knew they would be free people.[10]

Even without Jefferson's intervention, it is doubtful that Hemings thought being a slave was more at the core of her existence than being female; she could cease to be the one, never the other. Their numbers were still small when she was growing up, but there were free black people in Virginia, and their numbers would grow in the years after she returned to America.[11] The world sent her a very definite and hard message about enslavement at the same time as it conveyed another powerful message about what was to be her role in life as a woman—partner to a man and a mother. Those roles were tenuous because the law did not protect her in either of them. They were not, however, meaningless to her.

Having a child was perhaps the most serious matter that confronted women. Females who faced motherhood during Hemings's time— enslaved, free, black, white, and red—confronted the immediate issue of surviving the ordeal of pregnancy. They knew that even if they survived, at least some of their children would likely die because no society had figured out how to save its children from deadly childhood diseases that are of little import in the developed world today. The death of children was not the only stalker of slave mothers and potential mothers like Hemings. She and other enslaved women faced the added, unspeakable reality that they could be separated from their children by sale. Above all of slavery's depredations, the separation of children from their families crystallized the system's barbarity so clearly that slave owners claimed that it rarely happened or spent endless time talking about how loath they were to do it—just before they did it. While enslaved women knew that nothing could be done to ensure that they would never lose children to early deaths, and that this tragedy could affect all women, separation from children by sale happened *only* to them. That shaped their identities as women. Hemings, like other enslaved girls, must have dreamed of a future in which her motherhood would never be blighted by such a moment.[12]

THERE IS A more elusive set of influences to consider when thinking of the development of Hemings's expectations about her relationship with a man. Although a child of both Africa and Europe, who grew up surrounded predominately by European culture and values, Hemings had a connection to African culture that was actually quite close. She was raised by a woman whose mother was an African. We do not know how long Elizabeth Hemings had her mother, but parents can transmit cultural information about proper sex roles very early on in the lives of their children. Even if she was without her mother, Hemings grew up in a time and place where African women were very much present. The always entrepreneurial John Wayles was importing them, selling some, and keeping others. While the intermixture with Europeans had altered the family's African features, one doubts that all traces of African culture, conscious or unconscious, had been expunged from the family after only one generation. This is particularly so since the Hemingses' African heritage came through a woman, who as a mother in those days was primarily responsible for the care of her child, and was in a better position to transmit culture—language, religious beliefs, and values—to her children than a father was.[13]

Without precise knowledge of where Hemings's grandmother came from in Africa, it is impossible to say specifically what attitudes would have been passed down from mother to daughter to granddaughter about the proper place of females in relationship to men. Africa was and is a land of enormous cultural diversity. There were, however, some points of commonality across the ethnicities that were most typically part of the Atlantic slave trade. Women on the African continent were defined very much by their family relations and marital status, and they acquiesced in rules in order to gain the important status of wife, which led to the equally important, and perhaps even more important, status of mother in Africa's many matrifocal societies.[14]

Regarding the question of who would be the father of her children, Hemings, like girls of every race and status, had to consider what type of man she would end up with in life. Having sex with a man and going to death's door in order to bear children by him was thought to be a woman's duty. It was not an enterprise entered into lightly by any woman who had the opportunity to shape that experience. Not just any man who came along would do. Just as one can safely assume that enslaved men sought the prettiest wives they could attract, enslaved women took notice of the sometimes small degrees of status that existed among the men of their community. Slaves' imaginations allowed them to play out in their own minds hopes and preferences about the future courses of their lives, even if the chances of bringing them to fruition were limited. Had she been free and white, with greater power and potential mobility, Hemings would have had access to a wider variety of partners for legal marriage. In reality, she had even fewer chances to choose among a range of partners than had her brothers, whose personal mobility was far greater than that of the average enslaved man, and greater still when compared with that of the average enslaved woman. Her brother Robert found his wife in Fredericksburg, Virginia, when he was there working on his own.[15]

As a general rule, enslaved males had far larger engagements with the outside world than females had, which meant that they could more easily pick partners from surrounding plantations and towns. In fact, men carried out most of the interplantation traveling to see spouses. Account records from local stores in several Virginia counties show that enslaved "men outnumbered women by a large margin as store customers" and were the chief buyers of products for their wives and children. Views about a woman's proper place and, most likely, the demands of children meant that slave women had fewer occasions than men to leave, or were less able to leave, their home plantations in search of spouses in towns or on other nearby farms.[16]

Had Hemings never been in Paris, her choice of mates at Monticello would have been perhaps even more limited than that of other enslaved women on the plantation. Her racial background contributed to her identity and undoubtedly affected her views about who would be attractive as a companion and as father of her children. Race and American slavery were so intertwined that it may be hard to imagine that any slave could have separated the two and developed a sense of self and a set of priorities that confounded the rules about the way those defined as "white," and those defined as "black" or "mulatto," were supposed to feel and think. In slavery and outside of it, members of Hemings's family—female and male—developed a practice of having children with, and marrying when that was available, people who looked something like themselves, which is what most people in the world tend to do.[17] Jefferson probably resembled Hemings more than the average male slave on the plantation did, in terms of hair texture, skin color, and eye color. This is not to say that she would never under any circumstances have welcomed a partner with skin darker than her own or tightly curled hair, as allowances must always be made for the vagaries of attraction. It is human beings we are dealing with, after all, and no one has devised a precise formula or foolproof predictor of personal taste, and black couples and families come in all shades.

Although Hemings was probably not thinking in strictly legal terms about the racial makeup of the child she was carrying in Paris when she was deciding whether to come home with Jefferson, Virginia statutory law on racial categorizations, as Jefferson noted many years later, would make all of her children by him legally white. We know Hemings wanted to free her children from slavery, and Jefferson's actions show he wanted that as well. No one has ever said that Hemings thought it important to free them from blackness, too. However, that is exactly the route that three of her four children took when they left both slavery and the black community to live as white people. The one child of hers who did remain in the black community, Madison Hemings, married a woman who was fair-skinned enough that some of their children were able to pass into the white world. We do not know whether the Hemings-Jefferson offspring were raised to do that, but it would not be surprising, particularly given their father's stated values, if that was a part of a plan or at least a very strong hope.

While it is perfectly acceptable not to want one's children to be slaves, the notion of escaping from blackness may raise some hackles today, a reaction, it must be noted, that comes from the relative safety of the twenty-first century. It also comes after more than a century of the one-drop rule adopted in the wake of the South's defeat in the Civil War. In the decades following the end of slavery, southern whites became far more strident about racial classifications than they had been in Hemings's and Jefferson's time. The legal rule was supposed to send a message about the "contaminating" nature of blackness. Instead, blacks absorbed the concept and used it to forge political, if not always social, cohesion among themselves. This way of operating eventually turned blacks in the United States into a force to be reckoned with in ways unknown in other parts of the black diaspora (Brazil, for example) where the putatively "enlightened" sliding-scale approaches to race have effectively choked off political and social assaults on the doctrine of white supremacy. Frederick Douglass was clear about what the American linkage of race and slavery taught people of African origin like Sally Hemings years before the legalized one-drop rule, and this recognition explains how blacks of all shades were able to come together so forcefully in the nineteenth and twentieth centuries to work for racial justice for people of color. Douglass wrote,

> The father might be a freeman and the child a slave. The father might be a white man, glorying in the purity of his Anglo-Saxon blood, and his child ranked with the blackest slaves. Father he might be, and not be a husband, and could still sell his own child without incurring reproach if in its veins coursed one drop of African blood.[18]

Sally Hemings knew this and certainly would not have thought of herself as a white person, because she was not. But the political uses of black solidarity across the various shades, hair types, and facial features of all people with differing degrees of African ancestry, a very modern consciousness, would not necessarily have been available to her either.

Blacks in the eighteenth century who were in the position to do so—religious figures and community leaders in urban areas of the North, for example—did make appeals to people of African origin on the basis of their heritage. Free people joined organizations and secret societies that promoted black solidarity, and slaves felt loyalty to one another because of their shared oppression. Even with that, eighteenth-century people of African origin, like Hemings, did not have the same sense of African American identity as blacks in the twentieth and twenty-first centuries.[19] They could see themselves as black ("Negro" or "colored" the more common usage) and yet have a completely different understanding of what that actually meant in terms of how they should go about their personal lives. There was not then, as is there is not now, one way to be black.

Eighteenth-century African Americans were themselves from Africa or were, like Hemings, the recent descendants of people who had come to America as members of different ethnic groups with no idea that they were supposed to be part of a single entity called the black "race." That was an invention of whites. The process of melding together African people of diverse origins took place over time, driven, in part, by white society's need to destroy African identities so that blacks would fit more easily into the slave society they were creating on the American continent. The historian Michael A. Gomez emphasizes that slaves' "embrace of race . . . was not imposed upon the community but was a concept suggested by the logic and reality of the servile condition and adopted and fashioned by those of African descent to suit their own purpose."[20] That is certainly true. It is also true that, had it been left up to them, most Africans probably would have preferred to maintain even more of their distinctive ethnic identities than they were able to under the tremendous pressure from whites to give them up.

The Hemingses were in a more complicated position, with even fewer reasons than people who were "all black" or "all white" to believe in a world of fixed, bipolar racial categories. While they understood and accepted that they were part African, identity seems to have been a plastic rather than a static thing for them. Unmoored from any one racial destiny, their line could extend through blacks or through whites. Madison Hemings spoke openly of his "full-blooded" African great-grandmother without a trace of discomfort, and even with a touch of pride, when he did not have to mention her at all, much less emphasize her African heritage and that she may have come directly from the continent. She appeared right along with his English and Welsh forebears as a defining part of his heritage. At the same time he pointed to, and mildly disparaged, his sister Harriet's decision to marry a white man and live totally in the white world, which in American society required leaving blackness and, painfully for him, her family behind.[21]

Attitudes about race clearly played a role in this as well. The young Sally Hemings had been in a society where blackness, slavery, and a degraded legal and social status were inextricably linked. To be black, even to be free and black, was to live in a world with extremely limited horizons. Yet her sister had been married to Jefferson. She among all enslaved people would have felt the arbitrariness of the link between a notion of race and a severely restricted status. Life in France enlarged Hemings's sense of entitlement and belief that she should have some hand in shaping her future and that of her offspring.

We have the advantage today of knowing that the American story of blackness, slavery, and second-class status was going to end—or at least that slavery would end. We also have the example of a black community that has, by and large, bound itself together as a culture despite differences in skin color. It really has been left to specific individuals and families to decide how seriously they will adhere to color consciousness despite its patently obvious links to white supremacy.

As far as young Sally Hemings knew, the link between any trace of blackness and an assured diminished life might continue into the indefinite future. There was nothing on the horizon visible to her in France to suggest that matters would change in her lifetime or that of her children. She could not likely have foreseen that there would come a day when the words "black" and "power" or "black" and "beautiful" would flow naturally together and have a positive meaning and purpose that could direct the course of African American life. Under the circumstances of Hemings's life, given her society and her family history, what type of man would be most able to end slavery for her children along with all the problems associated with being a person with black skin in America? If not Thomas Jefferson, who? She may have thought him as good a white man as any other, perhaps even better in some ways. That was a judgment to ponder.

Calculating the Odds

Contingencies drive the making of history on scales large and small. To speak of the inevitability of any historical event or outcome is to ignore this salient fact. The same can be said of individual lives. Through a series of events, planned and unplanned, Sally Hemings was not in America when she had to think about what Jefferson offered. Unlike the vast majority of her enslaved cohort back in Virginia, freedom was within her grasp, and she ended up using the unique opportunity she possessed, not as an end in itself, but as a starting point for a discussion with the man who wanted to take her home with him. That Jefferson desired that at all, a further contingent element in Hemings's life, gave her leverage under their particular circumstances. Another man might not have cared enough to try to persuade her or would have dared her (and her brother) to do their worst: take their claim to the Admiralty Court. Hemings's discussion with Jefferson would have been meaningless if the pair had been in, for example, South Carolina and she had attempted to take her freedom and refuse to return to Virginia unless Jefferson assured her that he was going to provide what she thought would be a good life.

Any psychological influence Jefferson exercised over Hemings and her family was not total. Whatever he was to her back in Virginia, she had the will to challenge him in France—a very bold thing for a sixteen-year-old to try. Her gambit might not have worked on a man with a different personality—another contingency that shaped her life. It mattered greatly that Hemings was talking to Jefferson, a man who abhorred conflict, especially face-to-face. She probably knew this by the time they talked about returning to Virginia. She had had to pay close attention to him all her life, just as other enslaved people had to pay attention to the people who owned them. Living daily under the power of individual men and women, enslaved people could ill afford to see and deal with their owners as if they formed one, undifferentiated monolithic class. Timid men held slaves just as surely as overly aggressive men held them. Some slave owners were extremely intelligent, while others were as dumb as posts. Some preferred to fashion themselves as benevolent, while others were sadistic and reveled in their sadism. The quality of slaves' lives—if not their very lives—depended upon developing a sophisticated and pragmatic view of slave owners, and of white people in general. They knew how far they could go in exploiting, resisting, or relying upon the variable personal tendencies of both.

Hemings had not only her own observations of Jefferson to draw upon; a wealth of family history supplemented her knowledge. Whether she had had time in her young life to learn this fact about him or not, the truth is that few things could have disturbed the very thin-skinned, possessive, and controlling Jefferson more deeply than having persons in his inner circle take the initiative and express their willingness to remove themselves from it. To have this come from a young female, the kind of person he thought was supposed to be under the control of males, whether they were enslaved or not, was likely doubly upsetting. While Hemings was an item of property with a dollar value that he would have lost had she remained in France, Jefferson spent more money remodeling the various residences he rented in Paris, and later in New York and Philadelphia—investments he knew he was going to walk away from and leave to the landlord—than Hemings was worth to him in strictly monetary terms. This challenge was a far greater threat to his self-esteem and emotions than to his wallet. He had great confidence in his ability to charm and in his capacity to bring people to his side and keep them there. As we will see, he took her brother Robert's successful bid for freedom personally as if the man's willed separation from him were a failed connection of some sort, instead of a completely understandable desire for personal autonomy.

Her behavior suggests something of Hemings's own confidence—or vanity—that she believed she could hold Jefferson to his promises over what would be a very long period. Twenty-one years from 1789 was an eternity for a sixteen-year-old. Other children would extend the years. Then again, Hemings was a young person without the benefit of personal experience to provide a chastening dose of reality about how devastating to her and her children it would be if she turned out to have made the wrong calculation about Jefferson's character. She had to trust that he understood and valued what she was giving up by coming back to Virginia, and she staked both her and her children's futures on that critical belief about him.

According to her family story, with nine-year-old Hemings in the room, Jefferson promised his wife, Martha, that he would never marry again. Seven years had passed, and he still had no new wife, a long time by the standards of that day. As Hemings well knew, a Jefferson promise not to remarry was hardly a promise never again to have female companionship in his life. If Hemings thought Jefferson would continue to abide by his pledge, his desire that she return with him and talk of making a life with her made sense. She would be secure in her place at Monticello. No woman not already known to her would have any influence over the course of her life.

As the product of an interracial union, as a resident of a plantation where such unions were common, and as a Virginian, Sally Hemings knew how society at large would view her life at Monticello once she returned from France with Jefferson. Whites would, of course, be disdainful. One can imagine what other enslaved people at Monticello might have thought if they learned of the terms upon which she had given up her chance for freedom; as Michael A. Gomez has shown, the enslaved community tended to respond to their fellow slaves on the basis of how they conducted themselves. If upon her return Hemings presented herself as enemy to fellow blacks, she would be viewed as such. If she was friendly and acknowledged a common link to them, she could be accepted.[22]

Whatever the outside world felt, Hemings was apparently determined to make the outcome of her life with Jefferson different from the outcome of her mother's life with John Wayles, who had died and left Hemings and her five siblings to the mercy of his legal white daughter and her husband. Despite Jefferson's attempts to ameliorate their condition, what seems to have motivated Hemings as she talked with him in 1789 was that she and her siblings were legally enslaved. Freedom was clearly the preferable state, and she wanted substantially more for her offspring than favored treatment under slavery. The historians Dianne Swann Wright and Beverly Gray have said that Hemings wanted to bring her children "out of Egypt," which in the end is exactly what she did.[23]

Hemings had other concerns in addition to her children's future. Jefferson's promise to treat her well also figured in her decision to return with him. He knew what he had to say to her, and offered her a life as the companion to a wealthy and powerful man whom she knew well and could trust (he said) that he would do what he promised to do: take care of her in a place where she felt comfortable—at Monticello with her family—and provide something she very much desired for her children. He saw himself as offering what he thought most other young women at the time almost certainly wanted, a stable relationship with an acceptable man. What Hemings could have envisioned as a good life, and what Jefferson knew of that, must be measured by the kind of life that was actually possible for her to have. She knew that in Virginia marriage would be a legal impossibility for her, whether she was paired with Thomas Jefferson or anyone else.

The historian Brenda Stevenson has noted the methods that nineteenth-century planters used to promote matrifocal families within slave plantation communities, "routinely identifying the child's parentage solely with the mother, often denying any acknowledgement of the father's role—biological, emotional, social, or material"[24]—effectively erasing fathers from the lives of their children and diminishing their status as husbands. The extremely patriarchal Jefferson took a different route. He definitely saw enslaved men as the heads of their households, an attitude likely to be well known within the enslaved community. His Farm Book listings of slave households begin with a male's name, followed by a female's, and then their children's. When they do not, as other sources indicate, it was because the father of the children was a white man, and could not be listed as living within the woman's household, or the women had "abroad" marriages with men who did not live on Jefferson's farms. Perhaps even more telling about his attitude is that in the separate listing of births during any given year, after he wrote the child's name, he put the parents' names next. When the man's name was included (that is, when he was black and lived on one of Jefferson's plantations), it was customarily placed first. Writing of intact enslaved families in other documents, he referred to the man first and then "his wife" and children. When Jefferson contemplated blacks' future outside of slavery, he spoke of black men—not black women—as the prime movers of their society.[25] To him men of all races were natural leaders; women of all races, natural followers.

Hemings knew how Jefferson viewed women, and implicitly understood that if she were paired with an enslaved man she would have two men over her: her enslaved husband and Jefferson. She would be one step removed from the man who held power over both of them, and Jefferson would have no personal stake in her or the children she bore with another man. Paired with a white workingman, or another white man in Virginia, Hemings would be in a virtually identical situation, though a white man could seek to buy her and their children if he wanted to. That is what the Charlottesville merchant Thomas Bell did with Hemings's sister Mary, but not until after Hemings returned from France. None of the other white men with whom her sisters were involved took this route. Jefferson would have to agree, and he might not if he received a better offer or simply wanted to be recalcitrant, as Francis Eppes IV had been when Hemings's grandfather sought to buy her grandmother as a child.

The resolution of her conflict with Jefferson allowed Hemings to go home with the knowledge that she had a one-on-one relationship with the ultimate power at Monticello. The connection to John and Martha Wayles—an accident of biology over which she had no control—would no longer define her, and her family's, ties to Jefferson. She was now more than just the sister of Jefferson's wife and the aunt to his legitimate children. She would, in fact, be the mother of children he fathered. Their futures, and hers, now depended upon the dynamic of her interactions with Jefferson, which she could seek to structure directly. Her brothers and sisters were not just the biological aunts and uncles of Jefferson's legal family; they would be the aunts and uncles of the children in his second family with her. Her siblings would now see him as the father of their nieces and nephews. She herself would always be for Jefferson the woman who had given up something of enormous value on the basis of his promises. He was in moral debt to her. With all of this, the focus of the Hemings family's existence at Monticello would shift to Sally Hemings herself in a way that gave her a measure of influence over her life and the lives of her children, siblings, and extended clan.

Like other enslaved people when the all too rare chance presented itself, Hemings seized her moment and used the knowledge of her rights to make a decision based upon what she thought was best for her as a woman, family member, and a potential mother in her specific circumstances. She did not see Jefferson as the same type of man as her father, who had left his children in slavery, or she would never have trusted him. Elizabeth Hemings's fate would not be her own. Unlike Celia trapped on an isolated Missouri farm with Robert Newsom, with no family support, and no surrounding culture and law in her favor, and unlike the overwhelming majority of enslaved women back in Virginia, Hemings had room to maneuver. She was in the position to consider whether Jefferson was a man she could spend the rest of her life having children with or take her freedom in France, be rid of him forever, and perhaps find someone else.

Hemings was young, and she was taking a very risky and, some might say, foolish chance. Had she been a free white girl on the threshold of embarking upon a legalized relationship with a man of whatever age, she could have consulted her mother and father. The most obvious patriarch in her life was the one asking her to commit to living with him. If Elizabeth Hemings had been there, or if she had been able to communicate with her daughter about this, she could have advised her that the safer route to protecting her freedom and achieving it for her offspring would be to go to the Parisian Admiralty Court and seek refuge in its established law and custom rather than "implicitly" relying on Jefferson's promises.

Jefferson and Women, the Hemingses and Their French Options

Whatever one thinks of Sally Hemings's decision to trust Jefferson on this critical point, she had an opportunity, entirely lost to historians, to have seen him face-to-face when no one else was around and to make a judgment, on the basis not only of his words but of his demeanor, about the seriousness of his sentiments. Hemings and all her relatives knew a private Jefferson that we do not know. We know a Jefferson of the *Notes on the State of Virginia*, talking about the need to remove blacks "beyond the reach of mixture" and a late in life letter in which he disparages the very kind of relationship that he was so intent upon entering into in France and lived in for almost four decades.[26] We know something else just as well, or should by now: one must take with a grain of salt an individual's public pronouncements criticizing certain sexual behavior, particularly when offered gratuitously. For such statements can be as much about that person's inner struggle with socially forbidden private preferences as about their desire to voice a heartfelt sentiment for the benefit of mankind. They can also be about an attempt to deflect attention from an area where he or she is vulnerable. Even genuinely stated beliefs do not define the scope of private activities. People do things in private, have thoughts and feelings, that they do not want others to know about, and may honestly feel should not be replicated by members of society at large. "Do as I say, not as I do" is a well-known prescription in life, and Jefferson, like many human beings, was sometimes prone to offering it.[27]

Unlike other important men in history whose personal lives yield a great amount of information about their dealings with the opposite sex, Jefferson is a relative cipher. The woman with whom he spent the largest number of years simply could not be written about at all. Their son Madison, a very private man, gave limited details about the nature of his parents' relationship. Through some unknown months of courtship and ten years of marriage, Jefferson's wife left no letters that would reveal her assessment of him as a suitor or lover, or if she did, he destroyed them. He emerges as a father in his letters to and from his white daughters that, unsurprisingly, do not mention any romantic relations at all. The people who drew what has become the most familiar portrait of the private Thomas Jefferson were his grandchildren, who knew him best when he was an elderly man. Like most grandchildren, they could not easily, and probably would not even have wanted to, construct an image of their grandfather as a younger man in the grips of an attraction to a young woman who was not their grandmother. Because of their recollections and correspondence, the domestic Jefferson—as opposed to the public political figure—who comes most immediately to mind is a kindly, doting grandfather, living at a Monticello permanently suspended between 1809 and 1826, the years his grandchildren came of age and formed their most vibrant childhood memories of him and the place. Kindly, doting grandfathers can be sexual beings, too, but that is not their usual presentation to their grandchildren.

The closest we get to seeing Jefferson as a man in pursuit of a woman is in his correspondence with Maria Cosway. The letters that passed between them, always in danger of being read by her husband, give us some information about how he maneuvered in that realm, though not enough. Even if more explicitly revealing, they would not be a reliable guide to how Jefferson acted when he was serious about a union with a woman, because he could never really have been serious about Maria Cosway as a lifetime partner. That we have their letters at all supports this.

Compare his treatment of Cosway with that of his wife. As far as we know today, Jefferson kept no cache of letters to and from Martha Jefferson for posterity to pore over, interpret, and misinterpret. He wanted what happened between them to stay irretrievably private precisely because she was so important to him. The things that he valued most, that affected him most deeply and revealed his greatest points of vulnerability, he kept closely to himself. Jefferson wanted his relationship with Cosway to be a known part of his story in France; to appear before the world as a gallant and courtly lover in a vignette conveniently set far from home, community, and responsibility. Though Jefferson cared deeply for Cosway, it is highly probable that with every positive response to his attentions she confirmed her basic unsuitability as a woman he could take seriously on a long-term basis.

True to the conventions of his time, Jefferson believed that a wife, in contrast to the all too cosmopolitan Cosway, should be in the home, a place where a man's exclusive right to his wife's sexuality could be better protected. With Maria Cosway, Jefferson was caught in the conundrum faced by adulterous partners the world over: if Cosway could not be faithful to her present husband, as her affair with Jefferson indicated, how could Jefferson ever be sure that she would be faithful to him? That rather obvious question would have occurred to a man who called sex "the strongest of all the human passions"[28] and tended to view women as temptresses. Fidelity, so important to Jefferson, was a virtue that he could demand and expect from the virginal sixteen-year-old half sister of his deceased wife. If he could persuade her to come home, he could continue to own her—not in the metaphorical sense that one speaks of couples "owning" one another, but own her legally for the rest of his life. He did not have to rely on a marriage license or social shame to monopolize her sexuality, for she had much more to lose than a married white woman, like Cosway or one in Virginia who decided to stray. If she went outside of her relationship with him and put herself at risk of bearing another man's child, he could easily rationalize reneging on any promise he had made to her.

In the end, the word "husband" is the real key to the Cosway and Jefferson affair. Maria Cosway already had one. And unless Jefferson was prepared to take her away from her husband and live openly with her in adultery at Monticello—or become a very famous corespondent in a divorce action initiated because of an affair he started when he was in France on the business of the United States of America—Maria Cosway could only have amounted to an intense but fleeting diversion for Jefferson. The situation with Sally Hemings was far more serious for him than the Cosway interlude. He had two daughters whom he loved dearly. Yet, while speaking with Hemings of these matters, Jefferson knew that he was about to embark on a course of action that might hurt his daughters emotionally and, at the very least, perhaps even change the way they thought about him. Hemings was between sixteen and seventeen years old. Jefferson had fathered with his wife, Martha, at least six children, and Hemings's pregnancy showed that fertility was not a problem for him. It would not have been at all impossible for Hemings to have given birth to fourteen children as her mother did. As things turned out, she gave birth to seven.

JEFFERSON'S VISION FOR his life at Monticello with Hemings was far too weighty a matter to have been motivated by trivial, fleeting concerns. If Hemings accepted his vision, their relationship could not be kept secret. Everyone who lived there and interacted with them would know the realities.

Many years later, Israel Gillette, who had been enslaved at Monticello, said that he knew of Hemings's relationship with Jefferson from his "intimacy with both parties."[29] His recollections suggested that it was not just the presence of children who looked just like Jefferson—as his white relatives described them—but the way Hemings and Jefferson treated each other, Hemings's access to Jefferson, that told him what they were to each other.

One might say that Jefferson could expect his daughters to become inured to this type of relationship because their mother had experienced a similar one. Though this arrangement was a feature of life in his country, and families developed ways of dealing with it, it was not clear in 1789 that Patsy and Polly would be as sanguine about his connection to Hemings as their mother apparently was about John Wayles and Elizabeth Hemings. Not all white women reacted calmly upon learning that the men in their lives were involved with enslaved women. Indeed, a household in which a husband or father had taken a slave mistress could become the site of internecine domestic warfare conducted on levels low and high. Some women—wives and daughters—exacted reprisals against the women themselves—arguing for their sale and the sale of any children they bore. They, and other family members, fought the bequests their male relatives gave to the children they had with enslaved women. Sometimes silent acquiescence was the tack. "Unable to do anything about it, many a Southern white woman feigned ignorance of illicit, interracial relationships, at least those that occurred under their own roof."[30]

It is inconceivable, however, that on the self-contained and isolated farms and plantations throughout the South that any but the most dense white mistresses of households did not know when their fathers, husbands, or sons were having children with women on the plantation. Women have often felt obliged to play dumb for men's benefit; that has never meant that they were actually dumb—particularly not about sorting out situations and relationships affecting their own personal lives in the domestic sphere that was their domain. The nineteenth-century southern diarist Mary Boykin Chesnut's much quoted observation captures the spirit of denial required in a racially based slave society as slave owners dealt with one of the chief hazards of their business: "any lady is able to tell who is the father of all the mulatto children in everybody's household but their own. Those she seems to think drop from the clouds."[31]

This was a delicate matter for Jefferson as well as Hemings. Once she gave in and came home, the power she had in France would dissipate. He, on the other hand, had to tread lightly while that power existed. Throughout his public career the people whom Jefferson enslaved knew who he was, particularly the ones in the closest physical proximity to him and the guests he entertained and the friends with whom he traveled. They made up at least part of his domestic staffs in every incarnation of his public career, from Williamsburg to Washington. The Hemingses and other slaves understood that he was a leader among the men of his society and was honored as a great man not only in his home state of Virginia but throughout the new country. His reputation as a champion of freedom and liberty and, in France, his antislavery writings were integral parts of his public persona. In the end, after he had lost everything, and they had been auctioned off to pay his debts, some who had been enslaved at Monticello still made excuses for Jefferson's failure to live up to his image, saying that the money and effort he spent founding the University of Virginia left him unable to free all of his slaves, turning what they normally may have thought of as fault into an exaggerated, if somewhat misplaced, virtue.[32]

Visitors to the Hôtel de Langeac toasted Jefferson as the "apostle of liberty" and made much of his progressivism in the face of those who wanted to maintain the status quo in society. Imagine the stir if a slave of the "apostle" had shown up at the Admiralty Court in Paris, forced there because he had refused her request for freedom. Jefferson's image, which he so assiduously cultivated throughout his entire public career, would have been left in tatters. Not only would it have damaged him in the eyes of abolitionist friends (what would Lafayette think?); much more importantly, it would have embarrassed the United States at a very critical moment. The American revolutionaries had taken huge sums of money from the French to fight their battle for freedom. As Jefferson noted, by the end of the 1780s those loans had become a source of tension between the French and Americans because the new nation could not repay the money in a timely fashion, money that the French treasury, already in bankruptcy but unwilling to say so formally, sorely needed.[33]

To have Jefferson, of all people, act in direct opposition to France's Freedom Principle so that he could keep control over a sixteen-year-old enslaved girl would have been a spectacle for the ages. The word "irony" does not even begin to approach doing the situation justice. If the court had gotten the chance to see her, all would have been revealed instantly. It would not have taken a Voltaire to figure out what was going on. That was an outcome to be avoided at all costs. His years-long failure to register both Hemings and her brother, as French law required, would only have added to the debacle. Aside from whatever he felt for her, the Parisian Admiralty Court and Jefferson's special position and reputation in France gave Sally Hemings latitude to say, "I will go home with you, but only on certain conditions." The irony of Jefferson's predicament with Hemings was even deeper, for he was intimately involved with freedom suits, having represented a number of individuals seeking freedom during his days as a young lawyer. He lost his most well-known suit, *Howell v. Netherland*, but he knew that whoever represented Hemings would have prevailed where he had not been able to for Samuel Howell.[34]

Jefferson may have pointed out to Hemings and her brother the potential problems they might face by remaining in Paris. But this was middle age confronting the well-known optimism and sense of immortality of youth that produces that thin line between recklessness and bravery. Sally was particularly young in comparison with James, but her age is not the only thing to consider. Some people are more easily frightened than others at every stage of life. We cannot assume that because Sally Hemings was born enslaved and female she had a fear-driven personality. Her initial determination to defy Jefferson indicates she did not. By this time, whatever sense of entitlement she had as a Hemings had been added to all her experiences to date—traveling across an ocean, living away from the Hôtel de Langeac on her own (twice), learning a new language, accompanying Patsy to social events, and being a handsomely paid employee. The last experience was probably the most important. She worked alongside other French servants at the Hôtel de Langeac and knew she could work elsewhere. The fashion of having African and mixed-race servants gave her an advantage if she sought work as a *femme de chambre*. Failing that, she might have worked as a seamstress, though that would have given her substantially less money for rent, food, and clothing for herself and her child. Thousands of slaves—male, female, young, and old—ran away from slavery with nothing but the clothes on their backs and the hope that something, anything, would turn up and be better than their lives under slavery. Even enslaved people in America filed freedom suits knowing that, if they lost, they would have to return to the homes of their victorious and potentially spiteful owners.[35] Human beings, especially the young, take chances when much is at stake for them.

Hemings did not have to sort these matters out by herself. Her brother's presence in the household raises the question of just whose idea it was to stay in France in the first place. Madison Hemings was speaking of his origins, and how he and his siblings came to be free four decades before the Civil War ended slavery. His mother and, to a degree, his father were the heroes of his story. He did not mention Uncle James, who had died in 1801, four years before he was born. What happened in France involved not just Sally Hemings. If she knew that slaves were supposed to be free in France, James Hemings, who had lived there more than twice as long as she, knew the law as well and most likely told his sister. This is not to say that Sally needed James to tell her that being free was better than being enslaved. It is to say that she should not be thought of as a person alone. Her brother, an intelligent and spirited man, was an invaluable asset, and the plan to stay in Paris was evidently a joint effort between the two.

The very creative twenty-four-year old James Hemings had already been putting himself in the position to stay in France even before his sister arrived. His hiring of Perrault to be his tutor should be viewed against the backdrop of one important fact of life for French servants: they were a highly ambitious lot. As we noted in chapter 11, French was a second language to the majority of them. The better French they spoke, the better jobs they got, and those seeking new or different employment often advertised their facility in French or other languages. Hemings, immersed in the culture of Parisian servants for over five years, observed firsthand their customs, struggles, and preoccupations. He was literate in English, and Perrault's lessons evidently included enough tuition in French to teach him to read the language at a basic level, certainly enough to read postings or advertisements for services that could give him a sense of what people were looking for in servants. Before he left slavery and Monticello, and turned the kitchen over to his younger brother Peter, he wrote out an extensive list of the cooking utensils in a firm hand with very few misspellings.[36] Working with Perrault was a substantial investment of money and time for the future that made little sense if he thought his future was exclusively in Virginia. His timing is instructive. He hired Perrault when he was near the end of this apprenticeship, after he had gotten along well enough to make it through several years communicating with his French teachers. Money was not the issue. Jefferson had been giving him that even before he became chef de cuisine. Seeking to improve his French grammar would not have improved his cooking skills so much as made him more attractive to potential French employers.

And then there was Paris' small community of color, concerned enough about the welfare of its members to pass information around about the status of blacks in the country. Sally Hemings had a special reason for thinking of this community. She did not likely consider staying in France without thinking of what the future might hold in the way of marriage and companionship. Although only around a thousand *gens de couleur* lived in all of Paris, the vast majority of them, concentrated in a small number of neighborhoods, were males in their late teens and early twenties—exactly suitable for a young woman approaching her seventeenth birthday.[37]

Some among those unattached men, victims of the heavily skewed ratio of black males to females, surely would have welcomed a young and attractive woman like Hemings, though she spoke French only as a second language. It was not altogether inconceivable that the well-to-do mixed-race sons of white colonial fathers were potential mates, their social standing within their own hierarchical communities notwithstanding. In most cases, their mothers or grandmothers had been slaves, and though her white father had left her no property, Hemings's chief asset, along with her good looks, was that she could easily have fit into their caste. Being American may have made her seem even more exotically attractive.

The law against interracial marriage was not always enforced, so white men were in the available pool of mates for Hemings as well. She could not have known this, of course, but not long after she left the country, the Revolution abrogated the prohibitions against intermarriage. Even after the law was restored during the Napoleonic era, the French version of the one-drop rule went in reverse: people who had any European ancestry were allowed to marry white partners without restriction.[38] The rigid class system, however, made a formal marriage with a man from the upper classes virtually impossible. The most Hemings could expect from a white man at that level of society was to become his mistress and remain in France or travel with him to a French colony in the West Indies, Indian Ocean, or Senegal.[39]

At some point, the maxim "The devil you know is better than the one you don't know" likely came into play. But had Hemings decided to break away from Jefferson and start a new life with her brother, she would have had the chance to be the mother of children who were free at birth and she could have had a legal marriage and the social respectability that would elude her totally in Virginia living with Jefferson. None of her children would have felt compelled to leave her, one another, and their family history behind in order to escape the racism of nineteenth-century America. The descendants of Thomas Jefferson's oldest son and youngest daughter are unknown to us because they knew they could not live safely as people of African origin in the country their father helped found.

History provides a clear picture of what was just around the corner for France in the coming decade, and what James and Sally Hemings might have faced had they remained in Paris with revolution imminent, and some violence was already under way. Patsy Jefferson recalled seeing the "sixty thousand citizens flourishing swords, scythes, and pruning hooks"[40] march in the streets of Paris, and both she and her father resorted to gallows humor about people losing their heads. The memory of the charged atmosphere and the tumult in the city stayed with her for decades. Sally and James Hemings were there for all of this, too. Neither they nor anyone else could have known just how difficult matters would become in France—that much of the society they knew would be swept away by the Terror. The kind of upper-class Frenchmen for whom James Hemings was most qualified to cook, and the women whom Sally Hemings could have attended, soon would be under siege or dead.

Robert Darnton has argued that the French Revolution unleashed "a sense of boundless possibility," giving "ordinary people" the idea that they could act to influence their fate instead of being merely consigned to it.[41] Sally and James Hemings were no ordinary people. They had been born slaves and were now in a place that offered an opportunity for a brand-new life. Like many enslaved people during the American Revolution, the Hemings siblings had reason to welcome the dramatic change promised by the first stirrings of the French Revolution. Rather than being frightening, the talk of upending rules and creating a new type of society was likely energizing to these two young people. Tradition and the status quo represented comfort and safety to privileged white people, but they held nothing for the Hemingses except the continuation of slavery.

While a conflagration of major proportions loomed in France, there is no reason to suppose that James and Sally Hemings would have fared better in Virginia's racially based slave society than in Paris even with all its revolution-inspired troubles. If they had stayed in France, they would have joined the ranks of people of all races and cultures who throughout human history have braved unknown territory and built lives for themselves amid hostile, isolated, and barren wildernesses—as well as forbidding, cramped, and chaotic urban environments. The risks of hardship and failure are inevitable facts of life for free people of any color. Courage was not foreclosed to either of them.

Jefferson, however, was a very persuasive man. As we will see, his leverage over James Hemings brought the young man back to the United States and, for a time, to Monticello, until his emancipation. As for Sally Hemings, one wonders whether her threat to stay in France for the sake of freedom was not, in the end, merely a ploy she used to get what she really wanted: to go home with assurances that she could expect a certain type of life at Monticello with the rest of the Hemingses and Jefferson, along with his "solemn pledge" that *partus sequitur ventrem* would end in her line forever.

17

❀

"THE TREATY" AND "DID THEY LOVE EACH OTHER?"¹

AT FIRST GLANCE the terse presentation of how Hemings and Jefferson resolved the standoff between them at the Hôtel de Langeac has the look of a deal between two parties who, if not exactly operating at arm's length, were at least bargaining in a manner that seems unworthy of a man and a woman with any true emotional bond between them. Their son's description of the agreement as a "treaty"² calls to mind diplomats from two foreign nations drawing up terms for the cessation of hostilities or forming an alliance for trade or united defense against a common enemy. This runs counter to romantic conventional wisdom about the way women and men act when they are emotionally attached to each other and are embarking on a life together. In that convention, a particular conception of "love" occupies center stage; it blots out all talk of things practical and utilitarian, as if their very mention would cheapen the value of any truly heartfelt sentiments existing between the man and the woman.

Because Jefferson was more powerful than Hemings, and a vastly more important actor in world history, the temptation to focus on his thoughts and likely feelings is great, as though his legal ownership of her in America obviated the need to consider her actions in France. She, a mere object of his power, could never have influenced him or the course of her life, in any way. The historiography of slavery has long since moved beyond the notion that slave owners were deity-like in their omnipotence and that slaves really were actual chattel, like pieces of furniture lacking consciences and will. It is now well recognized that within their admittedly limited sphere, enslaved people helped shape the contours of the master-slave relationship, both as actors and as reactors.[3]

Whatever her situation in Virginia, Hemings had a sphere of influence much larger in France; Jefferson, a much diminished one. His power as a master was not coterminous with his whiteness. Although Jefferson was white wherever he went, he did not carry the legal powers of a Virginia slave owner wherever he went. One cannot speak seriously about the meaning and application of law without addressing the always pivotal question of *jurisdiction*—when and where the law speaks. Virginia slave law did not speak in France. There was, then, no way for Jefferson to legitimately exercise the power those laws gave him. Just as he did not carry his power as a master everywhere, the Hemingses did not carry their Virginia-induced powerlessness as slaves to France as if their legal condition had been truly grafted onto their skin, as white Virginians tried to make it. There was no such thing as an immutable slave character that endured beyond geographical, political, social, and legal boundaries.

Problems remain as we try to recover as much as we can of Hemings and Jefferson, the flesh-and-blood individuals operating in those final months in France. Unexamined conventional wisdom inhibits clear assessments of this extraordinary pair. In modern times a marriage is often treated as proof that love exists between the two people who join in matrimony. That Hemings was born into a society that did not allow her to have a legal marriage confuses and makes it hard to see, and easy to disparage, the idea of love and, what we may call, authenticity in any bond she formed. With no law to serve as a guide for how to think of her relationship, we assume all was chaos or insignificance. There are other stumbling blocks: the assumption that all black-white sex under slavery was degraded per se, the idea that Sally Hemings, an enslaved woman, was simply too indelibly degraded to be considered "lovable" by a man like Jefferson, and that Jefferson, a slave owner, was simply too implacably evil for Hemings to have loved. Under these rules, the "treaty" their son described could not have grown out of any non-meretricious attachment-based or "decent" sentiment. These notions—operating together or on their own—make up the very complex American response to matters involving not only slavery but even more particularly race and gender.

Love and the authenticity it supposedly gives to relationships are inherently difficult concepts to capture in any venue, but there is no question that slavery complicates matters almost exponentially, given the moral, social, and political implications of such a discussion. For modern observers the glaring problem with the idea of love between a slave and master is that southern apologists for slavery, near the end of the institution and long afterward, set teeth on edge with their endless talk about "the love" that existed between black and white in old-time Dixie, as if affection between discrete individuals could ever mitigate the inhumanity of the southern slave system or affect an individual's overall commitment to white supremacy. Human beings, creatures with the capacity to observe and reason, understand the concept of "exceptions"—that persons, things, or rules can vary from an accepted norm. *"This black person, that white person, is different from all the others."* It is quite instructive that all the talk never extended to love between males and females like a Sally Hemings and a Thomas Jefferson, who were eligible to engage in what people of their day would have thought of as "normal" heterosexual intercourse.[4]

Very importantly for Hemings and Jefferson, if we look closely at how we think we know when love and authenticity exist between a man and a woman, and when we are firm in our understanding that it did not and could not have existed, we can see the almost hidden hand of the law and the very open hand of white supremacy leading us to exalt the humanity of whites and to seriously discount the humanity of blacks in much the same manner as was done during slavery. This becomes clear when we try to get at the nature of Hemings's response to Jefferson at the Hôtel de Langeac by comparing her unprotected status in her relationship with him to that of her sister Martha Wayles, who was protected in her relationship with the very same man.

The Cover of Marriage

When Martha Wayles Skelton decided that she would marry and live the rest of what would be her altogether too brief life with Thomas Jefferson, she did not have to ask certain questions or make a "treaty" with him. Legal marriage itself was "the treaty," such an important one that society did not leave it to them to set their own basic terms. The deal between a man and a woman was the community's business as well as the couple's, and certain core terms were therefore set down as a matter of law, both religious and civil. By the time Martha and Thomas married centuries of English law (adopted in large measure in the new American context) had already set down the terms of engagement between men and women who were casting their lot together as married partners. Whether the couple loved each other or not, and for most of the history of marriage love was not the preeminent consideration, the parties had certain rights and obligations that were explicitly set forth.

Martha did not have to ask Thomas whether he would take good care of her. That was in the deal called coverture. He covered her with his protection and in return gained the right to control all of her property and to direct the course of her life. She ceased to exist as a separate legal person, hence Blackstone's famous description of marriage, the husband and wife became one, and the one was the husband.[5] Martha did not have to ask whether Thomas would take care of the children they had together and whether they would receive a patrimony from him. Laws about a father's duty of support and children's inheritance rights—a very elaborate array of rules—took care of that as well. Neither Martha nor Thomas had to wonder whether they were going to have sex, because that was part of the legal understanding of what made a marriage as well. In their time, marriage was the symbol of the union of male and female and what that union could achieve. If the two became one physically, and they were both healthy, they would produce children, which was what traditional marriage was supposed to be about. An unconsummated marriage was not a true one. If at some point one of the parties refused to have sex, that was considered abandonment of the marriage bed and was a ground for divorce.[6] No couple in Virginia eligible for legal marriage had to talk to their potential spouses about any of these matters at all.

This was, for Jefferson's time, an efficient system for the smooth operation of Anglo-American family relationships. Legal marriage existed for reasons that had absolutely nothing to do with slavery and white supremacy. Still, the availability of marriage to whites and the denial of it to enslaved black people served as yet another means of advancing both—strengthening and beautifying whites in their relationships with each other and weakening and degrading blacks in their relationships with each other and whenever they were involved with whites. With no opportunity for legal marriage, Sally Hemings, unlike her sister Martha, was operating without the benefit of any written rules. The plan for her life at Monticello with Jefferson was made up to suit their particular circumstances, and the carrying out of that plan depended not upon law but upon Hemings's ability to hold Jefferson in some serious fashion over the years and, more importantly, the quality of his personal character and his willingness to remain committed to her.

It is not all surprising, therefore, that Hemings and Jefferson talked of the very matters that were among the core issues addressed in the basic marriage contract for free couples in the world in which they lived: the treatment of the woman, the man's duty's and obligations toward the children, and what the children would receive from the man when they became adults, questions that men and women in every type of society from time immemorial have had to address. That the two would be having sex was implicit in the understanding that Hemings was going to have more children and that provision would be made for them as well as the one about to be born—the particular one that Hemings most wanted: their freedom.

That whites who wanted to marry never had to ask these most basic and practical questions moved their unions beyond the realm of more obvious deal making and horse-trading. Upper-class families did their share of negotiating about property matters before marriage, when they chose to do so. But for the most part the premarital negotiations that went on for white couples of means reflected their families' desire to help the new couple as they started out in life, augmenting the basic terms of the marriage contract.[7] With the need to negotiate the most elemental terms out of the way, Anglo-American legal unions evolved to the point where they could easily be portrayed as about something inevitably greater—more pure and romantic—than a deal (a "treaty," if you will) in which a man and a woman figure out how they are going to have steady access to sex and company in their lives with a partner acceptable to them, raise the children that come from that sex, and determine what they will do about their respective items of property.

An upper-class, married white woman in Virginia, no matter how her status was obtained—as part of a plan to unite large property holdings, to rein in the impulses of a headstrong girl, or to achieve a step up in her family's circumstances—could never have been a rape victim or degraded sexual object in her marriage. The marriage contract made her consent to sex implicit and all the resulting sexual activity "clean." A married white man, no matter how he came to be the husband of the bride—with the aid of family force or from a desire to gain wealth—could never have been a rapist or one who tainted the notion of true love in the relationship by bringing ambition for material or social gain into the plan for union. The law created a reality beyond itself and its purposes. It told a story about the lives of those whom it protected—men and women like Thomas and Martha—supposedly defining their basic natures and the quality of their characters, almost the very state of their souls.

The cover of legal marriage made every white "wife" an honorable woman, presumptively morally and spiritually superior to any enslaved woman, actually any black woman. This attitude prevailed among whites long after Hemings's time and shaped the way black people and their families and sexuality were viewed, the coupling of blackness with the degradation of slavery having done its work. As late as the 1950s, some newspapers in southern states refused to apply the honorific "Mrs." to even legally married black women. This had nothing to do with the disabilities of slavery—it had been abolished—and nothing to do with the protective veil of legal matrimony: these women had it. When all was said and done, "honor" and dignity were racially based. No black woman, even a lawfully wedded one, could ever have had either, or certainly their honor and dignity could not have been recognized on an equal footing with that of white women's in any public forum.[8]

Because they were legally married, the question whether Thomas Jefferson loved Martha Wayles Skelton as he first got to know her would never have been asked. We assume we know what he was thinking and feeling simply because he married her. Even raising the question might be considered an insult to their memory. The truth is that we do not know exactly what the young Thomas was thinking when he encountered Martha, the beautiful and rich widow. We do not even know when and where he first encountered her. What percentage of his initial attraction to her was that ineffable feeling that draws one human being to another in a heartfelt way that we all respect and honor as one of the highest expressions of our emotions? And what percentage of the attraction was the reality that a legal marriage to a woman whose father was very rich and well connected in the society in which Jefferson wanted to rise would bring him vast wealth that he might never have achieved on his own—a mercenary concern that is not a part of the kind of "love" that we long for and revere? The fact is we simply cannot know.

We know that Jefferson waxed enthusiastic about his prospective bride to friends during his courtship,[9] although he could not very well have gone on and on about his sexual attraction to her—apart from tasteful paeans to her beauty—and the virtues of her father's extensive land holdings and slaves. He would never have put cards on the table like that. With no letters from her and no diary, Martha left no trace of her thoughts during this period. So we do not even have Jefferson filtered through her observations. There is the testimony of their affection during their courtship from their great-granddaughter, who never knew either of them, and the statement, ironically enough, of one of his sons with Sally Hemings.[10] We do know from the way Jefferson conducted himself during his life with his wife—and from his actions at the end of their marriage—that he loved her profoundly and was utterly devastated by her loss. That was after the passage of ten years. It still does not get precisely at what the twenty-seven-year-old man was thinking as he first met and then planned to join his life with Martha Wayles Skelton.

What is left to us to do is to work our way back from what we know of the Jefferson marriage and add that to the actual fact of their marriage to reach a conclusion about his likely earliest feelings for her. The legal marriage, as an origin of their life together, gives us the freedom to feel comfortable saying we know for certain that the kind of romantic love we respect and understand existed between Thomas and Martha Jefferson, not as an outgrowth of their years together, but from the very moment they first interacted with each other. We take this freedom to know the quality of the Jeffersons' love even though the basic contours and expectations of their eighteenth-century marriage would be utterly foreign (and totally unacceptable) to modern sensibilities. In one extremely important area—property—it was not even acceptable to nineteenth-century sensibilities. The reforms of the Married Women's Property Acts that swept across the nation in the mid to late 1800s altered what Jefferson thought was a key component of his relationship with and marriage to Martha Wayles Skelton: the right as her husband to control her considerable property.[11]

After John Wayles died and his daughters inherited his thousands of acres and hundreds of slaves, Jefferson convened a meeting between himself and the husbands of Martha's sisters. He and his brothers-in-law decided on a plan of action for handling and disposing of the property.[12] In their time, that extreme display of paternalism, which essentially treated their wives like children, would be construed as evidence of their love for their spouses, a kind of love that would likely be incomprehensible to most modern Americans.

Even an attempted display of it in a current-day context might land the men in divorce court.

Hemings and Jefferson, slave and master, who had no chance for a legal union, were in a particular bind. The basic quality of their relationship, what they meant to each other in their daily intimate lives, not how the world outside characterized them, may have been better than that of many other legally married couples. As the legal historian Ariela Gross has noted, "Legal language is made up of words that *do things*. Saying 'I do' *makes* you legally married, if the words are said in the right setting."[13] Hemings and Jefferson were nowhere near the "right" setting when they were formulating a plan for their life together at Monticello. Without the safety blanket of legal marriage to gather up all our beliefs and fictions about love and unions between men and women, and with our knowledge of all that could legally happen between a master and a slave, there is an understandable uncertainty about exactly what a union between the two could really have been about. They do not fit any respectable couple that we can imagine, because they were absolutely not supposed to exist as a respectable couple.

Working Backward and Forward

When we work our way backward over the course of the thirty-eight years of Hemings and Jefferson's life together at Monticello to their beginnings in France, we come not to a wedding ceremony between a free white man and free white woman. We come instead to a white man who was the legal owner, under American law, of a young African American woman who believed that she was free under the laws of the country where they were living. We assume that Jefferson could not have forced himself upon Hemings's sister Martha without repercussion. He could have been arrested or his behavior might have caused her to reject him as a partner. Hemings, too, evidently cared how Jefferson treated her.[14] While it is certain that the Admiralty Court would have supported Hemings's bid for freedom, there was no assurance that Jefferson would have suffered any penalty (beyond mortification) if she had sought help from the authorities if he had forced himself upon her. It would have been her word against his; and at all levels of society, proving rape accusations has always been difficult for women. But even if Hemings had had no support from French authorities, a violent act or obnoxious pressure would likely have turned her against Jefferson and figured greatly in her decision about staying in France. The questions are whether Jefferson's ability to rape Hemings means we are to assume that he did it, and whether we are to take his ability to do it as the strict measure of how he felt about her.

For some, the reality that Jefferson "could have" raped Hemings is the only reality that counts. For it is here that we find, in concentrated form, the evil of slavery, the enormous power that one group had to control and wreak havoc in the lives of another. The problem with making what Jefferson "could have" done the sole question is that it suggests that the actual details of Hemings's life are meaningless. This way of viewing African Americans has survived slavery and hints that some present-day considerations of Hemings and Jefferson, which typically proceed as discussions about the nature of slavery, are really discussions about experiences supposedly universal to all black people throughout American history. The erasure of individual black lives—indeed, the assumption that the concept of individual as opposed to group identity is meaningless for blacks—makes it hard to accept any presentation of a black life that moves beyond well-set, predetermined, and very limited parameters. Making what *could* have happened to black people as a group the only question about a given black person's life saves one the effort of having to care about, discover, and analyze any of the details of that person's life. The *idea* of black people matters more than actual black people themselves. What is known about a defined group is very useful for predicting what might happen in the life of one of its members that is yet unfolding. When the person's life is over, however, what actually happened to him or her should take precedence over the almost infinite variety of things that could have happened. If we do not ignore specific information about Sally and James Hemings in favor of making a larger point about slaveholders' overall power, we have evidence that sheds light on the nature of the relationship between Hemings and Jefferson.

As to Sally Hemings, there is no one response to rape. It takes a huge liberty with her life, however, to assume that she was raped, and that she knew she could escape from her rapist forever, and for a time actually asserted her right to be free of him, but nevertheless decided to return with him to Virginia to live out the rest of her life having more forced sex. That construction too easily uses the fact that she was born a slave (and a black person) to presume an irreparably damaged, completely cowed, and irrational personality over one who had the capacity to know her circumstances and to intelligently use her knowledge to assess the risks and possible rewards of taking a particular action—in other words, to think. Her son, who was clearly proud of her, depicted her as a person who thought rationally about her situation and came to a conclusion. In the absence of any specific information about her to rebut his portrayal, all that is left is stereotype. Too many enslaved women, with far fewer opportunities than Hemings had in France, complained about, resisted, and ran away from rape at the threat and cost of their lives, to assume that willing and unconsidered submission was the automatic response of any enslaved woman—especially one who had an alternative.[15] An even more staggering notion is that Hemings, who showed such obvious concern for her children's future, would have "implicitly relied" on a man who had violated any trust she could have had in him by forcing sex on her. What would such a vicious act have told an intelligent person about the likelihood that Jefferson would be honorable enough to carry out his promises to her at some distant point in the future? Nothing about the institution of slavery warrants an assumption that an enslaved woman in Hemings's position in France would have operated at that level of mentality.

The historian Sharon Block describes the sexual coercion of enslaved women as a "process" in which some of the women tried to "bargain their way out of sexual assaults."[16] Their bargaining made it easy for those insensitive to their plight to portray any subsequent "sexual encounters" with their masters as having been based upon consent. Block rightly sounds a note of caution about drawing that conclusion in situations where enslaved women had no law or surrounding society to guide them or support their "bargaining" with their masters. The critical difference for Hemings, of course, is that her negotiations with Jefferson were conducted on French soil under the power of French, not American, law—which they both knew. She could speak to Jefferson in a different voice. Although Hemings ultimately decided not to invoke the formal machinery of law, her use of law as a basis for negotiating was not the act of cowed individual. It sounds much more like the handiwork of a smart, if overconfident, attractive teenage girl who understood very well how men saw her and was greatly impressed with her newly discovered power to move an infatuated middle-aged man. Her mother was not there to tell her that such spells rarely last forever.

Hemings and Jefferson did not exist in vacuum. What happened between them in France necessarily moved through the web of her enslaved relatives.

For seventeen years Robert and James Hemings had traveled with Jefferson, personally attended him, shaved him, and anticipated his wants and needs. Because of the extraordinary experience of living abroad with him for a substantial period of time in very intimate and singular circumstances, Sally Hemings was the logical extension of Robert and James; she was a female version perfectly suited to take their role as intimate personal caterers to Jefferson to a level where neither man could go—to his bed. How he dealt with her in that role mattered greatly. Her mother and siblings would have felt any of her misery he inspired, thus destroying the delicate ecology of the world he had built with the family. They would have had to carry on serving him, but in a changed climate, one that he would not have cared for. On the other hand, if they saw him acting in as decent a fashion as possible, that he was now bound to them by blood might have made at least some of them more inclined to see him in a positive light, thus shoring up the affective role that they certainly played in his life. As will be shown in the chapter to come, members of Hemings's family, free and enslaved, sometimes responded to Jefferson in ways that suggest they thought of him as more a version of an in-law than the rapist of their family member.

Her brother James knew the institution of slavery firsthand, including the special problems slave women faced. Aggressive as he was, we would not expect him to have exacted any direct reprisal if he believed Jefferson had raped his sister. We might think, however, that the rape of his sister would have meant something to him and affected his views about returning to Virginia with Jefferson, and his view of the man overall. Hemings, as we know, did return to America, and after he was a free man visited then Vice-President Jefferson, while he was in Philadelphia, talking to him about his past travel, his future travel plans, and life in general.[17] Until the end of his too brief life, he told people he always kept his work situations open so that if Jefferson wanted to hire him as a chef—for the right pay, of course—he would be ready to go.[18]

American slavery, in and of itself, would not make an enslaved man act with such callous disregard of his sister's life. Eighteenth-century enslaved siblings, perhaps echoing kinship traditions from Africa, were known to be especially close to one another.[19] We see this very clearly in the Hemings family's insistence on naming their children after one another down the generations. If they were not close before their time in France, James and Sally Hemings shared a very intense, life-altering experience together in an alien land. One cannot tell the sister's story without telling the story of the brother; his responses to her situation speak to the kind of man he was.

Certainly no white man in freedom, in the depths of villeinage, serfdom, or Arab enslavement, could be casually portrayed as so base and craven that he would pay gratuitous social calls on his sister's rapist and voluntarily make his sister's attacker his employer of first choice, because a white man would be presumed to have had a soul. One would have to offer very specific and persuasive evidence *about the man himself* to rebut that presumption, for the system of oppression a white man lived under would never be said to automatically signal the state of his individual character.

Enslaved men who lived on the same plantation with their sisters, wives, and daughters who were raped had little choice but to continue in the company of the men who raped them. They weighed responding to one horrific event against the likelihood of provoking other, more extensive horrific events that could destroy their families even more thoroughly. That was one of the deepest and harshest realities of slave life. James Hemings could be excused if he visited Monticello to see the rest of his family and deemed it better for their well-being to swallow any pride and stop by and visit with his former master who had raped, and was continuing to rape, his sister. After the Philadelphia visits, Hemings did return to Monticello to work for Jefferson as a paid employee, for a time, and was thinking about taking Jefferson's offer to be the White House chef just before his death.[19] But no other Hemingses were in Philadelphia when he visited Jefferson after his emancipation. Going to see Jefferson was merely going to see Jefferson. There is no indication that the Hemings family would have suffered reprisals if Hemings had simply never bothered to call on him.

IT IS, IN part, the uncertainly about the precise origins of the Hemings and Jefferson relationship that makes it hard to accept the idea that they were emotionally attracted to one another. Even if working our way back to the Hôtel de Langeac brings us to a beginning that was not presumptively pristine, as we view his origins with his wife, we find enough signs from both Hemings and Jefferson (him far more particularly) that these two people were emotionally attached to one another, and there is no reason to suppose that they were not from the very beginning. Saying that works no fundamental change in the nature of American slavery, even if many choose to treat Hemings and Jefferson as symbols of the institution—the violation of an entire people by the system of slavery, the violation of countless black women—reenacted in the lives of these two human beings, who because of their fame are easy to use as stand-ins for those larger phenomena.

Whatever the notion that Hemings and Jefferson may have loved each other makes us think of them as individuals, the idea of their love has no power to change the basic reality of slavery's essential inhumanity. For any who fear the effects of romanticizing the pair, the romance is not in saying that they may have loved one another. The romance is in thinking that it makes any difference if they did. Rhys Isaac, writing of Hemings and Jefferson (although the idea applies to Jefferson and Martha Wayles, too), has wisely cautioned, "We have to recognize that gender relations in past times and other cultures make 'love,' as we are inclined to idealize it, extremely problematic."[21] And how do we tend to "idealize it"? By demanding a great deal of the emotion, separating it out, and enshrining it above all others that move and direct the course of human affairs, viewing it as cure-all, able to end war, famine, disease—even beliefs in white supremacy. It is common to think of love as an always positive transformative force and, from our inevitably personal perspectives, transformative in just the ways we think are significant.

Love has been many things throughout history: the simple comfort of the familiar, having a person to know and being known by that person in return; a connection born of shared experiences, an irrational joy in another's presence; a particular calming influence that one member of the couple may exert on the other, or that they both provide to one another. A combination of all these and myriad other things can go into making one person wish to stay tied to another. Anyone who is not in the couple—that is, everyone else in the world—will not understand precisely how or why it works for two people.

The most intimate of situations, the one least likely to be observed by others—sexual compatibility—can also be a form of love. But in our Western culture (and some others, to be fair) sex is considered, if not exactly dirty or shameful, a somewhat guilty pleasure that must always be separated from more exalted love. This is especially true when a couple, like Hemings and Jefferson, for reasons of race, status, or gender are not supposed to be together, as if partners who do not have the imprimatur of law, society, and custom could never feel the emotion of love for one another. The invariable charge against such pairs is that they are inauthentic per se, because they are bound together purely for sex, rather than love.

We may turn once again to "Old Man Eloquent," John Quincy Adams, on *Othello* to make the point emphatically. After his earlier essay on the subject, mentioned in chapter 9, Adams confronted the issue of Desdemona's character again in a review essay written in 1836 in which he explained more fully the source of his objections to her.

> She absconds, from her father's house, in the dead of night, to marry a blackamoor. She breaks a father's heart, and covers his noble house with shame, to gratify—what? Pure love, like that of *Juliet* or *Miranda?* No! Unnatural passion; it cannot be named with delicacy. . . . Her admirers now say . . . that the color of *Othello* has nothing to do with the passion of *Desdemona*. No? Why, if *Othello* were white . . . she could have made no better match. Her father could have made no reasonable objection to it; and there could have been no tragedy. If the color of *Othello* is not as vital to the whole tragedy as the age of Juliet is to her character and destiny, then I have read Shakespeare in vain. The father of *Desdemona* charges *Othello* with magic arts in obtaining the affection for his daughter. Why, because her passion for him is *unnatural*; and why is it unnatural, but because of his color![22]

After noting that Shakespeare could not have intended to present Desdemona as an example of feminine virtue, because he has her "eloping in the dead of night to marry a thick-lipped wool-headed Moor," Adams wrote further of the black and white pair,

> Othello, setting aside his color, has every quality to fascinate and charm the female heart. Desdemona, apart from the grossness of her fault in being accessible to such a passion for such an object [Othello], is amiable and lovely; among the attractive of her sex and condition.[23]

In the end, the couple's individual personal qualities, which Adams concedes are excellent (aside from Desdemona's flaw in being able to become attracted to a person of another race), are totally irrelevant to the plausibility of their feelings for one another. The two could never connect on the basis of their mutually attractive innate human attributes. There was a barrier that could never be breached, and Adams makes clear what that barrier is when he intones, "I have said the moral of the tragedy is, that the intermarriage of black and white blood is a violation of the law of nature."[24] Even across the years, in other passages dripping with disgust, Adams's turmoil and conviction fairly leap off the pages of his essay. He well knew that intermarriage between the races was not *actually* against the law of nature, because if "nature" had cared whether blacks and whites mixed their blood, "nature" would have fixed it so they could not: black and white people would not be able to have children together. They could and did, of course, so the locus of nature's prohibition had to shift. Blacks and whites can have sex and produce children (a basic, biological function), but they can never experience together higher-order emotional responses; they can never love each other in a romantic way. Only a lower-order (animalistic) response—lust—can explain the lives of men and women who connect across the boundaries of race. Nature's loophole that allowed for black and white procreation was to be closed by refusing to credit (and certainly not to dignify) interracial couples' feelings for one another. Indeed, they and their feelings were to be subjected to extreme ridicule to discourage others from following their example. The statement about the inability of men and women of different races to love one another was (is) at its heart an expression of anxiety-driven aspiration rather than a description of reality.

Adams very openly grounded his belief in the impossibility of real love between Othello and Desdemona in his superstitions about race and the rules of human nature in a way that might make at least some modern readers uncomfortable. The fact is his views are not so different in practical effect from grounding the notion of the impossibility of love in inter-status and interracial contexts in superstitions about the power of law and social customs: that they operate (like Adams's human nature) as irresistible forces that inevitably control individual sensibilities. When they do not, it is the result of deep perversion: something is morally (in Adams's time) or psychologically (in our time) wrong with the people who transgress.

Neither view takes account of the almost infinite permutations of human personality and circumstances that make every person unique. Nor do they account for human beings' great ability to rationalize behavior until it fits, at least in the privacy of their own minds, the rules of whatever social game is being played. "What a stupendous, what an incomprehensible machine is man!" indeed.[25] Both approaches to the question of authentic love—faith in a version of human nature, faith in the plenary power of law and social custom—are troubling because they are deterministic and, like all deterministic formulations about the ways of men and women in society and history, diminish the human spirit and virtually require ignoring contrary evidence and the role of contingency and subjectivity in the lives of people and societies. They are even more problematic because one suspects that they are invoked to achieve a particular end: control. The idea of authentic love, and wielding the power to say when that can legitimately exist for some people and not others, emerges as a tool (with a romance all its own) used to ratify some aspect of an existing social order, or to make sense of one that is perhaps too difficult to comprehend or merely deeply disturbing. What one cannot understand, or put into a suitable category, simply does not exist.

It is an empirical, not just an intuitive or romantic, fact that law and social mores have never been able to stamp out constitutive elements of the human personality. The American slave society in which Hemings and Jefferson lived, with its tremendous grant of power to one group over another, grossly distorted the distribution of human emotions. One encounters vastly more instances of the negative ones that helped the institution along—some from Jefferson's own hand—than benign or positive ones that contradicted its basic tenets. Yet we would never expect law and even extreme social opprobrium to remove from a population jealousy, hatred, greed, sympathy, mirth, possessiveness—the entire palette of human emotions. If the shapers of law and social customs had that kind of power, social orders would stand forever. Cultures would never change. Very often the seeds of change are planted in the privacy of individual minds, homes, and bedrooms—any place where people retreat to escape from the demands of society's rules and to take on personae that are more suited to their own needs than those the external community would have them adopt.

In the Marriage Act of 1753 in England, parts of which Jefferson tried without success to bring to Virginia as one of his proposals for legislative reforms, parents were given the right to void the marriages of their minor children. Jefferson had his own reasons for supporting the law, but the original drafters' primary concern was that children might make matches that threatened the status of great families in the society. What if, one supporter asked, "'a young Girl of fifteen, for instance, one of the Daughters of a gentleman, happening to fall in Love with her Father's Butler' would marry him rather than 'her equal'; or that 'a boy of sixteen, heir apparent to an Estate, whose Fancy is captivated with his Mother's maid,' would marry her in order to 'gratify an impetuous passion.'"[26] As this supporter of the law recognized, being in vastly different social classes did not mean that males and females could never fall in love with their social "inferiors" or "superiors," for there was a deep and knowing understanding, no doubt born of familiarity with life and crises within English manor houses, about the ways of human beings when they were put in certain circumstances. Note the hypothetical's pairing of the daughter of a gentleman with his butler, and son of the lady of the house with her maid, instead of imagining a cross-class liaison between people who would not have encountered one another in a household on a daily basis.

This commentator knew that for males and females, it was a simple matter of proximity and opportunity, and positive law had to step in sometimes to protect society (those at the top of the hierarchy, actually) from the all too predictable course of human nature. Societies can effectively shape how, when, and whether people express and act on certain emotions in public. They cannot decree that individuals not have them, nor can they control what individuals do behind closed doors. A gentleman's daughter and his butler, or a lady's son and her maid, might feel as deeply for one another as they wanted, but they should not be allowed to translate their feelings into publicly supported actions that might disrupt the social order. Benjamin Rush, Jefferson's great friend and noted Philadelphia doctor, patriot, and signer of the Declaration of the Independence, understood the problem very well, and fretted about its operation in the United States. Anxious to maintain what he thought were the necessary "class divisions" in the emerging Republic, he pronounced it dangerous for men (the upper-class males with whom he was most concerned) to live alone; for these unmarried men, Rush said, were at great risk for crossing socially constructed barriers to form liaisons with women of lower classes. Sex, Dr. Rush believed, was a basic and natural part of life, but only legally established relationships could preserve it in its most wholesome form. He wrote, "While men live by themselves . . . they do not view washerwomen or oyster-wenches as washerwomen or oyster wenches, but simply as women."[27] Given this at once astute and banal observation, one would love to know what Rush truly thought upon hearing that his dear friend Jefferson, a longtime widower, had succumbed to the tendency that he outlined so plainly.

The reality Rush described had particular consequences for slaveholding societies. Hamilton W. Pierson, who took down the memoirs of Jefferson's overseer, Edmund Bacon, wrote his own memoir of his days riding circuit as a minister in the nineteenth century. He wrote of how common it was, more common than many wanted to believe, he said, to come upon farmhouses with bachelor or widowed white men living and having children with black women who had started out as their housekeepers.[27] More formal evidence of this can be found in legal cases from southern states that pitted the free white children of masters against their enslaved siblings in challenges to their slave owner fathers' bequests of freedom and/or property to their enslaved children. The facts recounted in the cases are telling. These fathers, usually widowers, lived with enslaved women, usually housekeepers with whom they were in close daily contact, as if they were married. The patterns of their behavior, and sometimes their words, show that these couples conducted themselves for all intents and purposes like married people, even though the law did not recognize their unions—the man providing a home and material goods, the woman cooking, cleaning, and taking care of the man. Interestingly enough, the judges hearing these cases often referred to how common, though lamentable in their view, these unions were.[29] For every case that made it to court, let alone to a published opinion, some multiple number of similar situations did not. Rather than air family business in public, some white family members accepted the emancipations of their enslaved relatives and whatever grants of property were made to them. It would not have saved Monticello, but Martha Randolph could have contested the emancipations of her siblings Madison and Eston and employed slave catchers to try to go and get her brother Beverley and sister Harriet, and bring them back to be assets in the hands of the executors of their father's estate. She chose to abide by her father's wishes.

The conflict between social rules and human impulses operated at all levels of society. Think again of Celia's George. If anyone should have absorbed the lessons of society's laws and rules, and adjusted his feelings accordingly, it was he. The relatively powerless, enslaved George should have known better than to fall in love with and feel possessive toward Celia and jealous of Newsom. But he did, and his love and possessiveness put in motion a chain of events leading to Celia's execution. Although George's responses are completely understandable, his "error" was to seek something beyond what his society would tolerate from him as an enslaved black man: the right to be in an exclusive relationship with the woman for whom he cared.

Jefferson was the complete opposite of George in terms of the power and freedom he possessed. Still, however he felt about Hemings, he would never have flaunted his relationship with her or made public declarations that would alienate friends like Benjamin Rush, offend the social order, and harm him politically, and it would be wildly romantic and naïve to make such actions the litmus test for his inner feelings. The very savvy and legacy-conscious Jefferson knew the way these things worked. As long as he did not issue a direct challenge to the announced values of Anglo-American society—he did not attempt to marry Hemings or legally establish his paternity of her children—he could do as he pleased, feel as he pleased at Monticello for reasons that were entirely his own. She and their children left slavery in ways designed to draw the least public attention possible to how Jefferson had lived for thirty-eight years. But, though he would never openly challenge society's expectations of him as a white man, society could not demand everything of him. To have freedom, privacy, and dominion over himself was why he had built his mountain home in the first place.

As for the transformation by love so important to modern sensibilities, we can see little trace of it in Sally Hemings, because of her status and relative invisibility in the record. One looks at Jefferson and sees none of the transformations that some, ignoring the clear limitations of his eighteenth-century Anglo-American heritage, might hope would naturally have flowed from his having loved her: giving up career and legacy and openly acknowledging her and their children, working to get himself in the position to free all of his slaves, recanting any disparaging comments about the nature of black people. Jefferson did none of those things. What he did instead was to ring down a curtain on his relations with Hemings and their children so heavy and thick that it took over a century and a half to effectively raise it. Any personal transformation that took place was conducted behind that curtain at Monticello, off-limits to all who did not see Hemings and Jefferson there and experience what it was like to occupy the same space with them.

Perhaps the most salient question for our times about Hemings, Jefferson, and love is about history, definitions, and who has the power to define. On the question of beginnings and love, some of the most important and often repeated stories illustrating the completely affectionate (as opposed to partially utilitarian) origins of Jefferson's relationship with his wife come to us from his legal white great-granddaughter, born many years after their deaths. Those stories have played a major role in defining Jefferson in relationship to his wife. For most of American history, Jefferson's biographers had the power to write the "official" record of his family life, and they essentially wrote the Hemingses out of it. Moreover, they accepted the Jefferson family's denial of Sally Hemings's connection to him, citing that family's insistent and much repeated alternative version of who she was at Monticello, a version that ultimately could not withstand the close scrutiny of either careful analysis or modern science.[30]

It is also true that a Jefferson great-granddaughter through the Hemings line told a similar story about Hemings and Jefferson's origins in France when explaining why her great-grandmother gave up the chance for freedom and came back to Virginia, saying, "Jefferson loved her dearly."[31] In other words, she and other family members answered the questions why Hemings trusted Jefferson and came back to Virginia with him, by referencing her confidence in her knowledge of that fact, a confidence that allowed her to take what seems a breathtakingly large risk. Other members of that generation had their own stories about their family. Of course, they were no more in Paris at the Hôtel de Langeac in 1789 than Jefferson's legal white descendants were present at their ancestors' beginnings in Williamsburg. There is, however, every reason to believe that both sets of descendants correctly described the state of affairs in their forebears' lives.

Jefferson wanted Hemings to come back to Virginia with him, so much so that he took to bargaining with her about this. He well knew that in Virginia there were many other women, enslaved and not, who could satisfy any merely carnal impulses as soon as he returned to America. The problem was, however, that they would not actually have been Sally Hemings herself, a requirement that was evidently very important to him. Her siblings and other relatives seemed to have gauged this. As suggested earlier, their attitude toward Jefferson after Hemings's return to Virginia is in perfect keeping with the idea that they believed he cared for her. If what had happened between them in France had been along the lines of more typical master-female slave sex, Hemings's expressed desire to stay in the country, especially after she became aware that she was pregnant, would have been exactly what Jefferson needed. He could have left her in Paris with her quite capable older brother, helped the pair financially, and found James Hemings employment, thus ridding himself of a potentially embarrassing problem in a way that actually bolstered, instead of hurt, his image. History, and his philosophe friends of the moment, would have recorded that Jefferson (breathing the rarefied air of Enlightenment France) so identified with the

Freedom Principle that he let go of two of his own slaves. He would have been a veritable hero.

Instead of doing that, Jefferson insisted on setting up an arrangement with a young woman that he knew could easily result in a houseful of children whose existence would be easily tied to him. He could not have foreseen in 1789 his eldest daughter's problematic marriage, which eventually required her to spend more time with him than was normal, and complicated his life at Monticello with Hemings and their children. Even without knowing that, his resolution of his conflict with her created many other potential problems for his personal life and reputation that were entirely foreseeable. He accepted the risks and forged ahead. During the decades that followed their time in France, and after an extremely hurtful public exposure that threatened his stature and legacy, this most thin-skinned of individuals persisted on his course, ignoring his family's wishes to send Hemings away, and having more children with her who were named in the same fashion as the older ones: for his important and favorite family members and his best friends.[32] James Madison Hemings was born almost at the virtual height of the public and political scandal surrounding Sally Hemings. Jefferson continued on, guided by his own internal compass and, no doubt, his awareness that the woman being vilified in the press had given up to him a thing whose value he understood: her freedom. He knew very well that these people, really, did not know what, and whom, they were talking about.

If sex had been the only issue, it would have been a far simpler and more practical matter, for himself and his white family when they returned to Monticello, for Jefferson to have installed Hemings in one of his nearby quarter farms at the base of the mountain and visited her there when the mood hit him. Then his daughters, their children, and visitors would have had scant opportunity to come upon either Hemings or her children who looked so much like him. Instead, Jefferson arranged his life at Monticello so that Hemings would be in it every day that he was there, taking care of his possessions, in his private enclave.

What most disturbed contemporary commentators about the arrangement at Monticello was not that the master had a slave mistress but that she was not sufficiently hidden away.[32] Hemings was a visible presence in his home when everyone knew that Jefferson had the resources to have her be someplace else. The racism and sexual hysteria this unleashed among white Americans was a thing to behold. It was common at the time, and remains so among many today, to construct whites who have sex with black people as inherently licentious, or as the victims of some version of sexual voodoo expressed crudely in the phrase "once you go black, you can't go back." If Jefferson had one enslaved African American mistress, he must have had a thousand. Yet, through all the talk during Jefferson's lifetime of his "Congo Harem," "Negro Harem," and "African Harem," only one woman's name emerged: Sally. Jefferson's enemies of the day could list each of Hemings's children, their order of birth and ages, what her duties were at Monticello, but they could never produce the name of another specific woman to be a part of his alleged seraglio.

From her side, it was Hemings who backed down from her decision to stay in France in return for a life at Monticello in which Jefferson would be a very serious presence. While she certainly had another compelling reason for wanting to remain tied to the mountain—her family—she was, for a time, prepared to forgo a life with them, although she may not actually have believed that she would *never* see her family again. Enslaved people who ran away often had thoughts of reunions with loved ones under changed circumstances. It is harder to interpret her actions once she returned to America and before she left Monticello upon Jefferson's death because in those years she was legally under his control. But during an almost twenty-year period of childbearing, she conceived no children during Jefferson's sometimes prolonged absences from Monticello as he acted as a public servant, indicating that she had no other sexual partners.[34] That could well have been at his insistence as much as her own personal desires. Still, the expectation of fidelity—on her part at least—suggests something about the nature of their relationship. Hemings was apparently not supposed to, or did not want to, be involved with another partner. Whatever she felt for Jefferson aside, she was not acting under the cover of Anglo-American marriage, which presumes that all the children of a marriage are the children of the husband. That legal presumption has enabled wives, in countless situations, to require husbands to pass along resources to children who were not their biological offspring. Hemings's connection to Jefferson, held together totally by whatever was going on between them, was her children's way out of slavery, so long as her children were his, too. She was apparently unwilling to do anything (as in having babies by other men) that might jeopardize that connection and bring the effects of *partus sequitur ventrem* back into her life.

Before Hemings died, she gave one of her sons as heirlooms personal items that had belonged to Jefferson, a pair of his eyeglasses, a shoe buckle, and an inkwell that she had kept during the nine years after his death. These artifacts—things she saw him wear and a thing he used to write words that would make him live in history—were seemingly all that she had left of him. Monticello and virtually all its contents were sold to pay debts or were in the control of his legal white family. These items were quietly passed down in the Hemings family until well into the twentieth century.[35] Slavery and racism worked such a distortion of human emotions (and continue to do so) that we may not feel comfortable attaching to this gesture the first inference that we would draw if the man whose belongings Hemings carefully saved and passed on to her offspring had been an enslaved black man or if she had been a white woman, even an unmarried white woman, handling a white man's possessions in this fashion. The meaning of her sister Martha's valediction to Jefferson—her unfinished copying of a passage from one of his favorite books, *Tristram Shandy*—is easy to discern.[36] Whether she knew the passage from her own reading, or whether she heard it first during the weeks that Jefferson helped to take care of her in her final days and may have read to her to keep her amused, she was attempting to tell him, and anyone who might read her transcription, what she felt as her life was ebbing away. It is both literal and literary, the very thing that historians love to see: words on a page that tell without much effort what the writer is saying. Words are not everything, and in the realm of deep emotion, quite often fail. Hemings's action, which at the very least exhorted her descendants to both remember Jefferson and her connection to him, indicate that she wanted them to know he meant something to her. She had, after all, lived with him for decades, and he had given her valued children whom he had let go to make their way in the world, something her father had not done for her and her siblings. Jefferson had kept his promises to her.

Distortion of human feelings is not the same thing as the total destruction of them. Sally Hemings, though enslaved, was a human being. Working backward to 1789 from either her death in 1835 or Jefferson's death in 1826, one can say that sixteen-year-old-old Hemings's instincts about how she might best shape her future in the context of her particular circumstances and needs were as sound as her older sister Mary's instincts about Thomas Bell, developing at the same time on another continent. Hemings could not have known this as she treated with Jefferson at the Hôtel de Langeac, but at the end of her life she would be able to say that she got the important things that she most wanted.

18

❧

THE RETURN

P ARIS HAD NOT seen anything like it for decades. The chill winds assaulting the city seemed a harbinger of terrible things to come. The temperature dropped so low that the Seine froze solid enough to support both the carriages that slid boldly across it and the ice skaters who came out daily and nightly to take advantage of the unprecedented weather.[1] James and Sally Hemings had not seen anything like it either, having grown up in a warmer climate, where freezing temperatures were not abnormal, but never so cold as what they experienced in the winter of 1788–89. This may have disconcerted them. Or the two young people could well have considered the spectacular arctic display a form of adventure, like the ice skaters gliding out onto the Seine. They were, apparently, able to do that. We know something of their health statuses from Jefferson's records. When the Hemingses needed medical attention, he put them under the care of doctors or nurses and recorded his payments for those services in his memorandum books. The lack of such notations during this period suggests that brother and sister made it through their last winter in Paris with no serious bouts of sickness. As noted in chapter 11, Patsy and Polly were not so fortunate. They were ill with typhus for parts of the winter.[2]

Whatever the Hemingses felt about that winter, Jefferson, the Parisian for a time, ever enamored of the sun and warm weather, was deeply distressed. Despite his close affinity for Paris, its customs, architecture, cultural life, and the people he met there, he could hardly abide its weather, a part of nature he watched with obsessive farmerlike zeal in every place he lived for any stretch of time. Almost from the moment he arrived, he had been

issuing periodic complaints to family and friends back home about just how
cold and how gray was the climate and atmosphere in the city. Although he
hated the cold, the insistent meteorologist in him was, nonetheless, excited
about the extreme winter as a weather occurrence. He ordered a new pair of
thermometers that could be placed outside and observed without "opening
the window" and would show the temperature to twenty degrees Farenheit
"below naught." He wrote to his brother-in-law about the "Siberian degree of
cold" the city was experiencing and noted that as early as November the temperature had plummeted to eight degrees.[3] If Jefferson was anxious before to
get himself, his daughters, and James and Sally Hemings back to America,
the hard winter probably deepened his resolve.

The aberrant weather was about more than these temporary immigrants'
personal and physical inconvenience. Distress was everywhere, the hard
winter having come upon the heels of a disappointing harvest and the institution of questionable economic policies that drove up the price of bread,
the staple of life for the country's poor. Thousands of people who had been
living in Paris and its countryside were barely able to hold on. Social life
began to break down under the weight of the unremitting deep freeze, star-
vation, poor housing, and a political system that was ill equipped to handle
the crisis. Beggars, always a part of the city's life, filled public spaces in even
greater numbers, giving evidence of social deterioration to all who traveled
the city's streets. The "people," however, were not merely helpless suppli-
cants. They were angry. The desperately poor, along with the faltering working and small middle classes, came out in great numbers to protest the
government's failures to deal effectively with the shortages, developing a
political critique along the way that would escalate into a full-fledged revolution by midsummer.[4]

One wonders whether the brutal winter, and the hardship it provoked in
the general society, gave the Hemings siblings any pause about staying in a
place where such things were even possible. That they contemplated staying in France at all suggests that they were an optimistic pair, not necessarily prone to thinking that because other people failed, they were destined
to fail, too. Life was looking up for them at the time, with a steady salary in
both of their hands, five years' worth of contacts and experience in Paris,
and an open avenue of freedom.

Volatile as the world outside their door must have seemed, the
Hemingses were really just witnessing the start of the revolutionary era in

France during that first half of the year. The violence in the country—the storming of the Bastille in July, bread riots, and the uprising of the peasantry in the villages surrounding the city—was a mere prelude to the more serious turn of events in the months immediately following their departure from France. Nine days after they left the city thousands of Parisian women marched to Versailles to protest the lack of bread, shouting within earshot of the royal family, *"du pain, du pain!"* The marchers, who had an extra measure of power because of the French military's reluctance to fire on women, were promised bread. Only mildly appeased, they insisted that King Louis and Queen Marie Antoinette return to Paris with them to ensure the fulfillment of the promise. The justifiably frightened couple had no choice but to go, and they left under the escort of the then still highly regarded marquis de Lafayette, a man known to both Hemingses as a frequent visitor to the Hôtel de Langeac, taking meals that James Hemings prepared.[5]

The Hemingses were in a country on the precipice of truly earth-shattering changes, but the person closest to them, who knew the most about what was going on both in the streets and in the government—Jefferson—apparently did not really believe that. After viewing the political response to the fall of the Bastille, he pronounced with his usual implacable optimism, three days after the event, that the "power of the States is now I think out of all danger." He seemed to believe that up until the time he left the country. "Tranquillity," he wrote to Lucy Paradise as late as September 10, "is pretty generally restored in this country," and then to Thomas Paine three days later,

> Tranquillity is well established in Paris, and tolerably thro' the whole kingdom; and I think there is no possibility now of any thing's hindering their final establishment of a good constitution, which will in it's principles and merit be about a middle term between that of England and America.[6]

Nothing could hinder this outcome except the hovering whirlwind that would descend soon after he left Paris. William Short, who knew him well, said that "Jefferson's greatest illusions in politics . . . proceeded from a most amiable error on his part; having too favorable opinion of the animal called Man."[7]

Jefferson enthusiastically supported the French Revolution, believing that changes were much needed in the country, and as with so many other things he deeply wanted to be true, he let his heart's desire influence what should have been a more dispassionate analysis of how matters might settle themselves in that conflict. This natural politician and statesman followed the activities of the political elite as well as the ordinary people, who he instinctively understood would be the elite's powerful counterpart, riding out into the streets to see the faces of the impoverished and enraged crowds that gathered to protest the government's fecklessness. Even amid what looked like impending chaos, he assumed that the people's wisdom would prevail and that all would be well in the end.

One of the more fascinating things to contemplate is what the enslaved people in Jefferson's world, particularly those close to him like James and Sally Hemings, made of the strange blend of aristocrat and egalitarian in him. Whatever the limits of Jefferson's personal egalitarianism, his ideas could not be, and ultimately have not been, contained within those limits. It is very likely that both Hemingses, like many during their time and afterward, understood that all who heard "all men are created equal" could make of those words what they wanted. We do not know what specific opinions he offered to the pair about the political and social turmoil in Paris, but he surely spoke to them, or commented within earshot, about the extraordinary events that were taking place around them. As the head of the household he could do no less, if only to give assurances about their personal well-being. Though they were not the likely objects of political hostility, during the same month that the Bastille was overtaken, burglars broke into the Hôtel de Langeac three times. Jefferson asked for additional police protection and then had bars and bells put on the windows to keep out intruders and to alert the people in the house if anyone tried to get inside. Even if the burglaries were not overtly political acts, they were another sign to the Americans that they were in the midst of difficult times and were, to some degree, vulnerable.[8]

The public turmoil aside, the Americans had their own business to attend to, some of which offered its own brand of trouble. It is more usual to think of Sally Hemings in conflict with Jefferson over leaving France. She was not the only cause of concern. Jefferson's own daughters were evidently giving him some moments of anxiety. While there is no question that he longed for home, and saw his leave as an occasion to put his financial affairs in order, his correspondence in 1788–89 clearly indicates that what worried him the most was that his daughters were coming of age in this foreign setting. Patsy was almost certainly the catalyst for his decision to seek a leave of absence. He was desperate to get her back home.

Although Patsy was still in her teens, she was, in Jefferson's view, of marriageable age. Much as he loved the French, he wanted her to make a match in her own country. His daughter was enjoying the gilded life in Paris perhaps a bit too much for his tastes, going out to balls where she danced with eligible bachelors, socializing with other young women who were doing the same, no doubt exchanging notes about the new world they had entered and the people, that is to say, young men, they encountered in that world. He had left America with no idea he would be gone for so long. Before he knew it, five of his daughter's formative years had been spent abroad, and she had been thoroughly acculturated. When Polly arrived in 1787, all the people who were the most important to Patsy were in France. Her mother was gone. While she probably longed to see her other relatives and Virginia, she could do that without having to remain there. Jefferson, however, meant to take her to Virginia for good and come back to France without her. Despite what he was saying to people back home, she was not ready to go and spoke of remaining in Paris and renting rooms at the abbey. That she was willing to stay in France without him shows just how far away from Virginia and his values she had grown.

With the young people in the house making noises about staying, Jefferson was the beleaguered patriarch confronted with various mini-rebellions breaking out in his domestic realm. He was, if anything, extremely effective when it came to tamping down dissension within the ranks, personal and political. He managed to sail through the difficult last months with the household intact, and the gathering of belongings at the Hôtel de Langeac accelerated after August 23 when he received word ("tho' not officially") from John Jay that he had permission to take his leave of absence and that his secretary, William Short, was to serve in his stead for the duration of his leave.[9] Once it was clear that the return home was imminent, the first order of business after packing was to find a suitable ship bound for Virginia. Jefferson immediately set out to do this, but the process turned out to be something of an ordeal itself—one that would not be over until the day in late October that he, James and Sally Hemings, and his daughters set foot on the *Clermont* bound for Norfolk, Virginia.

With a revolution breaking out and Jefferson feverish to find a ship to take them all back to Virginia, the Hemingses faced squarely the stark reality that if they were to go with him they would be leaving the chance for legal freedom and returning to legal slavery. There had been a long time to think this over during the course of Jefferson's preparations for going home. But Jay's letter put matters on a do-or-die footing for the siblings, and it was evidently during the roughly one-month interval between receiving the letter and leaving Paris that Sally Hemings, in the very early stages of pregnancy, and Jefferson had their most direct confrontation.

Fawn Brodie tied Jefferson's sudden illness in the days immediately after he got word that he could come home to his conflict with Hemings. About a week after receiving Jay's letter, he suffered a migraine attack that lasted for six days and confined him to bed.[10] For a man who hated confrontation and, as he confided to his friend James Madison, particularly hated face-to-face bargaining, being in conflict with Hemings over her decision to stay in France would have indeed distressed him greatly, particularly because he knew that he could not legally make her come home. If he were desperate enough (and lost all sense of himself), he could try to physically take hold of her and her brother, an absurd plan on its face. He could not enlist the police to help him force them out of the country. What basis could he cite? They knew the status of blacks in the country, and he knew he had not followed the law and registered the Hemingses. There is no reason to think the servants at the Hôtel de Langeac would have stood idly by while Jefferson played kidnapper if the Hemingses had asked for their help. It is quite clear that workers in Paris in 1789 tended to support one another and were not exactly in a deferential mood toward their "superiors."

A Jefferson attempt at force would have been as ironic and problematic as showing up in the Admiralty Court to argue against the Hemingses' freedom. As a twenty-eight-year-old, he had copied in his commonplace book "An Inscription for an African Slave." It is not known why, or for whom, he prepared the inscription—whether it was to be used for a specific individual or as an all-purpose one for the burial ground for enslaved people at Monticello—but it appeared just below one written for the headstone of his favorite sister, Jane. The inscription contained lines from William Shenstone's poem attacking the African slave trade. The stanzas express the longing of an African captured from the "bless'd" shores of his homeland and taken by "stern tyrant[s]" to toil for others.[11] He would not be "trading" slaves, but trying to impress James and Sally Hemings and put them on a ship to take them across the Atlantic to Virginia would have put

Jefferson in the position of the Barbary pirates he would fight a decade later as president.

Stress often made Jefferson physically ill.[12] Historians have long noticed (and he did too) that at pivotal moments in his life when he received unwelcome news or faced great pressure, his body responded negatively. When his mother died in 1776, he suffered a severe attack of migraine that confined him to his home for weeks. Although he never wrote, "I have developed a migraine because of the stress over my mother's death," the proximity in time of the two events and the pattern of his attacks suggest a causal relationship that says much about his personality and how he responded to serious emotional challenges.

Jefferson was, without question, a deeply passionate and emotional man behind his peaceful and amiable exterior. The uniform kindness that his son Madison Hemings recalled was one of the ways he controlled himself. Disarming people with niceness allowed him to retreat from the rough-and-tumble of daily life. Hemings also described his father as one who "hardly ever allowed himself to be made unhappy any great length of time."[13] Although he was generally a cheerful and optimistic man, when matters were not in order, or when he was faced with a tough and seemingly intractable problem, one that his engineer-like efficiency, superhuman work ethic, and dogged perseverance could not solve, he could break down or act in ways designed to render the problem invisible.

Although Jefferson's prolonged headache during those final weeks in Paris may have been brought on by a dispute with Hemings over her plan to stay in France, he had other important reasons to be anxious and ambivalent—namely, the things he had to deal with when he got there, including what to do about Hemings once back on their home turf. The trip to Paris had provided a respite from personal tragedy and the wrenching experience of his professional failure as the governor of Virginia. He had actually been seeking escape almost from the time of his wife's death, when one counts the months between September of 1782 and July of 1784 when he was away from Monticello almost all the time. Now he would go home and be very forcefully reminded, just by being there, of what had taken place on the mountain in the autumn of 1782.

It did not help that one of the reasons he needed to return to Virginia was very much connected to his wife. Possession of his father-in-law's tremendous wealth, combined with the social pedigree from his mother, had created a synergy propelling Jefferson to the forefront of Virginia's economic and social elite. He was sent there, however, with an almost equally tremendous debt and its radiating effects, with which he grappled like Sisyphus for the rest of his life. As he prepared to go home in 1789, the "Wayles debt," as he called it, threatened to overcome him financially.[14]

John Wayles's legacy operated on so many different fronts in Jefferson's life that it was impossible for him to totally detach from it. The predicament with Hemings powerfully emphasized that truth. Once home, his in-laws, relatives, and others who were close to him would learn that the Gordian knot of family relationships that already existed on the mountain among the Hemingses, Wayles, and Jeffersons had now become even more tightly wound. Along with a very complicated economic profile, Wayles had given Jefferson a legal wife and, now, a young mistress. He could not have apprehended it, but her name would become more firmly attached to his than that of any other member of his legal family.

Though Jefferson voiced certainty that he would return to Paris after his leave of absence, he had word from James Madison, two weeks before he received official permission to come home, that President Washington might ask him to join his administration.[15] Jefferson was adamant. He had no interest, he said, in a job that would take him away from his home for any length of time, and he seemed sincere in this. But it is perhaps significant that when the position of secretary of state was actually offered to him, he said he did not feel that he could ever refuse a request from George Washington. Madison's early query alerted him to the possibility that this inclination would be tested. So one can at least say that Jefferson's faith in his return to Paris was not as firm as it had been the year before when he originally conceived the plan to go home.

In his unfinished autobiography, which he decided to end just after his Paris years, Jefferson makes clear that he had had no intention of matching Franklin's eight and half years in France and that he planned in 1789 to "place [his] daughters in the society & care of their friends, and to return *for a short time* to [his] station at Paris" (emphasis added).[16] He could scarcely have contemplated anything else. Going back as minister to France on an open-ended basis could have meant a long-term separation from both of his daughters. His closeness to Patsy especially would not have allowed him to leave her on another continent for any extended period of time with an ocean between them. He had already lost one child under those circumstances, and the vagaries of mail carriage prevented him from finding that out until she was long dead and buried. As he was soon to learn, his life as a public servant would take him away from Monticello and his daughters for long stretches of time. He took comfort in the association of person and place. It was important for him to know—gratifying even—that when he was away his daughters were either at Monticello or within the vicinity of his home. The Atlantic Ocean was a different proposition altogether.

Because he never spoke publicly or wrote about Sally Hemings, and her association with the place and idea of Monticello, Jefferson's actions must substitute for his words. They make it clear: the association of person with place in Hemings's case was absolute. There was never any serious question about where she was going to be. As we will see, there would be several key moments between 1790 and 1805 when, but for his relationship with her, she should have been somewhere else. Jefferson did not want that, and the people around him knew it very well. The reason he did not want Hemings to be anyplace other than Monticello was never meant to be a part of his public legacy, for reasons of privacy and prudence.

Jefferson made a clear distinction between private and public life. When a correspondent who wanted to write about him asked him for the names of his grandchildren, he was incredulous. Why, he wanted to know, should the public care about the names of his grandchildren, and what did they have to do with anything that was going to be written about his life, which he took to mean a writing that focused on the only thing that should matter to the world at large: his acts as a public man.[17] Hemings, even more than his grandchildren, was very definitely of his private world, the very deepest part of it. If he destroyed letters from his legitimate white wife to keep the details of their intimate world private, there could be no record at all of his time with an entirely forbidden enslaved black woman.

As for prudence, Jefferson understood as well as any great man casting an eye toward posterity what types of things, fairly or not, could threaten what he took to be his legacy. Any out-of-marriage liaison that produced illegitimate children would be a threat to the way posterity viewed him; living with and having children with an African American enslaved woman, however, posed an exponentially greater one. That kind of thing was done, but the Anglo-American culture that formed Jefferson demanded that the men involved in those liaisons not lay their transgression before society in any open way. Then all could go about their business, pretending that what they knew was true was not true at all, but even entirely fanciful. The fictions of white society—the bedrock upon which white supremacy rested—could continue unchallenged. Jefferson knew his white country-men's attitudes quite well, and surely understood that in his time, and for a long time to come, they would forgive him almost anything but her. For one who wanted to be loved by "everybody," or as many people as possible, that was a risk never to be taken. He may not have been thinking of himself as a future president, but he readily comprehended that his involvement in the American Revolution, his turn as minister to France, and whatever he might be able to do in Virginia assured him a place in history.

Thus, Jefferson could openly express his longing for Monticello in a way that would be easily understood for what it generally and truly was: a desire for home, a place of memory existing alongside ambitious plans for the future where there was much to love and look forward to. But that desire would not be connected to Hemings specifically. What he knew, however, is that when he was away from Monticello, she was there and when he came home, she would be there, whatever others did or did not know about how she figured into his private construction of his life on the mountain—a process begun during what turned out to be his final months as minister to France.

Jefferson pressed on with his initial plan, making references in letters during the summer to his requirements for the trip that mentioned very gen-erally that he would be traveling with his "servants." Given the Hemingses' position, that could well have been just his assumption. By September 16, 1789, he was ready to be specific about his travel plans. He wrote to James Maurice on that day, telling him that he required "three masters births" for himself, Patsy, and Polly and regular berths "for a man and woman servant, the latter convenient to that of [his] daughters."[18] He was quite confident in the place he occupied in the lives of his traveling companions, for he then requested "a use of the cabbin in common with the others, and not exclu-sive of them which serves only to render [him] odious to those excluded," as if there were no doubt in his mind that he was the sun around which all four young people revolved.

JAMES AND SALLY Hemings left on Paris on September 26, 1789.[19] While there are indications that her brother James returned to the city after his emancipation, Sally Hemings never did. Her last carriage ride out of the city and her final look at the place where she had seen and done so much and where her life had been transformed forever put an irrevocable end to an important possibility. The twenty-six days that passed between the time of her departure from the Hôtel de Langeac and when she set sail with her brother and the Jeffersons on the *Clermont* marked the last period in which she would ever have a legal right to claim freedom on her own terms. Now her future was in Jefferson's hands. One must say in the hands of his *relatives* as well. He would be forty-seven on his next birthday in April of 1790. Hemings would be seventeen at some point in that same year. Almost three of her lifetimes could fit into his, and in their day Jefferson was long past being considered a young man. His own father had not made it past fifty, and there could have been no reasonable expectation that he would be given the gift of almost four more decades of life. If anything had happened to him, Jefferson's daughters, and, most likely, Francis and Elizabeth Eppes—if anything happened to Patsy and Polly—would have controlled Hemings's fate. There was no guarantee that these surrogates would have been at all concerned about what Jefferson had promised Hemings in Paris. The decision had been made, however, and they were now all on their way.

Adrien Petit came along to assist the Virginians who were retracing steps and seeing sites and terrain—churches and small villages—that they had seen before as they passed for the last time together through Normandy's rolling hills and green countryside. The night of the same day they left Paris, they lodged at an ancient Norman town along the Seine, Vernon, whose heart was the spectacular Collegiate Church Notre-Dame, dedicated in 1072, though not completely constructed until the seventeenth century.[20] After Vernon, the party proceeded to Bolbec, which Benjamin Franklin described in 1785 as a "market-town of considerable bigness" that was "thriving," its residents well dressed and in better physical condition than the people he had observed in other wine-growing regions.[21]

After a night in Bolbec, they went on to Le Havre, only to find a raging storm that delayed travel across the Channel to Cowes, where they were to meet their ship bound for Virginia. Almost as soon as the party arrived in the port city, Jefferson met up with Nathaniel Cutting, an American living in Le Havre, who was one of the people Jefferson had consulted about finding passage to the United States. The two men spent time together while the Virginians waited for fair weather. Cutting's diary records the time spent touring the city with Jefferson and his daughters and having tea with them at the Hotel L'Aigle d'Or, where the Jeffersons and Hemingses were staying. He made no specific mention of James and Sally Hemings except to note that "Jefferson with his daughters and servants rode round thro' the Citadelle" on their way to what would be a failed attempt to board a ship to cross the Channel. A break in the weather turned out to be temporary, and the party returned to the hotel.[22] Unless Cutting was following the normal practice of rendering servants invisible, the Hemings siblings were not involved in the Cutting-Jefferson excursions and were instead left to explore the town and find amusement by themselves.

Petit left the Americans to return to Paris on October 7 with a gift Jefferson gave him "for his extraordinary trouble."[23] There is no evidence he ever saw Sally Hemings again, but he would have a reunion with James Hemings and Jefferson, not in France, as they expected, but in the United States. The day Petit left, Jefferson wrote to William Short describing a disturbing event that had taken place the day before. He had gone in search of "a pair of shepherd's dogs." He continued, "We walked 10 miles, clambering the cliffs in quest of shepherds, during the most furious tempest of wind and rain I was ever in." He did not identify his companion, but it was not Nathaniel Cutting, whose diary makes no mention of the notable event Jefferson went on to describe. Cutting's entry for that day confirms that it was awful with a "squally, Dirty, tempestuous morning, and contrary Wind,"[24] but suggests that he did not see Jefferson until dinnertime. Given the nature of what he was doing, which might require someone to actually carry something for him, James Hemings was Jefferson's most probable companion. With no way to be the chef, during those days of transit, Hemings temporarily reverted to the position he had held when he first came to France: manservant to Jefferson. It is possible that Petit may have been along with them, although he was readying himself for his return to Paris the next day. Campaigning through rough terrain up and down cliffs in a blinding storm looking for puppies to buy would seem to go well beyond the limits of the job description, maître d' hôtel. The journey, long, arduous, and ultimately "fruitless," had an almost surreal coda. Jefferson wrote,

On our return we came on the body of a man who had that moment shot himself. His pistol had dropped at his feet, and himself fallen backward without ever moving. The shot had completely separated his whole face from the forehead to the chin and so torn it to atoms that

it could not be known. The center of the head was entirely laid bare.—
This is the only kind of news I have for you.[25]

They could not have known it at the time, but that gruesome scene of
suicide—one of the last images of France—was an ironic comment on
things to come.

"After being detained in Havre for ten days by contrary wind," the
Hemingses and Jeffersons left the city "before one o'clock in the morning" on October 8 and arrived at Cowes "at half after two in the morning"
on October 9.[26] They seemed to have worse luck with Channel crossings
than with the actual trips across the ocean, which were placid. Just as Patsy
had told of stormy conditions attending her trip with her father and James
Hemings when they crossed the Channel coming to France, Jefferson
painted a harrowing picture of the trip the other way, saying they all traveled under conditions that promoted "boisterous navigation and mortal
sickness."[27] They landed, and there they waited another two weeks before
the winds were favorable for sailing to Virginia.

Finally, on October 22, 1789, almost a month after they left Paris, James
and Sally Hemings boarded the *Clermont* and started for Virginia. In the
end, it was Jefferson's friend the painter John Trumbull who put his very
anxious friend together with a captain and a ship. Trumbull wrote from
London to say that he had gone aboard the *Clermont* to satisfy himself that
it was suitable, and he described the ship and its accommodations enthusiastically. It was, he said, "new and a good sailor" weighing "230 Tons" with
"two large staterooms"—one that would be convenient for Jefferson and
the other for his daughters. There was no mention of either James or Sally
Hemings, but Trumbull's description of the ship's "very good quarter Deck
for walking" reveals one important amenity the pair could take good advantage of to get a clear view of the Atlantic as they crossed it.[28]

There was a great deal more than the just the vast ocean expanse for
them to observe. On his trip to France Jefferson noted the wide variety of
ocean-based wildlife on display on the North Atlantic: numerous types of
seabirds near land, and sharks and whales out in the open sea.[29] With no
other passengers on board, it was easy to meet Jefferson's desire to have his
daughters' and Sally Hemings's quarters in close proximity to one another,
and for all the members of his household to have easy access to him. The
Clermont was a floating version of the Hôtel de Langeac (with someone else

beside Jefferson as the captain), as its former residents had a few more weeks to continue in the roles they had fashioned for themselves in Paris. This would be the last time that they, who had shared life as provincials abroad, building up a lifetime of memories, would live together as a defined unit. More importantly, every mile of the journey west made whatever personae the Hemingses created for themselves in France, as free or potentially free people, weaker and weaker. It is hard to think there was not some or even great trepidation in the hearts of these two young people (one who had a great deal riding on her young girl's poignant trust in a man) as they faced return to a place that was primitive not only in its physical and cultural aspects but in its understanding of might's relationship to right. The Jeffersons, on the other hand, as they sped toward America would merely become more powerful, their rights as masters and white people reconfirmed once they set foot on Virginian soil. Unlike the Hemingses, they had only the pleasures of living in Paris to lose.

A trip that was estimated to take nine weeks was made in about four, as Jefferson daily and dutifully noted the latitude and the "time from Paris by watch." With the benefit of favorable winds and the "fine autumn weather," Captain Colley decided to lay a straighter course across the ocean instead of the more circuitous route originally planned. They reached Norfolk on November 23 amid a shroud of fog. After waiting for it to lift, the captain maneuvered the ship into port into a "strong head wind" that was at the same time speeding along another vessel on its way out of port. The two ships narrowly avoided collision, and the outgoing vessel grazed the *Clermont*, taking off "part of [the ship's] rigging." They managed to make it safely to shore, but the mishaps continued.[30]

One of the chief advantages of travel on the *Clermont* was that some of Jefferson's enormous amount of baggage could be taken along with him instead of having to be shipped separately. In the weeks before he left Paris, he sent thirty-eight large packages to Le Havre to be loaded onto the ship for the trip home. His shipping list noted several trunks and other containers—"a leather portmanteau" (a large suitcase) and a "painted wooden box"—of "servts clothes," which carried James and Sally Hemings's apparel and belongings.[31] Other items of their clothing were packed away in the trunk and boot of Jefferson's phaeton. They had acquired numerous possessions during their stay abroad. The benefit of traveling home with them instead having them shipped separately turned into a near-catastrophe.

About two hours after they disembarked, before their belongings had been removed, the *Clermont* caught fire. The vessel was almost lost, along with all of Jefferson's public papers and everyone's personal belongs. For what must have been a harrowing period, the enslaved brother and sister faced the loss of almost everything they had accumulated during what could only have been (and would likely remain) the greatest adventure of their lives. They could have their memories, but they certainly wanted to be able to touch and share with their family the mementos of their days as Parisians—the dresses, suits, other items that would never be available to them in Virginia. Any presents brought home for their mother and siblings could have perished, too. Fortunately, the fire was doused, but not before the ship suffered substantial damage. Only the "thickness of the traveling trunks" saved the Hemingses from the loss of nearly all physical evidence that they had ever been in France.[32]

Although disaster on the *Clermont* was averted, the brother and sister were now back in a slave society. Moreover, they soon had news that suggested they would be there forever: Jefferson might not be going back to France after all. Madison's query about his willingness to join the government had been transformed into an actual request to serve as the first secretary of state of the United States of America. Word of the appointment was in the newspapers. It was also in the address of the committee of Norfolk politicians who formally greeted Jefferson on behalf of the town two days after he arrived there. His reply to the citizens of Norfolk suggests that he knew it might be difficult to turn down the request.[33]

James Hemings, of course, had a great deal to think and feel deeply about when he learned of Jefferson's possible new position, which would keep him in America if he accepted it. He had crossed the ocean with every expectation of going back to Paris and knew that he might have a second chance of obtaining freedom on his own. While Jefferson could look past his reluctance to accept the appointment and see the enormous honor it was that a man so esteemed as George Washington had selected him for it, the appointment meant nothing for James Hemings except the promise of a change of venue within the continental United States. New York, the national capital, was not Virginia, but it was hardly free soil like Paris. It was instead, like the Old Dominion, still very much a slave society. He would gain greater proximity to his family, and that was a benefit, but Hemings's actions after his emancipation suggest that proximity to family was not the only consideration for him. He had a broader conception of how he wanted to go through the world.

All of this had a meaning for Sally Hemings as well. Though she had no reasonable prospect of returning to France, news that Jefferson might accept a job that would take him away from Monticello to New York was a clear and serious reminder of the unpredictability of the life she had decided to come back to, how Jefferson could start out with one firm set of expectations and have them frustrated or altered because of others' actions. She was back in slavery now, bereft of any law to turn to and under his complete control, with no basis for bargaining with him about anything except the basis of whatever she knew about his feelings for her. Perhaps only he and she fully understood the reason for her renewed presence in the country—that it was at his instigation. Encouraging her to give up something he knew was valuable created a moral obligation on his part far beyond what any other member of his family could have really appreciated. At the same time, her brother's situation was different, seemingly even more heartbreaking. A door he thought was still open when he left Paris and crossed the ocean to come home was closing for him, and as far as he knew he might never see Paris again.

The British navy's bombardment of Norfolk during the Revolutionary War had effects that were still evident when the Hemingses arrived in 1789. There was a shortage of housing and, for a brief time, a question about where they all would stay, until some men at a hotel called Lindsay's graciously vacated their rooms in favor of the Jefferson party. Sally Hemings likely stayed with Patsy and Polly. James Hemings slept in a "hamac" in some part of the hotel. He had to do that only for a few days because the party left Norfolk on November 29 and proceeded to Richmond by way of Williamsburg, stopping at the homes of Jefferson's friends and relatives. After Richmond it was on to Eppington, the home of Elizabeth and Francis Eppes, who had sent Sally Hemings to Paris.[34]

It would probably take Tolstoy, who could think of his own illegitimate son by a peasant woman, a man who served as Tolstoy's coachman and lived on his estate, to truly realize, capture, and convey the mix of tragedy, absurdity, touching vulnerability, flawed humanity, hopeful expectation—the almost Shakespearean quality of the family gathering at Eppington during those days in December.[35] Elizabeth Eppes had sent her enslaved sister, the child of her slave-owner father, to live with her brother-in-law, another slave owner. That sister now came back home carrying her brother-in-law's child, extending the mixture of black and white, slave and free—and secrecy and rejection—into another generation.

Whether this was something Jefferson talked about in confidence to his in-laws is currently unknown, though he could not have had more sympathetic people to hear and understand his story. The Eppeses were entirely devoted to him, and their connection to the Hemings family was now well into its fifth decade, having started with Sally Hemings's African grandmother. They had seen this before and knew that, rather than being some wildly improbable circumstance, it was one of the things that happened in slave-owning societies when males and females lived in close contact with one another. John Wayles first connected the blood lines between the two families, so Elizabeth Eppes and her sister Martha had been in the same position with him that Patsy and Polly Jefferson were now in with their father. The shroud of secrecy that covers over many families' embarrassing and difficult entanglements descended.

It is not at all clear that Jefferson would have had to say anything to the Eppeses about Hemings as he passed the days with the couple at Eppington, or to Hemings's other half sister Anne Skipwith and her husband, whom he also visited before continuing on to Monticello. The most common picture of Hemings upon her return to America, drawn by Fawn Brodie's influential work, is that of a young woman, "big with child,"[36] whose condition was immediately apparent to all who saw her. Because we do not know when Hemings's child was born—"soon after her arrival," as her son said, could have been a few months—we do not know how far along in her pregnancy she was during that fall and early winter. Unlike women who have had multiple pregnancies, many first-time mothers do not even begin to "show" their pregnancies until they are into their sixth month—their abdominal muscles still firm and unchallenged by having carried a baby to term. Not all women experience morning sickness with every pregnancy. Even if Hemings was sick on board the ship, so were all the others periodically, at least before they got out into the open sea. Beyond that, this was a time when mysterious illnesses (bacterial and viral) struck people with some regularity. Sally Hemings's condition may not have been known to anyone but her, Jefferson, and, perhaps, her brother. If it was still a secret at this point, it was one that could not last.

PART III

ON THE MOUNTAIN

(OVERLEAF)

MILL'S ELEVATION OF THE SECOND MONTICELLO.

(Courtesy of Massachusetts Historical Society)

19

Hello and Goodbye

WORMLEY HUGHES, THE grandson of Elizabeth Hemings and the oldest son of Betty Brown, was eight years old when his uncle and aunt James and Sally Hemings came back to Monticello on December 23, 1789.[1] As an elderly man, he described their arrival to Jefferson biographer Henry Randall, who saw this as an event in the lives of Jefferson and his white daughters, not in the lives of the brother and sister traveling with him. Randall had spent a great deal of time at Monticello and its environs, talking with people who knew Jefferson in order to shape what would be his three-volume story of the president's life. He knew the name Sally Hemings, probably before he began work, but certainly after he very famously spoke with Jefferson's grandson about her as he did research for his book in the 1850s.[2] It is very unlikely that he did not know that she, too, was in the carriage that brought the soon to be secretary of state back to the mountain that December, and that her brother James was along as well.

Randall boasted of his familiarity with Jefferson's Farm Book and memorandum books, so he also knew that virtually all the individuals who served Jefferson atop Monticello were members of the same family, that the elderly man relating the story of what happened the day the Jeffersons returned to Monticello was a part of that family, and thus had an interest in the day's homecoming that went beyond his observations about the white master and mistresses returning to their domain. Hughes's mother's sister and brother—his grandmother's children—had come back from their long stay in a far-off land that was indeed a parallel world. This was, for him, a completely unprecedented type of family reunion.

Hughes's memory of his returning relatives was either dim or nonexistent. James Hemings had left the country when Hughes was three years old, and had been away from Monticello traveling with Jefferson or working on his own before then. Sally Hemings was at Eppington during those same years. But he had undoubtedly heard references to the pair and shared with his mother and the rest of his family excitement at their return. When Hughes spoke with Randall many years later, he was into his seventh decade as a black person in Virginia, and likely understood that Randall had no real interest in that aspect of the story, that his relatives were invisible to the historian—or at least were to be invisible in the record of Jefferson's life that he wanted to make—unless he could use their words or a story about them to bolster his preferred way of viewing and presenting his subject. For those goals Hughes's conversation with Randall did not disappoint.

The scene of jubilant slaves wildly celebrating the arrival of their long-absent master is a staple of southern apologias for slavery, offered as proof that slaves were contented, if not downright ecstatic, in their condition. Hughes's account, along with one given by Martha Randolph, is certainly in that vein. Both told essentially the same story from their different vantage points: members of the enslaved community at Monticello and the quarter farms at the base of the mountain were extremely happy to have Jefferson home. Hughes's account, as relayed by Randall, however, was even more dramatic in its portrayal of the slaves' expression of devotion to Jefferson.[3]

Because his original plans to come home were so long delayed, Jefferson's statement of what he desired in the way of "servants" at Monticello, where he planned to stay about two months, had been sent to Nicholas Lewis almost a year before his arrival. In addition to the "provision of garden-stuff . . . two months supply of bacon, corn & c," he named the people he expected to be there to attend him. "As for servants, Great George, Ursula, Betty Hemings will be there, of course, and if Martin and Bob can join us for the time it will suffice."[4] It was to be a low-key affair, coming home for a short time, setting his daughters up at Eppington, meeting with his brothers-in-law at Monticello to help settle the Wayles debt, going to New York to make reports and pay his respects to George Washington in the new nation's capital, and then returning to France for as short a time as possible.

Given the slave network's great efficiency at transmitting intelligence, it is likely that the black people on Jefferson's plantations knew not long after he set foot in Norfolk that he was on his way home. The only question was what day he would arrive. When they found out he was coming at a point so close to Christmas, when they would have had time "off" anyway, they asked to be allowed to leave work to greet him. They gathered first at the foot of the mountain and then moved farther along the road until they were about two miles out, near Shadwell. In Martha Randolph's telling of the story, as soon as the carriage appeared, amid great shouts of joy, "[t]hey collected in crowds round it and almost drew it up the mountain by hand." In Wormley Hughes's memory, when the carriage reached a certain point, the slaves, defying Jefferson's explicit orders not to, removed the carriage horses, then "pushed and dragged the heavy vehicle" to the top of the heavily forested red clay mountain.[5] If Randolph or Hughes mentioned to Randall who was driving the carriage, and his reaction to all this, the historian did not relay this information. James Hemings was almost surely the coachman that day. Randolph's and Hughes's memories reconverged on one specific point: as soon as the carriage came to rest near the house, and Jefferson opened the door and attempted to step out of it, his feet never touched the ground. He was immediately lifted into the air and carried into the main house while the slaves kissed him and strained to touch him all along the way.[6]

After noting the discrepancy between Hughes's account and Randolph's on how the carriage got up the mountain, Randall, in a fascinating and utterly instructive reversal of normal policy, flatly and happily declared the black man's account more trustworthy than that of the upper-class white woman's. "We consider old Wormley's authority the best on this point!" he wrote, clearly relishing Hughes's particular details about the "African ovation," as Randall termed what happened when Jefferson arrived at his mountain.[7] During the antebellum period in which Randall's book appeared, in 1858, it may have been good for sales, at least in the South, to highlight such an excessive display by slaves of their affection for their master—voluntarily turning themselves into beasts of burden *over their master's protests*—to reassure white southerners and to rebuke the implacable northern abolitionists who had named slavery a cruel and barbarous system. The blacks were eager to be slaves, and the benevolent whites only reluctantly took up the burden of being their masters. If the conditions existing in this "organic" relationship had really been cruel and barbarous, slaves would never have been so happy to see their oppressor.

Whether they actually pushed or pulled the carriage up the mountain or merely walked or ran alongside it, there is no reason to doubt that most of the enslaved people who gathered to greet Jefferson were truly happy to see him return. But, as with all stories, context is everything. It is just as likely that for the vast majority of them, who could not have known him in any real sense, Jefferson was more of an idea than a real person. Unlike the Hemingses, whose sons, brothers, daughters, and sisters lived and traveled with him, slaves down the mountain, particularly in the era before his retirement, would not have had the occasion for enough contact with Jefferson to have loved him in any meaningful sense—even had they had an inclination actually to do that. "Loving" from afar is the very definition of loving the idea of a person rather than the actual thing. He had been effectively gone from Monticello for almost eight years, nearly all of Hughes's lifetime on the date this memory was made. Moreover, Hughes was telling his story long after he had spent years taking care of Jefferson's horses and acting as the principal gardener at Monticello, and thus overseeing two of Jefferson's great passions—long after Jefferson had spent years fathering several of Hughes's first cousins, long after the days when Jefferson would put in a few token moments puttering in the garden some evenings with Hughes, and long after Hughes had dug Jefferson's grave.[8]

The filter through which Hughes's memories were reanimated and transmitted was idiosyncratic and deeply personal. He had associations and memories of Jefferson shared by no other members of the enslaved community on the road to Monticello that day. This does not make what he said untrue, although Randall tended to embellish stories, and it is entirely possible that he took what was Hughes's true story of a basic expression of respectful joy and turned it into an Albemarle County proslavery pageant play. The other enslaved people who greeted Jefferson, many older and far more knowledgeable about life than the young boy taking in that scene, had important reasons to be happy to see him besides irrational feelings of affection for one whom they knew largely by sight and reputation. The *idea* of Jefferson, what he represented, more likely fueled their enthusiasm.

Enslaved people's closest human associations and familiar surroundings often brought a form of stability and comfort. That was virtually all they had. Because they were treated as property, however, they understood the tenuous nature of their connections to persons and places. In fact, many of those present with Hughes that day were in that place because their original owner, John Wayles, had died and left them as the property of another man. They, or people of whom they knew, had been required to pull up stakes and move to accommodate their master's changed family situation. Even Jefferson's time in France, well short of an actual death, caused significant dislocations in the lives of the enslaved community. Many were leased out and thus separated from their families and homes with no idea when or if they would be reunited with loved ones in what had become their settled place in the world. To make matters more frightening still, that place—the farms that made up Monticello—had deteriorated significantly while Jefferson was away. The land was wasted and even the house itself, the very symbol of him, neglected and run down. None of this was hidden.[9]

Enslaved people were well familiar with the basic contours of agricultural life, as they formed the core ingredient to it and suffered under it. Farmers borrowed money and paid it back with the crop itself or the proceeds from the sale of the crop. Even the only minimally observant among the enslaved community understood that a failing farm lessened the owner's ability to pay creditors—those ever-present specters in the lives of Virginia planters. Unhappy and unfulfilled creditors led to voluntary sales of assets (very often, the slaves themselves) or foreclosures and auctions carried out under terms designed to suit creditors. In that most dire situation, the will of even a "benevolent" owner who wanted to keep a family together could be thwarted. Slaves regularly lost their mothers, fathers, children, and other relatives to this process.

Against that backdrop, the idea of Jefferson—healthy and returned—was a reason to cheer far beyond what he meant to them as a flesh-and-blood man, representing as he did that day their best chance for a degree of stability and a return to normality. Now that he was back, perhaps everyone else could come home, too. Those greeting Jefferson that day held many different images in their heads and hearts as they moved across land that the law (with the physical force to back it up) tied them to, whether they wanted to be there or not. They were cheering out of hope for themselves and the lives of their families within the very limited framework allotted to them, not necessarily, as Randall would have it, for their unlimited love for the man who owned them.

THE ALMOST FIFTY-FIVE-YEAR-OLD Elizabeth Hemings welcomed home her son and daughter who had been away in a distant place for years. Few Afro-Virginian women in her position ever experienced such a thing: to be able to listen to her children describe a world across an ocean that they had come to know intimately, perhaps bringing gifts and certainly bringing knowledge of a different language and culture from that faraway place. She, and no one else in her time, had the same expectations about maintaining easy contact with absent relatives that exist in the modern world. For all his wealth and power, Jefferson himself could not make a ship carrying a letter travel faster across the ocean than any other man could. Near the end of his stay in France, he sent the only letter he ever wrote to his younger brother, Randolph, while he was abroad, in which he makes clear that he did not even know how many children his brother had.[10] He communicated more with his sister and in-laws, with whom he was close, but those contacts, too, were invariably far apart in time. Even within those structural limits on communication, Jefferson at least was part of a social world in which all the immediate members of his family were literate, if some only marginally so. Words on a page connected them to people far beyond the sound of voices, conveying information and providing physical evidence that, within the time of sending and receiving, the correspondent was still present on earth.

Though Elizabeth Hemings lived in a world where oral communication was primarily the order of the day, her sons Robert and James Hemings could easily have written to one another while James and Sally were overseas.[11] If brother and sister did send any letters or packages to Monticello from France, no traces of them remain. Their communications, however, would not have been a part of Jefferson's record of his incoming and outgoing correspondence, so one cannot look to his papers to decide the matter. Those items would have gone the way of the vast majority of the documents and personal property of families who do not feel compelled to preserve their family history for posterity, or who try to do that but are thwarted by fires, floods, carelessness, and other mishaps. Jefferson's records do show that throughout the 1790s, Robert Hemings, when he was away from Monticello and after his emancipation, wrote at least five letters to Jefferson, and Jefferson wrote at least one letter to him. Given the fate of other letters that had a high probability of a mention of Sally Hemings—one would expect a brother to ask the man who was living with his sister how she and other family members were faring—it is not surprising that all of those letters are missing from the collection of Jefferson's correspondence.[12]

Even though the Hemings brothers knew how to read and write, Jefferson preferred to communicate with them, and other members of their family, by sending word through others. It would have been just as easy for the person who was supposed to deliver an oral message face-to-face to have given the Hemingses a letter from Jefferson containing the same information, if he had wanted to write to them. The circumstances of Robert and James Hemings suggest that Jefferson's preferences about this give a misleading view of his slaves' capacities. One might be tempted to say that he simply did not want to correspond with black people, or to be seen corresponding with his slaves, through the same means he used to send letters to whites. His messages to the Hemings brothers were usually sent at times when he did not know where they were, and an intermediary had to both find them and deliver the message. There is a good chance that Jefferson's white intermediaries might have felt demeaned by being asked to deliver letters to a black person. Relaying a verbal order from a master better maintained Virginia's social and racial hierarchy than carrying a letter intended for an enslaved person. He did write to other blacks, most famously to the almanac author and mathematician Benjamin Banneker. But the acclaimed Banneker was a special case, and the two men had no expectation of a continuing relationship. In later years Jefferson did correspond with Robert and James's younger brother John, who was literate, about work that he wanted to have done.[13]

As noted earlier, before he handed his duties as a chef off to his brother Peter, James Hemings compiled a very detailed list of the kitchen utensils at Monticello in clear and confident handwriting and spelling that showed a high degree of literacy, perhaps even above normal for that time. No one knows for whom the list was generated, but given that Peter would have been the one using the utensils and been responsible for keeping track of them, he probably knew how to read the list as well.[14]

While we know that Robert and James were literate and that Peter likely was too, we do not know about their other Wayles siblings, including their sister Sally. Her son Madison remembered asking his father's grandchildren to teach him his letters, which may lead to an entirely reasonable inference that his mother did not know them.[15] For if she had known, surely she would have taught her son. One could, of course, draw a similar inference about Robert and James Hemings in relationship to their sister and other siblings. It seems improbable that Sally Hemings's two oldest "full" brothers, who lived in the same place as their siblings, would have known how to read and write and not conveyed any information about literacy to their younger siblings—not even to tell them how to recognize letters in the alphabet. Although it is clear that whites placed a greater emphasis on the education of boys than of girls, there is no evidence that African Americans had the same attitude about this matter. In fact, literacy seems to have been for everyone who could obtain it.

Sally Hemings was much younger than Robert and James, and they were away with Jefferson for periods of her childhood. But she and James lived closely together under extraordinary circumstances in France. They were under no apparent prohibition from Jefferson on reading and writing, and were not overly burdened with work or minute supervision, as James Hemings's adventures with his French tutor, and Sally Hemings's relatively open work schedule during large stretches of her time in Paris, reveal. If only to improve the quality of their personal association and chances of survival in the country where they thought of staying, James Hemings would have had a great incentive to teach his sister the alphabet, and at least enough of the rudiments of reading and writing to be able to read lists and follow written instructions. They would have needed to pool their every available talent or ability in order to work together to survive.

This is a very delicate business to consider from our vantage point for a number of reasons. We live in a time when parents in industrialized countries and striving Third World societies understand that sooner is always better than later when it comes to education, that there really is no time to waste in preparing children for literacy. The notion has become so ingrained as to be thought almost primal. Education is the central preoccupation of our lives because it is that dividing line, not the line between being a free person and a chattel, that determines whether one's children will have good prospects in life rather than relatively poorer ones.

Without knowing Sally Hemings's expectations about literacy, when and how it was to be obtained, and her degree of familiarity with it or sense of urgency about it in her children's early lives, we can hardly say that her son's comment proves that she could neither read nor write at any level—especially since Hemings did not say how young he was when he asked to be taught his letters, or describe the circumstances surrounding his approach to Jefferson's grandchildren. He could easily have been a little boy anxious to identify with his white nieces and nephews, who were his age and going to a school that he knew he could never attend, but wanted to. Did he act on his curiosity before his mother, who undoubtedly had other critical things to teach him about the world that he was born into, thought to address this issue? Did her brothers, she, or other members of their family learn to read when they were six or seven or as teenagers? Great care must be taken with this because Hemings's comment raises questions about more than just the state of his mother's literacy and his relationship with his father. It goes to the very heart of the nature of the relations among the Hemings family and their understanding about their position in a slave society. There is every indication that they grasped the baleful position they had been born into, and knew that forces were actively working to keep them down. African Americans felt deeply about the denial of education to them. Literacy was a highly prized skill to be passed on, even if surreptitiously and even to people who were not in one's family. The Hemings family was very close. Siblings named their children after one another. They bought their relatives' freedom and supported one another in many ways. Yet a narrow reading of Madison Hemings's statement suggests that there was no Hemings family tradition of sharing educational achievements with one another, as there was in many other enslaved families; for if there had been, he would not have had to ask members of his father's white family instead of members of his mother's African American family to teach him his letters.

One must analyze Hemings's statement in light of what is known of enslaved people's general attitude about obtaining literacy and, more specifically, important details in his own personal life. There were a number of potential vectors of literacy within the Hemings family. Beside Robert and James, John Hemings, to whom Madison was apprenticed at age twelve, and was certainly in his life on a daily basis before then, knew how to read and write, as did his wife, Priscilla. If the Jefferson family had not saved John Hemings's letters, and all we had to consider was Madison Hemings's recollections, we would assume that John Hemings did not know how to read and write, because if he had known, surely he would have taught his nephew/apprentice a skill that he needed to ply the trade that he was supposed to be teaching him. That, of course, would be a totally wrong assumption. Mary Hemings could read and write; she signed legal documents, and she and her children by Thomas Bell, Robert and Sally, in nearby Charlottesville kept in close contact with their family at Monticello. James Hemings was dead by the time Madison was born, but Robert did not die until 1819. He lived in Richmond, but he, too, kept in contact with his family on the mountain.

A more detailed discussion of the Hemings children's relationship to the white Jeffersons will be left to a later chapter, but it is enough to say now that Madison Hemings's placement of the responsibility for his literacy *solely* in the hands of the Jeffersons when there were multiple other members of the Hemings family (and other enslaved people on the plantation) who could have taught him his letters seems more an attempt to wrestle with his complicated relationship with his father than a precise statement about who around him was available to teach him to read. Judging by his preface to Hemings's recollections, the man to whom he was speaking, S. F. Wetmore, was specifically interested in whether Jefferson had or had not contributed to Hemings's education, and was deeply critical because he felt the statesman should have done more.[16] It may never have occurred to him to consider that Hemings's black relatives had either the ability or the responsibility for teaching the young Hemings to read. Given his mother's family circumstances, and her personal history, it is more probable that Sally Hemings was literate at some basic level, understood her limitations, and felt it better to leave her children's tuition to Jefferson's grandchildren. There were distinct advantages to doing this. Not only were his grandchildren receiving rigorous formal training that could benefit her children, but encouraging her offspring's association with the Randolph children might further cement a connection to them that could be helpful in the long run. Madison Hemings did not say who among his father's grandchildren taught him, but he did name one of his children, Ellen Wayles, the same name as Jefferson's eldest granddaughter.

IN THOSE FIRST days after James and Sally Hemings returned, there was much news for their family to share regarding all that had taken place over the preceding five years. One of the first things to talk about was that there were now more of them. Mary Hemings, Betty Brown, and Thenia and Critta Hemings had all given birth while their brother and sister were away. Their oldest sister, Mary, was living with Thomas Bell, a relative newcomer to the area, having arrived in Charlottesville in 1784. Mary Hemings had been leased to him in 1787. Although the birthdates of their children are unknown, their youngest, Sarah (Sally) Bell, married in 1802.[17] This suggests that Hemings and Bell met sometime before she was leased to him; indeed that may have been the impetus for the transaction. While the

Hemingses and Jefferson were still at Eppington, Jefferson wrote to William Short reporting the recent news about Charlottesville, mentioning new people who had come to the area and noting that "A Colo. Bell is there also, who is said to be a very good man." He did not say who had told him about Bell, nor did he mention the context in which his new neighbor's name came up. But Bell had leased Jefferson's property—Mary Hemings. His name probably surfaced in a general discussion of Jefferson's business affairs or a general recitation of where members of the Hemings family were all living at the time. Bell was also among the notable citizens of Albemarle County who gave a public welcome to Jefferson when he returned to Charlottesville.[18]

Bell and Jefferson had met before that official event. Whether or not he had heard about Bell and Mary Hemings before their first meeting, he certainly knew of their relationship afterward. On Christmas Day 1789, two days after he came home, Jefferson went into town to buy "snuffers" from Bell's store.[19] It is not known whether James and Sally Hemings were along to see their eldest sister when Jefferson first visited Bell's store, although the holiday would have been the perfect occasion for a reunion with her after their years away from home. If they did not travel into Charlottesville with Jefferson, he would, as a simple matter of courtesy, have passed on to Mary news of her little brother and sister. Slavery, of course, mixed business with the personal in a very particular way. By the time of Jefferson's first visit, Mary Hemings had borne two children with Bell, Robert and the above-mentioned Sally. Her offspring, naturally, were of interest to her younger siblings. They were of interest to Jefferson because he knew Mary Hemings both as a person and as his property. Her children were additions to his capital.

Bell's store was attached to his home. So Jefferson undoubtedly saw Mary Hemings that day. Whether they spoke of it explicitly or not, it did not take much deduction on his part to figure out that she and Bell were lovers. There were new babies who had not yet been born when he left for France. One might say in our time that none of this was anyone's business but the couple's. In their time, it was *exactly* Jefferson's business. He had a right to know what was going on in Mary Hemings's life—from her as an item of his property, and from the man who had leased her, who had legal duties and obligations to him that arose from the leasehold agreement.

Jefferson's discovery of what was going on between Hemings and Bell made no difference to him. In fact, it may have been part of the basis of their instant affinity. He and Bell, involved with two enslaved African American sisters, took an immediate liking to one another and formed a deep friendship that was at once social, political, and business oriented. Given their respective situations, they had much in common and little ability (or need) to make judgments about the other's personal life. Bell has been a much neglected figure in Jefferson biographies. He truly was one of Jefferson's closest friends. He dined at Monticello, and Jefferson visited his home. Within two years of their first meeting, Bell was clearly like family, and Jefferson enlisted him in his very controversial effort to build support for the National Gazette, the newspaper he hoped fervently would provide effective opposition to Hamilton's economic and political program. Bell was a perfect Jeffersonian Republican. Neither a member of the gentry nor a yeoman farmer, he was what would be called a "middling" sort—a prosperous, intelligent, educated, and civic-minded man who had enough of a stake in society to make him want to be active in his community. He cared about what was going on, in his local government and in the new federal one, following both scenes and voicing his opinions. When he wrote or spoke to Jefferson about the political issues of the day, he offered the voice of the ordinary citizen, and Jefferson respected his opinions and came to trust him greatly. He enlisted him as his agent on business transactions and to sell the nails that enslaved boys made at Monticello. They socialized together, talked of quotidian things, including, no doubt, the ways—good and bad—of the sisters with whom each was living. Their connections to Mary and Sally Hemings gave their association deeper resonance, though not in a way that could ever be shared on paper.[20]

R. T. W. Duke, a white resident of Charlottesville, who knew several of Mary Hemings and Thomas Bell's grandchildren, described what he called the "'easy' morality" of Bell's and Hemings's day, not just in terms of what people actually did but in the way others reacted to them. He said that "no one paid attention to a man's method of living."[21] Their neighbors, Duke explained, would not have thought to raise a public fuss about the pair. His observation fits in with other known information about that era. Eighteenth-century people like Bell, Hemings, Jefferson, and their neighbors fit the popular conception neither of the Puritans nor of the later Victorians, though there is often a tendency to read the perceived values of one society forward and the other backward to cover the people who lived in the interim. There were standards of behavior, as there are in every period, but the era of Bell,

Jefferson, and Hemings was practical—more libertarian—about the ways of human beings and sex.

There was premarital sex, among all classes, but with the expectation that the couple would marry and avoid the stigma of illegitimacy. Fornication and interracial marriages were officially against the law, but neighbors were not going to bother people about their relations unless what they were doing somehow directly affected them or represented an aggressive threat to social mores. The couple usually had to act in a fashion that was annoying or troubling in some exceptional way before any persons in the community actively concerned themselves with their behavior.[22] Vigilante, and quasi-vigilante, activities are more likely to occur in communities living in fear of losing control in some fashion. There was no question who was in control of society in Albemarle County in the 1790s.

The stricter present-day "morality" of Duke's age—the one he contrasted with that of Hemings's and Bell's day—was the morality of a white South that had declared war on the blacks in their midst after the Confederate's defeat in the Civil War. Having had one form of control over blacks wrested from them, they desperately sought to reestablish other forms. Virginia fell into the total grip of Jim Crow. Interracial couples had a greater chance of being censured in Duke's era than in Hemings's and Bell's time, and laws regarding racial classifications became even tighter. It was not until the 1920s, however, that Virginia became the first state to adopt as a matter of law the so-called one-drop rule for deciding blackness.[23]

Twentieth-century Virginia legislators were more stringent in their beliefs about racial categories than Jefferson, who pronounced octoroons (individuals with one-eighth black ancestry) white, even though they, like his youngest son, Eston, could be visibly of African descent.[24] Duke's Charlottesville could not have countenanced a Thomas Bell living openly in town with a black woman and having children with her. He would never have become a justice of the peace or been appointed to a committee to study a proposal to bring public education to the town, as he was back in the 1790s while living with Mary Hemings.[25]

The Bell-Hemings union reveals something else about the nature of Charlottesville society, the workings of small towns, and family business in their time. We have no official record of Bell's ever having formally freed Mary Hemings or the children he had with her. Formal freedom required drafting a deed of manumission and filing it in the county courthouse, as Jefferson would do with deeds of manumission for Robert and James Hemings during the time Hemings and Bell were together. Alternatively, slaves could be freed by a will that would then be filed. One might understand how the recordation of one Bell deed might be lost, but that all three would have been lost seems unlikely. There is no gap in the records of Albemarle County deeds for that period. The most probable answer is that Bell freed his enslaved family only informally, and gambled that his will, which treats them as if they were already free, would be respected by his immediate white family and members of the community.

Bell's failure to act would be completely familiar to property and contract professors, as well as to legions of lawyers. The former have dozens of cases to analyze with their students and the latter are kept employed because of a simple fact: people often fail, in the most critical situations, to follow simple legal formalities even when the failure to do so could work catastrophic results for people they love. People often do things that make no sense. They postpone making wills and die before they get the chance, leaving it to the state to distribute their property and find guardians for their minor children. They purport to transfer land without a written document, a legal impossibility in countries following the English system of jurisprudence since the 1600s.

Bell apparently trusted that his legal relatives, and the surrounding community, who knew very well who Mary Hemings was to him, would not challenge his wishes as expressed in his will. Sure enough, as far as we know, no one rose to stand against his preferences, which is yet another example of how law works "on the ground," so to speak. When everyone, for whatever reason, agrees to look the other way, individuals can easily circumvent legal rules. Several decades later, Mary's sister Sally, who was also freed informally, appeared in the 1830 census as a free white person when she was neither legally free nor white. A few years after that, she appeared as a mulatto woman freed in 1826. Even though no formal papers had been filed, the community treated her as a free person. Still, Bell's was a risky strategy, and one wonders whether he might have been concerned about testing the limits of his community's tolerance. It was one thing for him to live with Hemings and have children with her when she was his property, but he might have gone too far if he had tried to live openly with her when she was a free woman. Had she been freed, of course, they still would not have been able to marry. Slavery provided a "polite" cover for what would otherwise be illegal fornication.

The coming years brought much travel between Monticello and Bell's house and store in Charlottesville. Mary Hemings's home was a meeting place—and no doubt a place of retreat—for multiple generations of Hemingses. According to family tradition, even after Bell died, Jefferson liked to come by the house to listen to Sally Bell's husband, Jesse Scott, play the violin. Scott was a member of a well-known and much celebrated mixed-race family of musicians. In that very convoluted and insular world, his family's connection to Jefferson was long-standing by the time of his marriage to Hemings and Bell's daughter. Jefferson had hired the "Scott Family" to play at his own daughter Martha's wedding, an event that took place two months after he first met Scott's future father-in-law that Christmas Day in 1789.[26] These multiple overlapping connections—business, personal, and family—ensured that there would be deep connections between the mountain and Main Street. Those bonds began to be forged in earnest during the period when the Hemingses started to reassemble at Monticello.

THOUGH ALL THE Hemingses had stories to tell in the last days of 1789 and the beginning of 1790, James and Sally certainly had more exotic and startling things to reveal to their family about their adventures abroad. One wonders about their states of mind in those early days. Theirs had not been a short vacation to a foreign land, dabbling in the local culture just long enough to get a taste of it before returning home and, at most, having their internal clocks disrupted by living briefly in a different time zone. They were out of their country long enough to have become part of a new one and to be changed in ways subtle and profound.

That certainly happened to Jefferson, who relished his time in the country and brought elements of it home in the form of his dress, furniture, appreciation for haute cuisine, wine, and, some said, even his mannerisms. Playing at being French meant one thing for Jefferson and another for the two Hemingses, James in particular. He had been in France as long as Jefferson and had every reason to remain attached to things French because it was his job to be a French chef. And while Jefferson merely added French culture to an already celebrated and secure persona, Hemings was a much younger man, with fewer social resources at his disposal. Having received a completely new identity in France, he now had a profession and experiences that set him apart from others.

Along with whatever cultural affectations and, perhaps, sense of superiority, attached to brother and sister because of their European adventure,
France lived in their memory as their time out of Virginian slavery and the
place where they could have lived free. They had to adjust to something very
different now, picking up where they had left off as slaves in a slave society.
If Jefferson and his daughters were at all discomfited by being thrown back
into "the Forest of Albermarle,"[27] they had not experienced so vast a change
in their statuses. Where they had once been powerful slave-owning white
Virginians, they were now powerful slave-owning white Virginians who
spoke better French and had firsthand knowledge of French culture.

The physical surroundings at Monticello told a symbolic story of the
social distance the siblings had traveled from a place of potential freedom
back to a slave society. They had returned from living at a grand and luxuri-
ous residence with indoor plumbing to an unkempt and run-down "great"
house that must have seemed a near wreck to them after the Hôtel de
Langeac. A few months after arriving home, Jefferson warned his in-laws,
the Eppeses, whom he had invited for a visit, that were they to come, they
would be "roughing it," indicating the poor condition of even his own living quarters.[28] There was no neighborhood full of well-appointed homes,
no street scenes to provide daily theater, no more balls for Sally Hemings
to attend as lady-in-waiting, no more sumptuous architecture. Instead, the
scene the siblings took in upon their arrival included the neglected "great
house" looming over tiny slave cabins dotting the landscape, providing a
stark reminder of what they had decided to return to.

Those poor dwellings housed the brother's and sister's relatives and other
enslaved people. It was, most likely, in one of those cabins that Elizabeth
Hemings learned that her daughter was now in the same position that she
had been in with the master of the household. Sally Hemings could tell her
mother why she believed her life and that of her children would be different
from the lives her mother and siblings had lived. Did Elizabeth Hemings
wish her daughter had made a different choice, to have opted for freedom
even if it meant she might be lost to the Virginia Hemingses forever?

Elizabeth and Sally Hemings surely discussed how the laws of slavery in France differed from the laws of Virginia. But that Hobson's choice
for families in slave societies was an especially tough one for females,
and Sally Hemings's predicament and her mother's more likely reaction to it, is explained very well by the historian Stephanie M. H. Camp's

observations about enslaved women's attitudes toward flight from slavery. Camp explained, "Paramount among women's reasons for not running away as fugitives more frequently were their family responsibilities and gender ideals among the enslaved. Women were enmeshed in networks of extended family and friends, and they played central roles in the black family." Enslaved women defined themselves as women "through their activities on behalf of their families." The "dense social relations" that informed their lives made it especially hard for them to leave their families behind. Many enslaved women did run away, but the special pressures they faced— the things they had to think about before they made their decisions—were ever present and insistent.[29]

One can easily see how women whose femininity was devalued by the society at large would want to latch onto a definition of self tied to something positive—being a source of support for loved ones—even if that meant putting self aside, and forgoing a chance for individual freedom. Self-sacrifice was a route to self-affirmation and respectability. Stephanie Camp quotes Molly Hornblow, who criticized her granddaughter for considering running away. "Nobody," Hornblow said, "respects a mother who forsakes her children."[30] In a culture where daughters were also expected to care for elderly members of their families, it was very likely that the sentiment ran in both directions to at least some degree. A daughter could also not be seen forsaking her mother. Jefferson, with his very traditional views about the role of women in family, probably reminded the sixteen-year-old girl coming into womanhood of her duties to her family as he sought to persuade her to come home with him. We do not know how Elizabeth Hemings felt about the way her daughter dealt with Jefferson and freedom or, for that matter, about how Jefferson had dealt with her daughter. Nor do we know whether she would have better understood it if her son had stayed than if her daughter had, but we do know that she had valuable information about what life was like as a slave woman attached to the master of a plantation. She could have told her daughter what to expect from Jefferson, other white people, and other members of the enslaved community. She had many more years to provide counsel because she lived longer than most people of her day, black or white, enslaved or free.

20

❧

EQUILIBRIUM

B Y THE BEGINNING of February 1790, if not before, James
Hemings knew with certainty that he would never go back to Paris
with Jefferson. After weeks of mulling it over and discussing it with
friends and family, Jefferson accepted the appointment as secretary of state.
That ended his term as minister to France, and he never saw Paris again.
New York, the capital of the new nation, was his next destination. Hemings
had not been anticipating an exact return to the life he had known in Paris.
Without his sister and Jefferson's daughters, things simply could not be the
same. He would not even return to the same house. Jefferson had decided,
before they left the city, that he could not afford so grand a residence as the
Hôtel de Langeac, and needed to find a less expensive alternative. Although
Hemings would not be going back to the same surroundings there, Paris,
a free society, versus New York, a slave society, was probably preferable to
him. He had to say goodbye yet again to his family at Monticello and to
whatever thoughts or plans he had about what he would do once he got
back to France.[1]

It was also clear that the configuration of slaves and masters who had
lived together overseas would never be reconstituted in the same way at any
place on American soil. At some point after the party's arrival in Norfolk on
November 23, their trek through Virginia stopping at the homes of various
relatives, and their return to Monticello one month later, Patsy Jefferson
encountered her cousin Thomas Mann Randolph. The two became engaged,
evidently sometime in January; one says "evidently" because it is not known
exactly how their courtship began or progressed. Jefferson's memorandum

books and letters trace his visits to others' homes during this period, but make no reference to Randolph or Tuckahoe. Jefferson learned of the couple's plan sometime in January and on February 4 received a letter from Randolph's father about the impending union. He quickly replied favorably to the match.[2]

Patsy, now called Martha, and Thomas had surely met as children, but cannot have known each other very well. She had been away from Monticello from the time she was eleven. Couples then and now do meet and fall in love at first sight, and that could have happened to this young pair, though that would not have been the only consideration in their time. As important as whatever love existed between them were the long-standing ties between the two families, ties that went back to the prospective fathers-in-law's own fathers and to Jefferson's family on his mother's side—he was a Randolph himself through her line.[3]

It helped that Jefferson knew Tom Randolph, though in a very limited fashion. While he was still in Paris, Tom had written to him from Edinburgh, where he was studying, and Jefferson spoke well of his daughter's future suitor.[4] Although this was not a case of a young girl's seeking to join her life's fortunes to a totally unknown quantity, it was nearly so. Martha's engagement to a man whom she could have known only as an adult for as little as three and, at most, seven weeks—four of which had been spent traveling from plantation to plantation when he would not have been with her all the time—is worth pausing over. Others who have chronicled Jefferson's life have done so, sometimes providing their own explanations for what really was an extraordinary turn of events.

Henry Randall insisted that the couple had met and courted in Paris. That could be the only reason for so swift an engagement in Virginia. He knew how intensely devoted Jefferson's eldest daughter was to him, a devotion he wrote movingly about in his biography. The idea that Martha could so hastily agree to leave her father's home—before she had even begun to reacclimate herself to that home—seems to have unnerved the historian so much that he promoted the idea of a European romance between the young lovers that all evidence indicates did not occur.[5]

The couple's granddaughter Sarah Randolph endorsed the idea of a meeting in the summer of 1788 as a possible start to her forebears' romance. She apparently based this on a letter from Thomas Mann Randolph Sr. to Jefferson dated November 19, 1787, in which he said he told his son to go

to Paris, as if a letter alone urging someone to go to a place, with no confirming after-the-fact circumstances, proved that the person actually went
there.[6] Thomas Jr. did not always do what his father said. That seems actually to have been the source of the great tension between them. At the end
of December 1788, Jefferson said he had not heard from Tom Randolph for
over a year and supposed that he had returned to America, which, in fact,
he had. The young man wrote to his mother the preceding May, saying he
was coming home, having decided not to go to Paris.[7]

Other, more modern considerations of this subject linked the quick
engagement and marriage to Jefferson's appointment as secretary of state.
Things had to move quickly because he had to assume his post and did not
want to miss the wedding.[8] There was also the marriage settlement to think
of. It had to be signed before the marriage took place, or it would have no
legal effect. That answers the question about the timing of the wedding
ceremony, not about how Martha came to accept so quickly a marriage proposal from a near-stranger on the very heels of her return from over five
years in another country. She gave herself no time to get settled and think,
and barely enough time to unpack. Love does that to some people, but it
is almost impossible to view this lightning-quick courtship and marriage
without taking note of its disappointing aftermath.

Unlike her sister Maria, Martha would not have a happy marriage. That
she and Tom had twelve children over a long stretch of time was most
likely due to the near-permanence of the marriage bond in those days and
the lack of a culture of and access to birth control. Martha could not have
refused Tom, even had she wanted to, though it was clear at some point that
she wanted no more children. After the birth of her ninth child, Benjamin
Franklin, she expressed the hope, in a day when abstinence was the only
sure route to preventing conception, that he would be her last. She had
three more after him. In the final period of her life, her family broken by
debt, she viewed her eldest son's growing family with great trepidation.
Children were more burden than pleasure.[9]

Jefferson has been seriously criticized for the failure of his eldest daughter's marriage, as if he were chiefly responsible for that. In the conventional narrative, for purely selfish reasons, he encouraged Martha's loyalty
to him over her husband, thus taking what was destined to be a happy marriage and wrecking it. On the other hand, Maria and John Wayles Eppes
were able to be happy because they resisted Jefferson's call to move to

Pantops, a farm near Monticello, and generally lived outside of his influence. Both couples were free adults who bear primary responsibility for
the way their lives turned out, both credit and blame—if any blame is to
be laid. Maria and John Eppes's marital happiness was not merely a function of Jefferson's absence. There is every reason to believe that these two
would have been happy wherever they were, because they loved each other
and were truly compatible. They, in contrast to Tom and Martha Randolph,
had known each other for many years before they married, and knew they
suited one another. A hard look at Martha and Tom's situation suggests that
Jefferson was never the major problem with their union. The details of the
Randolph marriage and family circumstances are worth considering closely
at this point because the fallout from their domestic woes shaped life at
Monticello—particularly the lives of Sally Hemings and her children from
1790 on.

All families have problems, of varying degrees of severity, but there has
been a marked tendency in the presentation of the life of Jefferson and
his white family to overlook some extremely serious issues the family had
to confront. There are clear indications from Thomas and Martha's eldest
son, Thomas Jefferson Randolph, and from other observers, that his father
was an unstable and physically abusive man. Jeff Randolph described him
as capable of being "more ferocious than the woulf and more fell than the
hyena."[10] No child says that about a father who is merely annoying or just
somewhat overbearing. Tom Randolph must have done things to members
of his family, hurt them in ways beyond being merely impecunious and
neglectful. Wolves and hyenas are associated with violence and aggression.
Indeed, Edmund Bacon remembers seeing Tom cane his eldest son when
he was a grown man, a wholly inappropriate act designed to humiliate as
much as to "correct."[11] By the time Bacon witnessed this, such things had
probably been going on for a long while and may have been worse before
the Randolphs moved to Monticello permanently in 1809.

Jeff Randolph denied Bacon's account of post-adult whippings from his
father in a broadside he published to refute some of Bacon's more embarrassing stories about life at Monticello. The man more ferocious than a wolf
and more "fell" than a hyena was transformed into a Virginian Saint Francis
of Assisi. Tom Randolph may well have been all these things—the sin-
ner/saint dichotomy always suppresses the complex nature of any human
being's life. Jeff Randolph was an old man by this time and could well have

been seeing his father through the nostalgic haze that often covers memories of earlier life. Moreover, his father had reportedly begged his forgiveness on his deathbed. It is also clear that Jeff Randolph thought of himself as the guardian of his family's reputation, and was willing to go to great lengths in that role even if it meant saying things that were not true.[12]

Thomas Mann Randolph is often written of as if his mental instability appeared only late in life—his poor financial circumstances and, again, Jefferson having driven him crazy. Evidence of Randolph's problematic temperament already appeared in the young man, soon after his marriage. In the months immediately following the wedding, Jefferson set up and tried to shepherd through negotiations with Tom's father to acquire one of his farms, Edgehill, as a family home for the newlyweds. Tom lost his temper during the negotiations and insulted his father so gravely that it caused a permanent rupture in their relations. They reconciled on the surface, but the elder man never really forgave or trusted his son again.[13] Two years later, when his sister was thrown into a scandal involving their brother-in-law Richard Randolph, Tom wrote to the embattled young man facing a criminal prosecution and trying to find a way to defend himself. He threatened his kinsman, saying that he would personally "wash out with your blood the stain on my family."[14]

Deviating from the well-documented typical pattern of youthful male aggressiveness in the late teens and early twenties that mellows, Randolph kept his rough edges well into his adulthood. He got into brawls. On one occasion, he struck his son-in-law Charles Bankhead in the head with an iron poker after Bankhead mistook him for a servant and cursed at him.[15] He could easily have killed him. His temper and lack of self-control affected not just the immediate objects of his wrath but also his relations with all who knew him. Imagine Jefferson sending a man a graphic letter threatening to kill him, getting into fistfights above the age of boyhood, or hitting someone in the head with a poker. It is not known whether Tom Randolph ever directed his physical aggression toward Martha. He, like other aggressive men, may have drawn the line at hitting women—or he may not have. Even if he never physically abused Martha, it cannot have been easy for a woman used to the placid environment of life with a father who modeled a version of manhood that emphasized control over one's emotions to be suddenly placed under the power of a man who had violent mood swings and felt no compunction about striking those who displeased him.

The family aggression replicated itself when Tom and Martha's eldest daughter, Anne, married the above-mentioned Charles Bankhead, who repeatedly beat her even while they lived at Monticello. At least one time, he beat her in front of her mother. When Martha Randolph told Jefferson about the incident, he appealed to Bankhead's father for support. They both tried to keep what had happened secret from Tom Randolph, fearing his reaction—although if there was ever a time to take a poker to a man, that was it.[16] Bacon's memory of Anne's travails at the hand of her husband gave rise to another Jeff Randolph cover-up. In the same broadside in which he disputed Bacon's claim that his father had caned him when he was an adult, Randolph flatly pronounced Bacon's story of "Mr. Bankhead's violence toward his wife" as "untrue," hiding his sister's suffering out of a sense of family shame, when he could have told the truth (Anne had done nothing shameworthy) or simply remained silent.[17] Instead, he saw himself as preserving the family honor by lying, for he well knew that his brother-in-law beat his sister. Moreover, Randolph had his own personal experience with Bankhead's violent tendencies. Decades before he denied that Bankhead beat his sister, Bankhead had almost killed Randolph, stabbing him when the two got into an altercation in a Charlottesville tavern. Bankhead's beastliness was so taken as a given that as Jefferson contemplated this horrible family situation, he was concerned not only about his grandson's life but about his granddaughter Anne's. Bankhead, he feared, would take things out on her physically after his fight with her brother.[18]

Bankhead also physically attacked a member of the Hemings family, Burwell Colbert, no doubt drawing the enmity of the clan. Ellen Coolidge wrote of the elderly Jefferson's indescribable anguish when he found out what had happened.[19] Their grandfather's home was undoubtedly a happy place for the Jefferson grandchildren; young people's resilience allows them to absorb an enormous amount of distress without despair while focusing on the good things that happened to them. But the presence of one, and then two, unpredictable and violent males at the heart of the Jefferson-Randolph household cannot be treated as a minor detail; aggression is never without consequence. Although both men were periodically exiled from the family, their difficult personalities and actions inevitably affected the lives of all family members and others who came into close contact with them.

It is completely understandable that Jefferson, upon viewing his daughter married to an unstable man with a ferocious temper, might well have wished to provide a haven for her without being open about why the haven was required. When he learned of the horror his granddaughter Anne was living with her husband, he begged her—to no avail—to come live at Monticello. When she refused, he confided with deep sadness to a friend that he always expected her "to die at [Bankhead's] hands."[20] We understand today much more about spousal abuse and that women like Anne stay in abusive relationships because they genuinely fear that their husbands will kill them if they leave. Often they are right. Bankhead was the sort who really might have killed Jefferson's granddaughter.

Great stigma attached to both serious marital discord and emotional illness. These were not the kinds of things a man so private as Jefferson cared to speak of in his letters, and his reference to Anne's problem shows that he was at a loss to do anything about her situation beside offering her a place of refuge. People were to carry on, entertaining friends and relatives, as if there were no problems at all. In the mid-1790s, Tom and Martha traveled from doctor to doctor looking for a cure to his unspecified or, perhaps, unknown illness.[21] Jefferson wrote as if the illness caused Randolph's depression, but it is also possible, given later descriptions of his emotional history, that depression was the actual root of the problem, and the difficulties with his "physical" health a mere byproduct.

While no one could have foreseen all of this at the couple's beginnings in 1790, more time and more opportunities to observe Tom Randolph—and hear what a wider range of people knew of him—might have given Martha at least the small consolation of being able to say, as the years passed, that she knew what she was getting into when she married him. If Jefferson can be faulted for anything relating to his eldest daughter's marriage, it is for not exercising greater vigilance about her entrance into what was, in his time, a permanent arrangement. In those first weeks after their return to America, his much vaunted possessiveness of Martha was nowhere in sight. She was vulnerable. Anyone would be disoriented after having spent almost six years away from home, five of them in a foreign country. She had gone from girl to woman in a different world. Yet her father quickly agreed to put her under the control of a man neither of them knew, understanding very well what marriage would mean for her. Not long after the wedding, he wrote to Martha saying that the happiness of her life now depended upon "continuing to please a single person."[22] This was not, as it is sometimes portrayed, merely a statement revealing Jefferson's personal misogyny.

Jefferson was speaking the plain truth. A married woman ceased to be her own person and was placed under the total dominion of her husband—by law. One who lives under the legal dominion of another, even if styled as a benevolent dominion or one grounded in "love," is not in control of his or her happiness. If Martha was too in love to think straight about this, it was her only surviving parent's job to think for her and suggest, at least, that they take their time. What was the rush, given all that was at stake?

At seventeen, Martha was younger than the average Virginia bride, and Tom was only twenty-one. When Tom's sister Judith was set to marry Richard Randolph, under the same circumstances, her mother, Anne Cary Randolph, objected strenuously. Cynthia Kierner has noted that Randolph "hoped to delay Judith's marriage and to keep all of her daughters single until, in her words, 'they were old enough to form a proper judgment of Mankind, well knowing that a woman's happiness depends entirely on the Husband she is united to.'"[23] Randolph's words, almost exactly tracking Jefferson's, were written several years before Tom and Martha's union. Having been a teenage bride herself, she knew very well what it meant to tie one's life to a man under the facts of social life as it existed for women in her time, having baby after baby (she gave birth to thirteen) with no satisfactory way out even if one were deeply unhappy in one's circumstances. Had she lived long enough to become Martha's mother-in-law, Anne Randolph would have understood perfectly the risk this young girl was about to take and would not have been at all surprised at how her married life turned out. She knew that there were many reasons why a seventeen-year-old girl, married much too soon to a twenty-one-year-old man, might become unhappy and wish fervently to return to girlhood in her father's home. Martha's circumstances were even more striking and poignant; within a nine-month period she went from living a carefree, almost giddy life in a grand residence in Paris, attending balls with her friends, to living in a virtual swamp in a barely adequate house in the middle of nowhere with a man she did not know.[24] Nothing about this signaled happily ever after.

One would not expect Jefferson to have had the same perspective on matters as Anne Cary Randolph. While her daughter's impending marriage caused her to reflect upon her own ambivalence about the way her life as a woman had turned out, he would have looked at Randolph's life and seen nothing at all amiss. What were women to do but get married, live under the direction of a man, and have his babies? Still, finding the *right* man was important, and it should have occurred to Jefferson that it might take Martha more than two or three weeks to do that.

It is very likely that Jefferson's habitual optimism and early life experiences overrode any reluctance to support his daughter's plan to get married so quickly when she did not have to. He had been brought as a little boy to live in Thomas Mann Randolph Sr.'s impressive residence, Tuckahoe. Although he was well used to gracious living from the time of his boyhood, Tuckahoe took that to another level. Well-appointed as it was, Shadwell did not rival his cousin's home. The boys grew up together for a time in that house, Randolph the young master of it, Jefferson a kinsman, but nevertheless a guest in those more opulent surroundings. When the son of the boyhood master of Tuckahoe asked for his daughter's hand, with the expectation that she would become the mistress of the place herself, Jefferson was not inclined to hesitate, even if he should have. The imprinted association of Tuckahoe with wealth and stability gave him the confidence to support the whirlwind engagement and marriage, even though he knew that Randolph Sr. carried a staggering amount of debt, inherited from his father-in-law, Archibald Cary. The trappings of Tuckahoe aside, Thomas Mann Randolph's family was neither wealthy nor stable.[25]

Most important of all, Martha's inexplicably quick courtship and marriage took place in a critical context. The very weeks that she met and married her future husband coincided with the period that Sally Hemings's condition became more obvious. If Martha's swift marriage was in any way her reaction to that, Jefferson was not in a good position to dissuade her from starting her own new life and household. He may indeed have been quite relieved. She was willing to go right away, and he was willing to let her go as fast as she wanted to. Family crises of this nature were not typically spoken of in the papers of white slave-owning families. It is unreasonable, therefore, to expect to be able to survey the family's written record of itself and hope to find an answer openly displayed, or to attribute any significance to the absence of a forthright treatment of such matters. If an answer is to be found in written records, it will be hidden away or referred to indirectly, which is exactly what happened with Sally Hemings and her pregnancy in 1790.

Following the trajectory of Hemings's life, and taking her seriously as a person, requires one both to notice when the trajectory veers and to look for an explanation for the change of course. It was a staple of life among upper-class slave-owning families that when the daughter of the household married, she was given a lady's maid to attend her in her new role as wife, usually a female whom she already knew and who had attended her before.[26] Through all the transformations that took place within the institution from the colonial period to the antebellum years, this phenomenon remained a constant to the point of cliché. Martha's grandmother Martha Eppes brought Elizabeth Hemings to her marriage. Her mother took Betty Brown as her lady's maid from the Forest with her when she married Jefferson. Sally Hemings, given her life up until 1790, could reasonably have expected, as she grew up, to follow in the footsteps of her mother and aunt and serve in the home of either Martha or Maria upon their marriages. Yet it was never to be.

Before Martha Jefferson wed Thomas Mann Randolph in February of 1790, her father drew up a marriage settlement earlier that month in which he gave her twenty-seven slaves.[27] Tellingly, he did not give her Sally Hemings, the young woman who had been her lady's maid for two years in France. That this very quickly created something of an issue for Martha was revealed in letters that passed between her, her aunt, and her father during the first half of that year. On July 2, 1790, while Jefferson was in New York serving as secretary of state, the newly married Martha wrote to him from Eppington, where she was living with her sister, "on the subject of a maid," saying that she needed one. Jefferson referred to this letter in one he wrote on July 25 to her aunt Elizabeth Eppes. Martha, along with Polly, now called Maria, had been staying with her at Eppington during the late spring and early summer of 1790 while Martha's husband got their home at Varina ready for them to live in later that season.[28] While there, she discussed with her aunt the fact that she needed a maid. Eppes had written to Jefferson on June 4 about the same issue, but her letter arrived after Martha's. Jefferson wrote, "Patsy has written me on the subject of a maid also, but adds that it will be time enough when we meet at Monticello. She will certainly never want any thing I can add to her convenience. I am in hopes, while in Virginia, to bring about arrangements which may fix her in Albemarle."[29]

Like other correspondence that holds a promise of a substantive discussion of Sally Hemings, both letters from these two women written almost exactly a month apart, on the same topic, are missing from the collection of Jefferson's letters. Although it is unlikely that either woman was totally candid or explicit about why Hemings would not be available to act as Martha's maid, there may have been some general reference to her unavailability and a discussion of who among the enslaved women at Monticello already known to Martha might be a suitable replacement.

The slaves Jefferson gave his daughter were from one of his outlying plantations, and she could not have known any of the women well enough to trust them so much as the women house servants she had grown up with at Monticello. The point, however, is that both women wrote to tell Jefferson that Martha needed and wanted a maid. Jefferson, for obvious reasons, did not suggest to Eppes or his daughter that Hemings could continue in her role as a "convenience" that he was willing to provide, though when he returned to Monticello that fall, he did act upon his daughter's request. He deeded Martha eight additional slaves, including the oldest daughter of Mary Hemings, Molly, who was about fourteen years old.[30] Mary Hemings had been an important house servant of long standing, and Martha knew her and her children. It made perfect sense in the context of slavery at Monticello to give the teenager to Martha to serve as the maid she said she needed. Molly evidently continued with Martha for many years.[31]

Hemings was Maria's maid, too, but her newly married sister was in far greater need of help in setting up what would be her new household with her husband than the thirteen-year-old who was back in her element with her beloved aunt, her cousins, and their slaves. The timing of Jefferson's exchange of letters with Betsy Eppes and his daughter about providing a maid for Martha is critical, especially in light of his November conveyance of additional slaves to his older daughter. He knew, at least as early as July of 1790, that Maria's circumstances were about to change drastically anyway. He had plans for her that would obviate the need for Sally Hemings to serve as her personal maid.

Earlier in the same month that Jefferson wrote to Eppes, as a partial result of some of his own very famous dealings with Alexander Hamilton, Congress had voted to move the capital from New York to Philadelphia on an interim basis before settling into its permanent home on the Potomac River. Even before the bill formally passed, Jefferson was so confident in its passage that he wrote to William Short on July 1, telling him to send his "baggage" from Paris to Philadelphia rather than to New York.[32] The thought that his younger daughter might join him there came quickly to

his mind, for in that same July letter to his sister-in-law, replying to her missive about getting Martha another maid, he informed her that he wanted
"to consult" with her about Maria and thought that could be "best done at
Monticello." He invited her and her husband to visit him there during the
coming fall. The Eppeses were apparently unable to join him for the face-
to-face consultation, but sent Maria along. In October, Jefferson wrote to
Elizabeth Eppes and announced that he was going ahead with the plan that
he had obliquely referred to earlier in July. He had decided that Maria would
remain at Monticello for the winter, but would join him in Philadelphia in
the spring and be placed in a boarding school.[33]

When Maria went to live with her father in Philadelphia, Sally Hemings
did not go with her. Instead, after a time, Jefferson hired a local woman to
attend his daughter. Just as he eschewed giving Hemings to Martha upon
her marriage, when Maria married seven years later, and Hemings was
still a very young woman, Jefferson did not give her to his younger daughter either, despite their lifelong intimacy with one another.[34] There was
no enslaved female with whom Maria was more familiar, and no role that
Hemings played until that time was of longer standing than being helper to
Jefferson's daughters. But they were going to get married and, presumably,
live away from their father. After Hemings's return from France, someone
very important had an interest in having her stay at Monticello: Jefferson.
Instead of giving Sally Hemings to Maria on her wedding, he gave her
another of Mary Hemings's children, Sally's fifteen-year-old niece, Betsy.[35]

It is not clear where Sally Hemings was in the spring of 1790. The most
reasonable estimate of the absolute latest month in which she could have
given birth was May, and it is not known how long her child lived. Martha
and Maria were supposed to go to Eppington right after Martha's wedding
at the end of February, and Jefferson left for New York at the beginning of
March, thinking his daughters and son-in-law would start right out for the
Eppeses. It seems unlikely, though not impossible, that Hemings would
have been expected to go with them if she was in the last stages of her pregnancy or had already given birth, and had a newborn (the Jefferson daughter's half sibling) to look after.

As things turned out, Martha and Maria did not get to Eppington for
another two and a half months—until the middle of May. At the end of
April they were at Tuckahoe, stranded there because they did not have their

own horses, and Tom did not want to borrow his father's to make the trip.[36] They explained this to a somewhat baffled Betsy Eppes, who told Jefferson that she and her husband could easily have supplied them with horses had they just written to say there was a problem.[37] Why the logistics of their trip had not been discussed and set before Jefferson even left is unclear. This seems another curious lapse in fatherly attention, though he may have felt it appropriate to step aside and let the new husband take matters into his own hands. If that was the case, Tom's performance was a portent of things to come.

Hemings was apparently at Eppington by summer's end, however. Tom and Martha sent for her there sometime in August, for Maria Jefferson referred to this in an undated letter to her brother-in-law written, most likely, before the last week in September 1790. Maria's language suggests that about six weeks had gone by since the last communication with her sister. Then she went on to mention Hemings. "We were at Cumberland when you sent for Sally but she was not well enough to have gone." Elizabeth Eppes's sister and Hemings's half sister, Ann Wayles Skipwith, lived in Cumberland County, and Eppes visited her sister regularly.[38] The nature of Hemings's illness is unknown.

There is no extant written explanation for why the Randolphs sent for Hemings. By midsummer the couple had concluded that Varina was ruining their health. Determined to move away as quickly as possible, they already had their eyes on Edgehill in Albemarle County. Monticello would be their way station until they gained ownership of it.[39] There was no urgency, at that late date, to take Hemings there to help put in order a house they expected to abandon shortly. If she was called to Varina to help, it was to help an overwhelmed Martha pack up to get ready to leave. The timing of the Randolphs' request, however, suggests that bringing Hemings to them was more likely about Monticello than about Varina.

At the beginning of August, Jefferson wrote to Martha, directing her to send word to Hemings's brothers Martin and Robert to make sure that they were at Monticello by September 1 to "have things prepared" by the time he got there.[40] Martha and Tom Randolph were likely planning to send Sally Hemings to Monticello, perhaps with one or both of her brothers, to help everyone get ready for Jefferson's arrival. He had told the young couple even before his August letter to expect him (and meet him) there near the beginning of September.[41] There was, then, at the end of the summer of 1790, a gathering of all the Hemingses who formed the basic foundation of the personal staff at Monticello. Everyone who was supposed to be there would be there when Jefferson arrived.

Gabriella Harvie and "Sarah Jefferson"

By the time Jefferson returned to Monticello that September, it was clear that his idea of finding a home for Martha and her husband in Albemarle might not work out, for reasons that strangely mirrored his own personal circumstances. He planned to talk with Thomas Mann Randolph Sr. about selling Edgehill to the newlyweds.[42] A complication arose in the form of Gabriella Harvie, Randolph Sr.'s seventeen-year-old soon to be new wife, whose turn through the Randolph household calls to mind the phrase "white tornado." Jefferson, forty-seven, and Randolph, fifty, boyhood friends and cousins, had both taken up with teenage girls of almost the exact same age—Jefferson, with a young girl from his household, Randolph, with a girl who lived on the plantation right next door. Like Jefferson, Randolph had probably known the young object of his attention all her life. It is also very likely that his children—some of whom were around Harvie's age, some older, some younger—had known her, too, for in the close-knit world of the Virginia gentry, the Randolphs and Harvies undoubtedly socialized. The Jeffersons knew Harvie as well. Her grandfather John Harvie had been one of Jefferson's guardians after his father died.[43]

This was a difficult circumstance for the Randolph children, especially the daughters. Whatever qualms she had had about marrying him (discussed in chapter 15), once married, Harvie almost immediately proceeded to wrap her much older husband around her finger (it did not take very long) and moved to ensure that any children they had would be favored over his previous large set. By the time she was finished, Randolph Sr. had seen fit to name his first son with her *Thomas Mann Randolph*, symbolically erasing his first son from his prior marriage. Though Virginia did not follow primogeniture, the symbolism of the first son as the head of his group of siblings remained. It was as if Randolph Sr. felt he was starting his life all over again. In a sense he was. His new bride was the same age as the woman he had married decades before. Between the time of his second marriage, at the end of 1790, and his death, in 1793, the couple had two children, a daughter who died in infancy and the son mentioned above.[44]

Had Randolph lived as long as Jefferson, he could have had as many children with Gabriella as he had with his first wife, Anne.

All this was a devastating blow to young Tom Randolph, whose struggles with depression and feelings of inadequacy could likely be treated today with medication and/or therapy. The saga of Randolph Sr. and Harvie also greatly alarmed Martha, who worried openly, and evidently without shame, about what this would mean for the distribution of property within her husband's family. She had married the presumptive scion of Tuckahoe, of which she would be the mistress, and now the current master of the plantation had decided he wanted a brand-new family. Martha wrote to her father about this matter in the very same July 2 letter in which she addressed the issue of requiring a maid.

Jefferson never responded to Martha in writing about the need to have a new maid, but he answered the part of her letter voicing concerns about Harvie in one of the most eloquent, wise, and deeply revealing pieces of prose that he ever wrote. Unlike other of his admonitions to young people that seem old-fashioned and stale, even for his own time, the universality and timelessness of parts of this letter to his daughter about how to respond to Harvie take him far beyond meaningless cliché and describe the human condition with a clarity that echoes across the centuries. He was able to achieve this, of course, because of his remarkable facility with language, but it was also because he was not affecting a pose or mouthing empty words or the kind of rote platitudes fashioned to suit any occasion that an older person might say to a younger one. He was speaking to his adored daughter from his heart, and he wanted her to really hear that, addressing her as one human being to another. Like all good writing, it was intended to, and does, operate on more than one level, for Jefferson was not just speaking about the problem with Harvie; he was speaking about himself, his daughter, and all who must live in society with others and who want to maintain some sense of peace and happiness—an equilibrium—while doing that.

> Every human being, my dear, must thus be viewed according to what it is good for, for none of us, no not one, is perfect; and were we to love none who had imperfections this world would be a desert for our love. All we can do is to make the best of our friends: love and cherish what is good in them, and keep out of the way of what is bad: but no more

think of rejecting them for it than of throwing away a piece of music
for a flat passage or two.[45]

While Martha may have reconciled herself to Harvie (she had no choice,
for she could not make Harvie disappear), she never ceased thinking about
the importance of property and inheritance to family life. Jefferson's white
family tradition has noted, with a faint hint of criticism, her keen interest
in her own children's ability to acquire property through their marriages as
if she thought this, rather than love, was the most important consideration
for their matches.[46] That mild note of censure seems a bit unfair, given that
acquiring and maintaining property was an ever-present obsession throughout Anglo-Virginian culture. Getting property had allowed a man like her
grandfather John Wayles, who was a "nobody" in English society, to become
a "somebody" in America. That process had replicated itself thousands of
times and would continue to do so in the future. Property was the engine
that drove the society, for good and for ill.

Randolph was a product of her time and place. In her day, even more
than in her children's day, when love began its ascendance as the primary purpose for unions between males and females, marriage was very
much about property and the eventual disposition of it. In that property-
obsessed and male-dominated society in which both Jefferson daughters
were raised, women were especially vulnerable, as their futures depended
upon the choices made by the men in their lives—fathers, then husbands
or whoever was the designated patriarch in the family. Living under that
regime and being women of the upper class, Martha and Maria Jefferson
did not have the same expectations about life as many modern women who
can leave home, take up a profession, support themselves, and chart a new
course if disappointed about a domestic situation. Their grandfather John
Wayles came to America with nothing but his talent, ambition, and skin
color. Because he was a man and white, he could enter a profession and be
befriended by other men who put him in the position to become a wealthy
landowner. If one job or venture did not work out, he could pull up stakes
and begin anew elsewhere. His was not a woman's story. Protected daugh-
terhood and well-made marriages that solidified and protected family property were women's routes to personal happiness.

If property and family were their chief sources of support, stability, and self-esteem, white women had to work (and hope) to maintain both. An awk-ward private arrangement at home was to be dealt with by adjusting one's attitude, something that women throughout the ages have been trained and expected to do when dealing with the men in their lives—their fathers, hus-bands, and lovers. That came with the territory of being a woman. As her father told her later on in a less inspiring passage in the letter described above, the more skillfully she handled difficult and personal family situa-tions, the more respect observers of the scene would have for her. Here was a message that one would expect Jefferson and other men of his era, white or black, as a matter of fact, to deliver, one that promoted a very traditional notion of virtuous womanhood. Women achieved respect by bearing the improprieties or transgressions of others in silence or without too obvious rancor. Jefferson and other men saw this as part of the balance of life: men had their trials to endure in the outside world, and women had their trials on the domestic front.

Some trials are more difficult than others, and realizing that things could always be much worse often shapes one's response to an unhappy situa-tion. The true nightmare scenario for an upper-class daughter in the world in which Martha Randolph lived was not a widower father in thrall to a slave woman who bore his children; it was the potential loss of property—the source of family wealth, social stability, prestige, and patrimony, along with the personal identity all those things provided—when her father remarried and had another set of legitimate white heirs. Having to manage an embar-rassing circumstance that was a well-known hazard of the way of life that they had chosen and was, otherwise, tremendously beneficial to them was one thing; facing the concrete effects of a deed, an inter vivos gift, a trans-fer of title, or a disappointing will or marriage settlement—all giving prop-erty to someone else's children—was quite another. Tom Randolph, and Martha, would have had nothing to fear if his father had chosen to take up with a seventeen-year-old enslaved girl instead of marrying a seventeen-year-old free white one.

Property united the past, present, and future, through the great events of life—birth, marriage, and death. This did not simply address itself to the passions and needs of one man and one woman in a particular generation; it affected generations to come. In their Anglo-Virginian world, both Jefferson daughters could fully expect that whatever was the meaning of Thomas Jefferson and Sally Hemings would die a mercifully restrained death with them. No marriage license, no white family acknowledgment, the only one that counted in their world, no grant of land, no intestate succession would bind them to their black half siblings. Once Hemings and Jefferson were "over," they would all go their separate ways forever—Jefferson's legitimate heirs, with the honor of a recognized connection to him and his property (they thought); the Hemings children, with their freedom and whatever he had given them over the course of the years under the heavy mantle of his discretion.

Unsettling as her father's relationship with Hemings may have been to Martha Randolph, the dispute with her father-in-law about Edgehill in 1790 through 1791 (and the eventual disposition of the famous family home, Tuckahoe, which went to Gabriella's Thomas Mann Randolph)[47] provided a stark lesson that he had actually done her and her sister a tremendous favor by becoming involved with a woman who was in no position to pull a Gabriella Harvie in her nuclear family. She cannot have looked at the marriage of her father's boyhood friend to a young woman who was exactly her age, a girl whom she knew personally, and not have wondered if a similar thing could happen in her life and what the fallout from it might be. There but for the grace of God—and Sally Hemings—she and her sister might have gone. No matter what her father had promised or thought at the time, neither she nor he (nor Sally Hemings, for that matter) knew for certain in 1790 that he was never going to meet another white woman he wanted to marry.

Martha Randolph observed firsthand over the years the poignant struggles, emotional and financial, of Thomas Mann Randolph Sr.'s daughters, brought on, in part, by the aftershocks from his remarriage. One of the most searing aspects of their father's union with Harvie—aside from its quickness, for their mother had died only the year before—was that Harvie immediately began to exercise the prerogatives of the wife of the household. Just months after her wedding, she redecorated the house, "painting the black walnut wall in the first floor parlor white."[48] Nancy Randolph, who had served as the mistress of the house after her mother's death, was summarily supplanted. One by one, the sisters sought refuge in others' homes: Nancy, very fatefully at her brother-in-law's home; Bizarre, Harriet, Jane, and Virginia, spending time with their brother and Martha at Edgehill and at Monticello, no doubt telling stories about their predicament. Harriet became a favorite of Jefferson's and was the probable source of the name for his and Hemings's daughters, one who died as an infant and one who lived.[49]

It is perhaps too facile to cast Harvie as the "evil teenage stepmother" for choosing to do what the Anglo-American property system gave her the perfect "right" to do. She was entitled to act as, because she was, the mistress of Tuckahoe, and could not reasonably have been expected to carry herself as if the first Mrs. Randolph were still alive and in the house. Even with that, Randolph Sr. bore some responsibility for the less than artful way matters proceeded. Thomas Jefferson was not Thomas Mann Randolph. If he had chosen a new bride, she might not have been at all like Harvie and even if she had been, she might not have been able to run Jefferson the way Randolph evidently let Harvie run him. Nonetheless, the risk of such a turn of events was always there. Jefferson, like any wealthy (or perceived to be wealthy) man, was "marriage material" for somebody until the day he died. As long as her father remained attached to Sally Hemings, Martha, her sister, and their children would be safe in the way that most mattered to them and others of their class during the eighteenth century.

Property was central, but there was an emotional component to the matter as well. Imagine Thomas Jefferson remarried in 1790 to a free and white Sarah Hemings by whom he had three white sons, William Beverley, James Madison, and Thomas Eston, with a "very beautiful"[50] daughter Harriet thrown in for good measure. Even if she had been the total opposite of Harvie, Jefferson's very ideal of a domestic "angel," the dynamics of his relationship with his older daughters and their children could not have remained the same with a Sarah Jefferson living and sleeping with him while presiding over his household.

Sarah Jefferson's primary duty would have been to secure her own and her sons' and daughter's places in her husband's heart, with the opportunity to do that every moment of the day. Under any circumstances, Jefferson's grandchildren would have been his absolute delight. But if they had been forced to compete with his legitimate white children who were in the same generation—the birth of an eldest grandson, Thomas Jefferson Randolph, followed six years later by the birth of an eldest son, William Beverley Jefferson—things would have been much different. Only if Beverley Jefferson had turned out to be an absolute disappointment could one have expected his father to favor his first grandson over his first son. Martha and her family would always have been welcomed to her father's home for visits long and short, but it is doubtful that she would have been able to move her husband and all her children there and

act as the mistress of Monticello if her father had had another legal family. That could not have been accomplished without diminishing the position of his wife, unless Martha's subordination to the new Mrs. Jefferson
in the running of the household had been made absolutely clear to everyone. Under those circumstances (unlikely to be satisfactory to either
woman), Martha would have had to, or wanted to, stay in her own home
with her own husband, thus losing some of the intimacy and familiarity that shaped the contours of her and her children's attachment to her
father over the years. Without even being able to see all the way down the
road, anyone who knew and valued the rules of family, property, and slavery in Virginia understood the differing levels of threat posed by a Sally
Hemings versus a Gabriella Harvie.

Martha and Tom eventually settled at Edgehill, but years after they
wanted to. Varina was somewhat worse than merely uncomfortable to
them, so it was decided that fall that they would live on the mountain for
a time. Accordingly, Jefferson wrote a memorandum to Nicholas Lewis,
who was still overseeing his farms and slaves, listing Sally Hemings, along
with her relatives, as one who would be available to attend to the needs of
his daughter and son-in-law, most likely using her skills as a seamstress.
Hemings was, by this time, just as he described her: one member (the third
on the list) of Monticello house slaves who could, if needed, do things for
his daughters.[51] He could not very well have told Lewis that she was really in
a position different from that of the rest of her kin and outlined any different course of treatment of her.

We have come to better understand, as our society's values have
changed and black people's position in the United States has improved,
that Jefferson and members of his white family are not to be taken as the
only, or even the best, sources of information about life at Monticello. What
they wrote, and did not choose to write, about their relations with their
human property does not define the total reality of either their lives or the
lives of those whom they enslaved. Members of the Hemings family, other
enslaved people on the mountain, and members of Jefferson's nearby community provided an answer to the question of why and how the trajectory
of Sally Hemings's life changed in 1790, just after she had returned to the
United States. Their answers provide a valuable framework in which to read
Jefferson's white family's letters and other documents that bear on the lives
of the Hemingses.

The explanatory power of an answer, or a story, if you will, is the truest and best measure of its credibility, how it illuminates without effort the meaning of the seemingly unrelated details, circumstances, and actions that exist in the world around it. It is most reliable when the providers of the answer or story had no ability to affect, or were even totally unaware of, all those details, circumstances, and actions. Madison Hemings, who described an event that took place in his mother's life in 1790—she had a baby who "lived but a short time"[52]—was not alive when Jefferson, his daughter, and sister-in-law wrote the letters that support his recounting of the important event that changed his mother's life that year. He certainly did not have access to Jefferson's family letters, which remained in his white family's hands long after he had left Virginia in the 1830s.

When Martha Randolph and Elizabeth Eppes wrote letters in the first half of 1790 saying that Martha needed a maid, and Jefferson responded by providing her with someone other than Sally Hemings and fixed Maria's life so that she would not need Hemings either, they did not know that eighty-three years later Madison Hemings would flesh out the meaning of what they were talking about and doing during that spring and summer. When, in 1802, Jefferson's neighbors, who assumed that all the children Hemings bore in the 1790s lived, said that she had five children and that her oldest child was about twelve, they had no knowledge of what Jefferson and his family wrote in 1790.[53] Had they been able to read those letters and had known of his actions that year, they would have immediately understood why Hemings eased out of her role as the personal maid to Martha and Maria Jefferson in 1790.

Even Ellen Coolidge could not escape the powerful gravity of an accurate answer. Just as her comments about maids in Jefferson's rooms unwittingly dovetailed with Madison Hemings's descriptions of his mother's role in life, she also unwittingly shed light on Hemings's situation in 1790. Coolidge asked plaintively, almost as if she, as a sixty-two-year-old woman, was still trying to sort this out herself, how it could be that her grandfather would have "selected the female attendant of his own pure children to become his paramour"?[54] Of course, men have conducted affairs with the housekeepers, nannies, and governesses to their children from time immemorial, and one would be hard pressed to characterize the *unmarried* ones among their number as presumptively evil.

The historian Nell Irvin Painter, in her study of the journals of Ella Gertrude Clancy Thomas, a long-suffering nineteenth-century southern

planter's wife, has written eloquently about the phenomenon of what psy-
chologists call "deception clues" and "leakages."[55] Both refer to the situation,
familiar to police interrogators, where a person seeking to hide damaging or
very painful truths accidentally reveals those hidden truths, or leaves clues
to them, in the stories he or she tells for public consumption. Coolidge
reflexively associated the start of the Hemings-Jefferson relationship with
the days in Paris when Hemings was, in fact, an "attendant" to Jefferson's
"pure children," inviting readers to conjure up images of Patsy's and Polly's
wounded girlhoods, while skipping over the many later years that Jefferson
could have "selected" Hemings.

Ellen had no personal memory of either her mother or Aunt Maria as
pure children attended to by Sally Hemings. By the time she was old enough
to pay any attention to Hemings, Jefferson's oldest "pure children" were
grown and married women, one of them, obviously, Ellen's mother. Maria,
married and moved away from Monticello in 1797, when Ellen was one,
and dead in 1804, when she was eight, was not much in Ellen's memory
at all. In a very poignant letter to her mother written in 1820, twenty-four-
year-old Ellen confessed that she had "almost entirely forgotten" her aunt.[56]
The Sally Hemings whom Ellen knew and remembered from her days at
Monticello was the mother of Beverley, Harriet, Madison, and Eston—all
born well after her days in France. Who had said, at the time of Coolidge's
letter, that Jefferson had chosen Hemings as his paramour *while she was
an attendant to* his children? It was, of course, Madison Hemings who said
that his father had "selected" his mother "during that time," and that was
how she came to have a baby in 1790. He did not say that in print, however, until fifteen years after Coolidge's letter. Coolidge (inadvertently) and
Hemings (deliberately), each unaware of the other's comments, put France
at the heart of both of their statements about the origins of Sally Hemings's
relationship with Jefferson.

In the end, right answers and true stories have a positive cascading
effect because they illuminate. They enable one to notice and make sense
of things that one might have ignored or thought incomprehensible without them, thus allowing for a clearer picture of the world one is surveying. Wrong answers and false stories obscure matters and have little or
no explanatory power. They shed no light on the facts, circumstances, or
actions in the world they purport to describe, because they are not really
of that world, and thus cannot help explain it. Instead, they tend to make

matters more confusing, by creating their own negative cascading effect, as other bad answers, weak, illogical, and/or simply false stories must be offered to shore up the original wrong answer's deficiencies.

The explanatory power of Monticello slaves' answer to the question of who Sally Hemings came to be to Thomas Jefferson, at the end of the 1780s, lies in how precisely it tracks and explains the otherwise inexplicable situation in 1790 described above. It accounts for all the other extraordinary things that happened to her over the years. Hemings had a very serious role in life—and a personal identity that grew out of it—and she suddenly ceased to have that role and identity and took on new ones. She was Jefferson's mistress, she had a baby, and she lost it. After that, she could do things for his older daughters, but she would never again be primarily attached to them.

That reality did not change. Years later, after Maria visited Monticello and needed to take an enslaved woman home with her to help with her infant for a time, she wrote to her father, then President Jefferson, that she had taken Hemings's sister Critta with her, understanding that the companion of her childhood was not eligible for that kind of service.[57] While Martha did end up living in Jefferson's home permanently during his retirement years, at the outset of both his daughters' married lives in the 1790s, he expected them to set up house with their husbands—not too far away from Monticello, he hoped—but away from it. Hemings, however, was supposed to remain tied to the mountain and to him. She was not going anywhere.

21

♦

THE BROTHERS

ROBERT AND JAMES HEMINGS had last seen New York when they were in the city just before James went to Paris. So they knew in general what to expect when they left Monticello with Jefferson on March 1, 1790. The three men started out with differing immediate destinations. Robert Hemings, with money from Jefferson, was to head for Alexandria to pick up horses and Jefferson's phaeton, newly arrived from France. James Hemings, on the other hand, went to Richmond with Jefferson, who had financial affairs to attend to in the town. After several days, the pair boarded a stagecoach for New York by way of Fredericksburg, stopping in Alexandria to meet Robert Hemings. They planned to continue north in Jefferson's carriage with the Hemings brothers alternating driving, and Jefferson perhaps taking the reins himself occasionally, because he liked to drive when he was bored or in a hurry.[1]

Their plan never materialized. A late winter storm blanketed Alexandria with a foot and a half of snow. After concluding that it was too dangerous to proceed on their own, Jefferson decided to ship the carriage by water, and the three men took a stagecoach with their horses being "led on" to New York. The trip sounds to have been beyond tedious: "The roads thro the whole were so bad that we could never go more than three miles an hour, sometimes not more than two, and in the night but one."[2] To relieve the boredom, Jefferson sometimes got out of the coach to ride one of the horses. The Hemings brothers probably did so as well, to find their own respite from the tedium. As they headed north, Robert Hemings was the advance man sent ahead—after Baltimore on to Philadelphia and then New York—to make arrangements for Jefferson's arrival in each city.³

On the Philadelphia leg of the journey, Jefferson called on Benjamin Franklin. The great Philadelphian was gravely ill, and would die on April 17, a month after Jefferson's visit. The last letter he ever wrote, in fact, was to Jefferson, answering his query about maps that had come up during their final time together.⁴ Robert Hemings almost certainly had at least seen Franklin many years before. He was with Jefferson in Philadelphia when he served with Franklin as a representative to the Continental Congress and wrote the Declaration of Independence. Though he knew of Franklin— practically everyone on at least two continents seemed to—it is less likely that James Hemings had ever encountered him. They were in Paris at the same time, but in deference to Franklin's advanced age and status—and perhaps because he did not yet have a suitable residence for entertaining before Franklin left the country—Jefferson usually went to the elder man's residence at Passy.⁵ There was no obvious reason for Hemings to have accompanied him on those journeys. After a short stay in Philadelphia, it was on to New York, where Robert Hemings was waiting for them.

Except for the surprise snowstorm, this was an altogether familiar situation. The Hemings brothers, one called home from his employment elsewhere, were once again compelled to travel with and serve Jefferson, as if time had stood still over the past five and a half years. One wonders how long it took the men to realize that things had changed; given all that had happened to them in the interim, they simply could not go on as they had before.

On the surface, James Hemings's situation had changed the most. He was a long time away from the mental and emotional requirements of the slave society he had just returned to. Although he had certainly lived a larger life in that society than most enslaved males even before he left the country, his experiences in France made it even less likely that he could fit back into his old self in quite the same way. It did not help that the move to New York was so sudden. This was a dizzying turnabout for Hemings. He had been in America just a little over three months, and he had assumed, for some part of that time, that he was on his way back to France.

Robert Hemings had never left America, but the preceding five and a half years had brought him to a different point in life as well. He had spent those years living on his own, working for wages, and, unlike his brother James, creating a life apart from Jefferson. This was the longest period that he had ever been separated from him since they had known each other. He had become Jefferson's traveling companion and valet when he was really a boy—only twelve. It is hardly speculative to say that he did as much growing up, and Jefferson did as much raising and training him during those early years, as he did being a real attendant to the much older man. He had known Jefferson primarily as a child or an adolescent would know an adult. Now, as they were back together in New York, he was a twenty-eight-year-old man with an adult perspective aided by the distance that Jefferson's absence had provided. He had more than learned the lesson that he could do without the man who legally owned him. Indeed, he could do without any owner at all.

Nothing in Virginia's slave society supported the way Robert Hemings had lived his life up until this moment, and much sentiment was against it. The pass system, which required slaves to have written permission to go out on defined missions or errands, was designed to maintain a nearly seamless connection between enslaved people and their legal owners. They were out for a specific purpose to go to a specific place, their very movements and use of time measured by the master's instructions. Owners looked askance at neighbors who gave slaves open-ended passes that allowed them discretion and some measure of control over their time and physical space. That interfered with the goal of subordinating slaves to the will of the master, as much as was humanly possible.[6]

It was, in fact, impossible to achieve complete and uniform subordination of slaves on a societywide basis. They resisted that in myriad ways, and slave owners themselves were sometimes weak links in the chain. Men like Jefferson, because of their own personalities, quirks, and senses of entitlement, wanted to be able, within reason, to construct their personal lives as they saw fit. Jefferson's way of life at Monticello called for a slightly different take on the master-slave relationship when it came to the older generation of Hemingses, particularly Robert and James. That he was also at a particular moment in his life—less rigid overall and caught up with his sense of himself as a leading man of progress living in a revolutionary era—no doubt shaped his views about how to deal with them. He did not have to be, or want to be, conventional in all aspects of his life. At the same time he clung to many of the comforts and verities of the patriarchal slave society that had formed him and shaped the contours of his own peculiar brand of unconventionality. Keeping the Hemings brothers in nominal slavery exactly fit his needs and self-image at the time. At various points in their lives, the two brothers were thus very much out in the world on Jefferson's general pass, so long as they heeded his call to come home.[7]

Despite that figurative tether, those times away from Jefferson allowed—actually required—the brothers to develop identities that had nothing at all to do with him. They did things and went to places he knew nothing about—had friends, enemies, and lovers who were unknown to him. They used their general passes in the treacherous environment of Virginia to create dual roles for themselves as enslaved men and employees. The practice of hiring the slaves of other men and women became more prevalent as the institution grew and matured; it allowed less wealthy people who could not afford to buy slaves to rent them, giving them an economic and personal stake in slavery that they would not have had otherwise. Not everyone was happy about this. Prospective buyers were often reluctant to purchase enslaved people who had ever been hired out, thinking that the experience of working for wages—even when they did not keep them—made them questionable as slave property. The split in authority between the "true" master and the hirer weakened enslaved people's links to both the idea and the fact of the primary master-slave relationship. It also highlighted their connection to free laborers. The two groups would inevitably compare themselves and see some points of commonality.[8]

Perhaps most ominously of all, hiring slaves out put a dollar value on their services, bringing home very forcefully to enslaved people (as if they did not already know this) that their labor had a specific economic value that could be determined. A hired enslaved carpenter knew that the hirer was paying his legal master for his labor. When the hire was over, he returned to his own home to do the same work. The value of his work, expressed by the hirer's payments to the master, did not disappear; it was merely being captured by his legal owner, just as surely as his body had been captured and held by men with superior numbers and force. Frederick Douglass wrote passionately about the extreme indignity of having to give his legal owner the money he had worked so hard for during the times he was hired out.[9]

The Hemings brothers had even greater reason to question their position in the world and what Jefferson meant in their lives. Unlike Douglass and most other slaves who worked for men who were not their legal masters, they chose their own employers *and* kept their wages. They knew exactly what their labor was worth and were used to personally benefiting from it. They were the embodiment of all that the law sought to prevent: enslaved African American men who had some control over their time and labor. Living like this in the middle of a generally closed slave society could only have made them special people in their own eyes and in the eyes of other members of their extended family—especially the female members. The Hemings brothers modeled aspects of traditional masculinity beyond the physical. They worked and made money, like other men—money they could give to their mother and sisters, or the other women in their lives, if they asked for it, or if they simply wanted to give it to them. The men were both resourceful and resources. Given his early close association with Jefferson, Robert Hemings, in particular, could not erase the thoughts his long separation from him almost inevitably raised. Why should he continue to be bound to Jefferson when he knew he could function on his own as a wage earner?

Jefferson let the Hemings brothers go and come back to him over the years because he felt confident that he could count on their loyalty no matter what. He was wrong about that—or he and the Hemings men just had differing conceptions of what one could reasonably demand as a show of loyalty. Robert and James Hemings and the rest of their family were products of Virginia's eighteenth-century slave society, before most slave owners adopted the strategically sentimentalized and self-serving notions of the master-slave relationship in the nineteenth century. Jefferson was somewhat ahead of his time in sentimentalizing his relationship with the Hemingses, for very obvious reasons. When he and other planters of his cohort called their slaves members of their "family," they were speaking the implacable and unsentimental language of the patriarch describing all the people over whom they exercised power, as well as displaying their notion of responsibility. Slaves had not yet taken their place in the "family," as they would during the antebellum period, as the adult "children" for whom some masters claimed they had feelings of love and impulses toward care. Southern members of the Revolutionary generation were firmly on the road to sentimentalizing their relations with slaves by the early nineteenth century; but during Jefferson's most intense time with the Hemings brothers—1774 through 1794—that process was only newly under way.[10]

That word "family" did not have the same application for everyone on Jefferson's plantations, because not every one of his slaves had true family connections to him. The young men traveling with him to New York to serve him there were actual, not metaphorical, family members—brothers to his dead wife and new mistress, and uncles to his children with Martha, as they were uncles to the child their sister already had or, more likely, was just about to bear. Jefferson had a degree of sentimentality toward them that grew out of all these ties that he did not have for other enslaved people on his plantations, and he evidently expected some reciprocity from these men and their other siblings in the form of love, gratitude, and attachment.[11]

Though the Hemingses and the Jeffersons were not the only enslaved and free families entangled by blood, it is probably true that few masters constructed their relations with their enslaved relatives as Jefferson did. From his place atop the pyramid, he could afford to indulge his sentimentality—styling himself as their "friend," keeping their sisters out of the fields and in the domestic realm, borrowing money from the brothers and paying it back as if they were just friendly acquaintances—without diminishing himself in any discernible fashion. The way Jefferson treated the Hemings brothers, no doubt, made him feel good about himself. He did not have to do any of this, as he well knew. Having the Hemings men live this way served some affective need on his part, for this was not solely an intellectual choice. He was aware that the young men who traveled ahead to Rouen, Philadelphia, and New York to put his life in order for him, and who found work on their own and supported themselves as workers, did not really need to live under his wing. His inclination to give them freedom, coupled with a hesitancy to give them the full measure of it, was a function of the possessive nature he displayed in so many other contexts. They were to be slaves, but slaves to him alone, as if he thought that made their enslavement less of a problem for them.

All this proceeded, apparently, without regard to the turmoil that a life configured in this way would naturally create in any person who had to live under those rules. If Robert and James Hemings did not accept the rightness of their enslavement, and they clearly did not, any gratitude they felt about being given part of what should have been theirs by right—to come and go as they pleased, to make a living, and to have a family like all other human beings—would quickly dissipate as they grew used to being self-sufficient men. Again, we may let Frederick Douglass express the complicated emotions at play when enslaved people were treated "benevolently." Of his owner he wrote,

He would, however, when I made him six dollars sometimes give me six cents, to encourage me. It had the opposite effect. I regarded it as an admission of my right to the whole. The fact that he gave me any part of my wages was proof, to my mind, that he believed me entitled to the whole of them. I always felt worse for having received anything; for I feared that giving me a few cents would ease his conscience and make him feel himself to be a pretty honorable sort of robber. My discontent grew upon me.[12]

The lives of Robert and James Hemings were even more complicated than Douglass's on this score, for there were many more ways in which Jefferson raised their expectations about what they had a right to have in life. It would have been a far simpler matter for Jefferson, and forestalled the conflicts that later arose, if he had given Robert and James Hemings fewer or no opportunities to develop identities apart from him. Their heritage almost surely affected the way they viewed their circumstances. The Hemings brothers knew that the man who controlled their lives had inherited a fortune that would have been theirs if they, the sons of John Wayles, had been born free white men. Robert was an eldest son in a world where that position meant something. There was nothing the brothers could do about it, but that did not prevent them—as Douglass would do years later—from considering the obvious.

For whatever this meant to Jefferson, the Hemings men could never have afforded to be sentimental about him in the way he wanted without giving up a great deal of themselves. They had to remain in slavery for this to work in the manner that best suited his emotional needs—living as the objects of his benevolence, protection, and grants of autonomy under the overlay of his will to control. Neither wanted to do that. They wanted their freedom. One wonders whether it ever crossed Jefferson's mind that they would want to be free, that these young men's experiences had created expectations that could never be fulfilled so long as they remained enslaved to him. After years of existing in this hybrid state, they would express the desire to leave him, or at least cut the legally created cord he used to bring them back at his discretion.

It happened many years later, but the example of James Hubbard, who was not a member of the Hemings family, is useful for considering how matters between the Hemings brothers and Jefferson unfolded in the early

1790s. Hubbard was a chronic runaway from Monticello, who in the first decade of the 1800s managed to string together fairly long periods when he was absent from the plantation. Jefferson dealt with runaways by selling them—a response perfectly in keeping with his preference for making conflict, or potential sources of it, disappear. He sold Hubbard while he was off on one of his escape attempts. The contract gave Jefferson extra money if he recovered him, so he had Hubbard recaptured, brought back to Monticello, "severely flogged" to set an example, and put in jail. He then suggested to Reuben Perry, the man who had bought Hubbard, that he immediately sell him because "the course he has been in, and all the circumstances convince me he will never serve any man as a slave."[13]

What slaves did, the things that happened to them, Jefferson was saying, affected the way they looked at life and their circumstances. This ran counter to the popular view, which Jefferson expressed later in his life, that slaves were perpetual children—people who never learned and grew. When in the midst of quotidian business, instead of when making pronouncements for public consumption, Jefferson revealed his true feelings and beliefs: experiences mattered to slaves. White society had to take active measures to keep them from engaging life in ways that would make them unfit for their condition. So there would be no school, no marriage, no unfettered ability to testify against white people, nothing coming from the white community that would make enslaved people see the world differently and be changed in the process. Enslaved people were left to build their own inner identities in opposition to the dominant society's assaults upon their humanity.

Hubbard had grown used to thinking he had a right to be free. He did not just think it; he acted upon the thought with some success. Even if he never ran away again, his mind-set had been forever altered because he had lived, very effectively for a time, in direct challenge to his enslavement. The Hemings brothers were not runaways in the same sense as Hubbard, but their time in the world away from Jefferson, and successes at independent living and decision making, also posed deep challenge to their enslavement. They met and embraced the challenge. Not long after their time in New York, both men took successful steps to disentangle themselves from Jefferson so that they could come back to him only when, and if, they wanted to. That was all to come; they still had to get through their time with him in New York.

New York

James Hemings and Jefferson arrived in New York on March 21, 1790. His older brother had secured lodging for the party at the City Tavern, where they remained for a brief period until moving to Mrs. Dunscomb's boardinghouse at 22 King Street, in lower Manhattan. There they would stay until they moved at the beginning of June to a house on Maiden Lane. The men immediately went about setting up their lives in this place, which was so different from Albemarle County and the Paris that James Hemings and Jefferson had left only recently. One of the first orders of business was settling accounts. Robert Hemings gave Jefferson the residue of the amount he had been given as expenses for his trip to the city. Jefferson repaid Hemings money he had borrowed at some earlier point on the journey.[14]

New York had already taken its place as the largest city in the United States; its multitudes crowded, for the most part, into the bottom of Manhattan Island.[15] The brothers had to adjust to this teeming environment while attending to a man who was decidedly—and probably very vocally to the Hemings brothers—out of his element. Jefferson did not care much for the place. It featured everything he hated about cities—cramped living conditions, noise, and citizens seemingly in perpetual contention with one another. It was not a place for the conflict averse. "I view great cities," he wrote to Benjamin Rush in 1800, "as pestilential to the morals, the health and the liberties of man." Though he conceded that they "nourish some of the elegant arts," the most "useful" among the arts could exist in other places with fewer downsides. Then there was the weather. There were only two seasons, he claimed. During the months he and the Hemingses were in New York, March until September, the weather went from cold to hot with no temperate springtime.[16]

New York was almost certainly disappointing to James Hemings after Paris. It offered little in the way of architecture, no beautiful parks to walk in, no stunning churches or cathedrals to admire and take refuge in. Most important of all for him and his brother, New York was a full-fledged slave society. The 1790 census counted 3,092 black people there—1,036 of them free, the other 2,056 enslaved. As it is for all poor and relatively powerless people, life was still a very difficult proposition for freed blacks because they were relegated to doing "most of the inferior labor of the town." There was indeed a great deal of all types of work to be done, for New York had already begun its ascent to its position as the financial capital of the United States. It was clear even by then that money, and those who made it, would rule the metropolis.[17] New York's economy was growing rapidly, and though the critique of slavery was growing louder, the number of slaves continued to grow during the years of economic expansion. Slave ownership became more diversified as the newly rich and upper middle class bought slaves as status symbols and to enhance their lifestyles, relieving housewives of drudgery and husbands of physically arduous tasks. Though slavery was an important part of the fabric of social life in New York, the numbers suggest that the Hemings brothers would have encountered many free black people as well. Although largely consigned to doing the dirtiest and most demanding jobs in the city, some became "shopkeepers, fruiterers, bakers, boardinghouse keepers or hawkers selling buttermilk or hot corn in the city's streets and markets." They mixed and jostled with newly arriving immigrants, fueling the political and social tensions that became a permanent feature of life in the urban North.[18]

Robert and James Hemings experienced the great diversity of black life in the city. African Americans were especially visible in the downtown area where they lived. From the time of the Revolution, when many of the city's blacks very rationally cast their fortunes with the English in the hope of achieving freedom, most free blacks lived in "Negro Barracks" on downtown streets like Church and Broadway. Both were very close to the Hemingses' first home on King Street and their second one on Maiden Lane. Just immediately north, the vast Negro (African) Burial Ground served as the final resting place for thousands of blacks (some estimates say almost twenty thousand) enslaved and free.[19]

Although the end of the twentieth century is often cast as a defining period of globalization, ideas, people, and goods moved across the Atlantic with great frequency (and with great impact) in the Hemingses' time as well. The shock waves from the French Revolution followed James Hemings from Paris to New York as blacks and their supporters in the city linked the struggle to end slavery in America to what was going on in the streets of Paris. Just a few months before he and his brother arrived in the city, "a crowd at the John Street Theater gave a thunderous ovation to an epilogue that linked the liberation of 'Afric's sable Sons' to the cause of international republicanism."[20] For myriad reasons, at the end of 1789 and the beginning of 1790, a number of New Yorkers made the abolition of slavery a major goal. Many were moved by their moral outrage against slavery's inhumanity, while others, especially European immigrants, simply did not want to have to compete with slave labor. New arrivals in the country often displayed their concern about this by adopting an actively hostile attitude toward the blacks who lived among them.[21] Whatever the motives for it, once again, James Hemings was in a city where the nature of liberty and freedom was the topic of ardent and very public discourse. This time, however, the discussion was specifically about the future of members of his race.

The brothers surely talked about the time James had spent in France, what he had done, and whether he expected to return to that country. One longs to know what they thought about Jefferson, for there could not have been any two people in the world at that point who knew him better. Their sister's relationship with him was a new and very important piece of knowledge, a circumstance to be considered from very different perspectives. James had, of course, been at the Hôtel de Langeac. He had either known about his sister and Jefferson all along, or it was something he found out near the end of their stay when the issue of remaining in France arose. Did he feel a useless pang of guilt for not having been able to intervene, and did Robert feel a useless negative judgment of James for the same reason? It is most likely that both men, the sons of a white man, simply viewed their sister's connection to Jefferson as a predictable event in life as they knew it. While the word was that Jefferson would never marry again, and both men may have believed that word, there was no reason for them to think that he was going to forgo female companionship for the rest of his life. They knew that southern slavery gave white slave owners who lost their wives several alternatives: never have sex again as long as they lived, take a new wife, take up with an enslaved woman on their plantation as a substitute wife in a steady relationship, frequent prostitutes in bawdyhouses, or spend the rest of their days rampaging through the slave quarters with multiple women—or some combination of all but the first choice. As for their little sister, the probabilities were always very high that she would end up with *some* white man. Jefferson may have appeared to the Hemings brothers to be at least as good as any other—with the added advantage of being the metaphorical devil they knew. And if they had any degree of trust in his word—that he was going to stick by his bargain with their sister—she was already better off than their mother, who had not obtained freedom for any of her children.

History had repeated itself, but only the future would tell if the replication was going to be exact. There was now a chance that a coming generation of Hemingses might escape living their entire lives enslaved to their close white relatives, because their sister had insisted upon that. Whether this made them feel more positive or negative toward Jefferson because he went along with this plan is unknown, but they surely had some opinions about it. If they expressed them to one another, what, if anything, did they say to Jefferson about their thoughts?

As with so many other aspects of slavery, it is difficult to fathom what conversations between these three men were like. One's first inclination is to think they never acknowledged to one another the complex nature of their relationships. That too comfortably—and strategically—limits the range of things one has to consider when imagining, as historians must, the lives of the Hemingses and Jeffersons. This may explain why, in a related vein, some have posited, even insisted, that Jefferson's wife did not know that Robert and James were her brothers, though Jefferson and people in their community knew. A Martha Jefferson ignorant of her father's relations is a less complicated personality—easier to fit into a perhaps preferred image of the innocent upper-class white woman who remained naïve about the ways of the world. That construction relieves us of the responsibility to *see* her knowing about her enslaved siblings, and then contemplate the persona that encompassed that knowledge. One sidesteps a deeply troubling aspect of the infinitely strange, but still in some ways familiar, world of slavery.

IT IS NOT clear exactly what Robert Hemings was supposed to be doing in New York, and whether he was really expected to have a long-standing formal role in Jefferson's household there. His brother was set to continue his job of several years, being Jefferson's chef. The most natural thing for Robert Hemings to have done was to reassume his place as Jefferson's valet, and that was probably his job at first. Curiously enough, that job did not entail shaving Jefferson, even though Hemings had been trained years before as a barber and Jefferson expected his manservant to shave him. Instead, Jefferson paid another man for shaving him during that first month in the city. Hemings may have been out of practice.[22] There is some irony in this, for Jefferson had arranged to have Hemings trained as a barber while waiting to go to France.

The brothers' formal roles were not their primary focus in May, their second full month in the city. Jefferson fell ill with one of his periodic migraine headaches at the very beginning of the month, and they directed their energy toward taking care of him. Although he described the attack as moderate, Jefferson's letters indicate that he was actually quite debilitated. Illness kept him pretty much housebound during the entire month and prevented him from writing any long letters—both serious matters for this normally energetic and communicative man. At the end of one shortened missive to his son-in-law, he described his "eyes" as being "too weak to" continue the letter. For most of this period, the brothers were Jefferson's main companions on a daily basis, nursing him to the extent that was needed, taking his orders, and running errands for him throughout the city.[23]

There were many things in Jefferson's life that might have brought on one of his stress-induced migraines, not the least of which is that he had just taken a serious position in a new government. He was still getting reaccustomed to being "home," that is, in the United States, but not the home that mattered to him most. He was reacquainting himself with America in an American city he despised. There was, too, the situation at Monticello with Sally Hemings, and the fact that he had recently and abruptly given a daughter away in marriage. Neither of his daughters had written to him since he left Monticello at the beginning of March—an almost two-month interval that must have seemed endless to him. Everything about his circumstances made him vulnerable to a physical breakdown. Robert Hemings went out to get his medicine and to pay the doctor he consulted. Peruvian bark (quinine), the usual remedy for his migraines, did not work this time. The headache, and the Hemings brothers' care of him, persisted.[24]

Robert and James Hemings were not alone in making Jefferson's life run as smoothly as possible. Through the fog of sickness, he managed to hire two additional people to work with them: Jacob Cooke to be a "house servant" and François Seche to be a coachman. This was in preparation for his move to the house at 57 Maiden Lane, which he had arranged to rent early on. These two men arrived in May, when the Hemingses and Jefferson had been in the city only a month and a half. It may have been clear by that time that Robert Hemings would not be staying, since Cooke and Seche seemed to combine the roles that he normally played. Did Jefferson really need a chef, a coachman, a house servant, and a separate manservant? He was long used to having help, but his recent experiences at the Hôtel de

Langeac had accustomed him to a very high level of personal maintenance. Even with that, the house on Maiden Lane was the very opposite of the Hôtel de Langeac—"small" and "indifferent," as Jefferson described it to his son-in-law and daughter, respectively. It was not the kind of place that really needed a large staff of servants to care for one person. There were, nevertheless, four by the time the Hemingses and Jefferson moved in at the beginning of June.[25]

That number diminished by one just several days after the move to Maiden Lane. Robert Hemings left New York for Fredericksburg to try to find employment there. Getting a paying job was not the only reason he wanted to go. While living in Fredericksburg on his own, he had met and married a woman named Dolly, and he wanted to be near her. Like so many enslaved women who married men who lived on other plantations or in nearby towns, Dolly Hemings was left alone to wait for Robert to visit whenever he could arrange it. The couple may have already had both of their children, Martin and Elizabeth, named for Robert's older brother and mother, respectively. Up until this time, Dolly was in a somewhat better position than other enslaved women because, for most of the time she knew him, her husband was at liberty to come and go on his own, and had disposable income to support their family. They now faced an unprecedented situation: her husband, off playing some ambiguous role in Jefferson's life, was well out of range for anything approaching a normal schedule of visits. No wonder Robert Hemings wanted to leave. Jefferson agreed to let him go, gave him money for his expenses back to Virginia, but held him to the same terms that always applied: Hemings was to tell whoever hired him that he would be available only until the time that Jefferson returned to Monticello and called him home. Sometime around June 7, Hemings set off. He had his reunion with Dolly in Fredericksburg, but whatever prospects he thought he had there did not materialize. So he went to Williamsburg and took a job working for a man named George Carter, going about his business while waiting for Jefferson to send for him.[26]

Hemings's desires to be with his wife and to find paid work are completely understandable. Why he had to leave New York to be able to do either one is less clear. Jefferson had no apparent problem paying the Hemingses wages. He paid James and Sally Hemings in France, and he paid James Hemings a salary in New York. It should have been possible to come to terms with Robert. Hemings's actions over the next few years provide a clue: he seems to have preferred working for people other than Jefferson. This may have influenced his choices about Dolly. As far as we know, he never made a move to have her join him at Monticello or in New York, for that matter. This is quite interesting, given that Jefferson bought the spouses of slaves whom he barely knew in order to reunite them with their families. It is hard to imagine that he would have refused a request from Robert Hemings to do the same thing. Dolly could have done housekeeping for Jefferson in New York or at Monticello. It is possible that the reticence about Dolly's joining him stemmed not from Hemings but from Jefferson. Perhaps Jefferson, French in so many ways in these years, had the same attitude toward the Hemings brothers as some members of the French upper classes who did not allow their household servants to marry. A servant with a spouse necessarily had divided loyalties: family concerns competed with the master's. Dolly Hemings's presence would have changed the dynamic between Jefferson and Robert Hemings, particularly since she was an outsider to life on the mountain and had not grown up knowing Jefferson and understanding the system he had established there.

Jefferson apparently did not think he was in great need of Robert's services in the household. By early April, just two weeks after they arrived in New York, he wrote to William Short, who was still living at the Hôtel de Langeac, asking him to implore Adrien Petit to come to New York to take over the running of his household.[27] If Petit agreed, which he eventually did, that would bring the total number of servants to five. Petit was used to running a much grander household, and with James Hemings, Cooke, and Seche on hand, and with all the washing for the household being sent out, matters could be very much under control without Robert Hemings.

After his brother left, James Hemings was solely responsible for handling the household expenses and making sure the domestic affairs were in order. As he could easily have expected, he soon had to do that in a house that was under construction. Jefferson, as always, immediately began a plan of remodeling the small house he had moved into; he put in a gallery and had cabinets and bookcases made. The bookcases alone cost more than a whole year's rent. His books were not even there yet, which distressed him greatly, but he was determined to be ready for them when they arrived.[28]

The two men settled into a period of intense involvement in a relationship whose characteristics differed markedly from those of any of its earlier incarnations. Jefferson's memorandum books for the rest of his time in New York tell a fascinating story of the daily exchanges between the two; they contain at least one reference to Hemings, giving him money for himself or some other purpose, almost every day.[29] With the household staff small compared with the one at the Hôtel de Langeac, and Jefferson's life less complicated—in Paris he had a wider array of cultural and social activities to spend money on—Hemings suddenly looms as a larger figure in the written record. He had always been close to Jefferson, but before going to Paris and while in the city, he was either surrounded by his brothers and sisters or was just one of a number of other French servants. This was yet a different turn in his connection to Jefferson, the first time he served as a paid employee to him in their native land.

Although his interactions with Jefferson were the most regular of all the employees at the house on Maiden Lane, Hemings was not the highest paid among them. That distinction belonged to Seche, though the gap between him and Hemings was much smaller than the one between Hemings and Cooke, the house servant. Apparently coachmen on both sides of the Atlantic were more highly paid, for Jefferson paid his coachman in France more than his cooks.[30] Whenever Hemings did anything in addition to cooking, such as "painting a shelf," he was paid. Even this does not really convey the total value of Jefferson's terms with the young man. Unlike his white servants, whose contracts expressly stated that they had to buy their own clothes, Jefferson continued to buy clothing for Hemings and to give him spending money—"necessaries for himself"—in addition to the wages he paid him.[31]

The steady salary put Hemings in virtually the same position that he had had in France in regard to salary, and it probably went a long way toward assuaging any disappointment or anger he felt about not returning there. He was in a somewhat better position because no servant was "above" him. He was in charge of the New York household. There remained the matter of formal freedom. There is evidence that Sally Hemings had a deal with Jefferson but no written reference to a specific "deal" between James Hemings and Jefferson upon their return to America has surfaced. Hemings's actions in France, and his sister's, suggest the existence of a joint agreement between the siblings to try to stay there. Just as Jefferson came to some understanding with Sally Hemings about coming back, he must have had some discussion with James Hemings. His treatment of Hemings in New York and Philadelphia, and the details of the written agreement they ultimately did make, suggests that the two had an understanding about Hemings's eventual freedom before they left France. The complicating factor was that Jefferson had brought Hemings to Paris to make him his French chef and had spent a good deal of money on the young man's apprenticeships. He felt Hemings owed him for that. From our modern view, we could easily see that Hemings had probably more than paid for his apprenticeships during the years he worked for Jefferson for nothing. That was not Jefferson's sense.

Had Hemings remained in France, and worked for someone else, he could have repaid Jefferson in currency. He could have done the same if they had returned to France, by coming to some arrangement about his salary, working for nothing until the "debt" was discharged and then remaining in the country when Jefferson went home. Jefferson, however, did not want money from Hemings. He wanted a French chef at Monticello. The only way for Hemings to adequately "repay" him was to go back to Monticello and train someone there—which is what he eventually did. George Washington's invitation to Jefferson to become secretary of state delayed their reckoning on this matter. Hemings's training of his replacement would have to wait until the end of Jefferson's stint in the new American government, which he thought would be relatively short.

Hemings was not in New York long. Three months after they arrived, Congress voted in July to move the capital to Philadelphia for ten years until a new one could be established on the Potomac River. This was apparently the result of a deal between Jefferson and his soon to be great rival Alexander Hamilton, with an assist from James Madison. One says "apparently" because neither Madison nor Hamilton ever wrote about what happened the night the bargain was made. But relying on the explanatory power of Jefferson's story—the way his recollections help make sense of the relationship between the placement of the capital and the adoption of Hamilton's program, historians have generally accepted that the famous "Dinner Table Bargain" was just as Jefferson described it.[32]

The details need not detain us here, but the historian Herbert Sloan cogently explained the essence of the matter: "to break the deadlock over Alexander Hamilton's [very ambitious] financial program, and, more important, to end the threat of disunion, Jefferson and Madison agreed to provide the additional votes necessary to pass the assumption of the state's debt and, on his side, Hamilton helped to arrange for the votes needed to place the permanent capital on the banks of the Potomac."[33] Foreshadowing the famous strategic political dinner parties of his presidency, Jefferson invited Hamilton and James Madison to his home for dinner to discuss the issue. Over Jefferson's good wine and the meal James Hemings prepared for them, the men discussed the fate of the nation's capital, coming to a compromise that Jefferson later regretted. Hemings had seen James Madison in Jefferson's home before and would do so many times again. Alexander Hamilton was more likely a new face to him. Over the course of the next few years, especially in Philadelphia, where Jefferson and Hamilton grew ever more hostile to one another, Hemings probably heard the name Hamilton quite a bit, though in tones less friendly than the ones likely used during that fateful evening in Jefferson's home.

Before the formal end of the summer, Hemings left New York, knowing that after a brief stay at Monticello he would have to help set up a new household in Philadelphia. Jefferson headed south with James Madison, adopting a leisurely pace as they stopped at various sites, Philadelphia for a few days, and other places, including Mount Vernon. It is not clear whether Hemings traveled with the pair or, if so, for how long. Once Jefferson and Madison reached Montpelier, Madison's Orange County plantation, Madison lent Jefferson a "servant" (again, their vernacular for "slave") for the one-day journey to Monticello. Jefferson noted that he paid for "oats," evidently for his horses and "servts breakfts" at an inn en route to his home, and that he gave a tip to Madison's servant before he went back to Montpelier. It is likely that the other servant who ate breakfast at the inn was Jefferson's coachman, Seche, who worked for him until the fall of 1792.[34] James Hemings apparently traveled to Monticello on his own, covering territory that was well known to him. What he found when he got there was a place and a family at the beginning of a transition, and it would turn out that Philadelphia was the last leg of his journey out of slavery.

22

PHILADELPHIA

T HE NATION'S CAPITAL now moved from New York to Philadelphia. James Hemings moved there, too, to continue his job as chef after a brief interlude at Monticello with his family in the fall of 1791. His early days in the city were somewhat unsettled because he could not immediately move into the house Jefferson had chosen to live in on High Street (Market Street).[1] Once again, the inveterate architect and builder had ordered extensive renovations, and they were not yet finished and would not be for weeks to come. He wanted a "book room, stable, and [a] garden house," added to the already well-appointed dwelling. The owner, Thomas Lieper, had actually "spared no expense" on the place, and if it was not quite the Hôtel de Langeac, it was far more than the "small" and "indifferent" residence that Hemings had come to know in New York. The interior was "expensively finished" with "stucco cornices, doweled floors, oversize window panes, and mahogany balusters and handrails."[2] By the time Jefferson was finished, Hemings was restored to the sort of opulent surroundings he had known in Paris—in very exalted company, as things turned out. President Washington lived on the same street, just three blocks away.[3] The new head of state was probably a familiar sight to Hemings as they both went about their business, sharing the same streets but living in their own respective worlds. All eyes were on the new president.

While waiting for the workers to complete enough of the renovations to allow them to move in, Hemings lived in a boardinghouse along with the other servants Jefferson hired for his new residence, giving him more new people to get used to. His duties as chef and servant in charge of household accounts started around January 8, 1791, the day Jefferson noted that he began to "dine at home."⁴ Even after the formal routine of Hemings's life got under way, matters were still in disarray. Work on the house continued, and Jefferson's staggering quantity of "books, household goods, furniture, paintings and papers" arrived at the end of October. There was no place to put the things at first, so he stored them at phenomenal expense on a Philadelphia wharf. Seventy-eight crates out of the eighty-six he had shipped from France were to be brought to High Street, while the other eight went to Monticello.⁵

In what must have been quite a memorable event, when the house was ready, Hemings saw "twenty-seven wagon loads" worth of Jefferson's possessions arrive at his door. That was not all. The items from the New York residence had to be incorporated into the house as well, a herculean task that took weeks to accomplish. The professional packing service Jefferson hired in France had meticulously prepared the crates to guard against damage on the transatlantic voyage. Unpacking was no easy thing. Each container cradled the goods inside in either "strong packing cloths; various kinds of paper, flannel . . . nearly 400 pounds of shredded paper, 624 bundles of rye straw and 36 bundles of hay for cushioning."⁶ Jefferson wrote to his daughter with almost childlike glee, "I am opening my things from Paris as fast as the workmen will make room for me."⁷ He was not doing that by himself. It is more likely that Hemings and the other servants who were on board by then were responsible for doing the bulk of this work when they were not about their basic duties.

Amid all the turmoil of his daily environment, Hemings continued to live his odd existence between slavery and freedom. Because Jefferson refused to hire a maître d'hôtel during the wait for Petit to arrive, he was, as he had been in New York, in charge of the household with no boss besides Jefferson. He was paid the same rate, or more, as the other servants and, unlike them, still received occasional gifts of money for his personal use. Jefferson continued to buy some of his clothes and even had clothing made for him by his own tailor.⁸ He was trying to make Hemings as comfortable in his condition as possible, perhaps because he knew what the young man had given up by deciding to come back to America.

Philadelphia, however, was no more Paris than was New York. What it lacked in exotic energy for Hemings, it more than made up for in the hopeful attitude of the African Americans living there. There was no easy place for blacks in the United States during these years, merely places that were less hard than others. Philadelphia was "less hard" than Virginia. It was, for a time, the locus of rising expectations for American blacks, though their hopes were often dashed, with all too brief bittersweet victories punctuated by disappointing setbacks and generally rough times. Pennsylvania had enacted the nation's first gradual emancipation statute in 1780. Though the first, it was also more timid in its effect than the similar laws that followed. The legislation did not liberate people currently in bondage; it freed children born after the passage of the act. Even those children were not immediately freed, for the law bound them to service to the men and women who would have owned them outright, but for the statute, until they reached the age of twenty-eight. That construction of the rules kept slavery in Pennsylvania decades after the statute was passed. In addition, many of the freed slaves and their children were forced into a form of long-term indentured servitude that resembled slavery.[9]

White supremacy and ideas about the sanctity of private property came together to mandate a compromise designed to end slavery, but to do so with the least amount of disruption to slave owners' lives. Blacks were bitterly disappointed by the gradual nature of the statute's self-described "step to universal civilization."[10] How could one speak of an evil that one was willing to tolerate for perhaps decades when it was in the power of the legislature to purge it? The question, of course, was whom did the legislators most mind hurting—present-day white slave owners who would suffer economic and psychological losses if the people they were enslaving were freed immediately, or present-day black slaves who were suffering under slave owners' power?

Despite favoring masters over slaves, the drafters of the legislation were actually serious about having people comply with the provisions they did enact. By the time Hemings arrived, they had already learned that a large number of masters were taking advantage of loopholes in the law. To curb the many "evils and abuses arising from ill disposed persons," the state passed another statute in 1788. It was designed to interdict masters' creative ways of skirting the law, including sending pregnant women out of the state until they delivered their children and selling out-of-state slaves who were in the twenty-eight-year period of servitude.[11]

New York would not pass its gradual-emancipation statute until 1799.[12] While Hemings was in the city, there were enough free blacks in his view to give him a sense of what it was like to live with relatively large numbers of free blacks, but with no positive state law providing a principle to guide the whole community. Now he was living in yet another society that had moved against the institution that formed the basis of his life with Jefferson. There was at least one similarity between the law passed in Pennsylvania and the *Police des Noirs*, as interpreted in the Parisian Admiralty Court. Both laws contained a registration requirement. There was a crucial difference, however. In Pennsylvania, in contrast to France, residency was a serious issue. The law was supposed to apply only to those who resided there. To establish some parameters for what that meant, the 1780 act mandated freedom for slaves whose owners resided in the state for more than six months.[13]

The law was passed during the time of the Second Continental Congress, when Philadelphia was the seat of the Revolutionary government. Because it was clear that some members of Congress were going to be slave owners, it was thought necessary to accommodate a way of life that was legally recognized throughout the rest of the country. Section 10 of the statute provided that "Delegates in Congress from the other American states, foreign Ministers and Consuls, and persons passing through or sojourning in this state, and not becoming resident therein" were exempted from the operation of the law.[14] The *Police des Noirs*, on the other hand, made no concession to foreign diplomats. France, one of the world's two great powers, could afford to be high-handed about these matters. The fledgling United States could not. Sectional tensions over slavery had to be smoothed over for the sake of union, and the new nation wanted to be able to receive emissaries from countries that might become allies.

By the 1790s, when the country had a formal government, with members of Congress, a president, a vice-president, and a cabinet, the terminology in section 10's exemption made no sense. Why allow members of Congress to keep their slaves in Philadelphia indefinitely, but not the president and secretary of state, or other slaveholding members who had come to serve in the government? President Washington, who had not lived under the law in Philadelphia, because he was away leading the Continental Army, was so worried about the language in the statute suggesting that his slaves might go free after six months that he asked a subordinate to study the law. If it was found to apply to him, he gave instructions to find some "pretext" to send the slaves home that would "deceive" his slaves and "the Public" in a way that allowed him to avoid the law's application. For this, he could tell a lie.[15]

While Washington was so worried about the gradual-emancipation statute that he took to shuttling slaves between Philadelphia and Virginia, Jefferson showed no signs of concern about the matter. He and Hemings stayed in Philadelphia for long stretches of time. In 1791, but for a one-month stay at Monticello and a one-month tour through upstate New York, the pair lived in Philadelphia continuously. In 1792 they were there for ten months and in 1793 for another eleven months.[16]

Jefferson had lived for over five years under a requirement that he register James and Sally Hemings, and he had ignored it successfully. Unlike Washington, he had seen and thought enough about law to know that, if tested, the statutory intent of the act of 1780 could rather easily be fleshed out in a way that kept him safe. While the exemptions did not, for the reasons mentioned above, include the term "secretary of state"—in 1780 there was no such title—it did designate men who came to Philadelphia to be part of the government in 1780 as people who were to be exempted from the law because they were not Pennsylvania residents. The law clearly intended to protect public servants of the national government from the application of the rule at a time when all public servants of the United States were "Delegates in Congress."[17] Jefferson knew that laws are words on a page to be interpreted by lawyers and judges, and he undoubtedly surmised that under no reasonable construction could the law have been meant to apply to men in his circumstance.

Two Supreme Court cases decided in the years after Hemings and Jefferson left the state, one favoring an enslaved man, the other, a slave owner, support the idea that Jefferson was exempt from the law. In *Butler v. Hopper*, the South Carolina congressman Pierce Butler tried without success to maintain his property interest in a man named Ben. Under the facts as presented in the case, Butler had lived in Philadelphia from 1794 until the dispute came before the Court in 1806. Although he went home to South Carolina for annual visits, he kept a house in Philadelphia, and even stayed there during a two-year period when he was not a member of Congress, but was serving as a representative in the South Carolina legislature.[18]

The Court rejected Butler's claimed exemption from the statute, saying he had "lost the privilege" when he "ceased to be a member of congress" for two years. Was he, when not a member of Congress, a mere "sojourner," Butler's alternative theory for exemption, during that two-year period? The Court found it unnecessary to address that question, because it accepted the findings of fact below: Butler was a resident of Philadelphia and not exempt from the law. He had actually lived in Philadelphia since the 1780s, in the famous "Butler mansion," and continued to do so until he died in 1822, even being buried in the city. There were more than enough incidental facts to prove Butler's deep connection to Pennsylvania. Jefferson was secretary of state the whole time he was in Philadelphia with Hemings. Unlike Butler, he had no gap in his public service to take him out of the exemption for public officials, and if he had, he would have spent it at Monticello, not in Philadelphia. Throughout his long public career, he hastened there every time he got the chance. There was no doubt where Jefferson considered home.[19]

In *Negro Lewis v. Holloway*, a slave brought suit against a member of the House of Representatives, Langdon Cheves, who remained in Philadelphia during a "recess of congress" that lasted for more than six months. Because Congress was not in session, the enslaved Lewis argued, the congressman was merely a resident and not entitled to the exemption. Lewis lost the case. The Court's opinion, written by Bushrod Washington, George's nephew, relied heavily upon the legislative intent of the act in light of the compromises over slavery that had made union possible. Washington found it inconceivable, "that the legislature of Pennsylvania could have intended to make a law, the probable consequence of which would have been the banishment of congress from the state."[20] Southerners would never have agreed to Philadelphia as a capital if they had ever been in danger of losing their slaves when they came there to serve the government.

Just as Hemings was aware of the law in France, he almost certainly knew about the very famous Pennsylvania law. Even enslaved people on plantations had heard of it and knew the reputation it gave the city. This was a place where liberty was possible, and hundreds of enslaved men and women escaped captivity to make it to the nation's temporary capital. Hemings would address that issue of freedom for himself at the very end of his stay in Philadelphia. In the meantime, he was once again in a place unlike any other he had ever lived. The striving community of color, around 2,150 blacks, vibrated with ambition, passion, and hope for the future.[21] These people were a part of Hemings's everyday life, and he got to know some of them as he went around the city, as well as those connected to his own household. Jefferson employed at least one other black servant in Philadelphia, and there may have been others among the shifting staff over the course of Hemings's time in the city.[22] Other blacks connected to the household were not a part of the staff. In January of 1791 Jefferson wrote, "Billy's wife (Mrs. Gardiner) begins to wash for me @ 20 a year." This was Henrietta Gardiner, the wife of William Gardiner, who had been the enslaved valet to James Madison. Gardiner, a free black woman, worked at Mary House's boarding establishment in Philadelphia. She remained Jefferson's washerwoman throughout his time as secretary of state. He hired her again when he returned to the city as vice-president, and she worked for him until he left in 1800.[23] That ended their association, for when he was elected president that year, the capital had moved to Washington.

Hemings and Gardiner were certainly in contact. Jefferson gave him money to pay her, and as the major domo in charge of running the household in those early days in Philadelphia, he was responsible for making sure that everything—pickups and deliveries—went smoothly.[24] Aside from being black people surrounded by whites, Hemings and Gardiner had points of association that made for a natural connection. Her husband, William Gardiner, had served Jefferson's friend Madison in the same way Hemings had served Jefferson. Servants in the households of people who associated as frequently as these two men often grew to know one another well.

Most important of all for Hemings, both Gardiners knew about slavery and freedom. William had accompanied Madison to Philadelphia in the early 1780s and lived with him there until 1783, when he refused to return home with Madison. After having lived among so many free black servants, Madison explained, his valet had become "too thoroughly tainted to be a fit companion for fellow slaves in Virginia." Madison did not force Gardiner's return, nor did he simply emancipate him, which he could have done. Instead, he opted for his version of "benevolence": he sold Gardiner in Philadelphia rather than down south.[25] When all was said and done, the opportunity to make money off of black bodies was American slavery's raison d'être. Selling Gardiner in Philadelphia was better than selling him farther south—he apparently became free later on—but emancipating him immediately was also a viable option. As long-term residents of Philadelphia, both Gardiners could tell Hemings things he needed or wanted to know about the black community—the places where black people met, what sort went there, where he could find respite and camaraderie.

In the midst of serious hardship, black Philadelphians were determined to forge a new identity for themselves through race uplift. They most often encountered opposition when they pushed too far, but when one door closed to them, they reflexively opened others. That is how the great Richard Allen came to found the African Methodist Episcopal Church, around the same time that Hemings came to the city. Disillusioned by the treatment of blacks in predominately white churches, Allen decided the only reasonable response was for black people to build their own churches and congregations. There they could be leaders and innovators on their own terms. They also formed independent institutions like the Free Africa Society (FAS) to promote black interests. James Forten had been born free and used that advantage and his talents to become a successful entrepreneur and proponent of abolition. Both men's reputations extended far beyond their city; literate blacks read about them, and those who could not read passed the word. That is why fugitive slaves knew to run to Allen for help when they made it to Philadelphia. He provided support and, often, helped the men and women find white lawyers to take freedom cases if they wanted to file them. Neither of these men could have succeeded in Hemings's Virginia, and the presence of both energized black Philadelphia during the 1790s.[26]

Blacks had their supporters among whites, too. No gradual-emancipation statute could have been enacted without them. The Quakers, in particular, were well known for bringing a spirit of abolitionism to the larger white community through the efforts of men like Anthony Benezet, a founding, and perhaps the most revered, member of the Pennsylvania Abolition Society (PAS), who worked hard for the statute. The PAS followed a "careful approach" to the effort, filing petitions and helping to bring cases on behalf of fugitive slaves and free blacks who had been kidnapped and taken into slavery. In the historian Richard Newman's words, "In an era when most political leaders avoided divisive issues, PAS strategy emphasized that government and its representative legal and political institutions should gradually attack the institution of slavery."[27] Its members, among the elite of Pennsylvania society, were heavily influenced by a republican ideology that sought community consensus and an Enlightenment philosophy that valued reason over emotion.

Benezet was among the most enlightened in the white community on the subject of race, and he spoke out against the idea of black inferiority. He even helped found a school for black children. Most of the other members of the PAS were not so forward thinking as he. They would not allow black people to join the organization until the 1830s, finding shared membership with people of color demeaning. While PAS members were unquestionably hostile to slavery, its very moderate members had no interest in blowing apart the racial hierarchy as they knew it.[28]

Dr. Benjamin Rush, Jefferson's dear friend and correspondent, is a good example of this phenomenon. Rush was an ardent member of the PAS, and he helped individual blacks on many important occasions, probably to the dismay of many in his community. A great champion of Richard Allen, Rush got Jefferson to give money to help build his AME Church. Yet, for all his determined efforts on behalf of blacks, Rush was capable of writing that blacks "excel[led]" whites "only in those things in which dogs & horses excel[led]" them. James Hemings was quite familiar with Rush, for he was a frequent guest at Jefferson's, and consumed Hemings's fare.[29]

This degree of confusion and hypocrisy within the white community put Philadelphia blacks on the road to freedom even as it ensured that racially inspired barriers would be placed all along their way. After the brief and hopeful period in the 1780s and 1790s while Hemings was in the city, the situation in Philadelphia began to deteriorate until in the 1830s free blacks explicitly lost the right to vote. They were officially second-class citizens.

To the North Country

Hemings had hardly settled into his new life in Philadelphia before he was on the road again. Acting on behalf of the American Philosophical Society, and to satisfy his own scientific curiosity, Jefferson in May of 1791 embarked on a tour of upstate New York and New England to study the Hessian fly, which posed a threat to the wheat crops of America. James Madison, to whom he was becoming ever closer, decided to accompany him on the journey. Again under the stress of politics and work, Jefferson was suffering another migraine attack and hoped to find respite during the journey.[30] His political rivals believed that he and Madison were really up to something else beside science: politics. The two men were making the trip, they said, to rally "northern support for their opposition to the Hamiltonian policies" that were gaining strength in George Washington's government.[31] Even the men's most sympathetic biographers have acknowledged that it would have been almost impossible for these two very ardent politicians to have avoided politics in one way or another—observing potential supporters, talking with local officials—as they moved across the towns and states on their itinerary.

For a month in the late spring of 1791, James Hemings ceased to be a chef and took up his old role as personal servant and coachman to Jefferson on his northern tour.[32] Did he want to go, or did Jefferson choose to take him because doing so killed two birds with one stone? Hemings could drive his phaeton and be his valet instead of using his coachman and bringing Hemings, or another of his house servants from Philadelphia, along to play the role of manservant. There was also a matter of trust. Jefferson had a history with Hemings and was used to relying on him in ways that he had not relied upon with his current coachman.

However it was decided that he should go on the trip, both Jefferson's and Madison's accounts of their tour suggest that there were majestic scenes to discover, and Hemings observed them as he drove the two men about upstate New York and New England. This was a positive opportunity for him, for he loved to travel. He also probably got an earful about the politics of the early American Republic as two of its chief architects chatted while they made their way through the North, tracking the Hessian fly and gauging the state of political affairs in the region.

The trip began in earnest in New York City, where Hemings and Jefferson traveled to meet James Madison, who had gone there in April. Hemings took Jefferson's and Madison's horses and Jefferson's phaeton from New York to Poughkeepsie, while the two politicians took their version of the scenic route, sailing up the Hudson to rendezvous with him there.[33] There is no mention in Madison's relatively spare notes on the trip that any one of his slaves or servants traveled with him, so it is likely that James Hemings attended both men on the journey.

Hemings knew Madison from Virginia and from his visits to Jefferson's home in Philadelphia. His association with Madison could have been even closer, for Jefferson, always eager to have his friends at hand, tried without success to persuade Madison to move out of his boardinghouse and into his spacious residence. Had he agreed to move, Hemings would have been chef to both of them on a daily basis. He did get to know Madison better on this extended tour. As a result of this trip, of all the Hemingses, James was the one who likely had the most personal contact with the man who was

Jefferson's closest political ally. He would not, however, live long enough to meet his nephew and Madison's namesake, James Madison Hemings.[34]

Hemings was now twenty-six years old, a young enslaved man traveling through rural New York on roads that he did not know in a place as American as his Virginia, but still foreign to him. The image of the young man traveling solo on unfamiliar roads in strange territory seems a metaphor for Hemings's life. It is perhaps incorrect, but one gets the impression of a somewhat solitary life for this man. There is no question that he had his own private world beyond the one he lived in with Jefferson—one largely known only to him that we simply cannot retrieve. He moved too freely away from Jefferson and his family for them to have known everything he did, where and how he spent his money, what people he knew, and what they meant to him.

The range of his travels and his efficiency in getting things done for Jefferson that required interaction with other individuals, oftentimes whites, suggest a man who knew how to make contact with people and fix them in his world as he needed, as he did his tutor in Paris. But the daily references to Hemings in the account books set the boundaries of his life firmly around the man who owned him; they give the sense of a claustrophobic existence devoted to seeing to the comfort of one individual, a man who had no wife and who happened to be emotionally needy and controlling.

One notices the lack of any mention of a woman in Hemings's life during this period. There may have been one, or some, and there was simply no reason for Jefferson to write anything about them, because Hemings never married and produced any children while at Monticello to be put down in the Farm Book. Jefferson's records do not account for Hemings's personal life outside of slavery. The life he had lived as an enslaved man up until this point had made it difficult for him to find time for a wife. This is, of course, the great difficulty in having to view Hemings's life through the records of the man who enslaved him. Despite his many years at Monticello, we do not know whether James's eldest brother, Martin, had a wife and children, though he certainly may have. Very often enslaved men and women at Monticello had abroad marriages, and Jefferson had no reason to keep track of their spouses and children. That Robert Hemings had children alive, probably as early as the 1780s, appears nowhere in Jefferson's records. He, unlike his brother James, was left in the United States to be on his own, and found a woman to marry while in his twenties. James Hemings's early twenties were taken up either traveling with Jefferson or living in a country where the opportunities to find a wife were drastically curtailed. As noted earlier, the overwhelming majority of people of color in Paris were young males like himself. That would have been a boon to his sister had she decided to stay there. It would not have been the same for him.

Now here James Hemings was again, in the spring of 1791, traveling by himself to meet up with two men who were companions to one another, but not to him. One wonders if he ever thought of simply continuing north, as he drove alone, or at any point when he was away from the two men he was driving around the countryside. After Jefferson and Madison rejoined him, the trio went as far north as Lake Champlain, and it would have been a relatively easy matter to have disappeared into Canada and take his chances there. When they crossed into New England, going through states where slavery had been abolished, Hemings could have balked at going back home with Jefferson.[35] He did not. His situation, working and receiving a steady salary, suited him for the time being.

In the midst of the spectacular scenery of upstate New York, on June 1, the travelers came upon what would have been to Hemings one of the most intriguing parts of the journey, one that had particular resonance for his life. They were at Fort George, near Lake George, a beautiful area with "mountains of considerable height the entire length of the lake." The one house found on the "East Side" of the lake was "owned & inhabited by a free Negro," in Madison's words.

> He possesses a good farm of about 250 Acres which he cultivates with 6 white hirelings for which he is said to have paid about $2^1/_2$ dollrs. per Acre and by his industry & good management turns to good account. He is intelligent; reads writes & understands accounts, and is dextrous in his affairs. During the late war he was employed in the Commissary department. He has no wife, and is said to be disinclined to marriage: nor any woman on his farm.[36]

This entry is in stark contrast to the rest of Madison's otherwise relatively spare and almost exclusively "scientific" travel journal. The future president was clearly fascinated by this man, whose existence was a total rebuke to his way of life on almost every level. There were certainly free blacks who had farms in Virginia in 1791, before and after that time, but probably few, if any, had such an extensive holding or employed so many white people. Actually, the man was a rebuke to the way of life for New Yorkers as well, for despite the movement toward abolition, slavery still had a firm hold in parts of the state.[37]

What Jefferson thought of the man is unknown, because he made no reference to him, but it is hard to believe that he and Madison did not talk about the man, given the closeness of their association on the journey and Madison's obvious interest in him. Jefferson devoted his journal entries, for most of the trip, almost entirely to descriptions of the flora and fauna observed along the way, noting how many land and water miles they traveled, along with rating the quality of the inns where they lodged on their journey. Aside from his writings about the Hessian fly, he concentrated on transcribing the vocabulary of the Unquachog Indians, whose language had disappeared so thoroughly that only "three persons . . . old women" could speak it. His only notation about the people at Fort George was that there were "very few inhabitants around the lake."[38]

More than all the other blacks whom people brought to Jefferson's attention to "prove" blacks' worthiness, this man, working his 250-acre farm, presented the single greatest challenge to Jefferson's, if not America's, imagination. Could the country incorporate not just a handful of genius almanac writers, poets, or painters, or musicians but legions of ordinary black men and women who wanted to enjoy the blessings of the American continent and political experiment—the rich land, access to credit to run a farm or build a business, and the ability to participate as a full citizen in a democratic system?

This black man was living the life that Jefferson dreamed of for free white men—a self-sufficient yeoman farmer with a basic education who was able to become a functioning and productive member of society. He gave other people jobs, white people, who if they worked hard and managed their money well, might be able to have their own farms, hire people, and continue the cycle. This "Negro" farmer would in modern parlance be called a "role model" or, not long ago, a "credit to his race." Despite the condescension often contained in those designations, they really have had a meaning in the African American community as blacks have gone about the business of trying to maintain a healthy self-image and build a culture in a hostile environment. Madison was impressed, and Hemings would have been too.

Return to Philadelphia: Petit and Banneker

After a journey of over eight hundred miles, Hemings returned to Philadelphia and settled back into his routine as chef and butler.[39] There were constant reminders of his life in France. The furniture Jefferson had bought there filled the renovated house, and at least part of the look of the interior of the Hôtel de Langeac was re-created right there on High Street. Letters from Jefferson's friends still in France arrived, and though Jefferson's records would not reveal this, it is possible that Hemings himself had communications from people he had met in the country. Other items evoked physically intimate memories for him. The bedding he had used in France and that of his sister Sally had arrived in the country just before he started the northern tour. Jefferson wrote to his daughter that he was shipping them home, that James's bedding was to be kept for him, and that Sally Hemings was to be given hers to keep.[40]

The most potent reminder of Paris arrived in July of 1791 when Adrien Petit came to Philadelphia, answering Jefferson's entreaty of the year before to come and be his "housekeeper" at a very generous salary. This was luring him back into the work force because after Jefferson left Paris he had retired from service and gone back to his native Champagne to live with his mother. He quickly became bored with his life there, telling William Short "qu'il meure d'ennui," and decided to take the offer, which was both an adventure and an opportunity.[41] Jefferson had grown accustomed to a certain style of living in France and wanted to re-create that to the extent that it could be done in the United States. Bringing the maître d'Hôtel de Langeac to the United States fit perfectly with his desire to be comforted in his immediate surroundings—having the same people in his circle following familiar routines and procedures. So intent was he on having Petit back in his household that he did not even bother to look for another person to fulfill that role. When Maria Jefferson came to live with her father in the fall of 1791, a small core of those who had resided at the Hôtel de Langeac, without Sally Hemings and Martha Randolph, was reunited.

Petit worked for Jefferson until he resigned his post as secretary of state in 1793, he and James Hemings re-creating the old division of labor that had existed at the Hôtel de Langeac. Petit was in charge of the overall running of the household, doing the grocery shopping and preparing the desserts, which Jefferson said was absolutely required of his maître d'hôtel.[42]

So Hemings and Petit collaborated on food preparation from before the meals were prepared to the end, for Petit's desserts had to complement Hemings's dinners. The two men likely accompanied one another on early morning excursions to the market to find the best fare for the table.

Petit's arrival, along with the French furniture and paintings, completed the Francophile cast to the house on High Street. Even Jefferson's coachman, François Seche, was of French extraction. Petit may not have been terribly comfortable in English, for all of the correspondence between himself and Jefferson was in French. So French was probably very much in the air as Hemings, Jefferson, and Petit interacted with one another in the household—out of both necessity (Petit's) and self-interest (Hemings's and Jefferson's). After over five years abroad, and a heavy investment in learning French, both Americans no doubt very much wanted to preserve as much of the language as they could. Jefferson, for a time, very noticeably kept the style of dress of a man who had spent time at the French court.

All of this contributed to the picture of Jefferson as a "cosmopolitan and artistic pacesetter" in a city that had become a more "sophisticated place" than it was when he first lived there as a young revolutionary.[43] The furniture, paintings, and knowledge of Jefferson's service in Paris alone would not have set his image so firmly in the eyes of those observing him. Hemings and Petit brought the food and language of France, the country's most distinctive treasures, to Jefferson's household. The interior of the house was designed to be viewed, and when Jefferson's guests, people as diverse in political views as Benjamin Rush and Alexander Hamilton, wandered through the dining room, or "salon," as Petit called it, and parlor admiring the paintings, they perhaps overheard snippets of French pass between Petit and Hemings, or when Jefferson made a request or gave an order to his transplanted maître d'.[44] The entirety of this presentation—French furniture, people, and food—enhanced the authenticity of Jefferson's effort to re-create a little part of Paris in the heart of Philadelphia. Here was definitely a case where the personal was political. The Francophilia displayed so openly in Jefferson's home gave ammunition to his political foes as the French Revolution grew more out of control and bloody. What probably seemed a charming affectation on his part at first took on a more sinister import as the 1790s unfolded.

The idea of home was never very far away from Hemings, as letters and packages were going to and coming from Monticello. Approaching

Christmases away from the mountain, in 1791 and 1792, each year Jefferson sent home boxes containing a football field length of linen and material for Sally, Critta, and Betsy Hemings. The 1792 packet included "2. peices of linen. 52. yards, 9. pairs of cotton stockings (3 of them small) 13. yds. cotton in three patterns, 36. yds. Calimanco, 9. yards of muslin." Whether he or James, or both of them, went shopping for all this is unknown. Jefferson also noted that "Bob" (Robert Hemings) was "to have a share of the linen." He had "promised" to send Hemings "a new suit of clothes" but "instead" sent him "a suit of superfine ratteen" of his own, which Jefferson had "scarcely ever worn." He mentioned that he had forgotten to buy stockings for Robert, and asked his daughter Martha to purchase some from "Colo. Bell's on [his] account."[45]

The most maddening aspect of James Hemings's story is that both his voice and the conversations he had with his family and people like Petit are lost to us. Their situation was extraordinary—a French white servant and an American black slave who had worked together for the same man on two continents. Both understood the position they occupied in Jefferson's life and were willing to use their knowledge to their advantage when the occasion warranted. James Hemings's time would come near the end of his stay in Philadelphia, whereas Petit's moment of truth with Jefferson came just a bit earlier, during one particularly incendiary time in the life of the household. Petit's days in Philadelphia were not easy. While he and Hemings apparently got along well, he had a difficult time with Jefferson's other employees, and it caused a great amount of turmoil in the household, becoming so intense that it disrupted the harmony that Jefferson always sought to maintain.

The coachman, Seche, along with his wife and children, lived in an "apartment" on the grounds of Jefferson's Philadelphia residence. Petit and Seche's wife fell into a simmering conflict that grew to full-scale war when the wife alleged that Petit engaged in sodomy and that he loved men. She had apparently said many other things to him that he found objectionable, but he was unwilling to ignore this. He wrote to Jefferson, who had gone with James Hemings to Monticello for a visit, saying essentially that it was either Seche's wife or him. If she was not immediately removed from the household, he would return to France.[46]

Jefferson's response to Petit was on par with his letter to his daughter after she wrote to him complaining about Thomas Mann Randolph's impending marriage to Gabriella Harvie, in terms of the clarity of the voice that comes through in the letter. When matters were really serious, Jefferson's tone in letters became almost conversational—not in the sense of employing informal language, which he did not, but in terms of his ability to convey effectively a true connection to the recipient of his letter. At those times, he managed to establish a sense of intimacy unhindered by the form of writing on a page, bridging the geographical distance between himself and whomever he was writing to, allowing the person to *hear* what he was saying and how he was saying it, not merely to read his words.

Even though he wrote back to Petit in French, Jefferson's "voice" comes through very clearly in the different language. His first sentence immediately reassured: "It was yesterday, my friend, that I received your letter of July 28." He did not address directly what Seche's wife had said, nor did he attempt to analyze any of the details that had set Petit off. Instead, he concentrated on making it plain that the matter would be handled entirely to Petit's satisfaction. He ended by eloquently invoking an expression of his long association with Petit and his regard for him, saying to his furious employee that since he had sought him out in France and waited a whole year for him to arrive he should know that he was not going to allow anyone to make him let him go so quickly, and then, finally, "je suis et serai toujours votre ami" (I am and always will be your friend).[47] That same day Jefferson wrote to George Taylor, who was handling his affairs in Philadelphia in his absence. Without mentioning the substance of the dispute, he instructed his agent to let Seche and his wife know where he stood. Taylor was to tell Seche that he "had such long experience of the fidelity of Petit, and value[d] him so much, that [he] would not have a moment's hesitation to say that no person shall stay about the house who treats him [Petit] ill."[48]

Petit, still in a tizzy about all this, evidently got the message from Jefferson's letter and knew his employer was on his side, for when Taylor talked to him about Seche he upped the ante and insisted that both the wife *and* the coachman had to go. Taylor thought this unfair. "I told him that as he alleged nothing against him [the coachman], it would not only be cruel but unjustifiable in me to discharge him. He declared that unless both were removed he would go to france."[49] This was a volatile situation that could easily have erupted into violence, a dispute between a man and a married woman whose husband would naturally take his wife's part.

Taylor instructed Seche not to go into the house or even speak to Petit, if that was possible. He was also directed to find another place for his wife and children to live. In the end, Petit would not budge from his position that the whole family had to go, and Jefferson's agent, with understandable nervousness, given that he was putting a man who had a family to support out of work, fired him. When he told Jefferson what had happened, Jefferson assured him, "What you have done . . . is exactly what I would have wished."[50]

There is little question whose side Hemings took once he returned to the city. This conflict had been brewing over the months before the final confrontation, and he probably already had chosen a side. His connection to Petit was far stronger and more long-standing than his connection to Seche and his wife. Petit referenced this shared history in the last line of his letter detailing his problem with the Seches when he told Jefferson that he wanted him to pass along his greetings to "Gimme" and "Salait" (Jimmy and Sally), the brother and sister serving as touchstones, reinforcing his own association with Jefferson.[51]

Whether true or not, Mrs. Seche's statement would in her and Petit's time, though not in ours, have been characterized as a "charge" or "allegation" or "accusation," as if Petit had engaged in sodomy, or really did love men, and had actually done something wrong. Sodomy was a crime, although no criminal prosecutions were brought for it in Philadelphia during the latter half of the eighteenth century, and no trials at all during the entire century. There was a fairly extensive subculture of men who engaged in same-sex activity in the city, who met in taverns and other establishments, but Philadelphians adopted a look-the-other-way attitude about the matter. Loving men, short of any kind of physical display of it, was not a crime, and it is fascinating that Mrs. Seche separated the two, suggesting that there was as early as the 1790s, as some scholars have posited and others have actively disputed, a consciousness in the general public of men who loved other men, not just men who engaged in same-sex activity.[52]

That Mrs. Seche thought to deploy homosexuality as a weapon in her conflict with Petit is also intriguing, given that there were other things she could have said. Was this a common taunt by women to men? Very little is known about Petit, and it is impossible at this juncture to know whether Mrs. Seche really believed that what she said was true, somehow knew it was true, or simply reached for what she thought might be a hurtful thing to say. Servants who worked closely with one another knew the backgrounds and activities of their co-workers. Indeed, Petit's reputation probably preceded him, as his arrival had been greatly anticipated for many months. Members of the household knew at least that Petit was a bachelor with no obvious sign of wife or children. They may well have heard that when Jefferson contacted him he had retired to the countryside to live with his mother and thought he was not living the life of a "normal" man, without understanding the nature of French society. As noted earlier, many French masters refused to hire, or fired, personal servants who married. Petit may well have loved men just as she said, or he may have been the victim of the excessive power that French masters exercised over their servants, a power that came back to haunt them during the 1790s when the "lower orders" exacted revenge upon those who had taken unimaginable liberties with their lives.

Petit's strong response conveys how serious a matter it was to him in the context of the world in which he lived. Still, to insist not only that Mrs. Seche be removed from the household but that her husband, who had not figured at all in his angry letter to Jefferson, also be put out of work for his wife's invectives seems an overreaction. Mr. Seche had a family to support, one who had suffered a grievous loss in the year before this, which Jefferson revealed when he noted that he paid the funeral expenses for one of the Seches children.[53] Was Petit incensed at Mrs. Seche for lying about him, or angry at her for bringing the truth of his life into the open? One wonders whether he would have repeated in a letter to Jefferson what she had said if her statement was true, unless the couple had threatened to say something to Jefferson themselves and this was Petit's preemptive move.

Jefferson showed no sign that he was bothered by what Mrs. Seche had said about Petit, beside the discomfort it caused his longtime employee. There is no indication he made any effort to investigate the truth or falsity of her statement, no show of concern that it posed any threat to his household. Either he did not believe Petit loved other men, already knew he did, or simply did not care one way or the other. His chief concern was to make sure that his maître d'hôtel, who had come all the way from France at his request, did not leave the country hurt. Above all, Jefferson could not abide domestic discord. One sees echoes of his response to the Petit-Seche battle in his handling of a later power struggle in the President's House. When one of his white servants, Edward Maher, complained about having to wear the same livery that Jefferson's black servant John Freeman wore, Jefferson's response was acid. He said that he had known and valued Freeman longer and better than

Maher, suggesting that the disgruntled man should simply put the livery on and fall into line.[54] The complaining Maher did not survive long in Jefferson's employ, and the master of Monticello was sanguine about his departure: "I like servants who will do everything they are wanted to do."[55]

In the end, the Seches, or at least his wife, badly misjudged how far they could go in baiting Petit and suffered for their miscalculation. They probably did not understand that Jefferson was not a prude and did not abandon friends or family easily. When his son-in-law's sister Nancy Randolph got into her famous trouble with her brother-in-law at Bizarre and became a social pariah, he continued to host her at Monticello—even when his daughter Martha refused to have Nancy in her home.[56] Jefferson's presence evidently had been sufficient to keep matters in the household from coming to the point of exactly the kind of poisonous domestic turmoil that he feared and loathed. Away at Monticello, he had had no way to keep the peace. Three days after he returned to Philadelphia with James Hemings, Jefferson closed the book on his time with his coachman from New York: "Pd Francis Seche for wages & board from Sep 1. to this day 19.D. He now leaves my service & John Riddle comes."[57]

IN PHILADELPHIA, James Hemings was at once at the center and periphery of momentous events in the life of the nation—at the center because of his physical proximity to some of the men who were making history, at the periphery because his race and status did not allow him to have a direct and personal hand in shaping those events. His impact on society came from being a member of the group whose past, present, and future in the country loomed over all serious discussions of where the nation would head in the coming years. In August of 1791 Jefferson received a letter from an African American who put the matter to him directly, not raising James Hemings's name specifically, of course, but seeking some clarification of what the future would hold for men like Hemings and his brothers and women like his sisters.

Benjamin Banneker, a free black man from Maryland was both a mathematician and astronomer. He prepared a scientific almanac that he sent to Jefferson, thinking that he would understand the spirit in which it was presented. He said that he was writing

> in consequence of that report which hath reached me, that you are a
> man far less inflexible in Sentiments of this nature [that blacks were

inferior beings], than many others, that you are measurably friendly and well disposed toward us, and that you are willing and ready to Lend your aid and assistance to our relief from those many distresses and numerous calamities to which we are reduced.[58]

Banneker went on to appeal to Jefferson on the basis of his words in the Declaration of Independence about the equality of mankind, suggesting that it served as a basis for him and other whites to "wean" themselves "from those narrow prejudices" which they had "imbibed with respect to" blacks and to work toward ending slavery. Banneker's approach to Jefferson can be seen as the formal start of black Americans' conflicted political engagement with him. Even before this time, and certainly long after it, blacks used the words of Jefferson's declaration as a promise, or as a tool of irony, to express the gap between American ideals and the reality of blacks' lives.[59]

Jefferson responded quickly and politely to Banneker, indicating that he was impressed with his work and that he hoped the conditions of blacks could be raised. He also promised to send the almanac to his friend Condorcet, the "Secretary of the Academy of sciences at Paris," which he did on the very same day he replied to Banneker. He had already heard about Banneker before the letter arrived, having been approached by Andrew Ellicot, the cousin of George and Elias Ellicot, the mathematician's chief benefactors, about allowing Banneker to become an assistant in surveying the land for the Federal District. Jefferson approved of the assignment, and Banneker began work during the first part of 1791.[60]

Eighteen years later, however, Jefferson sounded a different note about Banneker in letters to Joel Barlow and Henri-Baptiste Gregoire, the "Abbé Gregoire," questioning whether Banneker had had help in preparing the almanac he had sent to him.[61] Much had happened in the country, and to Jefferson, during those nearly two decades. Whether he had believed all along that Banneker's mentors had helped him is unknown. The astronomer was mixed race and could easily have fit Jefferson's profile of the African American "improved" by white blood. What is known is that the charge that Banneker may have received help in preparing his almanac did not originate with Jefferson. It appeared in print years before he hinted at it in his letters to Barlow and Gregoire, and it was conceived as a weapon to attack him. Thomas Green Fessenden, a prominent Federalist from New Hampshire, chided Jefferson mercilessly in a newspaper column as gullible,

saying that he had been taken in by Banneker and abandoned his supposi-
tions about blacks' inferiority after having encountered the "wonderful phenomenon of a Negro Almanac, (probably enough made by a white man)."
William Cobbett, a rabidly racist expatriate Englishman who wrote under
the pseudonym "Peter Porcupine," was even more sarcastic in his description of Jefferson's support of Banneker.[62]

Jefferson closely followed the writings of his enemies in the Federalist
press, and it is not possible that he did not know the tack they were taking on his dealings with Banneker. Being seen as one who supported black
aspirations was not the kind of thing any American politician of Jefferson's
day, or long thereafter, for that matter, wanted. There was no future in it.
Voicing a generalized antislavery sentiment was one thing—it fit with the
still resonant natural rights formulations that helped set aloft the Spirit of
'76—but championing blacks as individuals was another matter. It did not
help that for most of the first decade of the nineteenth century—from 1802
until his retirement in 1809—he and Sally Hemings had been the subject
of newspaper articles, cartoons, and ballads from one end of the country to
the next, even reaching across the Atlantic.

It may be difficult from this remove, when current-day fashion often casts
Jefferson as *the* extreme racist and political conservative of his age, to accept
that this was not his general reputation during most of his political career.
Without getting too far ahead of the story of how his political ambitions and
hopes for the future of the United States affected the Hemingses and his
other slaves, one can say at this point that the fallout from his dealings with
Banneker was an early and clear signal to one of the shrewdest and most
self-protective politicians of his era about how he could and should express
himself on the issue of slavery and race in public and in private.

At the time, Banneker and his supporters were thrilled to receive a letter
from Jefferson that from a modern-day perspective seems unremarkable—
even meaningless. Still, the letter was like tonic to blacks and whites who
opposed slavery. They very quickly arranged to have both letters printed
together in pamphlet form and distributed to advance the nascent cause
of abolitionism. There is no evidence that they approached Jefferson about
using his letter. However, one of Banneker's staunchest allies, Andrew
Ellicot, the commissioner in charge of building the Federal City, regularly
communicated with Jefferson. With his permission or not, after the pamphlets circulated, Jefferson became a target for those who put this exchange

together with his well-known support for the French Revolution and his antislavery sentiments written in the *Notes on the State of Virginia* and cast him as a dangerous political extremist.[63]

Much as it cheered Banneker and his supporters, Jefferson's reply to the black man enraged some prominent southerners. One, and apparently others, took his letter as a tocsin that he wanted to do away with slavery immediately, which was never the case. Every plan he ever conceived of along those lines contemplated a period of delay, as had been suggested by Condorcet and adopted by several northern states in the wake of the Revolution. One critic focused in on his signing off his letter, "I am with great esteem, Sir Your most obedt. humble servant," the entirely formulaic closing common in letter writing of that time. Indeed, that was how Banneker had closed his letter to Jefferson. The problem, of course, was that their mutually respectful letters and mirrored closings suggested equality between the two. Jefferson had let down the side by engaging Banneker in this fashion.[64]

In the realm of personal interactions, Jefferson had no problem with extending common courtesies to black people. He once rebuked his grandson for not bowing to a black man who had bowed to them while they were walking together on the street. Jefferson had returned the gesture and wondered aloud to his grandson why he let a black man be more of a gentleman than he. Throughout all the years Henrietta Gardiner was employed as his washerwoman, he invariably referred to her in his own records as "Mrs. Gardiner," never as Henrietta.[65]

Part of Jefferson's great skill as a politician lay in his ability to intuit and respond to how others would react to certain words or actions, not a trait that was easy for him to turn on and off, and it showed itself in many vastly different contexts. He would not have expected the black man to have assailed him for failing to bow or Mrs. Gardiner to have shown offense had he called her Henrietta, but it was easier to follow the policy of being nice and respectful if it really cost him little to do so. He apparently did not think these niceties in his one-on-one encounters with blacks cost him very much, for, in truth, they did not. Whether he styled himself as Banneker's "obedient servant," returned the bow of a black man, or called a black woman Mrs. Gardiner, he was still a white man who was the master of black people on his plantation and viewed as the social superior of all other blacks and the vast majority of whites.

George Washington, who was much more formal than Jefferson in every sense, did think such things mattered. He evidently did not easily recognize last names for black people. When he wrote of his manservant William Lee, with whom he seems to have spent more time than anyone else, he could not resist styling him "William (calling himself William Lee)."[66] In 1775 when he replied to the young poet Phyllis Wheatley, who dedicated one of her poems to him, he addressed her as "Miss Phillis," even though it was well known that she was married. Washington, as did Jefferson in his letter to Banneker, had kind words for her work. He could hardly be too critical of a poem containing the following couplet:

A crown, a mansion, and a throne that shine,
With gold unfading, WASHINGTON! be thine.[67]

Both Washington and Jefferson believed in white supremacy, because that was as much the currency of their time and place as was male dominance over females, but those who hold to that doctrine do not always express it in the same way. Washington was willing to go on record praising Wheatley's poetry, but would not address her with an honorific attached to her name. Jefferson went on record disparaging her poetry, but would not have hesitated to call her Miss or Mrs.

Given the nature of their association, it is hard to imagine that Jefferson did not mention to James Hemings his contact with Banneker as the matter unfolded, if only in a *"You're a black person, see what this other credit to your race has done"* fashion and to let James know that he had helped get Banneker a job surveying the Federal City. Whether Jefferson told him about it or not, Hemings almost certainly came to hear about the correspondence very soon—and perhaps read a copy of it—because it was widely circulated the following year in Philadelphia and other places where abolitionists had a presence. It was exactly the kind of thing any person of color would have been interested in at the time. Hemings was living in the home of a white man whom some blacks and their supporters looked to in their desperation for any glimmer of hope, no matter how small. Banneker told Jefferson that he was writing to him because he had the reputation of being a "friend" to black people. Jefferson's friendship with Benjamin Rush, who was well known in the black community, probably helped shape black Philadelphians' view of him.[68] They may also have heard that he had given money to help Richard Allen build a black church in Philadelphia. One cannot discount the possibility that the black people who dealt with Jefferson, like Henrietta Gardiner, and even James Hemings, circulated stories about him that suggested that he was, at least, approachable. Banneker had written from Maryland, but news traveled quickly and far in black circles. That is how fugitive slaves knew to run to Philadelphia and seek help from likely friends in the city.

Jefferson's very human contradictions have long bedeviled observers, but James Hemings and his family had to live with them. It formed the basis of their lives. Hemings would have immediately recognized Jefferson's instinct to be polite to Banneker, because he had witnessed such displays directed toward him and other blacks. He would also not likely have been surprised to see Jefferson's later waffling on Banneker's accomplishments after suffering public ridicule for having praised the astronomer. Nor would it have shocked Hemings to know that Jefferson suggested that Banneker's "white" blood and that of others offered to him as examples of black achievement might account for their talent. He and other members of the Hemings family were burdened by and benefited from Jefferson's construction of race and his ambivalent attitude about slavery and emancipation. That was one of the reasons he was in Philadelphia as a slave when Jefferson communicated with Banneker, yet poised on the threshold of making a radical transformation of his life.

23

EXODUS

Elizabeth Hemings and her children lived through the Age of Revolution. The end of the 1780s and the beginning of the 1790s saw the denouement of one, in America, and the beginnings of two others, in France and in one of its colonies, Saint Domingue. From the British invasion of Richmond to the malaria and smallpox-infested encampment at Yorktown and to the storming of the Bastille, several of Elizabeth Hemings's children had an ironic presence at galvanizing struggles for social transformation. Ironic, because these upheavals were not designed to bring about a revolution in their own particular circumstances; and if any people needed a transformation of their lives, it was the Hemingses and other American slaves.[1]

Although the American Revolution failed to end slavery in the South, or immediately to destroy it in the North, it did change, for a time, the nature of the conversation about the institution. In the wake of revolution, and talk of the natural right to freedom, Virginia liberalized its emancipation law in 1782, allowing individuals to free their slaves without the permission of the state. The rhetoric of political revolution was not the only influence. Religion played an important role as well. Denominations that had first appealed to nonelite white Virginians, Baptists and Methodists, the latter guided by the abolitionist and, for his day, antiracist sentiments of John Wesley, sent ministers throughout Virginia in the 1790s preaching the gospel. Methodists, in particular, urged any of their members who owned slaves to free them. A number of them did. In ways that might astonish

modern observers, black and white Virginians in the early Republic wor-
shipped together in Methodist services, sometimes with black men, often
still enslaved, acting as lay preachers. This, not surprisingly, drew the
enmity of those who feared alliances between ordinary whites and black
people of any status. When large numbers of upper-class white Virginians
began to join the church during the first years of the nineteenth century,
they insisted on marginalizing blacks, persuading any lower- and middle-
class whites who might think otherwise that racial affinity was vastly more
important than religious affinity. Soon churches that had urged their members to free slaves began to own slaves themselves.[2]

The revolution in Saint Domingue brought a flood of refugees into the
United States, many to Virginia towns like Richmond and Norfolk, telling
stories of the bloody and successful slave revolt. The specter of blacks killing whites for their freedom struck terror in the hearts of Virginians. By the
end of the 1790s, the small spirit of liberalization the American Revolution
had brought to race relations in Virginia began to dissipate in the wake
of white Virginians' fears that enslaved people would follow the course
they had taken with Great Britain: engage in armed conflict against their
oppressors.

At the beginning of the decade, however, the Hemingses lived in a
Virginia where more subversive ideas were being offered in the marketplace, with a small, but growing, population of freed blacks whose presence served as both provocation and inspiration. As to provocation, most
whites simply did not want these blacks without masters around. Their very
existence severed the link between blackness and slavery and reminded
the enslaved that freedom was a real possibility. Stifling the imaginations
of blacks—and of whites inclined to be sympathetic to them—became the
order of the day, discouraging thoughts that there could be any real change
in the way black and white Virginians went through the world together.
With most blacks laboring under the disabilities of slavery, life was made
hard for those who became free.[3]

As to inspiration, free blacks provided enslaved members of their race
with a hopeful example of what could be if they somehow managed to break
free. They saw them acting on their own as artisans and farmers, some failing under the weight of white hostility, others making decent lives for themselves. A cogent equation was projected: black did not have to equal slave.

Thenia and Mary Hemings

If any enslaved people were in a position to hope that they might benefit from the slight, but important, change in atmosphere in Virginia, it was Robert and James Hemings. They had existed on the cusp of freedom for many years, the younger brother literally a carriage ride away from it in France. They were not alone in being restless. Something happened at Monticello between 1790 and 1794 that never happened again. In that five-year period, five of the Hemings siblings, four who had played major roles at Monticello, decided they wanted to be somewhere else—one way or another.

The least well-known among this group was Thenia Hemings, John Wayles's oldest daughter with Elizabeth Hemings. In 1794, when she was twenty-seven years old, she was sold to James Monroe, along with her five daughters, Mary, Lucy, Betsy, Susan, and Sally.[4] Jefferson never wrote why he sold the family, but it was almost certainly at Thenia Hemings's request. She was, after all, a Wayles daughter, and Jefferson's attitude toward this group of siblings virtually rules out his having decided on his own to sell her away from her family on the mountain. Neither the sale nor the purchase of five little girls (age ten down to infants) would have given either Jefferson or Monroe much immediate value. The father of Hemings's children must have lived on Monroe's plantation or nearby, and the sale was carried out to unite her family. Most, if not all, of these children had been born while Jefferson was in Paris, and a number of the enslaved people at Monticello were hired out to neighboring farms.

Thenia Hemings had a direct connection to James Monroe dating from that period. Her brother Martin had hired himself out to Monroe as a butler or manservant even before other Jefferson slaves were rented out by Nicholas Lewis. Thenia had gone to work in a home in Staunton, Virginia, in 1786, but there is no indication of how long she was there.[5] The circumstances suggest that she might have worked at or near Monroe's after she returned from Staunton and formed a relationship with a man while there. Jefferson's memorandum to Nicholas Lewis written in November of 1790 and listing "Ursula, Critta, Sally, Bet, Wormeley and Joe," along with "Betty Hemings," as the "house-servants" at Monticello strongly suggests that Thenia Hemings was not at the plantation, or she would have been on that list with her mother and sisters. Everything that had happened in her family in the early 1790s told Thenia Hemings that, if she wanted to live with her husband and family, she had a good chance of having that happen. What time she had with them turned out to be far too brief; she died the year after her formal sale to Monroe.[6]

There was probably more than one reason for the exodus of Hemings siblings from Monticello in the first half of the 1790s. The world seemed to be falling apart there, or, one should say, it had never really been put back together again after Martha Jefferson's death. Jefferson had been gone from Monticello, effectively, for almost eight years. The appointment as secretary of state took him away from the mountain the overwhelming majority of the time he was in office. Except for his sojourn in France, he would never again be away from home for such a concentrated period as between 1790 and 1794, not even when he was the president. Given his absence, he could not exercise the same influence over the imaginative lives of those who lived on the mountain. The unsettled circumstances there brought opportunities for some family members and allowed them to think more expansively about what could happen in their lives. The situation at home, along with the subtle transformations taking place in Virginia's slave society, may well have emboldened members of the family to approach Jefferson about making the changes they wanted in their lives. And then, of course, there was Sally Hemings. Her siblings knew that she had successfully negotiated with him and that he was a man who might be reasoned with. Whatever they felt about the situation on the merits, Hemings's brothers and sisters cannot have looked at Jefferson in the same way as they did before he went to France. When they asked him for things now, it was in the context of a new connection between them.

Not all the members of the family had realistic prospects for the kind of changes that Robert and James Hemings were able to engineer. Gender and degrees of family affiliation mattered greatly. The most exact counterparts to Robert and James—Thenia, Critta, and Sally Hemings—could never have expected to persuade Jefferson to free them outright. If no free black man or white man sought to buy her, the most that Thenia or Critta Hemings could hope for from Jefferson is what Thenia accomplished, a sale to be united with an enslaved husband who lived elsewhere. As we have seen, Jefferson believed that women, all women, were supposed to be under the control of a man, preferably a white man. In fact, the first member of the family to formally break away at her own initiative was Mary Hemings. In

April of 1792 Jefferson wrote to Nicholas Lewis about her: "I am not certain whether I gave you power to dispose of Mary according to her desire to Colo. Bell, with such of her younger children as she chose. If I did not, I now do it, and will thank you to settle the price as you think best."[7]

Mary Hemings found one way to leave the mountain: exchanging masters—attaching herself to a man who never formally freed her or their children, but who ultimately acted more as her husband than as her owner. Yet this was not a clean break. Jefferson did not let all of her family go. In uniting one biological family unit—the Bells and their children—he broke apart another. "With such of her younger children as she chose" meant that her two older children, Joseph and Betsy (probably "Elizabeth," after her grandmother), had to stay at Monticello. In fact, Joseph Fossett was only twelve and his younger sister, Betsy, only nine when they were separated from their mother. The youngsters continued on, most likely looked after by their grandmother and aunts. Although they were geographically close, and there was always much contact between Monticello and Mary Hemings Bell's house, there were, no doubt, many painful nights for Joseph, Betsy, and their mother.

By the time Hemings was separated from Joseph and Betsy, as was noted earlier, her oldest children, Daniel and Molly, had already been given away. So having her offspring taken from her was nothing new. But nothing in the human makeup would allow a parent to view this as inconsequential. There could be no greater impetus to escape, however one could, a system that allowed such a thing to happen. It is almost inconceivable that Mary Hemings would not have chosen, if given the opportunity, to have all her children together with her. Although Bell may have wanted to buy only his son and daughter, Jefferson's instructions suggest that Joseph and Betsy were not for sale. Joseph Fossett became one of his most important artisans, and it is possible that Jefferson may have seen his potential and had plans for him early on. Like her brother, Betsy Hemings was kept on the mountain because Jefferson and his family were already looking to the future. The nine-year-old would be groomed for the role she eventually took on: Sally Hemings's replacement as the personal maid for Jefferson's daughters.

The most salient aspects of the Bell-Jefferson transaction were not written about. The deal was presented in a way designed to evade any understanding of its true meaning, guaranteeing that anyone who chose to rely primarily on the family letters of slave owners to tell the story of their lives with their slaves would never figure out what actually happened. In other business deals—who the parties really were to one another, what they were trying to accomplish and why, and where their real interests lay—were often presented in revealing detail, or in letters referring to the transaction. To see Jefferson and Lewis in operation in this circumstance (for it is unlikely that Lewis, who had leased Hemings to Bell and lived in the area, did not know their true relationship) is to view the shadow world of slavery at work. Here Jefferson was instructing his agent to sell a white man the enslaved black woman he was living with along with the two children she had borne him, writing in a manner that made clear that her two older children, who did not belong to the man, were not for sale.

One would never know that from any of Jefferson's letters to Lewis. A more curious reader, however, might wonder why Mary wanted to be sold to Thomas in the first place, and why being owned by Thomas Bell was preferable to being owned by Thomas Jefferson and living with all her children. One might also wonder why only her "younger" children were allowed to go, especially since one of the older children was not really that old. Even in the shortened childhood of slavery in general, and at Monticello specifically, a nine-year-old was still a child. Why separate Betsy from her mother without even an attempt to make her available for sale? That these "younger children" were born during Hemings's time in Bell's home might also raise an eyebrow.

Naturally, the Hemings family knew the story of Mary and Thomas Bell. In their world, however, their explanation for the underlying meaning of this cryptically rendered transaction would not likely have been accepted as valid for purposes of history. The Hemingses, and other American slaves, have a dubious distinction in Western civilization. They are the only victims of a historically recognized system of oppression who are made to carry the burden of proving beyond a reasonable doubt that things endemic to their oppression actually happened to them, as if enslaved people were a powerful government making accusations against relatively powerless, and presumptively innocent, people—slaveholders. This standard, borrowed from law, and others discussed more fully in chapter 3 hold sway in mainstream historical determinations of paternity in the southern slave system. Just as they did during slavery, these strategically restrictive standards protect masters against the claims of their black female slaves in order to preserve the racial integrity of white family lines—an interest often assumed to be of far greater importance than the family identity of African Americans. In the morality of this setting of the balance of interests, only Thomas Bell (and perhaps any of his contemporary *white* relatives who might claim the African American Hemingses as their relatives) had the power to make the story of Mary Hemings's life under slavery real within the pages of mainstream American history. By eventually acknowledging his children, he gave permission for everyone to see, and say, what Jefferson was really talking about in his letter to Lewis.

Martin Hemings

Elizabeth Hemings's oldest son, Martin, who had no Wayles connection and was less likely to have had children with a white person who could buy his freedom, evidently did not fare as well as his sister or his half brothers Robert and James during this period. On the surface the three oldest Hemings brothers' circumstances were alike. Jefferson reposed a great amount of trust in all three men and gave them privileges that others did not have. Their ultimate destinies suggest that all along there was, in fact, a profound difference in their situations: only Robert and James were destined to be emancipated by Jefferson. And when he did let them go and decided to have another personal servant, he did not replicate the relationship he had had with either Robert or James.

Martin Hemings had a very tense and fateful moment with Jefferson during one of his infrequent trips back to the mountain during the early 1790s. The first hint that he would not continue to live at Monticello came in a letter Jefferson wrote to Daniel Hylton in November 1792. Unlike that of his sister Mary, who had managed her departure in as smooth a way as possible, Hemings's eventual separation from the life he had known for almost two decades began in turmoil and ended in mystery.

> Martin and myself disagreed when I was last in Virginia insomuch that he desired me to sell him, and I determined to do it, and most irrevocably that he shall serve me no longer. If you could find a master agreeable to him, I should be glad if you would settle that point at any price you please: for as to price I will subscribe to any one with the master whom he shall chuse. Any credit may be given which shall be desired in reason. Perhaps Martin may undertake to find a purchaser.

But I exclude all idea of his own responsibility: and I would wish that
the transaction should be finished without delay, being desirous of
avoiding all parley with him myself on the subject.[8]

The last visit referred to in this letter had taken place earlier that
year. After an eight-and-a-half-month absence—from the end of October
1791 until the end of July 1792—Jefferson returned to Monticello from
Philadelphia.[9] He stayed there for a little over two months and then went
back to the capital, not to come home again until the following year. One
can imagine the difficulty these types of drop-in visits caused, especially for
slaves who were expected to snap to attention and deal with the extremely
self-absorbed and exacting Jefferson. He was, as we have seen, a man who
could not stand to live in a rented house without remodeling its rooms to
fit his specifications—even for the short time that he might be living there.
Rearranging the lives of the people who served in the house—so long as he
was, in his view, nice about it—would have been of no great moment.

Neither the cause nor the substance of his quarrel with Martin Hemings
was ever disclosed. It must have been extremely serious for Hemings to
have demanded to be sold and for Jefferson to have agreed to it with such
alacrity. Hemings had been the butler at Monticello for twenty years, since
he was nineteen years old. He was hardly a young man, and here he was
opting for a life away from the most obvious sources of emotional support—
not to gain freedom itself but just to be free of Jefferson. His departure
would represent a momentous break in his own life and a real change in
the structure of life at Monticello.

While Jefferson made clear that he wanted Hemings to find a master
of his own choice, and that he was willing to take any price in order to
help matters along, suggesting solicitousness toward the man, his anger
is palpable. There was here no viewing "every human being" for what it
was "good for" or "keeping out of the way of the bad" aspects of the person.
He was clearly furious at Hemings, and he fulfilled the truth of one of his
grandchildren's observations that he never talked about anything that he
did not want to talk about. He and Martin Hemings had gone past the point
of return, Hemings having said or done something so serious as to make
Jefferson want to sever contact as completely as possible.

Jefferson could have forced Hemings to continue at Monticello and, if
required, had him beaten into submission. Certainly, any attempt to bring

Hemings around by using the whip would have set off a chain reaction in a household staff made up entirely of Hemings's relatives. Whether they would have protested aloud or not, even a slight negative change in the atmosphere would have damaged the willed harmony that Jefferson sought to maintain everywhere he went. Then there was the matter of Hemings's younger half sister Sally. What would brutal treatment of her brother make her think of him? There was no need for a naked display of his power over Martin Hemings if the matter could be handled in a different way and keep some semblance of peace, and perhaps even make himself look good. The way Jefferson handled this, casting himself as the accommodating master, minimized the scope of the complaints that Martin Hemings's relatives could raise about what was happening. The substance of the dispute would never be detailed in print, but Jefferson's procedural "fairness" would be duly noted.

Unlike Robert and James Hemings, Martin did not, as far as we know, suggest that Jefferson free him or come up with a plan to buy his freedom as did his younger brother Robert within two years after this conflict with Jefferson. On the other hand, we should guard against assuming that because Jefferson never wrote down that something happened that means it did not happen. What the Jeffersons wrote about life at Monticello was only a tiny fraction of what actually occurred there over the years.

As it turned out, Hemings was not sold immediately. When Jefferson began to keep his Farm Book again in 1794 after twelve years away from permanent residence at Monticello, Hemings was listed as living there, but that was the last time he appeared in any of Jefferson's records regarding his slaves.[10] The only written trace of him after this time was a cryptic reference in one of Jefferson's letters to his daughter Martha in January of 1795. He spoke to her about some business that her husband was attending to for him in language that says all that needs to be said about what slavery was and meant to the people who lived under it:

> There remains on his hands Martin and the Chariot. If the latter cannot be disposed of without better wheels I would be obliged to him to take the greater and larger diameters of the axle, and the length of the Nut of the wheel, as also the height of the fore and hind wheels, that I may have a set of good wheels made here, and sent down.[11]

Martin Hemings and a "chariot": both to be "disposed of" by sale. It appears that Hemings was not able to find his own buyer among the people for whom he had worked during Jefferson's absences, if indeed he had wanted to work for them. There is no record that he was ever sold. He may have died during this period, or it is possible that he was simply let go at some point without a formal emancipation, to live as he had before, hiring himself to employers. The entirety of his life suggests that Hemings would never have been satisfied with any master. His aggressive attitude disqualified him from the status of the kind of faithful and loyal servant that Jefferson would reward by legally emancipating him. He was neither a woman going away to be taken care of by a white man nor a son of John Wayles. Lucia Stanton wrote of him as "the fierce son of Betty Hemings," and that description seems most appropriate.[12]

James Hemings

After Mary and Martin came James. About a year after Martin Hemings asked to be sold, Jefferson wrote a fascinating document that reveals how determined some members of the second generation of Hemingses were to press whatever advantages they had. It had most likely been a topic of conversation since before they left France, but it was at the end of their tenure in Philadelphia that the deal, reconciling Hemings's desire for freedom and Jefferson's wish to realize a return on his investment in having paid to have Hemings train as a chef, was put in writing. As fate would have it, Petit, Hemings's friend and co-worker from France, was involved in this and will be forever memorialized for it. Petit was the witness to the document that formalized Hemings's agreement with Jefferson to free him.

> Having been at great expence in having James Hemings taught the art of cookery, desiring to befriend him, and to require from him as little in return as possible, I do hereby promise and declare, that if the said James shall go with me to Monticello in the course of the ensuing winter, when I go to reside there myself, and shall there continue until he shall have taught such person as I shall place under him for that purpose to be a good cook, this previous condition being performed, he shall be thereupon made free, and I will thereupon execute

all proper instruments to make him free. Given under my hand and
seal in the county of Philadelphia and state of Pennsylvania this 15th
day of September one thousand seven hundred and ninety three.[13]

This document, signed and sent to Jefferson's son-in-law Thomas Mann
Randolph, a promise by a master to his slave, had no legal force. Although
enslaved people filed suit to uphold these types of documents, courts generally held them unenforceable either at law or in equity.[14] Hemings, literate and conversant in two languages and by that time a worldly man, knew
the rules of slavery and almost certainly understood that what Jefferson had
done was strictly personal. While this was not a legal document, one should
not underestimate what it meant to Hemings to know that it had been prepared in response to his discussions with Jefferson.

Promises do not have to have legal force to be important to the people
who make them. This was a piece of paper with Jefferson's signature on it
that put him on his honor, which was why it made sense to send a copy of it
to his son-in-law, who handled his business on many occasions. It marked
the seriousness of the venture and assured that if Jefferson broke the promise, someone whose esteem he valued (and that Hemings knew he valued)
would have knowledge and proof that he had done so. Also, if something
were to happen to Jefferson as the process unfolded, the paper would be evidence in the hands of his family of his intent on the matter. That Jefferson
kept a copy of it in his records shows that he wanted posterity to know that
he had done this as well. He could just as easily have written up a piece of
paper, given it to Hemings, and left it at that. There was no need for a witness to this extralegal document, either. That Petit was chosen, instead of
others in the household, seems especially fitting since this deal was apparently put in motion when the three men were still in Paris.

Jefferson did not likely draw up this agreement out of his own desire.
From his perspective, his word alone should have been enough, especially
since he knew the document had no legal validity. This was more likely
something he did to please Hemings. It has been suggested that he must
have been acting in response to a threat by the Pennsylvania Abolition
Society (PAS) to file a freedom suit on Hemings's behalf.[15] There is no indication that Jefferson ever felt threatened by the PAS or that credit for bringing him to this point belongs to benevolent, unknown whites and not to
Hemings and his courage and personal initiative. The PAS did have a record

of helping enslaved people bargain with masters about freedom, especially in the nineteenth century after Hemings's time in the city. But bargaining with masters about freedom was not a singular event in the world of slavery. Other enslaved people, in Pennsylvania, in Hemings's Virginia, and elsewhere, entered into bargains with their masters for their future emancipations, even when no white people were around to tell them what to do.

Given his residence in Philadelphia, Hemings did have the option of seeking the aid of the PAS or other abolitionists, black and white. If enslaved people from the South seeking liberation could make it to Richard Allen's church, he could have, too. One of the society's most prominent members, Benjamin Rush, a frequent guest at Jefferson's home and consumer of Hemings's fare, gave him direct access to the organization. He did not choose a legal confrontation. His situation in Philadelphia actually paralleled that of his and his sister's circumstances in France and raises the same questions: Why would a young woman come back to slavery at Jefferson's request, and why would a young man go along with Jefferson's proposal if it meant another two years as a slave instead of immediately filing suit against him to obtain his freedom as soon as possible? One should resist the temptation to say that when a person does not make the choice one would have made, that person must have been forced or tricked into it or deny that he had any choice at all.

His sister's possible motivations have been discussed at length in previous chapters. While it might seem clear enough from our perspective that almost two and a half more years as a slave would be a worse resolution than a possibly successful freedom suit, James Hemings's calculations evidently brought him to a different conclusion. It is not at all certain that a lawsuit could have been wrapped up more quickly than the time he ultimately spent at Monticello, or that he would have won. And while we do not have Hemings's words, we know enough about his life with Jefferson to that date—and enough experience with the meaning and fallout from litigation—to know that he would have had to weigh this matter very carefully.

Embarrassing Jefferson in Philadelphia, the site of his greatest achievement in life until that point, was to burn a serious bridge irrevocably, for he did not easily forgive those who wounded him personally. Hemings knew Jefferson extremely well—his strengths, vulnerabilities, and vanities. Taking the route he took allowed him to extricate himself from slavery with minimal rancor from a hugely influential man who, in a hostile world, could continue to be helpful to him in the future—but from a distance that Hemings could choose.

The language of the document is telling. Jefferson presents himself as "desiring to befriend" Hemings and announces his intent to "require from him as little in return as possible" as Hemings trained the new Monticello chef. The language of friendship lays the groundwork for a future association, which Jefferson definitely wanted and sought in the years after Hemings's emancipation. Referencing his "great expense" to have Hemings trained was also a justification for having him come back to Monticello as an unpaid trainer of a new cook to help Jefferson recoup his expenses. Finally, it was a not very subtle attempt to appeal to (or awaken) a sense of gratitude or guilt in Hemings. Whether this was a benevolent document (and whether that even matters, given the important end result that was achieved) is subject to debate.

The overall context in which the document appeared should also be considered. Jefferson, emotionally scarred from his battles with Alexander Hamilton, which he was losing at the time, had made a firm decision by the end of 1792 that he would retire when Washington finished his first term. He arranged to take a house about three miles outside of the city near the banks of the Schuylkill River, sending his furniture and, most important, his books back to Monticello, a clear sign of his seriousness because he cannot have expected to stay in Pennsylvania for very long without his books.[16] Before he moved to the country in April of 1793, it was clear to Hemings, and all members of the household, that their days in the state were coming to a close. After Jefferson left office, Hemings would return to Monticello with Jefferson, Petit would go back to France, and Jefferson's other employees would go on to new situations. By July, Jefferson had set on September as the end point for his term, and he told President Washington of his plans. It did not work out that way, for he was unable to resist Washington's request that he stay on until January.[17]

Though Jefferson's description of his house on the river makes the place sound charming, it may not have been for James Hemings, and one wonders how Petit felt about the change in scenery. This was clearly a place of needed respite for Jefferson. Here he escaped the scene of the bruising conflicts that had become integral to his position as secretary of state, while Hemings cooked and served him meals that he preferred to take outside under the trees surrounding his house whenever the weather allowed.

"I never go into the house but at the hour of bed," he wrote. Under his "high plane trees with good grass below," he would "breakfast, dine, write and receive . . . company."[18] His enthusiasm about this bucolic life and the almost childlike delight he took in being able to stay outside as long as he wanted are understandable. His generally pleasant letters home to his daughter and son-in-law hint at, but do not come close to telling, the story of the really titanic political machinations (some put in motion by him, others by Hamilton) that were going on before and during his idyll on the banks of the Schuylkill.

All this may have meant something quite different to James Hemings. Though he was only several miles outside of the center of the city, he apparently did not crave the semirural isolation that Jefferson found so appealing. He had come of age in cities, and when he was emancipated he went back to them to live—first Philadelphia and finally Baltimore. One does not get the sense of a man who ever longed for the quiet life on his own little farm. He had never been an agricultural worker, and nothing suggests that he had any particular competence in that arena, or wanted to obtain it. What he knew how to do best could more easily be done in an urban setting.

Jefferson's decision to move to the country might have been a life-saving one for both him and Hemings. By the beginning of August, five months after their departure from the house on Market Street, it was clear that something was going seriously wrong in Philadelphia. People began to come down with a mysterious illness that caused severe headaches and backaches, along with a high fever. After a few days, the skin of the victims turned yellow, and they began to vomit blood so dark that it looked black. This was the start of the yellow fever epidemic of 1793, which would end up taking five thousand lives in the city. From August to November "10 to 15 percent of the estimated 45,000 Philadelphians perished, while another 20,000, including most government officials, simply fled."[19]

No one knew where it came from or had any inkling that the "dense mass of" mosquitoes "that hung over the city like a cloud" were the vectors.[20] Many blamed the refugees who had only recently arrived in the city fleeing the revolution in Saint Domingue, and others, like Jefferson, believed that the city's cramped and sometimes dirty conditions were the culprits. Arguments over the fever's origins and the best treatment for it broke down along political lines—the Federalist faction blamed the émigrés, and the Republican faction faulted the noisome environment.[21] Jefferson's flight from political turmoil, and the distasteful prospect of having to run into his enemies on the streets of Philadelphia, succeeded in getting Hemings out of the city in the spring, long before the evenings of the summer and early fall of 1793, when the disease wreaked its worst damage.

The epidemic, a catastrophe for all, hit the black community hard in a number of ways. As the cases and death toll rose, and inhabitants left the city, some blacks stayed to help out in the crisis. Not all remained voluntarily. Many were conscripted and prevented from leaving so that they could dig graves and attend the sick. Of those blacks who stayed by choice, a good number saw this as a chance to perform a heroic deed that might change the way the white community viewed blacks overall. Committed "race" men like Richard Allen and Absalom Jones, who had both founded the African Methodist Episcopal Church, helped organize their efforts. Benjamin Rush had worked with these men before and urged blacks to stay, in part, because he thought they were naturally immune to the disease.[22] Jefferson alluded to this supposed immunity when he observed to his son-in-law, "The pure blacks have been found insusceptible of the infection, the mixed blood has taken it." What he thought more amazing was that "not a single instance of it occurred of anybody's *catching* it *out of Philadelphia*" (emphasis in the original).[23]

Blacks were not totally "insusceptible" to yellow fever, and a number of black Philadelphians who stayed behind to help caught the disease and died. Those who escaped death were repaid for their efforts when the crisis abated with charges that they had taken advantage of their sick patients, either robbing them or overcharging them for services. Richard Allen and Absalom Jones, ever vigilant to matters that affected their community, wrote a pamphlet refuting the charges and detailing the contributions of blacks to the relief effort. They also listed examples of the fees and payments for services that black nurses, drivers, and gravediggers rendered as they tried to help out during the crisis. There might have been people who acted inappropriately, they said, but the deeds of the minority should not have defined the character of the majority of blacks who risked their lives to help.[24]

When Washington talked Jefferson into staying in his position until the end of the year instead of leaving in September, he agreed to Jefferson's plan to go to Monticello for a visit that month instead.[25] James Hemings and Jefferson ended up leaving a week earlier than planned because

Jefferson's staff had dwindled down to one clerk, everyone else having fled to avoid the plague. In this harrowing time, the two men set out for Virginia knowing that they would not return to the house near the Schuylkill. Even though they did not know what caused yellow fever, all had noticed that the disease was seasonal—being particularly bad in the summer and disappearing in the cool weather. Hemings and Jefferson had reason to hope that by the time they returned, the epidemic would have abated or at least be in decline.

THEIR BRIEF SOJOURN at Monticello over, Hemings and Jefferson set off from Monticello on October 25, 1793.[26] They were not going back to Philadelphia. Germantown, just outside the city, had been designated the temporary seat of the government as officials tried to escape the ravages of yellow fever, whose depredations spared no one. Alexander Hamilton came down with the disease but recovered with some lingering effects, as well as Dolley Todd's young husband, who lost his life. A year later, the young and vivacious widow remarried and became Dolley Madison, a woman who would come to have her own place in Hemings family history.[27]

On their return Robert Hemings rode with them as far as Fredericksburg and then went back to Monticello with the horses. Jefferson gave him money there for his expenses and bought tickets for himself and James Hemings for the stagecoach to Baltimore. When they got there, they met President Washington, who was on his way to the capital himself. There is no mention of him in Jefferson's records, but Washington's ever-present body servant, William Lee, was probably along, and he and Hemings may have encountered one another before.[28]

Since no public stages went "further North," Jefferson had to hire a private driver—and was "fleeced," he said—to take him and Hemings on to Germantown, on a journey in which the weather ran the gamut from hot to cold to dusty to rainy. The pair arrived to find a town overflowing with escapees from Philadelphia and yellow fever. There was no place to stay. Jefferson reported that he, the secretary of state, "as a great favor" had gotten "a bed in the corner of a public room of a tavern" and had to stay there until "some of the Philadelphians" left the city.[29] Hemings was there with him, because no other place was to be had in the city, every available accommodation being full. They remained in those circumstances for several days until they found more permanent lodging and Hemings was able to settle back into his responsibility for taking care of the household. Jefferson paid him his month's wages and gave him money to purchase items for their daily needs.

Hemings's Germantown stay proved short. By December 1 he and Jefferson were back in a Philadelphia that was "entirely clear of all infection" with everyone ready to take up where they had left off. But Jefferson had no house, so he rented rooms in the home of Joseph Mussi on "the corner of Seventh and Market."[30] There was not enough space for Petit, who boarded at a nearby tavern. The men lived this strange existence—a chef with no kitchen to cook in, a master of the house with no house—for five weeks. Hemings may actually have enjoyed this, as it relieved him of some pressure, for Mussi's Italian chef prepared Jefferson's meals for the entirety of his stay. It also gave Hemings the chance to observe the differences and similarities in the preparation and, no doubt, taste of another of the world's great cuisines. The displaced chef, however, still had responsibilities, managing all of Jefferson's household expenses. Petit seems to have been primarily biding his time waiting to leave the country. As he had in France, Jefferson periodically borrowed money from his maître d'hôtel while he was in his service in Philadelphia. The men settled all their accounts in January of 1794, and Petit returned to his native land.[31]

From their very different positions in the world, both Hemings and Jefferson believed they were coming to a breaking point in their lives. Jefferson, frustrated and demoralized by the political setbacks during his time in Washington's administration, saw this as the end of his long public career and looked longingly toward Monticello as if he were going there to take a cure. Hemings had his own reasons to be eager. The sooner he began to train a new chef, the sooner he could return to Philadelphia, or wherever he wanted to go, as a free man.

Robert Hemings

Even though his younger brother seemed likely to gain his freedom first, it was the eldest son of Elizabeth Hemings and John Wayles who in the end received a formal deed of emancipation from Thomas Jefferson before any of the other Hemingses. Robert Hemings and his relatives surely knew of Jefferson's agreement with his younger brother, and this could only have raised his own expectations. Though he had not traveled as widely as James, Robert had taken his own serious steps toward freedom and needed a life away from Monticello. He was a husband and father whose family lived else-where. After the brief turn in New York, he returned to Monticello whenever Jefferson called for him, being his manservant, carrying messages back and forth between Jefferson, his daughter, and son-in-law, just as he had since boyhood. He even spent time in Jefferson's Philadelphia home.[32]

By 1794 his wife, Dolly Hemings, had moved from Fredericksburg to Richmond. At some point during that year, Robert Hemings and Dolly's owner, Dr. George Frederick Stras, worked out a deal. Stras would buy Hemings's freedom from Jefferson, and then Hemings would repay Stras. Robert's gambit seems to have taken Jefferson by surprise, and he was not happy about it at all. In fact, he was extremely angry at Hemings. He decided to go along with the proposal and wrote up a deed of manumission stating that he had "manumitted and made free Robert Hemings, son of Betty Hemings: so that in future he shall be free and of free condition . . . and shall be discharged of all obligation of bondage or servitude whatsoever. . . ."[33]

We get a glimpse of how Jefferson really felt about this in a letter he wrote to his son-in-law the day after Christmas.

> You will find by the inclosed that Bob's business has been hastened into such a situation as to make it difficult for me to reject it. I had certainly thought it just that the person whom I suppose to have debauched him from me, as well as the special inconvenience of my letting him go for 2. or 3. years to come, and a total abandonment of his services for 11. or 12 years past should have been known and oper-ated in estimating his value as a mulct on Mr. S. However all that has been kept out of view, and I have too much respect for the gentlemen who have valued him to have the subject revised. It remains therefore only to receive the money and deliver the deed, which you will find inclosed in the letter to Stras. I have made it to Bob himself, because Mr. Stras mentions it is for his freedom he is to advance the money, and his holding the deed will sufficiently secure the fulfilment of Bob's engagements to him.[34]

In some ways this document is more intriguing than Jefferson's earlier writing in which he promised to free James Hemings. The man who had the ultimate control in this situation placed himself in the position of one forced to do something that he clearly did not have to do; "Bob's business" "hastened" to the point that it would be "difficult" for him "to reject it," as if *he* were a victim of Hemings and Stras. Neither man could have forced Jefferson's hand on this matter. And then there was the characterization of Hemings's wish to be with his wife. The notion that the young man had been "debauched" from him by the woman's owner makes Hemings's very natural desire to be with his spouse and children sound an unsavory choice when compared with being Jefferson's manservant.

The most interesting language of all is the bitter lament about Hemings's valuation. Jefferson could not seriously have thought that it should have occurred to whoever valued Hemings to include as an item of value the fact that he had chosen to let Hemings work for other people over the previous "11. or 12 years." "Pay me for all the ways I chose not to use my property in years past," with no showing of how his "non-use" contributed to the property's value, was an extremely peculiar expectation on his part. He was counting all the way back to 1782, when he embarked on his odyssey away from Monticello after his wife's death, and he had allowed Hemings to hire himself out to others.

Jefferson did not mention what it had cost him to have Hemings apprenticed to a barber. This may well already have been included in the price. He cannot have been anticipating the loss of Hemings's services in that regard, for their time in New York shows he had not been using them; he paid someone else to shave him and dress his hair all the while Hemings was in the city. As to what he specifically referred to, unless he could show how Hemings's acting as a valet for other men over that time made him more valuable than he would have been had he acted as Jefferson's valet, the twelve years he decided to forgo personal use of Hemings's services were merely his lost opportunity. As for the wages Hemings made, and Jefferson did not collect, he had chosen to order things that way over the years, no doubt congratulating himself on giving the equivalent of a "gift" to the young man. He thought he was building emotional capital that would strengthen Hemings's loyalty to, and affection for, him. Allowing Hemings to have his own time away from Monticello and keep his money was Jefferson's own show of affection, and Hemings was supposed to see it that way and act accordingly: be content to remain in lifelong service to him on those "generous" terms. When Hemings failed to follow this plan, the now angry Jefferson wanted to monetize the emotional benefit he had gotten over the years so that he could take back the "gift" he had given Hemings, suggesting that Stras should have to pay for a thing he had never shown the slightest interest in having before: Robert Hemings's money.

Jefferson was, in truth, in a precarious position to begin with in terms of Robert Hemings's value. An enslaved person's history of having been hired out was often a liability upon an attempted sale. Two years after this episode, St. George Tucker, of the famed Virginia emancipation plan of 1796, sought to sell four highly skilled slaves who had been hired out to the city. He was stunned to find no takers. The man handling the sale, experienced in these matters, explained to Tucker that, having "so long hired their own time, and lived without controul," they were unattractive to potential buyers. Tucker eventually sold the slaves at a much lower price than he thought fair.[35]

Had Hemings been on an open market, Jefferson might have ended up with a price not far from the one he accepted from Stras had the extent of Hemings's freedom over the past decade been revealed to prospective buyers. Why would owners want to deal with a literate black man who had for twelve years been choosing his own employers, traveling at will, working where he wanted, and keeping his wages? Moreover, it was not true that what Hemings had been doing over the years amounted to a "total abandonment of his services." Hemings could not have abandoned anything without Jefferson's assent. He could have brought Hemings to France with him to be his manservant while his brother learned to cook, or he could have sent him to the fields if he had wanted to.

While on the surface Jefferson appears to be reasoning, his complaint makes sense only as an emotional outburst, rather than a well thought-out analytic dissection of the economic fairness of this transaction. He was not talking about the monetary value he had lost, nor was he really addressing the arbitrators who had valued Hemings. This was a complaint that grew out of his sentiment-driven pique that *Hemings* did not seem to value all the years he had let him essentially do whatever he wanted to do. Property often has a sentimental value, but the owner seeking to sell the property usually must say that outright or set a minimum price to reflect any non-economic, personal feelings that transcend more obvious economic considerations. The arbitrators did not know what it meant to Jefferson to have taken up his wife's twelve-year-old enslaved half brother, traveled and lived with him as part of a pair, and treated him, by the standards of the day, with great leniency. They also did not know that Jefferson had assumed there was some reciprocity of feeling from Hemings and that he experienced the purported mutuality of sentiment between them as a "value." Who but Jefferson had "kept" what all this meant to him "out of view"?

The arbitrators did not know any of this, but Jefferson surely expected Robert Hemings to know it, and he was deeply hurt that the younger man's knowledge seemed to make no difference to him. Despite everything, he wanted to go somewhere else. Money, which Jefferson could sometimes spend like the proverbial drunken sailor, was not the real issue. He simply did not want Hemings to want to go. Compare his attitude in this situation, carping about the price, with his attitude about the sale of Martin Hemings, an event unfolding at the same time. Martin and Robert Hemings had both occupied positions of trust in Jefferson's household, and both men had been allowed to work and keep their money. Jefferson pronounced himself willing to accept any price—to perhaps take a loss—in order to facilitate the sale to whomever Martin Hemings picked. There was no suggestion of try-ing to recoup the money that Hemings had made while out of his service for the same length of time as his younger brother.

Robert Hemings knew that Jefferson was angry and that his anger was not just about his dissatisfaction with the price. This transaction, proposed after Jefferson made the agreement to free James Hemings, raises an inter-esting question. Did Robert Hemings ever approach Jefferson on a one-on-one basis about working out a deal for his freedom? If he had let Hemings work for wages and keep them for himself, he could have let him work for wages to pay him with no middleman involved. Perhaps Hemings did raise the possibility with Jefferson, was rebuffed, and went to Stras as an alterna-tive. Whether the possibility was previously raised or not, Hemings sought to effectuate his emancipation working with a third party's involvement that automatically put the third party, Stras, on a par with Jefferson. He had been talking with someone besides Jefferson about his future. Glimpses of the tension this created are offered in the correspondence between Jefferson and his daughter Martha. Several weeks after Jefferson drew up the manu-mission deed, Martha wrote to him about Hemings:

> I saw Bob frequently while in Richmond he expressed great uneasiness
> at having quitted you in the manner he did and repeatedly declared
> that he would never have left *you* to live with any person but his wife.

He appeared to be so much affected at having *deserved* your anger that
I could not refuse my intercession so warmly solicited towards obtaining your forgiveness. The poor creature seems so deeply impressed
with a sense of his ingratitude as to be rendered quite unhappy by it
but he could not prevail upon himself to give up his wife and child.
(emphases in the original)[36]

This report of Hemings's feelings comes from an interested third party,
and it is a great loss to history that all the letters Hemings wrote to Jefferson
are no longer extant, for they might have allowed us to see exactly how
he approached his former owner in the aftermath of their difficult disen-
gagement. Hemings understood that Jefferson perceived his dealings with
Stras to be a form of disloyalty, and he correctly divined what his former
owner wanted to hear: an expression of devotion so wide that only his love
of his wife and child could get around it. Whether he actually felt that or
not, we will never know. Wearing "the mask" was often a necessary part of
life for relatively powerless people in those days. Whatever his feelings for
Jefferson, Hemings was interested in freedom for himself and his family.
He did not want to live in slavery with Dolly and their child (either Elizabeth
or Martin at the time) at Monticello, which very likely could have been
arranged. It is almost inconceivable that Jefferson, who bought and sold
men and women who were not Hemingses to unite their families, would
have balked at buying Hemings's small family. He would have kept his
manservant at Monticello and provided yet one more reason, in his eyes,
for the young man to have been grateful to him.

Jefferson's fertile and creative mind wandered everywhere and saw the
world not just as it was but how it could be, but for the conventions and
rules of society—some of which he approved, others of which he did not.
He knew that Robert and James Hemings were the sons of the man who
had given him his fortune, though we will never know if he ever for the
briefest moment allowed himself to ponder the ramifications of this. In
a world with any degree of morality, or even in another type of slave society, these young men would never have been his slaves and might have
had a share of that fortune. Jefferson had spent at least five years in a society where the mixed-raced children of slave owners sometimes shared the
property of their fathers, and he knew there was such a thing under the
sun. If he never talked to any of them, he almost certainly saw such people.

They often came to Paris to conduct business and were visible evidence that not every person of color occupied the same status. The laws of slavery, and the Anglo-American culture in which he and the Hemings-Wayles brothers lived, allowed—mandated—that John Wayles's wealth be transferred to his free white daughters and ultimately to his white son-in-laws, and not to his enslaved mixed-race sons and daughters. No "gift" or "privilege" Jefferson ever gave the Hemingses was in any way commensurate to what the law and cultural mores had taken away from them and transferred to him and his white family.

The brothers' course of dealing with Jefferson after their emancipations suggests that they had genuine affection for him at some level, but that was beside the point. They did not want to give their very lives to him any more than he would have wanted to give his life to them. Both men, very reasonably, were unwilling to make a show of love and devotion to Jefferson if it meant they had to remain slaves. Jefferson was like a planet whose gravitational pull holds some bodies in its orbit and constantly threatens to haul in other smaller bodies that happen to be passing by. His tendency toward possessiveness and controlling behavior undoubtedly had its own impact on the lives of Robert and James Hemings in ways we cannot recover, though his handling of their departure from Monticello gives important clues. Who knows how many lessons, admonishments, offers of advice, and stubborn opinions were offered to these two young men on their long journeys with Jefferson or during the many hours and times when they were completely alone with him? They were young boys when this began, and now they were men in a relationship that was to a great degree emasculating. Resistance, in the best way available to them, was the natural course.

When Robert and James Hemings broke away from Jefferson, they changed not just a lifestyle but their very statuses in life. No evidence of Mary Hemings's formal manumission, or that of her children with Bell, has been found. The official records of deeds in Albemarle County in the 1790s, which do record Robert's and James's emancipations, are intact. So there was no formal change in Mary Hemings's status when she went to live with Bell, who trusted his legal white relatives not to challenge his wishes regarding how she and his children with her were to be treated. No one knows Martin Hemings's ultimate fate, but he, too, wanted to break away. As for their sister Sally, none of the means her siblings used to leave the mountain were available to her if she ever thought of trying. She could never have said to Jefferson, "Sell me to another white man" or "Let me go out on my own and find a job." She could have said those things, but he would not have done what she asked. Her decision not to take freedom in France and to return to Virginia with Jefferson permanently fixed her in his orbit until he or she died.

How Robert and James Hemings engineered their freedom certainly became known to others on the mountain. Yet, over the years, no one else, not even other Hemingses, were able to replicate what these two brothers did in the 1790s. Not until just before his death did Jefferson prepare documents to free other slaves. When he freed five slaves in his will, two were his sons. His two older children—who chose to live as white people and would not have wanted formal and recorded documents proving that they were part black and had been born slaves—quietly left Monticello as soon as they became adults. Their uncles Robert and James Hemings were the only other enslaved people at Monticello who did not have to give their entire adult lives to Jefferson in order to obtain their freedom.

24

THE SECOND MONTICELLO

T
WENTY YEARS HAD passed. Girls had grown into women, boys
into men; and a new generation of Hemingses was coming of
age to participate in what would become a revised story of life on
the mountain. The man who had controlled their lives for all those years
had plans to alter the look of the place as he prepared to settle there for
good. The new story began with an ostensibly normal routine. In the middle of January 1794, Robert Hemings met his brother James and Jefferson
in Fredericksburg, Virginia, with fresh horses for the last leg of the trip
home from Philadelphia.[1] The brothers had performed this type of operation many times, and the rituals of deep acquaintance played out over the
trio's three-day journey to Monticello. And yet, this time things were different. Both of the young men riding on horseback those winter days were on
their way out of slavery at Monticello. It is not known precisely when Robert
Hemings first thought of the idea of having his wife's owner, Dr. Frederick
Stras, lend him money to purchase his freedom, but it was probably a plan
that unfolded over time. On the coming Christmas Eve, Jefferson would
sign a "deed of manumission" for Robert, who would then go to join his
family in Richmond to work off his debt to Stras.

James Hemings carried the promise of freedom, knowing that he had
one final task to perform to make sure that promise was fulfilled. The
agreement with Jefferson, now four months old, was undoubtedly known
to all the Hemingses, communicated the preceding September when James
had last been home, giving the family ample time to ponder his future. The
agreement was important for another reason: James was going to train his

younger brother Peter Hemings to take his place, ensuring that the legacy of his time in France would pass to another family member. While the terms of the pact expressly left it to Jefferson to choose James's successor, James himself may well have lobbied for his brother, for no one was better suited. At eighteen, John, the family's youngest, was the right age, but Jefferson had already marked the young man out for the profession that would make his name: that of carpenter, like his father before him. There had probably been little or no consideration of turning any of the Hemings females into cooks. Even though James had been away during the years Peter had grown to manhood, a natural affinity between the brothers might well have made the whole process go more smoothly. Whether they grew close because of this association or whether the affection was there all along, Peter Hemings named one of his sons after James.

No time was wasted. Just eleven days after James arrived at Monticello, Peter Hemings came home to begin his apprenticeship, having been away from the plantation, working for a local man named William Chapman.[2] Peter's arrival brought all five Hemings brothers together; it was the first time since 1782 that they could expect to be in one another's presence when Jefferson was not poised to take one of them off somewhere. Martin, at age thirty-nine, and John formed generational and genetic bookends to the three brothers in the middle—Robert, thirty-two, James, twenty-nine, and Peter, twenty-four. They were half siblings to one another and to the three Hemings-Wayles sons. Martin was nearing the end of his time on the mountain, and John would live there for another thirty-two years. While they could have been fond of one another, the twenty-one-year age difference between them and Martin's absence from Monticello between 1782 and 1790 would not have allowed for steady camaraderie between the two. But Martin knew his youngest brother, for he almost certainly returned to visit his mother and siblings, bringing money or other goods bought with his wages.

Jefferson had come home to Monticello in defeat, bested in the struggles over policy in Washington's cabinet. When his rivals Hamilton and Adams questioned the finality of his retirement, they did so at a distance, measuring what his presence on or absence from the scene might mean to their own political fortunes. The Hemingses knew Jefferson better than either Hamilton or Adams knew him, and had their own senses of whether he was really ready to leave the arena forever. The political battles in Philadelphia played out in newspapers that at least Robert and James Hemings, if not all the siblings, were able to read. The family had a personal stake in them because the courses of their lives depended upon where Jefferson wanted to be at any given moment. In fact, they were not at Monticello long—just nine months—before he was presented with a chance to return to public life. President Washington asked whether he would be willing to go to Spain as a special envoy, a significant overture, given that their final parting had been less than amicable. Though he was likely gratified by Washington's show of confidence, Jefferson, in the midst of a prolonged illness, declined the offer, citing what he thought was his totally broken health along with the "inflexibility" of his decision to leave public life.[3] Had he accepted, James Hemings would have accompanied him to serve as the chef in his Spanish household. It was perhaps this fleeting opportunity that prompted Hemings's determination to travel to Spain just a few years later.

Whatever the Hemingses' views on the question, Jefferson had styled himself in retirement, and for the moment everyone had to act as if he truly were. As he prepared for his new role, Peter Hemings could have had no expectation that it might take him to the kinds of places it had taken his older brother. On the other hand, who knew where this might lead? Peter could not help noticing that his two brothers who had been trained in a trade, and were the sons of John Wayles, were the two whom Jefferson decided to free. Perhaps this new job was a stepping stone. Although the thought would have been reasonable, timing in life is everything, and the timing was against Peter Hemings.

The youngest son of Elizabeth Hemings and John Wayles was simply born too late—in 1770—to take full advantage of his family status and gender. Robert and James Hemings came of age at just the right time to have the kind of close relationship with Jefferson that put them on the path to freedom in the 1790s. All the enslaved people in Jefferson's inner world were people he had helped mold, either by early and long association with them or by virtue of their youth—Jupiter Evans, Robert and James Hemings, Sally Hemings, and Burwell Colbert. These people would have viewed him differently (and he them) if they had had the chance to form personalities independent of him, before he brought them into his most intimate circle. Separated from his older brothers by eight and five years, respectively, and by two sisters, Thenia and Critta, Peter was a small child during the early period of the family's time at Monticello and did not have the occasion to be

Remains of Elizabeth Hemings's hearth.
(Courtesy of Monticello / Thomas Jefferson Foundation, Inc.)

Artifacts found at the Elizabeth Hemings archaeological site: furniture tacks, a shoe buckle, and a pencil. *(Courtesy of Monticello / Thomas Jefferson Foundation, Inc.)*

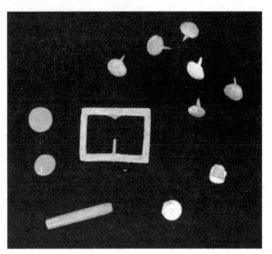

Pearlware found at the Elizabeth Hemings archaeological site. *(Courtesy of Monticello / Thomas Jefferson Foundation, Inc.)*

Fry-Jefferson map. Detail showing Beverley Manor and Treaty of Lancaster. *(Courtesy of Monticello / Thomas Jefferson Foundation, Inc.)*

Anne Cary Randolph, 1805–1808, Part A Household Accounts. Eight-year-old Beverley Hemings sells strawberries to his half niece Anne Randolph. *(Library of Congress)*

"A Philosophic Cock," 1804. *Federalist* satire of Jefferson's relationship with Sally Hemings. *(Courtesy of American Antiquarian Society)*

The president in 1805. *(Courtesy of the Fogg Museum, Harvard University)*

Photograph of Monticello, circa 1890. The photograph shows the outside
entrances into Jefferson's living quarters at the left side of the picture. *(Courtesy of
Holsinger Studio Collection, Special Collections, University of Virginia Library)*

John Hemings's campeche
lounging chair that he made
for Jefferson, circa 1818.
*(Courtesy of Monticello / Thomas
Jefferson Foundation, Inc.)*

Seed press made by John
Hemings. *(Courtesy of
Monticello / Thomas Jefferson
Foundation, Inc.)*

Filing press made by
Thomas Jefferson. *(Courtesy
of Monticello / Thomas Jefferson
Foundation)*

Revolving bookstand made
in the Monticello joinery.
*(Courtesy of Monticello / Thomas
Jefferson Foundation)*

Poplar Forest. John Hemings and his nephews—Beverley, Madison, and Eston Hemings—worked on the façade, roof, and interior of Jefferson's retreat.

(Courtesy of Thomas Jefferson's Poplar Forest)

Codicil to Thomas
Jefferson's will *(Courtesy of
Special Collections, University of
Virginia Library)*

EXECUTOR'S SALE.

Will be sold, on the fifteenth of January, at Monticello, in the county of Albemarle, the whole of the residue of the personal estate of Thomas Jefferson, dec., consisting of **130 VALUABLE NEGROES,** Stock, Crop, &c. Household and Kitchen Furniture. The attention of the public is earnestly invited to this property. The negroes are believed to be the most valuable for their number ever offered at one time in the State of Virginia. The household furniture, many valuable historical and portrait paintings, busts of marble and plaister of distinguished individuals; one of marble of Thomas Jefferson, by Caracci, with the pedestal and truncated column on which it stands; a polygraph or copying instrument used by Thomas Jefferson, for the last twenty-five years; with various other articles curious and useful to men of business and private families. The terms of sale will be accommodating and made known previous to the day. The sale will be continued from day to day until completed. This sale being unavoidable, it is a sufficient guarantee to the public, that it will take place at the time and place appointed.

THOMAS J. RANDOLPH,
Executor of Th: Jefferson, dec.

January 6, 1827—2t

The paintings and busts of THOS. JEFFERSON, dec. will not be offered for sale on the 15th of January next; but will be sent to some one of the large cities and then sold, after due notice.

BY AUTHORITY OF CONGRESS
WASHINGTON CITY LOTTERY,

Advertisement of executor's
sale at Monticello from
the *Charlottesville Gazette,*
January 13, 1827. *(Courtesy of
American Antiquarian Society)*

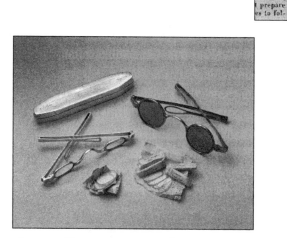

Thomas Jefferson's spectacles. Sally Hemings
kept another pair of Jefferson's glasses, among
other items, to pass on to her children *(Courtesy of
Monticello / Thomas Jefferson Foundation, Inc.)*

too closely connected to Jefferson. He was five years old when he came to the mountain, six in 1776 when his brother Robert traveled to Philadelphia with Jefferson, and thirteen when Jefferson left Monticello for seven years. When he returned, there was neither time nor reason for young Peter to develop an association with him, and by the time of Jefferson's first retirement, he was a grown man.

Hemings did share his family's easy association with his half sister Martha's husband and appears intermittently in Jefferson's documents, mainly in notations detailing various economic transactions. The first appeared in 1780, when he was only ten years old and Jefferson wrote that he had "Repd. Peter for shoe thread £9."—indicating that money, most probably from his older brothers, circulated among the Hemings siblings. Despite his relatively few references to him over the years, Jefferson thought highly of Hemings, proclaimed him extremely intelligent, and extolled his capabilities to others.[4] None of this would be enough, however, to make Jefferson free him.

With James Hemings acting as teacher, what had been the almost daily notations about him in Jefferson's records disappear. There is then no way to trace his day-to-day life after the beginning of 1794—either at Monticello or when he left Virginia as a free man. It is not even known where he lived on the mountain. Did he return from the Hôtel de Langeac and the house on Market Street to live in a slave cabin, or did he have a room in the house? Architectural evidence indicates that some enslaved people did live in the Monticello mansion. Thomas Jefferson Randolph said that during Jefferson's presidency his "confidential servant Burwell Colbert" lived there, and the source for the *Frederick Town Herald*, who knew enough to pinpoint Sally Hemings's role as a seamstress at Monticello, said she had a "room to her own" within the house.[5]

The Monticello of the 1790s was nothing like the place known to the throngs of modern-day visitors who come and see a house and grounds brought to a level of perfection that Jefferson himself never saw. James Hemings did not even live to see Monticello with a completed dome. The first house, never finished, was in bad condition after Jefferson returned from France, and his long absences during his days as secretary of state had left him no opportunity to begin to put things in order. Living standards for those in and around the house were severely compromised throughout the 1790s. Near the end of his first year home from Philadelphia, he told his friend and mentor George Wythe that he and his family were "living in a brick kiln," as he had started the process of tearing down the old to make way for the new.[6] It was not a safe environment, with bricks flying into the middle of a domestic routine that kept going no matter what. As work continued over the years, the house would be without even a roof for a time.

Although the kitchen where the Hemings brothers worked cannot have resembled what James had grown used to, he did have all his old cooking utensils, which had been sent over from France. They were far more advanced, varied, and costly than those typically found in Virginia. Jefferson had made the rounds of specialty shops in Paris, almost certainly with Hemings, seeking out and buying large amounts of French copper cookware. Much lighter and a better conductor of heat than ironware, it was designed for the French fare that was Hemings's specialty.[7] So the enslaved brothers set to work in a serviceable kitchen with state-of-the-art European equipment as the walls of Monticello began to come down around them.

Their first year together was difficult for every one on the mountain, being rainy most of the time and extremely cold in the winter. A smallpox epidemic in nearby Richmond, the state's commercial nerve center, brought travel in the area almost to a standstill, even interrupting the delivery of mail.[8] Jefferson's own prolonged illness confined him to bed at points. His poor health cannot have comforted members of the enslaved community, who well understood what might happen if he died. His daughters or, really, his sons-in-law, and whatever creditors swooped down for their share of property, would take his place and separate the enslaved people according to their respective needs. They already understood how changes in his fortunes and family structure could affect the lives of people enslaved on his plantations. Between 1784 and 1794, he had either sold or given away as part of marriage settlements to his daughters and sister over one hundred people.[9] While some of the sales were to unite family members, and Martha's settlement changed legal title but left most of the people in place, these transactions required many individuals to leave their homes. His death would have been even more disruptive. But he recovered near the end of the year; and life, work, and "pulling down" and "putting up" continued on the mountain.

The demolition and construction activities on the house were not the only distractions with which James and Peter had to contend, for Jefferson started several major projects at once. He transformed the landscape of the mountain by having enslaved people plant hundreds of peach trees to fence in his fields. Following the trend in Virginia, Jefferson was also making the switch from tobacco as a cash crop to growing grains like wheat, and he needed another source of income while he took his land out of production to replenish the soil and to prepare for this new type of agriculture. He wanted to find a new venture that would combine what he perceived to be his "interest and duty," which involved, he said, "watch[ing] for the happiness of those who labored for [his] own."[10] He settled on the nail-making business as the way to do this.

The historian Lucia Stanton has noted that, while in Philadelphia, Jefferson took an interest in the work of Caleb Lownes, a Quaker who argued for the reform of the city's penal system. Lownes criticized the operators of traditional prisons for failing to take into account that prisoners were human beings with "feelings and passions." They were, he said, too geared to "perpetually" tormenting the incarcerated. He had a different idea. Prisons should attempt to reform inmates by instituting a strict regime to train them to useful services. Corporal punishment would be eliminated, and replaced with character building through the incentive of paid work and other rewards. Lownes's prisons were to be a combination "school and manufactory."[11]

Lownes's theories were part of a larger movement of penal reform that Jefferson was well aware of, and he decided to work "out new humanitarian ideas about exercising power on his mountaintop." Stanton persuasively shows that Jefferson's nailery "was not just an adventure of industrial entrepreneurship. It was also an experimental laboratory for the management of enslaved labor in harmony with current ideas of humanitarian reform." Staffed, in Jefferson's words, by "a dozen little boys 10. to 16. years of age," the operations drew enough profit to allow him to get along until his farms made more money.[12]

Several of Elizabeth Hemings's grandchildren worked in the nailery, though they split duties between there and the house—Joseph Fossett, the brothers Wormley Hughes, Burwell and Brown Colbert, and James (Jamey) Hemings, son of Critta Hemings. When they were not working in the house—doing what besides occasionally breaking china is not clear—these first cousins joined other boys churning out thousands of nails a day. One thinks of Dickens and the children he wrote of trapped in the nineteenth-century workhouses that sprang up to power the Industrial Revolution.

There was no sense, in settings rural and urban on either side of the Atlantic, that the children of the laboring classes should be spared work. In fact, they had long been a part of the nail-making trade. In England boys and girls started at age seven in nail factories, bringing home whatever they could to support their families. Indeed, some of the children working in Jefferson's nailery looked very much like their English counterparts. Joseph, Wormley, Burwell, and Brown, and their other cousins, were almost certainly among the children whose appearances stunned noted Europeans who visited Jefferson in the 1790s. One, the comte de Volney, observed upon seeing them that they were "as white as [he was]."[13]

Nail making was boring and repetitive work at Monticello, performed cooped up for as long as twelve hours a day under strict supervision. George Granger's son, George Jr., was the foreman, but Jefferson involved himself directly in the daily work of the factory, counting the nails (which he probably enjoyed very much) and noting how many nails each boy produced and how much nail rod he wasted.[14] In keeping with his plan of increasing productivity through incentives, boys who performed well were given extra rations and more expensive clothing. Jefferson was thinking about the present and the future. Measuring these boys' performances, and giving them rewards for good ones, led to more nails immediately. It also told him what kind of men they might become, and how they would later fit into his plans for operation at Monticello. Isaac Jefferson, brother of the foreman, remembered that he and the other boys were allotted "a pound of meat a week, a dozen herrings, a quart of molasses, and a peck of meal"—twice the weekly ration for field hands.[15] George Granger, the only enslaved adult associated with the nailery, received one-sixth of the yearly profits of the operation.

This third generation of Hemingses represented a departure for the family. But for those members who were leased out during Jefferson's time in France—an anomalous situation—these youngsters were the first Hemingses employed in a form of labor specifically designed to bring income and profit to Monticello. Their aunts and uncles had all been personal servants to the Jeffersons, making their lives run more smoothly, but neither planting crops nor producing items for sale. Family-based connections would continue to matter, but this new generation of Hemingses, particularly Joseph and Wormley—and we may say John Hemings—were valued on the mountain not just because of who they were but because of what they produced.

Elizabeth Hemings

One important person was not at Monticello when James Hemings returned in 1794: his mother. At some point after 1791, Elizabeth Hemings went to live at Tufton, one of the quarter farms at the southern base of Monticello. No reason for the move has been found, but it suggests that by this time Hemings—approaching sixty—no longer had regular duties in the mansion. Enslaved women who grew too old to be productive in whatever tasks they performed when young often looked after the children of mothers at work in the fields. One of the enduring mysteries about Hemings's life is just what her actual duties had been, apart from motherhood and her connection to John Wayles and Martha Jefferson. Her eldest son had been the butler, the person traditionally in charge of supervising the household staff. Was Hemings, in deference to her age and status, a sort of über housekeeper, looming over all her children and ultimately responsible for the efficient running of the household? Or was she called into action to help her daughters only when required?

While the written record of Elizabeth Hemings's life at Monticello is frustratingly unrevealing, the archaeological record is rich and informative. At least since the 1970s, historians have recognized the critical role that archaeology can play in the study of American slavery. As the historian Patricia Samford put it, "[a]rchaelogical study of the detritus of daily life can provide a perspective on African-American life generally absent in the documents—the perspective of the enslaved themselves, visible through the structural footings of their homes, the broken ceramic bowls from which they ate their food, and the objects they used to give spiritual meaning to their lives."[16] The head of the archaeology department at the Thomas Jefferson Foundation, Fraser Neiman, and others have done extensive work at the site where Hemings lived after she came back to the mountain in 1795 and, perhaps, before. That work, combined with the documentary record, tells us a great deal about the way the matriarch of the Hemings family lived.

Hemings's residence must be considered in the context of the natural and planned landscape that surrounded her. Monticello was segmented by four roads, which Jefferson called "roundabouts," circling the mountain "at roughly constant elevation." The roundabouts were, in turn, linked to roads of varying slopes. This "internal transportation system" was both practical and aesthetic.[17] Jefferson viewed the roundabouts, along with the replacing of wooden fences with peach trees and a sunken fence (the ha-ha!) to cordon off fields and gardens, as part of his overall effort to create an ornamental farm. Beauty, rather than utility, was the main consideration.

The first roundabout enclosed the Monticello mansion and Mulberry Row, the area where Hemings's children and grandchildren lived. The second "encircled the kitchen garden and orchards planted on slopes just below the mansion." The third and fourth roundabouts "marked a transition zone between the ornamental and agricultural precincts of the Monticello Mountain landscape." It was in this zone, about "thirty feet south" of the third roundabout, that Elizabeth Hemings lived, situated somewhat apart from her children, and even farther from most of the currently known residences of other enslaved laborers.[18] A dense forest has reclaimed the spot today, but in her time the area was largely a cleared grass field interspersed with large trees. Her known neighbors were Robert Bailey, a Scot who served as the head gardener at Monticello during the 1790s, and "William Stewart, a white blacksmith from Philadelphia," who came later.[19] The composition of Hemings's "neighborhood" shows the problem with seeing slavery through the eyes of twentieth-century residential Jim Crow and displays the eclectic nature of Monticello's residents. A part English, part African enslaved woman lived next door to a Scot, and a white family who hailed from the North. A native of Italy, Antonio Giannini, a gardener at Monticello before Bailey, had relayed to Jefferson in Paris Elizabeth Hemings's message that her daughter had died.

There is little written record of what social relations were like in this multiethnic world. Jefferson's granddaughter Ellen focused on sex, painting a picture of easy sexual relations between the enslaved women at Monticello and Jefferson's "Irish workingmen."[20] Sex was not the only, or even the main, thing that linked them. Work was the focus, performed by blacks and whites while they shared the rituals of life in what was essentially a small town of around two hundred people. Jefferson's white workingmen taught enslaved people crafts and skills—some to Elizabeth Hemings's grandchildren. Wormley Hughes learned gardening from Bailey, and Joseph Fossett learned blacksmithing from Stewart, whom Jefferson pronounced "the best workman in America, but the most eccentric one."[21] He drank, not exactly unusual in those days, but Jefferson put up with the drinking because he was so gifted.

There is little doubt that, had she wanted to, Hemings could have lived in the midst of her children and grandchildren. By this time, however, she had been mother and grandmother to many. Peace and quiet, in a place of her own away from the demands of family, may have been her preference. She was not so far away that she had no easy access to her family, but she was at enough of a distance that some effort had to be made to visit. There was at least one other advantage to her location. Her living area was "at least ten times that of the people living along Mulberry Row."[22]

Hemings's dwelling fit the pattern of late eighteenth-century housing for enslaved people. Just as agriculture in Virginia was undergoing transformation, slave housing was changing as well. For most of the century, enslaved people lived in "'barracks-style' housing," with others who may or may not have been related to them. The floors of these houses featured numerous subfloor pits. These pits served as storage spaces for people who had no closets or trunks in which to keep their possessions. Being open, the pits left the contents visible to everyone—which was apparently the point. Each resident knew the other's pit and what was in it. That social knowledge, and the morality that grew up around it, worked as a check on theft among coresidents. The changing demographics of slavery—ratios of males to females became more equal, and slaves began to form families—caused a shift in housing patterns. Individual family dwellings replaced barracks, and subfloor pits disappeared. In keeping with this trend, Hemings, living alone, perhaps with containers for her possessions—had no subfloor pit.[23]

By modern standards, Hemings's house was almost unimaginably small—roughly 170 square feet. There is no evidence of a wooden floor, though she did have at least one glass window. The house was actually at the smaller end of the range of the typical square footage of slave quarters in Virginia—"from 144 to 672" square feet.[24] The size of slave housing depended, at least in some instances, on the number of people in the residence and the preferences of slave owners. Expectations about space and privacy were very different from our own, as were understandings about the usages of living space. For enslaved people there was, evidently, little sense of the interior of the home as a place where one spent much time, work being the center of their lives. For most of her adulthood, Hemings's daily life took place in John Wayles's house and, later, in Jefferson's. Her own home was primarily a place to sleep. Parlors, dining and sitting rooms, and multiple bedrooms were found in the homes of the elite, although even there people, including adults, were often expected to share bedrooms and beds. Because their houses were so small, Hemings and other enslaved people typically socialized, cooked, and took meals outside. One imagines that her large yard area, somewhat removed from the eyes of Jefferson and his family, was often a gathering place for the Hemingses.

Hemings and other enslaved people were not the only ones who lived in extremely tight quarters. A 1785 survey of one Virginia county showed that "more than 75 percent of the [white] settlers surveyed were living in one-room homes of less than 320 square feet."[25] Though whiteness and free status gave them a tremendous social advantage over blacks, the material lives of nonelite white Virginians were much closer to those of blacks than to those of people like the Jeffersons. Not only were their houses small; the homes of poor whites and even "many middling planters of English descent" had dirt floors and no glass windows.[26] One can well understand the deep resentment, even turmoil, this bred in them, for although they enjoyed the benefits of their society's enforcement of white supremacy, they were unable to rise, and Virginia's political system was designed to keep it that way. The extremely conservative state constitution, which Jefferson abhorred, left a full two-thirds of the white male population without the vote because of its stringent property qualifications.[27] Virginia's poor and mid-dling whites, the sort who would be working for Jefferson and living among the Hemingses, were in a worse position politically than their counterparts in other states. For example, Tennessee's constitution, which Jefferson lauded as the most perfect in the new union, provided for universal male suffrage in 1796. Even free black males could vote in the state until a con-stitutional convention in 1834 took the right away.[28] Thus, for roughly fifty years, free blacks in Tennessee (admittedly few in number) had the right to vote when large numbers of free white men in Virginia did not.

Archaeological work also allows a comparison between Hemings and her closest neighbor, William Stewart, that sheds additional light on her life. Both she and Stewart lived in log cabins "seated on a dry-laid stone founda-tion." Stewart's place was much larger than Hemings's, with almost "four times the floor space." Neiman suggests the difference cannot be attributed to the fact that there were seven people in the Stewart household, while Hemings lived alone. The residents of Mulberry Row had families, too, and their houses were smaller than Stewart's. The reason for the difference, of course, is that Stewart was a free white man, and the market created an incentive for Jefferson and other employers to give him and other white workers, particularly skilled ones, the best housing they could provide. If they did not, the workers could take their services elsewhere.[29]

Both Hemings and Stewart participated in the market and consumer revolution that took place in the latter half of the eighteenth century when Americans developed an unquenchable thirst for the imported British goods that filled country stores and vendue markets, which the historian T. H. Breen describes as a "combination of modern flea market and whole-sale auction." Peddlers, "mysterious and ubiquitous," traveled the country-side introducing people in isolated rural communities to "the pleasures of owning an ivory comb or colorful piece of ribbon."[30] Hemings, for example, accumulated a good quantity of consumer goods. She had creamware, pearl ware, and Chinese porcelain. This was not uncommon in the Chesapeake. Visitors to Washington's Mount Vernon remarked upon the incongruity of seeing china in the mean cabins of the enslaved. Slaves acquired these goods through different means, and the dating and usage gives clues as to how they obtained them. Evidence of heavy usage and old-style patterns suggest that much of the china in slave cabins consisted of castoffs from their white owners.[31]

Hemings's dinnerware, however, did not come from the Jefferson family, for the items do not match the records of the types of china the Jeffersons purchased. This is not surprising, given that her sons often worked for themselves and could give her money or buy her things on their own. Her dinnerware was not outdated. She continued to obtain items into the 1790s, favoring popular patterns of the day. For example, some of her por-celain plates were "painted with Nanking II–style motifs" that dated "from 1785–1800." She seemed to favor blue—even one of the chamber pots recovered was "painted in blue with a floral or Chinese motif"—and she had distinct preferences about the types of ware she used for different pur-poses. Plates and platters were mainly the more expensive pearl ware and Chinese porcelain, and her tea settings consisted mainly of less expensive creamware. Her pattern of consumption was the reverse of that of William Stewart, whose family spent more money on its tea settings and less on its dinnerware.[32]

Neiman suggests that the difference reveals Hemings's and the Stewarts' individual strategies for "social advertising." The striving Stewarts used their expensive tea set as a form of display to impress visitors, as the tea party was becoming a mark of a particular form of gentility. Hemings, on the other hand, preferred to impress at meal times, "while tea drinking was more an informal affair." But it is also likely that the Stewarts' five children influenced how much money their parents were willing to invest in the plates they used for their daily meals. Fancy tea ware could be safeguarded from rambunctious kids and brought out only on special occasions. As one might expect, given her son's and daughter's time in France, wine was also a part of Hemings's life. Wineglasses and wine bottles, English and French, were recovered from her home. But other than items related to meal consumption, not much else was found at the Hemings site besides "a half dozen upholstery tacks, two buttons, a woman's brass shoe buckle, and a slate pencil."[33]

Hemings had a garden and kept chickens, some of which she sold, along with produce and eggs, to Jefferson and his family, as did every other adult on the plantation, save for her daughter Sally. Given the nature of her relationship with Jefferson, it would have been odd indeed for her to have turned to him and asked, "Would you like to buy some string beans, or eggs, or chickens?" Tending the garden, raising animals, and looking after children may have been the main ways Elizabeth Hemings occupied herself in her declining years.

It is not known precisely what month Hemings returned to the mountain, but an important thing happened that year that made her return understandable. Sally Hemings gave birth to a daughter, Harriet, at the beginning of October.[34] Unlike her daughter Betty, who had a two-year-old, Edwin, Sally had no older children to help her during her pregnancy or after her baby was born. She had also lost her first child and may have had some difficulty with her pregnancy and the aftermath—she had, in fact, been sick in the months after she gave birth. That could only have increased anxiety about her and her child. Who better than her mother, a woman who had lost only one of twelve known children, that one well past infancy at age nine, to watch over her daughter as she began again her life as a young mother.

Jefferson's absences from Monticello between 1790 and 1794 defined Sally Hemings's earliest experience with motherhood. She had given birth in 1790 at age seventeen, and if he had been with her for any substantial amount of time, one might expect that she, a young woman at the very height of her potential fertility, would have had at least one other child within that period. But he was not at Monticello for any significant length of time. In 1791, he was away eleven months out of the year. He was gone for ten and one half months in 1792 and another eleven months in 1793.[35] His return in 1794 marked the real start of their time together in America, and, as we noted earlier, he was seriously ill for long stretches of time, the battles with Hamilton apparently taking their toll physically.

Harriet Hemings's birth also marked the beginning of another pattern that would adhere throughout Sally Hemings's life as a mother: her children would bear the names of people who were important to Jefferson. Harriet Randolph, the younger sister of Thomas Mann Randolph, was described as Jefferson's particular favorite among the females in his son-in-law's family. She spent time at Monticello in the mid-1790s, in the wake of the Randolph siblings' estrangement from Tuckahoe after their father's marriage to Gabriella Harvie. She continued to visit the mountain over the years and came there to give birth to one of her children. In the end, she would have a son named William Beverley, as Jefferson and Hemings did before her, a name that had a very poignant and particular meaning for Thomas Jefferson.[36]

There is no way to know whether naming this child Harriet was Jefferson's doing or Hemings's. But Harriet was neither a Hemings family nor a Wayles family name. Hemings knew and could have liked Harriet Randolph enough to name her child after her—but certainly not more than she liked her own mother, many sisters, and nieces, for whom this little girl could have been named. The Hemingses had a positive mania for naming their children after one another. It was their way of reinforcing family connections in a world that gave no legal recognition to enslaved families. The family continued in this steady pattern over the generations, well into the twentieth century. We do not know the names of all of her brothers' children, but Robert and Peter each named children after their siblings. Of her five female siblings, Sally Hemings was the only one who did not choose to, or did not get to, name *any* of her children after people in her family. It was not until her children began to have their own offspring that the name Wayles—first John Wayles Hemings and then Ellen Wayles Hemings—came back into her family line. In fact, two of her four sisters who had daughters named one of their own daughters after her. Her brother Peter and her nephew Burwell Colbert named one of their daughters Sarah. Hemings was apparently unable to return the honor to any of her relatives.[37]

Of course, naming children was important to white people, too. All of Jefferson's children with his wife had family names. Because his wife shared the name Martha with his sister, it is impossible to say whom the couple's first daughter was really named for: this was a happy and useful coincidence. The couple's two youngest children, both of whom died, were in succession named Lucy Elizabeth, a name that combined that of two Jefferson sisters, and Elizabeth, which was also the name of one of Martha's sisters. The two other daughters, Jane and Mary, were definitely the names of Jefferson's mother and sister. In the end, the balance clearly favored Thomas over Martha, as all of their children ended up with names that were held by people in *his* immediate nuclear family.[38] As with Sally Hemings and her children, this one-sided way of naming a group of siblings was the work either of a woman trying very hard to please a man or of a man who felt his children should bear his mark.

While Elizabeth Hemings's presence on the mountain allowed her to play the role of helpful grandmother, she was not the only resource available to her daughter. At some point in 1796, eight-year-old Edy Hern moved into Sally Hemings's household to help look after Harriet. Edy was the daughter of David Hern and his wife, Isabel, the woman who was originally slated to go to Paris with Maria Jefferson. Edy was replaced in 1797 by her younger sister Aggy when she turned eight years old.[39] According to Jefferson's specifications in the 1790s, enslaved children below the age of ten served as nurses for infants and very small children, apparently under the general direction of elderly enslaved women, but this did not require having the child move in with the enslaved mother. Hemings's duties as Jefferson's chambermaid and seamstress during this period did not likely require personal nurses for her daughter, particularly not ones who stayed overnight. This arrangement did provide someone to be with Hemings's child when she was with Jefferson.

JUST AS MONTICELLO as a physical entity in the 1790s differed markedly from its later incarnations, the social life of the place during those years was also different. The endless stream (horde) of visitors that marked Jefferson's retirement years, his passel of grandchildren, did not exist in the mid-1790s. There were many visitors, of course; the hospitality of the age required entertaining guests and putting up travelers who needed a place to stay while on the road. But it was nothing like what was to come. By the end of the 1790s, there were only three Jefferson grandchildren, and Martha and

Thomas Mann Randolph were not yet permanent residents of Monticello. The Hemings sisters undoubtedly had things to do, but by far the busiest people on the mountain during those years were Jefferson's workmen and nail boys, who were putting in motion his dreams for his house and for finding a path toward economic security in his new vision of a more "humanitarian" form of slavery. In those same years, an event in the lives of the Hemings family reinforced the basic impossibility of that vision.

Nancy Hemings and Her Children, Billy and Critta

While some of Elizabeth Hemings's children were about to or had left slavery and Monticello, another, Nancy Hemings, came back to the mountain in 1795, after a ten-year absence. When Jefferson was in Paris, his youngest sister, Anna, married Hastings Marks. Nancy Hemings and her two children, Billy and Critta, were part of the marriage settlement that Jefferson provided to the couple. Marks decided, sometime in 1795, that he wanted to sell Hemings, and may have been thinking of separating her family. Jefferson's sister told him of this because she knew that Hemings was an expert weaver and that Jefferson wanted to resume the "business of domestic manufacture." He noted that Hemings was "34. years of age" and, he believed, had "ceased to breed."[40] He wanted her to come back to the mountain and teach others how to weave, and begin his textile shop. Desperate to avoid sale to an unknown person, Hemings asked Jefferson to purchase her and her family. He flatly refused to buy Billy, who was fifteen, but said he was willing to buy Critta, age twelve, if Hemings insisted—as if there had ever been a chance she would not. In the end, Jefferson bought Nancy, and she returned to Monticello, and his son-in-law Thomas Mann Randolph purchased Critta. Unlike her brother, whose fate is unknown, Critta was at least within easy visiting distance of her mother at nearby Edgehill plantation, where she became a nurse to Martha Randolph's children.[41]

No matter how "close" the Hemingses were to Jefferson, no matter that he viewed some of them in a different light and did not subject them to certain hardships, their family remained a commodity that could be sold or exchanged at his will. As the years went by, the newest members of the family would become even further removed from the original connection that had made the Hemingses special in the first place, and would receive little benefit from their genetic heritage. In truth, Nancy Hemings, who was not a Wayles daughter, was never fully part of that connection to begin with. If she had been, Jefferson would not have given her to his sister. Robert, James, and Sally Hemings, living in whatever metaphorical greenhouse Jefferson had placed them in, could not save all their relatives from the most painful realities of slavery if doing that conflicted with Jefferson's, or his white family's, interests. After all, this whole problem arose because he chose to use Nancy and her children as wedding presents for the benefit of his sister. While it is true that he really did not have the money to buy Nancy and her children, and actually bought Nancy on credit, it would not have bankrupted Jefferson to have bought her son, too, or persuaded his son-in-law to purchase the youngster. That the sales of Nancy and Critta happened simultaneously indicates that Jefferson asked Tom Randolph to buy Critta so that she could be near her mother. But, in his view, Billy was essentially an adult, and his ties to his mother and sister did not warrant extra expenditures by him or Randolph.

In September of this same year, Jefferson recorded the deed of manumission he had drawn up for Nancy's half brother Robert.[42] It had taken Robert just nine months to pay his debt to Dr. Stras, and he became the first member of the Hemings family to obtain formal freedom. So, while this event, along with James's coming emancipation and the birth of Harriet Hemings, helped make a new story of the Hemingses' lives at Monticello, Nancy Hemings's separation from her son, Billy, shows starkly how the deeply tragic reality of slavery always remained the same.

25

INTO THE FUTURE,
ECHOES FROM THE PAST

O N FEBRUARY 26, 1796, James Hemings received thirty dollars from Thomas Jefferson "to bear" his expenses to Philadelphia.[1] This time Hemings was not going ahead to prepare for a Jefferson arrival. In fact, his departure had nothing to do with Jefferson at all. Two years and one month after he had returned to Monticello to train his brother Peter to be a chef, James Hemings was leaving slavery for good. Approaching the fourth decade of his life, he became the second member of the Hemings family to achieve formal freedom.

Although Jefferson had signed the deed of manumission three weeks earlier, Hemings had remained in place, perhaps preparing for his journey and saying a long goodbye to his family. There was undoubtedly much for him to do, leaving a life behind as he was. He would have had to find a place to live, a place to send his possessions, of which there were probably a good number. For about eight of the preceding ten years, he had been a paid employee in Paris, New York, and Philadelphia—places that gave him ample opportunity to acquire things. Certainly all of his belongings that Jefferson had shipped from the Hôtel de Langeac would go along with him now. These were, of course, strictly his own affairs, and Jefferson's records give no account of Hemings's preparations for his new life. Indeed, the only thing he left by way of a valediction that we have access to came from his old one: the list he prepared of all his kitchen utensils from Paris that would now be left in Peter's hands.[2]

James Hemings's choice of destination shows how different he was from his brother Robert, either by temperament or by experience. The elder brother was a family man of long standing, having developed a settled place for himself in Richmond, where his wife, son, and daughter lived. His settlement may not have been strictly a matter of choice, for we do not know when the rest of his family became free—whether it was before or after his own emancipation. By all appearances, however, Frederick Stras wanted to help Hemings. He seems like the sort who would have imposed lenient terms for the emancipation of Dolly and their children, for he was trying to unite their family. We do know that in 1802, Robert and Dolly's daughter, Elizabeth, became a legally married woman, which she could not have done had she still been enslaved.

Even long after all his family was emancipated, Robert Hemings chose to remain in Richmond, instead of seeking a new life in the North. Though nowhere near as populous as Philadelphia, the town did have its attractions. The 1800 census recorded 5,737 residents, which was large by Virginia standards. It was well situated on the James River, with a port that had a long history of shipping farmers' goods to other American cities and across the Atlantic to England. After it became Virginia's capital, in 1780, it grew quickly with lawyers and other functionaries of government arriving to take their place in society. Tobacco, wheat, coal, and the production of iron, in state-run industries, fueled its economy.[3]

Richmond's large black community, a little over two thousand enslaved and about six hundred free, had created a vibrant culture in the midst of oppression. Some free blacks managed to carve out stable existences, owning shops of various types. Others, like Robert Hemings, had their own fruit stands and hauling businesses.[4] Although Hemings was by no means prosperous, he so wanted to be his own man after a life spent acting at Jefferson's beck and call. We can see that in the image of Hemings—the former "privileged" manservant, now in his midthirties hawking fruit to passersby, braving all sorts of weather, exchanging money and pleasantries, and, on occasion, no doubt, encountering more hostile reactions from members of the public. Martha Randolph remembered seeing him often in Richmond, probably at his fruit stand.

Because of his former position, Hemings could have been, had he wanted to, something of a minor celebrity in Richmond, particularly when Jefferson occupied the highest offices in the country. There is no reason to believe that he would have wanted to divulge secrets about Jefferson, but he wouldn't have had to go that far to cash in on the public's desire to be connected to a famous and highly regarded person. *I just bought fruit from a man who used to be the confidential servant of Thomas Jefferson!* Hemings did, in fact, become the object of attention in the town after Jefferson's life with his sister was exposed by Richmond-based newspapers. It was from that scrutiny of him in 1802 that we learn that he had "some infirmity" in one of his arms, which explains why he did not ply his trade as a barber. By that time he had become a property owner, having half a lot on Grace and Seventh Street in Richmond. Isaac Jefferson recollected that Hemings had his hand blown off in a gun accident. He did not say when this happened, but it seems likely that it was by 1802, which accounts for the reference to his infirmity.[5] Jefferson perhaps exaggerated. A missing hand would not likely be termed "some infirmity."

Hemings was not alone in choosing to work on his own rather than going back into service. A number of freed blacks, often to the great annoyance of white observers who wanted them to work as domestics, preferred precarious lives as vendors, chimney sweeps, and laundresses to going back into the homes of white families on a daily basis. Hemings could have stayed on working for Stras or, with a letter of introduction from Jefferson and Stras, found a decent position in the home of another gentleman. He evidently wanted no more part of the kind of entangling alliances that had so defined his family—even to the point of blood.

Not that Hemings ever completely disentangled himself from Jefferson. Because his own family remained there, he visited Monticello on occasion. In 1799 Jefferson mentioned to his cousin and business agent in Richmond, George Jefferson, that Hemings had promised to obtain for him "a preparation of the lemon juice called in the W. Indies *center* but which he [Hemings] called by some other name."[6] There is no correspondence about this, so Hemings and Jefferson likely talked about the matter when Hemings was at Monticello. Later, when he wanted Hemings to buy him twelve bottles of the drink, he directed George Jefferson to relay the message to Hemings and then pay him for the beverage. After Hemings's report that he could not find the drink, Jefferson decided to settle on regular lemon juice and asked that some be sent to him, with either George Jefferson or Hemings to buy it and be repaid. A few days later Hemings found the sought-after center, and George Jefferson sent it Monticello.

Unbeknownst to George, Hemings had already sent along the lemon juice. He evidently told George this when he brought the news that he found the center, and he also told him that he didn't expect payment. The lemon juice was, Jefferson's cousin reported, "*a present from Mr. Hemmings*" (emphasis in the original).[7]

There are hints, however, that Hemings's sense of connection to Jefferson went only so far. In that same year, when Jack, an enslaved man whom Jefferson had hired, ran away from Monticello to visit his wife in Richmond, Jefferson wrote to his cousin George on May 18 to make inquiries about Jack. George wrote back to Jefferson on June 3, reporting that he had asked Robert Hemings whether he knew anything of the man and that Hemings said he did not. George then asked Hemings to speak with one of Jack's former employers to try to find out where he might be, but as of the date of his letter Hemings had not done so.[8] Whether or not this was Hemings's deliberate attempt to be noncooperative on Jack's behalf, his actions were dilatory and bought Jack that much more time away from slavery. By this record Hemings had no pressing interest in helping the Jeffersons apprehend a slave who had escaped from Monticello.

While free blacks like Hemings enjoyed some breathing room in Richmond, the many enslaved blacks living there also had an unusual amount of autonomy. Historians have long noted the difficulty of controlling enslaved people outside the context of rural plantation life, and Richmond with its large number of hired slaves was no different. The Hemings brothers had not been unique in traveling there to find work in the 1780s. Nor was Jack, the escapee from Monticello, unusual. Virginia's shift during the post-Revolutionary period, from growing tobacco to growing wheat, altered normal work patterns on plantations. The new crop required less labor overall than tobacco cultivation, creating longer periods when there was no work to be done in the fields. It was in the direct interest of slave owners to have their slaves gainfully employed instead of waiting idly for work on the farm. So they sent them to Richmond to find work there or be hired by other farmers, as Jefferson had done with Jack. These men, and sometimes women, usually turned all or most of their wages over to their owners. A few others, like the Hemings brothers, kept the money. Whatever their circumstances, the people who remained in town gained valuable information about how to maneuver in the world beyond the plantation.[9]

Their more independent existence emboldened Richmond's black residents in ways that often discomfited whites. In the same letter in which he groused about Robert Hemings's plan for emancipation, Jefferson, asking his son-in-law to hire some male slaves for him in the Richmond market for the coming January, stipulated that they be from "the country" and not from Richmond. He did not "chuse," he wrote, to have men from the city mix "with [his] own negroes."[10] Those Richmond "negroes" would come to Monticello with their city dwellers' heightened expectations and diverse experiences and wreak havoc in the limited and settled world of rural plantation life. He had had quite enough of that. In the sentences immediately following, Jefferson gave the bitter (to him) proof of the deleterious effects that cities had upon slaves: Robert Hemings, with confidence and contacts developed in Richmond, had wanted to leave him.

The town was, in Rhys Isaac's description, "a fickle, polymorphous segregated, non-segregated . . . fast-growing" place, where laborers, black and white, shared space with a much smaller number of privileged whites.[11] These poor and middling types were making their own rules in ways sometimes troubling to the town's more prosperous citizens, who preferred it if each social and racial group stayed in its designated place. At the same time, some better-off whites took advantage of the freewheeling attitude, particularly the great frequency of interracial socializing. Blacks and whites who worked together during the day continued their contact in bars and other gatherings at work's end.

James Callender, who in six years would become the scourge of Robert Hemings's sister Sally, spent time in Richmond at the end of the 1790s and early 1800s and was among the most vocal and expressive critics of its milieu. From his position as a columnist for the *Richmond Examiner*, the town's major newspaper, he railed against the "black dances" and barbecues often attended by white men of all strata of society. The rabidly racist Scottish émigré was outraged to see white men sitting in boxes at the local theater with their black girlfriends. As it turned out, his boss, Meriwether Jones, the editor of the *Examiner*, had a black mistress. When he and Callender fell out over Callender's exposé of Jefferson's life with Sally Hemings, Callender dubbed Lewis's paramour "Mistress Examiner." Of course, this sort of mixing went on in rural venues as well, but the openness in Richmond violated norms of secrecy-based decorum. It was one thing to carry on these liaisons with black women in the privacy of the home, quite another to appear with them in public.[12]

While the needs of the domestic economy and cultural mores shaped the social and racial climate in Richmond, news from the outside had an impact as well. Two world-defining revolutions—in France and Saint Domingue (Haiti)—put the issues of liberty and slavery into the public discourse in the most profound way—an especially important and difficult conversation in a fledgling country conceived in both liberty and chattel slavery. The two events had different implications for white and black Americans. Fresh from their own break with a monarchical system, most white Americans initially supported the French Revolution. As noted earlier, while James and Robert Hemings were in New York in 1790, those calling for the abolition of slavery, black and white, linked their struggle to the spirit of '89 in France. After the execution of Louis XVI and Marie Antoinette in 1793 and the excesses of Robespierre, the mood changed. French émigrés escaping the Terror brought news of France's spiral out of control, furthering skepticism about the new day dawning in the country of America's first ally. France and its revolution galvanized politics at the national level for all of the 1790s.

Saint Domingue, which came quickly on the heels of the French uprising, was a different story from the start, at least for many whites. The 1791 uprising there, and subsequent battle for control of what had been France's richest colony, raised the specter of slave revolts in the South. Although the United States had been born because Americans had fought—killed and been killed—to secure their liberty, many white Americans were alarmed about Saint Domingue. The black rebels apparently did not understand. Whites could fight and kill other whites for their freedom, and they could certainly fight and kill nonwhites for it. Blacks, however, were *never* to fight and kill whites for their freedom—their liberty not being worth that particular cost. Speaking of the evils of slavery in the abstract, instantly abolishing the institution in places with minuscule numbers of blacks, and enacting gradual emancipation plans along timetables suiting the needs of whites, kept the notion of white supremacy firmly in place. What was happening in Saint Domingue was altogether different, and the image of empowered blacks taking freedom on their own terms was a nightmare scenario for Jefferson and most other whites.

If whites were uneasy, blacks in Richmond and other places immediately identified with the rebels in Saint Domingue. By the end of the 1790s, the talk of the rebels' success on the island inspired an enslaved blacksmith,

Gabriel, to recruit black men—and lower-class whites, he hoped—to seize the armory at Richmond, take Governor James Monroe hostage, and force the end of slavery in Virginia. The evidently widespread plot, in place by 1799, was foiled, but the fear it struck in white Virginians changed the climate in the state. If the American Revolution prompted emancipation in the North, and brought liberalized emancipation to Virginia, Gabriel and Saint Domingue led to retrenchment. The charismatic blacksmith and many of his followers were hanged, along with some number of others who may not have been involved. "We were too lax," white Virginians explained, and local communities began to pass laws prohibiting, among other things, the congregation of enslaved blacks and free blacks, a pairing seen as the root of the "evil" of the uprising.[13]

One wonders what Robert Hemings knew of these matters. Dr. Stras, his erstwhile benefactor, was a French émigré. Robert and Dolly were connected to his household when the turmoil on the island began, and he certainly had thoughts about the matter. It is possible, indeed probable, that Robert Hemings, whose business brought him into daily contact with members of the public, actually knew Gabriel, or at least knew of him. The blacksmith apparently cut an impressive figure in the town, and the population of blacks was not so large that there could have been many degrees of separation between people of color. Information affecting their community could not have been kept from them. The slave/African American network being what it was, it is very likely that Hemings had heard something of Gabriel's plan to fight for freedom for all enslaved Virginians. Hemings already had his freedom. He just had to make the most of it in a community that was growing ever more wary of and hostile toward people like him and his family.

RICHMOND EVIDENTLY HELD no attraction for James Hemings. His brother had an established life there and was already in the town. It was not uncommon—indeed, it was even expected—that family members would pool their resources. In the years to come, when they had the chance, members of the Hemings family did exactly that, living together to cut down on expenses, taking in relatives, helping to secure loans for one another, and buying one another's freedom. The brothers may, in fact, have supported each other in ways that cannot be learned from the extant record. We cannot know the conversations the two had about what they planned to do in life after they were freed. Did one brother ever try to persuade the other of the benefits of life in the places where they chose to settle? On the other hand, one cannot assume that, because they were brothers, they necessarily got along well enough to live with, or close to, each other when they did not have to.

Given his life to date, Philadelphia made sense for James Hemings in a way that Richmond did not. More cosmopolitan than Robert, and with no known wife or children, he had a greater desire, and capacity, to test the outer limits of freedom. He was picking up where he had left off in 1794 in a place that he knew well from having lived there for three years. With any luck, any of his Philadelphia contacts would still be in the city and could be sources of aid and support—just what many others in his position were seeking. There was also Benjamin Rush, Jefferson's friend, who had enjoyed many of Hemings's meals and had a well-established record of aiding blacks independent of their association with any of his white friends. Hemings probably had a better basis for approaching Rush than any of the other free blacks who sought the doctor's help. The city was still considered a "refuge" for newly emancipated blacks and for fugitive slaves alike, with its small but growing middling class who through churches and civic organizations did what they could to help other members of their race. There was another group of likely interest to Hemings whose numbers had grown since he had left the city: French-speaking blacks—a few free, and the much larger number of enslaved people who were brought along with white refugees from Saint Domingue. Hemings would have known people like them when he was in Paris, and he, unlike other American blacks, would at least have had the chance to communicate with them in their native language, which many of them sought to preserve as long as they could.[14]

Whether the presence of this Francophone group, forced travelers as most of them were, provided the spark, or whether it was just his own wanderlust, Hemings did not stay in Philadelphia long; instead, he embarked upon a period of travel apparently within the United States and overseas. Again, we know this because of Jefferson. As it turned out, of course, Jefferson did not stay retired. He became vice-president of the United States to President John Adams in 1796. The office carried him back to Philadelphia, where he took up residence (as infrequently as decency would allow) after his election. In May of 1797 he wrote to his daughter Maria, "James is returned to this place, and is not given up to drink as I had before been informed. He tells me his next trip will be to Spain. I am afraid his journeys will end in the moon. I have endeavored to persuade him to stay where he is and lay up money."[15] Along with the completely delicious irony of seeing Jefferson tell another person to save money, this passage presents a fascinating look into James Hemings's state of mind in the aftermath of his emancipation. In the immediate post–Civil War period, whites, sometimes with disdain, commented upon the former slaves' seeming love of travel. People who had been forcibly detained on plantations, in servant quarters in urban areas, wanted to go. Freedom meant movement. Now many of these people, as whites probably did not think about or choose to acknowledge, were seeking to reconstitute families shattered during slavery. They were traveling to search for loved ones who had been sold away from them, often to distant parts of the country.

James Hemings knew where his relatives were, and they were not in Paris, his probable first destination after Philadelphia, nor were they in Spain. He was looking for something else—perhaps no more than any other person who wants to see the world and has the chance, though Jefferson's report indicates that he was particularly restless. Jefferson's endeavor to keep him in one place grew out of his own deep attachments—to familiar place, things, and people. Perhaps he and the younger man simply had different personalities. Hemings, with no wife and family to keep him in one place, seems to have preferred adventure and variety over stability and comforting familiarity.

Then there is the question of Hemings's drinking. Chefs in the eighteenth century were notorious drinkers. There is, however, no way to know whether Hemings was really an alcoholic at this point, for not all who drink, or even all who drink to excess at times, fit that category. The drastic report of his having given himself up to drink apparently came from someone who knew Jefferson well enough to know that he would be interested in a report on Hemings's condition—Henrietta Gardiner, perhaps, or Benjamin Rush, who long had an interest in the causes and effects of alcoholism. Whether his characterization of the report on Hemings was one of his customary exaggerations, or whether it was the person who had relayed the information who was exaggerating, the meeting with Hemings reassured Jefferson. He was apparently not there when Jefferson first arrived in Philadelphia, or else Jefferson would not have had to rely upon others to give him information about his former servant. Like his brother Robert, James Hemings still felt some vestigial connection to Jefferson. It is telling that when he returned to Philadelphia from his travels, evidently just long enough to start out again, he spent time with the man who had owned him, and still owned the rest of his family, save for Robert Hemings. That was a reality that he could not travel far enough to escape.

The First Son

When Jefferson returned to Philadelphia in 1797 to take office as vice-president, he was intent upon spending as little time in the city as he could. And the lightness of his duties in that office enabled him to follow his plan. So unlike his sojourn in the city when he was secretary of state, this stay saw him make no substantial investment in his living quarters. There was no beautiful house with a French chef and maître d'hôtel, only rooms in John Francis's hotel. Henrietta Gardner once again served as his laundress, and he made do during his entire tenure in office with only one manservant at a time. Not long after he left Monticello in February of 1797 to take the oath of office, he received word from his daughter Martha that "poor little Harriot," his child with Sally Hemings, had died at the age of two.[16] Hemings, now twenty-four years old, was once again childless.

Hemings was not to be childless long. Jefferson came home on July 11, 1797, and thirty-eight weeks after he arrived, Beverley, his first son who would live to adulthood, was born.[17] Although Jefferson never used the full name William Beverley in his writings, the evidence indicates that Beverley Hemings's first name was William. It was a convention of the day among many whites and blacks to refer to individuals by their middle names instead of their first names. John Wayles Eppes was known as Jack when he was a boy, but when he became an adult Jefferson sometimes referred to him as Wayles. Similarly, John Wayles Hemings, the son of Eston and Julia Hemings, was known as Wayles Hemings instead of John. Beverley's younger brother Madison, called Jim-Mad by family members, apparently reproduced the names of his first nuclear family in his own children. He did not mention the name of his first son, who died as an infant. His next child was named Sarah after his mother. There followed among his nine children James Madison, Harriet, Thomas Eston, and William Beverley.[18]

Here was a further forgone opportunity for Sally Hemings to give one of her children a name from her own family. There was another William Beverley on the periphery of her world, the nine-year-old son of Thomas Mann Randolph's sister Mary. His name, however, came from his father David Meade Randolph's side of the family. David and Mary certainly visited Monticello. But Mary was a married woman by the time of the family conflicts with her father's teenage bride, Gabriella Harvie, in the 1790s that drove her sisters, Anne (Nancy), Harriet, Jane, and Virginia, away from Tuckahoe—Nancy to Bizarre, Harriet, Jane, and Virginia to Varina and Monticello. Sally Hemings certainly knew of David and Mary Randolph and their children.[19] There is no reason to believe that she would have preferred naming her baby after their child instead of any one of her own brothers. Naming this boy Beverley was far more likely Jefferson's idea, and he had a good reason for it.

William Beverley was actually the name of an important man in Virginia history. The son of the historian Robert Beverley, he was a distant kinsman of Jefferson's through his mother's side, but that is not how Jefferson knew of him. Beverley was the well-known representative of the very wealthy, very land-rich Lord Fairfax, the only resident peer in Virginia during the mid-1700s. Fairfax had been granted a substantial amount of land in the colony, the so-called Northern Neck of Virginia. After disputes arose about the exact boundaries of Fairfax's property, the peer and the crown agreed to appoint a commission to do a survey. Each side would have commissioners and surveyors to represent its interests. William Beverley was one of the commissioners representing Fairfax's interests. These men, in turn, chose surveyors for what would be a grand expedition. Jefferson's father, Peter, was chosen as one of the surveyors for the crown, along with his great friend Joshua Fry, with whom he would later create the famous Fry-Jefferson map. At the end of the journey, the representatives returned to Tuckahoe, where the almost four-year-old Thomas Jefferson, his mother, and his sisters were waiting. Marking the Fairfax line was one of several epic adventures that spawned tales that Peter Jefferson told his son Thomas, who in turn passed them on, in vivid detail, to his grandchildren.[20]

Two years before marking the Fairfax line, Beverley had made history in another way. He and Thomas Lee were the commissioners from Virginia who, with commissioners from Maryland, negotiated the famous Treaty of Lancaster in which the Six Nations of the Iroquois deeded to Virginia all of the land that comprises what is now West Virginia. Actually, the Virginians claimed the deal covered much more territory—all the land extending to the Mississippi River. That was not the Indians' understanding of what they had sold, and a subsequent treaty, the Treaty of Logstown, was needed to clarify matters that could never really be clarified, given the white settlers' ultimate goal. Jefferson saw the Treaty of Lancaster, marked prominently on his father's map, as pivotal to Virginia's development and to western expansion in general. He had his own copy of the treaty, was intimately familiar with its contents, and told anecdotes in his *Notes on the State of Virginia* about events that had taken place during the negotiations. He listed the treaty at the end of the book as one of the critical documents that one had to know in order to understand Virginia history. William Beverley was also the proprietor of Beverley Manor, a section of land very near to, if not actually a part of, the land subject to the Treaty of Lancaster. It, too, is marked on the Fry-Jefferson map. Jefferson had one other reason to associate the name Beverley with his father. Peter Jefferson had left his eldest son four lots in a settlement called Beverley Town, which he had surveyed and laid out in 1756.[21]

Why, however, would Jefferson be thinking of William Beverley and his Treaty of Lancaster in the summer and fall of 1797 while he was at home with Sally Hemings when she was pregnant with Beverley? Several months before he returned to Monticello that July, Jefferson saw an item in a newspaper written by Luther Martin, a prominent Maryland Federalist, that riveted his attention. In the published letter, Martin attacked Jefferson for having written in the *Notes* that a Colonel Thomas Cresap, "infamous for the many murders he had committed" of Indians, had killed the family of the great Indian orator Logan. Martin charged further that Logan had never made the speech, ridiculing Jefferson's alleged credulity for believing that the Indian was capable of having done so. For the rest of 1797 and into 1798, Martin printed letters addressed to Jefferson in the papers, hoping to draw him out.[22] Martin had launched a serious two-pronged assault upon something that Jefferson held dear, for *Notes on the State of Virginia* presented Jefferson the philosopher, scientist, and historian commenting as an expert on his beloved Virginia. This was his personal masterpiece.

Jefferson would later claim that he had read only the first part of Martin's first letter, which may have been true or been simply his way to be grandly dismissive of his critic. Either way, the attack galvanized him and sent him to his research. After checking his own material, he began to write to others who might have information that would clarify matters.[23] Luther Martin had impugned his scholarship, but he had also, probably inadvertently, done something else. He opened the door to the lost world of Peter Jefferson and, as it turns out, John Wayles. In the latter half of 1797, Jefferson stepped through that door into the past. The Treaty of Lancaster, ironically concluded on July 4, 1744, produced a deed recorded in the proceedings of the Virginia Executive Council, and Jefferson had copies of Virginia's laws and documents at Monticello, which he consulted regularly when he was governor of Virginia.[24] Along with William Beverley's name, the deed contained the signature of the man who witnessed the signing of the treaty, Philip Ludwell Lee, the nephew and namesake of the man who had brought John Wayles to America. There was also the signature of the secretary of Virginia, Benjamin Waller, Wayles's old business partner and George Wythe's law teacher.[25] Both of Beverley Hemings's grandfathers had associations with men who had helped make the Treaty of Lancaster for Virginia.

The man responsible for setting up the treaty negotiations, who was originally set to represent Maryland and whose name was mentioned in the published proceedings of the treaty negotiations, because his property was a boundary line for the land subject to the document, was none other than the Indian trader and Indian fighter Colonel Thomas Cresap. Martin conveyed some of this information to Jefferson in January of 1798 in one of the eight letters he addressed to him on the Cresap matter over the span of several months—letters in which he lectured the author of the *Notes on the State of Virginia*, in a somewhat patronizing way, about the Six Nations, the Treaty of Lancaster, and other aspects of Virginia history.

If Jefferson truly never allowed himself to look at Martin's letters, he missed the specific reference to Cresap and the treaty. But it is almost inconceivable that Jefferson did not already know of the connection. Cresap was famous in Maryland and Virginia as an Indian fighter, a mapmaker, and a correspondent of Virginia governors and other Virginia officials. He was intimately involved in Indian affairs and disputes between the English and the French throughout the mid-1700s. Cresap's property bordered Indian territory. He had a trading post, sometimes called a fort, on the Great Wagon Road, which carried white settlers south and into what would become West Virginia. That pathway is also marked on the Fry-Jefferson map, adjacent to Beverley Manor, which the road cuts right through. A dispute about the treatment of Indians at Cresap's trading post was another impetus for the summit in Lancaster. There were always clashes at the border that threatened to erupt into serious confrontations. When the contest between the French and English entered this volatile mix, it led to the French and Indian War.[26]

After the Treaty of Lancaster putatively secured the western lands, Cresap helped form, and became an agent for, the Ohio Company along with Thomas Lee, Lawrence and Augustine Washington (George's brothers), and others. He and Christopher Gist, whose work influenced Joshua Fry and Peter Jefferson, became the faces of the Ohio Company. The company's purpose was to sell land and settle the Ohio territory, and it had a competitor in the form of the Loyal Land Company, an entity created by a number of prominent Virginians, including Peter Jefferson, Joshua Fry, Thomas Walker (Peter Jefferson's friend and physician), and the Reverend James Maury, Jefferson's teacher when he was a boy. Several principals of the company became Thomas Jefferson's legal guardians upon his father's death, in 1757, and later his mentors throughout his early career.[27]

Martin had an interest in what Jefferson had written about "Colonel Cresap" because he was married to the daughter of Michael Cresap, Thomas Cresap's son. Only Michael Cresap could possibly have been near Logan's family at the time of their deaths. As far as Martin was concerned, Jefferson had libeled his wife's father, though that appears to have been a pretext for attacking Jefferson. For his part, Jefferson had been clear from the beginning: if he had made an error in the *Notes* he would do a new edition and correct himself. As his research showed very quickly, he had, in fact, mistaken Colonel Thomas Cresap for his son Captain Michael Cresap. Even further, the evidence indicated that Michael Cresap had not personally murdered Logan's family, although Jefferson believed that his actions had led to the slaughter. After his intensive investigation, Jefferson wrote an appendix to the *Notes* removing references to Cresap as "infamous" for many murders and as the murderer of Logan's family. He did not change the language in Logan's speech saying that a "Colonel Cresap" had killed his family, nor did he back down from his view that Logan had actually given the oration.[28] It can be said in Jefferson's defense that there was often a very fine line between being an Indian fighter and one who was infamous for murdering Indians. Thomas Cresap did have the reputation that Jefferson charged him with, even though he was not involved in the murder of Logan's family.

It is extremely unlikely that any of these events would have been known to Sally Hemings in 1797 without Jefferson's mentioning them to her or that she would have cared enough about William Beverley to feel that Beverley was a more suitable name for her son than James, Robert, Martin, or Peter. The pattern of her children's names suggests that she was not in control of this process: Jefferson was. He was not present for Beverley Hemings's birth on April 1, 1798, having returned to Philadelphia at the end of December, as Luther Martin continued to harangue him about Cresap and Logan. By the time of Jefferson's departure, however, Hemings was well along in her pregnancy, past the point where the two would have discussed what to name their coming child. If it was a girl, Hemings would know what to do: name her Harriet after their daughter who had recently died. Jefferson had done this before, naming one daughter Lucy Elizabeth after an earlier daughter who died. The same had happened with his granddaughter Ellen Wayles, born in 1796, who was the second of that name. In fact, when Hemings and Jefferson did have another daughter who survived infancy, she was named Harriet. We cannot, of course, rule out the possibility that these two communicated with one another even when Jefferson was away.

But what about a boy—what would be a suitable name for Thomas Jefferson's first son? In truth, Beverley Hemings could not have had a more appropriate name. His younger brothers, Madison and Eston, would be named for important people in Jefferson's daily life. William Beverley, whose services to Virginia had suddenly been brought back to Jefferson's attention in 1797 by the Cresap matter and the need to revise *Notes on the State of Virginia*, represented ideas in Jefferson's head about the future of his country. Even Beverley, Virginia, laid out by Peter Jefferson, and Jefferson's patrimony from the town were connected to a notion of the future. Beverley Hemings wore the name of the man who had helped open the west to Virginians, perhaps his father's greatest obsession. This little boy, the most mysterious of the Hemings-Jefferson children, grew up passing through the foyer where his grandfather's map was prominently displayed, memorializing both William Beverley's name and his treaty. Did his father ever point this out to him? Did Beverley understand what the west meant to his father? Beverley Hemings would not, as an adult, join the throngs of people, black and white—his own younger brothers included—who made their way west to settle land "bought," stolen, and wrested away from the Six Nations

and other groups like them. Instead, he would remain safely ensconced on
the eastern seaboard, after leaving his mother and father to move into that
other brave new world, the world of American whiteness.

THREE MONTHS AFTER Beverley's birth, a perhaps unknowingly ironic
comment on the event arrived at Monticello. Jefferson received what has to
count as one of the most extraordinary letters in all of his correspondence—
a bolt seemingly out of the blue that appears to have stunned him. It came
from his protégé and dear friend William Short, who was still in Europe.
The two men had kept regular contact from the time Jefferson departed
France, talking politics, family, and careers. There is no indication, as of this
date, what Short knew about Jefferson's relationship with Sally Hemings.
The letter he wrote to his mentor that winter, however, shows that he would
not at all have been disapproving of their connection, at least not because
they were of different races. In fact, the interracial aspect of it may have
greatly pleased Jefferson's "adoptive son."

Until he became totally disillusioned later in his life about his countrymen's views of black people, and the possibility of ending slavery and
making blacks citizens, Short sincerely hoped for the abolition of slavery.
Evidently influenced by his time as minister to Spain in the mid-1790s, he
had an epiphany: intermixture between the races offered the best possible
solution to America's racial predicament. He wrote to tell Jefferson this at
the end of February 1798. Short was well familiar with the position Jefferson
had staked out in his *Notes on the State of Virginia*, so he understood he was
going against the grain in advancing this proposition. While making subtle
references to Jefferson's expressed views, indeed using echoes of Jefferson's
own language—for example, "deep rooted prejudices"—to press his point,
Short gently offered his friend a way out of his announced position, presenting reasons to break free from the habit of racial prejudice. Taking
great care, he noted that while some of "the most enlightened & virtuous
minds" (read Jefferson) expressed negative views about the idea of racial
mixture, there was still much to think about before the country closed off
that option because of its supposed "evils."[29] Short, who almost certainly
knew of the Hemingses' connection to the Wayles family—his double in-
laws—reminded Jefferson, as if he needed reminding, that racial intermixture was already prevalent within their slave society. He went on,

But even admitting that this mixture should change our hue & that all our Southern inhabitants should advance to the middle ground between their present color & the black (& this is granting more than can be asked as there are every where more whites than blacks) still they would not be of a darker color than the inhabitants of some of the provinces of Spain—& I do not see that these provinces labour under any inconvenience greater than the rest of the Spaniards or that the Spaniards in general labour under any inconvenience with respect to the rest of Europe, merely on account of their color—*Even in our own country there are some people darker, than the gradual mixture of the blacks can ever make us, & yet I do not know that they suffer from thence—I don't know if you ever saw, a Mrs. Randolph afterwards Mrs. Tucker,*—There is no country that might not be content to have its women like her—There is no sentiment from the contemplation of beauty that they would not be capable of inspiring equally with those who can boast the perfect mixture of the rose & the lilly. (emphasis added)[30]

This utterly astounding passage has a prominent eighteenth-century white Virginian extolling the beauty that could be produced by the mixture of black and white—beauty, he said, that equaled the combination of "the rose & the lilly." Short knew the exact significance of his choice of words, for this was a direct challenge to some of the best-known of Jefferson's passages in Query 14 of the *Notes*, which is why he tiptoed so gingerly. Short was speaking of Frances Bland Randolph Tucker, the mother of John Randolph of Roanoke and wife of St. George Tucker.[31] As far as we currently know, Frances Tucker was not part African American, but in Short's view she looked more like a black person than many mixed-race people he had seen. His willingness to use concrete examples to illustrate the soundness of his proposals about racial mixture could only have set off warning bells in the ultra-sensitive Jefferson. This was approaching ground he did not wish to cover. Although he lived daily surrounded by mixed-race slaves, Jefferson was careful *never* to personalize his comments about "amalgamation," to speak openly about the lives and family histories of the people he knew best. If Short was willing to talk about the beauty and virtues of a named upper-class white woman who was darker than some black people, might he not, if the conversation went any further, begin to speak of the beauty and virtues of black people who were almost as white as some white people—James and Sally Hemings, for example. For Jefferson to get a letter like this, just months after the birth of his mixed-race son, was quite remarkable. What on earth had prompted Short's declaration about the positive good of mixing races at that moment? Was he baiting Jefferson because he knew something about his life, or was this merely a spectacular coincidence?

Jefferson avoided any uncomfortable moments by refusing to engage Short on the subject—either to defend his comments in the *Notes* or to repudiate them. He apparently never, in any document found to date, even acknowledged what Short had said, although Short twice asked him for a response, explicitly in one letter and indirectly, but clearly, in a second.[32] Short wanted to draw his mentor out on the subject: to have him either defend his position on interracial mixture, in which case he could extend the debate and try to persuade Jefferson through examples that he was wrong, or repudiate his earlier writings and concede that Short's proposal had merit. In either case, Jefferson had been checkmated. If he answered Short by reiterating the views he expressed in the *Notes*, or by trying out the language he later used in his famous 1814 letter to Edward Coles about "amalgamation" producing "a degradation," he would invite the willing-to-be-specific Short to go further.[33] The younger man's mind would immediately turn to the Hemingses, and he could ask Jefferson point-blank whether he really believed that Robert, James, Thenia, Critta, Peter, and Sally Hemings were "degradations" produced by his father-in-law, John Wayles. And what of Elizabeth, Mary, Martin, and Nancy Hemings and Betty Brown, people whom Short knew from the times he spent at Monticello before he joined Jefferson in France? Were they all degradations, too?

There were things that Jefferson could say to Edward Coles that he could not say to William Short, because he bore a completely different relationship to the two men. In addition to being closely tied to Jefferson by the Wayles connection, Short had lived with the Hemingses and Jeffersons for over five years in Paris. If Jefferson tried out the "amalgamation equals degradation" formulation on Short, he would appear the perfect hypocrite or simply mindlessly hateful. Unlike Coles, Short had personally observed Jefferson living with two intelligent and attractive mixed-race African Americans working alongside with and being paid like free white workers— and the earth had continued to turn. Whatever he knew of Sally Hemings and Jefferson, Short had firsthand knowledge of Jefferson's general affection for her family. Why could not Jefferson's own experiences be replicated all over the United States? As Short observed, white people outnumbered blacks so greatly in the country that blacks, not whites, would be bred out. Virginia's way of determining race, as Jefferson well knew, relied on just such a known possibility: black families could become white.

On the other hand, if Jefferson recanted the position voiced in the *Notes* and sided with Short, he would be leaving for posterity a Rosetta stone that might help crack the code of a part of his life he wanted to remain totally private. He was already living the life Short recommended, but at a time long before it could ever be accepted openly. Three of his children would fulfill Short's prescription, melding into the white population as if Africa had never been a part of them.

In a letter written on his birthday, April 13, 1800, Jefferson acknowledged all the letters he received from Short in 1798 and 1799, save for his February 27, 1798, communication seeking comments on his suggestion that the way out of the American dilemma was to do essentially what Jefferson was doing: creating children who breached the color barrier. Instead, he changed the subject in a rather spectacular fashion—admitting to Short that he had been, for several years, without Short's knowledge, borrowing money from one of Short's accounts over which he held a power of attorney. He owed Short thousands of dollars, and he detailed the steps he was taking to repay the sum as quickly as he could. The Summary Journal of Letters shows that Jefferson received Short's February letter on June 22, 1798, but he had no intention of discussing this matter with his protégé.[34] He had to find his own private way out of the American dilemma as it unfolded on his mountain. Abstractions worked best in the republic of letters. What had to be done for Beverley, and then Harriet, Madison, and Eston who followed, was too serious for that—this was a concrete problem to be dealt with only in the real world.

26

♣

THE OCEAN OF LIFE

EOPLE IN CHARLOTTESVILLE and its environs had been talking
about Sally Hemings and Thomas Jefferson for nearly ten years,
gossiping as neighbors will. No matter how strenuously people
claim to be "above" such things, the romantic and sexual lives of others
have been of natural interest to humans from time immemorial. The situation at Monticello, however, would not have surprised the residents of
Albemarle County or the rest of Virginia, for that matter. Mixed-race people existed in great numbers, and they did not, as Mary Chesnut wryly
noted, fall "from the sky." They were the children of rape, the children
of casual encounters, and the children of men and women in long-term
relationships, like those of Thomas Bell and Mary Hemings and Thomas
Jefferson and Sally Hemings.

The difference for Hemings and Jefferson was that Jefferson decided to
resume his public career, and he did so at a singular moment in American
political history—a moment he had helped create. No politician, then or
later, had a better sense of the uses of newspapers and journalism than
Jefferson. From his earliest days as a young revolutionary, he involved himself in attempts to use the press to get "the message" out to the people at
large. He understood the concept of "talking points" and being "on message" centuries before those terms became part of our political vernacular.
In the late 1760s when the *Virginia Gazette* struck him as being too pro-
Royalist, he moved to have a new newspaper started to serve as a counter-
weight to what he thought was conservative pro-British propaganda.[1] This
was a precursor to his well-known debacle with the *National Gazette*, when

he and Hamilton waged internecine warfare through their rival newspapers even as they served in the same government. By the end of the 1790s, partisan politics was the order of the day, and each side had its publications waiting and willing to do battle for their cause.

In this take-no-prisoners environment, the closer Jefferson came to the ultimate prize in politics—the presidency—the more desperate his foes became. By all accounts, the talk of Jefferson's private life reached the newspapers at the very end of the 1790s. James Callender said that he had first seen hints of it in William Rind's *Virginia Federalist* in January of 1800. Rind wrote that he had "damning proofs" of what he called Jefferson's "depravity," but chose not to elaborate. The word did not stay in Virginia. Ten months after Rind's comment, a New York paper said flatly that Jefferson's "private life was far from spotless."[2] Earlier historians assumed that the innuendos about Jefferson from above the Mason-Dixon line were references either to the Betsy Walker affair, when he tried to seduce the wife of his friend, or to his affair with Maria Cosway, put into circulation by Hamilton, who may have learned of the connection from his sister-in-law, Angelica Church, who knew the pair in Paris. Although Church and Jefferson shared a lively and charged correspondence, she was nowhere near as close to the Virginian as she was to her brother-in-law, Hamilton, who some suspected was her lover. The two almost certainly talked to one another about Jefferson once he became Hamilton's determined foe in the 1790s.

We have in recent decades expanded the category of people who can be considered historical actors in the founding era, taking in the enslaved, servants, and people who are not founding fathers or related to founding fathers. Some of those enslaved at Monticello, as well as the white men who worked there, had as much valuable information about Jefferson as Alexander Hamilton or Angelica Church. We have no inkling of what members of the Hemings family thought about their relatives' connection to Jefferson. Were they ashamed or proud of the association? They could have gone either way. Jefferson was considered a great man, but this phenomenon of generational concubinage that had yet to bring about the emancipation of family members may have been distressing. Did they talk about this to outsiders? If so, there would have been no way to keep the knowledge within the strict confines of the house at Monticello.

It is hard to believe that James Hemings, during his years in Philadelphia—with and without Jefferson—never breathed to a soul the true nature of his connection to Jefferson in all its aspects. One can imagine an entirely predictable conversation with a companion, platonic and otherwise.

James, what were your parents' names?
Elizabeth Hemings and John Wayles.
You're very bright skinned. Were either of your parents white?
Yes, my father was white.
You don't have to talk about this if you don't want to, but why don't
    you live with him? Did your father sell you?
No, Mr. Jefferson married my father's oldest daughter, and when he died,
    Mr. J. inherited me and my brothers and sisters.
My goodness: the things that happen in slavery! How do you and
    your brothers and sisters feel about Mr. Jefferson?
Well . . .

The more time Hemings spent with a person, and the closer he grew to her or him, the greater the temptation would be to tell the person who he really was, for his sister's life was intimately bound up with his own life story. It was, in fact, part of the reason he was back in the United States and not in Paris.

We can posit the same of Robert Hemings living in the household of Dr. Stras in Richmond. These two men must have had a fairly close relationship for Stras to do something for Hemings that Jefferson did not think to do: help him set up a plan for his emancipation. It is virtually impossible to keep a secret that more than one person knows, and after too many people know, it can no longer be called a secret. Under the circumstances, it is just as likely that the talk about Jefferson's "far from spotless" personal life referred to what he was doing *at the time*, and not just his attempt to seduce his best friend's wife or his fleeting sixteen-year-old affair in a foreign land with a foreign woman. Far more people on American soil in the 1790s knew about Jefferson and Hemings than knew about Jefferson and Cosway.

So it was clear by January of 1800, and probably before, that there was a chance that Jefferson's relationship with Hemings might become a source of public trouble for him. The most sensational sex scandal to date had been Alexander Hamilton's admission of his adulterous affair with Maria Reynolds, an act from which he never really recovered.[3] The astute Jefferson understood that Hamilton's mistake, if he had wanted to remain a public figure, was in talking about the matter. Had he remained silent or, at most, opted for the ever useful, but quite transparent, "Why, I won't dignify such trash with a response," he might have been able to salvage a national career for himself. That is, if he had not also rushed headlong into publishing a bizarre diatribe against John Adams.[3] He was a brilliant man, still young, who could have looked forward to making additional contributions to the nation.

It is natural to think first of what the gossip meant to Jefferson because he obviously had a great deal at stake, as did the nation. He was in the midst of trying to become president of the United States when the first blind items about his private life had begun to circulate in public. But this talk was likely far down on Jefferson's list of preoccupations in 1800 as his political future was being decided by the American electorate and while he waited, far longer, as it turned out, than he had expected, to find out whether he would become president.

The Hemingses had things at stake, too, but none of national import. Sally Hemings's brother Robert and his wife lived in what would become the epicenter of the scandal. The Richmond newspapers carried the story to the outside world, and Robert probably learned very early on that his sister's story—even if not given in detail at first—had reached beyond Charlottesville. What might this mean for her? He and other family members would be entirely justified if they feared that all the talk might become too much of a problem for Jefferson and his white family, and Sally and her child—there was only Beverley in 1800—might be sent away. Enslaved people were well aware that slave owners almost always made decisions on the basis of the needs of their white families, not the enslaved people they called "family" in the paternalistic sense or those enslaved people who really were part of their biological family. Whatever they may have thought Jefferson felt for Hemings, there could be no guarantee of what he was going to do about this until he did it.

The election was close—an actual electoral tie—until after thirty-six ballots in the House of Representatives, Jefferson was elected the third president of the United States on February 17, 1801. He was already in Washington, having come there in December to finish out his duties as president of the Senate and to await the election results. With that behind him, he immediately set about making plans for his administration and for his life in the President's House. There was no question whom he wanted to be his chef.

A Life Unravels

James Hemings had returned from his travels and settled in Baltimore. Why he was there instead of in Philadelphia remains a mystery. Although the city did have a large free black population, with opportunities for work, it was located in a southern slave state, and appears to have been more like an expanded version of Richmond than a city like Philadelphia. Baltimore's large and busy port carried many people to and from the United States, and it was a possible point of departure and return for Hemings during his travels. He may have simply decided to settle there after one of his trips. Jefferson knew where he was, and five days after his election he wrote to a Baltimore resident and innkeeper, William Evans,

> You mentioned to me in conversation here that you sometimes saw my former servant James, & that he made his engagements such as to keep himself always free to come to me. could I get the favor of you to send for him & to tell him I shall be glad to recieve him as soon as he can come to me?[4]

Evans's comments about Hemings had given Jefferson every indication that the younger man was anxious to work for him again. Hemings had no difficulty finding jobs, but apparently acted as if his employment was temporary until Jefferson sent for him. Jefferson was so confident about Hemings's arrival that he wrote to the French envoy, Philippe de Létombe, the same day he wrote to Evans that he was looking for a maître d'hôtel from "among the French in Philadelphia," adding, "I have a good cook: but it is pour l'office, & to take charge of the family [meaning his servants in the President's House] that I am distressed."[5]

Three days after writing to Evans, he received a letter from another of his former employees, Francis Say. Say also lived in Baltimore and was in contact with Hemings. As Jefferson had told Evans in his letter of February 23, Say had come to him earlier seeking employment, and he, too, mentioned that James Hemings was anxious to work for him again. Say was reporting on what Hemings was now saying about working for Jefferson and repeating his own offer to serve the new president.[6] This was a delicate business because Jefferson wanted to hire only Hemings, not Say, who drank and quarreled too much with his wife for Jefferson's taste. When he got serious about contacting his former chef, he decided to write to Evans instead of Say. After asking Evans to have Hemings come to work for him, he asked the innkeeper to try to persuade Say not to ask him for a job.[7] The man who wanted to be loved by everybody—the president-elect of the United States—did not have the heart to tell Say that he did not want to hire him. Before Evans could get to him, Say wrote,

> I have spoke to James according to your Desire he has made mention again as he did before that he was willing to serve you before any other man in the Union but sence he understands that he would have to be among strange servants he would be very much obliged to you if you would send him a few lines of engagement and on what conditions and wages you would please to give him in your own hand wreiting.[8]

By February 27 Evans had received Jefferson's letter. He responded saying that he had immediately passed along Jefferson's message to Hemings, who said in return that he was working in a tavern for a "Mr. Peck" and that it was "out of [his] power" to quit "for a few days." Evans pressed him to be specific about the date he could leave. Hemings told him that he would think about it and get back to him later that evening, but he did not. Evans explained what happened next: "I sent for him a second time, the answer he returned me, was, that he would not go until you should write to himself—"[9] Evans's communication about Hemings trailed off with that suggestive dash, and then he promised to try to persuade Say not to ask Jefferson for a job.

This awkward correspondence clearly suggests a power struggle between Hemings and Jefferson that hints at feelings that may have existed between the two for years. Lucia Stanton has persuasively suggested that Jefferson offended Hemings by summoning him as he had in years past when Hemings was first a boy and then an enslaved man.[10] He was an adult free man now. He could read and write. He knew that Jefferson spent hours at his desk writing to everyone under the sun. Why not a line formally asking him to come to Washington? Being the president's chef de cuisine was a serious job. Why not spell out in writing all that was expected?

The great likelihood is that just as Hemings may have been offended by Jefferson's mode of communication, Jefferson was probably annoyed by Hemings's delays and demand for a writing. Here he was, a new president, "distressed" at the prospect of filling positions in an administration, and a man he had known since he was a little boy was proceeding as if they were truly operating at arm's length. He had been Jefferson's chef de cuisine in Paris, New York, and Philadelphia. Jefferson had paid him a salary just as if he had been a free white worker. Having James Hemings as his chef de cuisine should have been easy, yet Hemings was making it hard, demanding what Jefferson would have thought of as a symbolic show of respect. From his perspective, the real show of respect might have been his confidence in Hemings's ability to handle such an important position, and his quick indication to Létombe that he already knew he had "a good cook" for the President's House.

The interesting, but unanswerable, question is whether Jefferson would have responded to Hemings, had he written to him in the first instance instead of conveying his own sentiments through third parties. Hemings knew where Jefferson was just as well as Say. Why not mail the president-elect a letter, or send it by his friend? Indeed, why hadn't he come to see Jefferson himself, as Say had done? If Hemings wanted to play the game of employer-employee, wasn't it equally incumbent upon him to write to Jefferson seeking a position, as legions of other people would soon do?

After all these years, Hemings undoubtedly had complex feelings about Jefferson, and it is likely that Jefferson had complex feelings about him as well. It could hardly have been otherwise. Hemings's behavior in this episode hints at some of those feelings and his state of mind at the time. His insistence that Jefferson write to him before he accepted an important job he said he wanted suggests that he had not moved fully beyond his former persona—not just as an enslaved man but as a person who had been the object of Jefferson's special "benevolence." For all his desire for the trappings of a formal engagement in the world of free labor, Hemings cast the older man more as father figure than as prospective employer, like a child who expects the parent to be formal in a given situation, but retains the option of informality for himself because of the parent-child relationship. Jefferson was "a miser with his time,"[11] and when he saw Hemings's reluctance to commit to the job, he quickly turned elsewhere. It was March, and he wanted his chef to start in April. With the aid of Létombe and Carlos

Martínez de Irujo, the Spanish ambassador to the United States, Jefferson settled on Honoré Julien, former chef to George Washington, as the most suitable candidate. He then conducted the negotiations for Julien's hiring wholly through Létombe—wages, terms, and starting date. He apparently never wrote to Julien himself.[12]

While the possible effects of Hemings's time with Jefferson during his enslavement must always be taken into account, it is also crucial to consider his individual personality and experiences. He had been a chef, or in training to become a chef, for almost half his life. With the necessary caveats about relying too much on stereotypes, one can at least say that this profession has been known to produce some quite outsized egos. Ego, stubbornness, and a taste for dramatics may have been an inevitable part of the job, given the creativity and, particularly in the eighteenth century, hard physical labor required of a chef de cuisine. Hemings had been trained in Paris, which gave him every reason to be proud. How many other Americans, black or white, had done that in the eighteenth century? He was special, and one detects in Hemings's demand from Jefferson the workings of a male prima donna. Recall that he beat his tutor Perrault when the hapless man dared to ask for, or asked for in the wrong way, the money that Hemings owed him. Now that he was legally free, he would have from Jefferson the dignity he deserved.

Former enslaved man, well-traveled, highly trained African American chef—all these various identities bundled into one frame made for a very complex and vulnerable man. Jefferson likely knew this about James Hemings, and, under the circumstances, his withholding attitude seems a little petty. For all his eighteenth-century limitations, Jefferson was smart enough to have figured out that Hemings's request was about more than just a piece of paper. But he would not give in. Perhaps Jefferson's nonresponsiveness was more than simple stubbornness or the arrogance of the former master. This was, in fact, a very delicate moment in his life. The presidency had been won, but there was no guarantee that the steady drip of indelicate items about his private life would simply go away. Things of that nature do not get better. They only get worse—especially when there is more information to be known, and a great incentive for others to find it out and publicize it. Jefferson would hardly have been paranoid if he had believed that his enemies were out there; they were, even if he did not know at this time which one would turn out to be the most virulent. Because he guarded his reaction to the public revelations about Sally Hemings so closely over the years, we cannot gauge the level of Jefferson's concern during the period just before the major storm of publicity broke. He cannot have been totally unconcerned, because this was something over which he had no control. Opening up a direct correspondence with Sally Hemings's brother in this climate may not have been what he wanted to do.

It is still a fascinating spectacle, however, seeing Hemings and Jefferson talk to one another through surrogates, each sending messages that the other was supposed to decipher through the filter of third-party communication. Jefferson received Evans's letter on February 28, and his response was a masterpiece of Jeffersonian control and subtlety, all the more so because he probably figured that Hemings would actually see the letter. He was about to leave for Monticello.

> I cannot go without thanking you for the trouble you were so good as to take as to James & Francis. I supposed I saw in the difficulties raised by James an unwillingness to come here, arising wholly from some attachment he had formed in Baltimore; for I cannot suspect an indisposition towards me. I concluded at once therefore not to urge him against inclination, and wrote to Philadelphia, where I have been successful in getting a cook equal to my wishes.

And then, after a few words about his relief that Francis Say would not be coming to Washington, he added,

> I would wish James to understand that it was in acquiesance to what I supposed his own wish that I did not repeat my application, after having so long rested on the expectation of having him.[13]

In other words, this was Hemings's fault, and Jefferson wanted Evans to tell him that (or have Hemings read it) while delivering other peevish messages to the younger man. First, Jefferson expressed his confidence that Hemings's reluctance to leave Baltimore could not possibly be related to him, since he obviously had not done anything wrong in not writing to Hemings as he asked. He refused to credit the legitimacy of Hemings's feelings about this and instead suggested that an "attachment," likely romantic, held Hemings in place. The "attachment" cannot have been a job, because Hemings had repeatedly stated his willingness to leave his employers to work for Jefferson. Jefferson's turn here is somewhat reminiscent of his complaint that Dr. Stras had "debauched" Robert Hemings from him by way of his having fallen in love with Stras's servant, Dolly. In both instances there is the intimation that the men's sexual passions had overridden what Jefferson took to be their reason. Why else would they not want to work for him?

And then to a man who had been trained by some of the best cooks in France, and who had every reason to be proud of his accomplishments over the years, Jefferson announced that he had found another chef whose talents were "equal to [his] wishes," that is, a chef just as talented as Hemings. He did not have to say *that*. This would be the last of the multiparty communication about getting Hemings to become the chef at the President's House. Had Hemings accepted, he would have been the first African American to play that role, and we have missed all the stories that could have sprung from that engagement. This was, however, not the end of the story linking the two men.

If James Hemings and Jefferson ever wrote to one another after this episode, Jefferson kept no record of it. But they must have communicated, because Hemings came back to work at Monticello sometime in August while Jefferson was on his summer vacation. Whatever difficulties they had had were resolved to some degree, and Jefferson hired Hemings at twenty dollars a month, twice his normal salary. Twenty dollars was also what Jefferson had originally thought to pay Honoré Julien, but bargaining brought the salary up to twenty-five dollars a month. Julien had already started, and having two cooks in the same kitchen was out of the question.[14] Even though Jefferson had a cook at Monticello, Peter Hemings, he evidently wanted to reach some rapprochement with James—perhaps going back to the old routine, with James working at Monticello when Jefferson came home and finding work on his own when Jefferson went back to Washington. That would still have given him substantial employment, for Jefferson fully intended to spend as much time at Monticello as he could. He would not repeat his behavior as secretary of state when he came home only one or two months each year.

Hemings was now in a less favorable position than he would have been had he taken the job at the President's House. As Jefferson's Washington-based chef, he, like Honoré Julien, could have remained in Washington and perhaps sought temporary work when Jefferson went home for vacations.

Now he was going back to Monticello, getting a salary, to be sure, but in the same surroundings he had escaped five years earlier.

Hemings did, however, have the consolation of family, one that had changed in composition since he had left the mountain. His half sister Betty Brown, who almost rivaled her mother in terms of the age gap between her first and last child, had given birth to two more children, Robert and Mary. According to Jefferson's eldest grandson, the father of these two children was likely Jefferson's nephew Samuel Carr. Hemings's sister Sally had lost her daughter Harriet, given birth to Beverley, lost another daughter in 1799, and had another, Harriet, in May of 1801.[15]

While a good salary and being in a familiar place might, on the surface, seem to have provided Hemings with some measure of comfort, the familiar place remained a slave plantation. He was free, but his family was not. With all the places he had been to, all the things he had been able to do, how did it feel to know that his mother and the rest of his family, save for Robert, had absolutely no chance to go with him, even had they wanted to. What did he think seeing his youngest sister locked in a cycle of having Jefferson's babies every two or three years? If they had stayed in France, she might have had a real husband. Her children would have been free from birth and not have had to depend upon their father's living long enough to see them to adulthood or bank on the kindness of Martha and Maria, who might actually have despised their half siblings and their mother. Instead, gossip mongers were now starting to spread stories about his sister. The September 14 issue of William Rind's *Virginia Federalist*, printed in Richmond, gave the most explicit information to date about Jefferson's relationship with her. According to the paper, sources said that "Mr. J," a man very high in office, had "a number of yellow children and that he is addicted to golden affections," presumably meaning Hemings's yellow-skinned sister.[16] Robert Hemings was likely the first in the family to know that his sister's life had been exposed, even though her name did not appear. It was only a matter of time before more specific stories appeared, but James Hemings would not live to see them.

About five days after the item about Jefferson and Sally Hemings appeared in the *Virginia Federalist*, James Hemings left Monticello. There was no reason for him to stay, because Jefferson was about to go back to Washington, and there was no need for a chef at Monticello when he was not in residence. Before Jefferson left, he paid Mrs. Snead, the midwife who had delivered his daughter, Harriet, born just four months earlier.[17] What no one knew at the time, of course, was that as one life in the Hemings family was just beginning, another was about to end.

WHEN JAMES HEMINGS left that September of 1801, it was probably the last time any of his family on the mountain saw him alive. Sometime near the end of October, or early November, Jefferson received word at the President's House, evidently through the network of the black community, that Hemings had killed himself. The news appears to have stunned Jefferson, and he wrote to William Evans for confirmation of what he had heard and to find out what he could about the matter. Evans wrote back to Jefferson with the terrible news. Hemings had, in fact, "committed an act of suicide." Evans told Jefferson that Hemings had been "delirious for some days previous to his having committed the act, and it is as the General opinion that drinking too freely was the cause."[18]

Jefferson wrote to Thomas Mann Randolph in December, saying that he had previously written to James Dinsmore, a white Monticello workman, about James Hemings's "tragical end."[19] Jefferson's letter to Dinsmore is no longer extant, so we may never know what he said to him about any additional information he had found out. When the Hemingses at Monticello learned of James's death is unknown. The slave communication network, however, known for its speed and reach, may have brought news to Monticello around the same time Jefferson learned of it. It is possible, in fact, that it was an inquiry from the mountain that prompted Jefferson's letter of inquiry to Evans. His passing reference in his letter to his son-in-law about Hemings's "tragical end" hints that people on the mountain already knew of the death.

James Hemings "tragical end" often appears in Jefferson scholarship as a cautionary tale, and a not so subtle justification for Jefferson's failure to free his slaves. *See, if he had freed more of them, they would have all gone crazy and killed themselves.* It is also framed as a matter of failure on Hemings's part. He was given a chance, and because he was not truly prepared for freedom, he failed. If he was not prepared, then none of Jefferson's slaves was prepared. In the end, not freeing them was a true blessing.

It is entirely possible that when James Hemings's African grandmother was being transported across the Atlantic Ocean to the West Indies, or directly to Virginia, she shared a vessel with other Africans who made the choice to jump overboard rather than live in the world that their European captors had planned for them. The vast majority did not make that choice. If we feel compelled to think of the captives' differing reactions in terms of strength versus weakness—and it is by no means clear we should—it makes more sense to speak of the uncommon strength of the people who stayed alive than to speak of the "weakness" or "failure" of those who could not endure what no human being was supposed to endure.

Hemings did not experience the Middle Passage. But he did live in a society that treated him and others like him inhumanely, with no clear prospect of changing that in his lifetime. How does one rest comfortably in such a place? How could Hemings, who had seen the world and knew a great deal of what was in it, without guilt, move ahead with a family forcibly held back? Five years after his death, Hemings's home state would pass a law providing that black people emancipated in Virginia would have to leave the state within one year or be reenslaved unless their owners petitioned the government to allow them to remain. Some masters did that, and in other instances the law was ignored. But that official show of contempt for a people who had built Virginia from its earliest days says volumes about the world Hemings lived in. He carried this extra burden along with all the normal struggles that attend human life.

Even outside of Virginia, there was no place in the United States where Hemings and his extended family would have been treated as full human beings. There probably was no place in the Western world where that could have happened, though he had lived in a city that offered at least some breathing room. Hemings might have lived longer, had he and his sister taken the chance to work together to build a life in Paris. Though racism was alive and well in France, there was a substantive difference between the treatment of mixed-race people there and their treatment in the United States. That did not change the condition of the entire race, but the extra social space might have made a difference to an individual as sensitive as James Hemings. By the end of his life, starting over in Paris was a moment that had passed. There would have been a great difference between putting down roots there in 1788 or 1789 with a sister who could have helped pay the rent and make a home and stepping alone into the uncertainty of postrevolutionary France.

That said, it is also true that Hemings had lived with all the problems of being black in America up until that moment. How did he become so despairing in the fall of 1801 that he felt he simply could not draw another breath? What comes immediately to mind is the missed opportunity in Washington. It appears that he did want to be chef de cuisine at the President's House all along. That he left his job and came back to Monticello shows that he had no deep animosity toward Jefferson. When this episode began, he was working in a Baltimore inn, a place that provided a living, but where he had no prospect of doing the kind of cooking that he had been trained to do, and had done, in Paris, New York, Philadelphia, and Monticello. Jefferson might have been casual and republican about his attire during this period, but he spared no expense on food and wine. He spent a fortune on both during his time in the President's House and was said to have set one of the best tables in the country. Had he accepted Jefferson's offer, Hemings would have been in charge of all this, but his hesitancy had destroyed this opportunity. There was no way to fix things. Jefferson was not going to fire Honoré Julien and his wife, who had both left Philadelphia to come work for him. Hemings had missed the chance of a lifetime.

The bungled job negotiations were important. But other, more serious underlying problems haunted Hemings. Depression and suicide are complex phenomena, even with the medications we have today. Predispositions to either can be exacerbated, or ameliorated, by circumstances that are often out of one's control, and it seems as primitive to think of this in terms of weakness or failure as to believe that the mentally ill are possessed by evil spirits. Enslaved people suffered from depression and sometimes committed suicide, as did free blacks. Even prosperous free whites, to the bewilderment of those around them, sometimes killed themselves when they came to believe there would be no awakening from whatever nightmares had seized their minds. Hemings's life was probably more difficult because he had no wife and family to succor him and to support in return. He seems to have been on his own—alone—in the most profound way. With that said, the fact is that the personal demons, or physiological idiosyncrasies, that drove Hemings to kill himself will remain unknown to us.

The record on James Hemings goes poignantly silent after the final letters about his death. We do not know whether his family sent for his body and had him buried in the slave cemetery at Monticello or whether he rests in a grave in Baltimore. The person who lived in Jefferson-related documents as "Jame," "Jim," "Jamey," or "Gimme," from the time he was a small boy, formed no part of the stories Jefferson's white family left for posterity. He first appears in Jefferson's memorandum books as "Jamey," a seven-year-old enslaved boy given a small sum of money by the man who had just married his half sister and owner. Isaac Jefferson remembered him as "Jim," a teenager riding on horseback to Williamsburg with the family of the newly minted governor Jefferson in the midst of America's Revolutionary War. Then he was the intrepid "James" traveling on his own to Rouen, France, to find accommodations two days after he and Jefferson had arrived in that country. Adrien Petit, whom he met in France and who was probably the first white person he had worked with as an equal, knew him as "Gimme" as they collaborated on two continents to run Jefferson's household. We do not know what his sister Sally and the rest of his family called him—though "Jimmy" seems a good bet, the French Petit not likely to have derived "Jimmy" from "James" without having heard him called that. We do know, however, that he and his name were cherished. The name James was given to several nephews and passed down the family perhaps long after all memory of the man had been lost. Besides that, and a few of his recipes preserved at Monticello, his chief legacy is his story. James Hemings's was a singular life: an eighteenth-century Afro-Virginian who lived abroad in France, who was passionate and intellectually curious enough to hire a tutor to teach him to speak and think in a different language, who was literate, who became a chef de cuisine, who negotiated his freedom, and who continued to journey far and wide after he became a free man. Surely it broke his family's hearts to lose him.

Exposure

"It is well known that the man, whom it delighteth the people to honor, keeps, and for many years has kept, as his concubine, one of his slaves. Her name is SALLY." With those words published in the September 1, 1802, issue of the *Richmond Recorder*, James Callender opened the door to Sally Hemings's world at Monticello, or at least the world as he chose to portray it.[20] It had been almost thirteen years since she and her brother had returned to Monticello. James was tragically gone. The first anniversary of his death loomed, and this now twenty-nine-year-old mother of two faced a crisis that her sixteen-year-old self could never have imagined when she came back to America with Jefferson. She had no doubt expected a private life. This was exposure in the most public and hostile way. The cruelty Callender directed toward her continued over the course of several months.

Callender's informers were Jefferson's neighbors in Charlottesville and people in Richmond, and one gets a sense from what he got right and what he got wrong how familiar his informants were with life at Monticello. In his original piece he spoke of Hemings's and Jefferson's "son" "Tom," who was "ten or twelve years of age." He also said that Hemings had gone "to France in the same vessel with Mr. Jefferson and his two daughters." In his column of September 15, he mentioned that she had five children.[21] His next piece revealed that a man in Richmond had "bet him a suit of clothes or any sum of money" that the story was true, but pointed out that Callender had made an error in his first story: Hemings had not gone to Paris with Jefferson but traveled later.[22] Of course, that man clearly was not talking off the top of his head, for that was a specific detail about a long-ago event that no one could have guessed. The next column purported to correct information about Tom's age. "He is not *big enough* at least our correspondent thinks so, to have been in existence fifteen or sixteen years ago. Our information goes to twelve or thirteen years (emphasis in original)."[23]

Sally Hemings did not have five children in 1802. She had, however, given birth five times, but three of her children had died. The people talking to Callender may have been close enough to know when she got pregnant— there would have been reason to gossip about that—but were not closely following her children's lives after that time.[24] The mountain was full of fair-skinned enslaved children of all ages, some of them Hemingses who probably resembled one another. Who from the outside could, or would want to, be keeping track of who belonged to whom?

One strongly suspects that Callender's informants actually told him that Hemings had lost children, and he simply felt that saying Jefferson had five children with an enslaved woman sounded better than just two, for that clearly established the relationship as long-standing. What seemed to bother him, and later commentators who joined in, was the apparent stability of the relationship, which suggested that Hemings was something like a wife to Jefferson. That, they believed, was an insult to white women, for this was, in modern terminology, a zero-sum game. If he chose to live with a particular African American woman, that inevitably meant he rejected all white women. Awful as he was, Callender was no fool. Telling his readers, in the midst of articles meant to be jeering and hostile, that Hemings had once had five children, but that only two survived, might actually have triggered some empathy with her. Nearly all of his readers would have known someone who lost a child, or lost one themselves, in a world where diseases carried away the offspring of all classes and races. Only the lowest of the low could have failed to sympathize with a mother who had endured such losses.

As his biographer Michael Durey pointed out, Callender had a particular penchant for exaggeration, a not unhelpful trait for a polemicist. At one point he said that Hemings had up to thirty "gallants of all colors."[25] Five or six would not have been enough; she had to have thirty of them in *all* colors. He dubbed Hemings and Jefferson's purported eldest son "President Tom" and made him an important part of his series—President Tom who bore "a striking, though sable" resemblance to Jefferson, President Tom who was "putting on airs." It was the perfect way to ridicule Jefferson, a child with his same name, a sable Tom Jr. who strutted about full of himself—showing the clear dangers of racial intermixture. That's what happens when you mix the races, he was saying, you get these ridiculous creatures who do not know their place. Not one of the other supposedly five living children was ever mentioned. Neither four-and-a-half-year-old Beverley nor the infant Harriet could have served Callender's needs so well.

Callender's discussion of President Tom indicates that his multiple informants were, in a somewhat confused way, trying to fix Hemings's first child's age and, thus the beginning of her relationship with Jefferson, by reference to her trip to France. They were simply going on when they remembered Hemings's first child was born—when the gossip started—sometimes mixing up when she went to France with when she returned. That is the reason for Callender's language in his "correction" of himself, saying that Tom was not "big enough to have been in existence "fifteen or sixteen years ago." Using fifteen or sixteen years as a marker for this child's "existence" would have taken things back to around 1787, when Hemings had gone to France. Of course, she did not have a baby when she went there. She had her baby when she returned. Had that child lived, he or she would indeed have been twelve years old.

Hemings could have expected the usual run of gossip about her and Jefferson. As the mistress of the plantation owner, she would have had all eyes fixed on her—the eyes of the enslaved, as well as any others who knew of her circumstance. She could not have expected to have her name in the newspaper with a virulent Scotsman branding her a "slut as common as the pavement," suggesting that she lived in the pigsty at Monticello.[26]

His hatred for her was unreasoning and unbounded. Why? And why had Jefferson brought this man into her life, anyway?

The basic outline of Jefferson's history with Callender is straightforward and familiar. He noticed Callender's undeniable talent for polemics during the mid-1790s and thought the ardent Republican might be useful in his struggles with the Federalists. Callender had shown that he was willing to go to almost any length to hurt those with whom he disagreed—a trait that should have given Jefferson pause about getting involved with him. Unfortunately, it did not. The 1790s for Jefferson was life during wartime. The Federalists had to be stopped no matter what. To all appearances, Callender was a comrade, and Jefferson optimistically (naïvely) thought their shared political beliefs a sound basis for a connection in times of war. Callender would only go after those whom he was supposed to go after—the much hated Federalists. Although Jefferson later played down the closeness of their connection, his early financial support of Callender, and encouraging words and gestures, put him into the position of being something of a mentor to him.[27] Being mentor to James Callender, however, was like walking a cobra on a leash. Jefferson never had any reasonable prospect of knowing when Callender might turn on him.

By the end of the 1790s, Callender's sharp pen and criticism of the Adams administration got him sent to jail in Richmond under the power of the Alien and Sedition Acts. Jefferson resolved to pardon everyone convicted under the law when he became president. Callender had served his term before Jefferson took office and had to pay a $200 fine. Jefferson ordered the federal marshal David Meade Randolph, brother-in-law to Thomas Mann Randolph, to give Callender back his money. Randolph hesitated, infuriating Callender, who perversely saw Jefferson as responsible for Randolph's behavior. He grew angry when Jefferson failed to answer one of his letters and demanded a patronage job—postmaster of Richmond. Even as he seethed about the perceived ingratitude of Jefferson and the Republicans—he really had suffered for doing their bidding in the climate of the Alien and Sedition Acts—he decided to give himself insurance. After his release from jail, he went to Charlottesville to find out if the hints in the newspapers about Jefferson and an enslaved woman were true. He also made inquiries in Richmond.[28]

When Jefferson learned of Callender's rising anger, he thought additional money might mollify him. It did not. He wanted to be postmaster

of Richmond, the only thing that could repay him for the time he had
spent in jail for having roasted the Republicans' enemies in the pages
of the *Richmond Examiner* and his other publications. Callender went to
Washington and met with James Madison, but the meeting satisfied no one.
When told of this, Jefferson sent his secretary Meriwether Lewis, of later
Lewis and Clark fame, with an additional fifty dollars to give to Callender,
along with a promise to help him get reimbursed for the fine he had paid.
This inflamed him further, for he now realized that there was no chance
that Jefferson would give him a job in his administration.[29]

Callender's fine was repaid, but his rage was now out of control. He felt
used, and that was not all. James Callender's hatred of blacks was full-blown
and vicious. He was genuinely horrified that the man who had once been
his hero and benefactor had an African American mistress and children by
her. Jefferson, a traitor to the white race, had been unworthy of his respect
from the beginning. In his fury, Callender sought to humiliate Jefferson by
making Hemings a special target, when she had not done anything to him
at all. As noted earlier, Callender had made part of his career in Richmond
excoriating the white men of the town for being involved with black women.
He claimed then that he was concerned only about married men who were
committing adultery, giving a pass to bachelors. Despite what he said, the
passion he repeatedly brought to his denunciations and the things he said
about black people in general make plain that it was interracial mixing, not
adultery, that really infuriated him.[29]

Jefferson had been a widower for two decades. It is highly unlikely that
he ever frequented Charlottesville taverns and dances with Hemings or
took her to the theater, like the men of Richmond whom Callender assailed.
Jefferson and Hemings's world was private. Her life centered on caring for
his rooms and his belongings—a space Jefferson guarded closely. Although
she may have traveled to Philadelphia, Washington, and Poplar Forest, in all
events she was strictly of Jefferson's domestic world. Not that consistency
would have mattered to Callender, but his attack upon Jefferson the bachelor and Hemings the completely private person made no sense, given his
earlier posture about attacking only married men who publicly broke their
marriage vows.

There is no record of what Jefferson ever said to his white family
about Callender's writings in 1802, and no record of what the Hemingses
thought. Just as Jefferson's white neighbors knew about the exposure of

the relationship, members of the enslaved community knew as well. The only question that any of these people could have had at this point was what Jefferson would do next. This crisis had implications for his public and private lives, the former more than the latter. For most people who did not live at or in the environs of Monticello, this was a revelation. For the people who lived there, it was not. By the time of Callender's exposé, both the Hemings and the Jefferson families, and other relatives close to them, had had at least twelve years to adapt themselves to Sally and Thomas's lives at Monticello. They did it in the way that all families, at one time or another, are forced to deal with potentially embarrassing situations involving their loved ones; they closed ranks. One of the great strengths (and great weaknesses) of the institution of the family is that family members protect or, depending upon the situation, cover for one another. Members are anxious, sometimes to the detriment of themselves or other individuals in the family, to present a united and, usually, positive front to the outside world.

If one were to drop down into the middle of any seemingly bizarre family situation, one would wonder how these people could possibly live in those circumstances. The people living in it, however, would have had years to fit themselves into whatever strange configuration one found them in. A thousand tradeoffs, exchanges, and accommodations would have been made, completely away from the view of outsiders. The family adjusts and endures. In the eighteenth and nineteenth centuries, it had no choice.

Slavery simply provided families in the South with many more ways to be bizarre than in regions where it never took hold or was abandoned early on. Fathers owning sons, brothers giving away brothers as wedding gifts, sisters selling their aunts, husbands having children with their wives and then their wives, enslaved half sisters, enslaved black children and their free little white cousins, living and playing together on the same plantation—things that by every measure violate basic notions of what modern-day people think family is supposed to be about. This was one of the myriad reasons why slavery was a horrific thing. These weird family situations actually violated emerging norms for the family in the eighteenth and nineteenth centuries, which is why southern whites of that time worked so assiduously to hide this aspect of southern life.

One of the more difficult things for modern-day observers to accept is that Jefferson's daughters knew of his relationship with Hemings, in much the same way that their mother was said to have lived with John Wayles and

Elizabeth Hemings without knowing they were having multiple children together. The people of their time, however, at least the ones who wrote about it, absolutely assumed that these women knew. In fact, much of the commentary about Jefferson and Hemings dwelled on his daughters' likely feelings about this over the years. Their contemporaries never entertained the notion that the women of the household did not know what was going on in their own houses. They understood their community and its mores, and knew that such situations were not uncommon. Martha and Maria's father's fame and position in society could not protect their family from things that were endemic to the institution of slavery.

Jefferson's white daughters, like white women all over the South in their time, were expected to adjust to the men in their lives, not the other way around. They loved him dearly, and would not have stopped doing so for any conceivable reason—certainly not for having a mistress. It is hard to see through the heavy prism of the Victorian age that followed Jefferson's time, but celibacy was not an expectation among the people of the eighteenth century. Martha and Maria could no more force that on their father than they could have made him marry a white woman he did not want to marry, a thing that would have been to their distinct disadvantage anyway. After the deep disappointment in the 1790s, described earlier, when her father-in-law remarried and destroyed her chance of becoming the mistress of Tuckahoe, Martha Randolph had lived a somewhat unsettled existence, moving between Monticello, Eppington, Varina, Belmont, Edgehill, and, finally, back to Monticello.

The Randolph-Harvie marriage was a socially acceptable union that had been, in fact, personally disastrous for Martha and her children, who would have grown up in and inherited the grand house Tuckahoe, had Thomas Mann Randolph not remarried. Maria Eppes, who married in 1797, was in a much more stable situation with her husband and lived about a hundred miles from Monticello. By the time Callender began ranting about Hemings, these women had likely made all the necessary adjustments. Sally Hemings was a woman they knew, their mother's half sister with whom they had grown up. This was in all ways a family matter, and, as so often happens, they may have resented the intrusion of outsiders more than what was going on in their family. What neither Martha nor Maria had bargained for, however, was that Jefferson's decision to return to public life would result in making their privately made accommodations about their family life known to the world.

As for the Hemingses, all they could do was watch and wait to see whether this new public phase would compel Jefferson to make a change. Would Hemings and her children remain at Monticello and things continue as they had, would Jefferson simply end their association, or would he send her, Beverley, and Harriet away? Following so closely upon James Hemings's heartrending death, the family must have felt that a plague had been visited upon them.

27

✿

THE PUBLIC WORLD AND THE
PRIVATE DOMAIN

WHEN JEFFERSON WENT to live at the President's House in
1801, he took no member of the family who had been the most
intensely involved with him for the preceding twenty-seven
years. Hemingses probably visited him, including Sally, for there was periodic traffic between Jefferson's two households during his eight years in
Washington. At least every six months, David Hern Jr., an enslaved man
at Monticello, traveled to the capital and back, carrying letters, plants, new
horses for Jefferson, and other items. Even Robert Hemings, who had been
with the new president at the start of his national career in Philadelphia
in 1776, may have come to see the man with whom he had spent so
much time and who was now at the pinnacle of his power. But the closest the family came to having a full-time representative there was Edith
(Edy) Hern Fossett, the fifteen-year-old who came to Washington in 1802
to be an apprentice cook to Honoŕe Julien, the man who had taken the
job that Jefferson had originally intended for James Hemings. Sometime
in the early 1800s, perhaps before she left Monticello, she married Joseph
Fossett, the son of Mary Hemings. This Hemings in-law would remain at
the President's House for six years.[1]

Jefferson never gave a good account of why none of Fossett's relatives
by marriage were chosen for her assignment, or to work alongside her in
other capacities. When he was governor of Virginia, he took almost his
entire household staff to Williamsburg and Richmond. Although he did
not repeat this when he went to Philadelphia as secretary of state, he had a

good reason. His daughters were still living on the mountain. Martha and her husband had yet to settle into a habitable place, and Maria would not join him in Philadelphia for several months. Both Jefferson daughters were married by the time he became president, and the Hemings women were in "idleness" at Monticello when he was away.

Jefferson did give an explanation of sorts for his choice when he expressed his preference for having white servants in the President's House. It was easier, he said, to sever ties with them were they to "misbehave"—an odd statement, given the facts of life in his Washington household. He actually had a number of black servants there, enslaved and free, and it is unfathomable that he really believed that Peter, Sally, and Critta Hemings, and Betty Brown, or any of the younger generation of Hemingses, for that matter, would have behaved so atrociously in Washington that he might have wanted to "exchange them." As for Peter Hemings, we have no reason at all to think that his evidently agreeable personality made Jefferson leave him at home. There was likely something else. While he enjoyed Peter's cooking and thought highly of him overall, he apparently did not believe James's younger brother his equal in talent and, thus, up to the task of being chef in the President's House. There is no hint that Critta Hemings ever gave anyone a problem, and the few reports of Sally Hemings give the impression of a sweet and reasonable person. Betty Brown may have been another matter. A Jefferson granddaughter at one point described her as being "a greater virago than ever,"[2] suggesting that she had been one for a long time, but Brown was not so much trouble that Jefferson made any move to get rid of her. She did have small children, but Edith Fossett and Frances (Fanny) Gillette Hern, Fossett's sister-in-law who joined her in Julien's kitchen in 1806, would have small children, too. Between the two of them, five youngsters were born in the President's House, including James Fossett, evidently named for Joseph Fossett's tragically lost uncle.

Why Jefferson did not bring Sally Hemings to Washington on a full-time basis is obvious. Living with her anyplace other than Monticello would have caused all sorts of complications, not the least of them cute babies running around who looked just like him. And having a woman in the President's House whom he favored, but who lacked the recognized power of a wife, could have created all sorts of jealousy and tension among the domestic staff—the kind of thing Jefferson sought to avoid at all cost. This was particularly so since at least five white women—the wife of Jefferson's chef, the wives of two other servants, and two laundresses—lived at the President's House. Each of the wives, at various times, worked for Jefferson, too.³ This was the largest group of white women at any of Jefferson's residences when he was in public life. There had been one female cook at the Hôtel de Langeac before James Hemings took over as chef and before Sally Hemings arrived. There was, of course, the ill-fated Mrs. Seche, the wife of his coachman in Philadelphia who had tangled with Adrien Petit, whom Jefferson had brought all the way from France to be his housekeeper. The presence of five white women, and the children of one of the women, changed the usually male dynamic of Jefferson's away-from-Monticello households, and one suspects that the situation would have been potentially volatile had Sally Hemings and her sisters lived in the President's House.

Jefferson's white daughters had grown up with the Hemings women and were used to their special status. Their family history allowed them to put these women in context. Very importantly, they had the luxury of viewing them from their positions as the unquestioned mistresses of Monticello whenever they were in residence. The middling and lower-class white women in Jefferson's presidential household could have had no ingrained understanding of how these women fit into Jefferson's world, and no firm basis for security about their status in his eyes. There would almost inevitably have come a moment when Jefferson would have had to arbitrate some dispute between these free white women and the enslaved African American women whom he had encouraged all their lives to see themselves as having a special relationship to him. Mrs. Seche's dispute with Petit, and the trouble it caused Jefferson, comes most immediately to mind as an example. There Jefferson was forced to choose between one servant to whom he had long-standing ties and another who was only recently of his world. Petit was nowhere near as close to Jefferson as the Hemings women. If they had been mixed in with his Washington "family," and he made the wrong choice about one of them, an "anti-Hemings" choice, he would not only have upset his household in Washington; the hard feelings would have traveled all the way back to Monticello. There were always benefits and burdens to having his household staff on the mountain composed of one family. Whatever he did for, or to, one member would be known and judged by the others. Under the circumstances it was far better to have a staff made up of people who were on relatively equal footing in terms of their associations with him.

A complement of reasons, of varying strengths lay behind Jefferson's choice to leave the Hemingses at home when he went to Washington. His evolving sense of himself and his position in the world also influenced his relationship to the family. Jefferson had been remaking his image from the time he was elected vice-president in 1796. With his ascent to that office, the age of the plain, austere Jefferson had arrived, and he carried it through his presidency and beyond. Much has been made of his shift from the somewhat Frenchified southern aristocrat, to the plainly attired, unassuming embodiment of republican simplicity and virtue, his straight hair undressed and unpowdered. Was it all an act, an example of Jeffersonian duplicity and hypocrisy? If it was an act, it was a useful one. Politics is theater, and the successful politician is the one who can skillfully bring just the right symbolism to the cultural and political moment at hand. Jefferson understood that political power was shifting to the so-called common man, and that it was therefore critical to do away with the most obvious trappings of Old World elitism.

Even as his Federalist opponents ridiculed this new homespun version of Jefferson, the voters took to it. They were not dumb. They knew he was a wealthy man compared with them, but they apparently appreciated that he at least made the effort to appear as one of their own—thus acknowledging that they were the country's political future. This cost Jefferson little, as his new persona easily took him into what today would be known as shabby chic—like the modern-day trust funder so confident in his social position that he uses duct tape to wrap up his worn docksiders when he could easily buy a thousand new pairs. Certainly the Federalists ultimately did themselves no favor by making sport of Jefferson's attempts to appear in solidarity with the common people. The fun all ended for them, of course, with the election of 1800.

This new incarnation of Jefferson not only affected his public conduct but also altered the way he deployed his personal servants. Members of the Hemings family, and others enslaved at Monticello, had been the most obvious evidence of his high position in society. What could have been more elitist than having Robert and then James Hemings following him about as his manservant? In later years his grandson-in-law Nicholas Trist, in keeping with that generation of the family's habit of saying things about Jefferson's life that were patently untrue in order to control his image, claimed that Jefferson "usually" did without a "body servant." According to Trist, his famous in-law followed the motto that one was "never to allow another to do for you what you can do for yourself." It was, therefore, Trist explained, "incompatible with the sentiment of Manhood, as it existed in him, that one human being should be followed about by another as his shadow."[4] Leaving aside the fact that Jefferson could probably have handled a plow as well as—and probably better than—many of the men *and* women he had tilling his fields, Trist's statement erases significant portions of the life and efforts of Jupiter Evans, Robert and James Hemings, and Burwell Colbert. All of these men were, at one time or another, Jefferson's body servants. Evans and the Hemings brothers were before Trist's time at Monticello, but he knew that Colbert was, in Jefferson's later years, virtually his "shadow." The notion that Jefferson had no use for such things was born in the 1790s, and with it came a change in the trajectory of his life with the Hemingses. There were still other factors.

As many historians have also noted, Jefferson's overall attitude regarding slavery underwent a subtle shift after his return from France. The young man who had been very vocal, for one of his station and place, on the subject of emancipation, fell pretty much silent from his middle age on. In earlier times he had spoken of legislated gradual emancipation when the idea was anathema to the overwhelming majority of his class cohort, and while in France he contemplated importing German workers to live and labor at Monticello along with slaves who would be freed and transformed into something akin to European tenant farmers. In a letter of 1789, he wrote,

> I will settle them and my slaves, on farms of 50. acres each, intermingled, and place all on the footing of the Metayers . . . of Europe. Their children shall be brought up, as others are, in habits of property and foresight, and I have no doubt but that they will be good citizens.[5]

Jefferson ceased such talk in the 1790s. He was a national figure with his base in Virginia, where there was no strong clamor for abolitionist politics at any level of white society. Actually, no clamor existed at the national level either. Despite his protests to the contrary, once Jefferson saw in the early 1790s that his vision for America after the Revolution might actually be thwarted by Hamilton and his followers and what would become the

"Federal party," there was really little chance that he was going to walk away from politics altogether. Although he wrote to others about his seeming contentment during his first retirement, he later confessed to his daughter Maria that he had been deeply unhappy for long stretches of time during that period.[6] He loved Monticello, but he simply did not find enough there to occupy his time, particularly when there were really pressing things he wanted to have happen on the national political scene. Jefferson was not ready for retirement until he had been in the position to try to accomplish what he thought should be accomplished for the United States. His election in 1800 allowed him to do that. Building the nation was Jefferson's true obsession, not the end of slavery and definitely not the racial question.

As he retreated from the antislavery rhetoric of his youth, and grew comfortable in his role as the champion of the common man (the common white man), Jefferson, like others of his type, began to accommodate himself to the institution of slavery. As was discussed earlier, Lucia Stanton has detailed his plans for his version of a kinder, gentler slavery at Monticello with his experiments with the nail factory. He also brought in overseers who eschewed violence in favor of incentives as a way of motivating enslaved workers; for unexplained reasons, however, the men did not remain in his service. Jefferson was again, in all of this, ahead of his time—on the leading edge of adopting the sort of paternalism that would in the coming decades turn his white grandchildren's generation into full-throated apologists for the peculiar institution.

One of the signs of the change in Jefferson is that he never again put an enslaved man from Monticello in the position that Martin, Robert, and James Hemings occupied. Their relative freedom in the 1770s and 1780s made sense in the heady days of the American Revolution and the pre–Saint Domingue early American Republic. Jefferson was not inclined to free these men totally—he never really wanted to let go of anyone who had ever been close to him—but they were able to move about as if they were free. This cannot have been a matter of his greater affection for these three men than for the ones he encountered later. There is no reason to believe that he felt closer to Martin Hemings than to Burwell Colbert. He probably liked him less, but he gave the elder Hemings a much wider range of operation than he did Colbert, who was thoroughly of the home.

Colbert was thirteen when Jefferson became vice-president, seventeen when he became president, and Jefferson had already singled him out as a special favorite. Although he worked in the nailery, he was not indispensable there, and certainly could have attended Jefferson in Philadelphia and Washington. In the 1770s his uncle Robert at age twelve was following Jefferson around on horseback and acting as his manservant. In the 1780s it was sometimes the teenage James Hemings. John Freeman, the man Jefferson hired to fill a role that Colbert could have played at the President's House—that of footman, waiter, and traveling attendant to Jefferson—was only three years older than Colbert and did not have the advantage of long acquaintance with Jefferson. Ironically enough, Freeman became a member of the Hemings family through his marriage to Colbert's sister Melinda.[7]

Bringing Colbert to Washington would not have been a case of taking a person who had no knowledge of service and putting him out of his league. Colbert, his brother, and cousins also worked in the house at Monticello and knew what it meant to serve there. By the mid-1800s Colbert had experience as a painter and glazer, but there is no indication that he was allowed to leave Monticello and ply his trade for others during the months that Jefferson was away. Instead, Jefferson told his overseer to give him spending money whenever he asked. This was the difference between treating a person as an adult versus treating him as a child, which, after all, is what paternalism is about.

It appears that Jefferson did not want his particular "favored" slaves to see and get used to the outside world. Just as he did not want "city negroes" at Monticello, at a certain point he no longer wanted his favorite Monticello "negroes" to go to the city. This was particularly true of Colbert, whose presence in Washington would have made the most sense. After all, what had been Jefferson's experiences with the young man's uncles? The end result of their autonomy and forays in the world at large was that each of them grew restless in his service and anxious to end his formal association with him. When they wanted to leave, he was not emotionally prepared to thwart them, though he easily could have. So he avoided this possible "bad" scenario by leaving the person who most reasonably could have played a role in Washington at home and making him stay there.

The only other enslaved people Jefferson brought from the mountain to live and work in the President's House were teenage girls, all of them to be trained as cooks. The first, Ursula, who joined the Hemings family when she became the wife of Wormley Hughes, was a member of another important family at Monticello with ties all the way back to Jefferson's wife. She was the granddaughter of George and Ursula Granger, the "King" and "Queen" of Monticello and the niece of Isaac of the famed memoir and photograph. George Granger was the only black man to serve as an overseer at Monticello, and his wife, Ursula, had been the head cook before the Hemings brothers took over the position in the days after Jefferson returned from Paris. Ursula, it will be remembered, served as a wet nurse for Jefferson's eldest daughter when her mother was unable to produce enough milk for her and the Jeffersons feared the infant might die. Ursula's "good breast of milk," as Jefferson put it, saved her life.

At the dawn of the nineteenth century, the Granger family faced its own catastrophe. George and Ursula, and their eldest son, George Jr., all died in less than a twelve-month period in 1799 and 1800. After falling ill, each consulted a black doctor in a nearby county who gave them medicine that the Jefferson family believed poisoned them. Jupiter Evans, who also died in 1800, had consulted the same doctor, who, in Martha Randolph's words, "absconded" after learning of Evans's death.[8] Given her family history, and the still fresh tragedy that must have devastated her, the remaining members of the Granger family, and the other members of the enslaved community at Monticello, Jefferson's idea to have the fourteen-year-old Ursula Granger come to Washington and train to be Monticello's new cook, like her grandmother and namesake before her, appears a sentimental choice.

Jefferson's plan did not work. Ursula lasted less than a year. She was actually a few months pregnant when she came to the President's House, a fact no doubt unknown to Jefferson when he decided to bring her to Washington. Indeed, Ursula's child, not Martha Jefferson Randolph's son James, was the first child born in the President's House.[9] Being pregnant, and a first-time mother with an infant, was not the best way to begin an apprenticeship to a French chef. She apparently did not fare well as a cook trainee and went home to resume life as an agricultural worker, and to have nine more children with her husband, Wormely Hughes. Her efforts in Washington were not totally lost, because she often helped out in the kitchen when she was not in the fields. Edith Fossett and Frances Hern were her replacements, and these "two good girls" as Jefferson's maître d'hôtel at the President's House, Etienne Lemaire, called them, succeeded where Ursula apparently failed. In fact, Fossett became the head of the kitchen at Monticello when Jefferson retired from politics in 1809, Peter Hemings having moved on to other trades, including that of a brewer. It was Fossett's cooking that visitors to Monticello like Margaret Thornton and Daniel Webster would extol in the years to come.

With his very traditional views about the natures of men and women, Jefferson probably saw these teenage girls as less likely to cause problems than teenage males, at least not the kind that would make them grow restless and want to go out into the world. All of them had ties to men at Monticello that they might not have wanted to break. It is true that Sally Hemings, a teenager, had rebelled temporarily in France, but her situation in Paris was quite different from that of Ursula's, Edith's, and Frances's in Washington. The nation's capital had no law that provided an easy avenue to freedom, no revolution was brewing just outside the walls of the President's House, and the three teenagers in Washington had no older brother there helping them think they could build a life away from Jefferson.

The presence of Hughes, Fossett, and Hern may have fueled the rumor that Jefferson kept a "stable of mulatto slave girls"[10] at the President's House, and had an African harem, for his sexual pleasure. We do not know about Ursula Granger's mother, but, as noted earlier, the Grangers were not mixed race, and we have no reason to believe that Ursula would have been thought of as a "mulatto." Precision, however, was not the point of these exercises, or perhaps Ursula represented the "African" part of the contingent. Some of Edith Fossett's children passed for white, so she was likely fair-skinned, as was her husband, Joseph. The members of Frances Hern's family, the Gillettes, were also described as mixed race.

Whatever these young ladies' skin color, President Jefferson lived under a cloud of suspicion about his relations with African American women. Because many whites saw engaging in interracial sex as something akin to a malady or an indelible character flaw, having sex with black women would be a recurring event for him, a terrible and mighty thing beyond his control. After the Hemings revelations, Jefferson, they said, was *the kind* of person who would do *something like that*. This racist formulation cast any African American woman in his vicinity as his likely mistress, with no consideration of how that might have distorted the lives of the women involved. If these women had children, they belonged to him. The great irony, of course, is that just as Jefferson moved to make the Hemingses strictly a part of his private world, his return to the public domain forced his private life with one family member out into the open.

"His Mechanics"

As the locus of Jefferson's relations with the Hemingses shifted strictly to Monticello, John Hemings and Joseph Fossett—son and grandson, respectively, to Elizabeth Hemings—became the family's new face at Monticello at the turn of the nineteenth century. Unlike their older relatives, these two young men, particularly Hemings, grew close to Jefferson, not as personal attendants but as craftsmen whose skills he respected. They began to come into their own in their separate fields during Jefferson's presidency— Hemings, the carpenter and joiner, and Fossett, the blacksmith and metalworker. These two young men, from very different pathways, became the most important enslaved artisans on the mountain.

In many respects, the less well-known Joseph Fossett's progress through life is the more poignant, for the theme of separation from family permeated the line of his mother, Mary Hemings, throughout their time at Monticello and afterward. Their experiences show starkly how tenuous the Hemingses' "privileges" really were. Fossett's elder brother and sister, Daniel and Molly, had been given as wedding presents in 1787 and 1790 when young Joseph, born in November 1780, was seven and then ten.[11] We most typically think of the pain of the mother and child separated, but enslaved children suffered, too, when their brothers and sisters were taken from them. While children of all races and classes lived with the loss of siblings through death, young Joseph and his enslaved cohort knew they could lose their family members through the normal operations of the systems of slavery and property.

When Daniel and Molly were taken, Joseph was old enough to know, and presumably miss, his older brother and sister. If fears of death brought nightmares to all young children who buried siblings, Joseph Fossett, at seven and ten, could lie in bed at night and fear that his time to be given away might come. Although Molly had served as Martha Randolph's maid from around 1790, and probably came to Monticello when Martha visited, Daniel, whose last name was Farley, was farther away in Louisa County with Jefferson's sister Anna Scott Marks. The removal of Daniel and Molly from Joseph Fossett's daily life provided a harsh first lesson regarding his family's true position in the world. Jefferson often spoke of the transfers of enslaved people between and among his white relatives as keeping slaves "in the family," as if that mitigated the harshness of family breakups. Whatever he felt he had to tell himself in these situations, one seriously doubts that Mary Hemings and her children really considered Anna and Hastings Marks, or Martha and Tom Randolph, as members of *their* family.

Around the same time his brother was given away, Joseph, along with his sisters Molly and Betsy, went to live in the home of Thomas Bell, who had leased their mother while Jefferson was in Paris. Two years after Molly was given to Martha Randolph, Joseph faced another loss when Bell bought his mother and the two children she had borne him during the time of the lease. Mary Hemings was forced to choose between the possibility of freedom for herself and her two youngest children and living in bondage with all four of the children left to her. She decided, of course, to remain with Bell, perhaps calculating that this offered the best chance to rescue her other children in the future. Joseph and Betsy's aunts and uncles almost certainly stepped in to help raise the twelve- and nine-year-olds. That was a tradition born of necessity in enslaved families, for they always lived with the reality of separation and had to have ways of taking care of their own. It appears that these early and recurrent reminders of the fragility of family bonds in slavery, rather than breaking his sense of family, made Joseph Fossett more determined to keep his family together. As things turned out, he would need every ounce of that determination in the years to come.

Fossett was twenty when Jefferson became president. One of the original nail boys in the Monticello plantation factory, he distinguished himself for his efficiency in churning out product for Jefferson. Like some of his other Hemings cousins in the nailery, he worked part-time in the house, a scene that united him with his sister Betsy, who had become Sally Hemings's replacement as Maria Jefferson's maid. The siblings lived together, for they were listed in the Farm Book in 1794, two years after they were separated from their mother, as making up their own household.[12] When Betsy Hemings left the mountain in 1797, when Maria got married, Joseph, then approaching seventeen, became the last of Mary Hemings's children to remain at Monticello.

Fossett's skill in the nailery suggested to Jefferson that the young man had a particular talent for metalworking. He therefore put the sixteen-year-old under the training of George Granger Jr. to become a blacksmith. Within a year of Granger's death, in 1799, Fossett became the next foreman of the nail factory. He also came under the tutelage of the extremely talented, but equally erratic, William Stewart, the blacksmith from Philadelphia who lived next door to Fossett's grandmother Elizabeth Hemings. Jefferson hired him in 1801, and from the beginning Stewart established a reputation for weirdness. When he was on his way to Monticello to begin work, he stopped in on Jefferson's cousin George to ask for part of his salary in advance. George wrote to Jefferson in alarm, saying that his new workman "was either very much intoxicated or, is actually a madman." He knew nothing of what Stewart was supposed to do at Monticello, and when he tried to get the information from him, the workman was so "incoherent" that George could not figure out what he was saying.[13] Stewart nevertheless had a genius for metalworking and did masterly work at Monticello and passed on his skills to Joseph Fossett, among others.

While Fossett continued at his trade, his wife, Edith, continued at the President's House. The couple saw each other infrequently, for Jefferson typically left his trainee cooks behind when he went home to Monticello on vacations. The difficulties posed by having a long-distance marriage got to be too much for Fossett. Not long after Jefferson came home for his summer vacation in 1806 without Edith, Fossett left the mountain to go and see her. Lucia Stanton suggests that John Freeman and John (Jack) Shorter, two of Jefferson's African American servants who had come to Monticello with him, had told Joseph something about his wife or their young son, James, that caused him to set out immediately for the capital.[14]

When he found out that his blacksmith was gone, Jefferson wrote to Joseph Dougherty, his coachman at the President's House, alerting him to the possibility that Fossett might be on the way there and telling him that he had "sent Mr. Perry in pursuit of a young mulattoe man named Joe, 27. years of age, who ran away from here the night of the 29th inst[ant] without the least word of difference with anybody, and indeed never in his life recieved a blow from anyone." He went on to say that Fossett might "possibly trump up some story to be taken care of at the President's house till he can make up his mind which way to go" and noted that Fossett might "make himself known to Edy only, as he was formerly connected with her."[15] The pair's connection was "former" only to the extent that Jefferson had pulled them apart by bringing Edith to Washington.

This episode is intriguing on a number of levels. First, there is Jefferson's incredulity that Fossett would run away when in his view his blacksmith had had a good life at Monticello to date. There was some dim awareness that Fossett might be going to see his wife, but that did not appear to register as a reason important enough to make him leave. Jefferson was a very cagey correspondent, and there was almost certainly more to this episode than appears in his letter. Did Fossett simply leave after asking Jefferson for permission to visit his wife and being refused? If Jefferson did refuse the request, why? Abroad marriages were common at Monticello and on other plantations, and enslaved people were given permission to visit spouses who lived apart from them. Washington was farther away than a neighboring plantation, but enslaved people at Monticello traveled back and forth from the capital with no supervision.

Jefferson knew that no matter how loyal enslaved persons appeared, no matter what "benefits" they received under slavery, there was always the underlying reality that they were not really happy to be enslaved. We see this in Jefferson's instant and serious response—quickly employing a slave catcher to apprehend Fossett, instead of saying, "Oh, he's just going to see his wife. He'll be back." He clearly thought Fossett was gone for good, the stop at the President's House to see his wife just a way station on his flight to freedom, perhaps taking her with him.

Fossett got to spend little time with Edith, for he was apprehended while leaving the grounds of the President's House not long after he arrived. He spent the night in jail, and then Perry brought him back to Monticello. Etienne Lemaire was sympathetic to the "poor unhappy mulatto," saying that he deserved "a pardon" for running away or, rather, running to see his wife, but we do not know how Jefferson received Fossett upon his return to the mountain.[16] Madison Hemings described Jefferson as one who did not allow himself to be made unhappy for any great length of time. If anger and disquiet created a quotient of unhappiness in him, he apparently forgave those rather quickly who made him angry. The surest evidence that Jefferson bore no long-term rancor against Fossett is that less than a year later—when he could take his brilliant, but drunken, blacksmith William Stewart no longer, and fired him—he made Joseph Fossett the head of Monticello's blacksmith shop.[17]

From 1807 on, Fossett was at the very center of activity on the plantation, and he was a pivotal figure for many. He made things that were indispensable to life on a farm in the early nineteenth century—shoes for horses, tools for tilling the earth. When these items had to be repaired or needed sharpening, people returned to him, and not just members of his immediate community. Fossett's shop on Mulberry Row served farmers and other residents in the area, bringing the Monticello community, enslaved and free, into contact with the world outside the plantation, countering the isolation that might otherwise have attended life on top of the mountain.

When Jefferson was in residence, he spent a good deal of his time holed up in his bedroom/office writing, engaging the world through the republic of letters. Fossett's blacksmith shop, strategically located on Mulberry Row and directly adjacent to Jefferson's wing at Monticello and the homes of his relatives who worked in the house, was the exact counterpart to Jefferson's more cloistered world. This was the republic of face-to-face communication, with all the glories and hazards of unguarded talk and revealing facial expressions and gestures. People of different statuses and races met to solve the problem at hand—a too dull plow, a broken horseshoe—even as all the mores and tensions of that slave society shaped their interactions. Here was a venue in which to discuss the latest serious news of the area and to gossip. Whether Fossett would have volunteered information about his aunt Sally is unclear. That depended upon how he felt about her and Jefferson. It is inconceivable, however, that during his years as the head of the blacksmith shop dealing directly with Jefferson's white neighbors the subject never arose. Until he left public life in 1809, Jefferson's relationship with Hemings was fodder for the political fights of the day. Even after he returned home, his neighbors continued to talk, and it is very likely that many who made the trip up the mountain hoped to catch a glimpse of the woman who was, at the time, the most well-known enslaved person in America.

The Monticello blacksmith shop was more than just a social center: it was a business that turned a modest profit for Jefferson. It made money for Fossett, too. Following the practice begun with his nail factory, Jefferson wanted to create incentives for his artisans to work harder and better. So Fossett received one-sixth of the profits of the shop, in the same way that the Grangers had before. He was also allowed to do work on what was considered his own time and keep whatever money he made. He gave good value. Jefferson's overseer Edmund Bacon, who began work at Monticello in 1805, said that Fossett "could do anything it was necessary to do with steel or iron,"[18] combining his own natural talent with the teachings of

William Stewart. One sees in Fossett and his uncle John Hemings, the carpenter and joiner, the way slavery exploited one of the noblest aspects of the human character: the desire and capacity to be creative. Talented artisans like Fossett and Hemings took pride in their capabilities and their work, and each had the artist's will to perfection. They went beyond what they had to do, having fallen in love with their creations. Yet their creativity, which necessarily required some inner freedom from the restraint of convention, flowered in an atmosphere of coercion. This was the nature of the society they lived in, and Fossett and Hemings were better rewarded for their talent than many others, but the cruel reality at the heart of their lives remained.

Woodworking was in John Hemings's blood, his father, Joseph Neilson, having plied the trade at Monticello during the 1770s. He learned to be a professional joiner, however, from two white workmen whom Jefferson brought to the mountain, David (Davy) Watson and James Dinsmore. Watson had deserted the British army to remain in Virginia, and he was in the mold of William Stewart. Isaac Jefferson remembered him as a heroic drinker, who would "get drunk & sing," sometimes wasting a week at a time when he was on a bender, leaving Hemings to pick up the slack.[19] His first stint at Monticello came in the early 1780s and lasted for two years, before Jefferson embarked on the journeys that took him to Paris. Watson returned to Monticello in 1793 and stayed another four years. It was during this time that Jefferson gave the first inkling of his plans for the then seventeen-year-old Johnny Hemings, as he was wont to call him. In the midst of a set of elaborate instructions sent to his son-in-law Tom Randolph from Philadelphia, the secretary of state wrote, "As to the house joiner, I mean Johnny (Betty Heming's son) to work with him." Then, later in the year, "Johnny is to work with him [Watson] for the purpose of learning to make wheels and all sorts of work."[20] His free white laborers might stay or go, depending upon their whim and opportunities. As a result, Jefferson had to tolerate a good deal more bad behavior from them. Having skilled— and captive—enslaved artisans saved money and held out the promise of greater stability.

After Watson came James Dinsmore, a native of Ireland, who gave Hemings another close association with a person from a foreign culture. Dinsmore was William Stewart minus the alcoholism, a man of exceptional talent in whom Jefferson reposed a great deal of confidence. Another Irish-born joiner, John Neilson (whose relationship to Joseph Neilson is unknown), joined Dinsmore and Hemings in 1805, and he also came without any raging personal problems. James Oldham rounded out the trio of Jefferson's white master joiners for several years at the beginning of the 1800s. Jefferson respected him, too, but was particularly pleased with the collaboration between Dinsmore and Neilson and wrote with characteristic hyperbole, but nevertheless genuine enthusiasm: "They have done the whole of that work in my house, to which I can affirm there is nothing superior in the U.S."[21] John Hemings honed his skills in the company of these men, making furniture in the plantation joinery that had every kind of tool and device a carpenter or joiner could ever need, for no one was more serious about building than Jefferson. Because Jefferson always had projects in mind, Hemings had almost endless opportunities to learn on the job.

In this place where work and personal lives fused, Oldham played a critical role in the lives of John Hemings and his family that had nothing to do with woodworking. In 1804 Critta Hemings's son James (Jamey) was a seventeen-year-old worker in Jefferson's nail factory, having started there at the age of ten when operations at the nailery first began. After George Granger Sr. died and George Jr. came down with the lingering illness that would kill him, Gabriel Lilly was hired as the overseer at Monticello and took charge of the nail factory for a time. Lilly was as brutal as he was uneducated. He, too, drank excessively, making liberal use of Monticello's well-stocked wine cellar when Jefferson was away in Washington. He could neither read nor write, and violated all of Jefferson's precepts about using incentives, rather than violence, in the nail factory. James fell ill one day and could not work, enraging Lilly, who resorted to the whip to try to beat work out of the youth. Oldham wrote to Jefferson about what happened: "The barbarity that he maid use of with Little Jimmy Was the moost cruel, to my noledge Jimmy was sick for thre nights and the moast part of the time I raly thot he would not of Livd he at this time slepd in the room with me."[22] In addition to the information about James Hemings, this missive reveals much about Oldham's level of education and the physical closeness of whites and blacks during slavery. James was sleeping in the same space with Oldham. Through this intimacy Oldham was well aware of James's condition, and he attempted to intervene on James's behalf, explaining that the young man was too ill to work, and "Begd. [Lilly] not to punish him." Lilly did not listen and took his anger out on James and "whipd. him three times in one day, and the boy was rely not able to raise his hand to his Head."[23]

This was too much for young James Hemings, who had probably never been whipped by anyone, besides his mother or grandmother, in his life. He decided to escape. As far as the record shows, it was about six months before Jefferson heard anything of him. Oldham, who hated Lilly and felt the overseer had abused him, too, left Monticello not long after this episode and moved to Richmond, where he encountered the young escapee.[24] Hemings had almost certainly thought first of seeking out family when he left Monticello, and his uncle Robert was a natural contact there. His mother, her siblings, and other relatives may have helped him leave, since this was, quite possibly, the first time anyone in their family had been treated this way. Being hit repeatedly with a whip was not only painful and scar inducing; it could even kill. It was not unheard of for slaves to die during "correction," and the sociopath Lilly appears to have been so unable to govern himself that they would have been justified in fearing that he might inflict a serious, if not fatal, injury upon this young man.

As far as the record shows, Jefferson's chief communication about Hemings in Richmond came from Oldham, not from his uncle Robert. James may have contacted his uncle upon his arrival in Richmond, but chosen not live with him. Robert Hemings's home would have been the first natural place to look for James or to inquire into his whereabouts, as the young man well knew. He evidently had no intention of returning to Monticello. Rather than staying at his uncle's home, he lived instead with a man named James Right, who surely knew, but evidently did not care, that he was harboring an escaped slave. Hemings obtained money for rent and food by working on a boat that traveled between Richmond and Norfolk.[25]

A man named John Taylor had originally told Oldham that Hemings was in Richmond, and the two discussed whether to put the young man in jail. Oldham, who had been sympathetic to Hemings from the time this matter started, decided that it would be better to take Hemings to live with him until he heard word from Jefferson about how to proceed. Knowing how all this started, Oldham apparently did not really believe that Hemings's actions amounted to a criminal offense that merited spending any time in jail. He quickly became the mediator between Hemings and Jefferson, who pronounced that he could "readily excuse the follies of a boy."[26] Hemings had told Oldham that he was willing to continue "to serve" Jefferson, but that he had left because of the way Lilly had treated him. He would return, he said, only if Jefferson would never again put him under Lilly's direction.

Jefferson quickly agreed to these terms and promised that Hemings would no longer be under Lilly's supervision and that he could work with "Johnny Hemings and Lewis [another enslaved joiner] at house-joiner's-work."[27]

Jefferson gave in to Hemings's ultimatum because he could see the reasonableness of it. He was not at all happy about what Lilly had done, though it would take a demand for a too steep raise in wages to make him get rid of Lilly the following year. This situation, however, threatened domestic harmony at the most intimate level—down to the bedroom, and Jefferson had to do something. James Hemings was the child of the valued house servant Critta, the namesake of her tragically lost older brother, the nephew of Jefferson's mistress and of men who had been his personal servants, the cousin to his children Beverley and Harriet, and the grandson of Elizabeth Hemings and John Wayles. He and his first cousin Burwell Colbert had been nail boys together, the two very youngest in the group, and may have had a special connection. What would Burwell Colbert think of this? All these multiple identities shaped the way Jefferson saw what Lilly had done. The Hemingses, naturally, had every reason to despise the overseer and could only have been up in arms about the brutality he meted out to their young relative. Jefferson's initial resolution of this conflict acknowledged his own concerns, but also preserved his relations with the Hemings family and maintained the atmosphere he had created on the mountain. Harmony and efficiency were his constant watchwords.

Jefferson showed this in another violent episode involving a member of the Hemings family that happened just the year before the Lilly-Hemings confrontation. In 1803 Brown Colbert, Burwell's younger brother, was almost killed by a fellow worker in the nail factory. The eighteen-year-old Colbert, who apparently had a mischievous streak, had been teasing Cary, another youth. Seeking "a most barbarous revenge," Cary took a hammer, approached Colbert from behind, and "struck him with his whole strength." The blow fractured Colbert's skull, sending him into convulsions and then a coma.[28] There must have been chaos on Mulberry Row as word quickly spread of what had happened. Even minor head wounds are notoriously bloody, and this could only have presented a grisly and terrifying scene. Colbert underwent an operation to remove parts of his skull that had lodged in his brain, a horrific thing to contemplate given the medical knowledge and almost total lack of sanitary conditions of the day. One hopes that he was still in a coma when the operation was performed because those were the days before anesthesia. Jefferson's son-in-law Tom Randolph, who reported this to him, claimed to have assisted in the very complicated operation. He also had Cary put in jail.

The attack made Jefferson livid. He told Randolph to leave Cary in jail and then issued what has become one of the most often quoted passages in scholarship about his attitude toward slaves and slavery. "It will be necessary for me to make an example in terrorem to others in order to maintain the policy so necessary in the nail boys." He wanted Cary sold farther south or "in any other quarter so distant as never more to be heard of among us. It would be to the others as if he were put away by death."[29]

This heated response, born of Jefferson's obsession with maintaining order among his workers, and his use of the words "in terrorem" and putting Cary "away," as if he had died, have shaped the presentation of this episode in Jefferson scholarship. What is not considered is what this event signaled to the Hemingses as well as to other members of the enslaved community. Cary had not struck out at his real oppressors, the people who were enslaving him or even the brutal overseer, Lilly. Cary had almost killed one of their own, and he had done so not in self-defense but out of anger over a childish prank. As far as every enslaved person knew after this episode, Cary was the kind of person who might inflict a mortal wound upon his fellow slaves if they angered him. There is no reason to suppose that any enslaved person at Monticello, besides Cary's most extreme partisans, would have failed to see the gravity of his transgression or focus on Cary's banishment to the exclusion of thinking of the young man he had almost killed, and what the near loss of him meant to his family and his community. Why would the Monticello enslaved community be sanguine about having to live with a would-be murderer in their midst, or ever want to run into him anywhere in the immediate vicinity? Cary had to go. Colbert recovered, but did not stay on the mountain very long. Two years later he asked Jefferson whether he could be sold so that he could live with his wife, who had a different owner. Decades later he would go even farther away from Monticello, leaving Virginia entirely for Liberia, where he and other members of his family would perish while hoping desperately that they had finally found a promised land.

James Hemings's interaction with the violence of slavery, followed by his half year in freedom, left him determined not to return to Monticello. After agreeing to Hemings's condition about being removed from Lilly's oversight, Jefferson told Oldham to put Hemings on a stagecoach and send him home. Oldham relayed Jefferson's direction, and Hemings seemed agreeable to it, but he then asked whether he might take a moment and go to see his uncle Robert. Oldham agreed, and the young man never returned. The last reported sighting of him during this period was on a boat on the James River.[30] Whether he went to see his uncle is unknown.

What happened next, or what did not happen, is revealing. Jefferson simply let him go, a response that reiterates that not all enslaved people were the same in his eyes. Even though the multiple associations mentioned above did not prevent Jefferson from holding Hemings in slavery and making him work cooped up in a plantation factory ten hours a day, they did shape his reaction when the young man ran away after being beaten within an inch of his life. Lilly was notorious for using the whip, and had Jefferson freed every slave his overseer abused, he would have lost a good part of his work force. In his brutal treatment of James Hemings, however, Lilly had overstepped a serious boundary, and Jefferson made amends for that by letting Hemings go. This may well have been at the request or suggestion of James's mother, Critta, and all his aunts and uncles, who certainly had opinions and preferences about this.

Whatever the genesis of Jefferson's decision, the way he handled this episode speaks volumes about his view of power, the way to wield it, and his relations with members of the Hemings family. Other slaveholders would surely never have tolerated Hemings's defiant refusal to return to Monticello unless Jefferson had taken him out of the control of Lilly. He would have been apprehended and brought back to the plantation in chains, if needed. Jefferson clearly had the right under law to do just that, with the authority to apply corporal punishment upon Hemings's arrival if he desired. This takes us back into a consideration of the gulf between what Jefferson had the power to do and what he was inclined to do, as influenced by his personality and his particular relations with individual enslaved people.

While Jefferson had virtually unlimited power over the Hemingses, he felt personally constrained in the use of that power. He did not for a moment have to listen to Hemings's preference for a new supervisor and vow not to return to Monticello until his preference was granted. And when James tricked Oldham and disappeared down the river instead of returning to Charlottesville on the stagecoach as Jefferson had directed, Jefferson had the power to be draconian in his response. That he was willing to "forgive the follies of a boy" for running away does not explain why he allowed James Hemings to escalate the gravity of the situation by dictating terms to him and then defying him even after Jefferson had been amenable to those terms.

Though Jefferson never wrote why he did not take a firmer hand with Hemings even after he had defied him, the end result of his actions suggests the answer. His extreme forbearance gave the family who ran his household, including his mistress and his children, and his favored artisans, one more reason to have a sense of gratitude toward him while deepening any affection they may have had for him. He probably congratulated himself for his own sense of fairness on this occasion: he had done a good thing. It is too easy to cast this as simply another example of Jeffersonian manipulation—a calculated stunt designed to impress. As a mere stunt, it was a rather expensive one, for unlike his uncles Martin, Robert, and James, the younger James Hemings did not merely provide creature comforts to Jefferson. He was a healthy working male slave who made a product that brought income to Monticello. It was no small matter to let him go. If it was manipulation, it was the type of manipulation that all human beings engage in as we try to keep order in our existences by pleasing the people closest to us and maintaining our own internal sense of ourselves as just and fair actors.

It may be difficult from our vantage point to believe that Jefferson had an internal sense of justice and fairness, depending as he did on a labor system that was constitutively unjust and unfair. By holding upward of two hundred "souls," as he called them, in bondage, he worked injustice and unfairness in their lives every single day. James Hemings should never have been in Lilly's pathway, working in Jefferson's nail factory against his will, for no pay, subjected to violent coercion to make him work. Lilly had simply gone too far. If he had struck Hemings once or twice, matters would not have gotten to the point that Jefferson allowed Hemings to leave the plantation. But Jefferson did have his own sense of fairness within the confines of his inhumane way of life, and he showed it in the way he resolved the crisis with James Hemings. The proviso to this, however, is that Hemings's identity created the necessary spark to Jefferson's impulse for this level of fairness.

Although Hemings never again appeared in the Farm Book's listing of slaves, this was not the end of his dealings with Monticello. Jefferson's memorandum book records a payment to "James Hem." in 1815 for finding the eyepiece of a telescope for him.[31] Hemings apparently lived in informal freedom, coming back to see his family on the mountain as he desired and dealing with Jefferson on apparently cordial terms. There is also no hint of any hard feelings between Jefferson and Robert Hemings, who almost certainly played some role in his nephew's life during the half year he lived in Richmond as an escapee from Monticello.

"The Incomparable Sally"

Jefferson's enemies, fastening on the public interest in the private lives of leaders, continued to refer to Sally Hemings throughout Jefferson's presidency. Despite the outraged and moralizing tone of some of the references, it is highly probable that stories about the president and his beautiful young mistress made many men in the country secretly admire more than revile him. "Dusky Sally" and "Black Sal" appeared sporadically in the press. No other enslaved person was so well known, yet truly unknown, to the American populace. There were not only prose newspaper references. For some reason, the story moved many to verse, and it is these offerings that give the true flavor of the psyches of the men—and we can assume they were all men—who composed them. John Quincy Adams, then a senator from Massachusetts and Jefferson's occasional dinner guest at the President's House, who presumably should have had other, more constructive things to do, devoted himself with an intensity that was rather unseemly to periodically writing and publishing anonymously satirical poems about the president and his mistress, including "The Discoveries of Captain Lewis," a "lampoon" of the Lewis and Clark expedition that contained references to "Dusky Sally." At other times Adams turned classical, composing another long, racially hostile, and dull effort, "Ode to Xanthias Phoceus," in October 1803 for the *Port-Folio*, a magazine out of Philadelphia. Adams was quite proud of this latter poem, writing to his brother Thomas that the work "produced some sensation in this quarter" and predicting that it would "not pass unobserved in other parts of the union."[32]

The Adams family bore a different relationship to the Hemings story than others who were just reading about it in the newspapers. They—at least John and Abigail, for certain—had seen Sally Hemings. She had lived in their London home for several weeks when she was a young girl, and they were in a position to describe her to their son John Quincy. It is often said that John Adams did not believe that Jefferson and Hemings were lovers. But if he did not, he was probably the only member of the family who did not. Abigail certainly believed it. She and Jefferson exchanged a series of letters in 1804 when Adams sent her condolences after learning about the death of Jefferson's daughter Maria. By this time it had been conclusively proven (through the publication of Jefferson's own letters after he and his supporters flatly denied that he had supported Callender) that he had been giving Callender money even as the aggressive Scot launched vile personal attacks against Abigail's husband. Jefferson, ever the optimist and seeker of affection, believed that Abigail had forgiven him, when she was merely expressing her sincere regret at the death of his daughter. The renewed correspondence quickly deteriorated as politics crept into the discussion. At one point Adams expressed her feelings to her estranged friend in blunt terms. She told Jefferson, among other things, that she had always thought he had been a good friend, an "affectionate father," and a "kind master" until she had read Callender's writings, but that she could no longer hold those opinions of him.[33] Callender had said nothing that touched on Jefferson's role as a father and slave master other than that he had a long-term relationship with one of his slaves, under the eyes of his daughters Martha and Maria. Adams's statements about Jefferson as a father and a master could not have been a reference to anything else but the revelations about him and Sally Hemings.

Abigail Adams could count. Callender had said in 1802 that Hemings's first child was about twelve years old, and her time in France had figured in his stories. Anyone familiar with Jefferson's personal history, as Adams was, knew this indicated that Jefferson's relationship with Hemings started in Paris. Moreover, Adams even had a tangential connection to it. The girl whom she had encountered as what she took to be a still immature sixteen-year-old, the girl she had thought to send back home, had gone on to Paris and become Jefferson's mistress. Adams's letter ended for many years Jefferson's communication with the woman who had once been his dear friend. She had ventured into territory that no one could touch, much less explore. Writing to Benjamin Rush in 1811, who was in the midst of bringing about the famous postretirement reconciliation of Jefferson and Adams, Jefferson told the doctor how deeply Abigail had hurt him, explaining why it was nearly impossible for him to resume friendly relations with her.[34]

Neither John Quincy Adams nor his wife, Louisa, much liked Jefferson. Yet they continued to enjoy his hospitality, sitting at the president's dinner table, very much aware of the missing companion—Hemings—who could not be present. Actually, Louisa, a high-riding snob, went far beyond disliking Jefferson; she despised him, pronouncing him "ungainly, ugly and common" and ridiculing his casual manner and presentation, believing it demeaned the office of the presidency.[35] She was particularly upset by one example of Jeffersonian openness. Jefferson was notorious for his ostentatious courtesy to the Native American delegations that visited the President's House to discuss what they undoubtedly suspected were the terms of various efforts to drive them from their land. On one occasion Jefferson invited the wives of the chiefs, an act that caused great consternation among many who thought it put the Indians on the same social level as whites, and was a particular insult to the white women in attendance. Louisa was acid in her response, linking Jefferson's respectful and cordial treatment of the Native American women to his relationship to Sally Hemings. "Perhaps this is the first *step* toward the introduction *of the incomparable Sally*" (emphasis in the original).[36]

Jefferson almost certainly never let on that he was aware of just how much the Adamses disliked him or that he knew that John Quincy was the author of some of the verses that mocked Sally Hemings. At the end of his time in Washington, however, he could not resist using his very dry wit to get in a dig at the younger man. He ran into Adams at the celebration of James Madison's inauguration in 1809. Adams told his wife that he had seen the now former president, who was in high spirits because he was leaving office, and reported on their quite ironic—intentionally so on Jefferson's part—conversation. He clearly suspected, or knew, that Adams was behind some of the verses that appeared in the *Port-Folio*, one of the most famous literary magazines of its time, and he wanted Adams to know that he knew. Adams's report to his wife shows he got the message.

> I had some conversation with him in the course of the evening, in the course of which he asked me whether I continued as fond of POETRY as I was in my youth. I told him yes; that I did not perceive I had lost any of my relish for good poetry, though my taste for *amatory verses*, was not so keen as it had been when I was young. (emphasis in the original)[37]

28

❧

"Measurably Happy": The Children of Thomas Jefferson and Sally Hemings

TRADITIONALLY, THE YEAR 1809 has been seen as the end of one era at Monticello and the beginning of another, signaled by Jefferson's retirement from public life and return to his beloved mountain home, leaving behind the rough and tumble of politics. But one could also make the case for 1807 as marking the more pivotal end of an important era on the mountain, for that was the year Elizabeth Hemings died. The exact date of the seventy-two-year-old matriarch's death is unknown, though Lucia Stanton has suggested that it was likely during Jefferson's summer vacation. Had he been in Washington, some family member would have written to him with the news.

At the time of Hemings's death, only eight of her known twelve children definitely lived, for Martin Hemings's whereabouts after 1794 are unknown. She already had over thirty grandchildren and at least four great-grandchildren. That latter number would grow much larger by the end of what would be the family's final two decades on the mountain. The Jefferson family never wrote substantively of Hemings, and her grandson Madison provided the only memory of his grandmother in her later years, the sole record of any words she spoke. He was about three years old, having been born in January of 1805, and he was in her home as she lay dying. While eating a piece of bread, he offered his grandmother some, and she declined, saying, "Granny don't want bread any more." She did not live very long after that.[1]

This vivid childhood memory, fixed in Hemings's mind because it was so closely associated with his grandmother's death, reveals the closeness, or sense of duty, of his family. The little boy was most likely in his grandmother's cabin because his mother was there, visiting or helping to take care of her mother, who was on her deathbed. We can be certain she would not have been alone in this task, for Elizabeth Hemings had so many daughters and daughters-in-law that there was plenty of help to go around. Although her remaining sons, Robert and Peter, could help in their own ways, caring for the sick and dying was women's work, as was helping to bring children into the world—tasks that were hardly foreign to Hemings herself. Now the time had come for those whom she had borne and raised to minister to her and bring the cycle of life to a close.

Hemings had lived far beyond the normal life expectancy of her day, and the brief conversation with her small grandson linked those who had experienced the height of the slave trade in Virginia to the generation that would fight the Civil War and destroy the American slave system. Elizabeth's lost mother represented the direct tie between Africa and Virginia. Madison Hemings's future sons would grow up to fight for the Union, one said to have perished along with almost thirteen thousand other Union prisoners of war in the infamous Andersonville prison at Fort Sumter, in Georgia.[2] Hemings lived to see two of her sons formally emancipated and one daughter, Mary, informally freed living in a house she owned. And she had good reason to be hopeful that her daughter Sally and her children would make it out of slavery, too. Her sons and grandsons were highly skilled workers whose talents provided them some measure of security in a system that was basically insecure—so long as Jefferson remained alive.

It is not known whether Hemings, or her children, besides her son John, were religious. Her grandsons Madison and Eston Hemings, perhaps under the influence of their father, never joined a church when they moved to Ohio in the 1830s—a highly unusual omission, given that they had identified themselves as part of the black community. Church membership in that area was de rigueur among their generation of free blacks, not just for religious purposes, but for the social support that church membership provided.[3] One does not have to be religious, however, to embrace the famous words of the apostle Paul as he neared the end of his life, words that have sounded in many African American funeral orations and eulogies over the years: "I have fought the good fight. I have finished the course. I have kept the faith." All that we know of her suggests that Elizabeth Hemings had done the same within the confines of the inhumane system that governed her life from the moment she drew her first breath until the day she drew her last.

ELIZABETH HEMINGS'S DEATH was actually an emphatic punctuation mark to a series of devastating personal losses for the enslaved community at Monticello and for Jefferson as well. Along with the deaths of Jupiter Evans and the members of the Granger family at the end of 1799 and 1800, Thomas Bell, Mary Hemings's partner and Jefferson's longtime friend, died in 1800, leaving his property to Hemings and their children, Robert and Sarah.[4] And then there came the terrible tragedy of James Hemings's death in 1801. There were losses among the Jeffersons, too. Mary Bolling, Jefferson's older sister, died at the beginning of 1804. But the death that affected him the most deeply—shattered him, actually—was the loss of twenty-five-year-old Maria Jefferson Eppes in that same year.

Like her mother, Maria had always had problems with pregnancy and its aftermath. She gave birth to a daughter during the winter, fell ill, and never recovered. Jefferson, still in Washington awaiting the end of the legislative session, was struck with anxiety when he heard of her difficulties, for it brought back all the memories of the poignant struggles of the mother whom she so closely resembled. Maria had been staying at her sister's home at Edgehill, just a few miles from Monticello. After her father suggested that she be brought back to the mountain, where she might be more comfortable, slaves made a litter and carried her up to the place of her birth. Jefferson arrived home on April 4, 1804, to find his daughter in a much weakened state, though she rallied a bit, buoyed by his presence. He remained hopeful, but Maria died just thirteen days after he arrived.[5]

Jefferson was disconsolate, seared by his personal loss and, no doubt, the sense of the unfairness of it all. Her mother had died early, at thirty-four, but even Martha Jefferson had nine more years on earth than her daughter. While their sadness could not have approached that of Maria's father, husband, sister, and small son, Francis, members of the enslaved community may have felt some sense of loss, too. Maria had not been as much of a presence at Monticello in recent years as her sister, Martha, but many people there had known her from her childhood. Although we do not know how Sally Hemings felt about her niece, theirs had been a long association, and even outright enemies can regret the death of an antagonist. Despite the differences in their statuses, she and Maria had shared a great adventure, two young girls crossing the Atlantic as a pair to live and learn in a new culture and language. Now James was gone, and so was Maria. Of the five Virginians who had known the world of the Hôtel de Langeac, the Champs-Elysées, and the Bois de Boulogne, and were familiar with life in Paris just before and during the fall of the ancien régime, only Sally Hemings, Jefferson, and Martha Randolph remained.

There was death and then there was life. Though it could in no way have lessened Jefferson's pain at the loss of his daughter, Sally Hemings gave birth to their third child, a second son conceived during the month and a half Jefferson was at Monticello after he came home to attend to his daughter, Maria.[6] She was a mother again, this time to a child who would grow up to care for her in her final days and keep her story alive for the generations of their family and for history. This boy was named James Madison Hemings, apparently not at the direction of Jefferson himself, though he could hardly have objected to the name.

According to Madison Hemings, Dolley Madison suggested that he be named after her husband, promising his mother a present if she did. Hemings said this conversation occurred at the time of his birth, but like many people recounting family stories—for example, Martha Randolph's apparent blending of the layout of the second Monticello with the first when detailing the events surrounding her mother's death—Hemings collapsed the timing of an encounter his mother had with Dolley Madison. As it turns out, Dolley Madison was not at Monticello on January 19, 1805, the day Madison Hemings was born, but she and her husband were at Monticello during the preceding September when his mother was in her sixth month of pregnancy with him.[7] Dolley evidently made the comment—if it's a boy name him after my husband, and I'll give you a gift—when Sally Hemings was pregnant, not on the very day she gave birth.

Hemings recounted this event not for any evident pride in the name James Madison but because it was an instance in which his mother was poorly treated—a thing not easily forgotten. Dolley reneged on her promise, even though she knew that Hemings had named her little boy Madison.

This is exactly the kind of slight a mother might point out to her children to alert them about the character of an individual with whom they had to come into contact over the years, whether she wanted to or not. Most interesting of all, Hemings linked Dolley's bad act to the attitude whites had generally exhibited toward blacks up until that moment in history: they had been careless and arrogant people who took liberties with others. They made promises to nonwhites that they thought nothing of breaking. The only white person who appears to have been exempted from that blanket condemnation was his father: Jefferson had kept his promises to Hemings's mother to give her a good life and free their children.

Neither James nor Dolley Madison was naïve, and James certainly was no more a prude than Jefferson. By 1805 both he and Dolley, who took a keen interest in the private lives of others, surely knew of Jefferson's enslaved mistress, Sally. There is an indication that Dolley's suggestion of a name for Hemings's child may have created some competition within the Jefferson household. Almost a year to the day after James Madison Hemings was born, Martha Randolph, while visiting her father at the President's House, gave birth on January 17, 1806, to James Madison Randolph.[8] In one year's time, Jefferson had a son and grandson named for his close friend.

The year of Madison Hemings's birth was a particularly delicate time for Jefferson. Callender had been dead for two years, but New England Federalists continued to use Jefferson's private life as a form of background music to their relentless critique of his presidency. This, even though his resounding victory in the election of 1804—in the face of Callender's exposé—clearly showed that the majority of the American electorate apparently did not care about the issue. Voters may have enjoyed reading about it—been titillated by it—but stories about Jefferson's mistress were irrelevant to the question whether he should be president, especially after the triumph of the Louisiana Purchase had many of them looking west to a new future. The Federalists, of course, would soon have a real issue with which to beat Jefferson about the head and shoulders: the passage of the Embargo Act of 1807, which began his ultimately ill-fated attempt to use economic pressure rather than war to deal with British attacks on American interests on the high seas.

The embargo and its attendant legislation aimed to prevent any shipping from American ports, with the goal of punishing Great Britain and France, each of which in the midst of the Napoleonic Wars was trying to stop the neutral United States from trading with its enemy. The logic was that if the Europeans lost American goods, they would see the advantages of coming to reasonable terms with the new nation. But America paid a tremendous price for this policy. The embargo had a devastating effect upon the American economy.[9]

In the face of this serious national crisis, and the policy debate about the efficacy of a measure that was bringing financial ruin to many, carping about Jefferson and his slave mistress could only have appeared trifling. But in the interlude after his reelection and before the embargo, attacks on Jefferson for his alleged atheism and his relationship with Sally Hemings were the only weapons at the Federalists' disposal. As often happens when no life-defining policy matters are at stake in the country, or when the party out of power feels particularly impotent, the political discourse turned to an obsessive investigation of and focus upon the supposed "character" of the chief executive. And because character in the United States is almost always measured by sexual behavior and religious beliefs, Jefferson, who later declared, "I am of a sect by myself, as far as I know,"[10] when pressed to declare his religious views, and who had a still-growing number of children with Hemings, was a prime target for a character-based assault.

That Jefferson was willing to have another child with Hemings in the midst of this intense public scrutiny is not surprising. He did not change course easily, nor did he abandon people close to him because of the criticism of others. His deep sense of loyalty and, it must be said, his great comfort with himself, and eerily fixed belief in the rightness of his decisions, would not allow others to make him second-guess his dealings with people about whom he had made up his mind. It is quite telling that he turned to Hemings during one of the most heartbreaking periods of his life, when he was a veritable portrait of emotional devastation. Madison Hemings's conception in the harrowing six weeks Jefferson was at home to attend to his daughter shows that this extremely sensitive man sought the comfort of the familiar with the person who understood better than anyone besides his daughter Martha what Maria had meant to him.

It was a rare moment when the very private Jefferson gave vent to his true emotions in his correspondence, but the tone and content of his letters in the aftermath of Maria's death show a man bereft. Several months after her death, he wrote to John Page, a dear and longtime friend, that he had lost "the half of all [he] had" and his "evening prospects" now hung "on the slender thread of a single life," meaning, of course, his daughter Martha.[11] At the time Jefferson wrote those words, he had six grandchildren whom he adored and who were far from "nothing" to him. His children with Sally Hemings, two at the time of this letter, could never belong to him as Martha and Maria did, or as his grandchildren did, for that matter. They were being raised to leave him and, perhaps, even their mother if they chose to go into the white world.

BEYOND THE STEADFASTNESS of Jefferson's attachments to those about whom he felt deeply, his life with Sally Hemings pertained to Monticello, the place where he ruled. To allow what was being said in the press to work a change in his behavior in this intensely private realm was to lose control of himself and this place. Journalists and his political enemies would be the masters of Monticello, not he—a thing he would never have countenanced. This new child offered evidence that he had not been in the least chastened by the criticism. And he could not reasonably have expected that his defiance would remain hidden, for it was clear that someone close to Monticello was giving information to the press. When one gets past the juvenile and generic "Congo harem" references, much of the information that appeared in the newspapers about Hemings and Jefferson was accurate. In the same year that Madison Hemings was born, a Boston newspaper published an article that contained detailed information about the Walker affair, and the efforts to avert a duel over it, that none but a well-connected source could have known. That same piece mentioned Beverley by name, said he was the eldest of the Hemings-Jefferson children, and mentioned that Sally Hemings was John Wayles's daughter.[12] This was not the product of random guessing. Jefferson simply kept living the way he had always lived, following his own internal compass.

Even as he was battered in the papers, Jefferson suffered an additional crushing personal loss, which brought uncomfortable personal issues to the fore. In 1806 George Wythe, his law teacher, mentor, and friend, was apparently murdered by his grandnephew George Sweeney. Wythe had been married twice, but had no children. His will left his house and other property to Lydia Broadnax, a free woman of color who was his housekeeper, and property to another former slave Benjamin, who predeceased Wythe. To Michael Brown, a fifteen-year-old African American boy who lived with him as a ward, he left bank stock with the instructions that Jefferson was to take charge of Brown's finances and his education. Sweeney apparently coveted the property and tried to get around the provisions of the will by poisoning the beneficiaries. Broadnax survived, but Wythe and Michael Brown did not.[13]

A year after these events Broadnax, suffering the lingering effects of her brush with death, wrote to Jefferson, alerting him to her "distressed situation" and, with great embarrassment, asking whether he would be willing to provide her with some financial assistance. She appealed to him on the basis of their "old and intimate acquaintance" and her knowledge of Jefferson's benevolence. Jefferson had been in Washington when the letter arrived, but he attended to her entreaty as soon as he returned home. He wrote to his agent George Jefferson, in Richmond, where Broadnax lived also, directing him to give her fifty dollars, a good sum in those days, along with other instructions about handling his affairs. Interestingly enough, when he noted his directions to George in his memorandum books, he listed the other transactions but made no mention of having told George to give Lydia Broadnax money.[14]

The exact nature of Michael Brown's connection to Wythe and Broadnax is unknown. It has often been assumed that he was Wythe's son and that Broadnax was his mother. No evidence exists to support either conclusion, however, though Wythe's treatment of the pair was extraordinary. Whether Brown, who was described as "yellow" skinned, was his biological son or not, Wythe treated him as if he were, taking pains with his education. Certainly asking his own favorite and most famous pupil, the current president of the United States, to become Michael's guardian shows the depth of his affection for the boy.

Once again, a member of Jefferson's close circle had died an unnatural death, leaving him stunned. He wanted a memento of his old teacher and asked William Duval, who had informed him of Wythe's death, if he might be sent a profile of Wythe that Broadnax owned to make a copy. Broadnax sent Jefferson the original. He expressed his sorrow that Wythe, who lingered for several days before dying, lived his final hours knowing that the young man who Jefferson knew he regarded as a son had already died. He also said how much he regretted that Michael's tragic death "deprived [him] of an object for the attentions which would have gratified [him] unceasingly with the constant recollection & execution of the wishes of [his] friend."[15]

How would Jefferson have carried out Wythe's final request about his involvement with Michael Brown? Would he really have brought the African American boy to Monticello or to the President's House to continue his studies, or would he have used the money from Wythe's estate to hire tutors for him? Brown at Monticello would indeed have been an interesting and problematic sight. Had Brown lived, and Jefferson accepted his dear mentor's charge, he would have been attending to the education of George Wythe's African American surrogate son, even as he had mixed-race sons and a daughter of his own flesh.

By 1806 Beverley was eight years old, Harriet five, and Madison nearly two. Two years after the Wythe tragedy and the near-miss of a Jefferson/Brown pairing, the last of the Hemings children arrived, Eston, born a month after Jefferson's sixty-fifth birthday. This was truly an occasion, for it marked the first time that Jefferson had been home for the birth of one of his four children with Hemings who survived. Eston was also the first child that Hemings bore without her mother's presence, another likely milestone in the life of the now thirty-five-year-old woman. And, yet again, Hemings did not—or was not able to—name her child after a member of her family. This youngest son was instead named for Thomas Eston Randolph, a favorite Jefferson cousin, the son of his maternal uncle William Randolph. Born and raised in England, he had come to the United States in the 1790s, apparently holding fast to the culture of that isle. One of Jefferson's granddaughters, long after Randolph had left the country of his birth, referred to him as that "most English of Englishmen."[16]

Though Randolph was younger than Jefferson, the two men struck up a friendship that involved all the generations of the Jefferson family. In fact, Jefferson described Thomas Eston Randolph's family and his as being "almost as one," and that was no Jeffersonian exaggeration. Randolph married Thomas Mann Randolph's younger sister, Jane, who was also very close to Maria Jefferson. The couple had their own son named Eston and a daughter Harriet, born the year after Jefferson and Hemings's daughter Harriet. Another Thomas Eston daughter, Mary, would grow up to marry Maria Jefferson Eppes's son, Francis. Randolph and Jefferson went through some rocky periods in later years, as often happens when friendship and family get mixed with business, but their tie was never really broken. Indeed, in Jefferson's final days, Thomas Eston Randolph, with great emotion and sensitivity, volunteered to sit up at night with his dying cousin and friend.[17]

The names of the Hemings children brought them into these convoluted Jefferson/Randolph/Eppes family connections, but not on the basis of equality. They certainly knew they carried the names of people important to their father and had some thoughts on what this meant. But like most enslaved children in their position, the times and their circumstances gave them ample reason to be realistic about all that this did not mean. Their father, an Anglo-American man of the eighteenth century, with a legitimate white child and grandchildren, was going to go with them only so far down the road.

The Hemings children's older cousins Robert and Sally Bell had been in a completely different position. They had no competition, because their father, Thomas Bell, was apparently without any known white children, legitimate or otherwise. We will never know, but one wonders whether a Thomas Bell with white children would have taken property from them (which is what sharing entails) and given it to his mixed-raced enslaved children and his mistress. He certainly would not have been able to do that without formally freeing Mary Hemings, Robert, and Sally and making them eligible to receive his property. He was able to get away with informally freeing them and relying on his relatives, the law's deference to his expressed will, and his community's acquiescence to see things through. If he had had legitimate white children, that would have been next to impossible.

Madison Hemings remembered that his father, elderly even by today's standards, was kind to him, his brothers, and his sister, as he was to everyone. He was "not in the habit," however, of showing his younger children "partiality or fatherly affection." He also mentioned that Jefferson's grandchildren taught him to read and write, implying that Jefferson took no interest in his formal education.[18] Hemings's statement is often transformed into saying that Jefferson *never* showed any partiality or fatherly affection to him and his siblings. That cannot have been what Hemings meant, at least not regarding partiality, for he also detailed many of the ways that he and his siblings' lives were different from others' on the plantation, differences that were direct products of Jefferson's decisions. Hemings may have wanted more from his father, but these decisions clearly showed that Jefferson favored his children with Hemings over other enslaved children on the plantation.

Hemings revealed what he meant by "fatherly affection" when he offered, by way of comparison, Jefferson's treatment of his grandchildren toward whom he was "affectionate." Jefferson was well known for his attentiveness to his grandchildren, playing games with them and, like many grandparents, being more indulgent with them than he had been with his daughters when they were young. We get a sense from Madison Hemings that Jefferson rarely played with or cuddled his youngest children, things that the young boy Madison noticed and perhaps longed for. Very tellingly, his point of reference for Jefferson's shows of fatherly affection was not his half sister Martha. Instead, Hemings compared himself to Jefferson's grandchildren, who were around his same age.[19] Imagine a six-year-old with a father who is always kind to him, but who seems to ration his affectionate gestures, viewing that same father freely expressing his affection for his grandchildren who were around the six-year-old's age. This scene, almost unfathomable to the modern American mind, has been played out countless times in feudal and slave societies the world over—biological children living within the eyeshot and touch of fathers from whom they were separated by class, race, or legal status. All three of these factors distanced the Hemings children from Jefferson. These four individuals had to forge, very early on, singular identities as they lived in what could only be characterized as a form of limbo.

Madison Hemings suggested what that identity was when he said that he and his siblings were "measurably happy" during their childhoods because they grew up free from the "dread" of being enslaved all their lives.[20] Their knowledge of their parents' intended future for them, and their father's capacity to bring that future about, gave them a distinct way to see themselves. They were not truly like the others enslaved at Monticello, though their father listed them in his Farm Book and wrote of them as if they were. Here was that not infrequent case where seemingly neutral documents badly mislead. Both the Farm Book and Jefferson's nearly rote and veiled references in his letters calling Beverley and Madison, and then Madison and Eston, John Hemings's "two assistants" or "two apprentices"—always unnamed—hid a vital truth of their lives, and of his as well.[21] The phrases "his assistants" and his "two apprentices" suggest obscurity and hint at their unimportance relative to their uncle John, when the young men buried beneath these titles were the very opposite of unimportant. They were Jefferson's sons who were going to receive what no other enslaved people at Monticello ever received: emancipation with his blessing upon reaching adulthood so that they could live the prime of their lives as free men. Their father, for whom everything and everyone had a place, put them in the nearest compartment that fit their circumstances, knowing all along that even that would be temporary. And when the two oldest Hemings children left Monticello, he used the language of slavery in his Farm Book to describe their departure. Both Beverley and Harriet, whom Jefferson arranged to be put on a stagecoach with the equivalent of about nine hundred dollars in today's terms, "ran away."[22] This event had been expected and planned for since the day they were born, so they had not run away in the conventional sense. This was the beginning of the fulfillment of the plan set in motion thirty-two years before in France.

So the Hemings siblings had childhood identities as a special band of people who were destined to go, to leave behind two states that were coterminous for them: childhood and slavery. Even though their father was the master of it, Monticello would never be theirs, any more than *he* could ever really be "theirs." They grew up in anticipation, with a present connection to their father, but moving toward a future where their connection to him would live only in their memories and whatever they wanted to tell their families about him. The situation would be even more stark for those of the children who planned to go into the white world. If Beverley and Harriet had thought all along that they would live as white people when they became adults, they knew early on that their father could live only in their memories for, depending upon whom they married, it might be unwise to tell their spouses or children who Jefferson was to them.

One wonders whether Jefferson ever told Beverley, Harriet, Madison, and Eston that by Virginia law they were white, a law that he explicated, in needlessly complicated algebraic form, in an 1813 letter to a man named Francis Gray, who had asked him about racial designations in Virginia.[23] He might not have had to tell them. Their mother probably knew. Enslaved people were often familiar with some of the basics of law, especially the laws of slavery and property that related to them. Isaac Jefferson, for example, was quite precise about the source of Jefferson's fortune, saying that Jefferson was personally wealthy primarily in knowledge; his wealth in land and slaves had come to him through his legal marriage to Martha Wayles Skelton. One did not have to be a legal scholar to know that enslaved status was determined by the status of one's mother, or even that people who were less than one-quarter black were considered white. This was the kind of information that mixed-race slaves, and even the whites around them, would have been interested in knowing and talking about. If these children grew up thinking of themselves as legally white, their connection to racially based slavery would seem even that much more tenuous to them. Their future was not just out of slavery but out of one putative race into another.

The Hemings children did not venture into this future unguided, for Jefferson had a direct hand in shaping their progress through life and the way they viewed themselves. In fact, so many things are known about the Hemings siblings that bear the mark of Jefferson's actions that Madison Hemings's picture of his life with his father seems more a description of Jeffersonian ambivalence than of rejection. There is a predictable sameness to their lives that has the unmistakable shadings of a plan, from their names, their hobbies (the violin), and the trade they would be trained to follow.

Other than running errands when they were small, all the Hemings children remained out of the realm of service and never had the occasion to develop an identity as servants. In another time, and in a different household, Harriet Hemings might have been considered a perfect personal maid for one of Jefferson's numerous granddaughters. Instead, Harriet "learned to spin and weave" in Jefferson's small textile operation, though his overseer remembered that she never worked very hard.[24] Her father gave her something to do that did not automatically signal a subservient status—to him, the outside world, and to her and her siblings. After all, his mother and sisters had been spinners. Susan Kern has pointed out, in writing of the Jefferson females, that they used spinning primarily as a "polite hobby." Jefferson bought his mother a spinning wheel and sent her wool and cotton for spinning.[25] Certainly the republican revolution that brought forth the cult of republican wife and motherhood idealized women who produced homespun, lessening their family's dependence upon foreign manufactures. Like all daughters, Harriet probably spent a good deal of her time under her mother's direction learning to sew and to do other domestic tasks. Harriet Hemings was prepared at Monticello to be a successful wife and a mother, which is exactly what she turned out to be.

Jefferson followed a similar, gender-appropriate pattern with his sons. The boys were trained to become the types of workers he admired the most—carpenters and joiners, instead of blacksmiths, gardeners, or hostlers. Jefferson placed all three under the direction of his most trusted artisan, John Hemings, who became a surrogate father to each one. Madison Hemings remembered becoming apprenticed to his uncle at age fourteen, but Jefferson's records indicate that the Hemings brothers began to assist

John Hemings sometime after the age of ten. A Jefferson Farm Book entry in 1810 lists twelve-year-old Beverley as a workman along with his uncle. Six years later, in September of 1816, when Madison was four months shy of his twelfth birthday, Jefferson wrote to his overseer Joel Yancey at Poplar Forest, telling him when he would be arriving at the plantation. "John Hemings & his two aids will set out so as to be at Poplar Forest the evening before us."[26] The "us" included Jefferson and his daughter Martha and his sons' uncle Burwell Colbert. The "two aids" were the eighteen-year-old Beverley the nearly twelve-year-old Madison. Neither Beverley nor Madison at ages eleven or twelve would have been expected (or allowed) to do dangerous carpentry work, but carrying their uncle's tools, watching him work, and getting used to the world of carpentry before they actually tried their hand at it made perfect sense. The extremely talented and literate "Johnny" would teach them everything they needed to know.

Still, a Jefferson with working-class sons seems incongruous. Why not train them to be at his level in society? As Rhys Isaac has observed, class, along with race and status, governed the way Jefferson viewed his children.[27] He had less to be concerned about with Harriet, who as female was not really his counterpart. Great beauty and a genteel (gentle) manner would be enough for her to attract a decent mate— at almost all levels of society. She could be successful at womanhood with just the rudiments of an education. As for his sons, Jefferson knew they would not grow up to be thought of as gentlemen in the same way that he was thought of as a gentleman. Unlike their grandfather John Wayles, whose whiteness allowed him to escape the lower class, Beverley, Madison, and Eston were of African origin. Had it been widely known that they were his sons, that part of their heritage would have to be known, too. This man, at the very pinnacle of the social pyramid, had children who had been born at the lowest status in society. The basic imperative was not to bind them to himself, or to try to make them junior versions of the public Thomas Jefferson, but to get them out of that status and, one suspects, he hoped, into a different race.

In the letter to Francis Gray in which he explained how much white blood it took to turn a black person white, Jefferson declared that freeing a person who was one-eighth black, like his children, would make that person a free white citizen of the United States.[28] There was, of course, no reference to the Hemings children in this letter. It seems highly unlikely, however, that they were far from his mind when he issued the unnecessary (Gray was not interested in questions of U.S. citizenship) and emphatic pronouncement about the effect of emancipation upon people like his offspring.[29] He knew that, when they became adults, he was going to make them the best thing he could think of, free white American citizens.

The historian Peter Onuf has noted how much Jefferson's plan for the emancipation, and then the colonization, of American slaves resembled his situation with his children, in that it required the separation of parent from child. Jefferson acknowledged the difficulty that posed, but suggested that the great prize to be won—freedom for the generations to come—should not be thwarted out of sentimentality about the relationship between one parent and one child.[30] This may have been a rationalization on his part, a way to explain why he had children who could never belong to him in the way children were supposed to belong to their parents—and why in the end that was still a good thing. One was to think of what freedom would mean to future generations. As things turned out, Jefferson's calculations were right; his grandchildren who lived as white people used the privilege of whiteness and prospered greatly. We will never know what, if any, emotional toll this deferral of familial connection took on him, Sally Hemings, and their children. There is no way around the fact that their predicament at Monticello—and there is no better way to characterize the situation with Hemings and Jefferson, their children, and Martha and her children—carried no prospect of a harmonious resolution that could be equally satisfactory to all.

Jefferson did not separate himself from the Hemings children. Choosing to make his sons carpenters and joiners guaranteed that he would at least be able to oversee their work and development. With no other artisan at Monticello did he spend more time than with John Hemings. During the years of Jefferson's retirement, where John Hemings was, Beverley, Madison, and Eston—when he was old enough—were, too. When Madison Hemings astutely observed that Jefferson had "but little taste for agricultural pursuits" and preferred instead to be among "his mechanics,"[31] he was talking, in part, about himself and his brothers.

Although Madison Hemings, an obviously very reserved and private man, gave a rich account of his life at Monticello, we really cannot gauge from his recollections alone what life was like for all of his siblings, especially not Beverley and Harriet. The world of siblings is not static. Each one enters the unit at different stages in the lives of the parents and the life of the family itself. That is even more so when there are large gaps in ages between siblings, years in which the family's circumstances can change drastically. Beverley Hemings was seven years old when his little brother, Madison, was born. He was a full decade older than Eston. By the time Madison grew old enough to really pay specific attention to how Beverley and Jefferson interacted—say, when he was nine or ten, and that estimate may be generous—Beverley was well into his teens, certainly past the point of playing games on the lawn with anyone. Although Harriet was only four years older than Madison, that was still enough to create a gap in his knowledge about how Jefferson dealt with her when she was small.

Where one ends up in life is very often determined by where one starts, and it is, perhaps, significant that Beverley and Harriet Hemings entered their family and Monticello at a very different time in the life of the family and of the place than their younger brothers. They took paths in life quite different from those of their younger siblings. Both left Monticello to enter the white world immediately, with no apparent consideration of spending any time in the black community. They took white spouses and left blackness completely behind. Although their youngest brother, Eston, eventually followed them into that world, it was only after it became apparent that his children's lives would be severely circumscribed if they continued to live as people of color.

Beverley Hemings had almost five years at Monticello with Jefferson before Callender exposed his parents' life together. He was a first son, not the type of person whom a man who knew he would never have white sons could easily or totally have resisted. It would have been one thing for Jefferson to have had a "forbidden" first son living on another of his plantations, quite another to watch this small replica of himself running through the foyer at Monticello. This was the boy who, according to one recollection, would grow up to ascend balloons, one of his father's great interests from the time he had heard of them until the day he died.[32] Beverley bore so many marks of his father that it is not at all likely that Jefferson was ever completely indifferent to him. One of the few specific comments about him hints at an independent streak. In July of 1820 Edmund Bacon wrote a note to Jefferson asking him whether he knew that Beverley had not been coming to the carpenter's shop for about a week. The now twenty-two-year-old, a year past the time of his promised freedom, apparently decided to take the week off. Jefferson did not respond to his overseer in writing. There is thus no indication whether he knew from John Hemings or Beverley that he had been absent from the shop, or whether he knew anything about it at all.

The person who was most like a full legal white son to Jefferson, of course, was his much adored first grandson and namesake, Thomas Jefferson Randolph. But Jeff Randolph bore neither a physical (other than height), intellectual, nor temperamental resemblance to his grandfather. His some-what exacting mother worried when he was a boy that he was not very smart. He himself complained that he had been sent to inferior schools in his youth and was never sent to college. Jefferson, who helped direct his education, resigned himself early on to the reality that his grandson was not cut out to be a scholar.[33] If Randolph was not an intellectual like his grandfather, he turned out to have been different from Jefferson in another way: he was a sound business manager, who worked tirelessly and successfully to keep his family afloat in the fallout from his grandfather's disastrous financial affairs.

Jeff also had more of his father's mercurial and aggressive personality. Although Jefferson preferred incentives to whipping people, he never totally banned whippings on his plantations. He did not, however, administer them himself and spoke ill of overseers because he suspected they actually enjoyed inflicting cruelty. Jeff Randolph, on the other hand, had no com-punction about personally wielding the whip. He even whipped an enslaved man in front of his young nephew visiting from Massachusetts, Thomas Jefferson Coolidge. Coolidge recounted the incident in his memoirs and seems to have been horrified by the whole southern way of plantation life. But Jeff Randolph had another trait that must have greatly disappointed his grandfather. According to his sister, Jeff had an "aversion to music," about which his grandfather was passionate.[34]

The great irony, or tragedy, is that at least one, if not all, of the Hemings brothers—separated from Jefferson by the gulfs of race, class, and status—may have been more like him substantively than Jeff Randolph was. One wonders whether there was not some attempt to take these boys and turn them into some version of himself. He loved to build. They would build. He loved music and the violin. They would love music and play the vio-lin. As far as the record shows, the youngest, Eston, seemed to have iden-tified with him the most, and with good reason. He was said to be a near copy of Jefferson facially and physically in terms of his height and build. We do not know Beverley's profession, but music was also the passion of Eston's soul, so much so that he learned to play the violin and the piano and made his living as a musician. Although he never spoke publicly about Jefferson, he kept alive his connection to him by changing his name from Eston Hemings to E. H. (Eston Hemings) Jefferson when he went into the white world. He also carried a bit of Jefferson with him in his professional life, a private remembrance that had to remain unknown to his audience. Jefferson did not care much for popular music, but there were several songs he liked enough to copy down in his notes, one a tune called "Money Musk." Decades later, Eston would make "Money Musk" one of his signature tunes as he played at society events throughout southern Ohio.[35]

Even more important than the fallout from Callender's exposé was the move of Jefferson's daughter and grandchildren to the mountain in 1809. Beverley and Harriet Hemings were eleven and eight years old, respectively, when this happened. Unlike Madison and Eston, who were four and a little over one in 1809, they knew a time when the Randolphs were not continuously at Monticello. Martha and her children had always visited during Jefferson's vacations, but having them move into the household full-time was an important psychological step for all involved. There can be great comfort in knowing that visitors are eventually going to go home. Having the Randolphs as permanent fixtures at Monticello and Martha as the mistress of the plantation necessarily changed the dynamic of life there. Matters were even more delicate because the move was made under unhappy circumstances.

The Randolphs' final settlement at Monticello has been portrayed either as the natural coming together of a happy family under the benevolent authority of the patriarch or as a sinister outcome engineered by a manipulative Jefferson. It was neither. This was, instead, the end result of a slow-motion, across two decades, catastrophic failure. Martha and her children would never have been back at Monticello if Thomas Mann Randolph had been successful and stable and if her marriage had been happy. It is doubtful that Martha and her children would have spent months out of the year there even before this final move, if the family had been in happy circumstances. As discussed in chapter 20, there was, from the very beginning, good reason to think the union between Martha and Tom might not succeed, and the ensuing years simply bore that out.

A Thomas Mann Randolph, in a strong financial position, could more easily have resisted this public display of the failure of his marriage and his inadequacies as a provider. Even if Martha had been unhappy in marriage, and had wanted to escape it by choosing to be the housekeeper to her father, instead of wife to her husband, she would not have been able to involve her children in this unless Tom had consented. On that point the law was clear: children belonged to their fathers. If Tom had been a wealthy patriarch, there would have been no reason for the Randolph offspring to be anywhere other than under his roof.

As things stood Jefferson had become the sole financial support for his daughter's family, a precarious situation that seems to have humiliated his son-in-law and left him few avenues to make demands regarding his family. This, however, was not Jefferson's fault. He did not make Tom Randolph unsuccessful. Nor did he cause the younger man's apparent mental instability and tendency toward aggression, circumstances that had to have shaped the family's view of him. It is often noted that Jefferson adamantly opposed his son-in-law's plan to start over by moving his family farther south. He doubtless wanted to keep his daughter and grandchildren close to him, a not unusual desire. But if he, like others, harbored doubts about Randolph's overall mental health, it is easy to understand why he would have been anxious about having his daughter go too far out of his sight, or the potential range of his help.

What this meant to Sally Hemings and her children is clear. With Jefferson in retirement and in the daily company of Martha (the most important person in the world to him) and her offspring, there was little chance that he could treat his children with Hemings fully as his own. Martha's status as the mistress of Monticello surely made things more awkward for Hemings and Jefferson at times, but it posed no fundamental challenge to their identity as lovers. Martha had no basis for competing with Sally Hemings in that realm.

The Hemings children and Jefferson's grandchildren, however, bore a different relationship to one another. This was, in modern parlance, a zero-sum game. Whatever Jefferson did for Beverley, Harriet, Madison, and Eston would come out of whatever he was supposed to be doing for his legal white grandchildren. To raise the Hemings children up was to lower the Randolph grandchildren, and Maria's son, Francis Eppes, as well. What would these children think if they saw their grandfather tousle Madison Hemings's hair or put his arm affectionately around his daughter Harriet? She, in particular, posed a problem. Jefferson already had a daughter and numerous granddaughters. Although they had the satisfaction of being of a superior social class and, in their biased view, a superior racial stock,

Harriet Hemings had a basic advantage in the one area where women the world over are encouraged to compete: she was, in the words of one observer, "very beautiful" and, in another's, "very handsome."[36] Jefferson's eldest granddaughter was thought attractive, but her mother, Martha, was variously described as plain or even homely. Jefferson's daughter and granddaughters may have looked down upon Harriet, but the sense of competitiveness about appearance is a great leveler, even if not expressed openly. As Deborah Gray White and others have shown, despite their more important social status and greater power, white plantation mistresses were often jealous of enslaved women who were as attractive as, or more attractive than, they. Indeed, Jefferson had to be especially careful in how he treated Harriett, when his daughter and his granddaughters were about.

Jefferson had another important reason to be on special guard. While his affair with Hemings certainly helped keep Martha free of a stepmother and legitimate half siblings, the kind of people who could have been rivals for his unfettered affection and property, his eldest daughter had suffered greatly because of the way the world viewed his personal life.[37] The public exposure during his presidency, at the exact moment when the eyes of the world were upon him, went far beyond anything any of them could have expected to have to endure when Martha first had to accommodate herself to her father's life. Her precipitate marriage in 1790 brought the hope of a future with the new man in her life and offered the promise of emotional refuge. During the following nearly two decades, that bright future withered and the refuge crumbled. She returned, not even as a widow, to the home of her girlhood. The two most important men in her own life, her father and husband, each in his own way, had made her life difficult. Though he would not send Hemings away, as Jefferson's grandson said Martha wanted him to, Jefferson would not repay her forbearance with a final indignity: treating the enslaved mixed-race children of his affair as if they were the same as her free white ones. If Maria Jefferson Eppes had taken second place in her father's affections, Beverley, Harriet, Madison, and Eston Hemings could never have expected their father to place their interests above those of Martha Randolph and her offspring. Their hopes for true and deep family connections within the context of a nuclear family lay in their expectations for the future their mother and father had planned for them.

29

❧

RETIREMENT FOR ONE,
NOT FOR ALL

WHILE JEFFERSON MAY have left public life, the public life never really left him. A virtual horde of visitors began to descend on the mountain almost as soon as he came home in March of 1809—nineteen years after he left home on a similar March day to begin his political career in 1790. The flow of people did not cease until his death in 1826. They came from all over—strangers, friends, and family—to catch a glimpse or be in the presence of the lion in winter. Some were quite bold about this, peering through the windowpanes at Monticello, watching him as he went about his life, as if he were, indeed, the main attraction at the zoo. A large number wanted more than just a glimpse. They came to stay at Monticello as complete households—parents with children and, sometimes, servants in tow, relying on Jefferson's radical hospitality.

It seems clear that many of these people simply wanted to tour the beautiful Virginia countryside, see Jefferson's much talked-about home and its famous resident while, in Jefferson's overseer Edmund Bacon's words, saving themselves "a tavern bill."[1] Martha Randolph had that sense as well. Jefferson, however, preferred to see the attention as a token of his countrymen's esteem and turned aside suggestions that he find ways to discourage the aggressive visitations. His openhanded nature and hatred of direct confrontation prevented him from doing anything that approached being openly inhospitable, though the deluge of visitors added greatly to his already strained finances. All of them, along with whatever horses they brought, were put up and fed at his expense. Some even stayed for weeks at a time. Once, he roundly scolded Bacon after discovering that his frugal overseer was rationing the feed for his guests' horses as a cost-saving measure. He made him restore full portions.[2]

It was not just the money that caused tension in Jefferson's retirement household. Martha Randolph and her daughters resented the constant presence of company. The enslaved laborers no doubt resented them as well. Although Monticello did not legally belong to them, some, like Betty Brown, had spent far more actual time there than Jefferson. The mountain was theirs in a way that mattered greatly. They had created a community born of years of shared experiences and dependence upon one another—and now here came another set of masters and mistresses to get used to for however long they chose to stay. This community had ample reason to feel besieged by the multitude of demanding strangers interrupting daily routines and expectations.

While these visitors would have had no great effect on the daily lives of the enslaved agricultural workers at Monticello, Edith Fossett, Joseph Fossett's wife, whose cooking so impressed Jefferson's visitors, was no doubt the most sorely tasked. She had to prepare multiple meals a day for these people, and do it at a consistently high level. But Fossett was probably not the one who had to make the greatest adjustments. What she was now doing at Monticello was a continuation of her job at the President's House, held for almost eight years. She was used to hard and constant work. And as the cook, she had a measure of control over her activities, working within a rather defined set of parameters. Because she approached artistry in her work, Fossett surely liked cooking and could have the occasional sense of satisfaction of having achieved perfection and the benefit of compliments for having done so.[3] Although she is often referred to as Jefferson's "cook," that title really does not do justice to Fossett's training and experiences, for she, just like James Hemings, was trained for years by a real French chef.

It was the other household servants—the Hemings women and their children—who saw the biggest increase in their daily responsibilities, with fewer possibilities for psychological rewards. Changing linen, making beds, and lighting fires for guests, though less labor-intensive than cooking—left less room for creativity and love of craft than being a chef or a cook. By every measure, the end of Jefferson's formal employment actually marked the start of a new era of drudgery for those who worked in the house. His long absences during his almost two decades of public service after he returned from France left Sally Hemings and her female relatives with little to do when he was away. The men, artisans, always had work—whether Jefferson was there or not. With his daughters returning to their homes when he went back to Washington, and no reason for many visitors to come to the mountain when the center of attention was away, the Hemings women were idle during Jefferson's presidency. Indeed, it is hard to imagine just how these women occupied themselves during the many months when there were no daily household duties to perform.

Because her "formal" employment focused on taking care of Jefferson's chambers, Sally Hemings's work routine necessarily became steadier when he returned permanently to the mountain. It is not likely, though, that she personally attended visitors to Monticello. Even before the name Sally became linked with "Jefferson," and it would have been imprudent to have her interact with curious and likely-to-gossip strangers, her female relatives and their children are the ones who appear in the record as performing the tasks of domestic service. She had ceased being connected to Martha after their return from France, and Martha had a personal maid and complement of enslaved people from her own plantation, Edgehill.

Besides what her son Madison said she did, and the description from a newspaper account in the early 1800s that correctly pegged her as a seamstress for the family, Hemings did help her sisters bottle cider when the season arrived. Neither of those tasks would have required much contact with guests. We know that Hemings's female relatives, like all the other adults at Monticello, kept gardens or raised animals because all of them sold produce or chickens and eggs to the Jefferson family. Hemings did not enter the market with the Jeffersons. Whether she spent any of her time gardening is thus unclear. Her son Beverley, showing an early sign of the entrepreneur at age eight, did sell three quarts of strawberries to the household in 1806.[4] It seems improbable that the youngster planted the fruit himself, so he likely gathered them wild or had been given a section of a family member's garden to call his own. Many later years, after he had left Monticello to begin life as a white man, his teenage brothers, Madison and Eston, would sell to their father cabbages they had grown.

Sally Hemings evidently spent most of her time during Jefferson's retirement years looking after her children—seeing them through childhood illnesses and helping them prepare to become adults. This African

American enslaved mother was in a singular circumstance. She had children who would not be slaves once they reached adulthood. They might not even live as African Americans. Hemings's task was probably not so much about how her children would speak or carry themselves, for there is little reason to believe her speech and presentation were all that different from what theirs turned out to be. As noted earlier, antebellum and postbellum writers and commentators grossly exaggerated the distance between the speech patterns of black and white southerners, in their determination to enforce, even on the written page, a supposed uniform norm of essential racial differences. Hemings had had ample time and occasion to know the ways of whites and, in her case, a particular type of white person to serve as models of behavior for her children. In his late-in-life recollections of Monticello, her great-nephew Peter Fossett spoke with extreme condescension about some of the whites he encountered after leaving Monticello. In his eyes, they were merely crude people, who knew nothing of the rules of etiquette he had learned through his observations of life at Monticello.[5] Sally Hemings, of course, had seen much more of that type of world than her great-nephew. There is no way to know whether she was as snobbish as he about this sort of thing, but she certainly had the opportunity to be.

Hemings, like other mothers of girls, would have spent considerable time teaching her daughter, Harriet, to sew and mend clothing while doing a great deal of that herself. Harriet learned spinning along with the other enslaved girls, probably under the direction of her aunt Nancy, who had been brought back to Monticello in the 1790s for the express purpose of starting Jefferson's small textile operation. Sewing, spinning, and weaving were staple signifiers of feminine virtue, made even more important by the embargo and War of 1812, which disrupted the country's trade with Europe. As it had been just before the American Revolution, homespun became a potent symbol of American self-sufficiency and independence from foreign goods. While his daughter was learning to spin and weave, Jefferson was extolling the virtues of homespun to correspondents like John Adams, at the very beginning of their famous rapprochement in 1811. He praised it as an important example of the "economy and thriftiness" of America's "household manufactures."[6]

Although Sally Hemings was likely the primary influence in the life of her daughter, an important masculine influence began to shape their daily lives once her sons—Beverley, Madison, and Eston—reached the age of twelve or so. They were put under the direction of her brother John, who undoubtedly ended up being something of a surrogate father to them. Though their mother continued to have an important role in their lives, their apprenticeships to their uncle marked the beginning of their transition into manhood. Hemings and his wife, Priscilla, were extremely devoted to one another and, as far as the record shows, had no children of their own. So Jefferson's decision to put his sons in the daily care and under the tutelage of their uncle was not only a sound practical move; it served an important affective goal as well. Standing in Jefferson's place, the much respected carpenter and joiner could be the father they could not have, and they could be like sons to Hemings.

The Monticello joinery was an active place, where John Hemings and his assistants made desks, chairs, and tables, often from Jefferson's designs and from his own inspiration. When Jefferson saw items he liked, such as the Campeche or "siesta" chair for lounging made popular in New Orleans in the early 1800s, he turned to Hemings. Jefferson had wanted a Campeche chair for many years, but was unable to obtain one until 1818. Even before the chair arrived, he described it to Hemings, who made his own version. When the much sought-after object arrived at Monticello, Hemings made at least two more after studying the genuine article. Given whom he worked for, Hemings had to be extremely versatile. In 1814, when the seventy-one-year-old Jefferson grew tired of making his thrice-a-year visits to Poplar Forest on horseback, he drew up plans for a landau, a coach that could seat at least four people. Hemings built the vehicle's body, Joseph Fossett did the necessary iron work, and Burwell Colbert painted it. The vehicle was a source of great pride to Jefferson—and the men who actually worked on it probably felt the same way. Others were less than impressed with a design that seems to have owed a bit too much to Jeffersonian quirkiness.[7]

Perhaps Hemings's grandest achievement, however, was one that did not survive long at all. In 1825 he made a desk for Jefferson's granddaughter Ellen, who had married Joseph Coolidge and moved to Boston. His great time and effort ultimately came to nothing, for the desk was lost at sea on its way to her. Hemings wept at the news. Jefferson reported his utter devastation to Ellen. Hemings had apparently seen the desk as his masterpiece, and Jefferson said that he was as torn apart by the loss as Vergil would have been had his *Aeneid* perished in a fire.[8]

Hemings occupied important space in the lives of Jefferson and his family. Like his nephew Burwell Colbert, he received an annual gratuity and was allowed to have a line of credit at the local store to purchase his own clothing.[9] There was no artisan on the plantation Jefferson respected more, or with whom he worked more closely. About a dozen letters of their correspondence to one another survive, indicating the importance they attached to keeping in contact. The two must have been an interesting sight in conversation—Jefferson, who was six feet two and a half inches tall, and Hemings, who stood just under five feet six inches. As an amateur woodworker himself, Jefferson approached his discussions with Hemings from a more personal vantage point than if he had been less interested in the process of woodworking and building. The two men talked about the work Hemings did for Jefferson, and they very likely discussed whatever items Jefferson worked on himself.

The connection between Hemings and Jefferson spilled over into their immediate families. Jefferson's younger grandchildren, in particular, were close to Hemings, calling him "Daddy" and his wife, Priscilla, who was their nurse, "Mammy." Priscilla Hemings, who, like her husband, was religiously devout, traveled to the President's House to care for the Randolph children when Martha Randolph visited her father there. Edmund Bacon remembered that she had complete charge of the young Randolphs and said that "if there was any switching to be done, she always did it."[10] This was a time when corporal punishment of children was generally expected, and this enslaved woman was allowed, probably directed, to spank Jefferson's grandchildren when they fell outside of the basic norms of behavior that small children of all races were expected to observe.

The Randolph children, whose father was at various times estranged from the family, may have been in special need of male attention from someone younger than their grandfather. Although Jefferson was known for his attentiveness to them, as Madison Hemings remembered, he spent an enormous amount of time during his retirement in his study, reading the countless letters he received, replying to many of them, and initiating his own correspondence.[11] In addition to whatever plantation matters he had to deal with and note in his Farm and Garden Books—along with attending to visitors—this was also Jefferson's time for planning and building the University of Virginia. He simply did not spend as much of his day romping with his grandchildren as some memories of Monticello might indicate.

When they were not in school, the joiner's shop at Monticello was a favorite place for some of the younger Randolphs. They pestered Hemings to make things for them, requests he sometimes turned aside for a while, reminding them that his primary duty was to their grandfather. Hemings had a clear internal sense of the nature and extent of that duty, mentioning to one of the Randolph children that he was saving a large stock of wood to make Jefferson's coffin, an act that he did eventually perform.[12]

We can see the extent of Hemings's identification with Jefferson in an episode at Poplar Forest in 1821. During one of his extended stays at the plantation, he wrote to Jefferson about the activities of Nace, the foreman and gardener at the plantation. After noting that he did not care much for complaining, Hemings said he felt he had to say something because Nace was taking "everything out of the garden," carrying it back to his cabin, and hiding it. When Hemings asked Nace for vegetables, he claimed that he was saving them for Jefferson. Other residents of Poplar Forest revealed Nace's real game: he was taking the vegetables into nearby Lynchburg and selling them in the market.[13]

While Hemings's act of informing on Nace at first glance appears traitorous to a member of the enslaved community, the truth is more complicated. Hemings and his nephews, who were not at Poplar Forest year-round and would not have had their own gardens, evidently got their vegetables from Jefferson's kitchen garden. By taking all the vegetables for himself, Nace was "hurting" not just Jefferson but also Hemings, who had no access to a valuable foodstuff that Nace was appropriating for monetary gain. Hemings faced the common dilemma of members of any subordinated group within a given society. Certain individuals within the group are often willing to commit bad acts that seriously harm their fellows. They then rely upon the group members' natural inclination to stand together in the face of oppression to keep doing whatever they are doing. Of course, the individual bad actor has no real loyalty to the community, or else he or she would never deliberately hurt one of its members. Such persons are motivated by the kind of extreme selfishness that can be found in any race, class, or other subsection of the human population. Often the oppressed community closes ranks and will continue to suffer rather than expose the bad actor to the wrath of their common oppressor—unless the problem passes some threshold of intolerability. Then they can either exact retribution themselves or have the oppressor deal with the one who is causing the problem. That is what seems to have happened with Hemings and Nace.

Nace erred by going too far. His greed adversely affected members of his own enslaved community. Had he been willing to share, there would have been no problem. The difficulty with community policing of Nace's activities was that he was the foreman at Poplar Forest and in a position of power. The only ones "above" him were the overseer and Jefferson, the community's oppressors. We really do not know what steps Hemings took before bringing Jefferson into the matter. His letter suggests, however, that writing to Monticello was a last, desperate resort.

EVEN BEFORE JEFFERSON left office, his life as a public man began to intrude upon his private world at Monticello, and he took what steps he could during his presidency to protect himself. The front line in the battle was his private chamber, which he guarded almost obsessively. A visitor to his home, Margaret Bayard Smith, described it as his "*sanctum sanctorum.*" It is not that no one ever went into Jefferson's private living quarters, though he did create the strong presumption that the area was generally off-limits. Anna Maria Thornton, a visitor during his presidency, noted with great interest, and some bewilderment, that the multiple doors leading to Jefferson's bedroom suite were always locked and that he used only one entrance himself—the door leading into the library. He did allow visitors. Thornton was eventually given a tour, and Isaac Jefferson and Edmund Bacon mentioned having conversations with Jefferson in his living area. And, of course, in the daily life of the place, Sally Hemings, Burwell Colbert, and, probably, many others were in Jefferson's bedroom and living area for one reason or another over the five decades he lived on the mountain. Two entrances into his living quarters from the outside may have on occasion doubled as service entrances as well as a means for Jefferson to have quick access to the outdoors. These entrances also allowed his world with Sally Hemings, and perhaps even with their children, to remain resolutely separate from the world he lived in with others.[14]

As more strangers came to visit Monticello and wander freely about the grounds, it became clear that the very open nature of the house posed a problem. The picturesque walkway just off the south piazza next to his chambers created a bird's-eye view into his living chambers. With the help of John Hemings, Jefferson took steps to rectify this problem during his presidency. Hemings built, and James Dinsmore also worked on, what Jefferson called "porticles"—structures attached to the exterior of his private living area. The porticles, with their louvered blinds, blocked outside views into his bedroom chamber and study and enclosed the two small private porches on the western and eastern flanks of Jefferson's bedroom that essentially extended his living area. The porticles, or Venetian porches, as they are also known, preserved at least some of the sense of being outdoors, allowing him to look out, but preventing those outside from seeing in.[15]

Jefferson never said why he built them and, in the process, destroyed the perfect geometric symmetry of Monticello's Palladian design. There are no porticles on the north side of Monticello. Indeed, later owners of Monticello thought them ugly and tore them down, but they have since been restored. It has been suggested that Jefferson got the idea of building them after the exposure of his relationship with Sally Hemings.The bedroom shades and the closed blinds of the porticles made it harder to see into his living area when she was there.[16] Whether that was the impetus or not, her ability to enter his rooms from the steps of the outside porches leading into his quarters created privacy for them both. Ellen Coolidge's claim that no female servant could have entered Jefferson's rooms without being seen by anyone is patently untrue. Hemings never had to enter Jefferson's rooms from the entrance hallway on the inside of Monticello that visitors and other members of his family traversed. If Hemings, or anyone else, for that matter, used one of the two sets of outside steps leading into his bedroom suite late enough at night, no one in the house would have known she had entered. Only sentinels keeping watch over those two outside entrances twenty-four hours a day, seven days a week, could have done that. As far as we know, such sentinels never existed at Monticello.

Changing the physical structure of the most intimate part of his home, however, was not enough to ensure privacy when Jefferson really wanted it. In Paris he had had his hermitage for work and relaxation in solitude, and he needed something similar in the United States. Poplar Forest, in Bedford County, about ninety miles from Monticello, was Jefferson's second home during his retirement. It was part of the land that he and Martha inherited upon the death of her father. This is where the Jeffersons retreated after his narrow escape from the advance of Tarleton's troops on Monticello in 1781 and where he began to write *Notes on the State of Virginia*, an obscure place where no one would come looking for him, an aspect that had changed little even into the nineteenth century. Obviously, it was not obscure to the people who lived there, for Poplar Forest was a working plantation with an enslaved labor force that provided steady income for Jefferson's family. Here he grew tobacco, long after he had switched to wheat at Monticello. Enslaved people traveled back and forth between the two plantations, and families were sometimes split up in the process. A number of teenage boys were taken from Poplar Forest to work in Jefferson's nail factory at Monticello, and their female counterparts also came there to learn spinning and weaving until he opened a weaving shop at Poplar Forest and they stayed there to learn.[17]

The remoteness of the place clearly appealed to Jefferson, and amid the travails of his presidency, he began to build a house in what had once been a dense forest of poplar trees. He started in 1806, and the building was finished in 1809, just in time for his retirement. Because few people knew he even had a second home, this was the ideal place to go to escape the throngs at Monticello. It was, indeed, a very Jeffersonian solution, an act of circumvention rather than confrontation. Instead of suggesting, directly or indirectly, that people leave Monticello, he simply decided to leave Monticello to *them* periodically. At first he went alone, but in later years he sometimes took his older grandchildren, who developed a love-hate relationship with the place. They, like he, enjoyed escaping the overabundance of company, but the members of this younger generation were not always happy with the long sojourns.[18] Whether Sally Hemings was ever there with him is unknown, because there is virtually no chance that any persons in the Jefferson household would ever have mentioned that in their correspondence.

The house Jefferson built there was, for him, an architectural delight. Later occupants, including his grandson Francis and his wife, Mary, were less impressed. Made of brick, and in his favorite shape, the octagon, the house had a series of inner octagon-shaped chambers surrounding the main living room. With characteristic enthusiasm he pronounced it "the best dwelling house in the state, except that of Monticello." Given that he built it for privacy, he allowed that Poplar Forest was particularly suited to "the faculties of a private citizen" and was in that way actually better than Monticello.[19]

Jefferson could never really have been a private citizen, for he had sought to graft himself onto the public mind for nearly two decades. Although he may have done that in the name of furthering his political ideals and preferences for the direction of the new nation, he wanted to make himself the symbol of those ideals and could not easily have been separated from them. Despite that, he took the firm view that public officials should be judged on their actions as public men alone. His private life was not really the public's business. One understands clearly now why he was so adamant about drawing and maintaining the public/private distinction, but it was an unrealistic notion then, as it is today. While there should indeed have been limits to how much people wanted to know about him, as a student of history, he understood that the lives of famous men are always subject to scrutiny. This new era of modern American politics, an era he helped usher in, had not changed that fact of human nature. Even he was interested in the personal and sexual lives of other leaders.

The noted Harvard professor George Ticknor, who visited Monticello during Jefferson's retirement, remembered the former president's great fondness for a collection of memoirs of what Ticknor called "documents of regal scandal."[20] Ticknor sought to explain Jefferson's surprising and slightly frivolous (to Ticknor) attachment to the volumes as an example of his well-known hatred for monarchy. That may have been true to an extent, but it sounds very much like an earlier version of reading *Playboy* for the articles. Given what he knew of the world, Jefferson could not reasonably have expected to be able to control the public appetite for information about him. Just as many longed to come to see him even after his public life ended, the interest in his private life continued.

About two years into Jefferson's retirement, Elijah Fletcher, an educator on his way to his installation as president of New Glasgow Academy, gave an account of his visit to Monticello and Charlottesville. Fletcher, of Vermont, sounding every bit the stereotype of the puritanical New Englander, admitted that he had always been dubious of what he called Jefferson's "moral conduct"—probably gleaned from what he had read in Federalist newspapers. But, he said, Jefferson's neighbors in Charlottesville gave him additional cause for concern on that score. They were more than willing to talk about the master of Monticello, and what they knew of life there, including Sally Hemings. Fletcher wrote,

The story of black Sal is no farce—That he cohabits with her and has a number of children by her is a sacred truth—and the worst of it is, he keeps the same children slaves—an unnatural crime which is very common in these parts. This conduct may receive a little palliation when we consider such proceedings are so common here that they cease here to be disgraceful—[21]

Jefferson's children were thirteen, eleven, six, and three at the time Fletcher visited, and his commentary reiterates a point that cannot be emphasized enough: the Hemings children's situation was not in and of itself unique. Many mixed-race children had white fathers who also legally owned them, because interracial sex on plantations was not uncommon. When healthy men and women had sex, they almost invariably had children, given the lack of effective birth control and societal attitudes toward abortion. What made Beverley, Harriet, Madison, and Eston Hemings different was that their father was a *famous* white man, and many people cared enough about him to pay attention to what he was doing. Jefferson's fame, however, did not immunize him and his family from the constitutive attributes of the slave system. The other difference that Fletcher could not have known is that the two eldest children were readying to leave the status that so upset him, and the two youngest would follow in their turn.

Jefferson's retreat, Poplar Forest, actually played a role in preparing Beverley, Madison, and Eston Hemings for their lives outside of slavery. John Hemings had done work on the house from the very beginning, and all throughout Jefferson's retirement, Hemings worked on the house's exterior and interior, doing the woodworking and making the furniture to Jefferson's specifications. When Beverley and Madison Hemings came of age and became his apprentices, they, and later Eston, all traveled to Poplar Forest to learn carpentry and joining by working on their father's house. During their teenage years all three were away from the mountain and at Poplar Forest, sometimes for long stretches of time.

It is common to think of Jefferson's trips to Poplar Forest as involving merely his granddaughters. The Randolph family letters set the domestic scene, telling of the tedium of the journey—sometimes broken by picnics along the roadside with Jefferson carving the meat and dishing out the food—and stays in inns along the way. Then there was the scene at

the house, with the girls studying Latin and conversing with their grandfather when he was not working and they were not receiving visitors occasionally and going to the homes of others. Naturally, in their own minds,
they were the centerpiece of this tableau. The young women did, however,
often write of Burwell Colbert, who invariably traveled with Jefferson, and
of John Hemings, whom they liked very much, passing along these men's
regards to wives and family left behind. Their correspondents at Monticello
followed the same course, sending messages and greetings from family
members to these men.[22]

Jefferson's granddaughters apparently never mentioned, in any correspondence available to date, the other people from Monticello who were
also present at Poplar Forest when they made their visits: Beverley, Madison,
and, in later years, Eston Hemings. The scene brought together four
Hemings males of different generations who likely got to know one another
better than they would have had they been together only at Monticello with
more levels of people between them. Colbert's job was to help Jefferson as
needed and keep the house clean. John Hemings was there to work, along
with his nephews, on the house itself, the interior and outside. In the isolation of Poplar Forest, their nephews had the same level of contact with
the Jefferson granddaughters as they did. It is simply not possible that the
Randolph girls did not encounter their grandfather's sons on a daily basis,
or that Jefferson did not have lots of contact with them as he supervised and
commented on their work, proceeding right before his eyes.

The Randolphs' practice of keeping the Colbert and the John Hemings
families apprised of one another's well-being did not extend to conveying
messages from Sally Hemings to her still young sons or from her sons to
her. The Hemingses may have communicated on their own, or Jefferson
could have written letters, kept no copy of them, and sent them by the
enslaved people who went back and forth between the two plantations.
But the absence of any references to the well-being or activities of Beverley,
Madison, and Eston Hemings when they were at Poplar Forest is telling. It
fits perfectly with the apparent Jefferson-Randolph family convention that
Jefferson's children with Sally Hemings were to exist, as much as possible,
in modern parlance, off the radar screen.

The pattern of life that ensued at Poplar Forest perhaps helps put into
context Madison Hemings's decision to name one of his children "Ellen
Wayles."[23] This was no random act—the Hemingses were very serious and

deliberate in the naming of their offspring. Although Hemings could well have been reaching back to honor his grandfather John Wayles's mother, Ellen Wayles, it seems more likely that naming his daughter grew out of the nature of his dealings with and view of Ellen Wayles Randolph. At the same time, it is not at all surprising that there would be an asymmetry in how these two people presented their connections to the outside world. Given the way race has been lived in the United States, and given what Ellen thought was at stake for her white family, even if she and Madison Hemings had cordial relations in private, she would feel compelled to deny her true connection to him—indeed to write of him and his siblings as if they were almost strangers to her.

In her letter claiming that her uncle Samuel Carr, not her grandfather, was the father of Madison Hemings and his siblings, Ellen writes with all the authority and sangfroid of one used to having her word treated as the final say on matters. It is, at the same time, a rather poignant document, considering what we know of how Hemings apparently viewed her. The letter, ostensibly just to her husband, Joseph Coolidge, was clearly meant to be shown to others. The strategic passing around of letters was considered a genteel way among upper-class families to convey important information to members of their class without going into the newspapers. In the letter, written in 1858, Sally Hemings was not a woman Ellen knew growing up. She did not have a specific role and function in the Monticello they both shared over the years. She was a woman Ellen barely knew anything about except that she had served as her mother's lady's maid in France almost a decade before Ellen was born. Beverley, Harriet, Madison, and Eston were Hemings's nameless "children," rather than people Ellen knew well from both Monticello and, in case of the sons, Poplar Forest. Beverley Hemings used to play the violin at the dances the Jefferson granddaughters hosted as young women at Monticello. Yet, by 1858, Sally Hemings and her children might as well have been enslaved people living on another plantation whom Ellen saw on intermittent visits.[24]

A number of Jefferson's letters to his overseer at Poplar Forest, Joel Yancey, and our knowledge of John Hemings's whereabouts make plain that these young men spent at least as much total time at Poplar Forest as Jefferson's granddaughters. Sometimes they came with Jefferson, at other times they left a few days ahead of time to be there when he arrived, and at still other points they were already in residence when the party from

Monticello descended. Jefferson's letters to Yancy and the letters of his granddaughters show that the Hemings brothers and the granddaughters were there at the same time. For example, in September of 1816, when Beverley was eighteen and Madison was four months shy of his twelfth birthday, Jefferson wrote to Yancy, "John Hemings & his two aids will set out so as to be at Poplar Forest the evening before us." In November of 1818 he noted, "I shall carry up Johnny Hemings & his 2.assistants early in the year and they will work there till the fall." The following June he wrote, "I shall be able to leave this for Poplar Forest about the 7th of July, and shall bring with me one glass of one kind to repair damages to the house, while two boxes of another kind will go up from Richmond by the first boat from Lynchburg. Johnny Hemings and his assistants will go when I do; the other carpenters something later."[25]

For each of these and other letters making reference to Hemings and his helpers, there are letters from one or more of Jefferson's grandchildren indicating that they or their mother were at Poplar Forest at the same time as these men. For example, Ellen Coolidge's letter to her mother of July 18 explains Jefferson's reference to repairing the "damages to the house." He had been told that a hail storm had come through Bedford and that, in Ellen's words, "all the glass on the north side of the house" had been "demolished." Her postscript confirms Jefferson's plan of July 7 to have the rest of the Monticello carpenters join John Hemings and his nephews later.[26]

If his granddaughters' letters totally "disappear" Beverley, Madison, and Eston Hemings, Jefferson's letters to his overseer are only marginally more open, following the practice of keeping these young men as anonymous as possible. The problem for him, and his grandchildren, was that the Hemings children had names that were virtually indistinguishable from the rest of their family. William Beverley, George Wythe, Harriet, Benjamin Franklin, James Madison, Meriwether Lewis, Thomas Eston—all of these names were connected to Jefferson, either through blood or because of his association with and affection for those individuals. Each name was appropriate for his children or grandchildren, and James Madison was indeed the name of a son and grandson.

Names signify identity. Jefferson did not mind that the Hemings children bore names that signaled their identity to anyone knowledgeable about his family and associations. He evidently wanted that. Neither he nor his family, however, wanted to carry that signal of identity into posterity by indiscriminately putting the Hemings children's names into their letters. Beverley, Madison, and Eston are, depending upon the year, John Hemings's "two assistants" or "two aids" or "two apprentices." In 1825, when writing to his grandson Francis Eppes, who was living at Poplar Forest when a fire damaged the roof, Jefferson reported that he would send Hemings and his "two aids" to help repair it. By that time Beverley was gone, and thirteen-year-old Eston had taken his place. Had it not been for Jefferson's will, and the serendipity of Madison Hemings's recollections, we would never have known who the two nameless "aids" and "assistants" at Poplar Forest were. The law absolutely mandated that Jefferson give the names of the people he was granting freedom, so he could not be evasive in that document.[27]

BURWELL COLBERT'S CLOSENESS to Jefferson in his retirement brought advantages, along with acute hazards. Because Jefferson decided to have two homes, Colbert was required to have two homes as well. Of the two men, only Jefferson really needed to escape Monticello and free himself from importuning guests. That was Jefferson's problem, not Colbert's, and the younger man had to endure long and frequent separations from his wife, Critta, and their children.

Burwell and Critta Colbert had done something that was highly unusual among Africans Americans, whether enslaved or free. They married one another despite being half first cousins. Burwell was the son of Betty Brown, and Critta was the daughter of Betty's half sister Nancy Hemings. Whether the taboo against marrying cousins was a holdover from some of the West African cultures from which most enslaved people in the United States hailed, or whether it was something that developed in America, is unknown. But this type of incest was one cultural affect that blacks determinedly resisted picking up from whites, who saw no problem marrying their first cousins, let alone second or third ones.[28] We cannot, of course, recover the details of the Colberts' courtship, and the two young people could easily have had other reasons for falling in love, but one wonders whether the impetus to break this very strong taboo was the lack of suitable partners. The Hemingses tended to pair with other mixed-race people, and there may not have been enough of them who were both unrelated and attractive to them in their immediate environment. As we noted earlier, Colbert apparently did not travel as freely as his uncles Martin, Robert, and James Hemings. There is no record of his having a separate life in Richmond or Fredericksburg, from which he could have drawn a partner. Because of gender conventions, Critta Hemings, a woman enslaved on the nearby Randolph plantation from the time her mother returned to Monticello in the 1790s, also had fewer chances to go very far searching for a husband.

Whatever the basis of their attraction, the evidence indicates that the Colberts were deeply devoted to one another, and both suffered during the enforced separations when Colbert attended Jefferson and his granddaughters at Poplar Forest. Colbert had to receive secondhand reports of the well-being of his family through messages sent in Jefferson's granddaughters' letters. In 1816 Betty Brown sent word to her son that his daughter, for whom she was caring, was still as ill as she had been when he left. One can only imagine that the father would rather have been with his wife and daughter comforting them both than keeping house for Jefferson and his granddaughters.[29]

In 1819 Colbert was at Poplar Forest when he learned that his wife had died, an event that devastated him. He was, Ellen Coolidge wrote, "overwhelmed with grief" at the news. Her words on this subject, however, show with great clarity the vast gulf she placed between herself and the newly widowed and grieving man, for whom she claimed to have had sympathy. It is difficult to imagine that one could find a better window into the mind-set of the soi-disant "good white slave owner." Ellen's reaction to the death of Critta Colbert, who had been her nurse for a time, is worth quoting in some detail. Her letter reveals her and her sisters' attitudes toward the Colbert daughters, Susan, Emily, Martha, and Thenia.

> I have been recollecting that some time ago, when I was lamenting very seriously that I had not secured one of her [Critta's} elder children Mama promised I should have any one of them not disposed of. Susan and Emily I believe Cornelia and yourself had taken at that time, and I think I pitched on little Martha as subject to no prior claims. I hope with all my heart this is the case, for I am more than ever anxious to have it in my power to befriend, and *educate as well as I can, one of these children*, and if I remember right Martha is a little sprightly black-eyed girl, whom I have often noticed with pleasure. I think her poor mother would have liked this disposition of her, I believe she preferred me to

the rest of the family. If however Mary or any of the rest of you should have a prior claim why then Mama's promise will hold good for little Theana. (emphasis added)

When speaking of Burwell, she added,

[I]f he should be averse to the distributing of all his children, I am willing to waive the claim I spoke of altogether, or else to promise that if I should ever quit my family of which there is scarcely a possibility, I will then surrender my rights. or if Mama should be unwilling to deprive herself of the last of a family which has a hereditary right to be highly valued, I will say and think no more about the matter.[30]

One thinks immediately of the thirty-six-year-old man, alone in his room, or being comforted by his uncle John and his first cousins Beverley and Madison Hemings. He is riven with pain at the loss of his wife, the mother of his children, who were being talked about as if they were puppies being picked from a litter by Ellen and her sisters. To be sure, Ellen speaks of wanting to educate "one" of Colbert's children, and that good intention alone no doubt allowed her to think of herself as a humane person even as she casually detailed the parceling out of another couple's children in a manner that would have broken her own parents' hearts had she and her siblings been treated similarly.

Ellen could easily have educated one of Colbert's children without "pitching" a "claim" to the child, as if there were no way for her to conceptualize the Colberts except as possessions. Actually, Jefferson's grandchildren did teach enslaved people at Monticello to read. In 1816, while on a visit to Poplar Forest, seventeen-year-old Cornelia Randolph asked her mother to send a dictionary that she had intended to give to John Hemings, but had left behind at Monticello. Beverley and Madison Hemings were at Poplar Forest, too, and would have had access to the dictionary as well. Cornelia, however, took an interest in Hemings's education, but without pitching claims to him in any way.[31]

Ellen did suggest that she would relinquish her "claim" upon little Martha Colbert if she married and moved away from her family. That would have been some small consolation to Colbert, but he knew that the fulfillment of this promise was entirely up to Ellen. And what of Ellen's sisters—had they promised to leave Susan and Emily Colbert at Monticello when and if they ever married? No matter how frequently it happened, no matter how endemic it was to a system that treated human beings like property, enslaved people never got used to having their children claimed by others as possessions.

We will never know, because he left no record, what Colbert really thought of the family who viewed his children and the rest of his extended family as items to be parceled out among themselves. As we will see, Jefferson's will kept him pretty much under the influence of the Randolph family until he died. But because he was so close to Jefferson and, unlike his aunt Sally, an acceptable enslaved person to write about openly, Colbert appears regularly in Randolph family stories and correspondence. He has also appeared in Jefferson scholarship from the earliest days as an exemplar of the kind of slave that southerners found most appealing. He and Sally Hemings were the only enslaved people who were ever said to have lived in the house at Monticello, though it is possible that others, James Hemings, for example, did as well.[32]

One must be wary of the "faithful darky" stories beloved by so many generations of slavery's apologists, because they seldom involve a sophisticated consideration of a given enslaved person's possible motive in playing the role of the "faithful darky." Colbert was very likely making calculations about how best to proceed, given his circumscribed position. It will be recalled that Jefferson had singled him out for special treatment as early as the 1790s, when Colbert was still in his early teens, most probably in preparation for the role he played in Jefferson's retirement: his faithful manservant who could be counted on to put his interests first, to keep his secrets, and to appear happy to do both. It would have taken a strong person, indeed, to resist what appears to have been Jefferson's sustained effort, from Colbert's early adolescence, to make him think he was special to Jefferson.

Although it seems that Colbert had a genuine fondness for Jefferson and that Jefferson was fond of him, it must be remembered that affection usually carries a complement of self-interest. We often gain from displaying it to another. The most immediate reward is reciprocity. Jefferson gained Colbert's loyalty and discretion. For his part, Colbert could have affection for Jefferson but never lose sight of the man's ultimate utility for him. And as long as he responded to Jefferson's displays in the expected fashion, the Randolphs might continue to "value" the Colbert family enough to keep them as close together as possible. Mutual affection was practical, if not symbiotic, for the two men in their respective circumstances.

We get some sense of the nature of the relationship between Colbert and Jefferson in two separate events where each one thought the other in danger of dying. In July of 1819, just a month before his wife's death, Colbert, while at Poplar Forest with Jefferson, fell gravely ill with some "obstruction of the bowel" that caused him enormous pain and prevented him from sleeping for two days. The doctor called in to attend to him bled him until he almost passed out. He also prescribed laudanum, which may have exacerbated Colbert's intestinal problem, but did ease his pain enough to allow him to sleep.[33]

Ellen Randolph's letter describing Colbert's illness and the toll it took on him and on her grandfather is deeply revealing. Jefferson was beside himself with worry throughout this entire episode. "I never saw any body more uneasy than Grandpapa, and his constant anxiety by convincing me still more of his extraordinary value for Burwell, increased my own fears and feelings to a degree that surprised even me."[34] Ellen creates a vivid picture of a distraught Jefferson, who on other occasions reviled doctors, now waiting anxiously for the local physician to arrive and help Colbert. While she was concerned about her grandfather's manservant, she was still more concerned about the effect Colbert's illness was having on her grandfather, fearing what would happen if he woke up one morning and found Colbert dead. And then Ellen witnessed something else that seemed to startle her but that is wholly unsurprising, given the relationship between the two men.

> John Hemmings paid him attentions which were really affecting. I always believed him an excellent creature but I think better of him now then [sic] ever. I really believe that at one time his advice and application of a warm bath, by the temporary relief it procured, enabled Burwell to stand against the violence.[35]

Hemings's attentiveness to and concern for his sister's child would be considered completely normal in a culture that placed a high value on extended kinship networks. This lesson in family feeling and responsibility set an example for Beverley and Madison Hemings, who would have witnessed the same display as Ellen. In fact, it is probable that they, too, were involved at least in some way in their uncle's care, and also saw their father's response to their cousin's suffering. Helping a severely weakened grown man, who was just a shade under six feet tall, into a warm bath may have required more than just two hands.[36]

Nineteen-year-old Israel Gillette, of Monticello, who would later give his recollections of life on the mountain, took over for Colbert during his illness. He did so well, and pleased Jefferson so much, that Ellen said that she had to "abuse" him "every day to prevent him from thinking hereafter, that the complaints I have no doubt we *shall* have cause to make, are without foundation—is not this being very prudent and shewing great judgement and forethought."[37] This may have been a joke—or perhaps not. She may have actually thought that toying in this manner with a person over whom she had nearly plenary power made good sense.

Jefferson's report of Colbert's illness shows the folly of thinking that his letters express the sum total of his emotions about a given subject. Much more was always going on under the surface in the mind and life of this very complicated man, much more than he was willing to share openly. He did sometimes give vent to his deep feelings about matters and people, but he may have thought it unseemly to put down for posterity the degree of his emotional vulnerability to an enslaved person. Instead, his letter describing this episode speaks in a matter-of-fact fashion, "we have been near losing Burwell . . . but he has got about again and is now only very weak." As the historian Jefferson Looney has noted, it is only through his granddaughter's description of his frantic concern that we learned how deeply the possible death of Colbert affected Jefferson.[38]

Colbert had equal cause to be anxious about Jefferson six years later. John H. I. Browere, described as an "itinerant sculptor" by Dumas Malone and a "vile plaisterer" by Jefferson's granddaughter Virginia, appeared at Monticello in the fall of 1825. Browere, a New Yorker, asked the elderly and now frail Jefferson to allow him to take a life mask. Against his better judgment and that of his family, Jefferson decided to go along with the procedure. The "artist" positioned Jefferson on his back on a sofa. Perhaps to steady himself while doing this and to help him rise when he wanted to sit up, Jefferson rested one hand on a nearby chair. Members of his family at one point stepped out of the room, leaving Colbert with Jefferson and Browere. Browere, who was apparently not very skillful, covered Jefferson's face and neck with plaster that hardened too quickly. The mask began to impair Jefferson's breathing and prevented him from speaking. Already in a weakened state when Browere arrived, and now furthered enfeebled by the loss of oxygen under the plaster, he could not stand up. Finally, he remembered the chair, lifted it up and banged it on the floor, alerting Burwell and Browere to his distress. Panic ensued. Colbert was at complete attention, though really unable to do anything. Browere immediately attempted to remove the mask, but because he had not put sufficient oil on Jefferson's face, the plaster stuck to his skin. Jefferson groaned and even sobbed as sections of the cast were pulled off his face.[39]

Jefferson described the ordeal to Madison with a wry undertone that disguised the fact that the "life mask" had almost become a death mask.

> He was obliged to use freely the mallet and chisel to break it into pieces and cut off a piece at a time. These thumps of the mallet would have been sensible to a loggerhead. The family became alarmed, and he confused, till I was quite exhausted, and there became a real danger that the ears would separate from the head sooner than from the plaster. I now bid adieu for ever to busts and even portraits.[40]

In Jefferson's description "the family" was alarmed; he, merely exhausted and resigned. Actually the family members—including, in Jefferson's patriarchal sense, Colbert—were more than alarmed. They were furious. According to Jefferson family accounts, after the cast was removed, Colbert hurried to help Jefferson up. He was holding the weakened man in his arms and glowering ominously over Jefferson's shoulder at the hapless Browere when other members of the household rushed into the room upon realizing there was a problem.

Amazingly, instead of gathering up his materials and leaving forthwith, Browere stayed long enough to dine at Monticello. Jefferson rallied and appeared at the table that evening, but he was described as "tormented by the chattering of the magpie [Browere,]" who was so boorish and insensitive that he actually joked about having almost killed the former president of the United States. Even more astonishingly, when word of the fiasco became generally known, and Browere feared his reputation might suffer, he asked Jefferson to write a testimonial for him, which for some inexplicable reason he agreed to do.[41]

While professional negligence was at the heart of Jefferson's near-death experience, the episode was a stark reminder to all those enslaved at

Monticello that their continued settlement at this place now depended upon the life of one who was slowly fading away. The Hemingses, to be sure, were not the only long-term residents on the mountain who were about to have their lives transformed when the inevitable arrived. But no family had longer, closer, more complicated—and more compromising—connections to the man whose existence was the only thing that stood between the vast majority of them and the auction block. What would become of their family and the enslaved community at Monticello when he was gone?

30

ENDINGS AND BEGINNINGS

T HE SEEDS OF disaster had been planted early, though just how early is hard to say. If we think in terms of distinct financial events as paving the way for the Hemings family's tragic endings at Monticello, we might start with the time the family arrived on the mountain in the 1770s. Before they came to Jefferson as part of the assets of John Wayles's legacy, Jefferson had no extensive experience with all that could go wrong with the liabilities side of a ledger. His father had been able to provide a comfortable, even sophisticated, style of living for his family while leaving his heirs assets that exceeded the value of his liabilities. His mother's debts were relatively small, and easy to settle, although he took a long time to do that.

Jefferson's engagement with the Wayles debt really began his lifelong and frustrating struggle with creditors. The legacy itself worked almost as a Faustian bargain for him, not because of its inherent nature but because of his. For Jefferson the glass was always half full; his basic optimism tended to make him accentuate the positive, while eliminating the negative. So when he received Wayles's thousands of acres and 135 slaves and added them to his own, not insignificant holdings, it solidified his inner view of himself as an extremely wealthy man. And he had good reason to think that way if one considered only the totality of his assets—the half full glass. The Wayles inheritance did, in fact, make him one of the largest property owners—in both land and enslaved people—in Virginia. That never meant, however, that he was free from danger. Judicious planning, frugality, and considered attention to detail were required to manage both the benefits and the burdens that came with what Wayles had left to his daughter and, by extension, to him.

It is not that Jefferson failed to recognize the perils of debt. But other than make him worry at times, and voice exasperation at the way his creditors harassed him, his knowledge did not typically order his daily behavior. He did periodically take steps to try to alleviate his financial problems, initiating schedules to repay creditors after selling land and enslaved people. And in what must have been one of the most bittersweet moments of his life, he sold in 1815 his personal library, consisting of 6,847 books, to the Library of Congress to replace its collection, just 3,000 books, lost when the British burned Washington during the War of 1812.[1]

In most respects, Jefferson was not so different from other Virginians of his class for whom indebtedness was a way of life. But he had more expensive tastes and an obsession with building that strained his finances in ways far beyond the ordinary. He also had a penchant for plans that would supposedly generate enough income to bring him into solvency. Though he realized he had to cut expenses, he clearly placed greater emphasis on getting more money as a way of escaping debt than effectively managing his spending. This strategy has trapped many a debtor into a lifetime cycle of often unnecessary financial instability—waiting to win the lottery or for "the ship to come in" before taking effective control of their economic lives. His nail operation had been profitable until a flood of cheaper British nails destroyed his market. Then he also sank thousands of dollars into a flour mill that turned into "a disaster of mammoth proportions."[2] It is easy to understand his preferences along these lines. A nail factory required a building and turned out a product he could physically count. It had mechanical implements that made an item needed for other building. The flour mill had to be designed and built—another mechanical operation. Both can be seen as large-scale versions of the gadgets Jefferson so adored. Why not play with them? Cutting back on expenses was never so alluring; that would just mean doing without something he wanted. And since he was, in his own mind, basically wealthy, why should that really be necessary? Had Jefferson been less of an optimist—some might say more of a realist—he might never have taken his persona as a wealthy man so much to heart, treating his outstanding debts and obligations as external to his world, instead of as integral parts of his overall financial state.

Though he famously told James Madison that the debts of one generation should not be transferred to succeeding ones—because "the earth belongs . . . to the living"—there is no evidence that Jefferson ever seriously doubted that the wealth of one generation should go to its progeny. His odd decoupling of the concept of assets from liabilities, benefits from burdens, may explain something almost unfathomable: though he kept meticulous records of his daily expenses—how much he spent, usually for what purpose, and where he was when he spent it—he never totaled up his expenses and compared them to his income. Double-entry bookkeeping was not for him, and, as a result, he never really grasped his extremely perilous financial condition.[3] He seemed to live totally in the moment, keeping all hints of a day of reckoning off the page—and thus invisible. Indeed, at several key moments in his life, Jefferson was brought up short, shocked to find that he owed thousands of dollars that he had no idea he owed. One suspects this was a case of not wanting to know. Had he ever really acknowledged how deeply in debt he was at a given time, he would have incurred the responsibility of doing something about it. Instead, he walked through life assuming that all would work out in the end; and since he thought of himself as a good and well-intentioned person, who was often generous to a fault with others, that would surely count for something in the overall scheme of things.

The historian Herbert Sloan, in his detailed exploration of Jefferson's handling of his finances, raised the deep tragedy at the heart of this story with characteristic insight and understatement. "Jefferson's attitude toward his debts, his belief that in time things would right themselves, his certainty that, if allowed to do things his way, everything would turn out for the best, had significant consequences for others."[4] The "others," as Sloan explained, who would suffer the most grievously when Jefferson's time and luck ran out, were the enslaved on his farms, including the Hemingses, whose lives were inexorably linked to his fortunes. Under the rules of his society, which supposedly justified the plantation way of life, the patriarch who governed had a corresponding duty to protect those who lived under his dominion. The price of failure was the humiliation of the patriarch and his legal family, but it also involved the actual decimation of the families of the enslaved—husbands, wives, children, brothers, sisters, mothers, and fathers—scattered to the four winds.

Jefferson's salary as president should have been enough to help put him on the road to financial security. Despite this, he retired to Monticello in even more dire financial straits than when he had taken office, stunned by the new debts accrued in eight years. The way he conducted the business of the presidency was the heart of the problem. He spent lavishly, out of his own pocket, on the much storied dinner parties—or "campaigns," as he called them—that he hosted for members of Congress and other government offi-cials. This was not frivolity. These affairs had a serious public purpose for Jefferson and were critical to the way he governed. There he presided over a roundtable, eschewing waiters, serving the food to his guests himself, "being mother," as it was called.⁵ The exquisite wine and choice French fare and his casual manner displayed in this intimate setting were central to his plan to build the Republican Party as a bulwark against Federalism that would out-last his tenure in office. The development of the United States along the lines he thought preferable was Jefferson's true obsession. It operated to the detriment of any real consideration of ending slavery in the country or at Monticello. It even operated to the detriment of his legal white family. Much as he spoke of his family as the center of his universe, he, like many public men before and after him, arranged his life so that he spent large amounts of time away from his family doing what he thought was the real business of his life. Not only did his family lose time with him; his only surviving legal daughter, Martha, still with school-age children, would end up without her own home—the object of pity and charity.

How much the enslaved people closest to Jefferson, like Sally Hemings and Burwell Colbert, who were with him when no one else was around, knew of his financial circumstances upon his return to the mountain and in the years that followed will remain unknown. Though he may never have con-fided in either, a worried look or furrowed brow can communicate volumes. Even the free whites and unfree blacks who were not intimately involved with him could sense the precarious state of his finances, without knowing the full extent. Conversations overheard, strained silence at the mention of certain topics, bills delivered from persistent and familiar commercial outfits, can send messages almost as explicit as those directly conveyed.

The enslaved at Monticello, portrayed in early Jefferson scholarship as childlike and simpleminded, were anything but that. One has only to read the memoirs of men like Isaac Jefferson and Israel Gillette, with their dead-on observations about the financial states, family relationships, and histo-ries of the whites in their world, to know that they were not. They could never have afforded to ignore any visible signs of turmoil. Knowing white slave owners was their business, for their lives, and the lives of their loved ones, were in the hands of these fallible people, who could be expected to put the interests of the enslaved last when and if things began to fall apart.

The sale of Jefferson's personal library was a major indication that all was not right in the Monticello household. While it was, without question, a great thing for the country, the seed of the magnificent institution that we know today, anyone at all familiar with Jefferson knew how deeply he loved his books, collected over the four decades after the fire at Shadwell destroyed his first library. Isaac Jefferson saw Jefferson's library as central to his persona. One of his most vividly expressed memories of Jefferson was as the man whose "mighty head" was full of information gleaned from the books strewn about his room, eager to consult them when asked a question he did not know the answer to. Seeing Jefferson's books, the source of his strength, packed away in crates and loaded onto wagons moving down Monticello's roundabouts was like seeing Samson's shorn locks upon the floor. That effect did not last, however, for, as he famously proclaimed, Jefferson could "not live without books." Not long after he said goodbye to one library, he began to build another.[6]

There were indeed other mixed signals at Monticello as Jefferson continued to live outwardly as if he had no serious money problems. The economic fallout from the War of 1812 and poor harvests plagued him during the first ten years of his retirement. The horde of visitors, who it can truly be said helped eat him out of house and home, made matters worse. Sometimes as many as a dozen uninvited guests would show up to dine and stay with him. Jefferson might have been able to avert final ruin had he sold his slaves and a good portion of his land and retreated to his home at Poplar Forest to adopt a much less lavish lifestyle. Monticello was not a prosperous farm. Many of the enslaved people there worked on his building projects instead of in the fields. The large numbers of household servants— all Hemingses—were not making products that could be sold. In fact, as things careered out of control, members of his white family floated to him the idea of a move to Poplar Forest. It was far too late for that. In 1819 land prices collapsed, and the sale of his property, real and human, would not have saved him. Virginia's economy did not begin to rebound until the 1830s, years after his death.[7]

Jefferson would never even have considered so drastic a course between 1809 and the 1820s, because he would have seen no need for it. Along with his preference for discovering income-producing activities over drastically cutting expenses, he also embarked upon another surefire losing financial strategy during his retirement: borrowing money to pay off other loans. Any modern-day observer doing the same with multiple credit cards will immediately recognize the morass Jefferson had entered. This was not only a bad practice on its face. It obligated Jefferson to the man who helped him get the bulk of the loans, Wilson Cary Nicholas. This unfortunate relationship really sealed Jefferson's fate, and the fates of nearly 150 people—Hemingses among them—whose lives would be thrown into utter turmoil and despair because of what happened between Jefferson and Nicholas.

Nicholas, a governor of Virginia between 1814 and 1816, was the president of the Richmond branch of the Bank of the United States. His brother was the president of the Farmer's Bank. They were the sons of Robert Carter Nicholas, who had been an associate of John Wayles and whom Jefferson had known for many years. With Wilson Nicholas's help, Jefferson secured hefty loans during the first decade of his retirement from both Nicholas brothers' banks. Wilson Nicholas was also "family," the father-in-law of Jefferson's grandson Jeff Randolph. There is no question that Nicholas helped Jefferson secure the loans on easy terms because of their family connection. But in 1818 it was Jefferson's turn. Nicholas asked him to cosign two $10,000 notes from the Bank of the United States. From today's perspective it appears absurd for Nicholas to have sought the endorsement of a man he knew from personal experience had no money and was living life on credit. It was, of course, Nicholas's knowledge that the Jefferson name carried weight that made him ask for this favor.[8]

Although Jefferson hesitated over Nicholas's request—he really did not want to sign the notes—he felt he could not refuse his friend and his grandson's father-in-law, especially since Nicholas had been solicitous toward him. It turned out to have been one of the single worst mistakes of Jefferson's life, for him and for those enslaved on his plantations. While on a visit to Poplar Forest, he heard the baleful news. Nicholas was in default. He assured Jefferson that he would be protected, saying that he would never forgive himself if his friend suffered because of his failure. Nicholas's promise to feel bad if Jefferson was hurt because of him surely provided small consolation, given that if he was wrong about his ability to protect Jefferson, the already financially imperiled former president would have $20,000 plus interest added to his indebtedness. As it happened, Nicholas could not protect Jefferson: he lost everything in the Panic of 1819 and died while visiting his daughter and son-in-law at Tufton, one of Jefferson's quarter farms. Jefferson thus became liable for the $20,000.[9]

As Herbert Sloan has pointed out, it was not just the $20,000 that was the "coup de grace," as Jefferson put it, but the interest on the debt, some $1,200 a year that Jefferson had to pay the Bank of the United States, money that he simply did not have. This fiasco could not have remained hidden from those enslaved at Monticello, for it was the kind of thing people gossiped about. What could cause more talk than the spectacle of a former governor of Virginia, the president of a bank, losing everything in a financial tidal wave along with other, ordinary people? If there was ever any notion that Jefferson might free his slaves, that chance was more than lost after this debacle.

The fact is there really is no reason to suppose that Jefferson would have freed his slaves even if he could have. In the first place, doing so would have deprived his daughter and grandchildren of property, something he would never do, particularly since his son-in-law was in even more desperate straits than he. He had been taking care of Martha Randolph and her family for most of her married life. Jefferson always suffers in comparison with Washington on the question of emancipating slaves, but the differences between the two men's situations are obvious and stark. Washington had no legal biological white children, and his stepchildren were part of a family that was extremely wealthy in its own right. Inheritance is a central component of private property regimes, and for many people the right to leave property to one's offspring is the whole point of having property. The right to inherit creates expectations of its own, and George Washington would have had to be willing to disappoint the expectations of a George Washington Jr. and a set of siblings—not to mention their mother—if such offspring had existed. Recall the young Martha Randolph's great frustration with her father-in-law's decision to remarry and start a new family. That marriage took property away from her husband and, by extension, from her own children.

The first president, who actually dithered about emancipating his slaves up until the last moment, died in 1799, when Virginia's economic climate was far better than it was in the 1820s, when Jefferson died.[10] Moreover, traces of the fallout from the American Revolution were still influencing attitudes about emancipation. The combination of the revolt on Saint

Domingue, which happened before Washington's death, and Gabriel's rebellion, which occurred after it, changed the atmosphere in Virginia significantly. The post-Revolutionary enthusiasm for the rights of man that had created a critique of slavery had long faded by the 1820s, and Jefferson's Virginia was already well on its way toward a full embrace of proslavery ideology. Jefferson discerned early on in his career that, no matter what some members of his society said about the evils of slavery, a legislative abolition of the institution in Virginia, and in the South as a whole, was as close to a political impossibility as anything could be. Accepting that reality, he set his sights on things that he could actually accomplish.

Most important of all, however, is that Jefferson really had made his personal peace with slavery by the time of his retirement, and much of what he experienced in the final phase of his life only reinforced his sense of complacency. Even as the extension of easy credit from the Richmond and Washington banks allowed him to maintain his lifestyle with no serious thought of making drastic changes, his closest relationships with enslaved people on the mountain worked to similar effect. The Hemingses, of course, cannot be considered, in modern parlance, "enablers," in the manner of the banks, for Jefferson controlled their lives. Still, the way he constructed his life with them did allow him to avoid facing the basic realities of slavery.

It is more common to think about Jefferson and slavery in intellectual terms, what he tried to do about it as a young man in the House of Burgesses and what he said about it in the excised portions of the Declaration of Independence, in the *Notes on the State of Virginia*, and in his various letters over the years. Slavery, however, had an emotional salience in Jefferson's life that far outstripped its meaning as an intellectual topic for discussion, or even as a political issue. When that is understood, much that seems perplexing and exasperating about him—that he said one thing on the subject but did something else—becomes totally comprehensible, if no less exasperating.

We can discover slavery's ultimate meaning for Jefferson only by examining intensely the nature of his relations with the people whom he enslaved and by considering what those relationships meant in his day-to-day life. Rather than being a necessary evil or a problem to be solved, a thing to feel tortured about, slavery—as Jefferson lived it with the Hemingses, in particular—provided him with constant reinforcing positive benefits. We see this most clearly in his retirement, the longest period of his continuous residence at Monticello and, not coincidentally, the very period that many consider to mark the nadir of his expressed attitudes about slavery.

Jefferson had returned to Monticello at the age of sixty-six, not an age associated with making dramatic changes in one's personal life. His longing for home had been a longing for stability, familiarity, and peace. There was surely a sense of vulnerability and a need to be cared for as he approached his declining years. He characteristically was able to escape thoughts of his financial worries by burying himself in a positive project: building the University of Virginia, an idée fixe that sustained him through his most despairing moments. He was happy when his grandson Jeff became more involved in helping him manage his farms, and greatly relieved when he was able to turn the whole business over to the younger man. What was left, and what he helped to perpetuate at Monticello during the final seventeen years of his life, were circumstances perfectly suited to his personality and most deeply felt needs.

There was his white family, Tom Randolph's failure having brought his daughter Martha and her children back into his domestic fold. But slavery provided him with other things that were great comforts. It gave him a beautiful younger mistress and children, who could be shaped into some version of his private self—woodworker, musician, and sometime gardener. It provided him with a steady companion in Burwell Colbert, whom he styled as a "friend," who acted as if he genuinely cared for Jefferson and whom Jefferson cared for in return. It gave him artisans whom he could be among and whose work he admired. Jefferson could monopolize all these people's time, talents, and attention to his heart's content, which he could not do with the whites in his life.

Consider first his artisans and the workers with whom he was in close contact. Joseph Fossett and John Hemings, in particular, headed the shops that were doing the kind of work that most interested Jefferson. Wormley Hughes was in charge of Jefferson's gardens. What Susan Stein has called "the collaboration" between Hemings and Jefferson intensified between 1809 and 1826, as Hemings worked both at Monticello and at Poplar Forest.[11] Jefferson was not a passive bystander, an owner/employer who issued orders and then stood back. He involved himself in Hemings's work because he cared about the outcome and, as a woodworker himself, was deeply interested in the process. That Hemings had charge of Jefferson's three sons also made their relationship deeper and more complex. There is no reason to doubt that part of John Hemings's apparently intense loyalty to Jefferson stemmed from the fact that Jefferson had entrusted to him his sons, who were also Hemings's nephews. This intersection of bloodlines and slavery, and the way Jefferson chose to handle the intersection, was just one more way that slavery distorted human relations.

Jefferson's engagement with Joseph Fossett during his retirement was not as personally intense as his engagement with Hemings. He did make keys and locks, a simpler version of the metalworking that Fossett did in his blacksmith shop, but building things was by far Jefferson's favored activity. The evidence regarding Fossett's feelings about Jefferson is more ambiguous. He did, after all, run away during Jefferson's presidency, and we cannot know certainly that he intended only to go to Washington to see his wife and then return to Monticello. At that point Jefferson clearly did not have the confidence that Fossett would return. That is why he took immediate steps to have him apprehended and brought home. Making Fossett the head of the blacksmith shop a year later, giving him a percentage of the profits earned there, and allowing him to work on his own time and keep the money he earned were Jefferson's ways of making Fossett more "comfortable" in his enslavement and Jefferson more "comfortable" owning him.

Wormley Hughes was twenty-eight years old when Jefferson retired. He had served many roles at Monticello, including working in the nailery and on several of Jefferson's building projects. After Jupiter Evans's death, he took charge of Jefferson's stables, a task that he enjoyed because he loved horses. By the time of Jefferson's retirement, he was the head gardener at Monticello, apparently having learned his craft from Robert Bailey, the man who had lived next door to his grandmother for a time. Hughes thus had charge over two things Jefferson loved: horses and his gardens. Jefferson kept a Garden Book from 1766 until 1824, when his health began to fail drastically. The bulk of the entries note the day various plants bloomed, when various fruits and vegetables came to the table, and what types and quantities of plants others, enslaved people, planted. In his retirement he became more personally involved in the activity, famously writing in 1811. "[T]ho' an old man, I am but a young gardener." Jefferson would sometimes come out in the evenings and work in the garden Hughes tended, no doubt encountering the younger man and talking about the whole operation. The two men laid out flower beds on Monticello's west lawn and worked closely enough together that Jefferson recommended that he be given his freedom.[12]

Burwell Colbert and Sally Hemings occupied similar places in Jefferson's life. They had to work together as a team in order to deal effectively with Jefferson, particularly as he grew older. Both were familiar touchstones as the years advanced. Colbert, who was only ten years younger than his aunt Sally, named a daughter after her. Both Hemings and Colbert had come into Jefferson's personal orbit when they were young and impressionable people who could be molded into the kind of companions that he wanted to have. They belonged to his closely guarded intimate world, though Colbert had a decidedly more public face as Jefferson's manservant. Wherever Jefferson went during his retirement—to Poplar Forest, to Madison's Montpelier, to the homes of other friends—Colbert went, too. Hemings's place in Jefferson's life was more resolutely private and contained, not at all the kind of thing that either he or his white family would have referred to. Acting as a substitute for a wife, sleeping with Jefferson, and having his children created the ultimate form of intimacy between the two over a very long period of time. Certainly by the time of his retirement, Hemings and Jefferson had a long history together and were well used to one another's ways.

In contrast to Joseph Neilson (John Hemings's father), James Dinsmore, William Stewart, James Oldham, and the many other white artisans and workers who came in and out of Jefferson's life, none of the people mentioned above—Colbert, Hughes, Fossett, and John and Sally Hemings—could leave him unless he was willing to let them go. He was not willing to do that until after he had died. With the exception of Sally Hemings, Jefferson could easily have freed these Hemingses during his lifetime and kept them on as paid workers. John Hemings, Colbert, and Hughes would almost certainly have worked for Jefferson as an employer rather than as a master. Although Fossett did run away, that was under the parameters of slavery. Being the paid head of Jefferson's blacksmith shop, while continuing to live with his wife and children would have been a different matter altogether.

For all the reasons discussed earlier, it would have been extremely problematic if Jefferson had attempted to free Sally Hemings and have her live at Monticello as his mistress. Jefferson, Thomas Bell, and many other slaveholders used slavery to cover their relationships with enslaved women. The very patriarchal Jefferson could easily rationalize holding Hemings in slavery as keeping her within what he would call the protection of his family. Again, he saw women, slaves, and children as suitably disabled under law, people who should not be free in the way white men or even emancipated black men were free. Given the gender conventions of the day, that Jefferson wanted to maintain control over Sally Hemings, a woman, makes far more sense than keeping control over men he apparently respected. Jefferson knew that all of these men could take care of themselves, and he felt it necessary to hold them in a status that mixed the attributes of the free laborer with those of the slave. He could not, while he was alive, bring himself to follow things to their logical conclusion.

The problem for Jefferson was that giving any of these people freedom would have created the possibility that they could leave him, just as Robert and James Hemings had done in the 1790s. One supposes that if any of the men had tried to leave after Jefferson had freed them, he could have punished them by refusing them access to their spouses and children. Colbert's and Hemings's wives were Randolph family slaves, so Jefferson would have had to enlist the aid of his daughter and son-in-law to carry out such a prohibition. That would have required summoning and sustaining over the years an amount of negative energy that was uncharacteristic for Jefferson, since it would have made him look mean and small in the eyes of others, something he always tried to avoid. A freed Sally Hemings would most likely have had to leave the plantation and be out of the constellation at Monticello, if not Virginia. The only way for a man to control a free woman was to marry her, which he could not do. Selfishness and self-absorption seem far too inadequate as reasons for the way Jefferson treated these members of the Hemings family. There is often great power in simplicity, and the simple, terrible fact is that the law vested Jefferson, and other slave owners, with the powers of a tyrant, as he said himself. This domestic tyrant tried to mitigate the meaning of that reality by being as benign as he could. That made it easier for him to see himself as a good man as he indulged his impulses and met his needs—economic, social, and affective—through his control of these family members, to whom he was tied by years of intimate acquaintance, experiences, and blood. He created his own version of slavery that he could live in comfortably with the Hemingses. It suited him. There was never any serious chance that he would have given this up.

NEARLY THIRTY-FIVE YEARS had passed since Wormley Hughes had witnessed the return of his cousins James and Sally Hemings to Monticello after their years in France with Jefferson. As noted earlier, as an elderly man, Hughes would describe the enthusiastic response of those enslaved at Monticello to the return of Jefferson, whose continued existence offered the best assurance that they might be able to remain in place with their families. Now, in 1824, one of the most famous episodes in the life of the mountain, and the country, helped put what happened on that Christmas Eve in 1789 into perspective.

The marquis de Lafayette, Jefferson's old friend from the days of the American Revolution and Paris, made his triumphant return to America for about ten months in 1824 and 1825, stopping at the sites of old Revolutionary War battles and being feted and honored everywhere he went. There was scarcely a chance that he could have come to America and failed to visit the man with whom he had shared many memories and much correspondence. Indeed, their letters—Lafayette's announcement that he wanted to see Jefferson and Jefferson's invitation for Lafayette to stop by—passed each other in the mail not long after the Frenchman arrived in the country.[13]

The ten days Lafayette spent at Monticello in November of 1824 produced numerous recollections, including that of Peter Fossett, son of Joseph and Edith Fossett. The young Fossett, then nine years old, was part of the last generation of Hemingses to live at Monticello. His siblings and first and second cousins, numbering more than a dozen, were the first Hemings cohort to grow up with either no memories or only faint ones of the matriarch of the clan, Elizabeth Hemings. Peter Fossett echoed the observations of newspaper accounts of Lafayette's arrival on the mountain. A number of citizens of Charlottesville who had come up to witness the event gathered on the front lawn, along with those enslaved at Monticello. When Lafayette reached Albemarle County, Jefferson sent him the landau that John Hemings had built for the final leg of his guest's journey to Monticello. At the sound of a bugle, which alerted those milling about on the lawn that Lafayette and the honor guard accompanying him were near, the crowd hushed and parted as they waited for Jefferson to emerge from the house and greet his old friend. The now eighty-one-year-old man moved gingerly down the steps, walking slowly at first, then more quickly, toward Lafayette. Fossett recalled the words spoken as the two old compatriots fell into each other's arms and wept, "My dear Lafayette" and "My dear Jefferson."[14]

The emotional valence of that deeply human moment resonated among those assembled. Tears welled and then flowed, even among the people who had virtually no stake in these proceedings: the enslaved community at Monticello. One says "virtually no stake" because they were given the day "off" in honor of the special celebration that was to be held at the soon to be officially opened University of Virginia.

The journey to the new university the following day provided another occasion for a member of the Hemings family to comment upon Lafayette's visit. Robert Scott, the twenty-one-year-old grandson of Mary Hemings and Thomas Bell, and thus Peter Fossett's first cousin, was living as a free man in the house that his mother, Sally Jefferson Bell, had inherited from her father, Thomas. Although Bell apparently never formally freed Sally or her brother Robert, but instead simply left them property as if he considered them free, his white family and the white community had gone along with that informal path to emancipation. Thus, Sally Bell Scott and her children escaped *partus sequitur ventrem*. That is how Scott came to be watching from his home on Main Street as the landau passed by, carrying Jefferson, Lafayette, James Madison, and James Monroe on their way to the university's famous rotunda for the dinner. Either because it was true, or out of his sense of personal connection to Jefferson, who often visited Scott's home to socialize and hear him play the violin, Scott recalled that "Mr. Jefferson was by far the most distinguished looking of the four." As it turned out, Scott would get an even closer look at the French general because he and his relatives, a famous family of musicians, were invited to Monticello to play for Lafayette and his party. It is not at all improbable that their musician relatives already on the mountain accompanied them. Beverley Hemings, who played at the parties Jefferson's teenage grandchildren threw, had left the mountain by 1824. But his younger brothers, Madison and Eston, could easily have joined their cousins.[15]

Lafayette almost certainly saw and spoke to Sally Hemings. She, Jefferson, and Martha Randolph were the only people on the mountain who had seen the general in Paris, making Hemings the only enslaved person on the plantation who had laid eyes on the Frenchman's native land in the 1780s. He had been a guest at the Hôtel de Langeac and eaten her brother James's cooking many times. Whether he remembered the now fifty-one-year-old woman who had been a teenage girl in Paris or her brother, now dead for twenty-three years, is unknown. Hemings, however, had every incentive to remind Jefferson's guest of her own days in Paris and her memories of him there, if only to be polite.

Lafayette's visit presented an opportunity for nostalgia as much for Sally Hemings as for Jefferson and Martha Randolph, evoking memories of her time in Paris and how that had helped shape her life over the decades. It had a particular and poignant meaning now for she was probably still feeling the effects of the departure of her two eldest children, Beverley and Harriet, not quite two years earlier. This was what she had asked of Jefferson long ago in Paris—to have her children leave slavery after they became adults and were old enough to leave her. Jefferson's records indicate that Beverley left Monticello a few months before Harriet in 1822, most likely to prepare the way for his sister, who would not have been expected to live in a city by herself. Jefferson arranged to have Harriet put on a stagecoach with fifty dollars when her time came to depart.[16]

Now, as the celebration of Lafayette's visit unfolded, only two of Sally Hemings's children, Madison and Eston, remained. It would have been almost impossible for Lafayette, over the course of his ten days on the mountain and upon his return visit at the end of his stay in America, never to have encountered these two young people—the nearly twenty-year-old Madison and the nearly seventeen-year-old Eston—as they moved about Mulberry Row, just outside the "great house" at Monticello. He may actually have gone into the joinery where they both worked. Jefferson showed important visitors around Monticello, and the place where his most valued artisans worked was a likely site to showcase. All of Jefferson's children with Hemings were said to resemble him, one of the sons so much that a person coming upon the young man at dusk dressed as Jefferson would have assumed that it was Jefferson himself. That could well have been Eston. A group of men who knew him in Ohio later visited the University of Virginia and, upon seeing a statue of Jefferson, remarked that the likeness was a close image of Eston Hemings. If Eston, now in his late teens, had experienced the growth spurt that would take him near his father's height of six feet two, he certainly would have been difficult for Lafayette to miss, since he would have towered over most of the people on the mountain. Madison was shorter, in the neighborhood of five feet ten, but facially the two brothers were younger versions of Jefferson, a resemblance that Lafayette, who had known Jefferson many years, would have noticed.[17] The Frenchman could easily have figured out, with the wisdom of a worldly man, and perhaps with a sense of relief, that his old friend had not spent the past nearly four decades alone.

Lafayette came to the mountain with his private secretary, Auguste Levasseur. Both men were quite interested in the subject of slavery, in general, and slavery at Monticello, in particular. Jefferson evidently told his French visitors that enslaved workers had built the landau that had brought Lafayette to Monticello. Levasseur complimented the vehicle's construction, saying that it was "a powerful argument against those who pretend that the intelligence of negroes can never be raised to the height of the mechanic arts." Levasseur strongly favored emancipation, wanting to turn slaves into servants. At the same time, going a little over the top, because he clearly revered Jefferson, he wrote that the "good appearance and the gaiety of the negroes at Monticello attested the humanity of the master; if so noble a character had need of an attestation. . . ."[18] He talked with some of the people enslaved on the mountain, and his report of what they told him about their lives appear as a somewhat ironic bookend to Wormley Hughes's description of the way they responded when Jefferson returned from France. Indeed, Levasseur may well have spoken to Hughes himself, who as the head gardener would have been one of the African Americans visitors saw when they called upon Jefferson for any length of time.

Aside from the fact that it would not have served their interests to speak ill of Jefferson to strangers, whether he grasped it or not, the people Levasseur spoke to presented him with a very clear-eyed and hard view of the reality of their lives. Given the balance of power in Virginia, they understood that a major, positive change in their situation was unlikely for the foreseeable future. They were happy to work at Monticello in the meantime, because they knew that as long as Jefferson remained alive, there was a good chance that they would not be sold away and separated from their families.[19] Of course, Jefferson was not going to live forever, as they well knew. The "gaiety" Levasseur observed and the happiness they described to him were thus very tenuous forms of the emotion indeed.

Levasseur's report on Monticello's enslaved community confirms that the spontaneous display of affection and love for Jefferson in 1789 grew out of an underlying anxiety that existed within enslaved people. The death of a master—hated or "loved"—was almost always a calamity for them, as creditors came to satisfy debts, and children and other relatives took their share of the property, human and otherwise, that the decedent left behind. Jefferson's almost eight-year absence from Monticello in the 1780s had kept alive the fear that such a calamity might befall the enslaved community.

Thirty-five years later, in 1824, Jefferson was still a vital presence at Monticello. But he was definitely a man of very advanced age for those days. As he lived in his twilight, the enslaved people on his plantations were marking time to a painful day of reckoning. His daughter Martha's presence may have stirred some hope of continuity. Monticello had been her home for more than a decade and a half, so why would she leave it? She had no legal white siblings to share her father's property. In the end, this turned out to be far worse than a false hope for anyone on the mountain who might have held it. A full-fledged cataclysm was in store.

By the time of Lafayette's visit, Monticello was in physical decay, as was the man who had willed it into existence. It was not enough to build a mansion; the mansion had to be maintained, and Jefferson's shattered finances did not allow him to do that. Visitors noted the house's and grounds' worn and tattered appearance. Jack McLaughlin has posited that adequate maintenance of the exterior of the structure would have required painting it every six years to protect the wood from the elements, particularly rain and the general humidity of Virginia's climate. If that was ever done, there is no record of it.[20] Matters were made worse by the sheer number of people who moved through the house—Jefferson's relatives and the endless parade of visitors who wore down the interior just in the normal business of living.

Although Jefferson himself had been in poor condition for a number of years, his stamina and will to go forward were so great that he continued to strike observers as hale and hearty for a man of his age. Late in his life, visitors like Daniel Webster remarked upon his continued vitality, and even his son Madison remembered his father as a generally robust man until near the very end. There were the usual infirmities of old age, along with at least two harrowing accidents. When he was seventy-nine, he fell and broke his arm and wrist. Later, with his arm still in a sling from the previous accident, he was thrown from his horse Eagle as he forded a stream. He would have drowned had he not been able to hold on to the bridle and been dragged out of the water as the horse climbed onto the banks. After that accident his family wanted Burwell Colbert to ride with him, but Jefferson declined. Having fallen into the habit of riding alone, he said that he would prefer not to ride at all if he could not ride in solitude.[21]

The most notable illness that Madison Hemings recalled occurred in 1818, and the treatment for it may have contributed to Jefferson's slow decline and the eventual failure of his health. Long troubled by what he called rheumatism, Jefferson went to Warm Springs, Virginia, to bathe in the mineral waters to help ease his pain. Whatever relief he gained was

offset by a viral or bacterial infection that caused him to break out into painful boils. The application of large amounts of sulfur and mercury apparently ended the outbreak—or the disease just ran its course. Whatever
claims might be made for sulfur as a medicine, mercury in all but trace
amounts is an unqualified poison. Certainly the exposure to large amounts
can cause permanent physical damage, and Jefferson suspected that the
course of treatment for his illness at Warm Springs had permanently damaged his health.[22]

The mounting evidence of Jefferson's mortality was as alarming to members of the enslaved community as to his white family, if not more so. Only
a handful of enslaved people, all Hemingses, could have had any reasonable assurance that they would still have their loved ones around them after
Jefferson died and his estate was distributed. The men Jefferson eventually
freed all knew he was going to free them upon his death, because he had
told them he would. Each passing day brought the overwhelming majority
of those enslaved at Monticello closer to the moment when community and
family ties would be severed forever.

The white family at Monticello, Jefferson included, had been pondering
various ways to avoid a total collapse. According to Martha's later recollections, Jefferson lay in bed one evening worrying about his financial state
when the idea of a lottery for the sale of property hit him "like an inspiration from the realms of bliss."[23] Lotteries had been previously used in
Virginia to dispose of burdened private estates and to raise money for public causes. Tickets were sold at low prices with the land as the prize. Then
as later, many people opposed lotteries on religious and moral grounds as a
form of gambling. In fact, Jefferson himself had publicly positioned himself
over the years as an opponent of speculative enterprises. That he resorted to
this scheme shows the depth of his fear during this period.

If it is ironic that Jefferson embraced this species of speculation in his
most desperate hours, it is also ironic that just two years earlier he had
hosted the great French (and honorary American) patriot Lafayette, who
was himself in such dire financial straits that he had to borrow the money to
come to America. While on his visit, the U.S. Congress, which had already
given Lafayette money in 1803, voted to give him an additional $120,000.
That was about $13,000 more than what would turn out to be the total
amount of Jefferson's indebtedness when he died. Jefferson, reeling under
the weight of his own debts, congratulated Lafayette on his good fortune,

saying with an empathy born of true experience that he hoped it would help the Frenchman sleep better at night and give him "surplus . . . days of ease and comfort through the rest of [his] life."[24]

When the bill to allow the lottery was submitted to the Virginia legislature, it was initially rejected. Jefferson's supporters were stunned. How could the state he had served in so many capacities reject his plea for help, especially since it took no money from the public till? As he recalled, he had come into public service "as soon as of age . . . in 1764." Sixty-one years, he felt, should have counted for something. The lottery's supporters marshaled their forces and reintroduced the measure, which then passed. Jefferson had it in his mind that it would not be necessary to include Monticello in the proceedings. His grandson remembered that he turned "white" when told that the work of his life would, in fact, have to be part of the scheme. That news was made a bit more palatable because Jefferson was assured that he would have a life estate in the house and that his daughter would be able to stay there for two years after his death.[25] An alternative plan surfaced to help him, but, in the end, all the exertions were to no avail. Even in the midst of this high drama, Jefferson continued to be consumed with his duties as the rector of the University of Virginia, which had opened in Charlottesville in 1825, no doubt consoling himself in one of the "dreams of the future," which he famously said he preferred to thinking about the past. Thinking of the past that had led him to this excruciating present was likely unbearable.

The Hemingses had no direct hand in all the plans and designs to save the plantation. Instead, those who were Jefferson's personal servants were involved in caring for an increasingly sick man. In addition to prostate problems, which had left him in debilitating pain that required daily doses of laudanum, he began to suffer periodically from diarrhea, a fact that he had kept from his white family members, not wanting to alarm them.[26] By March of 1826, as he approached his eighty-third birthday the coming April 13, Jefferson knew he was reaching the end. He prepared his will on the sixteenth of that month and then a codicil the next day that granted freedom to five members of the Hemings family. Burwell Colbert was listed first. He was given his freedom and three hundred dollars. Next came John Hemings and Joe Fossett, who were to be freed as of a year after his death, with all the tools of their trade. All three men were given life estates in houses and one acre of land, with the stipulation that they be near their wives and most likely place of employment, the University of Virginia. The will continued,

> I give also to John Hemings the service of his two apprentices, Madison and Eston Hemings, until their respective ages of twenty-one years, at which period, respectively, I give them their freedom; and I humbly and earnestly request of the Legislature of Virginia a confirmation of the bequest of freedom to these servants, with permission to remain in this State, where their families and connections are, as an additional instance of the favor, of which I have received so many other manifestations, in the course of my life, and for which I now give them my last, solemn, and dutiful thanks.[27]

With this document Jefferson fulfilled the promise made to Sally Hemings thirty-seven years before in Paris. The emancipations of their two oldest children, Beverley and Harriet, had taken place in secret. They simply disappeared into the white world. The emancipations of Madison and Eston were altogether public, and the way their father accomplished this suggests he knew that freeing these two young men might raise eyebrows. As always, the context is important. Talk of Jefferson's relationship with Sally Hemings had never ceased over the years. His overseer Edmund Bacon made it clear that people were paying attention to Jefferson's actions toward the Hemings children. People in the area noticed, he said, Harriet's departure in 1822 and attributed it to her being Jefferson's daughter, and they likely knew when her brother left in the months before her.[28] Mixed-race children were the inevitable result of America's racially based slave system, and freeing these children, if done in a quiet and discreet manner, was considered the "decent" thing to do. That posed a severe problem for one of the most famous persons in the nation, a man who never intended to make a public declaration—explicitly or implicitly—about his enslaved mistress and their children.

Creditors' interests took precedence over emancipations, so the list of people to be freed had to be very small and the people on it chosen with extreme care. Except for being Jefferson's sons, Madison and Eston Hemings should, by all rights, have come after their cousin Wormley Hughes and their uncle Peter Hemings, both skilled and talented men. Hemings, after all, was Martha Jefferson's half brother, whom Jefferson had known for over fifty years. He had freed Peter's older brothers Robert and James decades earlier. James did not live long to enjoy his freedom, but Robert, who died in 1819, had twenty-three years as a free man. How, then, to explain why two obvious youngsters were on a list with men who had rendered services to Jefferson for more years than the pair had been alive and why others had been passed over? If there is any thought that Jefferson's mind and instinct for maneuvering were in any way impaired in those final months, his will dispels it.

Jefferson's language suggests that he was freeing Madison and Eston not because they meant anything to him but because they were connected to John Hemings. He was giving his older valued servant something: their services. One difficulty, however, was that Jefferson almost certainly knew, as readers of the will would not have, that Madison was already past his twenty-first birthday. The condition precedent to his emancipation had already come and gone, and John Hemings would not have his "service." Eston, approaching his eighteenth birthday, could have served his uncle for three years. But even that was a small reward to John Hemings compared with the lifetime of freedom that Eston would enjoy. Jefferson was a careful drafter, and as a lawyer he knew he could have written this provision in a way that granted the young men freedom if they agreed to work with their uncle until they became adults. Putting this in terms of giving services to John Hemings deflects the question why these young men mattered enough to Jefferson for him to do this momentous thing. As it turned out, neither Madison nor Eston was required to work for his uncle. Jefferson's family gave Eston "his time" when Jefferson died, instantly abrogating the terms of his will. It is almost inconceivable that the family would have done this without Jefferson's prior instruction.

We will probably never know what discussions took place between Jefferson and members of his white family who stood to lose if the talk about his enslaved children resurfaced at this critical juncture. Jeff Randolph was still pressing ahead with the plans for raising money from the public to help retire his grandfather's debt and save his lands. Despite an outpouring of support from many people in Virginia, there remained significant opposition to helping the dying statesman. Hard as it may be to imagine today, given what the institution has become, there was great skepticism about Jefferson's university, for both economic and religious reasons. He had spent a good amount of social capital in championing what he wanted to be a determinedly secular institution, with a library as the center of the grounds rather than a chapel. He and his family had to tread very carefully under the circumstances.

The beginning of Jefferson's end started in June of 1826. The story of his final days was presented in the recollections of his white grandchildren, and their reflections illustrate the difference between the slave society that their mother and grandfather had been born into and the one that the younger Randolphs knew. While the Jefferson family memories of Martha Jefferson's death in 1782 make no mention of the enslaved women who surely helped care for the dying woman, enslaved people played prominent roles in Jefferson's grandchildren's recorded memories of his death. Edmund Bacon's 1857 recollections reflect the change as well. In what was fast becoming antebellum southern society, enslaved people were no longer to be hidden. Instead, the presentation of slaves as integral, intimate members of the plantation "family" emerged as an argument in support of the peculiar institution.

As Jefferson faded, his grandson Jeff Randolph and the others remembered, "he would only have his servants sleeping near him."[29] Randolph makes clear that more than one enslaved person was deeply involved with Jefferson's care in his final days. That is not surprising. There were more than enough Hemingses to stand watch, and in those intense moments the attention of the entire place was riveted on the man who for over five decades had dominated the consciences, imaginations, and lives of everyone who lived on the mountain. Randolph did not name all the "servants" who attended Jefferson, but it is almost certain that they included, at the very least, Burwell Colbert and Sally Hemings, the only two people said to have taken care of his rooms and him. As is often the case with those on their deathbeds, Jefferson had trouble sleeping, and people took turns sitting up with him during the day and at night. He did not want to be alone, and insisted that his enslaved caregivers make pallets so that they could sleep in the room with him overnight. Only they were allowed in his bedroom after dark, and anxious members of the Randolph family took to making secret forays into his bedchamber to check on their own loved one.[30]

This is what it had come to. The people who had nursed him from the beginning of his life, whose energies he had harnessed for his own use up until this moment, were now called upon to care for him as he faced his last days on earth—sitting up with him at night, sleeping on pallets around his bed to be ready to hear when he called out in need, in fear, or out of simple loneliness. These African Americans, whom he had sentimentalized as having the best hearts of any people in the world, had given their lives to him—followed him about, cleaned up after him, no doubt worried about him, for his sake and their own—slept with him, and borne him children. He had held them as chattel, trying, in the case of the Hemingses, to soften a reality that could never be made soft. While he claimed to know and respect the quality of their hearts, he could never truly see them as human beings separate from him and his own needs, desires, and fears. In the end, all he really knew of their hearts was what they were willing to show him, and they carried enough knowledge in their heads to know his limitations and the perils of giving too much of themselves in the context of their society. The world they shared twisted and perverted practically everything it touched, made entirely human feelings and connections difficult, suspect, and compromised. What could have been in the hearts of any human beings living under the power of that system was inevitably complicated, inevitably tragic.

JEFFERSON AND THOSE around him wished fervently that he would live to see the fiftieth anniversary of the signing of his Declaration of Independence. Early in the morning of the Fourth of July, before the sun rose, he called out to the servants who were in the room with him, apparently telling them something he needed to have done. He talked for a while and then went back to sleep. By midmorning, when members of his white family were in the room, he looked over at his grandson Jeff Randolph and tried to communicate a request. Randolph did not understand what he asked for, but Burwell Colbert did. Jefferson wanted to be raised higher on his pillows. After Colbert adjusted the pillows, the dying man was satisfied. About an hour later, Jefferson fell unconscious. An hour after that, he stopped breathing altogether.[31]

In a coincidence often thought providential, John Adams died later on that same day in Quincy, Massachusetts, uttering before he died, "Thomas Jefferson still survives." The statesmen could not have engineered a more dramatic exit from the public stage, and in the case of Jefferson this stunning turn of events has received more attention than what immediately followed. As he wished it, the funeral of one of the most important men in history was a private ceremony in the graveyard at Monticello. John Hemings had been preparing for Jefferson's death for days, if not weeks, using the wood he had long been saving to make Jefferson's coffin. There is no extant record of who prepared Jefferson's body for burial, but if it was not Burwell Colbert, it was probably female members of the enslaved community, for preparing bodies, like bringing children into the world, was generally considered woman's work. Wormley Hughes dug Jefferson's grave. His family members and slaves carried his body to the cemetery for what was a simple ceremony, a gathering of the Monticello community enslaved and free and people from nearby Charlottesville. There was at least one report of acrimony between Jeff Randolph and his father, even in the midst of mourning Jefferson. James Madison did not attend, and two of Jefferson's favorite granddaughters, Ellen Coolidge and Cornelia Randolph, could not make it home for the funeral.[32]

Martha Randolph, not surprisingly, appears to have been in a state of shock, and the same was probably true for many of those who lived at Monticello. This was not only the death of a man; everyone understood that this was the death of an entire community. Members of Jefferson's white family were devastated by his loss and their own fears as they contemplated their financial ruin, but, whatever happened, they were still free and white. Even with the humiliation and pain they felt at the loss of status and wealth, they had the basic attributes of privilege that would ensure that they could fall only so far. They had merely lost property; they were not the property that was going to be sold to pay their father's and grandfather's debts.

What Sally Hemings and other Hemingses felt as they watched, or imagined if they were not at the funeral, Jefferson being lowered into his grave is unknown. One can safely speculate that there were many varied and complex responses among them. They were of one family, but they bore different relationships to him—ranging from the small children who barely knew him to the woman who had had seven children by him. Fifty-two years before Wormley Hughes dug Jefferson's grave, his mother, Betty Brown, had come to Monticello as the fifteen-year-old lady's maid to Martha Jefferson. Fifty-one years before John Hemings crafted Jefferson's coffin, his mother, Elizabeth Hemings, and all of her children were assembled on the mountain. Their presence there was as long as, and more continuous than, Jefferson's and his white family's. That continuity and stability were never of their own making, and they could not have expected to be able to control their own destinies. What was about to happen to the family now could not really have surprised the adults among them, however. The older Hemingses—Betty Brown, Mary (from her home in Charlottesville), and Nancy—were old enough to remember the death that had taken the Hemingses from one home and placed them at their current one, albeit under different circumstances. When John Wayles died, other enslaved families faced separation as Jefferson decided where and how to settle them. That the Hemingses would come to Monticello was likely a foregone conclusion. The specter of imminent bankruptcy brought much more uncertainty about the family's overall future during these days.

There was something else, of course. Jefferson legally owned the Hemingses, but he and his white daughter and grandchildren were also blood relatives to some of them. He had lived for thirty-eight years with a female member of the family. When Jefferson died, Beverley, Harriet, Madison, and Eston Hemings lost their biological father. Sally Hemings lost the man with whom she had cast her lot when she was only a teenager. A situation common enough in their world seems almost unthinkable in ours. Aside from assuming that Sally Hemings was happy that Jefferson had kept his promises and that her children would be free people, we have little to go on in trying to imagine what the now fifty-three-year-old woman felt when Jefferson was gone. Something is perhaps revealed in the items she decided to take with her when she left a Monticello that was soon to be stripped of everything: a pair of Jefferson's glasses, an inkwell, and one of his shoe buckles, things that she had seen him wear and use and that she knew were important to him. Keeping these items, and eventually giving them to her son as mementos, was a charge by the woman who apparently never spoke to outsiders about Jefferson, to keep alive the memory of her, and her children's, connection to him. This was, however, only for her family. In the end she was as private about him as he was about her.

It is often said that Americans lack a sense both of tragedy and of irony. Fawn Brodie very rightly called what happened on the mountain in 1826 and its immediate aftermath "The Monticello Tragedy." It was certainly that, but obviously much more. It was a national tragedy—the natural result of America's engagement with the institution of slavery, the doctrine of white supremacy, and the nature of human frailty. The relationship of the Hemingses to the tragedy of slavery was unique only because they happened to be owned by one who made himself a public man, but wanted to keep private the world he really lived in with this particular African American enslaved family. There is deep irony in this, too. What Jefferson accomplished for his children, and some of their relatives, was just what he stated could not be accomplished in the nation as a whole.

When freeing Burwell Colbert, Joseph Fossett, John Hemings, and Madison and Eston Hemings, the man who said that he believed it impossible for blacks and whites to live together in the United States, and that people of African origin should be repatriated to another country, asked the legislature to allow these men to remain not just in America but in Virginia. By the time Jefferson died, the American Colonization Society was up and running, and a few slave owners were freeing their slaves and making provision for their transportation to Liberia. They were acting on their deeply felt beliefs. What were Jefferson's likely true beliefs? The answer depends upon whether one chooses to pay more attention to what people say than to what they actually do. Why not send the men he freed to Liberia? Burwell Colbert's brother, Brown, would later opt to go there on his own. Jefferson gave the right answer to the question that likely never crossed his mind. The Hemingses should be allowed to remain in Virginia, he said, because that is where their "families and connections" were. That, of course, was the answer to the question why all other African Americans, most of whose ancestors had come to America before or around the same time as the African woman who had borne Elizabeth Hemings, should be allowed to remain in the United States. Many of these people were the children, grand-children, or great-grandchildren of white men—just like the men he freed. Their families and connections were in America, too. In truth, Jefferson did not mention race as the basis for the right to a home in America at all. Long-standing family ties and memories created the right. As was often the case, the public rhetorical Jefferson was very different from the down-to-personal-business Jefferson, the one he seldom wanted anyone to see.

The personal Jefferson had dominated the lives of the Hemingses. Their family connections to him, first through his wife and John Wayles and then the connections he created on his own with Sally Hemings, shaped the course of the family's existence. They also ensured that the world the Hemingses lived in with Jefferson would not be forgotten by their descendants and would remain a subject of fascination to the outside world. That is certainly not what Jefferson and his white family wanted. But, thankfully, they were not mas-ters and mistresses across all space and time, and there is more to the world than law. The power of memory, love, and the strength of family kept alive the Hemingses' story. That we remember them today is the best and most fit-ting tribute to the no doubt terrified and unknown African who arrived on the shores of Virginia so many years ago to begin this family's saga.

EPILOGUE

J EFFERSON'S DEATH MERELY set the stage for the final catastrophe. While history has marveled at the near-simultaneous deaths of the Sage of Monticello and the Sage of Quincy, many years later Peter Fossett, who was still a young boy when Jefferson died, put this stunning coincidence into some perspective. He understood the importance of what had happened on July 4, 1826, but noted that "sorrow came not only to the homes of two great men . . . but to the slaves of Thomas Jefferson." He was not just talking about the loss of Jefferson. Both old patriots had lived more than their biblical three score and ten, and human beings are born to die. They are not born to endure what Fossett and his family endured six months after the fiftieth anniversary of the signing of the Declaration of Independence. In January of 1827, Peter Fossett, all of eleven years old, stood alone on an auction block and was sold away from his mother, father, brothers, and sisters. Many of Fossett's siblings and cousins, some as young as eight years old, suffered the same fate.[1]

Unlike the first generation of Hemingses who experienced the death of Martha Jefferson, this generation of the family clearly would not survive Jefferson's death intact. Half a year after his death, the contents of Monticello, along with "130 VALUABLE NEGROES," were auctioned off. Whatever anxiety the Hemingses felt during this period, they were somewhat better off than other members of the enslaved community, who had no prospect of having anyone in their families freed. Indeed, the fates of the vast majority of those enslaved at Monticello are unknown. Jeff Randolph, the principal executor of Jefferson's estate, had refused an offer from a man in Georgia to buy a large number of them.² Sale to the Deep South was a nightmare scenario for most enslaved people, and there was great relief that this did not happen.

White members of the local community had determined the monetary worth of each person enslaved at Monticello. Lucia Stanton has suggested that the prices of some of the slaves were kept low to enable family members to purchase them, which is what occurred in several instances. Daniel Farley, the eldest son of Mary Hemings who had been given to Jefferson's sister in the late 1780s, bought fifty-six-year-old Peter Hemings, his mother's half brother, for one dollar. The older man was listed as free in the 1830 census and continued to ply his trade as a tailor for the rest of his life. Jesse Scott, the son-in-law of Mary Hemings, bought her son, Joseph Fossett's wife, Edith, and their two youngest children, William and Daniel, for just over five hundred dollars. Scott evidently had borrowed money, using some of the property his wife had inherited from her father as collateral, a decision that would have serious consequences decades later. The imperative of the moment was to keep as much of the family together as possible.³

Fossett could not have bid on his wife and children even if he had had the money, because he would not be a free man until July 4, 1827. The truth is that he did not have the money to purchase them all, the cost running in the thousands of dollars. Instead, he made arrangements with as many members of the white community as he could to purchase his older children and hold them until he could buy them himself. John R. Jones, the man who bought Peter Fossett, broke his promise and balked at selling the youngster to his family.⁴

Burwell Colbert attended the auction that January day as well. In addition to spending thirty-one dollars for a mule, he bought "a carving knife, tea china, and portrait engravings of Jefferson and the Marquis de Lafayette." Colbert had numerous children, but because his deceased wife, Critta, had belonged to Martha Randolph, they were not part of Jefferson's estate. We do not know whether he had yet received his three-hundred-dollar legacy. Given the appraised value of the younger, more productive members of the Hemings family, his bequest would not have been much help. In addition, he did have children of his own to think of. His mother, Betty Brown, was listed as having no value and was in no immediate danger of being moved from her cabin on Monticello. He had no reason to fear for his aunts Critta and Sally, who were not part of the auction either. He may have already known that Francis Wayles Eppes intended to purchase the freedom of Critta Hemings, his nurse for a brief period and the half sister to his mother, so that she could live with her husband, Zachariah Bowles, which he did the same year of the auction.[5]

Sally Hemings's situation was convoluted and mysterious, as it had been since her return to America, but one can piece together what happened. Many years later, in 1873, Israel Gillette stated that Jefferson had freed seven slaves, including Sally Hemings and all her children. Of course, he freed only five people in his will. Beverley and Harriet Hemings simply left Monticello as white people with no formal emancipation. Who were the other two? Jefferson evidently made oral bequests of freedom as well. Members of his family told Henry Randall that Jefferson had directed his daughter to free forty-five-year-old Wormley Hughes, if he wanted to be free. For very obvious reasons, no one in the family would report to a historian an oral instruction from Jefferson to free Sally Hemings if she wanted it. Eight years after her father's death, Martha Randolph directed that two of her father's slaves, Sally Hemings and Wormley Hughes, and one of her own Randolph slaves, Betsy, the wife of Peter Hemings, be given "their time," even though all had been living as free people since Jefferson's death. "Giving time" was a customary way of emancipation that avoided having to make a request to the legislature or county court to allow the enslaved person to remain in the state. Martha explained that she had to free them this way because otherwise they would have been forced to leave Virginia. She knew full well, however, that there was an alternative. She could have asked the legislature, of which her son had been a member, to let Sally Hemings stay in Virginia. This, she was unwilling to do, and her father was apparently unwilling to do it either.[6]

Whether or not Sally Hemings knew it by the time of Jefferson's death, the man with whom she had returned to America those thirty-six years earlier had never been one for martyrdom. He believed, he said, in taking life by the "smooth handle." Putting the name Sally Hemings in his will, along with their two children, would have been the very opposite of smooth. Indeed, it would have exposed a truth for which, as far as he knew, white America would never forgive him. While the names Madison and Eston Hemings were probably known only to people in Jefferson's home territory, the name Sally when connected to that of Jefferson was known throughout the country, thanks to Callender and those who followed, like John Quincy

Adams. Formally freeing Hemings, while also emancipating two people obviously young enough to be their children, would have told the story of his life over the past thirty-eight years quite well. Instead of remaining a discreetly handled family matter, stories of "Dusky Sally," "Black Sal," or the "African Venus" would have come roaring back into the public view.

In truth, it is not at all clear that Jefferson would have thought that formally freeing a fifty-three-year-old woman was the right thing to do, and Virginia law reveals some white Virginians' thinking on the subject of emancipating older enslaved people. The 1782 Virginia law that allowed private manumissions specifically forbade the freeing of slaves under the age of twenty-one and over the age of forty-five without making express provision for their support.[7] The fear, and probably accurate prediction, was that slave owners would work their slaves for their entire productive lives and then free them when they no longer wanted to provide food and shelter for people who were too old to work. These freed/discarded former slaves would then become public charges. Critta Hemings was also older than her sister, Sally, but her source of support was her husband, a man of some means. When he died, Critta Hemings Bowles was given a life estate in their ninety-six-acre farm just north of Charlottesville. Burwell Colbert was only forty-three, and his three-hundred-dollar legacy and life estate in a house and one acre of land would have been enough provision even had he been older. John Hemings was fifty and Joseph Fossett forty-six, both over the statutory limit. But not only were they established tradesmen—Fossett's blacksmith shop was well known in the community—they, too, had been given places to live and enough land to grow their own food.

What would Jefferson have had to do in order to free Sally Hemings formally? First, he would have had to put her name in his will, and then detail how he was going to make provision for the woman who many knew, and others believed, had been his longtime mistress. Then he would have had to ask the Virginia legislature to allow her to remain in the state. That entailed asking the men in a body that he had sat in as a young man, a body from which he had launched his public career, to give a public endorsement of his nearly forty-year cohabitation with an African American enslaved woman. Given what had initially happened with the lottery, there was no guarantee that the legislature would have granted such a petition. Opposition to the lottery had been framed in terms of morals and concerns about Jefferson's reputation. For most white Virginians, interracial mixing was not only a legal issue but also a moral one, and stories of Jefferson's involvement in it had been bandied about for years. In the eyes of many, helping Jefferson make provision for his slave mistress would have raised an issue of even greater concern than lotteries. If the legislature said no, Hemings, at age fifty-three, under law would have to leave Virginia. If the legislature said yes, its members would have to go home and explain their votes to their wives and constituents, who might not have taken kindly to the official endorsement of what they called amalgamation.

Jefferson's will had both public and private dimensions. It was a public document, with a public effect, but it was also a last statement to Martha Randolph and his legal white grandchildren. It is all but impossible that any but the youngest among them in 1826 would not have known about Jefferson and Hemings. As in all families, knowing and keeping secrets within the family is one thing. There is little doubt that Jefferson and the Randolphs would have seen a public indication that he did indeed have a "shadow family" as a deep betrayal of his legal one. That was never a likely scenario under any circumstances, and certainly not under those in which Jefferson left Martha and her family. One has only to read the spare 1836 will of this woman who had been born into one of the wealthiest families in the country, who had grown up in luxury on two continents, to get a sense of how far she had fallen. At the end of her life, she had almost no material possessions or wealth to pass on, unlike her mother, whose death left Martha's father a wealthy man. [8] The way Sally Hemings departed Monticello is, then, a study in avoidance. It avoided harm to Jefferson's legacy, it avoided embarrassment and hurt to his white family, it got around the 1782 law's prohibition of freeing slaves over forty-five without stating how they were to be provided for, and it avoided the operation of the 1806 law that would have required a request for permission for Hemings to remain in the state.

After Jefferson's death Sally Hemings and her sons went to live in a rented house on Main Street in Charlottesville, not far from her sister Mary. Later her sons would buy their own homes, and she would live with her son Madison. Word spread of her informal emancipation, for she and her sons were listed in the 1830 census as free white people, even though it is inconceivable that the census taker did not know who she was. Her honorary whiteness did not last, however. Three years later, in a special census of 1833, conducted to count the free blacks in the community for purposes of determining which of them wanted to be resettled in Africa, Hemings described herself as a free mulatto who had lived in Charlottesville since 1826. She and her sons declined to return to Africa. They continued to live in downtown Charlottesville, participating in the life of the growing town until her death in the 1830s. Her two eldest children, Beverley and Harriet, kept in contact with their family. But as the years passed, the choices the children of Sally Hemings and Thomas Jefferson made would separate their lines forever. Three would live in the white world, and one would remain in the black world. The end result of their individual decisions show clearly what it has meant to be white in America and what it has meant to be black.[9]

Monticello was not sold until 1831, when a local citizen, James T. Barclay, bought it and 550 acres for $7,500. The house had been deserted well before then. After her father's death, Martha Randolph and her youngest children went to live for a time with her daughter Ellen in Boston. Some of the older members of the Hemings family, who had spent their entire lives in one place, clung to the familiar setting of the mountain that was now "theirs" in a way that it had never been before. The place was empty, and no one was making demands upon them. Betty Brown, the first Hemings to arrive at Monticello, was now in her seventies. It was never likely that she thought of going too far away from what had been her home until she absolutely had to. Her son Burwell Colbert, who kept the keys to the house at Monticello, came up periodically to see her, and to clean the house and make sure the yard was in order. Although the dwelling was empty, he felt compelled to perform the tasks that had defined his life for over twenty years. From his home at Shadwell at the base of Monticello, the place of Jefferson's birth, he ventured out into the world as a painter and glazer, working at the University of Virginia and for people in the community who had known Jefferson. He started a new life at age fifty-one when he married a twenty-year-old local free woman, Elizabeth Battles, and began to raise a second family.[10]

John Hemings, the youngest living child of Elizabeth Hemings, suffered the devastating blow of the loss of his beloved wife, Priscilla, in 1830. He lived three years after her, apparently experiencing extreme depression. He began to drink heavily, which he had not done before, and he stopped working altogether. Martha Randolph claimed that "liberty . . . was no blessing to him." But like his ill-fated older half brother James, who had lived five years as a free man, John Hemings was more than just an enslaved person. He was a devoted husband who had lost his wife. He was a talented artisan whose eyesight had been failing for a number of years to the point that he could no longer perform at the level of perfection to which he aspired. His family had been torn apart. And, it must be said, he had lost Jefferson, who, as Lucia Stanton eloquently put it, "had called forth his talent." All these things contributed to his sense of alienation. There is no reason to suppose that slavery would have salved these deep wounds and given him a renewed sense of meaning in his life.[11]

Although both Joseph Fossett and Wormley Hughes had children who were sold at auction, what happened to Hughes's family shows that he was much closer to Jefferson and his white family than one might gather from the fact that he was only informally freed. It also indicates that the memory of George and Ursula Granger, the former overseer at Monticello and Martha Randolph's wet nurse, still resonated within Jefferson's family. Hughes's wife, Ursula, was their granddaughter. She and seven of their children had been sold to local members of the Charlottesville community. Just a few days after this event, Jeff Randolph bought all of them back and reunited them at his Edgehill home, not far from Monticello. Within the next two years Jeff bought eighteen members of Wormley and Ursula Hughes's extended family. Jeff's mother-in-law was at first perplexed and then aghast at his actions. She flatly accused her son-in-law of putting the interests of the Hughes family ahead of those of his own children. Hughes himself continued to work for two more generations of the Jefferson-Randolph family until his death in 1858.[12]

Joseph Fossett's family situation was the most personally devastating. Though his half sister and brother-in-law Sally and Jesse Scott had bought his wife and their two youngest children for him, his daughters Maria and Isabella, ages twenty and eight, were sold to purchasers unknown. His daughter Patsy ran away from the man who bought her, and there is no record of her life after that. After his manumission, through his diligence and hard work, Fossett was able to gain ownership of five of his children and four of his grandchildren. To avoid application of the 1806 law, he kept them in legal bondage until he decided in 1837 that it was time for a change. In September of that year, he formally emancipated his own family members. Then around 1840, he, like many other African Americans, his nephews Madison and Eston Hemings included, left Virginia's slave society behind to make a new life in Ohio. The Fossetts' departure was not without heartache, for the couple's older daughters were not with them, and their son Peter was still owned by John Jones, who continued to refuse to sell him to his parents. So they went to Ohio without him. A miraculous reunion would eventually take place, but only after decades of struggle, heroics, and faith. One can merely imagine what Elizabeth Hemings, the African and English enslaved woman, would have made of the way her many descendants acquitted themselves as they journeyed through the harshness of American life.[13]

Acknowledgments

This project could not have been completed without the help of numerous friends, colleagues, and individuals who were unknown to me when I first started. I am touched beyond words by the generosity of those who spent time reading and commenting upon my work. They should not suffer for being kind. While I owe them for all the ways they enriched my effort, I am responsible for any errors that appear in this book.

There have been two constants from the beginning of my time writing about Monticello: Peter S. Onuf, the Thomas Jefferson Foundation Professor of History at the University of Virginia, and Lucia (Cinder) Stanton, Shannon Senior Research Historian at the Thomas Jefferson Foundation. I met one within days of meeting the other, without knowing that they were friends, back when I was writing my first book about Tom and Sally. From that time forward, I have relied on them, above anyone else, as sounding boards and sources of information about Jefferson, the Hemingses, and Monticello. Peter read an early, uncompleted version of this manuscript and then reread the whole thing at the end, employing his sharp eye, luminous humanity, and wide-ranging knowledge. Cinder also read and critiqued sections of the manuscript. She has always been a model of patience and reliability in responding to my near-endless and, often, bizarre queries, bringing me back to earth when needed.

Ronald Hoffman and Sally Mason of the Omohundro Institute of Early American History and Culture went beyond the call of duty reading the first section of the manuscript. Sally provided a wonderful line edit, and Ron suggested additional pertinent scholarship to consult. Their dual (and sometimes dueling) comments were frank, insightful, and always given with great wit and sensitivity—an unbeatable combination.

The same can be said of Edmund S. Morgan, Professor of History Emeritus at Yale, who read the first two sections of the manuscript. Like any great teacher, Ed asked questions that made me think more deeply about what I had written and immediately identified areas that needed further consideration. His encouraging words, and those of his wife, Marie, came at just the right time to spur me on to complete the last section of the book.

The late Winthrop Jordan read and commented upon the first section of the manuscript until he became too ill to continue. Gentleman that he was, he actually apologized to me for being unable to continue. What an honor it was to have as a supporter and friend the man who made me know, as a twelve year old, that I wanted to write history. *White over Black* helped set the course of my life. So I am eternally indebted to Win for much, in addition to his help with this work.

Jan Lewis, my friend and now colleague at Rutgers, brainstormed with me for hours about life at Monticello and continued her habit of bringing good things to my life by suggesting that Kenneth A. Lockridge of the University of Montana might be able to answer a question I had posed. From that one inquiry grew a voluminous correspondence that could fill a small book itself, in which Ken and I discussed (and argued gently) about Jefferson and Hemings. Ken also gave invaluable critiques of large swaths of the manuscript. Confirming the smallness of the world, before I contacted Ken, his longtime friend, the ever delightful Rhys Isaac of Latrobe University, read chapters, peppering me with questions and comments that helped refine my presentation.

For getting me quickly up to speed on blacks in France in the eighteenth century, I thank Sue Peabody of Washington State University Vancouver and Pierre Boulle of McGill University. Sue and Pierre read my chapters on France with extreme care and seriousness. Their observations, writings, and the source material they introduced me to gave me new ways to think about the Hemingses, race, and the workings of law in society.

I was especially fortunate to receive the very considered thoughts of Martha Hodes of New York University and Stephanie M. H. Camp of the University of Washington. Both women do work on race, women, and American slavery that I admire enormously. Barbara Heath of the University of Tennessee read my first chapter and gave me several critical reminders about the geography of early Virginia, and answered queries about the lives of enslaved people at Poplar Forest. I thank William Nelson of New York University for allowing me to present an early chapter before the NYU's Legal Colloquium and Francis D. Cogliano at the University of Edinburgh for his comments.

As always, my colleagues at New York Law School have been supportive of all my scholarly endeavors. My library assistant, Grace Lee, was enormously creative and helpful in finding anything I asked for. Associate Dean Stephen Ellmann asked me to present a chapter at one of our weekly Faculty Scholarship Luncheons, where I received helpful feedback from our dean, Richard Matasar, Leni Bensen, Carlin Meyer, Arthur Leonard, and the late Denise Morgan. Denise's premature death was a devastating blow to all who knew her as well as to the legal academy and profession. The world lost a truly wonderful person and a dynamic scholar. William LaPiana, Seth Harris, and Edward Purcell read more of the manuscript and gave me valuable critiques. Gemma Jacobs, my faculty assistant at NYLS, was, as always, a cheerful and efficient aid to my professional life. Her counterpart at Rutgers, Christina Strasburger, is in the same mold, and has been indispensable to me as I have settled in there.

Barbara B. Oberg and J. Jefferson Looney, the editors of *The Papers of Thomas Jefferson* at Princeton and *The Papers of Thomas Jefferson (Retirement Series)* at Monticello, respectively, made documents readily available to me and were always eager to answer questions. Members of their staff, Linda Monaco at Princeton and Lisa Francavilla at Monticello, endured comments like "Didn't I read a letter where someone said to TJ on some day that . . . " and would immediately find exactly what I was talking about. Now that this book is finished, Jeff Looney and I can move on to our own special Jefferson project.

I thank Jeanne Niccolls of the Fairfax County Park Authority, which runs the Sully Historic Site, for helping me find information about John Wayles. I also thank Elizabeth Nuxoll of *The Papers of John Jay* and Kate Ohno of *The Papers of Benjamin Franklin* for giving me access to unpublished material from their archives, and for all that I learned from them about Jay and Franklin and their dealings with enslaved people in Paris.

I am grateful for the support and help of others at the Thomas Jefferson Foundation and those associated with it. Dan Jordan, the foundation's president, and Andrew O' Shaughnessy, the director of the International Center for Jefferson Studies, deserve special mention for fostering, in the spirit of

Jefferson, a climate of intellectual inquiry and engagement. Susan Stein, Fraser Neiman, and Leni Sorenson made helpful suggestions about ways to think about the project. Jack Robertson and Anna Berkes of the Jefferson Library assisted me whenever asked. Liesal Nowak was of incalculable help as I gathered images for the book. Beverly Gray and Dianne Swann-Wright, who work with Cinder Stanton on the foundation's Getting Word project, gave me information and much to think about over the years. I also thank Octavia Starbuck and Gale Pond at Monticello's sister site, Poplar Forest, for their help.

I spent a great deal of time in archives and benefited enormously from the suggestions and efforts of the people who worked in them. The staff at the Special Collections division of the University of Virginia Library was a great resource whenever I visited, helping me find what I asked for and pointing out things I would never have found on my own. The staffs at the Virginia Historical Society and the Library of Virginia were similarly outstanding, helping me ferret out documents even when I had incomplete information about what I was searching for. Elaine Grublin of the Massachusetts Historical Society, Cindy Brennan of the American Antiquarian Society, Christopher Linnane of the Fogg Museum at Harvard University, and the staff of the Digital Services department at the University of Virginia provided me with images in an extremely prompt fashion. Elyse Reider ran interference for me with the Europeans.

I give special thanks to the superb genealogist Denise Harman of Lancashire, England, who did research for me on the Wayles family. The ultimate professional, her work was meticulous and creative, smoothing the way for my own trip to Preston, Lancashire, to delve further into the record and to have the privilege of meeting her. I also credit the staff of the Lancashire Records Office for their great courtesy to me and my son on our visit. They offered me suggestions about sources that I knew nothing of, and gave me valuable insights into the world in which Wayles was born.

Guy Holborn, the librarian at Lincoln's Inn in London, helped me search for any traces of John Wayles's legal career in England in the records available to him, including the archives of the other Inns of Court. He also told me what I needed to look at on my own in the National Archives at Kew in order to continue the search. Jo Hutchings, Lincoln Inn's archivist, helped with this process, as did Theresa Thom, the librarian at Gray's Inn.

It isn't often that historians get to spend time with the descendants of the people about whom they write. I have been fortunate to meet many descendants of Thomas Jefferson and Sally Hemings, other branches of the Hemings family, and descendants of Jefferson and his wife, Martha. I thank Julia Westerinen; her late husband, Emil; their children, Dorothy, Art, and Marshall; Shay Banks-Young; Shannon Lanier; Edna Jacques; and Lucian Truscott IV for talking with me about their families. Jane Feldman, not a Jefferson or Hemings by blood but the family's de facto official photographer, also receives my thanks.

I must credit others who have helped me sustain along the way. I owe much to Vernon Jordan. I have no words to express what his friendship and support have meant to me over the years. Loretta Lynch, a friend since law school, has been with me through thick and thin. Natalie S. Bober, who brings Jefferson to life for young people, is an inspiration. Richard Holbrooke has been a constant cheerleader, pulling me out of the eighteenth century to go to lunch occasionally. I thank Paul Golob, of Henry Holt Times Books, for reasons he well knows but that don't have to be explained here.

I can't say enough good things about Robert Weil, my one-of-a-kind editor at Norton. Bob actually edits manuscripts and cares deeply about his authors, books, and his craft. With great patience and fortitude, he helped bring this ship to shore. His assistants, Tom Mayer and Lucas Wittmann, were models of efficiency and good humor as we worked. I am deeply grateful to my copyeditor, the incomparable Otto Sonntag, who floored me with his thoroughness, great ear for language, and wide-ranging knowledge. Faith Childs, my agent, believed in me and this project from the beginning and helped shepherd me through the intricacies of trade publishing. She has been both protector and friend.

Finally, a project like this makes one think of one's own family. My brothers, Alfred Gordon Jr. and Jay Gordon, and I lost our father, Alfred Sr., in 2007. Our mother, Bettye, having died in 1990, we are without the "cover" we've known from the beginning of our lives. As life has it, I have now become part of the "cover" of others. I thank with all my being the people to whom this book is dedicated: my husband, Robert; my daughter, Susan; and my son, Gordon. They endured my absences, mental and physical, as I once again gave myself over to total obsession. What they have taught me about the meaning of family is the foundation for this work.

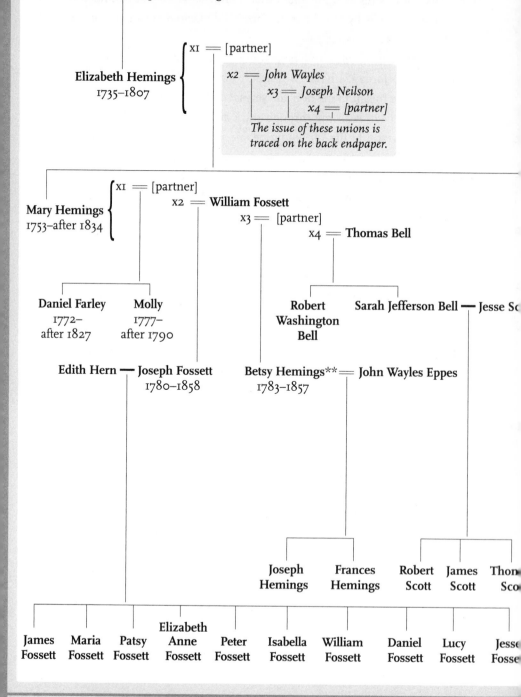

African woman ═══ Captain Hemings

Elizabeth Hemings
1735–1807
{ x1 ═══ [partner]

x2 ═══ John Wayles
x3 ═══ Joseph Neilson
x4 ═══ [partner]

The issue of these unions is
traced on the back endpaper.

Mary Hemings
1753–after 1834
{ x1 ═══ [partner]
x2 ═══ William Fossett
x3 ═══ [partner]
x4 ═══ Thomas Bell

Daniel Farley
1772–
after 1827

Molly
1777–
after 1790

Robert
Washington
Bell

Sarah Jefferson Bell — Jesse Sc

Edith Hern — Joseph Fossett
1780–1858

Betsy Hemings** ═══ John Wayles Eppes
1783–1857

Joseph
Hemings

Frances
Hemings

Robert
Scott

James
Scott

Thom
Sco

James
Fossett

Maria
Fossett

Patsy
Fossett

Elizabeth
Anne
Fossett

Peter
Fossett

Isabella
Fossett

William
Fossett

Daniel
Fossett

Lucy
Fossett

Jesse
Fosse

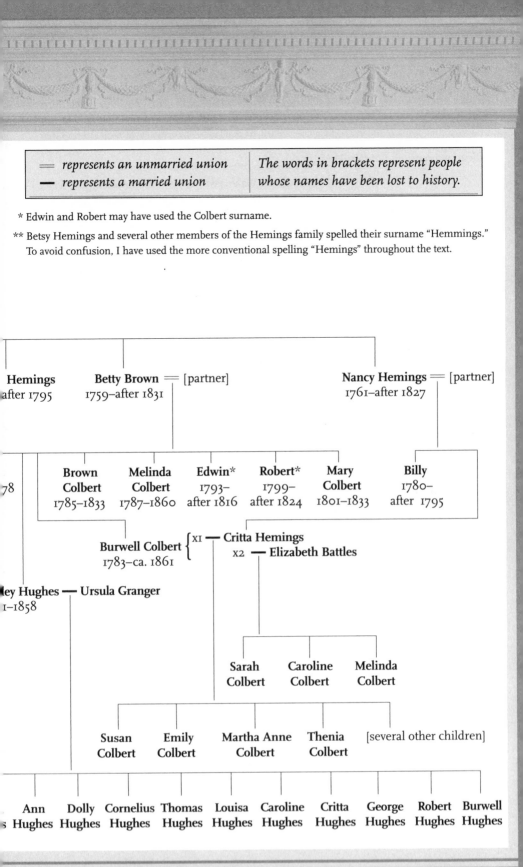

=	represents an unmarried union	The words in brackets represent people
—	represents a married union	whose names have been lost to history.

* Edwin and Robert may have used the Colbert surname.

** Betsy Hemings and several other members of the Hemings family spelled their surname "Hemmings." To avoid confusion, I have used the more conventional spelling "Hemings" throughout the text.

Hemings
after 1795

Betty Brown ═ [partner]
1759–after 1831

Nancy Hemings ═ [partner]
1761–after 1827

78

Brown
Colbert
1785–1833

Melinda
Colbert
1787–1860

Edwin*
1793–
after 1816

Robert*
1799–
after 1824

Mary
Colbert
1801–1833

Billy
1780–
after 1795

Burwell Colbert
1783–ca. 1861 { X1 — Critta Hemings
X2 — Elizabeth Battles

ley Hughes — Ursula Granger
1–1858

Sarah
Colbert

Caroline
Colbert

Melinda
Colbert

Susan
Colbert

Emily
Colbert

Martha Anne
Colbert

Thenia
Colbert

[several other children]

Ann
s Hughes

Dolly
Hughes

Cornelius
Hughes

Thomas
Hughes

Louisa
Hughes

Caroline
Hughes

Critta
Hughes

George
Hughes

Robert
Hughes

Burwell
Hughes

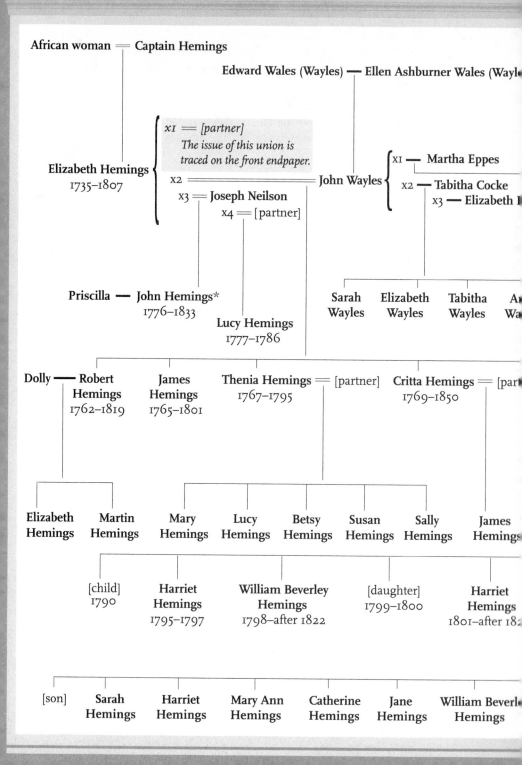

THE HEMINGS FAMILY TREE—2

African woman ═══ Captain Hemings

Edward Wales (Wayles) ─── Ellen Ashburner Wales (Wayl

x1 ═ [partner]
The issue of this union is traced on the front endpaper.

Elizabeth Hemings
1735–1807

x2 ════════════════════ John Wayles

x3 ═ Joseph Neilson

x4 ═ [partner]

x1 ─── Martha Eppes

x2 ─── Tabitha Cocke

x3 ─── Elizabeth I

Priscilla ─── John Hemings*
1776–1833

Lucy Hemings
1777–1786

Sarah Wayles

Elizabeth Wayles

Tabitha Wayles

A
Wa

Dolly ─── Robert Hemings
1762–1819

James Hemings
1765–1801

Thenia Hemings ═══ [partner]
1767–1795

Critta Hemings ═══ [par
1769–1850

Elizabeth Hemings

Martin Hemings

Mary Hemings

Lucy Hemings

Betsy Hemings

Susan Hemings

Sally Hemings

James Hemings

[child]
1790

Harriet Hemings
1795–1797

William Beverley Hemings
1798–after 1822

[daughter]
1799–1800

Harriet Hemings
1801–after 18

[son]

Sarah Hemings

Harriet Hemings

Mary Ann Hemings

Catherine Hemings

Jane Hemings

William Beverl
Hemings

= represents an unmarried union	The words in brackets represent people
— represents a married union	whose names have been lost to history.

* John Hemings and several other members of the Hemings family spelled their surname "Hemmings." To avoid confusion, I have used the more conventional spelling "Hemings" throughout the text.

** These four other children died very young: a daughter Jane, an unnamed son, and two daughters, both named Lucy Elizabeth.

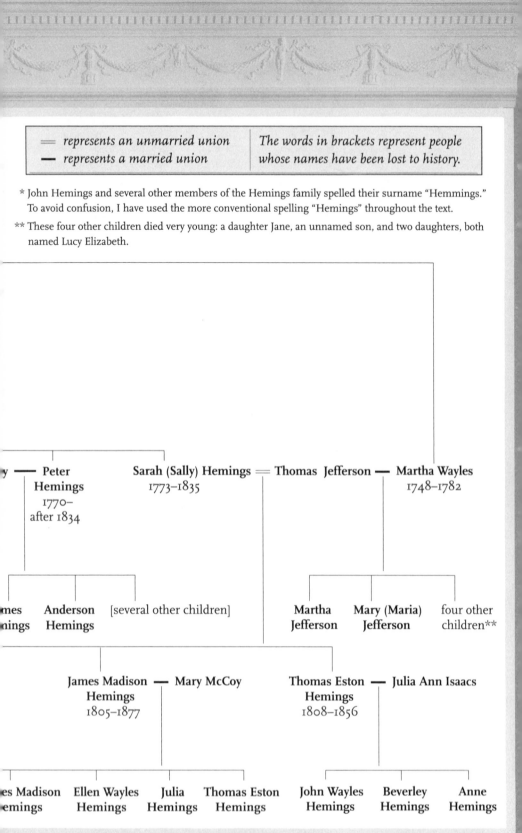

y —— Peter Hemings 1770– after 1834

Sarah (Sally) Hemings 1773–1835 == Thomas Jefferson —— Martha Wayles 1748–1782

mes ‌ Anderson ‌ [several other children] ‌ ‌ ‌ ‌ Martha ‌ ‌ Mary (Maria) ‌ ‌ four other
nings ‌ Hemings ‌ ‌ ‌ ‌ ‌ ‌ ‌ ‌ ‌ ‌ ‌ ‌ ‌ ‌ ‌ ‌ ‌ ‌ ‌ Jefferson ‌ ‌ Jefferson ‌ ‌ children**

James Madison —— Mary McCoy
Hemings
1805–1877

Thomas Eston —— Julia Ann Isaacs
Hemings
1808–1856

es Madison ‌ Ellen Wayles ‌ Julia ‌ Thomas Eston ‌ ‌ ‌ John Wayles ‌ Beverley ‌ Anne
emings ‌ ‌ ‌ Hemings ‌ Hemings ‌ Hemings ‌ ‌ ‌ ‌ ‌ Hemings ‌ ‌ Hemings ‌ Hemings

NOTES

Abbreviations

Brodie, *Thomas Jefferson*	Fawn M. Brodie, *Thomas Jefferson: An Intimate History* (New York, 1974)
Family Letters Project	Family Letters Project, Thomas Jefferson Foundation, *The Papers of Thomas Jefferson: Retirement Series*, at http://www.monticello.org/papers/index.html
Farm Book	*Thomas Jefferson's Farm Book, with Commentary and Relevant Extracts from Other Writings*, ed. Edwin Morris Betts (Princeton, 1953)
Gordon-Reed, *TJ and SH*	Annette Gordon-Reed, *Thomas Jefferson and Sally Hemings: An American Controversy* (Charlottesville, 1997)
LOC	Library of Congress, Washington, D.C.
LVa	Library of Virginia, Richmond
Malone, *Jefferson*	Dumas Malone, *Jefferson and His Time*, 6 vols. (Boston, 1948–81)
MB	*Jefferson's Memorandum Books: Accounts, with Legal Records and Miscellany, 1767–1826*, ed. James A. Bear Jr. and Lucia C. Stanton, 2 vols. (Princeton, 1997)
MHi	Massachussets Historical Society, Boston
Papers	*The Papers of Thomas Jefferson*, ed. Julian P. Boyd et al., 35 vols. to date (Princeton, 1950–)
SH	Sally Hemings
SJL	Summary Journal of Letters
Stanton, *Free Some Day*	Lucia Stanton, *Free Some Day: The African-American Families of Monticello* (Charlottesville, 2000)
TJ	Thomas Jefferson
VHS	Virginia Historical Society, Richmond
ViU	University of Virginia Library, Charlottesville
VMHB	*Virginia Magazine of History and Biography*
WMQ	*William and Mary Quarterly*

1: Young Elizabeth's World

1. Willie Lee Rose, "The Domestication of Domestic Slavery," in Willie Lee Rose *Slavery and Freedom*, ed. William W. Freehling (New York, 1982).

2. Perhaps the earliest-known usage of the phrase, and certainly the most widely disseminated, was the headline for an Evan Thomas article in *Newsweek* published to coincide with Independence Day celebrations: "Founder's Chic: Live from Philadelphia," *Newsweek*, July 9, 2001. The phrase and phenomenon have sparked discussions in both scholarly and popular venues. See, e.g., David Waldstreicher, "Founder's Chic as Culture War," *Radical History Review*, no. 84 (Fall 2002): 185–94; H. W. Brands, "Founder's Chic: Our Reverence for the Founding Fathers Has Gotten out of Hand," *Atlantic Monthly*, Sept. 2003.

3. Wesley F. Craven, *White, Red, and Black: The Seventeenth-Century Virginian* (Charlottesville, 1961), 29–30; Edmund S. Morgan, *American Slavery, American Freedom: The Ordeal of Colonial Virginia* (New York, 1975), 49. Although Morgan notes that the first permanent settlers were sponsored by the Virginia Company, "a joint stock company [whose] members hoped for a profit," he allows that those who formed the company at least styled themselves as having a higher calling, but with a spirit and an objective that might offend modern-day sensibilities: bringing civilization to the "heathen savages" while saving the lower orders in England "from idleness and crime." See also Edmund S. Morgan, "Headrights and Head Counts: A Review Article," *VMHB* 30 (1972): 361–71, describing how the system of headrights and land patents promoted "landgrabbing" and resulted in huge concentrations of property in the hands of a very few people; Anthony Parent, *Foul Means: The Formation of a Slave Society in Virginia, 1660–1740* (Chapel Hill, 2003), whose first chapter, "The Land Grab," echoes Morgan's characterization and gives a detailed and entirely unsentimental description of how land was acquired in early Virginia that shows how many of the great families of the Old Dominion obtained their wealth and positions; and Robin Blackburn, *The Making of New World Slavery: From the Baroque to the Modern, 1492–1800* (London, 1997), 227, which describes the headright system as one in which, in keeping with the "biblical maxim 'to him that hath shall be given,'" planters "with capital, and the necessary application," could "accumulate both land and labour."

4. *Farm Book*, 130; "The Memoirs of Madison Hemings," in Gordon-Reed, *TJ and SH*, 245; Parent, *Foul Means*, 36; Blackburn, *Making of New World Slavery*, 227.

5. A plethora of books and articles are devoted entirely, or in part, to the evolution of Virginia's slave society in the seventeenth and eighteenth centuries; many of them have become classics in American historiography. See, e.g., Morgan, *American Slavery*; Allan Kulikoff, *Tobacco and Slaves: The Development of Southern Cultures in the Chesapeake, 1680–1800* (Chapel Hill, 1986); Philip D. Morgan, *Slave Counterpoint: Black Culture in the Eighteenth-Century Chesapeake and Lowcountry* (Chapel Hill, 1998). The origins debate has prompted its own line of scholarly inquiry. See, e.g., Winthrop D. Jordan, "Modern Tensions and the Origins of American Slavery," *Journal of Southern History*, 28 no.1 (Feb. 1962): 18–30; Russell Menard, "From Servants to Slaves: The Transformation of the Chesapeake Labor System," *Southern Studies* 20 (1977): 355–90; Alden T. Vaughan, "The

Origins Debate: Slavery and Racism in Seventeenth-Century Virginia," *VHMB* 97, no. 3 (July 1989): 311–54. For a critique of the historical writings about the origins of slavery, see Nathan I. Huggins, "The Deforming Mirror of Truth: Slavery and the Master Narrative of American History," *Radical History Review*, no. 49 (1991): 25–48. For a discussion of the debate in the context of legal history, see Thomas D. Morris, *Southern Slavery and the Law, 1619–1860* (Chapel Hill, 1996), 8–14.

6. Philip Morgan, *Slave Counterpoint*, 9.

7. James B. Walvin, *Black and White: The Negro and English Society, 1555–1945* (London, 1974); F. O. Shyllon, *Black Slaves in Britain* (London, 1974); F. O. Shyllon, *Black People in Britain, 1555–1833* (London, 1977); Philip D. Morgan, "British Encounters with Africans and African Americans, circa 1600–1780," in *Strangers within the Realm Cultural Margins of the First British Empire*, ed. Bernard Bailyn and Philip D. Morgan (Chapel Hill, 1991), 157–219; Ira Berlin, "From Creole to Africa: Atlantic Creoles and the Origins of African-American Society in Mainland North America," *WMQ*, 3d ser., 53 (1996): 51–88; Ira Berlin, *Generations of Captivity: A History of African-American Slaves* (Cambridge, Mass., 2003), chap. 1.

8. See Winthrop D. Jordan, *White over Black: American Attitudes toward the Negro, 1550–1812* (Chapel Hill, 1968), 7–11.

9. T. H. Breen, "Creative Adaptations, Peoples and Cultures," in *Colonial British American: Essays in the New History of the Early Modern Era*, ed. Jack P. Greene and J. R. Poole (Baltimore, 1984), 202, discussing intellectual historians' engagements with "study of white attitudes about blacks and Indians," and noting, "West Africans possessed an image of the white man that was extremely unflattering. Blacks seem to have associated the color white, at least on human beings, with a number of negative attributes, including evil."

10. Ibid., 200.

11. Philip Morgan, *Slave Counterpoint*, 62–70.

12. T. H. Breen and Stephen Innes, *"Myne Owne Ground": Race and Freedom on Virginia's Eastern Shore, 1640–1676* (New York, 1980).The authors argue that there was a "possibility of a genuinely multiracial society . . . during the years before Bacon's Rebellion in 1676." Nathaniel Bacon led a group of lower-class whites and blacks in a revolt against his relation by marriage, Governor William Berkeley, and his upper-class supporters. The property-poor rebels wanted land that belonged to a Native American group with whom the white government officials, who had already gathered their large estates in land, had made agreements. This show of solidarity between poor whites and blacks taught the upper class at least two valuable lessons: (1) if they wanted to continue to rule, they had to drive a wedge between the two groups who might have reason to join together against them; and (2) it was in their interest to have a thoroughly subjugated work force, i.e., slaves who would be in no position to demand a share of benefits within Virginian society.

13. "Whereas some doubts have arisin whether children that are slaves by birth, by charity and piety of their owners made pertakers of the blessed sacrament of baptisme, should by virtue of their baptisme be made ffree, *its is enacted* . . . that the conferring of baptisme doth not alter the condition of the person as to his bondage or ffreedom; that diverse

masters, ffreed from this doubt, may more carefully endeavour the propagation of christianity by permitting . . . slaves . . . to be admitted to the sacrament." *An act declaring that
baptisme of slaves doth not exempt them from bondage* (Act II, Sept. 1667), in William Waller
Hening, comp., *The Statutes at Large, Being a Collection of All the Laws of Virginia from the
First Session of the Legislature in the Year 1619*, 13 vols. (Richmond, Va., 1809-23), 2:260.

14. *Negro Womens children to serve according to the condition of the mother* (Act XII, Dec. 1662), in
Hening, comp., *Statutes at Large*, 2:170. For an extensive and informative discussion of how
Virginians constructed racial and sexual identities, see, generally, Kathleen M. Brown, *Good
Wives, Nasty Wenches and Anxious Patriarchs: Gender, Race, and Power in Colonial Virginia*
(Chapel Hill, 1997). This is the theme of the entire work, but chap. 8 deals directly with the
time period that laid the foundation for the world that Elizabeth Hemings and her African
mother encountered in the first half of the eighteenth century in Virginia.

15. Brown, *Good Wives*, 132; Warren M. Billings, "The Cases of Fernando and Elizabeth
Key: A Note on the Status of Blacks in Seventeenth-Century Virginia," *WMQ*, 3d ser., 30
(1973): 467-74. Fernando was a slave seeking freedom because "he was a Christian and
had been several years in England." Key was the daughter of Thomas Key and a slave
woman. She brought suit, citing the English common law rule that said that children followed the status of their fathers. Fernando lost his case, but Key was successful after a
nonsuit was entered against her opponents.

16. Winthrop D. Jordan, "American Chiaroscuro: The Status and Definition of Mulattoes in
the British Colonies," *WMQ*, 3d ser., 19 (1962): 183-200. See also Joel Williamson, *New
People: Miscegenation and Mulattoes in the United States* (New York, 1980), 134-35 on scientific racism.

17. Gordon-Reed, *TJ and SH*, 245. Port Anne (College Landing), a mile from Williamsburg's
center, functioned "throughout the eighteenth and part of the nineteenth century as
Williamsburg's major port, linking it to local and European trade routes via the James
River." Capitol Landing, a mile to the north, linked "Williamsburg to the Chesapeake
by way of Queen's Creek and the York River." Andrew C. Edwards, *Archeology at Port
Anne: A Report on Site CL7, an Early-17th Century Colonial Site* (Colonial Williamsburg
Archeological Report, 1987).

18. Philip Morgan, *Slave Counterpoint*, 81.

19. Henrico County Deed Book, 1744-48, April 29, 1746.

20. Henrico Co. Deeds & Wills, 1725-1737, no. 2, part 1, Nov. 17, 1733.

21. Ibid. Both names recur in the Hemings family line. Sarah appears more frequently, but
that could be due to simple preference. For the will of John Wayles, see *Tyler's Quarterly
Historical and Genealogical Magazine* 6 (1924-25): 269.

22. Henrico Co. Deeds & Wills, 1725-1737, p. 277. Cited in note 19 above.

23. Frederick Dorman, *Ancestors and Descendants of Francis Epes I* (Petersburg, Va., 1992).
See, generally, Morgan, "Headrights and Headcounts"; Parent, *Foul Means*, cited above.

24. Parent, *Foul Means*, 42-47, discussing the "coup" that black headrights were for the "great
planter class" for the period their use was allowed, noting that William Byrd and Ralph
Wormeley's "applications accounted for 44.2 percent of black headrights used in patent-
ing land from 1635 to 1699" (p. 44). The practice conflicted with the Board of Trade's
desire to promote homesteads over land speculating, and eventually the practice was outlawed, but not before vast acreages were taken up by large planters.

25. Dorman, *Francis Epes I*, 58.

26. See Rhys Isaac, *The Transformation of Virginia, 1740–1790* (Chapel Hill, 1982). Edward A. Wyatt IV, "Newmarket of the Virginia Turf," *WMQ*, 2d ser., 17 (1937): 481–95, noting that horse "racing appeared in southern Virginia at an early date; a race is known to have been held at Colonel Eppes's store at Bermuda Hundred in 1678" (p. 482). The family continued to be associated with Newmarket well into the nineteenth century.

2: John Wayles: The Immigrant

1. Jefferson Family Bible, LVa, listing the date of the Wayles and Eppes marriage as May 3, 1746. For a discussion of white women's property rights in Virginia, see Linda L. Sturtz, *Within Her Power: Propertied Women in Colonial Virginia* (New York, 2002).

2. Malone, *Jefferson*, 1:153

3. Jefferson Family Bible, LVa.

4. *MB*, 329 n. 15. The Forest was said to have been burned down during the Civil War. "Historical and Genealogical Notes," *WMQ*, 6 (1897): 63. In 1728 Parliament enacted a statute designed to better regulate the profession of law, which in England was and is separated between solicitors, who prepare cases in the offices, and barristers, who argue cases in court. The 1728 law required registration of every man trained as a solicitor, when he entered the profession, and with whom he trained. *The Attorneys and Solicitors Act of 1728* (2 Geo. 2, c.23). Wayles does not appear on any of these lists. He was thirteen years old when the statute was passed, well before the age that he would have been in training, and he was in America by 1740. Had he been trained as a solicitor, his name should have appeared some time in the 1730s. Nor does Wayles appear in any of the archives of the Inns of Court, whose records of barristers go back to the 1500s. Lists, even those required by law, are compiled by human beings and are therefore fallible, as are the people who search them. But other evidence strongly suggests that Wayles received his legal training after he came to Virginia. *Attorney Admitted to the Court of Common Pleas*, CP 69/1, CP 70/1. National Archives London.

5. Lancashire Record Office, Records of St. Mary's Parish, St. Mary Ref. PR3262/1/2, Jan. 1714–March 25/1724.

6. Daniel Defoe, *A Tour through the Whole Island of Great Britain*, ed. Pat Rogers (Exeter, 1989), 195, 193.

7. Melinda Elder, *The Slave Trade and the Economic Development of Eighteenth-Century Lancaster* (Halifax, 1992), 19, 30, 169–70. Elder cautions that Lancaster's participation in the trade may be undervalued because many Lancaster merchants cleared "a number of their vessels from or via Liverpool" in the last decades of the eighteenth century, minimizing the amount of Lancaster-based capital that helped fuel the trade. Ibid., 171–73, 210.

8. Ibid., 210.

9. Lancashire Records Office, Records of St. Mary's Parish, "Will of Edward Wayles of Lancaster, Butcher, Admon. By Elizabeth Wayles, Widow, unto John, Thomas, Edward, and Anne Wayles the natural children of said Edward."

10. Genealogical Notes of the Lee Family, Papers of Richard Bland Lee, MSS1 L5153 b 13-16, VHS.

11. "Virginia Gleanings in England," *VMHB* 19 (1911): 289. Charles Campbell, "Life of Isaac

Jefferson of Petersburg, Virginia, Blacksmith," *WMQ*, 3d ser., 8 (1951): 580. Available evidence suggests that Isaac Jefferson's family name was Granger. In later years he aparently used both Granger and Jefferson. I will use the name Jefferson when referring to him but will use Granger when referring to his relatives. Monticello Research Department, Thomas Jefferson Foundation.

12. Virginia B. Price, "Constructing to Command: Rivalries between Green Spring and the Governor's Palace, 1677–1722," *VMHB* 113 (2005): 2–45; Jesse Dimmick, "Green Spring," *WMQ*, 2d ser., 9 (1929): 129–30; *Virginia Gazette*, Sept. 1, 1738; A. B. Shepperson, *John Paradise and Lucy Ludwell* (Richmond, Va., 1943).

13. Will of Philip Ludwell of Westminster, Middlesex, May 6, 1767; Prob. 11/928, Records of the Prerogative Court of Canterbury; Prerogative Court of Canterbury and Related Probate Jurisdictions: Will Registers. For the reference to Wayles in the *Virginia Gazette*, see discussion and notes at pp. 19–20. Paul C. Nagel, *The Lees of Virginia: Seven Generations of an American Family* (New York, 1990), 127–30.

14. The will of Philip Ludwell, cited above, n. 13, gives Corbin's and Nicholas's titles. See also "Williamsburg—The Old Colonial Capital," *WMQ* 16 (1907): 33, describing Nicholas's close friendship with the popular royal governor Botetourt. Wayles and Waller were described as "Esqrs. Attorneys at Law." Waller was also a representative in the Colonial Assembly in 1752, along with Carter Burwell.

15. Richard Corbin to Philip Ludwell, May 7, 1767; Richard Corbin to Philip Ludwell, Aug. 13, 1764, M 2287 Special Collections, Alderman Library, University of Virginia; Corbin to Lucy Ludwell, May 28, 1768, "Corbin Papers from Colonial Williamsburg," M 2287 Special Collections, Alderman Library, University of Virginia; Robert Carter Nicholas to an unknown correspondent, Jan. 5, 1770. "Understanding after I parted with you that Mr. Wayles & Mr. Waller seem very desirous that the division of Col. Ludwell's Estate should be immediately completed. . . ." Lee Family Papers, 1638–1867, 1L51f190–415, sect. 94–114, VHS.

16. John M. Hemphill II, ed., "John Wayles Rates His Neighbors," *VMHB* 66 (1958): 302–6.

17. "Williamsburg—The Old Colonial Capital," 9, 10.

18. Ibid., 10–11, 23. See also Carville V. Earle, "Environment, Disease, and Mortality in Early Virginia," in *The Chesapeake in the Seventeenth Century: Essays on Anglo-American Society*, ed. Thad W. Tate and David L. Ammerman (Chapel Hill, 1979), 96–125.

19. Malone, *Jefferson*, 1:62; "Williamsburg—The Old Colonial Capital," 14.

20. A. G. Roeber, "Authority, Law, and Custom: The Rituals of Court Day in Tidewater Virginia, 1720 to 1750," *WMQ*, 3d ser., 37 (1980): 29–52. See p. 30, on how "the 'Dignity and Decorum' of court rituals—the dramaturgical exercises—in which propertied authority and communal custom defined the shared values of the culture by means of law."

21. *Virginia Gazette*, March 1744; *Virginia Gazette*, Oct. 24, 1745.

22. Minutes of the Executive Council of Virginia, April 1741, LVa.

23. Maria (Taylor) Byrd to William Byrd III, April 1760, MSS1B996b13 Byrd, VHS.

24. Maria (Taylor) Byrd to William Byrd III, Sept. 23, 1739, MSS1B9963b10 Byrd, VHS.

25. Purdie & Dixon's *Virginia Gazette*, Aug. 13, 1767; ibid., May 18, 1769; Rind's *Virginia Gazette*, May 15, 1769; Purdie & Dixon's *Virginia Gazette*, May 16, 1771; Rind's *Virginia Gazette*, May 23, 1771; Purdie & Dixon's *Virginia Gazette*, Sept. 24, 1772; Rind's *Virginia Gazette*, Oct. 8, 1772.

26. Jacob M. Price, "The Last Phase of the Virginia-London Consignment Trade: James Buchanan and Co., 1758–1768," *WMQ*, 3d ser., 43 (1986): 64–98. See Richard B. Sheridan, "The British Credit Crisis of 1772 and the American Colonies," *Journal of Economic History* 20 (June 1960): 161–86, quoting John Wayles's description of how easy credit affected Virginians consumption of "luxury" items.

27. For documents related to the failed *Prince of Wales* venture, see *Papers*, 15:642–67. Note in particular Farrell & Jones to Wayles and Randolph, Feb. 3, 1772, announcing that the *Prince of Wales*, one of two ships bound for Virginia, was carrying 400 enslaved Africans, and John Wayles letter to Farrell & Jones of Sept. 24, 1772, confirming the arrival of the ship with "280 slaves." The voyage took longer than expected, which may have accounted for the large number of deaths. On April 3, 1773, Farrell & Jones wrote to Wayles & Randolph saying that "the mortality amongst the slaves could not be prevented."

28. Papers of William Jones, Somerset Record Office, Somerset, Eng.

29. *Hemphill*, ed., "John Wayles Rates His Neighbors," 302–6.

30. Ibid., 303.

31. Ibid., 305.

32. Ibid. John Wayles, Benjamin Waller, and Richard Hanson advertised themselves as the attorneys for John Lidderdale, arranging for the sale of land and enslaved people in an advertisement in the *Virginia Gazette* on Feb. 22, 1770. Ironically, on that same day the paper carried a notice of the destruction by fire of TJ's home at Shadwell.

33. TJ to Daniel Hylton, March 17, 192, *Papers*, 23:290.

34. Hemphill, "John Wayles Rates His Neighbors," 305.

35. Land Office Patents No. 32, 1752–56 (vols. 1 and 2, pp. 1–715), p. 675, Feb. 14, 1756 (500 acres); ibid., (reel 30) (1,000 acres); 254 acres between Angola Creek and Great Guinea Creek, Land Office Patents No. 33, 1756–61 (vols. 1, 2, 3, and 4, pp. 1–1095), p. 371 (reels 31–32), Feb. 14, 1756; ibid., p. 1054 (reels 31–32), Aug. 7, 1761, LVa; *Executive Journals of the Council of Virginia*, vol. 5, Nov. 1, 1739–May 7, 1754, p. 454, LVa.

36. Purdie & Dixon's *Virginia Gazette*, July 7, 1766; Woody Holton, *Forced Founders: Indians, Debtors, Slaves, and the Making of the American Revolution in Virginia* (Chapel Hill, 1999), 39–43, does not mention Wayles's involvement but gives a concise description of the political and economic interests at conflict in the trial.

37. Purdie & Dixon's *Virginia Gazette*, Sept. 9, 1766.

38. Ibid., Jan. 1, 1767.

39. Ibid., Jan. 8, 1767.

40. Ibid., Oct. 10, 1766.

41. Ibid., Oct. 17, 1767.

42. Ibid.; "Old Virginia Editors," *WMQ* 7 (1898): 9–17, 15.

3: The Children of No One

1. John Wayle's will, April 15, 1760, *Tyler's Quarterly Historical and Genealogical Magazine* 6 (1924–25): 269.

2. Jefferson Family Bible, LVa.

3. *Farm Book*, 15, 18; Stanton, *Free Some Day*, 177 n. 178; Lucia Stanton, "Monticello to Main Street: The Hemings Family and Charlottesville," *Magazine of Albermarle County*

History 55 (1997): 125. Mary Hemings's grandson described her as an octoroon, which is almost certainly incorrect. If Mary Hemings's father had been white, she would have been a quadroon like her siblings Robert, James, Thenia, Critta, Peter, and Sally Hemings. Hemings's situation is interesting. She is alternately described as Mary Hemings or Mary Bell by herself, Mary "Wells" by Thomas Bell, or Wales by a historian of Charlottesville. See Edgar Woods, *Albermarle County in Virginia, Giving Some Account of What It Was by Nature, What It Was Made by Man, and Some of the Men Who Made It* (1901; reprint, Berryville, Va., 1984). As was noted earlier, Mary was the name of John Wayles's sister. Madison Hemings, who knew Mary, does not mention her as a Wayles daughter. As of now, there appears to be no demonstrated oral history among the descendants of Mary Hemings that she was a Wayles daughter. It may well be that Mary Hemings's father was white and that the talk about Elizabeth Hemings and John Wayles led members of their community to assume that any of her older and lighter-skinned children belonged to him.

4. Morgan, *Slave Counterpoint* (Chapel Hill, 1998), 81. "As early as the second decade of the eighteenth century, Virginia's slave population began to grow from natural increase, an unprecedented event for any New World slave population." Morgan also notes (p. 87), "Whereas women in eighteenth-century England began childbearing in their midtwenties slave women in eighteenth-century North America tended to be in their late teens when they conceived their first child."

5. Wayles's will, cited above, n. 1.

6. *Farm Book*, 24.

7. See Thomas D. Morris, *Southern Slavery and the Law, 1619–1860* (Chapel Hill, 1996), 230–37, on the subject of exclusion of testimony of blacks.

8. Robert F. Bennett, then senator from Utah, commenting on the strength of candidate George W. Bush, listed the possible catastrophic things that could derail Bush's nomination. "Unless George W. steps in front of a bus, some woman comes forward, let's say some black woman, comes forward with an illegitimate child that he fathered within the last 18 months, or some other scenario that you could be equally creative in thinking of, George W. Bush will be the nominee." Bennett's remarks caused a furor, and he apologized for them. *New York Times*, Aug. 17, 1999, sec. A, p. 12, col. 1.

9. Stewart E. Stark, "Estoppel in Property Law," *Nebraska Law Review* 77 (1980): 756, 759–69.

10. Laurel Thatcher Ulrich, *A Midwife's Tale: The Life of Martha Ballard, Based on Her Diary, 1785–1812* (New York, 1991).

11. Joshua D. Rothman, *Notorious in the Neighborhood: Sex and Families across the Color Line in Virginia, 1787–1861* (Chapel Hill, 2003), 4.

12. Ibid., 4–5.

13. David W. Blight, *Race and Reunion: The Civil War in American Memory* (Cambridge, Mass., 2001).

14. Charles F. Robinson II, *Dangerous Liaisons: Sex and Love in the Segregated South* (Fayetteville, Ark., 2003), 49–50.

15. Thomas Jefferson Randolph's recollections, ViU:1874.

16. Journal of John Hartwell Cocke, Jan. 26, 1853, in John Hartwell Cocke Papers, Box 188, Alderman Library, University of Virginia.

17. See, generally, Philip J. Schwarz, *Slave Laws in Virginia* (Athens, Ga., 1996).

18. *Boston Repertory*, May 31, 1805; Campbell, "Life of Isaac Jefferson," 566–82, 567–68; Gordon-Reed, *TJ and SH*, 245.

4 : Thomas Jefferson

1. Purdie & Dixon's *Virginia Gazette*, March 12, 1767.

2. *Papers*, 3:532; Martha Jefferson's Account Book, Feb. 27, 1772 (Account Book with Record of Cases Tried in Virginia Courts, 1768–69), LOC.

3. Jefferson's Family Bible, LVa.

4. Thomas Jefferson, *Autobiography, in Writings* (New York, 1984), 7–8; Malone, *Jefferson*, 1:430, 21, 21–33; Brodie, *Thomas Jefferson*, 41–45.

5. Susan Kern, "The Material World of the Jeffersons at Shadwell," *WMQ*, 3d ser., 62, no. 2 (2005), at http://www.historycooperative.org/journals/wm/62.2/kern.html, 14–18.

6. Merrill Peterson, *Thomas Jefferson and the New Nation* (New York, 1970), 9.

7. Douglas L. Wilson, ed., *Jefferson's Literary Commonplace Book* (Princeton, 1989).

8. Brodie, *Thomas Jefferson*, 43.

9. Kern, "Material World of the Jeffersons," 14.

10. Ibid.

11. Ibid.

12. Henry S. Randall, *The Life of Thomas Jefferson*, 3 vols. (1858; reprint, New York, 1972), 1:33.

13. TJ to William Fleming, March 20, 1764, "11. o'clock at night," *Papers*, 1:16.

14. Susan Kern, "The Jeffersons at Shadwell: The Social and Material World of a Virginia Plantation" (Ph.D. diss., College of William and Mary, 2005), 1:87–92, discussing the implications of Jane Jefferson's history of childbearing.

    TJ never referred to Jupiter as "Evans." However, his son's name was John Jupiter Philip Ammon Evans. See Stanton, *Free Some Day*, 22. In several listings, including his 1801 record of vaccinations of enslaved people and some of his grandchildren, TJ did refer to Philip Evans as "Phil Ev." Evans was thus the family name during slavery. See *Papers*, 35:34.

15. Campbell, "Life of Isaac Jefferson," 577; Martha Jefferson Carr to TJ, March 27, 1787, *Papers*, 15:655.

16. Thomas Worthington's diary, entry for Jan. 25, 1802, LOC.

17. Gordon-Reed, *TJ and SH*, 247.

18. Campbell, "Life of Isaac Jefferson," 577.

19. Brodie, *Thomas Jefferson*, 34.

20. TJ to Giovanni Fabbroni, June 8, 1778, *Papers*, 2:196; Malone, *Jefferson*, 1:90; Gordon-Reed, *TJ and SH*, 15, 51.

21. Malone, *Jefferson*, 1:129, 120; the indenture between Richard Corbin, Robert Carter Nicholas, John Wayles, and Benjamin Waller and Philippa Lee, wife of William Lee, dated Nov. 5, 1770, in Lee Family Papers, VHS.

22. *MB*, 34, 35.

23. Purdie & Dixon's *Virginia Gazette*, Feb. 22, 1770.

24. Malone, *Jefferson*, 1:157–58.

25. See, e.g., *Farm Book*, 77. Betty Brown was listed along with her children. Thomas Jefferson Randolph identified his uncle Samuel Carr as the father of Brown's children. If he was telling the truth, these were most probably her two youngest, born in the late 1790s. See Gordon-Reed, *TJ and SH*, 254.

26. *Howell v. Netherland*, 1770 Va. Lexis 1: Jeff. 90, p. 2. Samuel Howell ran away with his younger brother. Wade Netherland placed a notice in the *Virginia Gazette* (Aug. 8, 1770) of Howell's escape. After describing Howell as a "sensible fellow and good sawyer," he mentioned that "Samuel lately brought a suit in the General Court for his freedom, which was determined against him."

27. See also Annette Gordon-Reed, "Logic and Experience: Slavery, Race and Thomas Jefferson's Life in the Law," in *Slavery and the American South: Essays and Commentaries*, ed. Winthrop Jordan (Jackson, Miss., 2003), discussing *Howell v. Netherland*.

28. Jefferson, *Autobiography*, 9; *MB*, 1:285.

29. Gordon S. Wood, *The American Revolution: A History* (New York, 2003), 3–62.

30. *The Works of Samuel Johnson*, 16 vols. (Troy, N.Y., 1913), 14:93–144.

31. Sidney Kaplan and Emma Nogrady Kaplan, *The Black Presence in the Era of the American Revolution*, rev. ed. (Amherst, Mass., 1989). See also Sylvia R. Frey, *Water from the Rock: Black Resistance in a Revolutionary Age* (Princeton, 1991); Ira Berlin and Ronald Hoffman, eds., *Slavery and Freedom in the Age of the American Revolution* (Charlottesville, 1983).

32. Parent, *Foul Means*, 147.

33. Benjamin Quarles, *The Negro in the American Revolution* (1961; reprint, Chapel Hill, 1996), vii; "Two Dawns of Freedom," in R. Jackson Wilson et al., *The Pursuit of Liberty: A History of the American People*, vol. 1, *To 1877* (New York, 1984), 121–40.

34. Malone, *Jefferson*, 1:169.

35. See, generally, Allan Kulikoff, *Tobacco and Slaves: The Development of Southern Cultures in the Chesapeake, 1680–1800* (Chapel Hill, 1986), 300–312.

36. *Farm Book*, 18; *MB*, 1:341.

37. *De Ende v. Wilkinson's Administrator*, 1857 VA. Lex. 55, 2 Patton & H. 663.; *Synder v. Grandstaff* 96 VA. 473 (1898).

38. *How Slaves May Be Emancipated*, Laws of Virginia, 1723, chap. 4.

39. *MB*, 329 n. 15; *Farm Book*, 9, 18, 15.

5: The First Monticello

1. This is a nod to Andrew Burstein, *The Inner Jefferson: Portrait of a Grieving Optimist* (Charlottesville, 1996). The first chapter of the book is entitled "The Well Ordered Dreamworld," referring to Monticello. Rhys Isaac, "The First Monticello," in *Jeffersonian Legacies*, ed. Peter S. Onuf (Charlottesville, 1993). The title of this chapter and the concept of there being two physical and social "Monticellos" are taken from Isaac's essay. A chapter below, entitled "The Second Monticello," will complete the set.

2. *MB*, 30. See also n. 48.

3. Rhys Isaac, "Monticello Old and New," in *Sally Hemings and Thomas Jefferson: History, Memory, and Civic Culture*, ed. Jan Ellen Lewis and Peter S. Onuf (Charlottesville, 1999), 116–17.

4. *Malone and Jefferson: A Conversation with Anne Freudenberg* (Charlottesville, 1981).

5. Jack McLaughlin, *Jefferson and Monticello: The Biography of a Builder* (New York, 1988), 154–55.

6. Ibid., 156–57.

7. *MB*, 212 n. 20; McLaughlin, *Jefferson and Monticello*, 153, 161.

8. *Farm Book*, 3. Betty Brown was listed as one of Jefferson's "proper slaves" as of Jan. 1774, distinguishing them from the enslaved people who were to come into his possession as a result of the distribution of Wayles slaves upon his death. This indicates that John Wayles had given Brown to Martha before his death, most likely upon her wedding. See also Stanton, *Free Some Day*, 124.

9. See, e.g., *MB*, 263, 285, 297.

10. Ira Berlin, *Generations of Captivity: A History of African-American Slaves* (Cambridge, Mass., 2003), 113–19.

11. Stanton, *Free Some Day*, 105.

12. See Kathleen M. Brown, *Good Wives, Nasty Wenches, and Anxious Patriarchs: Gender, Race, and Power in Colonial Virginia* (Chapel Hill, 1996), chap. 4, discussing the early construction of slaveholder attitudes about women of African descent; Stephanie M. H. Camp, *Closer to Freedom: Enslaved Women and Everyday Resistance in the Plantation South* (Chapel Hill, 2004), 64.

13. "Memorandums on a tour from Paris to Amsterdam, Strasburg and back to Paris," March 3–April 22, 1788, *Papers*, 13:27–28.

14. TJ to William Drayton, July 30, 1787, *Papers*, 11:647–48.

15. G. Ugo Nwokeji, "African Conceptions of Gender and the Slave Traffic," *WMQ*, 3d ser., 58 (2001): 47–68.

16. See, e.g., TJ to Martha Jefferson Randolph, Dec. 13, 1792, *Papers*, 24:740–41; Stanton, *Free Some Day*, 106.

17. "Critta Hemings," Monticello Research Department.

18. Gordon-Reed, *TJ and SH*, 254; Brodie, *Thomas Jefferson*, 288. While denying that his grandfather had fathered children by Sally Hemings, and asserting that Peter Carr had fathered *all* her children (a claim destroyed by DNA testing of Hemings and Carr descendants in 1998), Thomas Jefferson Randolph named his uncle Samuel Carr as the father of "Betsy" Hemings's children, meaning Betty Brown, who in addition to her older children had three relatively late in life children, Edwin, Robert, and Maria.

19. Stanton, *Free Some Day*, 106–7.

20. Ibid., 119.

21. *MB*, 371, "Recd. From the Forest 4 Doz. 10 bott. Of Jamaica rum (Note I shall keep a tally of these as we use them by making a mark in the margin in order to try the fidelity of Martin."

22. Stanton, *Free Some Day*, 35–51; Monticello Research Department; Campbell, "Life of Isaac Jefferson," 566–67. On the question of family names, it has become apparent that many of the enslaved families at Monticello had last names that Jefferson and his family either did not know, simply never used, or were not in the habit of using—Gillette, Granger, Hern, and Evans, for example. Jefferson was not alone in this. As Herbert G. Gutman showed, throughout slavery slave owners were very often totally unaware (or, again, acted as if they were) that their slaves had surnames. See *The Black Family*

in Slavery and Freedom, 1750–1925 (New York, 1976), chap. 6, "Somebody Knew My Name." Laws' failure to recognize slaves surnames no more means that they did not have them than that the law's treatment of them as real estate actually turned enslaved people into land. Slaves kept these names alive in their own families and consciousness and handed them down. Why would it have been otherwise, given the nature of their surrounding society? One could understand why a peasant during feudal times might be content to call himself "John of Surrey," when last names were not the convention in the surrounding community. It would make no sense in the context of the world that Jefferson's slaves lived in, particularly since some slaves were called by their last names—the Hemingses and the Hubbards, for example. By the late eighteenth century and early nineteenth, first and last names were a matter of course throughout the society in which blacks lived and moved. Black families, as had white families, picked their own last names to try to fix the boundaries of their families as best they could.

23. TJ, *Notes on the State of Virginia*, in Merrill D. Peterson, *Thomas Jefferson: Writings* (New York, 1984), 267.

24. Stanton, *Free Some Day*, 34–40; TJ to Nicholas Lewis, July 11, 1788, *Papers*, 13:343.

25. Monticello Research Department records on the hiring of Critta and Thenia Hemings.

26. Stanton, *Free Some Day*, 104.

27. Thomas Jefferson Randolph, draft letter, Dec. 25, 1873, VI:U8937.

28. See, e.g., *MB*, 419, entry for June 7, 1776, "Pd for shoes for Bob 8/."; 420, entry for June 25, 1776, "pd. For 2pr. Stockings for Bob 15/."; 423, entry for Aug. 19, 1776, "Gave Bob 3d."

29. *Farm Book*, 24; Gordon-Reed, *TJ and SH*, 245; *Papers*, 9:624n.

30. Stanton, *Free Some Day*, 115.

31. Woods, *Albermarle County in Virginia*, 29.

32. Brodie, *Thomas Jefferson*, 84.

33. Stanton, *Free Some Day*, 115.

34. Ibid., appendix (Hemings family tree); Monticello Research Department, on Betsy Hemings and her son Fossett Hemings. The oral history of some lines of Mary Hemings's descendants indicates that Joseph Fossett was the son of Thomas Jefferson. Jefferson freed Fossett in his will. In the Fossett descendants' view, the name Fossett was just given to Joseph by Jefferson or someone who assumed that William Fossett was his father. While anything, within the laws of physics, is possible, the prime difficulty with this idea is that Joseph Fossett, and his contemporary relatives of the time, acted as if the name Fossett had real meaning in their lives. Joseph Fossett wore his last name when he did not have to. He and other enslaved people knew that last names signified paternity. Fossett named one of his sons William. Again Joseph's nephew Joseph Hemmings named his son Fossett. In short, the Hemingses of the generation still in slavery were very serious about naming their children, because it was the only way to achieve some semblance of formality in their family relations. It seems unlikely that they would have accepted a name of a true outsider foisted upon them by mere whim.

If Mary Hemings was, in fact, Jefferson's mistress before Sally Hemings—indeed, before Martha Jefferson's death—his relations with her must have been of a character completely different from that of his relations with Sally Hemings. He repeatedly did the thing that most effectively encapsulated the heinous nature of slavery, the thing that every mother dreaded: he separated Mary Hemings from four of her six children, giving three of them away as wedding presents. The one child of hers that he did free, Joseph Fossett, he freed not as soon as he left childhood, as he did with his children with Sally Hemings, but when he was a forty-six-year-old man. Jefferson made no provision for Fossett's children, and the supremely determined father then spent years buying back his children—children who would have been Jefferson's grandchildren.

35. Sarah N. Randolph, *The Domestic Life of Thomas Jefferson*, ed. Dumas Malone (New York, 1958), 44.

36. Martha Jefferson to Eleanor Conway Madison, Aug. 8, 1780, *Papers*, 3:532.

37. TJ, *Autobiography*, in *Writings*, 3; Brodie, *Thomas Jefferson*, 44; Mclaughlin, *Jefferson and Monticello*, 46–47.

38. Jefferson Family Bible; Campbell, "Life of Isaac Jefferson," 567; Stanton, *Free Some Day*, 33–34.

39. Martha Wayles Skelton, 1772–1782, Part B Household Accounts, Thomas Jefferson Papers Series 7, Miscellaneous Bound Volumes, LOC. March 5, 1777, "made 100 lbs. of soft soap"; March 20, 1777, "made . . . hard soap not weighed"; June 23, 1773, "brewed a cask of beer"; Dec. 16, 1772, "brewed a cask of beer—20 gallon cask."

40. Campbell, "Life of Isaac Jefferson," 566.

6: In the Home of a Revolutionary

1. *Papers*, 1:121–35.

2. Brodie, *Thomas Jefferson*, 99–103; Malone, *Jefferson*, 1:181–82.

3. *MB*, 419–20.

4. TJ, *Autobiography*, in *Writings*, 45–46; Richard Henry Lee to TJ, Sept. 27, 1776, *Papers*, 1:522; TJ to John Hancock, Oct. 11, 1776, ibid., 1:524; Richard Henry Lee to TJ, Nov. 3, 1776, ibid., 1:589.

5. TJ to William Phillips, June 25, 1779, *Papers*, 3:15; TJ to James Monroe, May 20, 1782, ibid., 6:184.

6. TJ to John Page, June 1779, *Papers*, 2:279.

7. Campbell, "Life of Isaac Jefferson," 568.

8. Ibid., 569–70.

9. Dunmore's proclamation of Nov. 14, 1775, Purdie & Dixon's *Virginia Gazette*, Nov. 25, 1775; Woody Holton, *Forced Founders: Indians, Debtors, Slaves, & the Making of the American Revolution in Virginia* (Chapel Hill, 1999), 155–56.

10. *Farm Book*, 29. Lucia Stanton has noted the change in TJ's characterization of the actions of the enslaved men and women who left his plantation to join the British forces. His first notations in the Farm Book describe them as having "fled to the enemy" or "joined enemy." Later he characterized these slaves as having been "carried off." TJ to William Gordon, July 16, 1788, *Papers*, 13:363–64; Stanton, *Free Some Day*, 53. Cassandra Pybus has challenged Jefferson's estimates of the number of slaves who were "taken from Virginians" by the British forces. After noting that historians have relied on Jefferson's statement that at least "30,000" slaves were taken from Virginia alone, Pybus reminds

us that Jefferson made the comment while he was in Paris away from the scene and that his letter gives no hint of how he had arrived at that number. Without entering the larger debate about exactly how many African Americans joined the British, we should note that Pybus argues that Jefferson, as time wore on, was careless in his statements about how many slaves *he* actually lost to the British. Only twenty-three left, but by 1786 he said that "thirty" had been gone, including in that number four slaves who had actually been recovered, one who died soon after his return, two who were sold, and one who was given away. The other three were slaves who had never been accounted for and were not included in his 1783 listing of losses. Catherine Pybus, "Jefferson's Faulty Math: The Question of Slave Defections in the American Revolution," *WMQ*, 3d ser., 62 (2005): 243–64.

11. Campbell, "Life of Isaac Jefferson," 569; Malone, *Jefferson*, 1:339.

12. Malone, *Jefferson*, 1:336–41.

13. Campbell, "Life of Isaac Jefferson," 570–71.

14. *MB*, 507. According to the oral history of some descendants of Wormley Hughes, Jefferson was his father. As with the Fossett family oral history, the first question that comes to mind when considering this is why Wormley had the last name Hughes, instead of Brown, which was the last name of his mother, Betty. Betty Brown had several children with the last name Colbert. One of those children she named after herself—Brown Colbert. Pulling names out of a hat did not seem to be the family's style. Wormley was, in fact, extremely close to Jefferson and was informally freed, along with Sally Hemings, at Jefferson's instruction.

While Joseph Fossett's family was dispersed after the 1827 auction at Monticello, Jefferson's grandson Jeff, just days after Hughes's wife and four youngest children were sold at the event, purchased all of them and brought them to live together at his Edgehill plantation. Was this family-based remorse? As will be discussed later, it is more likely that Hughes's wife, Ursula, was the impetus for this action. Further reason to doubt that Hughes was Jefferson's son is that the Randolph family acquiesced in Henry Randall's apparently extensive interviews with him as he prepared his biography of Jefferson. It is near inconceivable, given their extreme secrecy and sensitivity about Jefferson's children with Sally Hemings, that they would have directed (allowed) Hughes to talk to a man who was writing a book about their family if Hughes were, in fact, Jefferson's son.

The oral tradition of Mary Hemings's family holds that Jefferson had children by three enslaved women, including their ancestor, Mary, and Sally Hemings. These individuals did not name the third woman, but given the Hughes tradition and Wormley's relationship with Jefferson, the most likely third woman they were talking about was Betty Brown. In the 1940s Pearl Graham spoke with these Hemings descendants and Charlottesville residents (not Hemings family members) who knew descendants of others enslaved at Monticello. They all painted a picture of Jefferson as promiscuous with "colored women." He had a habit, they said, of accosting one of his mistresses, a laundress, on her way back from doing her work. See Lucia Stanton "Through the Other End of the Telescope: Jefferson in the Eyes of his Slaves," *WMQ*, 3d ser., 57 (2000): 145.

This picture of the sexually predatory Jefferson contrasts sharply with Madison Hemings's portrayal of him. He stated that he and his sibling were the only children Jefferson had with an enslaved woman. If Jefferson had been involved with Mary Hemings or Betty Brown, it would have been some years before he began his relationship with Madison's mother, Sally. Still, it seems unlikely that he would not have known that his uncles, whom he saw every day, were actually his brothers.

In sum, there is simply not enough information at present to support the idea that Joseph Fossett and Wormley Hughes were Jefferson's sons. Given that so many slave owners had children with enslaved women, and the "better" among this group freed their children, it is natural (and right) to consider all possibilities when a slave owner frees, formally or informally, a much younger person. But not all the slaves Jefferson freed, or the ones he was very fond of, were his children. We should avoid treating interracial sex as something akin to an addiction or chronic disease—if he had sex and children with one enslaved African American woman, he must have had sex and children with others. The standard for coming to this conclusion must remain the same for each individual case—not primarily for Jefferson's sake, but for the sake of the enslaved people who had lives and identities that must be treated with as much care and respect as the lives of those who enslaved them. For a discussion of Randall's relationship with Jefferson's grandchildren, see Lisa Francavilla, " 'Holding in Trust for the Use of Others': Jefferson's Grandchildren and the Creation of the Jefferson Image," a paper presented at the 2006 annual meeting of the Society for Historians of the Early American Republic, Worcester, Mass.

15. See, e.g., *MB*, 507, for March 30 reference to Betty Brown; 508, for April 5 reference to James Hemings.

16. Malone, *Jefferson*, 1:354–60; Emory Evans, "Executive Leadership I Virginia," in *Sovereign States in an Age of Uncertainty*, ed. Ronald Hoffman and Peter J. Albert (Charlottesville, 1981).

17. *MB*, entry for April 15, 1781, "Our daughter Lucy Elizabeth died about 10. o'clock A.M. this day."

18. Henry S. Randall, *The Life of Thomas Jefferson*, 3 vols. (1858; reprint, New York, 1972), 1:338–39.

19. Stanton, *Free Some Day*, 170 n. 78.

20. TJ to William Gordon, July 16, 1788, *Papers*, 8:364.

21. Ibid.

22. Pybus, "Jefferson's Faulty Math," 243–64.

23. George Wythe to TJ, Dec. 31, 1781, *Papers*, 6:144. Wythe offered to help TJ recover "other servants belonging to [TJ]," if he would send him "a description" of them.

24. *MB*, 519, "Our daughter Lucy Elizabeth (second of that name) born at one o'clock A.M."

25. TJ to James Monroe, May 20, 1782, *Papers*, 6:186.

26. Randall, *Life*, 1:382.

27. Malone, *Jefferson*, 1:396.

28. McLaughlin, *Jefferson and Monticello*, 188.

29. See photograph in first insert. Gordon-Reed, *TJ and SH*, 128–29.

30. Lucia Stanton and Dianne Swann Wright, "Bonds of Memory: Identity and the Hemings Family," in *Sally Hemings and Thomas Jefferson: History, Memory, and Civic Culture*, ed. Jan Ellen Lewis and Peter S. Onuf (Charlottesville, 1999), 173.

31. Hamilton W. Pierson, *Jefferson at Monticello: The Private Life of Thomas Jefferson*, from *Entirely New Materials, with Numerous Facsimiles* (1862), 106–7.

32. Ibid.

33. Gordon-Reed, *TJ and SH*, 252.

34. Brodie, *Thomas Jefferson*, 168.

35. See "The Room in which Martha Jefferson died," wiki.Monticello.org, for a discussion of the problems with Martha Randolph's recollections of what happened when Jefferson was led from the room when his wife died. In Martha's account, her aunt Martha Carr led Jefferson with "great difficulty . . . into his library." The library in the first Monticello was upstairs. The author of the article posits that it seems unlikely that Martha Carr led "a full-grown man on the verge of collapse up an extremely narrow stairwell." Martha recalled that her father had been working in a nearby room as her mother lay bedridden for five months. It seems more likely that Martha Jefferson was in what is now Jefferson's bedroom downstairs, and the room where he worked while she was ill was one over from the room that became Jefferson's library in the second Monticello. Martha Randolph's memory blended the layout of the first Monticello with that of the second.

36. Randall, *Life*, 1:382.

37. Andrew Burstein, *Jefferson's Secrets: Death and Desire at Monticello* (New York, 2005), 160–72.

38. Ronald Hoffman, in collaboration with Sally D. Mason, *Princes of Ireland, Planters of Maryland: A Carroll Family Saga, 1500–1872* (Chapel Hill, 2000), 371–72, discussing the toll that six pregnancies during ten years of marriage took on Mary Carroll, the wife of the Maryland senator and planter Charles Carroll, the only Roman Catholic to sign the Declaration of Independence.

39. TJ, *Autobiography*, in *Writings* (New York, 1984), 46.

7: "A Particular Purpose"

1. TJ to Elizabeth Blair Thompson, Jan. 19, 1787, *Papers*, 11:56–58.

2. Jefferson himself characterized his time in Paris as an escape in an indirect way that muted the pain of his wife's loss. "An unfortunate change in my domestic situation by the loss of a tender connection who joined me in esteeming you, occasioned me to wish a change of scene and to accept an appointment which brought me to this place and will keep me here some time." TJ to Geismar, March 3, 1785, *Papers*, 8:10. Jefferson confided to his sister-in-law, "This miserable kind of existence is really too burthensome to be borne, and were it not for the infidelity of deserting the sacred charge left me, I could not wish it's [*sic*] continuance a moment. For what could it be wished? All my plans of comfort and happiness reversed by a single event and nothing answering in prospect before me but a gloom unbrightened with one chearful expectation." Only the prospect of caring for his daughters offered any respite from his torment. TJ to Elizabeth Eppes, October 3?, 1782, *Papers*, 6:198.

3. Thomas Jefferson, *Autobiography*, in *Writings* (New York, 1984), 46. At the time of the second appointment, Jefferson was facing an inquiry about his conduct as governor, recuperating from a nasty fall from his horse, and concerned about his wife's always precarious health. He had sequestered himself (Edmund Randolph's critical characterization) at his Bedford estate, vowing never to return to public life. TJ to Edmund Randolph, Sept. 16, 1781, *Papers*, 6:117; Edmund Randolph to TJ, Oct. 9, 1781, ibid., 128.

4. Jefferson's memorandum books and his letters offer the surest way to track his movements and those of members of the Hemings family who traveled with him. *MB*, 522–54,

details his travels during the two-year period after his wife's death as he awaited word that he was to proceed to France. See also Stanton, *Free Some Day*, 107–8.

5. James A. Bear Jr., *The Hemings Family of Monticello* (Ivy, Va., 1980), 7.

6. TJ to Daniel Hylton, July 1, 1792, *Papers*, 24:145; TJ to Martha Randolph, Aug. 8, 1790, ibid., 17:327.

7. *MB*, 536 n. 82.

8. *MB*, 542, entries for Feb. 1, 3, 10, and 13.

9. TJ to William Short, May 7, 1784, *Papers*, 7:229.

10. William Short to TJ, May 14, 1784, *Papers*, 7:253, 255.

11. Ibid., 256.

12. Ibid., 256–57.

13. Thomas D. Morris, *Southern Slavery and the Law, 1619–1860* (Chapel Hill, 1996), 338–40. Morris notes that Virginia was the first to pass a statute to require slaves to carry passes. "A magistrate could order twenty lashes inflicted on a slave who was off 'his masters ground without a certificate from his master, mistress, or overseer.'" There were no penalties to the master for violating, but the law sent the message that all white members of society had a duty to help control the blacks within their midst. Virginia's large black population gave white Virginians (and South Carolinians) a special interest in keeping tabs on black people.

14. Ibid., 339.

15. George Green Shackelford, *Jefferson's Adoptive Son: The Life of William Short, 1759–1848* (Lexington, Ky., 1993), 3; Malone, *Jefferson*, 1:433.

16. William Short to TJ, May 14 [15], 1784, *Papers*, 7:256.

17. TJ to David Humphreys, June 21, 1784, *Papers*, 7:311.

18. See *MB*, 553, entry for June 30, 1784; TJ to Nicholas Lewis, July 1, 1784, *Papers*, 7:356.

19. *MB*, 554 n. 61, entry for July 5, 1784: "Sailed from Boston at 4. o'clock A.M. in the Ceres Capt. St. Barbe."

20. *MB*, 555, Jefferson's diary of the voyage.

21. *MB*, 556, entries for July 27, 28, 1784 (see also n. 63); TJ to James Monroe, Nov. 11, 1784, *Papers*, 7:508 ("I therefore went ashore at Portsmouth where I was detained three or four days by a fever which had seized my daughter two days before we landed"); Martha Jefferson to Eliza House Trist, [after Aug. 24, 1785], ibid., 8:436–37.

22. *MB*, 556, entry for Aug. 1, 1784.

23. TJ to James Monroe, Nov. 11, 1784, *Papers*, 7:508.

24. *MB*, 557, entry for Aug. 3, 1784.

25. Martha Jefferson to Eliza Trist, [after Aug. 24, 1785], *Papers*, 8:437; *MB*, 557, entry for Aug. 6, 1784.

26. Malone, *Jefferson*, 2:5, 8; Edward Dumbauld, "Where Did Jefferson Live in Paris," *WMQ*, 2d ser., 23 (1943): 64–68.

27. *MB*, 559, entry for Aug. 20, 1784; 630 n. 33, entry for June 26, 1784; 567 n. 13.

28. Malone, *Jefferson*, 2:6–7; Marie Kimball, *Jefferson: The Scene of Europe, 1784 to 1789* (New York, 1950). Humphrey's fraternal relations with TJ broke down under the weight of Humphrey's very conservative Federalist political views that made him anathema to the by then President Jefferson, who recalled him from a diplomatic post overseas in 1801.

29. *MB*. 571 n. 26. See also Malone, *Jefferson*, 2:8, 131.

30. *MB*, 554 n. 60. See also *Papers*, 8:269–73.

31. *MB*, 567 n. 11.

32. TJ to James Monroe, March 18, 1785, *Papers*, 8:43.

33. *MB*, 569, entry for Dec. 1, 1784.

34. James Currie to TJ, Nov. 20, 1784, *Papers*, 7:539; Elizabeth Wayles Eppes to TJ, Oct. 13, 1784, ibid., 441; Francis Eppes to TJ, Oct. 14, 1784, ibid., 441–42. The SJL indicates that Jefferson learned of his daughter's death when the Currie letter arrived in Jan., brought to him by Lafayette. The Eppes letters did not reach him until May. See also (p. 539) Julian Boyd's highlights on Currie's horrifically insensitive letter, in which he comments on the weather, on a history of ballooning that TJ wrote to him about, and on politics and then, at the end, mentions that TJ's daughter died of whooping cough; TJ to Francis Eppes, Jan. 13, 1785, ibid., 601–2. The SJL refers to this letter, which has not been found, but the entry describing what was in the letter indicates that he told his brother-in-law of his "wishes to have Polly brought were not [his] return not very distant." See also Malone, *Jefferson*, 2:12–13.

35. TJ to Francis Eppes, May 11, 1785, *Papers*, 8:141. TJ writes to his in-laws, "I must have Polly," and inquires whether there is "any woman in Virg. [who] could be hired to come." Elizabeth Eppes wrote to TJ on July 30, 1786, indicating that she was resigned to the fact that Polly should be sent to him. *Papers*, 15:629. TJ to Elizabeth Eppes, Dec. 14, 1786, ibid., 594. He wrote that same day to Francis Eppes, telling him to "address her [Polly] to Mrs. Adams who will receive her and advise me of her arrival." Ibid.

36. See, e.g., Francis Eppes to TJ, Sept. 14, 1785, *Papers*, 15:623–24; Elizabeth Eppes to TJ, Sept. 22, 1785, ibid., 624. See below, chap. 9, for a discussion of Polly's trip with Sally Hemings.

37. *MB*, 570 n. 22; 558, n. 73.

38. *MB*, 609, entry for Feb. 2, 1786.

39. TJ to Antonio Giannini, Feb. 5, 1786, *Papers*, 9:254.

40. Malone, *Jefferson*, 2:6. While in Paris, Jefferson never tried his hand at writing personal letters in French. His friends wrote to him in the language, and he wrote back in English. See, e.g., Madame de Tessé to TJ, Jan. 21, 1787, *Papers*, 11:60-61; Madame de Tott to TJ, early Feb. 1787, ibid., 117; TJ to Madame de Tessé, Feb. 28, 1787, ibid., 187; TJ to Madame de Tott, Feb. 28, 1787, ibid., 187–88. It is possible that his official correspondence was drafted by William Short. He did write to his servant Adrien Petit in French, but Petit was not well educated, and Jefferson may have worried less about impressing (or failing to impress) him.

41. Antonio Giannini to TJ, June 9, 1786, *Papers*, 9:624.

42. Malone, *Jefferson*, 1:430.

43. *The Autobiography of Colonel John Trumbull, Patriot-Artist, 1756–1843, Containing a Supplement to the Works of John Trumbull*, ed. Theodore Sizer (New Haven, 1953), 35.

44. Philip Mazzei to TJ, April 17, 1787, *Papers*, 11:297–98.

45. Ibid.

46. Ibid.

47. TJ to Philip Mazzei, May, 6, 1787, *Papers*, 11:354.

48. Bear, *Hemings Family*, 10.

8: James Hemings: The Provincial Abroad

1. Henry Adams, *History of the United States of America during the Administration of Thomas Jefferson*, 2 vols. (New York, 1986), 1:101.

2. *Letters of Mrs. Adams, the Wife of John Adams*, ed. Charles Francis Adams, 2 vols. (Boston, 1848), 1:193; Martha Jefferson to Eliza House Trist, Aug. 24, 1785, *Papers*, 7:437.

3. See David Garrioch, *The Making of Revolutionary Paris* (Berkeley, Calif., 2002), 67, discussing the "corporate" nature of French society. "The corporate system was central to the Parisian labor market. Anywhere up to two-thirds of the adult male population and a smaller proportion of the adult female population were grouped into over 120 officially recognized trade corporations, while another 16 or 17 trades had a guild structure but no legal standing." In other words, working people were used to banding together to assert their rights.

4. Ibid., 246–47, on the spread of elite culture to the masses and on Madame Moreau, a seamstress who ran a literary salon.

5. Margaret C. Jacobs, *Living the Enlightenment: Freemasonry and Politics in Eighteenth-Century Europe* (Oxford, 1991).

6. See, e.g., *MB*, 369, 572, 573, 593, 605, 569, 577, 608, 627.

7. Garrioch, *Making of Revolutionary Paris*, 244.

8. Ibid.

9. Sue Peabody, *"There Are No Slaves in France": The Political Culture of Race and Slavery in the Ancien Régime* (New York, 1996), uses the phrase "Freedom Principle" to describe the announced French position on the status of slaves in France. In her new, more comparative work, she refers to the principle as "Free Soil."

10. Ibid., chap. 1.

11. For a discussion of the basic function of the parlements of France, see William Doyle, *Origins of the French Revolution* (Oxford, 1980), 68–70. See also Georges Lefebvre, *The Coming of the French Revolution* (Princeton, 1947), 17. See, generally, Peabody, *"There Are No Slaves"*; Pierre H. Boulle, "Racial Purity or Legal Clarity?: The Status of Black Residents in Eighteenth-Century France," *Journal of the Historical Society* 6 (2006): 19–46.

12. See Peabody, *"There Are No Slaves,"* 73 (the "deluge"). Peabody notes that for the rest of his life Poncet de la Grave continued to "wage his personal war against licentiousness," which had always been focused on efforts to stamp out interracial relations and prostitution (p. 139). "Crank" is a pejorative term, but it seems apt for one who, because he equated a man and a woman who wanted to marry and raise a family with prostitution, was largely responsible for the 1778 law that banned interracial marriage. Of course, Poncet de la Grave was not alone in his concern about having blacks in France. See Boulle, "Racial Purity," 23, citing a letter from the minister of the marine written in 1763, expressing the need to curb the number of blacks in France because their "communication with the whites" was resulting in "mixed blood, which increases daily."

13. Peabody, *"There Are No Slaves,"* 4 (on the populations of England and France).

14. Ibid., 111–20; Boulle, "Racial Purity," 25–27.

15. *Déclaration pour la police des noirs*, Aug. 9, 1777, reprinted in Pierre Boulle, *Race et esclavage dans la France de l'Ancien Régime* (Paris, 2007), 255–58.

16. See C. L. R. James, *Black Jacobins: Toussaint L'Overture and the San Domingo Revolution*

(New York, 1963), 47–48; Laurent Dubois, *A Colony of Citizens: Revolution and Slave Emancipation in the French Caribbean, 1787–1804* (Chapel Hill, 2004), 46. "The plantation economy, and the traffic in humans that sustained it, produced fortunes in France." Boulle, "Racial Purity," 27.

17. *Déclaration pour la police des noirs.* Article 1 provided, "Faisons défenses expresses à tous nos sujets, de quelque qualité et condition qu'ils soient, même à tous Étrangers, d'amener dans notre Royaume, après la publication et enregistrement de notre présente Déclaration, aucun noir, mulâtre, ou autres gens de couleur, de l'un ou de l'autre sexe, & de les y retenir à leur service; le tout à peine de trois mille livres d'amende, même de plus grande s'ily echoit." Article 2 made clear that the declaration was meant to cover even free blacks: "Défendons pareillement, sous les même peines, à tous Noirs, Mulâtres ou autres gens de couleur de l'un & de l'autre sexe, qui ne seroient point en service, d'entrer à l'avenir dans notre royaume, sous quelque cause & prétexte que ce soit." Article 4 provided for the creation of a "dépôt" to house blacks pending their return to the country.

18. Article 13: "Les dispositions de notre présénte Déclaration seront exécutées nonobstant tous Édits, Déclarations, Réglements, ou autres à ce contraires, auxquels nous avons dérogé et dérogeons expressément." Had there been any express provision in law for immunity for diplomats, the clear language of this article would have abrogated it. They were quite serious about this matter and even discussed how to handle matters if "princes of the blood" were found to have violated the rules. See Peabody, "*There Are No Slaves,*" 125. If they were willing to confront members of the royal family, it is doubtful that they would have hesitated to confront Jefferson about either of the Hemingses.

19. Article 9 provided for the registration of blacks who came into the country. "Ceux de Nos Sujets, ainsi que les Étrangers, qui auront des Noirs à leur service, lors de la publication & enregistrement de notre présente Déclaration seront tenus dans un mois, . . . de se présenter par-devant les Officiers de l'Amirauté dans le ressort de laquelle ils sont domiciliés, & s'il n'y en a pas, par-devant le Juge Royal dudit lieu, à l'effet d'y déclarer les noms & qualités des Noirs, Mûlatres, ou autres gens de couleur . . . qui demeurent chez eux le temps de leur débarquement, & la colonie de laquelle ils ont été exportés." Article 1 established the fine for noncompliance with the law "le tout à peine de 3,000 liv. d'amende, même de plus grand peine s'il y échoit." At the time of its publication, the declaration gave every French subject and foreigner who had a black slave or servant one month to register the person. If one month passed without registration, the master "could only keep the said blacks in their service with the consent of the latter." The provision caused much confusion and led to the publication of clarifying *arrêts*, which were not substantially more helpful. There is no record of cases involving foreigners and their slaves, but it is probable that if an American slaveholder brought a black slave to France, a court inclined to deport blacks who arrived after 1777 would have been satisfied to have them sent back to the United States. The important thing was to get them out of France.

20. Pierre Boulle, *Race et esclavage*, 127. "Ainsi, aucune déclaration n'est faite par Thomas Jefferson, le ministre plenipotentiaire des Etats-Unis de 1784 à 1789, au sujet de ses deux serviteurs de couleur, James et Sara Hemings, bien que le ministre Sartine, quelques années plus tôt ait clairement spécifié que la loi s'appliquait aussi aux ambassadeurs." (Jefferson the minister plenipotentiary of the United States, 1784–1789, did not declare his servants of color, James and Sarah Hemings, even though Minister Sartine, some

years before, had clearly specified that the law applied to ambassadors.) Sue Peabody, who has also done extensive work with the registers of blacks, confirmed to me that Jefferson did not register either Hemings sibling.

21. See Peabody, *"There Are No Slaves,"* chap. 8, "Erosion of the *Police des Noirs,"* 121–36.

22. See Doyle, *Origins*; William Doyle, "The Parlements of France and the Breakdown of the Old Regime, 1771–1788," *French Historical Studies* 6 (1970): 415–58, on the parlements' role in opposition to royal authority. For a highly critical view of the parlement, see Thomas Carlyle's classic, extremely retrograde and dated but entertaining, *The French Revolution: A History* (New York, 2002), 72–76, 88–89.

23. The drafters of the *Police des Noirs* correctly assumed that the Parlement of Paris would not register the act if it was seen to be regulating slaves. So the declaration proscribed conduct "based upon skin color alone, not slave status." Peabody, *"There Are No Slaves,"* 106. See also Boulle, "Racial Purity," 28, on the Parlement of Paris' likely objection to a law that mentioned slavery. Peabody, *"There Are No Slaves,"* 5 and 134–36, on the Parisian Admiralty Court's commitment to the Freedom Principle.

24. Peabody, *"There Are No Slaves,"* 135.

25. Ibid.

26. Ibid.

27. It is probably impossible to come up with a precise figure for the number of blacks in Paris during the Hemings siblings' time there. In *Race et esclavage*, 126, Pierre Boulle used the registrations of Parisian blacks between 1777 and 1790 and counted "765 non-Blancs personnes de couleur à Paris et en banlieue entre les années 1777 et 1790." That figure is probably better seen as a minimum, since there is evidence of widespread noncompliance with the law on registration. Boulle notes the "relative absence de déclarations issues de la haute noblesse." See also his table (p. 128) listing the statuses of male and female *gens de couleur* in Paris.

28. Boulle also analyzed the neighborhoods where blacks lived and found that, for the most part, blacks lived in the richest neighborhoods. Ibid., 137–38 (map of Parisian neighborhoods with the concentration of blacks).

29. Peabody, *"There Are No Slaves,"* 84–85. Boulle, *Race et esclavage*, 138.

30. See Cissie Fairchilds, *Domestic Enemies: Servants and Their Masters in Old Regime France* (Baltimore, 1983), 158–59, on the high value of mixed-race servants and those of African origin and on the reasons for the preference. See also Sarah C. Maza, *Servants and Masters in Eighteenth-Century France: The Uses of Loyalty* (Princeton, 1984), 206–8.

31. Perrault to TJ, Jan. 9, 1789, *Papers*, 14:426.

32. John Jay to William Temple Franklin (unpublished), Nov. 11, 1783; Sarah Van Brugh Livingston to William Temple Franklin (unpublished) (undated). I thank Professor Edmund Morgan for bringing this correspondence to my attention and graciously sending me copies of it. I also thank Elizabeth M. Nuxoll, editor of *The Papers of John Jay*, and Kate M. Ohno, one of the editors of *The Papers of Benjamin Franklin*, for providing me with relevant correspondence and for sharing their insights about this matter.

33. Peabody, *"There Are No Slaves,"* 97–103, on Henrion de Pansey; 103–5, on the motives of other lawyers involved in freedom suits.

34. Ibid., 103. In discussing *Roc v. Poupet*, a freedom suit brought in 1770 in which the lawyer for the slave submitted his expenses to the court, Peabody notes that "evidence

concerning slaves' sources of money to pay lawyers is rare." Ibid., 177 n. 86. More work must be done on this question, but one can speculate that the submission of a bill to the court in 1770 suggests that the legal culture had evolved in a way that suited both law-yers' needs and the preferences of the Admiralty Court. By 1770 the court's position on the freedom suits should have been clear to everyone who held slaves in Paris; a master who resisted the slaves' desire for freedom was going to lose. Fee shifting is seen as a way of affecting the behavior of the litigants—if the law is clear, the party in the wrong has an incentive to settle and not waste court resources fighting the inevitable. If there is no case to be made, the party who wants to sue will think twice before wasting the court's time. The court's action in *Roc v. Poupet* was in perfect keeping with the overall goals of fee shifting. This outcome might be attractive to lawyers who could make rela-tively easy money doing rote petitions with an entirely predictable result. The case sug-gests that Jefferson might have had to pay Hemings's lawyer had the young man filed a freedom suit.

35. See Jacqueline Sabattier, *Figaro et son maître: Maîtres et domestiques à Paris au XVIIe siècle* (Paris, 1984), 24–27. See, generally, Jean-Pierre Gutton, *Domestiques et serviteurs dans la France de l'ancien régime* (Paris, 1981); Olwen Hufton, "Women and the Family Economy in Eighteenth-Century France," *French Historical Studies* 9, no. 1 (Spring 1975): 6; Fairchilds, *Domestic Enemies*, 54–58; Maza, *Servants and Masters*, 164–67. See also, e.g., *MB*, 681 for James Hemings's salary, and 691, for Sally Hemings's salary.

36. See Fairchilds, *Domestic Enemies*, 13–20, on the history of wages and customs about wages.

37. Peabody, "*There Are No Slaves*," 105.

38. Ibid., 119, quoting Antoine de Sartine, one of the architects of the *Police des Noirs*, who linked the posters about and published accounts of successful freedom suits as a reason for the new law.

39. Marcel Dorigny and Bernard Gainot, *La Société des amis des noirs, 1788–1799: Contribution à l'histoire de l'abolition de l'esclavage* (Paris, 1998); TJ to Brissot de Warville, Feb. 11, 1788, *Papers*, 12:577–78.

40. Daniel Resnick, "The Société des Amis des Noirs and the Abolition of Slavery," *French Historical Studies* 7 (1972): 558–69.

41. Martha Jefferson to TJ, May 3, 1787, *Papers*, 11:334.

42. Paul Bentalou, Aug. 9, 1786, *Papers*, 10:205.

43. Ibid.

44. TJ to Paul Bentalou, Aug. 25, 1786, *Papers*, 10:296.

45. See Peabody, "*There Are No Slaves*," 19, 39, 49, 90, 119, 154 n. 71, discussing the various parlements' reactions to royal declarations; Laurent Dubois, *A Colony of Citizens*, 147, on Bordeaux and the slave trade.

46. See, generally, Peabody, "*There Are No Slaves*," and Boulle, *Race et esclavage*.

47. Peabody, "*There Are No Slaves*," 129–30.

48. William Short to TJ, May 14, 1784, *Papers*, 7:254.

49. Winthrop D. Jordan, *White over Black: American Attitudes toward the Negro, 1550–1812* (Chapel Hill, 1968).

50. Peabody, *"There Are No Slaves,"* 3.

51. Boulle, "Racial Purity," 35.

52. Ibid., 38.

53. Shelby T. McCloy, "Negroes and Mulattoes in Eighteenth-Century France," *Journal of Negro History* 30 (July 1945): 279–80.

54. Boulle, "Racial Purity," 39.

55. McCloy, "Negroes and Mulattoes," 280 n. 17. I follow Louverture's spelling of his name.

56. Alain Guédé, *Monsieur de Saint-George: Virtuoso, Swordsman, Revolutionay: A Legendary Life Rediscovered*, trans. Gilda M. Roberts (New York, 2003), 18, 3; Dominique-René de Lerma, "The Chevalier de Saint-Georges," *Black Perspective in Music* 4 (1976): 3–21.

57. Ibid.

58. Alexandre Dumas, *My Memoirs*, trans. E. M. Waller, 3 vols. (New York, 1908), vol. 1, xx; Gilles Henry, *Les Dumas: Le secret de Monte-Cristo* (Paris, 1999), 55.

9: "Isabel or Sally Will Come"

1. TJ to Francis Eppes, Aug. 30, 1785, *Papers*, 15:622 (supplementary letters).

2. See, e.g., TJ to Martha Jefferson Carr, Aug. 20, 1785, *Papers*, 15:620–21, expressing his growing impatience with delays in sending his daughter—"It is upwards of 10. months since I have had a letter from Eppington; this is long for a parent who has still something left there"; Francis Eppes to TJ, Sept. 14, 1785, ibid., 623; Martha Jefferson Carr to TJ, May 5, 1786, ibid., 618–19.

3. Francis Eppes to TJ, Oct. 23, 1786, *Papers*, 10:483; Martha Jefferson Carr to TJ, Jan. 2, 1787, ibid., 15:633; Elizabeth Wayles Eppes to TJ, March 31, 1787, and Mary Jefferson to TJ, ca. March 31, 1787, ibid., 11:260—"I should be very happy to see you, but I can not go to France and hope that you and sister Patsy are well"; Stanton, *Free Some Day*, 59, 108.

4. Francis Eppes to TJ, April 14, 1787, *Papers*, 15:636.

5. Stanton, *Free Some Day*, 195 (family tree of the Hern family).

6. Gordon-Reed, *TJ and SH*, 240; *Farm Book*, 13.

7. Elizabeth Wayles Eppes to TJ, May 7, 1787, *Papers*, 15:356; Abigail Adams to TJ, June 26, 1787, ibid., 11:501 (Jefferson's SJL records this letter as received on June 30, 1787); Abigail Adams to TJ, June 26, 1787, ibid.; Abigail Adams to TJ, June 27, 1787, ibid., 502 (Jefferson's SJL records these letters from Adams as received on June 30 and July 6, respectively).

8. *Farm Book*, 13, 18.

9. Pierson, *Jefferson at Monticello*, 107–8.

10. Elizabeth Eppes to TJ, May 7, 1787, *Papers*, 15:637; Stanton, *Free Some Day*, 108.

11. TJ to Elizabeth Eppes, July 28, 1787, *Papers*, 11:634–35.

12. Abigail Adams to TJ, June 26, 1787, *Papers*, 11:502.

13. Abigail Adams to TJ, June 27, 1787, *Papers*, 11:503.

14. Abigail Adams to TJ, July 6, 1787, *Papers*, 11:551.

15. See discussion of SH's probable birthdate, in chap. 14, below.

16. Abigail Adams to Mrs. Shaw, March 4, 1786, *Letters of Mrs. Adams, the Wife of John Adams*, ed. C. F. Adams, 2 vols. (Boston, 1840), 2:125.

17. John Quincy Adams, "Misconceptions of Shakespeare, upon the Stage," reprinted in James Henry Hackett, *Notes and Comments upon Certain Plays and Actors of Shakespeare* (New York, 1863), 224–26.

18. *Fanny Kemble's Journals*, ed. Catherine Clinton (Cambridge, Mass., 2000) 127.

19. Ibid.

20. Joseph Tate, *Digest of the Laws of Virginia* (Richmond, Va., 1823), sec. 11 S. 3, p. 127. The age was raised to twelve, Patton and Robinson, *Code of Virginia*, tit. 54, chap. 191, sec. 15, 715, quoted in Diane Miller Sommerville, *Rape and Race in the Nineteenth-Century South* (Chapel Hill, 2003), 44, 276–77 n. 8.

21. Francis Eppes to TJ, April 14, 1787, *Papers*, 15:636.

22. Paul Bentalou to TJ, Aug. 9, 1786, *Papers*, 10:205.

23. Andrew Ramsey to TJ, July 6, 1787, *Papers*, 11:556.

24. Abigail Adams to TJ, July 6, 1787, *Papers*, 11:551.

25. Ibid.

26. Brodie, *Thomas Jefferson*, 217.

27. Boulle, *Race et esclavage*, 255.

28. *MB*, 594 n. 87, discussing TJ's expenses.

29. Sue Peabody, *"There Are No Slaves,"* 90–91.

30. Passports issued by Jefferson, 1785–89, *Papers*, 15:485; TJ to Abigail Adams, July 1, 1787, ibid., 11:514–15.

31. Abigail Adams to TJ, July 6, 1787, *Papers*, 11:550–51; TJ to Abigail Adams, July 10, 1787, ibid., 572.

32. TJ to Abigail Adams, July 1, 1787, *Papers*, 11:514. See also *MB*, 677 n. 93, detailing expenses for tickets for Petit, SH, and Polly Jefferson.

33. Malone, *Jefferson*, 2:135.

34. Brodie, *Thomas Jefferson*, 218.

35. Conor Cruise O'Brien, *The Long Affair: Thomas Jefferson and the French Revolution, 1785–1800* (Chicago, 1996), 23–25.

36. TJ, *Notes on the State of Virginia*, in *Writings* (New York, 1984), 288.

37. Malone, *Jefferson*, 2:135.

38. Abigail Adams to TJ, July 6, 1787, *Papers*, 11:551; Abigail Adams to TJ, July 10, 1787, and John Adams to TJ, July 10, 1787, ibid., 574. Adams sent this letter to TJ with an enclosure detailing the items bought for Polly Jefferson and SH. The items "For the Maid Servant [SH]" were as follows:

    12 yards. calico for 2 short Gowns & Coats
    4 yd. half Irish linen for Aprons
    3. pr Stockings
    2 yd linning
    1 Shawl handkerchief

39. Harriet Jacobs, *Incidents in the Life of a Slave Girl, Written by Herself*, ed. Nell Irvin Painter (New York, 2000), 182, 184.

40. Abigail Adams to TJ, July 6, 1787, *Papers*, 11:551

41. Abigail Adams to TJ, July 2, 1787, *Papers*, 11:551, referring to Polly's complaint that, after not having come for her himself, TJ had sent "a man she [could not] understand" to get her.

10: **Dr. Sutton**

1. TJ to Abigail Adams, July 16, 1787, *Papers*, 11:592.
2. *MB*, 681.
3. See, e.g., ibid., 649, entry for Jan. 2, 1787; 655, entry for Feb. 28, 1787; 675, entry for July 12, 1787. There are numerous other references throughout the *MB* to money given the Hemingses.
4. TJ to Abigail Adams, July 16, 1787, *Papers*, 11:592; TJ to Mary Jefferson Bolling, July 23, 1787, ibid., 612; TJ to Elizabeth Wayles Eppes, July 28, 1787, ibid., 634.
5. TJ to Elizabeth Wayles Eppes, July 28, 1787, *Papers*, 11:634. TJ and Polly did not have much time alone together. She arrived at her father's house on July 15. Her sister came and stayed with her for a week, and then they both went back to school. Jefferson told his sister-in-law that Polly was "established in the convent, perfectly happy." Although both Jefferson girls enjoyed their time in France, it seems doubtful, given all that she had been through and Adams's description of her state of mind while in London, that Polly was not still in a period of adjustment after just two weeks in France.
6. Stanton, *Free Some Day*, 109; "Brief Biography of Sally Hemings," Monticello.org. The *MB* lists SH among the household servants at the Hôtel de Langeac. See, e.g., *MB*, 690, entry for Jan. 1, 1788; 718, entry for Nov. 3, 1788; 725, entry for Feb. 2, 1789. Perhaps because he believed he was at the end of his time in Paris, TJ stopped listing the names of each servant and the amount he or she was paid. He simply recorded the lump sum that he gave Petit to pay their salaries. The lump sum remained the same for the rest of his time in Paris, indicating that JH and SH continued to receive the same wages. See, generally, *MB* from March through Sept. 1789.
7. TJ to Joel Yancey, Jan. 17, 1819, *Farm Book*, 43.
8. Sue Peabody, "*There Are No Slaves*," 15–16. The case, which the judges decided on the basis of customary law that favored freedom, sparked officials to call for the first regulations of slavery in mainland France.
9. Francis Eppes to TJ, Aug. 31, 1786, *Papers*, 15:631; Martha Jefferson Carr, Jan. 2, 1787, ibid., 633.
10. *MB*, 408, entry for Sept. 27, 1775; 409, entry for Nov. 6, 1775 (TJ pays for lodging and nursing Robert Hemings during inoculation); 471, entry for Sept. 28, 1778.
11. Michel Antoine, *Louis XV* (Paris, 1989), 991; Voltaire, "De la mort de Louis XV et de la fatalité (1774)," *Oeuvres complètes de Voltaire*, vol. 29, *Mélanges VIII (1773–1776)*, new ed. (Paris, 1879), 301, 299. "Que conclure de ce tableau, si vrai et si funeste? [What to conclude from this scene, so true and so disastrous?] Rois et princes nécessaires aux peuples, subissez l'inoculation si vous aimez la vie; encouragez-la chez vos sujets si vous voulez qu'ils vivent." After the death of Louis, "le seul roi de France qui soit mort de cette funeste maladie nommée *variole*, ou *petite vérole*," After all this, it was time for France to realize that all over the world, other societies had embraced inoculation as a way of protecting their people.
12. Eugenia W. Herbert, "Smallpox Inoculation in Africa," *Journal of African History* 6 (1975): 539–59.
13. Elizabeth A. Fenn, *Pox Americana: The Great Smallpox Epidemic of 1775–82* (New York, 2001).

14. Malone, *Jefferson*, 1:99–100; *MB*, 388 n. 56, 524 n. 42.

15. Genevieve Miller, *The Adoption of Inoculation for Smallpox in England and France* (Philadelphia, 1957), 23. TJ to Benjamin Rush, Jan. 16, 1811, *The Works of Thomas Jefferson*, ed. Paul Leicester Ford, 12 vols. (New York, 1904–05), 9:296. In 1806, ten years after Edward Jenner developed vaccination as an alternative to inoculation, by using the cowpox virus "vaccinia" instead of the live smallpox virus, TJ wrote excitedly to him, hailing his discovery and counting it, too, as a major advancement in human progress. TJ to G. C. Edward Jenner, May 14, 1806, LOC, 27806. He became a vaccinator himself, personally vaccinating slaves at Monticello.

    In August of 1801, Jefferson had vaccinated (calling it inoculation) six enslaved people, including Joseph Fossett and Burwell Colbert. Fossett, then twenty-one, and Colbert, eighteen, became the source of protection for others at Monticello. After their eruptions appeared, Dr. William Wardlaw took the virus from them and vaccinated, among others, Jefferson's grandchildren, Ellen and Cornelia, and other members of the enslaved community, including Critta Hemings and Wormley Hughes.

    Jefferson kept up the program of vaccinations as cowpox virus became available when the disease broke out in the area. Age did not matter. Cornelia Randoph was approaching three when she was vaccinated. Beverley Hemings was four and his sister Harriet just a year old when Jefferson vaccinated them in 1802. There were two more rounds of vaccinations on the mountain. Jefferson vaccinated Beverley's and Harriet's younger siblings, Madison and Eston, in 1816. The final round was conducted five months before Jefferson died in 1826. There is great poignancy in this. According to the oral history of Eston Hemings's family, he died of smallpox. What his father probably did not know when he vaccinated Eston is that, unlike inoculation, vaccination does not guarantee lifelong immunity to smallpox. In a small percentage of people it may not provide immunity at all, and the protection tends to wear off in everyone over time, so that booster shots are needed to maintain it. See "List of Inoculations," *Papers*, 35:34–35 (forthcoming). TJ's list of "Vaccinations," unpublished. I thank Barbara Oberg, the editor of *The Papers of Thomas Jefferson*, for making these lists available to me.

16. Kenneth Kiple, ed., *The Cambridge World History of Human Disease* (Cambridge, 1993), 1011.

17. Ibid. Mary J. Dobson, *Contours of Death and Disease in Early Modern England* (Cambridge, 1997), 270–71. See Charles Leach, "Hospital Rock," *Hog River Journal*, Winter 2004, on the "Suttonian Method" in the American colonies. The Suttons' influence also extended into Canada. They had trained "James Latham, a British Military surgeon," who "variolated 303 people, including prominent members of English and French families in Quebec City and, later, in Montreal, without fatality." John W. R. McIntyre and Stuart Houston, "Smallpox and Its Control in Canada," *Canadian Medial Association Journal* 161 (1999): 1543–47.

18. *Virginia Gazette*, Sept. 8, 1768, while discussing the events leading up to anti-inoculation riots in Norfolk that sparked a legal case that would involve TJ, referred to "the apparent success of Sutton," as if there were no need to explain to its readers who Sutton was and what he had done.

19. Guenter Risse, "Medicine in the Age of Enlightenment," in *Medicine in Society: Historical Essays*, ed. Andrew Wear (Cambridge, 1992); Steve Lehrer, *Explorers of the Body* (Garden City, N.Y., 1979), chap. 8.

20. Voltaire, *Lettres philosophiques* ("Lettre XI. Sur l'insertion de la petite vérole), *Oeuvres complètes de Voltaire*, vol. 22, *Mélanges I*, new ed. (Paris, 1879), 445, chiding the French for their failure to adopt inoculation "est-ce que les Français n'aiment point la vie? est-ce que leurs femmes ne se soucient point de leur beauté?"

21. David Van Zwanenberg, "The Suttons and the Business of Inoculation," *Medical History* 22 (1978): 71–82. See also Hervé Bazin, *The Eradication of Smallpox: Edward Jenner and the First and Only Eradication of an Infectious Disease* (London, 2000), 17, saying that the Suttons' "philanthropy" was not extensive. See, generally, Van Zwanenberg, "Suttons"; *MB*, 685; J. M. Peebles, *Vaccination a Curse and a Menace to Personal Liberty, with Statistics Showing Its Danger and Criminality* (Los Angeles, 1913). There is merit to the view that the Suttons' creative marketing ability and business sense were as much the reason for their fame as their true skill or creativity as innovators. They were good at recognizing what was best about various procedures surrounding inoculation, adopting them, and then aggressively promoting their newly refined method. This takes nothing from their achievements, but it is an old and familiar story; very often it is not the originator of an idea but the one who comes in and refines it and is willing to do what it takes to promote knowledge of the refined product who profits most. See, e.g., Miller, *Adoption of Inoculation*, 61 n. 53, debunking the claim that the Suttons were the first to use a lancet in inoculation.

22. *MB*, 685, entry for Nov. 7, 1787.

23. Peebles, *Vaccination a Curse*, 16.

24. Van Zwanenberg, "Suttons," 81–82 n. 17.

25. R. Hingston Fox, *Dr. John Fothergill and His Friends: Chapters in Eighteenth Century Life* (London, 1919), 81.

26. Van Zwanenberg, "Suttons," 76 n. 17, 77.

27. Antoine, *Louis XV*, 991. But see Dorothy Porter and Ray Porter, *Patient's Progress: Doctors and Doctoring in Eighteenth-Century England* (Palo Alto, Calif., 1969), 128–29, describing Robert Sutton alone as King Louis's doctor.

28. *MB*, 409, 471.

29. Bazin, *Eradication of Small Pox*, 18 n. 18; Stanton, *Free Some Day*, 110; Miller, *Adoption of Inoculation*, 230.

30. Daniel Sutton, *The Inoculator; or, Sutton on the System of Inoculation Fully Set Forth in Plain & Familiar Language* (London, 1796).

31. Fenn, *Pox Americana*, 36.

32. Bazin, *Eradication of Small Pox*, 17.

33. *Papers*, 6:viii.

34. Frank L. Dewey, *Thomas Jefferson: Lawyer* (Charlottesville, 1986), 19, 56. TJ had firsthand knowledge of the community stake in the process of inoculation. In 1768 he was involved in the criminal case arising out of the riot that had taken place in Norfolk, Va., when a doctor attempted to keep an inoculated person in a residence instead of the "pest houses" that were specifically set up to shelter people with dangerous diseases. The rioters burned their neighbor's house to the ground. Jefferson was hired to prosecute the rioters and to defend those who had created the "nuisance" by performing the inoculation in an ordinary neighborhood setting. He won the case. Nine years later, while in the House of Burgesses, he served or a legislative committee that created and helped pass a law "allowing inoculation anywhere if a majority of the neighbors within two miles consented, and

if the proper quarantine were maintained." Dewey devotes an entire chapter to TJ's work on the case, citing it as an example where his position as a public figure merged with his private interest in science and progress.

35. See, generally, Sutton, *Inoculator.*

36. Ibid., foldout insert at end of the book.

37. Ibid.

38. Fenn, *Pox Americana,* 34–35. Adams was inoculated along with his brother. The men shared the experience with nine other patients, who he said suffered more than he. When he broke out in the pox, he stopped writing to Abigail, fearful of transmitting any infected material on the pages of his letter. Abigail's inoculation was far less of an ordeal.

39. Sutton, *Inoculator,* 80–83.

40. Malone, *Jefferson,* 1:245.

41. Gordon-Reed, *TJ and SH,* 245.

42. Yvon Bizardel and Howard C. Rice Jr., "Poor in Love Mr. Short," *WMQ,* 3d ser., 21 (1963): 516–33, esp. 517–18.

11: The Rhythms of the City

1. Howard C. Rice, *L'Hôtel de Langeac: Jefferson's Paris Residence, 1785–1789* (Paris, 1947), 7–8. See TJ to James Madison, Sept. 25, 1788, in *Papers,* 12:202, discussing the expectation that he would maintain the same "stile of living" that Franklin had established and that his governmental allowance gave him "500 guineas a year less to do it."

2. Rice, *Hôtel de Langeac,* 8, 13–14.

3. Ibid., 11, 13; McLaughlin, *Jefferson and Monticello,* 211.

4. Malone, *Jefferson,* 2:20; *MB,* 674 n. 83

5. Eugene Genovese, *Roll, Jordan, Roll: The World the Slaves Made* (New York, 1972), 328–65; John W. Blassingame, "Status and Social Structure in the Slave Community: Evidence from New Sources," *Perspectives and Irony in American Slavery,* ed. Harry P. Owens (Jackson, Miss., 1976); Morgan, *Slave Counterpoint,* 353–58. See, generally, Stephanie M. H. Camp, "The Pleasures of Resistance: Enslaved Woman in the Plantation South," *Journal of Southern History* 68 (2002): 3, recounting enslaved men's and women's efforts to create a space for themselves "away from slaveholding eyes" where they could be themselves among their own.

6. *Farm Book,* 77. Stanton, *Free Some Day,* 106,

7. Stanton, *Free Some Day,* 151.

8. Marie de Botidoux to Martha Jefferson, Nov. 1789–Jan. 10, 1790, Special Collections, ViU.

9. Maria Jefferson to Kitty Church, May 7, 1789, *Papers,* 16:xxxi.

10. Fairchilds, *Domestic Enemies,* 54–58, 68–69.

11. David Garrioch, *The Formation of the Parisian Bourgeoisie, 1690–1830* (Cambridge, Mass., 1996), 309–10.

12. See photograph in first insert.

13. Martha Jefferson to Eliza House Trist, in *Papers,* 8:437.

14. Garrioch, *Making of Revolutionary Paris,* 22; Alistair Horne, *Seven Ages of Paris* (New York, 2002); Colin Jones, *Paris, Biography of a City* (London, 2004);

15. TJ to Montmorin, July 8, 1789, *Papers,* 15:260.

16. Garrioch, *Making of Revolutionary Paris*, 23.

17. Ibid.

18. McLaughlin, *Jefferson and Monticello*, 211.

19. Eugen Weber, *My France: Politics, Culture, Myth* (Cambridge, Mass., 1991), 93.

20. Fairchilds, *Domestic Enemies*, 105–6, notes "the difficulties faced with language" and describes how the stereotype of the inarticulate servant formed the basis of many comic scenes in plays and the literature of the day.

21. Petit to TJ, Aug. 3, 1790, *Papers*, 17:298; Petit to TJ, July 28, 1792, ibid., 24:262.

22. Fairchilds, *Domestic Enemies*, 50–51. Despite the government's geopolitical contests, "'À l'anglaise' was the fashion in the Parisian beau monde."

23. From Perrault, *Papers*, 14:426.

24. Rice, *Hôtel de Langeac*, 10, 13.

25. *MB*, 690.

26. Ibid., 718; Fairchild, *Domestic Enemies*, 54–58; *MB*, 730 n. 47.

27. *MB*, 686 n. 20.

28. TJ to Martha Jefferson Randolph, March 28, 1787, *Papers*, 11:251.

29. Pierson, *Jefferson at Monticello*, 107.

30. See, generally, Sabattier, *Figaro et son maître*; Gutton, *Domestiques et serviteurs*; Fairchild, *Domestic Enemies*; Maza, *Servants and Masters*, on wage rates and positions.

31. Gordon-Reed, *TJ and SH*, 248.

32. See Maza, *Servants and Masters*, 110–11, on prejudices against female servants.

33. Virginia Cope, "'Verily Believed Myself to Be a Free Woman': Harriet Jacobs's Journey into Capitalism," *African American Review* 38 (2004): 5–20.

34. Fairchild, *Domestic Enemies*, 54–58.

35. Ibid., 56–58, wage tables; Pierre Boulle, "Les Gens de couleur à Paris à la veille de la Révolution," 162–63.

36. Bear, *The Hemings Family*, 9.

37. Mary Jefferson to Thomas Mann Randolph, Oct. (?), 1790, LOC 11992. This letter was more likely written at the beginning of Sept., as both parties were at Monticello during the end of Sept. and entire month of Oct.

38. Martha Randolph's will, April 18, 1834, Family Letters Project.

39. Brodie, *Thomas Jefferson*, 234.

40. Francis D. Cogliano, *Thomas Jefferson: Reputation and Legacy* (Charlottesville, 2006), 74–105.

41. Gordon-Reed, *TJ and SH*, chap. 3.

42. *MB*, 731, entry for April 29, 1789.

43. Brodie, *Thomas Jefferson*, 233.

44. *MB*, 716, entry for Oct. 7, 1788.

45. Stanton, *Free Some Day*, 109.

46. TJ to James Madison, Jan. 13, 1821, *Republic of Letters*, 3:1828.

47. TJ to William Short, Jan. 22, 1788, *Papers*, 15:483.

48. Martha Jefferson Randolph to Ann (Nancy) Cary Randolph Morris, May 26, 1827, Family Letters Project.

49. R. Premaratna et al., "Acute Hearing Loss Due to Scrub Typhus: A Forgotton Complication of a Reemerging Disease," *Clinical Infectious Diseases* 42 (2006): e6–e8.

50. Scholars have speculated that a bout with typhus caused Beethoven's deafness. Tony Miksanek, "Diagnosing a Genius: The Life and Death of Beethoven," *Journal of the American Medical Association* 297 (2007): 2643–44.

51. Ellen Randolph Coolidge to Joseph Coolidge, Oct. 24, 1858, Family Letters Project. See also Gordon-Reed, *TJ and SH*, 259. Readers should note that there was an error in the transcription of this letter in the earliest editions of the book that was corrected in later printings. It formed no part of my analysis and discussion in the main text. The full letter itself appeared only in the appendix to the work. The relevant passage is the quoted material in the text to which this endnote refers. I devoted a chapter (pp. 78–104) of my book to TJ's grandchildren's alternative vision of life at Monticello. Without rehashing that discussion, a couple of things are worth mentioning.

    In my first take, I focused primarily on what I thought, and still think, was the most important information conveyed in Coolidge's account: that Samuel Carr had fathered all of SH's children. My analysis at the time (later borne out by DNA tests on descendants) made clear to me that Coolidge's statement was untrue. Coolidge's letter nevertheless remains important because the DNA results reveal the level of desperation that TJ's white family felt about his relationship with SH—that they would resort to picking relatives to name as her lover. As I think of it now, the passage in which Coolidge claimed that no female slave had ever gone into TJ's room when he was there and that anyone who went into his room would have been seen by others also lays bare their anxiety. It is just the kind of "never" or "always" formulation that should provoke skepticism.

    Coolidge was presenting herself as an eyewitness to SH's access to her grandfather, offering that because she lived at Monticello (and was a legal descendant and thus had the right to tell the "official" family story), she could be trusted to know that they were never alone in his room. That it was impossible for her to have known that struck me then, and strikes me now, as patently obvious. Unless she was physically attached to him or SH, it was not humanly possible for Coolidge, or anyone else besides TJ and SH, to know whether they were ever alone in a room together over the near two decades that the pair was having children together. Coolidge was a contemporary of SH's children, the first two of whom were conceived before she was born and the others when she was an infant or a child herself. She could not possibly have known whether SH was in TJ's room or not when those children were conceived. Coolidge and her siblings spent large amounts of time at Monticello during their childhoods, moving there permanently in 1809 after all SH's children were born. By the time the last child, Eston, whose descendant was the subject of the DNA test, was conceived in 1807, Coolidge was at least old enough—eleven—to be observant of her world. Coolidge did not, as an eleven-year-old girl, spend her time running back and forth between the outside and interior entrances to her grandfather's bedroom twenty-four hours a day making sure that no one went inside. For that is what she would have to do in order to know the thing she said she knew and reconstruct, at age sixty-two, the memory of her eleven-year-old self having done that impossible thing. Nor would TJ's guests—who were nowhere near as numerous during his preretirement years, the period when SH was conceiving her children—be standing by the indoor and outdoor entrances to TJ's bedroom morning, noon, and night, watching to see whether anyone went inside.

52. Gordon-Reed, *TJ and SH*, 259.

12: The Eve of Revolution

1. I've borrowed this image from Carlyle, *The French Revolution*, 59, describing the fiscal policy of "Comptroller Calonne."

2. See Doyle, *Origins*, 45–53.

3. Ibid.

4. TJ to Abigail Adams, Feb. 22, 1787, *Papers*, 11:174; TJ to James Monroe, Aug. 9, 1788, ibid., 8:489.

5. Doyle, *Origins*, 76–90; Lefebvre, *The Coming of the French Revolution*, 102–9.

6. TJ to Anne Willing Bingham, May 11, 1788, *Papers*, 8:151.

7. Garrioch, *The Making of Revolutionary Paris*, 291: "In the last years of Louis XV's reign and under Louis XVI there was a growing condemnation of 'despotism,' even though the government was more responsive to 'public opinion' than ever before." See also Doyle, *Origins*.

8. See Robin Blackburn, *The Overthrow of Colonial Slavery, 1776–1848* (London, 1988), 173–75; Dubois, *A Colony of Citizens*, 99–104, discussing the effort to allow *gens de couleur* a measure of representation in the National Assembly.

9. Mirabeau quoted in Dubois, *Colony of Citizens*, 99–100. See also his useful "Chronology" at the end of the book. See, generally, Shelby T. McCoy, "Further Notes on Negroes and Mulattoes in Eighteenth-Century France," *Journal of Negro History* 39 (Oct. 1954): 284–97.

10. Malone, *Jefferson*, 2:221; Dubois, *Colony of Citizens*, 100.

11. TJ to Maria Cosway, Oct. 12, 1786, *Papers*, 10:443. TJ and Cosway have been written about in numerous works. Perhaps the best treatment of the story is in Brodie, *Thomas Jefferson*, 199–215. Although at times she makes too much of the couple's dealings when Cosway returned to Paris after a time in London after their initial meeting, Brodie's informed depiction of the romantic mores of ancien régime Paris, and TJ's response to it, is nuanced, insightful, and lively—even when she overreaches. See also Marie Kimball, *Jefferson: The Scene of Europe, 1784 to 1789* (New York, 1950), 168–69; Malone, *Jefferson*, 2:70–78; Burstein, *The Inner Jefferson*, 75–99; John P. Kaminski, ed., *Jefferson in Love: The Love Letters between Thomas Jefferson and Maria Cosway* (Madison, Wis., 1999).

12. When he was in his twenties, TJ propositioned—she claimed repeatedly—Elizabeth (Betsey) Walker, the wife of one of his best friends, John Walker. Walker's father, Thomas, had been TJ's guardian after Peter Jefferson's death. The younger men became like brothers, with TJ standing as a groomsman at his friend's wedding and acting as godfather to his child. When Walker found out about TJ's actions many years later, a duel was only narrowly averted when mutual friends of the two men acted as intermediaries in intense negotiations to resolve the dispute; it was an intervention perfectly in keeping with the tightly knit world of upper-class communities in eighteenth-century Virginia. Some years after the resolution, in the early 1800s, TJ and Walker achieved a rapprochement of sorts, with TJ making small gestures at the right moment that seemed designed to show that he was genuinely sorry about what had happened. Walker accepted them. See Malone, *Jefferson*, vol. 4, appendix "The Walker Affair"; Brodie, *Thomas Jefferson*, 57, 79; Gordon-Reed, *TJ and SH*, 141–46.

13. Brodie, *Thomas Jefferson*, 225, 253; Gordon-Reed, *TJ and SH*, 187; D. S. Neff, "Bitches,

Mollies, and Tommies: Byron, Maculinity, and the History of Sexualities," *Journal of the History of Sexuality* 11 (2002): 431. Neff argues that Byron understood that "castrati and eunuchs had a very real proclivity for heterophilic and homophilic sexual attachments." The poet claimed that "Italian women preferred castrati 'for two reasons—first they do *not impregnate* them—and next as they never . . . spend—they go on "in eterno" and serve an elderly lady at all times.'" See also n. 136, citing Angus Heriot, *The Castrati in Opera* (London, 1956), confirming castrati's status as "lady-killers" who were in demand because "their embraces could not lead to awkward consequences."

14. For example, the Royers and their daughter do not figure in either Malone's or Brodie's biographies of Jefferson, although both discuss his affair with the duchesse de La Rochefoucauld. Short's biographer George Green Shackelford, in an otherwise detailed biography does not mention Short and Royer either: *Jefferson's Adoptive Son: The Life of William Short, 1759–1849* (Lexington, Ky., 1993).

15. Yvon Bzardel and Howard C. Rice Jr., "Poor in Love Mr. Short," *WMQ,* 3d ser., 21 (1964): 516–33.

16. Ibid., 518, 523.

17. Ibid., 520, 519, 523, 523–26, 526–28.

18. Ibid., 531–33.

19. James Maury to TJ, Sept. 17, 1786, *Papers,* 10:389. Maury notes that his mother "some how or other" had heard that Patsy was "in a Convent, which has made her very uneasy and I am afraid she will not easily forgive you"; TJ to James Maury, Dec. 24, 1786, ibid., 628, asking him to assure his mother that the convent was a "house of education only" and that the nuns did not attempt to influence the girls.

20. Ellen (Eleanora) Randolph Coolidge's Recollections of Martha Jefferson Randolph, [after 1826], Family Letters Project.

21. See *MB,* 730 n. 47; Brodie, *Thomas Jefferson,* 239; Stanton, *Free Some Day,* 110.

22. *MB,* 730 n. 47; Ellen Coolidge, *Recollections,* Family Letters Project.

23. Daniel Roche, *The People of Paris: An Essay in Popular Culture in the Eighteenth Century* (Berkeley, Calif., 1987), 66.

24. Ibid.

25. Archibald Bolling Shepperson, *John Paradise and Lucy Ludwell of London and Williamsburg* (Richmond, Va., 1942), 202–5; Herbert E. Sloan, *Principle and Interest: Thomas Jefferson and the Problem of Debt* (New York, 1995), 41–42. See Lucy Ludwell Paradise to TJ, Aug. 2, 1788, *Papers,* 13:457, calling Jefferson "My dear Protector" and, Aug. 17, 1788, ibid., 522, "What happiness should I enjoy, could I see Mr. Paradise as thoughtful, regular, Active and Industrious as you are"; Lucy Ludwell Paradise to TJ, Aug. 21, 1788, ibid., 533–34.

26. See above, chap. 2.

27. TJ to John Jay, Nov. 19, 1788, *Papers,* 14:215–16.

28. *MB,* 279, entries for April 6, 16; 734, entry for May 25. It is very likely that he bought other items of clothing for her that were included in his occasional listings of his pay-ments for clothes "for servants." See, e.g., 694, entry for Feb. 21, 1788; 729, entry for April 23, 1789.

29. Brodie, *Thomas Jefferson,* 239; O. J. Wister and Agnes Irwin, eds., *Worthy Women of Our First Century* (Philadelphia, 1877), 20.

30. Stanton, *Free Some Day,* 110.

31. Wister and Irwin, *Worthy Women*, 20

32. Mary Jefferson Eppes to TJ, Feb. 2, 1801, *Papers*, 32:537; TJ to Mary Jefferson Eppes, Feb. 15, 1801, ibid., 593.

33. *MB*, 734. See also n. 57.

34. Clifford D. Panton Jr., *George Augustus Polgreen Bridgetower, Violin Virtuoso and Composer of Color in Late 18th Century Europe* (Lewiston, N.Y., 2005), 5, 17.

35. See Londa Schiebinger, "Anatomy of Difference: Race and Sex in Eighteenth-Century Science," *Eighteenth-Century Studies* 23 (Summer 1990): 387–405. Schiebinger notes that as scientific "'evidence' mounted that women and blacks lacked native intelligence, proponents of equality collected examples of learned European women and learned Africans" (p. 399). These exceptional people had to meet standards set by people who were their opposites. "Of course, European males generally set the standards of scholarly excellence. Learned women or blacks had to excel in those arts and sciences recognized by the white male academy—fields such as classical music, astronomy, Latin or mathematics" (p. 400).

36. "Bridgetower, George (August Polgreen)," *Baker's Biographical Dictionary of Musicians*, rev. ed. (1992). See also Panton, *Bridgetower*.

37. Gordon-Reed, *TJ and SH*, 245; Stanton, *Free Some Day*, 101.

38. TJ to Nathanial Burwell, March 14, 1818, *The Writings of Thomas Jefferson*, ed. Andrew A. Lipscomb and Albert E. Bergh, 20 vols. (Washington, D.C., 1903), 15:165–67, quoted in Brodie, *Thomas Jefferson*, 447.

13: "During That Time"

1. Gordon-Reed, *TJ and SH*, 246. See also below, chap. 20.

2. TJ to Martha Jefferson Randolph, Dec. 23, 1790, *Papers*, 18:350.

3. TJ to Francis C. Gray, March 4, 1815, LOC, 36173; TJ, *Notes*, in *Writings* (New York, 1984), 267.

4. TJ to James Madison, May 25, 1788, *Papers*, 8:202.

5. Elizabeth Fox Genovese, *Within the Plantation Household: Black and White Women of the Old South* (Chapel Hill, 1988); Catherine Clinton, *The Plantation Mistress: Woman's World in the Old South* (New York, 1984).

6. Gordon-Reed, *TJ and SH*, 246; Burstein, *Inner Jefferson*, 144–49; *Republic of Letters*, 1:7, quoting Jefferson.

7. Campbell, "Life of Isaac Jefferson," 573; TJ to Isaac MacPherson, Aug. 13, 1813, in TJ, *Writings* (New York, 1984), 1286. This contains TJ's very famous statement against patents on ideas.

8. Malone, *Jefferson*, 2:17.

9. Gordon-Reed, *TJ and SH*, 254; Campbell, "Life of Isaac Jefferson," 567–68. Among other comments, Henry Randall remembered TJ's grandson saying that SH was "decidedly good looking."

10. There is no official record of when SH died, but her son Madison gave his mother's year of death as 1835, linking it to the time before he left Virginia. It is possible that the sixty-eight-year-old Hemings misspoke or that the newspaper that carried his story made a mistake in recording what Hemings said about the date. In his memoir of his trip

through the United States, Count Francesco Arese, a visiting European who spent time in Charlottesville in 1837, claimed to have seen her and referred to her as "very pretty . . . although she was no longer young." She would have been in her sixties. Apparently SH, or at least the story of "his pretty Negress," as she was described in the book's index subheading under "Jefferson, Thomas," surely one of the more arresting index entries for him in any historical work, had become an important enough part of the town's history to be talked about to visitors as if she were a natural wonder. Count Francesco Arese, *A Trip to the Prairies and in the Interior of North America [1837–1838], Travel Notes,* trans. Andrew Evans (New York, 1834), 29, 214.

11. Gordon-Reed, *TJ and SH,* 54.

12. TJ, *Notes on the State of Virginia,* 267.

13. Ibid., 269; William Peden, "A Bookseller Invades Monticello," *WMQ,* 3d ser., 6 (1949): 633.

14. *Papers,* 9:295; *MB,* 554 n. 60. David Humphreys had gone back to America in 1786, and Charles Williamos had died in 1785.

15. *MB,* 635 n. 6; 689, Jan. 1788 notation for "Trumbull's servants"; 741, entry for Aug. 31.

16. Yvon Bizardel and Howard C. Rice Jr., "Poor in Love Mr. Short," *WMQ,* 3d ser., 21 (1963): 523, 527–28.

17. Ibid., 519.

18. TJ to John Trumbull, June 1, 1789, *Papers,* 15:164.

19. TJ to William Short, March 29, *Papers,* 11:253; Bizardel and Rice, "Poor in Love Mr. Short," 523. Although the older man told his young friend to follow his "inclinations" about the time he spent in the countryside, TJ's tone suggested resignation rather than active support of Short's preferences. Their mutual friend the aristocratic Madame de Tessé was aware of Short's situation, but "*grande dame* that she was, politely refrained from mentioning a girl in her bantering allusions" in her letters to Jefferson about Short's spending so much time there instead of being in Paris. She teased TJ by saying that Short much preferred Saint-Germain to the city. TJ and Madame de Tessé were very close, and what could not be said in letters was very likely commented upon during his many visits to her home.

20. See, e.g., TJ to Maria Cosway, Jan. 9, 1789, *Papers,* 16:144–46. He notes that he had not heard from her for a while, but this could be because he had not written to her. He blamed illnesses in his family for failing to communicate for over two months. That was certainly true, but he had written to other people—to Madison and John Adams multiple times. He wrote to Angelica Church as much as he wrote to Cosway during that period— exactly once. TJ's tone is always gallant and flirtatious, but their correspondence at this point, from his side, does not sound like one deeply in love with another. See *MB,* 680 n. 3, suggesting that Cosway's second stay in France during TJ's residence there did not amount to a real renewal of their affair.

21. For a discussion of historians' use of Maria Cosway as antidote to SH, see Gordon-Reed *TJ and SH,* 184–90. For the best treatment of the subject, see also R. R. Burg, "The Rhetoric of Miscegenation: Thomas Jefferson, Sally Hemings, and Their Historians," *Phylon* 27 (1986): 128–38. I did not find this article until I began research for this book and, unfortunately, did not know to discuss it in my first book about the scholarly treatment of SH and TJ. Burg's dead-on and scathing analysis of the way TJ biographers

viewed and wrote stories about Jefferson and the various women in his life (Betsy Walker, Maria Cosway, and Sally Hemings) is essential reading for anyone interested in the way racial attitudes, conscious or unconscious, often affect the writing of American history.

22. TJ to Anne Willing Bingham, May 11, 1788, *Papers*, 12:152.

23. TJ to Dugald Stewart, June 21, 1789, *Papers*, 15:204.

24. TJ to Elizabeth Eppes, July 28, 1786, *Papers*, 11:634; TJ to Maria Jefferson, April, 11, 1790, ibid., 16:331.

25. Rhys Isaac, "Monticello Stories," in *Sally Hemings and Thomas Jefferson: History Memory, and Civic Culture*, ed. Jan Ellen Lewis and Peter S. Onuf (Charlottesville, 1999), 120.

26. TJ to Maria Cosway, April 24, 1788, *Papers*, 13:103; Brodie, *Thomas Jefferson*, 230-31. See also Isaac, "Monticello Stories," 122; E. M. Halliday, *Understanding Thomas Jefferson* (New York, 2001), 100–104.

27. Kaminski, ed., *Jefferson in Love*, 23.

28. Martha Jefferson to Eliza House Trist, [after Aug. 14, 1785], *Papers*, 8:437

29. Melvin Patrick Ely, *Israel on the Appomattox: A Southern Experiment in Black Freedom from the 1790s through the Civil War* (New York, 2004), 290–95.

30. Nell Painter, *Sojourner Truth: A Life, a Symbol* (New York, 1997).

31. Peter Bargaglio, "An Outrage upon Nature: Incest and Law in the Nineteenth Century South," in *In Joy and in Sorrow: Women, Family, and Marriage in the Victorian South, 1830–1900* (New York, 1991).

32. TJ, *Notes*, in *Writings*, 238.

14: Sarah Hemings: The Fatherless Girl in a Patriarchal Society

1. Jefferson Family Bible, LVa.

2. Brenda E. Stevenson, *Life in Black and White: Family and Community in the Slave South* (New York, 1996). See also Peter Kolchin, "Reevaluating the Slave Community: A Comparative Perspective," *Journal of American History* 70 (Dec. 1983): 579–601, tracing the evolution of attitudes about the nature of life in antebellum slave communities.

3. Lucia Stanton, *Slavery at Monticello* (Charlottesville, 1996), 16. "Between 1784–1794 [TJ] disposed of 161 people by sale or by gift." Lucia Stanton, "'Those Who Labor for My Happiness': Thomas Jefferson and His Slaves," in *Jeffersonian Legacies*, ed. Peter S. Onuf (Charlottesville, Virginia, 1999), 148, 162. The post-Revolutionary/early Republic periods, in which the Hemingses lived at Monticello, witnessed the transformation of the southern slave society. Ira Berlin, *Many Thousands Gone: The First Two Centuries of Slavery in America* (Cambridge, Mass., 1998), 264–65, describing the "massive exodus" of the slave population from the upper South as the interstate slave trade transferred thousands of slaves to the lower South, separating and traumatizing thousands of enslaved individuals and families; Steven Deyle, *Carry Me Back: The Domestic Slave Trade in American Life* (New York, 2005), 41, noting, "The domestic slave trade was also a part of a larger economic transformation commonly referred to as the market revolution taking place in America in the first half of the nineteenth-century." See, generally, *Farm Book* for listing of slaves.

4. Campbell, "Life of Isaac Jefferson," 568.

5. Fawn Brodie, "Thomas Jefferson's Unknown Grandchildren: A Study in Historical Silences," *American Heritage* 27 (Oct. 1976): 23–33, 94–99.

6. Philip D. Morgan, *Slave Counterpoint: Black Culture in the Eighteenth-Century Chesapeake and Lowcountry* (Chapel Hill, 1998), 540–48; Stevenson, *Life in Black and White*, 251–52.

7. *Journal of William Maclay, United States Senator from Pennsylvania, 1789–1791* (New York 1927), 265–66, entry for May 24, 1790; Jack Shepherd, *Cannibals of the Heart: A Personal Biography of Louisa Catherine and John Quincy Adams* (New York, 1980), 113–15; *The First Forty Years of Washington Society, Portrayed by the Family Letters of Mrs. Samuel Harrison Smith (Margaret Bayard)* (New York, 1906), 6.

8. Kierner, *Scandal at Bizarre*, 75; Paul C. Nagel, *The Lees of Virginia* (New York, 2006).

9. Henry Lee to Richard T. Brown, Paris, Aug. 24, 1833, unpublished letter at Stratford Hall, Home of Robert E. Lee. Interestingly enough, the bulk of Lee's letter is spent retelling the Walker story. Not surprisingly, it is clear that TJ's attempted seduction of the married Betsy Walker, a white woman, was for Lee a greater offense than having children with an enslaved African American woman. The scandal engulfed Lee personally and professionally, for he and his wife's sister had not only engaged in adultery but also broken the laws against affinity-based incest. After being denied a government appointment because of his affair, in the same letter in which he sought to explain what had happened between him and his sister-in-law, Henry bitterly compared himself with TJ. Why was it, he asked incredulously, that "the well known example of Mr. Jefferson, the sage, the patriot, the light of philosophy, the friend of freedom, the apostle of liberty, the redeemer of the Republick," should not have been enough to erase him from the hearts, minds, and esteem of the public? "Around the shady sides of Monticello," he raged, "his [TJ's] offspring wander with skins as tawny as their soil & eyes bright with hereditary lust." Not only was the Sage of Monticello bad, Henry posited; his children were bad, too.

10. Kierner, *Scandal at Bizarre*, 75.

11. *MB*, 729, 734.

12. Jefferson's acquisitive nature is well known. Susan Stein has cataloged the astounding array of possessions he accumulated while in France. See *The World of Thomas Jefferson at Monticello* (New York, 1993).

13. Peter S. Onuf, *Jefferson's Empire: The Language of American Nationhood* (Charlottesville, 2000), 149–51.

14. Dubois, *A Colony of Citizens*, 177–83; Campbell, "Life of Isaac Jefferson," 570. Isaac Jefferson's anecdote about Cary gives an insight into TJ's personality and tendency to want to maintain peace at all cost. The idea of a houseguest stalking into a kitchen to see what is on the menu and then if they "didn't have what he wanted—obliged [everyone else] to wait dinner till it was cooked" and beating a young slave boy who transgressed in some fashion, or other slaves who displeased him, rather than taking the matter up with TJ, astounded Isaac Jefferson, as was made clear by his statement that "Col. Cary made freer at Monticello than he did at home." Tolerating Cary's sociopathic behavior seems more than mere hospitality on TJ's part. In fact, it was almost a perversion of the notion of hospitality, since the term implies at least a degree of mutual respect between the guest and the host. Throughout the ages, bullies have known what they are doing (and whom they safely can do it to), and one wonders what Cary actually thought of TJ after he allowed him to carry on in this fashion in his home before all the members of his household.

15. Memoirs of Thomas Jefferson Randolph, 4, Special Collections, ViU; Gordon-Reed, *TJ and SH*, 155.

16. Niccolò Machiavelli, *The Prince*, trans. and ed. William J. Connell (Boston, 2005), 91.

17. TJ to Anne Cary, Thomas Jefferson, and Ellen Wayles Randolph, Mar. 2, 1802, in *Writings*, 1102.

18. Lucia Stanton, "'A Well-Ordered Household': Domestic Servants in Jefferson's White House," *White House History*, no. 17 (2006): 5–6.

19. Martha Jefferson Randolph and Thomas Mann Randolph to TJ, Jan. 31, 1801, *Papers*, 32:528.

20. See Stanton, *Free Some Day*, 122, quoting Ellen Coolidge on Jefferson's idea of his relationship with Burwell Colbert.

15: The Teenagers and the Woman

1. Jefferson Family Bible Record, LVa.

2. Morgan, *Slave Counterpoint*, 534–35.

3. TJ to James Madison, May 7, 1784, *Papers*, 6:267; *Republic of Letters*, 1:228–29, 242, 264; Irving Brant, *James Madison*, 6 vols. (Indianapolis, 1941–61), 2:283; Gordon-Reed, *TJ and SH*, 115; *The Papers of James Madison*, ed. William T. Hutchinson and William M. E. Rachal, 17 vols. (Chicago and Charlottesville, 1962–91), 6:182 n. 28.

4. TJ to James Madison, Feb. 20, 1784, *Papers*, 6:546.

5. TJ to Madison, April 22, 1783, *Papers*, 6:262, expressing his desire that Floyd and Madison get together and saying that he "often made it the subject of conversation, more exhortation, with her [Floyd] and was able to convince myself that she possessed every sentiment in your favor which you could wish. But of this no more without your leave." Julian Boyd notes, p. 262 n.1, that this paragraph "was entirely written in cipher" and had to be decoded by the editors.

6. Brant, *James Madison*, 2:283–87; James Madison to TJ, Aug. 31, 1783, *Papers*, 6:335. A passage in the letter that had referred to Floyd was "heavily scored out by Madison" at a later point. Boyd, *Papers*, 6:335 n. 1. TJ was sympathetic about his friend's "misadventure which has happened from whatever cause it may have happened" and assured him that "the world still presents the same and many other resources of happiness, and you possess many within yourself." He then counseled, "Firmness of mind and unintermitting occupations will not long leave you in pain."

7. Jean Edward Smith, *John Marshall: Definer of a Nation* (New York, 1996), 73, 85–86; Morgan, *Slave Counterpoint*, 534–35.

8. Kierner, *Scandal at Bizarre*, 29; Edith Tunis Sale, *Manors of Virginia in Colonial Times* (Philadelphia, 1909), 122; Jefferson Randolph Anderson, "Tuckahoe and the Tuckahoe Randolphs," *Register of the Kentucky State Historical Society* 35 (1937): 29–59.

9. Martha Hodes, *White Women, Black Men: Illicit Sex in the Nineteenth-Century South* (New Haven, 1999).

10. Thomas R. R. Cobb, *An Inquiry into the Law of Negro Slavery* (Philadelphia and Savannah, 1858), 98–100. There have been many studies of European attitudes toward black women. See, e.g., Jordan, *White over Black*; White, *Ar'n't I a Woman?*, 27–46, on the "Jezebel" stereotype.

11. Sloan, *Principle and Interest*, 14–17. On the question of the value of the Wayles fortune, see ibid., 254 n. 15; on the decision to take the Wayles assets, see ibid., 15–16.

12. Ibid., 16.

13. TJ to Nicholas Lewis, July 11, 1788, *Papers*, 13:343.

14. "Critta Hemings," Monticello Research Department, Thomas Jefferson Foundation, Inc.

15. TJ to Nicholas Lewis, April 12, 1792, *Papers*, 23:408.

16. See Hemings family tree in this book; Lucia Stanton, "Monticello to Main Street: The Hemings Family and Charlottesville," *Magazine of Albemarle County History* 55 (1997): 100.

17. Melton A. McLaurin, *Celia: A Slave* (Athens, Ga., 1991), provides the most extensive treatment of the legal case that grew out of Celia's killing of Robert Newsome. See also Annette Gordon-Reed, "Celia's Case," in *Race on Trial: Law and Justice in American History*, ed. Annette Gordon-Reed (New York, 2002), 48–59.

18. Gordon-Reed, "Celia's Case," 49.

19. Ibid., 50.

20. Ibid., 51–52.

21. Ibid., 57.

22. Walter Johnson, *Soul by Soul: Life inside the Antebellum Slave Market* (Cambridge, Mass., 1999).

16: "His Promises, on Which She Implicitly Relied"

1. TJ to Andre Limozin, May 3, 1789, *Papers*, 16:86.

2. Gordon-Reed, *TJ and SH*, 246.

3. Kierner, *Scandal at Bizarre*, 56–57; White, *Ar'n't I a Woman?*, 85–86, 126.

4. TJ, *Notes*, in *Writings*, 180.

5. Stanton, *Free Some Day*, 105.

6. See White, *Ar'n't I a Woman?*, 20, Genovese, *Within the Plantation Household*, 172–77. Both White and Genovese make the point that, however white society chose to see them, enslaved women maintained their own sense of themselves as women, developing their own sense of style and understanding about what role they were to play in the society they were forced to live in. See also Stevenson, *Life in Black and White*, 234–37, discussing how "gender socialization from their mothers" taught female slaves how they were to behave as women.

7. See Michael A. Gomez, *Exchanging Our Country Marks: The Transformation of African Identities in the Colonial and Antebellum South* (Chapel Hill, 1998), 1, referring to "Denmark Vesey's insurrection" as the "ultimate form of resistance." Historians of slavery have, in fact, expanded the definition of what acts can be considered forms of resistance to slavery as it has become clear that counting up actual slave revolts was an unfair and inadequate way to measure enslaved people's responses to their situation. With respect to women in particular, the headings in the index to White's *Ar'n't I a Woman?* (p. 242) tell the story that resistance is defined as "aggressive behavior," "feigning illness," "schemes and excuses," "uses of poison," and "work slow-downs." In his introduction to *Slave Counterpoint*, xxii, Philip Morgan explains the lack of a separate chapter on slave resistance by saying, "In work and in play, in public and in private, violently and quietly, slaves struggled against masters."

8. White, *Ar'n't I a Woman?*, 88–89. Infanticide was "atypical." Stevenson, *Life in Black and White*, 244–45, takes the same view: "a few slave mothers went so far as to commit infanticide." See Stephanie M. H. Camp, *Closer to Freedom: Enslaved Women and Everyday Resistance in the Plantation South* (Chapel Hill, 2004), and Morgan, *Slave Counterpoint*, 542, on the greater prevalence of mothers running away with children.

9. Morgan, *Slave Counterpoint*, 526.

10. Thomas Gibbons to Jonathan Drayton, Dec. 20, 1802, William L. Clement Library, University of Michigan, Ann Arbor, copy at the Thomas Jefferson Foundation Library. Gordon-Reed, *TJ and SH*, 171, 245.

11. Morgan, *Slave Counterpoint*, 665–66; "An Act to Authorize the Manumission of Slaves," *Laws of Virginia*, 1782, chap. 61.

12. Despite all their talk of their paternalistic attitudes toward their slaves, a wealth of recent scholarship has shown the extremely limited nature of that paternalism as massive numbers of slaves, "members of the family," were sold as the circumstances of their owners obliged. See, e.g., Johnson, *Soul by Soul*; Deyle, *Carry Me Back*; Adam Rothman, *Slave Country: American Expansion and the Origins of the Deep South* (Cambridge, Mass., 2005).

13. See above, chap. 1. Gomez, *Exchanging Our Country Marks*, a book devoted to tracking and analyzing the process through which Africans became African Americans, stops at 1830 because, by then, "a translation [had] taken place, consistent with the demographic evidence, that delineates the demise of a preponderant African sociocultural matrix and the rise of an African American one in its place." SH died in the 1830s, and her mother, Elizabeth Hemings, lived until 1807, when her youngest daughter was thirty-four years old; both lived their lives almost totally within the African sociocultural matrix Gomez describes. See also Morgan, *Slave Counterpoint*, 459–77; Ira Berlin, *Generations of Captivity: A History of African-American Slaves* (Cambridge, Mass., 2003), 134.

14. Stevenson, *Life in Black and White*, 233–34; Morgan, *Slave Counterpoint*, 553–55. One configuration of male-female relations that was quite widespread across the continent was the practice of polygamy, in which "wives were generally subordinate to their husbands." John Thornton has noted the "oft repeated assertion that African wealth was measured in wives, in the sense that polygamy was indicative of prestige and that such wives were often in labor forces." John Thornton, *Africa and Africans in the Making of the Atlantic World, 1400–1800*, 2d ed. (Cambridge, 1998), 86. Elizabeth Hemings's mother would likely not have expected to be the sole wife of a man, an understanding that would have given her very different perspectives on her life as a woman, whether positive or negative, from a woman whose culture promoted monogamy. There is an overall sense that in the West and Central African countries from which the majority of American slaves were brought, male dominance was very much the norm, and many slaves carried that attitude with them across the ocean. Of course, African men were not alone in their preference for dominance over females. That can almost be called a universal tendency among males. See also White, *Ar'n't I a Woman?*, 106–18, discussing West African conceptions of motherhood.

15. Bear, *The Hemings Family*, 9.

16. Barbara J. Heath, *Hidden Lives: The Archaeology of Slave Life at Thomas Jefferson's Poplar Forest* (Charlottesville, 1999), 51.

17. Stanton, *Free Some Day*, 106; Lucia Stanton and Dianne Swann Wright, "Bonds of Memory Identity and the Hemings Family," in *Sally Hemings and Thomas Jefferson: History, Memory, and Civic Culture*, ed. Jan Ellen Lewis and Peter S. Onuf (Charlottesville, 1999), 170–72.

18. Frederick Douglass, *The Life and Times of Frederick Douglass* (Hartford, Conn., 1882), 28. On the history of racial classifications, see Peter Wallenstein, *Tell the Court I Love My Wife* (London, 2004); Robinson, *Dangerous Liaisons*, 655. Ariela Gross has cautioned against taking too much stock in "statutes and appellate opinions as evidence of social beliefs about race—for example, 'one-drop-of-blood' rules of racial identification as evidence of the growing power of biological racism—[she] found that the legal rule articulated by statute or high court often made little difference at the local level. Ancestry rules did not usually decide actual cases." Ariela Gross, "Beyond Black and White: Cultural Approaches to Race and Slavery," *Columbia Law Review* 101 (Apr. 2001), 654.

19. For works devoted to the various modes of black activism during the eighteenth century, see, e.g., Benjamin Quarles, *The Negro in the American Revolution* (Chapel Hill, 1961); Robert Colley, *Slavery and Jeffersonian Virginia* (Urbana 1973); Sidney Kaplan and Nogrady Kaplan, *The Black Presence in the Era of the American Revolution*, rev. ed. (Amherst, Mass., 1989); Sylvia R. Frey, *Water from the Rock: Black Resistance in a Revolutionary Age* (Princeton, 1991); Woody Holton, *Forced Founders: Indians, Debtors, and the Making of the American Revolution in Virginia* (Chapel Hill, 1999).

20. Gomez, *Exchanging Our Country Marks*, 220.

21. Gordon-Reed, *TJ and SH*, 245, 246. Hemings's seeming pride that his grandmother was a full-blooded African was not unusual. Michael Gomez endorses John W. Blassingame's findings on how many enslaved men and women viewed Africans with respect. See Gomez, *Exchanging Our Country Marks*, 191, 236, referencing Blassingame's *The Slave Community: Plantation Life in the Antebellum South* (New York, 1972), 39–42.

22. Gomez, *Exchanging Our Country Marks*, 235–36.

23. Stanton and Wright, "Bonds of Memory," 178.

24. Stevenson, *Life in Black and White*, 222. Although Stevenson's book centers on slavery in one county in Virginia, it can be seen as a corrective to the notion that a female-headed household is necessarily a dysfunctional one. Because the legacies of slavery are still with us, there has been much discussion about whether current-day dissolution of black family life can be attributed to blacks' experiences during slavery. The famous Moynihan report fingered the black "matriarchy," with its purported roots in slavery, as the source of problems in the black community. Herbert Gutman's important work *The Black Family in Slavery and Freedom, 1750–1925* (New York, 1976), a direct response to the Moynihan report, suggested that enslaved people more often lived in nuclear families than was thought. Subsequent work, including Stevenson's, suggests that perhaps Gutman went too far in the opposite direction from Moynihan and understated the effect that the sales of slaves had on the lives of enslaved families.

25. See, e.g., *Farm Book*, 28.

26. TJ to Jared Sparks, Feb. 4, 1824, in *Writings*, 1486–87.

27. None of this is unique to our age. Throughout his life, Jefferson, with the utmost sincerity (who knew more than he about the perils of debt), advised against spending more money than one had. Yet he did that to the very end of his days. The last letter he ever

wrote was not the one famously thought to be his final one—the very eloquent and stirring missive to Roger C. Weightman in which he had to decline, owing to his poor health, an invitation to participate in the fiftieth anniversary of the signing of the Declaration of Independence. His last letter was an inquiry about a shipment of expensive wine that he had ordered, even as he faced financial ruin and the loss of his beloved Monticello. He was absolutely right to have ordered the wine, since he was not going to save Monticello by doing without it. There was no point in suffering more than he already was, the time to have listened to himself having long since passed. If he had lived the preceding forty years not spending money that he did not have, or lending money to others that he did not have, the troubles of his old age would have been greatly lessened. TJ to Roger Weightman, June 24, 1826, in *Writings*, 1516–17; J. Jefferson Looney, "Thomas Jefferson's Last Letter," *VMHB* 112 (2004): 178.

28. TJ to John Banister Jr., Oct. 15, 1785, *Papers*, 8:636.

29. Gordon-Reed, *TJ and SH*, 252.

30. White, *Ar'n't I a Woman?*, 40–43.

31. C. Vann Woodward, ed., *Mary Chesnut's Civil War* (New Haven, 1981), quoted ibid., 40–41.

32. Lucia Stanton, "The Other End of the Telescope: Jefferson through the Eyes of His Slaves," *WMQ* 3d ser., 57 (2000): 146.

33. See above, chap. 12.

34. Peabody, *"There Are No Slaves,"* 101–3. *Howell v. Netherland*, 1770 Va. Lexis 1; Jeff. 90 (April 1770). See also Annette Gordon-Reed, "Logic and Experience: Slavery, Race and Thomas Jefferson's Life in the Law," in *Slavery and the American South: Essays and Commentaries*, ed. Winthrop Jordan (Jackson, Miss., 2003).

35. There is, of course, extensive literature on enslaved people who succeeded in liberating themselves from their enslavement, or attempted to do so. That literature makes clear that these individuals ran whether there was a chance, let alone a guarantee, that life outside of slavery was going to be a certain way. See, e.g., *Runaway Slave Advertisements: A Documentary History from the 1730s to 1790*, ed. Lathan A. Windley, 4 vols. (Westport, Conn., 1993); Morgan, *Slave Counterpoint*, 696; Peter H. Wood, *Black Majority: Negroes in Colonial South Carolina from 1670 through the Stono Rebellion* (New York, 1974), 239. Washington University in St. Louis maintains an online database of hundreds of freedom suits through the St. Louis Circuit Court Historical Records Project at http://stl courtrecords.wustl.edu.

36. James Hemings's inventory, see photograph in the first insert.

37. Pierre Boulle, "Les Gens de couleur à Paris à la veille de la Révolution," 1:160–61.

38. Jennifer Heuer, "The One Drop Rule in Reverse?: Interracial Marriages in Napoleonic and Restoration France," forthcoming article.

39. One of the more popular novels of early nineteenth-century France was *Ourika*, based on the true story of a young woman from Senegal who is taken in by a French family. *Ourika* seeks to move above her station, and the novel recounts her struggle in Paris. Claire de Duras, *Ourika: An English Translation*, trans. John Fowles (New York, 1994).

40. Wister and Irwin, *Worthy Women of Our First Century*, 20–22.

41. Robert Darnton, "What Was Revolutionary about French Revolution?," quoted in David Brion Davis, "American Equality and Foreign Revolutions," *Journal of American History* 76 (Dec. 1989): 735.

17: "The Treaty" and "Did They Love Each Other?"

1. For the past decade, I have traveled the country, speaking about Hemings and Jefferson. I do not recall a setting where this question was not asked explicitly or implicitly.

2. Gordon-Reed, *TJ and SH*, 246.

3. The question whether historians should focus on the hegemony of the slaveholding class—the power they exercised over slaves and the larger society—or examples of the agency that enslaved people exhibited in the face of that attempted hegemony is part of a continuing conversation among those who write about slavery. See Ariela Gross, "Beyond Black and White," 664, referring to the "circularity of the 'hegemony v. resistance' debates that have sometimes dominated slavery studies."

4. Gordon-Reed, *TJ and SH*, 166–69, discussing "Mammy love."

5. W. Blackstone's *Commentaries on the Laws of England*, vol. 1 (Oxford, 1765), chap. 15.

6. Hendrik Hartog, *Man and Wife in America: A History* (Cambridge, Mass., 2002), 2–3, 23–24, on law's shaping of the meaning of marriage.

7. See above, chap. 3, on the marriage settlement of John Wayles and Martha Eppes. See also "Marriage Settlement for Martha Jefferson," *Papers*, 16:189.

8. See Hodding Carter, "Mrs. Means Married Women," from *Where Main Street Meets the River* (1953), reprinted in *Reporting Civil Rights: American Journalism, 1941–1973* (New York, 2003), 134–40. Carter describes a meeting with a "Negro woman" who came into his office to complain because the *Democrat-Times* refused to refer to married black women as "Mrs.," "instead giving their unadorned names, as Lucy Jones and Mary Smith" and "listing only the initials of their husbands as if their first names could not be learned." Carter wrote, "I might have brushed her aside with the usual comment that this was the established policy of the paper and of most Southern papers from time immemorial. Or I might have evaded the issue by saying that I would like time to think about it since if I complied, I would be violating one of the longest lasting of deep Southern taboos."

9. From Mrs. Drummond, March 12, 1771, *Papers*, 1:65–66; TJ to T. Adams, June 1, 1771, ibid., 71–72.

10. Sarah N. Randolph, *The Domestic Life of Thomas Jefferson*, 25–26; Gordon-Reed, *TJ and SH*, 245.

11. For a discussion of the implications of the Married Women's Property Acts, see Norma Basch, *In the Eyes of the Law: Women, Marriage, and Property in Nineteenth-Century New York* (Ithaca, N.Y., 1982). Basch and other historians have emphasized the limited nature of the reforms—they were not meant to completely overthrow traditional notions about marriage and the relationship between husbands and wives. Though a given law may have limited application, it may also carry a powerful symbolic message that shapes the attitudes of the public. See also Lawrence Friedman, *A History of American Law* (New York, 1985), 209–11, 295–96.

12. Sloan, *Principle and Interest*, 15–16; *Papers*, 1:100, 103.

13. See Gross, "Beyond Black and White," 649.

14. Gordon-Reed, *TJ and SH*, 246.

15. White, *Ar'n't I a Woman?*, 7–8, 76–77; Stevenson, *Life in Black and White*, 236–37.

16. Sharon Block, *Rape and Sexual Power in Early America* (Chapel Hill, 2006), 67–74.

17. TJ to Maria Jefferson, May 25, 1797, *Papers*, 29:399.

18. TJ to William Evans, Feb. 22, 1801, *Papers*, 33:38.

19. Morgan, *Slave Counterpoint*, 548–49.

20. Francis Say to TJ, Feb. 23, 1801, *Papers*, 33:53.

21. Rhys Isaac, "Monticello Stories," 119.

22. John Quincy Adams, "The Character of Desdemona," in Hackett, *Notes and Comments upon Certain Plays and Actors of Shakespeare*, 235.

23. Ibid., 237, 247–48. It is not uncommon today to hear interracial couples described, jokingly some might say, as having a malady: "jungle fever." But, of course, humor is often used as a soft way to communicate a hard message. Americans clearly prefer to characterize the attraction between black and white couples, as opposed to the attraction between intraracial couples, as an inherently more degraded—or less serious—form of love.

24. Ibid., 247.

25. TJ to Jean Nicholas Demeunier, June 26, 1786, *Papers*, 10:63.

26. Holly Brewer, *By Birth or Consent: Children, Law, and the Anglo-American Revolution in Authority* (Chapel Hill, 2005), 325–26.

27. Clare A. Lyons, *Sex among the Rabble: An Intimate History of Gender and Power in the Age of Revolution, Philadelphia, 1730–1830* (Chapel Hill, 2006), 353.

28. Hamilton W. Pierson, *In the Brush; or, Old-Time Social, Political, and Religious Life in the Southwest* (New York, 1881).

29. See Bernie D. Jones, "'Righteous Fathers,' 'Vulnerable Old Men,' and 'Degraded Creatures': Southern Justices on Miscegenation in the Antebellum Will Contest," 40 *Tulsa Law Review* 40 (2005): 699–750; Adrienne D. Davis, "The Private Law of Race and Sex: An Antebellum Perspective," *Stanford Law Review* 51 (Jan. 1999): 221–88.

30. Randolph, *Domestic Life*, 25–26. See, generally, Gordon-Reed, *TJ and SH*, "DNA: The Author's Response."

31. Fawn Brodie, "Thomas Jefferson's Unknown Grandchildren," 176.

32. Gordon-Reed, *TJ and SH*, 196–201.

33. Ibid., 170–71.

34. Ibid., 100–102, 216.

35. Nellie Jones to Stuart Gibboney, July 29, 1938, Aug. 10, 1938; Stuart Gibboney to Nellie Jones, Aug. 1, 1938, Nov. 1, 1938, correspondence in the University of Virginia Library, Accession No. 6636-a-b, Box No. Control Folder, Folder Dates 1735–1961. Nellie Jones was Madison Hemings's granddaughter. She wrote to Gibboney, the then president of the Thomas Jefferson Memorial Foundation, offering to donate mementos that her great-grandmother Sally Hemings had saved and given to their son: a pair of his glasses, an inkwell, and a silver buckle. Gibboney referred the matter to Fiske Kimball, then "Chairman of the Restoration Committee." Kimball wrote to Gibboney on Oct. 28, 1938, "Nellie Jones: This very resptctable [*sic*] colored woman writes a letter much more intelligently than members of our own race. Her story was very straight (except that I was not aware that Jefferson took any slave to France—but that's not the crucial point. [*Oh, but it was!*] I see no harm in letting her send on the things, for inspection as she is willing to do. It might be that the buckle is identical with one of the buckles we have, which would thus authenticate the whole lot. As to purchasing them, and fixing a price, we really have *quite enough of these little mementoes* so that it would be indifferent whether we bought any more" (emphasis added). On the strength of that analysis Gibboney wrote to Jones,

saying, "Under the circumstances, therefore, we will not be interested in buying these relics, but we will keep your letters in our file in case we hear of someone who would be interested in acquiring them, should you not dispose of them yourself in the meantime." It is not clear what the state of affairs was in 1938 with respect to "relics," but it is hard to imagine that the museum devoted to TJ's life could really have had too many pairs of his eyeglasses lying around.

36. Burstein, *The Inner Jefferson*, 61–62.

18: **The Return**

1. Colin Jones, *Paris: The Biography of a City* (New York, 2005); Alistair Horne, *Seven Ages of Paris* (New York, 2002), 155; David Garrioch, *The Making of Revolutionary Paris* (Berkeley, Calif., 2002), 45; Malone, *Jefferson*, 2:205–6.

2. *MB*, 723 n. 31; Malone, *Jefferson*, 2:206.

3. In a postscript to that same letter written on Dec. 15 that he was unable to send until Jan. 11, because of lack of a "conveiance," he reported (no doubt after receiving his new thermometers) that the temperature had dropped to "9 ½ degrees below zero." TJ to Francis Eppes, Dec. 15, 1788, *Papers*, 14:358.

4. Horne, *Seven Ages of Paris*, 155–56. See William Doyle, *Origins*, 168, suggesting that "as many as 30,000 more immigrants than usual may have been present in Paris as a result of the economic crisis." See also Doyle's chap. 12, outlining the state of affairs in 1788–89 in Paris.

5. TJ to Andre Limozin, May 3, 1789, *Papers*, 15:86; William Short to TJ, Oct. 8, 1789, ibid., 511; Thomas Carlyle, *The French Revolution*, 212; Georges Lefebvre, *The Coming of the French Revolution*, 199–205.

6. TJ to Lucy Paradise, Sept. 10, 1789, *Papers*, 15:412; TJ to Thomas Paine, Sept. 13, 1789, ibid., 424.

7. William Short to John Hartwell Cocke, Aug. 12, 1826, Cocke Papers, University of Virginia, quoted in "Thomas Jefferson and William Short," at Monticello.org.

8. TJ to Montmorin, July 8, 1789, *Papers*, 15:260.

9. John Jay to TJ, June 19, 1789, *Papers*, 15:202. TJ's SJL lists the letter as having been received on Aug. 23.

10. Brodie, *Thomas Jefferson*, 243; *MB*, 247; TJ to John Trumbull, Sept. 9, 1789, *Papers*, 15:407.

11. *MB*, 247.

12. See, e.g., Brodie, *Thomas Jefferson*, 43, 114–16. For a discussion of TJ's health problems in later years, see Andrew Burstein, *Jefferson's Secret Death and Desire at Monticello* (New York, 2005), The relationship between TJ's physical illnesses and stress was not strictly a psychological matter. Modern scientists have noted, and are still attempting to understand more clearly, the role that stress plays in compromising the human immune system, making certain people more prone to illness during times of emotional upheaval.

13. Gordon-Reed, *TJ and SH*, 246.

14. Herbert E. Sloan, *Principle and Interest: Thomas Jefferson and the Problem of Debt* (New York, 1995), 13–14.

15. James Madison to TJ, May 27, 1789, *Papers*, 15:153; TJ to James Madison, Aug. 29, 1789,

ibid., 369; TJ to James Madison, Jan. 9, 1790, ibid., 16:92–93 ("I expect with anxiety the President's ultimate determination as to what is to be done with me. I cannot bring myself to be indifferent to the change of destination, tho' I will be passive under it"); Malone, *Jefferson*, 2:248–49.

16. TJ, *Autobiography*, in *Writings*, 98.

17. TJ to Joseph Delaplaine, April 12, 1817, LOC, 37369.

18. TJ to James Maurice, Sept. 16, 1789, *Papers*, 15:433.

19. *MB*, 743–47.

20. Ibid.

21. Jared Sparks, *The Life of Benjamin Franklin, containing the Autobiography, with Notes and a Continuation* (Boston, 1848), 509.

22. "Extract from the Diary of Nathaniel Cutting at Le Havre and Cowes," *Papers*, 15:490, 494

23. *MB*, 745.

24. TJ to William Short, Oct. 7, 1789, *Papers*, 15:509; "Extract from the Diary of Nathaniel Cutting," ibid., 495.

25. TJ to William Short, Oct. 7, 1789, *Papers*, 15:509.

26. TJ to Madame de Corny, Oct. 14, 1789, *Papers*, 15:520; *MB*, 745.

27. TJ to Madame de Corny, Oct. 14, 1789, *Papers*, 15:520.

28. *MB*, 747; John Trumbull to TJ, Sept. 22, 1789, *Papers*, 15:468.

29. *MB*, 555. In addition to keeping a daily log of the latitude, longitude, distance traveled, temperature, and wind direction, TJ noted sightings of sea creatures observed each day.

30. TJ to William Short, Oct. 23, 1789, *Papers*, 15:527; *MB*, 747; TJ to Nathaniel Cutting, Nov. 21, 1789, ibid., 551–52; *MB*, 747; Martha Jefferson Randolph's reminiscences, *Papers*, 15:560–61.

31. TJ to William Short, Oct. 4, 1789, *Papers*, 15:506; "List of Baggage Shipped by Jefferson from France" [ca. Sept. 1, 1789], ibid., 375–77. See also Stein, *The World of Thomas Jefferson*.

32. TJ to John Trumbull, Nov. 25, 1789, *Papers*, 15:560; Martha Randolph Jefferson reminiscences, ibid., 560.

33. "Address of Welcome of the Officials of Norfolk," Nov. 25, 1789; "Jefferson's Reply to the Foregoing Address of Welcome," Nov. 25, 1789, *Papers*, 15:556, 556–67.

34. Martha Randolph Jefferson's reminiscences, ibid., 560–61; *MB*, 748, 748–49.

35. William L. Shirer, *Love and Hatred: The Tormented Marriage of Leo and Sonya Tolstoy* (New York, 1994).

36. Brodie, *Thomas Jefferson*, 248.

19: Hello and Goodbye

1. *Farm Book*, 24; *MB*, 749.

2. Gordon-Reed, *TJ and SH*, 254.

3. Henry S. Randall, *The Life of Thomas Jefferson*, 3 vols. (1858; reprint, New York, 1972), 1:552, Martha J. Randolph on the homecoming; Wormley Hughes on the homecoming, ibid., 552–53.

4. TJ to Nicholas Lewis, Dec. 16, 1788, *Papers*, 14:362.

5. Randall, *Life*, 1:552, 553.

6. Ibid., 553. See also Stanton, "The Other End of the Telescope," 56 (2000): 139–52, 150–51. Stanton, who with Dianne Swann Wright has collected a multitude of family stories from the descendants of people who were enslaved at Monticello, as well as some stories from TJ's white descendants, has found that the story of TJ's return has survived for two hundred years among black and white families, who interpret the meaning of the recollection differently. TJ's white descendants tell it as an example of the extreme loyalty of slaves. The descendants of slaves tell it as a story that illustrates TJ's dependence upon their family members.

7. Randall, *Life*, 552.

8. Stanton, *Free Some Day*, 133–36, 143–44.

9. Malone, *Jefferson*, 2:253.

10. TJ to Randolph Jefferson, Jan. 11, 1789, *Papers*, 14:433–34.

11. See Morris, *Southern Slavery and the Law*, 347–48, discussing the southern attitude about teaching slaves to read, noting that "half of the slave states did not prohibit teaching slaves to read and write." Virginia, for example, never made it completely against the law to teach slaves to read. Unlawful assembly laws were directed chiefly at stopping the creation of schools for blacks. Whites were interested primarily in black labor and rarely had the incentive to teach blacks to read. Those blacks who did learn often taught others.

12. See *Papers*, 28:223, listing the dates the letters were written and the dates they were received as recorded in the SJL.

13. Gordon-Reed, *TJ and SH*, 139–40, 149.

14. First page of James Hemings's inventory of kitchen utensils (in the first insert).

15. Gordon-Reed, *TJ and SH*, 247.

16. "Life among the Lowly," *Pike County (Ohio) Republican*, March 13, 1873.

17. See Hemings family tree in this book; Lucia Stanton, "Monticello to Main Street, 123.

18. TJ to William Short, Dec. 14, 1789, *Papers*, 16:26; "Address of Welcome by the Citizens of Albemarle and Jefferson's Response," Feb. 12, 1790, *Papers*, 16:177.

19. *MB*, 749.

20. Thomas Bell to TJ, June 12, 1797, *Papers*, 29:427; Stanton, "Monticello to Main Street," 123 (although Bell's grandson's recollections refer to visits that would have taken place after Bell's death, it is apparent from the tenor of the two men's letters, and the fact that Bell's store was attached to his home, that TJ visited Bell's home in the 1790s as well); TJ to Thomas Bell, March 16, 1792, *Papers*, 20:758–59; TJ to Archibald Stuart, Dec. 2, 1794, ibid., 28:214; TJ to Thomas Mann Randolph, Aug. 20, 1795, ibid., 28:214, 439; James Madison to TJ, Dec. 25, 1797, ibid., 29:591.

21. Stanton, "Monticello to Main Street." 100.

22. See, generally, Joshua Rothman, *Notorious in the Neighborhood*, on the attitudes in TJ's immediate community about interracial relations.

23. Robinson, *Dangerous Liaisons*, 101.

24. TJ to Francis C. Gray, March 4, 1815, LOC, 36173.

25. See Edgar Woods, *Albemarle County in Virginia* (1901; reprint, Berryville, Va, 1984), 276, listing Bell as a magistrate, one of the "County Officers" in 1791. In 1794 he was part of a commission to "study how to reinstate" records that were lost owing to the "wanton ravages of the British troops near the close of the Revolutionary War" (p. 25). The following year Bell was chosen with, among others, Wilson Cary Nicholas, to study the question of

public education. Other jurisdictions were hesitant even to talk about it, because it would require raising taxes. The matter died a quick death. Ironically, in 1849 the issue arose again, and Thomas Jefferson Randolph was one of the leading opponents of bringing public education to Charlottesville, which put him on the opposite side of Dr. William H. McGuffey, a professor at the University of Virginia, which Randolph's grandfather, of course, had founded (p. 90).

26. Stanton, "Monticello to Main Street," 100; Gordon-Reed, *TJ and SH*, 138.
27. TJ to William Short, Dec. 14, 1789, *Papers*, 16:26.
28. TJ to Elizabeth Eppes, July 25, 1790, *Papers*, 17:266.
29. Stephanie M. H. Camp, *Closer to Freedom*, 36–37; Morgan, *Slave Counterpoint*, 542.
30. Camp, *Closer to Freedom*, 37.

<h3 align="center">20: Equilibrium</h3>

1. TJ to George Washington, Dec. 15, 1789, *Papers*, 16:34–35; TJ to James Madison, Jan. 9, 1790, ibid., 92–93; George Washington to TJ, Jan. 21, 1790, ibid., 116–18; TJ to George Washington, Feb. 14, 1790, ibid., 16:184.
2. Thomas Mann Randolph Sr. to TJ, Jan. 30, 1790, *Papers*, 16:135 (TJ received the letter on Feb. 4); TJ to Thomas Mann Randolph, Feb. 4, 1790, ibid., 16:154–55.
3. See Malone, *Jefferson*, 1:19–20, on the early relations between the Jeffersons and Thomas Mann Randolph Sr., and 2:250–53, on the marriage of Martha Jefferson and Randolph Jr.
4. See, e.g., Thomas Mann Randolph Jr. to TJ, Aug. 16, 1786, *Papers*, 10:260–61; TJ to Thomas Mann Randolph Jr., Aug. 27, 1786, ibid., 205–9.
5. Randall, *Life*, 1:558.
6. Randolph, *Domestic Life*, 138–39.
7. TJ to Thomas Mann Randolph, Feb. 28, 1788, *Papers*, 14:367–68 n. Julian Boyd effectively sorted out the question whether the couple met in Paris in 1788. His conclusion that they did not is persuasive. Additional evidence that the couple did not meet and fall in love in France is that after her father announced that he was taking a leave of absence, Patsy Jefferson spoke to friends about her wish to stay in France during her father's leave of absence. *MB*, 730 n. 47.
8. Jack McLaughlin, *Jefferson and Monticello* (New York, 1988), 241–42.
9. Dolley Payne Todd Madison to Anna Payne Cutts, Aug. 28, [1808], University of Virginia Press, 2004, http://rotunda.upress.virginia.edu/dmde/DPM0178. See, e.g., Martha Jefferson Randolph to Ann Cary Randolph Morris, Jan. 24, 1828, Family Letters Project, stating "that poor Jefferson [her son] is about to have another addition to his family is merely the usual annual occurrence."
10. Thomas Jefferson Randolph to Dabney S. Carr, July 11, 1826, Carr-Cary Papers, quoted in Lewis, "The White Jeffersons," *Sally Hemings and Thomas Jefferson: History, Memory, and Civic Culture*, ed. Jan Ellen Lewis and Peter S. Onuf (Charlottesville, 1999), 134. Jefferson's overseer Edmund Bacon remembered the incident when Randolph hit his son-in-law in the head with an iron poker after he mistook him for a slave in the failing light of dusk one evening. Pierson, *Jefferson at Monticello*, 99.
11. Pierson, *Jefferson at Monticello*, 99.
12. Thomas Jefferson Randolph, "The Last Days of Jefferson," Special Collections, ViU.

13. William H. Gaines, *Thomas Mann Randolph, Jefferson's Son-In-Law* (Baton Rouge 1966), 32–34.

14. Cynthia A. Kierner, *Scandal at Bizarre*, 38–39.

15. Pierson, *Jefferson at Monticello*, 99–100.

16. Gaines, *Thomas Mann Randolph*, 106–7.

17. Thomas Jefferson Randolph, "Last Days of Jefferson," Special Collections, ViU.

18. Elizabeth Trist to Nicholas Trist, Feb. 13, 1819, Family Letters Project.

19. Ellen Coolidge to Henry S. Randall, March 13, 1856, Coolidge Letter Book, Special Collections, University of Virginia.

20. TJ to Wilson Cary Nicholas, March 8, 1819, LOC, 38312.

21. Gaines, *Thomas Mann Randolph*, 39; Malone, *Jefferson*, 3:175.

22. TJ to Martha Randolph, April 4, 1790, *Papers*, 16:300.

23. Kierner, *Scandal at Bizarre*, 22.

24. Thomas Mann Randolph to TJ, May 25, 1790, *Papers*, 16:441. Randolph describes the bad state of affairs at Varina. "We have 2 small houses with 2 rooms in each, which might have been rendered very commodious, had they not been situated at a distance from each other." He makes clear that the home was unsuitable and the couple wished to move elsewhere as soon as possible. The excessive heat was making him ill.

25. Susan Kern, "The Material World of the Jeffersons at Shadwell," *WMQ*, 3d ser., 62, no. 2 (2005), at http://www.historycooperative.org/journals/wm/62.2/kern.html; Kierner, *Scandal at Bizarre*, 19–20. See also Philip Hamilton, *The Making and Unmaking of a Revolutionary Family: The Tuckers of Virginia, 1752–1830* (Charlottesville, 2003), 100, discussing how Thomas Mann Randolph's daughter took the cue from her parents about the importance of a "glittering lifestyle . . . to their reputation." See Martha Jefferson Carr to TJ, Dec. 3, 1787, *Papers*, 15:640, noting the death of Archibald Cary and the dire financial straits in which he had left his family.

26. Stanton, *Free Some Day*, 124.

27. Marriage settlement for Martha Jefferson, *Papers*, 15:189–91.

28. TJ to Elizabeth Wayles, July 25, 1790, *Papers*, 17:266; Thomas Mann Randolph to TJ, May 25, 1790, ibid., 16:441, in which Randolph tells his father-in-law that his Martha was staying at Eppington while he prepared "for her coming to Varina."

29. TJ to Elizabeth Wayles, July 25, 1790, *Papers*, 17:266. The SJL notes that TJ received Martha's letter on July 2. He did not get the letter from his sister-in-law until July 8, as he notes in the body of his reply to her.

30. See Stanton, *Slavery at Monticello*, at 16, reproducing a copy of a missing page from Jefferson's Farm Book.

31. See Martha Jefferson Randolph to Anne Cary Randolph Morris, Jan. 22, 1826, referring to Molly Warren as one of her long time house servants. Family Letters Project.

32. TJ to William Short, July 1, 1790, *Papers*, 16:588–90.

33. TJ to Elizabeth Eppes, July 25, 1790, *Papers*, 17:266; Elizabeth Eppes to TJ, Aug. 11, 1790, ibid., 331; TJ to Elizabeth Wayles Eppes, Oct. 31, 1790, ibid., 658. Jefferson was unable to realize his plan to have his younger daughter join him in Philadelphia during the summer of 1791, and Maria did not make it to the city until the fall of that year. *MB*, 836–37.

34. Marriage settlement for Mary Jefferson, *Papers*, 29:549–50.

35. Ibid., 550.

36. Thomas Mann Randolph to TJ, April 23, 1790, *Papers*, 16:370; Martha Randolph to TJ, April 25, 1790, ibid., 384.

37. Elizabeth Eppes to TJ, May 23, 1790, *Papers*, 6:209 n.

38. Mary Jefferson to Thomas Mann Randolph, Oct. 1790 [?], LOC, 11992. Mary Jefferson's letter to Randolph is undated. The estimated date appended to the top appears to be incorrect. Jefferson indicated that his family had arrived at Monticello on Sept. 22, 1790. TJ to James Madison, Sept. 23, 1790, *Papers*, 17:512 n. There would have been no reason to write to her brother-in-law in Oct., because they were together at Monticello. On Anne Skipwith's illness, see Mary Jefferson to TJ, July 20, 1790, *Papers*, 17:239; Elizabeth Eppes to TJ, Aug. 11, 1790, ibid., 331.

39. TJ wrote to Thomas Mann Randolph Sr. in July about the situation at Varina, hoping that they could "arrange together a matter which our children have at heart. I find it is the strong wish of both to settle in Albemarle. They both consider Varina too unhealthy, a consideration too important, nor to overbear every other." TJ to Thomas Mann Randolph, July 25, 1790, *Papers*, 17:274.

40. TJ to Martha Randolph, Aug. 8, 1790, *Papers*, 17:327.

41. TJ to Martha Randolph, July 17, 1790; TJ to Mary Jefferson, July 25, 1790; TJ to Thomas Mann Randolph, July 25, 1790, *Papers*, 17:327, 214, 275.

42. Malone, *Jefferson*, 2:252–53. See also TJ to Martha Jefferson Randolph, April 26, 1790, *Papers*, 16:386–87. He did speak with Randolph about the property. Thomas Mann Randolph, Jr. to TJ, Nov. 11, 1790, ibid., 18:43.

43. Gaines, *Thomas Mann Randolph*, 32. In a letter dated July 17, 1790, TJ makes clear that Martha and Gabriella Randolph knew each other: "Former acquaintance, and equality of age, will render it easier for you to cultivate and gain the love of the lady." *Papers*, 17:215. TJ's completely tone deaf comment provides a very telling insight into his worldview and, probably, that of other men of his time. He seemed to believe that because Martha and Gabriella were the same age and knew each other, it would make it easier for them to get along, when in fact the whole situation was always very likely to do the opposite. He could not have been looking at the matter from his daughter's perspective. By Jefferson's logic, Harvie and the sisters of Martha's husband should have gotten along famously. Instead, from the very beginning, they entered into a female version of a metaphorical duel to the death, which Harvie ultimately won. Many years after her victory, when Nancy Randolph, whom she had driven away from Tuckahoe, fell on hard times and scandal, a then remarried Harvie teamed up with Nancy's longtime tormentor, John Randolph, to try to completely destroy her former "step daughter's" reputation. Kierner, *Scandal at Bizarre*, 114–15. What TJ evidently did not see (or chose to ignore) was that Gabriella's marriage to Martha's father-in-law confused expectations among these young people (Thomas and his sisters included), both economically and psychologically. It put Gabriella in control of this age cohort's fortunes and patrimony. The quickness of the courtship and marriage after the death of the Randolph children's mother, and the two family's physical proximity to one another, no doubt raised uncomfortable questions about just when the elder Randolph first started thinking about Gabriella.

44. Kierner, *Scandal at Bizarre*, 29.

45. TJ to Martha Jefferson Randolph, July 17, 1790, *Papers*, 17:215.
46. George Green Shackelford, "Mr. Jefferson's Grandchildren," *Magazine of Albemarle County History* 33/34 (1975–76): 163–72, at 171.
47. Kierner, *Scandal at Bizarre*, 29.
48. Ibid., 29–30.
49. Gordon-Reed, *TJ and SH*, 198–99, on Harriet Randolph.
50. Pierson, *Jefferson at Monticello*, 110. Edmund Bacon described Harriet Hemings as having been "very beautiful."
51. Malone, *Jefferson*, 2:320; TJ to Nicholas Lewis, [ca. Nov. 7, 1790], *Papers*, 18:29.
52. Gordon-Reed, *TJ and SH*, 246. The oral history of the very numerous and prominent members of the Woodson family maintains that the child Hemings bore in 1790 did not die, as Madison Hemings said. They believe their ancestor Thomas Woodson was that child and that he was sent away from Monticello in 1802, after the public exposure of TJ's liaison with SH. My own analysis of the matter (ibid., 67–77) tended to support Madison Hemings's version of his family's story: SH had a child in 1790, but that child did not live. There are no records of a child named Thomas linked to SH in TJ's Farm Book, even in the years before SH and TJ's relationship was exposed to the public. TJ was not keeping the Farm Book between 1790 and 1794, which explains why there was no record of a birth to SH in 1790. Once he resumed making notations in the Farm Book—again well before Callender's exposé and when he thought he had retired from public life—he listed the names and birthdates of all of SH's children except an unnamed daughter who did not survive infancy. That child was mentioned in a letter to his son-in-law in 1799. Other Jefferson documents are revealing, as discussed in note 15 to chap. 10. Jefferson began his program of vaccinations against smallpox at Monticello in 1801. He kept a separate record, apart from the Farm Book, detailing his progress. Unlike today, with our modern storage capacity, the timing of vaccinations on the mountain depended upon the availability of the cowpox virus. Jefferson vaccinated his children Beverley and Harriet in 1802, and Madison and Eston in 1816. All four are listed as children of Sally Hemings. There is no Hemings child named Tom on the list, as he certainly would have been had he existed. Again, these vaccinations began well before Callender ever wrote about a child named Tom at Monticello. The DNA testing conducted on the Hemings, Jefferson, Carr, and Woodson descendants in 1998 found a connection between the Hemings family member and the Jeffersons tested, no connection between the Hemings family and the Carrs, and no connection between the Woodsons and any of the other families who were tested. The *Nature* article announcing the results of the DNA test needlessly confused the issue by giving the impression that it was absolutely clear that SH bore a child in 1790 who grew up to become Thomas Woodson. The article completely ignored both Madison Hemings's statement that his older sibling had died as an infant, and the fact that TJ's records contain no mention of a child named Thomas who belonged to SH. That is why there was no DNA match. The supreme, and very telling, irony is that the article accepted SH's maternity of a child with no scientific or contemporary documentary evidence from Monticello, or known members of her family, supporting the idea that she had a child named Thomas Woodson. That notion was put forth in the midst of a study that was done because the mountain of contemporary evidence supporting TJ's paternity of SH's children was deemed insufficient—only scientific corroboration of his paternity would be good enough.

"Irony" is perhaps not the word to use to describe how this matter unfolded. It is, in fact, perfectly in keeping with past and present racial hierarchies for blacks' stories to be accepted when they affect only other black people, but to treat their stories with super, super skepticism when they say things about white people that other whites find to be problematic. Thus, blacks can say who their black ancestors were and be "believed" on their word alone. Their statements about their white ancestry have to be backed up by scientific proof or support from the white ancestor or that ancestor's other white family members. Even before the DNA analysis, the weight of the evidence was against the idea that SH had a son born in 1790 who lived long enough to have descendants whose DNA could be tested in 1998. With that as the backdrop, the DNA results were not at all a surprise to me. At the same time, it seems clear that the Woodson family is connected to the Hemingses. The story is too strong, and from too many disparate sources—people who did not even know each other—for there not to be some connection. The only question that remains is exactly what that connection is.

53. Gordon-Reed, *TJ and SH*, 73–74.

54. Ellen Randolph Coolidge to Joseph Coolidge, Oct. 14, 1858, Family Letters Project.

55. Nell Irvin Painter, *Southern History across the Color Line* (Chapel Hill, 2002), 82. Sorting through all this is a difficult, but necessary, task. In that same work Painter writes of the skill with which "Aristocrats" (still speaking in the context of southern slavery) kept secrets and notes how extremely devoted they were to keeping up appearances. All too often, Painter argues, historians have accepted the well-constructed and controlled images contained in the documents created by elite families. Troublesome sexual behavior, alcoholism, family violence, incest, and mental illness that remain hidden in these pages, or only obliquely referred to, surface in oral histories or the comments of persons less close to the situation and, in a few cases, court records. It is the difficult task of historians to "examine sources more critically" and to "transcend complete reliance on the written record" (pp. 37–38).

56. Ellen Randolph to Martha Randolph, Sept. 13, 1820, Family Letters Project.

57. Maria J. Eppes to TJ, April 21, 1802, *The Family Letters of Thomas Jefferson*, ed. Edwin M. Betts and James A. Bear Jr. (1966; reprint, Columbia, Mo., 1986), 224.

21: The Brothers

1. *MB*, 750, 752, 753; TJ to Thomas Mann Randolph, March 28, 1790, *Papers*, 16:277–78; Campbell, "Life of Isaac Jefferson," 568.

2. TJ to Thomas Mann Randolph, March 28, 1790, *Papers*, 16:277–78.

3. *MB*, 753 (Jefferson purchased only two tickets to Baltimore), 754 ("gave Bob exp. To Philada").

4. *MB*, 754 n. 17.

5. Malone, *Jefferson*, 2:9.

6. Morris, *Southern Slavery and the Law*, 338–39.

7. See chap. 7.

8. Sara S. Hughes, "Slaves for Hire: The Allocation of Black Labor in Elizabeth City County, Virginia, 1782–1810," *WMQ*, 3d ser., 35 (1978): 260–86; Morris, *Southern Slavery and the Law*, 339.

9. Frederick Douglass, *Narrative of the Life of Frederick Douglass, an American Slave, Written by Himself* (1845; reprint, Whitefish, Mont., 2004), 69.

10. Philip D. Morgan, *Slave Counterpoint*, 284–96. A lively debate has taken place about the nature of paternalism—whether it truly existed and how and whether it matters if it did. There is more of a consensus that the nature of the relations between slaves and masters changed over time and that before the America Revolution slaveholders tended to be unsentimental patriarchs who understood that they were dealing with a hostile labor force, rather than sentimental paternalists who, having decided to accommodate themselves to slavery, sought to justify it by styling themselves as "benevolent" fathers to enslaved men, women, and children. For exemplars of differing schools of thought about the nature of slaveholders, see James Oakes, *The Ruling Race: A History of American Slaveholders* (New York, 1982) and *Slavery and Freedom: An Interpretation of the Old South* (New York, 1990); Eugene D. Genovese, *The Political Economy of Slavery: Studies in the Economy and Society of the Slave South*, 2d ed. (Middletown, Conn., 1989); Eugene D. Genovese and Elizabeth Fox-Genovese, *Fruits of Merchant Capital: Slavery and Bourgeois Property in the Rise and Expansion of Capitalism* (New York, 1983); Mark M. Smith, "Time, Slavery and Plantation Capitalism in the Antebellum American South," *Past and Present*, no. 150 (Feb. 1996): 142–68. Perhaps the most famous portrayal of paternalism, arguing that slavery was essentially a benevolent system, was advanced by Ulrich Bonnell Phillips, in *American Negro Slavery: A Survey of the Supply, Employment and Control of Negro Labor as Determined by the Plantation Regime* (Baton Rouge, 1966).

11. While there is much to dispute about his excoriation of TJ in *The Long Affair: Thomas Jefferson and the French Revolution, 1785–1800* (Chicago, 1996), Conor Cruise O'Brien, with his keen intelligence, observational skills, and sharp writing style, zeros in on one of the less explored aspects of TJ's personality: he loved to be in a home where he was surrounded by his "children and house slaves," with which the latter, O'Brien says, he had "veiled and equivocal relationships." Whatever negative things he had to say about mixing the blood of black and white, TJ deliberately chose to live surrounded by mixed-race people whom he relied upon for virtually all his needs.

12. Douglass, *Narrative of the Life of Frederick Douglass*, 69.

13. Stanton, *Free Some Day*, 73–78, 79–82; TJ to Reuben Perry, April 16, 1812, *Farm Book*, 34–35. Deed to Reuben Perry, [Sept. 3, 1812]. Stanton notes that the deed is misdated in the Betts edition of the Farm Book; it should be 1811.

14. *MB*, 754–55.

15. Edwin G. Burrows and Mike Wallace, *Gotham: A History of New York to 1898* (New York, 1999).

16. TJ to Benjamin Rush, Sept. 23, 1800, *Papers*, 32:167; TJ to Elizabeth Wayles Eppes, June 13, 1790, *Papers*, 16:489.

17. Graham Russell Hodges, *Root and Branch: Africans in New York and New Jersey, 1613–1863* (Chapel Hill, 1999).

18. Burrows and Wallace, *Gotham*, 350.

19. Ibid., 249.

20. Ibid., 348.

21. Paul A. Gilje, "Between Slavery and Freedom: New York African Americans in the Early Republic," *Reviews in American History* 20 (June 1992): 163–67.

22. *MB*, 756; TJ placed an advertisement in a Philadelphia newspaper in 1791 for "a Genteel servant who can shave and dress well, attend a gentleman on horseback, wait at table and be well recommended," *MB*, 815 n. 33.

23. For TJ's references to his illness, see TJ to Thomas Mann Randolph, May 9, 1790, *Papers*, 16:416; TJ to Martha Randolph, May 16, 1790, ibid., 429; TJ to Mary Jefferson, May 23, 1790, ibid., 435; TJ to Thomas Mann Randolph, May 23, 1790, ibid., 436; TJ to William Short, May 27, 1790, ibid., 443, TJ to Peter Carr, June 13, 1790, ibid., 487, TJ to Elizabeth Eppes, June 13, 1790, ibid., 489, Nicholas Lewis, June 13, 1790, ibid., 492.

24. *MB*, 756 n. 32.

25. *MB*, 757 n. 33; TJ to Thomas Mann Randolph, March 18, 1790, *Papers*, 16:278, TJ to Martha Jefferson Randolph, April 4, 1790, ibid., 300. See also *MB*, 755 n. 23; 758 ("removed to Maiden Lane No. 57").

26. *MB*, 758 n. 42; Bear, *The Hemings Family*, 7.

27. TJ to William Short, April 6, 1790, *Papers*, 16:319.

28. Malone, *Jefferson*, 2:257.

29. See, generally, *MB*, 758–65, containing numerous references to giving "James for hhd. exp."

30. *MB*, 762. See, e.g., *MB*, 725.

31. *MB*, 763. In May he noted, "Francois Seche comes into my service on same terms as Jacob Cook," a few days before he wrote of Cook when he came into his employ, "He clothe himself & wash"—pays for his own washing (p. 757). That same month he gave "James for pr. Shoes 9/" and bought another pair in June (p. 759). Before Robert Hemings left, he also bought shoes for him (p. 757). The following months saw a daily dispensing of money to Hemings for the expense of running the household and numerous other transactions that are not always specified. Some of the payments were for his salary on account or in partial payments. Others payments were just for spending money. "Gave James for himself 32/" (p. 759), "James . . . necessaries for himself 18/9" (p. 764). Just before they left New York, he gave James £3 14s.

32. Jacob E. Cooke, "The Compromise of 1790," *WMQ*, 3d ser., 27 (1970): 523–45; Kenneth R. Bowling, "Dinner at Jefferson's: A Note on Jacob E. Cooke's 'The Compromise of 1790,'" *WMQ*, 3d ser., 28 (1971): 629–48 (Cooke's rebuttal, pp. 640–48); Norman Risjord, "The Compromise of 1790: New Evidence on the Dinner Table Bargain," *WMQ*, 3d ser., 33 (1976): 309–14.

33. Sloan, *Principle and Interest*, 125–26, 225–32.

34. *MB*, 765 n. 79, 766–67.

22: Philadelphia

1. Malone, *Jefferson*, 2:321.

2. Susan R. Stein, *The Worlds of Thomas Jefferson at Monticello* (New York, 1993), 44.

3. Malone, *Jefferson*, 2:321.

4. *MB*, 808.

5. Stein, *Worlds*, 45

6. Ibid., 46.

7. TJ to Martha Randolph, Jan. 20, 1791, *Papers*, 18:579.

8. See, e.g., *MB*, 808, 810, 812, listing Hemings's wages along with those of TJ's other servants; *MB*, 818, 832, 880, noting money given to James for clothes.

9. *An Act for the Gradual Abolition of Slavery, March 1, 1780*, in *The Statutes at Large of Pennsylvania from 1682 to 1801*, comp. James T. Mitchell and Henry Flanders (Harrisburg, 1896–1915), 10:67–73; Gary B. Nash and Jean R. Soderlund, *Freedom by Degrees: Emancipation in Pennsylvania and Its Aftermath* (New York, 1991), 176–77.

10. Nash and Soderlund, *Freedom by Degrees*, 113.

11. *An Act to Explain and Amend an Act, Entitled "An Act for the Gradual Abolition of Slavery," March 29, 1788.*

12. *An Act for the Gradual Abolition of Slavery (1799) New York.*

13. *An Act for the Gradual Abolition of Slavery, March 1, 1780.*

14. Ibid.

15. Henry Wiencek, *Imperfect God: George Washington, His Slaves, and the Creation of America* (New York, 2003), 31–36.

16. *MB*, 768–71, 808–32, 836–41, 861–77, 880–901, 904–12.

17. Pennsylvania act, sec. 10. It would have been an odd thing, indeed, if the legislature of Pennsylvania had created a law that allowed its citizens to keep slaves born before March of 1780 for life, so long as they registered them, but then tell elected officials from other parts of the country, who were exempt from the registration requirement, that when they came to Philadelphia to serve their constituents and brought slaves they had to set them free after six months.

18. *Butler v. Hopper*, 4 F. Cas. 904 (C.C. Pa 1806) (No. 2241)

19. Ibid.

20. *The Commonwealth ex. rel. Negro Louis v. Holloway*, 6 Binn 213 (Pa. 1814).

21. Nash and Soderlund, *Freedom by Degrees*, 18.

22. See, e.g., *MB*, 839, 860, 901. Robert Hemings was in the city for a time.

23. *MB*, 808 n. 7.

24. See, e.g., *MB*, 814.

25. Ralph Ketchum, *James Madison: A Biography* (Charlottesville, 1971), 148.

26. Gary B. Nash, *Forging Freedom: The Formation of Philadelphia's Black Community, 1720–1840* (Cambridge, Mass., 1988), 100; Harry V. Richardson, *Dark Salvation: The Story of Methodism as It Developed among Blacks in America* (Garden City, N.Y., 1976); Daniel A. Payne, *History of the African Methodist Episcopal Church* (1891; reprint, New York, 1969); Julie Winch, *A Gentleman of Color: The Life of James Forten* (New York, 2002).

27. Richard S. Newman, *The Transformation of American Abolitionism: Fighting Slavery in the Early Republic* (Chapel Hill, 2002), 4.

28. Nash and Soderlund, *Freedom by Degrees*, 113–15. It is also likely that they shied away from acting formally with blacks on behalf of the black community if that meant that any whites might suffer. Interracial cooperation has always posed a threat to those who have wanted to maintain the status quo on race in America.

29. Nash, *Forging Freedom*, 117; Rush quoted in Susan E. Klepp, "Seasoning and Society: Racial Differences in Mortality in Eighteenth-Century Philadelphia," *WMQ*, 3d ser., 51 (1994): 487 n. 48.

30. Malone, *Jefferson*, 2:359.

31. "Notes on the Lake Country Tour," *The Papers of James Madison*, ed. William T. Hutchinson and William M. E. Rachal, 17 vols. (Chicago and Charlottesville, 1962–91), 14:25; "The Northern Journey of Jefferson and Madison," *Papers*, 20:438.

32. *MB*, 819 n. 49.

33. Ibid.

34. Gordon-Reed, *TJ and SH*, 197.

35. For Hemings's and TJ's itinerary on the journey, see *MB*, 819–25, and *Papers*, 20: 453–73.

36. "Notes on the Lake Country Tour," *Papers of James Madison*, 14:27.

37. Graham Russell Hodges, *Root and Branch: Africans in New York and New Jersey. 1613–1863* (Chapel Hill, 1999), 163–64.

38. "Northern Journey," *Papers*, 20:471–73, 467–70, 454.

39. *MB*, 823–25; see also n. 78, suggesting that perhaps the daily entries from May 17 to June 19 might be a more accurate listing of the mileage than the final report cited at 823–25.

40. TJ to Martha J. Randolph, *Papers*, 20:381.

41. *MB*, 829 n. 91: William Short to TJ, Feb. 18, 1791, *Papers*, 19:291.

42. Lucia Stanton, "'A Well-Ordered Household': Domestic Servants in Jefferson's White House," *White House History*, no. 17 (2006): 14.

43. Stein, *Worlds*, 43.

44. Ibid.

45. TJ to Martha Randolph, Dec. 4, 1791, *Papers*, 22:377; TJ to Martha Randolph, Dec. 13, 1792, ibid., 24:740–41.

46. Adrien Petit to TJ, July 28, 1792, *Papers*, 24:262.

47. TJ to Adrien Petit, Aug. 13, 1792, *Papers*, 24:294.

48. TJ to George Taylor Jr., Aug. 13, 1792, *Papers*, 24:295.

49. George Taylor to TJ, Aug. 26, 1792, *Papers*, 24:326–27.

50. Ibid.; George Taylor to TJ, Sept. 1, 1792, ibid., 340. TJ to George Taylor, Sept. 10, 1792, ibid., 365.

51. Adrien Petit to TJ, July 28, 1792, *Papers*, 24:262.

52. Clare A. Lyons, "Mapping an Atlantic Sexual Culture: Homoeroticism in Eighteenth-Century Philadelphia," *WMQ*, 3d ser., 60 (2003): 119–54, par. 30.

53. *MB*, 830.

54. Stanton, "'Well-Ordered Household,'" 12–13.

55. Ibid., 13.

56. Kierner, *Scandal at Bizarre*, 84, 109.

57. *MB*, 880.

58. Benjamin Banneker to TJ, Aug. 19, 1791, *Papers*, 22:49.

59. TJ to Benjamin Banneker, Aug. 30, 1791, *Papers*, 22:97–98.

60. See *Papers*, 22:52–54, detailing TJ's relations with Banneker.

61. TJ to Henri-Baptiste Gregoire, Feb. 25, 1809; TJ to Joel Barlow, Oct. 8, 1809, *The Works of Thomas Jefferson*, ed. Paul Leicester Ford, 12 vols. (New York, 1904–05), 9:309–10, 10:261.

62. Thomas Greene Fessenden, *Democracy Unveiled; or, Tyranny Stripped of the Garb of Patriotism*, 2 vols. (New York, 1805), 2:52n, cited in *Papers*, 22:54.

63. See, *Papers*, 22:54 n.; Silvio A. Bendini, *The Life of Benjamin Banneker* (New York, 1972); Gordon-Reed, *TJ and SH*, chap. 2.

64. Gordon-Reed, *TJ and SH*, 139.

65. Ibid., 139–40. There are numerous references to Gardiner in TJ's account books between 1790 and 1800; see, e.g., *MB*, 808 n. 7, 814, 980, 1019.

66. Philip D. Morgan, "'To Get Quit of Negroes': George Washington and Slavery," *Journal of American Studies* 39 (2005): 404.

67. Ibid., 415.

68. Annette Gordon-Reed, "Engaging Jefferson: Blacks and the Founding Father," *WMQ*, 3d ser., 58 (2000): 171–82.

23: Exodus

1. For discussions of the late eighteenth-century revolutions, see, e.g., David Brion Davis, *The Problem of Slavery in the Age of Revolution, 1770–1823* (Ithaca, 1975); James, *Black Jacobins*; Robin Blackburn, *The Overthrow of Colonial Slavery, 1776–1848* (London, 1988).

2. *An Act to Authorize the Manumission of Slaves*, Laws of Virginia, 1782, chap. 61; Ira Berlin, "The Revolution in Black Life," in *The American Revolution*, ed. Alfred F. Young (DeKalb, Ill., 1976), 349–82; McColley, *Slavery and Jeffersonian Virginia*; Ralph Waller, *John Wesley: A Personal Portrait* (New York, 2003); James Haskins, *The Methodists* (New York, 1992); Cynthia Lynn Lyerly, *Methodism and the Southern Mind, 1770–1810* (New York, 1998).

3. Berlin, "Revolution in Black Life," 362, 364; Ira Berlin, *Slaves without Masters: The Free Negro in the Antebellum South* (New York, 1974); Frey, *Water from the Rock*.

4. Stanton, *Slavery at Monticello*, 16.

5. "Thenia Hemings," Monticello Research Department files, Thomas Jefferson Foundation, Inc.

6. See Hemings family tree in this book.

7. TJ to Nicholas Lewis, April, 12, 1792, *Papers*, 23:408.

8. TJ to Daniel Hylton, Nov. 22, 1792, *Papers*, 24:657

9. *MB*, 836, 877.

10. *Farm Book*, 30.

11. TJ to Martha Randolph, Jan. 22, 1795, *Papers*, 28:249; Stanton, *Free Some Day*, 179 n. 204.

12. Stanton, *Free Some Day*, 119.

13. "Agreement with James Hemings," Sept. 15, 1793, *Papers*, 27:119–20.

14. See, e.g., *Sawney v. Carter*, 27 Va. 173 (1828); *Shue v. Turk*, 56 Va. 256 (1859). But see *Elias v. Smith*, 6 Hum. 33, and *Lewis v. Simonton*, 8 Hum. 185, cases from Tennessee allowing for the enforcement of contracts for emancipation made between slaves and masters.

15. Paul Finkelman, "Treason against the Hopes of the World," *Jeffersonian Legacies*, 205.

16. *MB*, 891 n. 28.

17. "Notes of a Conversation with George Washington," Feb. 7, 1793, *Papers*, 25: 153–54.

18. TJ to Martha Randolph, July 7, 1793, *Papers*, 25:445–46.

19. Martin S. Pernick, "Politics, Parties, and Pestilence: Epidemic Yellow Fever in Philadelphia and the Rise of the First Party System," *WMQ*, 3d ser., 29 (1972): 559.

20. Ibid.

21. Ibid., 562–63.

22. See J. H. Powell, *Bring Out Your Dead: The Great Plague of Yellow Fever in Philadelphia* (Philadelphia, 1993), xi. 96–101, detailing African American involvement with the epidemic.

23. TJ to Thomas Mann Randolph, Nov. 2, 1793, *Papers*, 27:299. TJ gave his earliest descriptions of the disease to James Madison and then to his son-in-law Thomas Mann Randolph. TJ to James Madison, Sept. 1, 1793, *Papers*, 26:7; TJ to Thomas M. Randolph, Sept. 2, 1793, ibid., 20–21.

24. Powell, *Bring Out Your Dead*, 100–101.

25. TJ to George Washington, July 31, 1793, *Papers*, 26:593–94; "Notes of a Conversation with George Washington," Aug. 6, 1793, ibid., 627–30; TJ to George Washington, Aug. 11, 1793, ibid., 659–60; George Washington to TJ, Aug. 12, 1793, ibid., 660.

26. *MB*, 903.

27. Malone, *Jefferson*, 3:141; Ketchum, *James Madison*, 378–82.

28. Malone, *Jefferson*, 3:146.

29. TJ to James Madison, Nov. 2, 1793, *Papers*, 27:297; TJ to Thomas M. Randolph, Nov. 2, 1793, ibid., 299.

30. *MB*, 904 n. 69.

31. Ibid., 910.

32. Bear, *The Hemings Family of Monticello*, 7. See also Thomas Mann Randolph to TJ, April 30, 1791, *Papers*, 20:328; Mary Jefferson to TJ, May 1, 1791, ibid., 335; TJ to Daniel Hylton, July 1, 1792, ibid., 24:145.

33. "Deed of Manumission for Robert Hemings," Dec. 21, 1794. See photograph in the first insert.

34. TJ to Thomas Mann Randolph, Dec. 26, 1794, *Papers*, 28:225–26.

35. Hamilton, *Making and Unmaking of a Revolutionary Family*, 83.

36. Martha Randolph to TJ, Jan. 15, 1795, *Papers*, 28:247.

24: The Second Monticello

1. *MB*, 912.

2. Ibid. TJ noted, "Peter comes home from working for Chapman," on Jan. 27.

3. Edmund Randolph to TJ, Aug. 28, 1794, *Papers*, 28:118; TJ to Edmund Randolph, Sept. 7, 1794, ibid., 148.

4. *MB*, 499; *Farm Book*, 421; TJ to James Barbour, May 11, 1821. TJ does not mention him by name, but the "servant of great intelligence and diligence" was Peter Hemings, who had been taught brewing by a London brewer who had relocated to Virginia.

5. Thomas Jefferson Randolph, "The Last Days of Jefferson," Special Collections, ViU; Brodie, *Thomas Jefferson*, 352–53, quoting the *Frederick Town Herald*, reprinted in the *Richmond Recorder*, Dec. 8, 1802. The editor of the paper employed a curious formulation of Callender's writings about SH's alleged son, "Tom," noting that the boy Callender "called" Tom did indeed look like Jefferson, as if they were skeptical of Callender on this point.

6. TJ to George Wythe, Oct. 23, 1794, *Papers*, 28:181.

7. Stein, *The Worlds of Thomas Jefferson*, 81.

8. TJ to Edmund Randolph, Feb. 3, 1794, *Papers*, 28:15–16; TJ to James Monroe, March 11, 1794, ibid., 34–35.

9. Stanton, *Slavery at Monticello*, 16.

10. Ibid.

11. See Lucia Stanton, "Rational Plantation Management at Monticello," in forthcoming collection of essays from Univ. of Virginia Press, quoting Lownes.

12. TJ to Jean Nicolas Demeunier, April 29, 1795, *Papers*, 28:341.

13. Stanton, *Free Some Day*, 114.

14. *Farm Book*, 110–11. See Stanton, "Rational Plantation Management," on TJ's method of keeping daily tabs on the output of each nail boy.

15. Charles Campbell, "Life of Isaac Jefferson," 581.

16. Patricia Samford, "Archaeology of African-American Slavery and Material Culture," *WMQ*, 3d ser., 53 (1996): 88.

17. Fraser Neiman, Leslie McFaden, and Derek Wheeler, "Archaeological Investigation of the Elizabeth Hemings Site (44AB438)," http://Monticello.org/archaeology/publications/hemings.pdf, 5.

18. Ibid.

19. Ibid., 6. As this book was going to press, an additional home site was found in the vicinity of the Elizabeth Hemings site.

20. Ellen Randolph Coolidge to Joseph Coolidge, Oct. 14, 1858, Family Letters Project.

21. TJ to George Jefferson, Dec. 3, 1801, *Farm Book*, 425.

22. Fraser, McFaden, and Wheeler, "Elizabeth Hemings Site," 54.

23. Ibid., 16–17.

24. Samford, "Archaeology," 94.

25. Ibid.

26. Ibid., 92–93.

27. Peter S. Onuf, *Jefferson's Empire*, 68.

28. Charles H. Wesley, "Negro Suffrage in the Period of Constitution-Making, 1787–1865," *Journal of Negro History* 32, no. 2 (April 1947), 143–68 at 154; James W. Patton, "The Progress of Emancipation in Tennessee, 1796–1860, *Journal of Negro History* 17, no. 1 (Jan. 1932), 67–102 at 68–69.

29. Neiman, McFaden, and Wheeler, "Elizabeth Hemings Site," 17.

30. T. H. Breen, *The Marketplace of Revolution: How Consumer Politics Shaped American Independence* (New York, 2004), 140.

31. Samford, "Archaeology," 95.

32. Neiman, McFaden, and Wheeler, "Elizabeth Hemings Site," 50–51.

33. Ibid., 52.

34. *Farm Book*, 31.

35. See Gordon-Reed, *TJ and SH*, 195–96.

36. Ibid., 196–201.

37. See Hemings family tree in this book.

38. Malone, *Jefferson*, 1:430.

39. *Farm Book*, 50, 51, 52.

40. TJ to William O. Callis, May 8, 1795, *Papers*, 28:346.

41. Stanton, *Free Some Day*, 124.

42. "Deed of Manumission for Robert Hemings," Dec. 21, 1794, *Papers*, 28:222. See photograph in the first insert.

25: Into the Future, Echoes from the Past

1. *MB*, 936.
2. James Hemings's inventory of kitchen utensils at Monticello, *Papers*, 28:610–11. See photograph in the first insert.
3. Midori Takagi, *"Rearing Wolves to Our Own Destruction": Slavery in Richmond, Virginia, 1782–1865* (Charlottesville, 1999), 17, 10, 13–14.
4. Ibid., 22–23; Marianne Buroff Sheldon, "Black-White Relations in Richmond, Virginia, 1782–1820," *Journal of Southern History* 45 (1979): 28–29.
5. Michael Durey, *With the Hammer of Truth: James Thompson Callender and America's Early National Heroes* (Charlottesville, 1990), 158; Campbell, "Life of Isaac Jefferson," 567.
6. TJ to George Jefferson, June 21, 1799, *Papers*, 31:135.
7. George Jefferson to TJ, July 8, 1799, *Papers*, 31:148; TJ to George Jefferson, July 12, 1799, ibid., 148; George Jefferson to TJ, July 14, 1799, ibid., 148; TJ to George Jefferson, July 25, 1799, ibid., 149.
8. TJ to George Jefferson, May 18, 1799, *Papers*, 31:111; George Jefferson to TJ, June 3, 1799, ibid., 118.
9. Takagi, *"Rearing Wolves,"* 22–23; James Sidbury, *Ploughshares into Swords: Race, Rebellion, and Identity in Gabriel's Virginia, 1730–1810* (Cambridge, 1997), 184–219.
10. TJ to Thomas Mann Randolph, Dec. 26, 1794, *Papers*, 28:225.
11. Rhys Isaac, review of Sidbury's *Ploughshares into Swords*, in *Journal of Social History* 33 (2000): 1020–21.
12. Durey, *With the Hammer of Truth*, 154.
13. Extensive literature on Gabriel's revolt references the importance of Saint Domingue in the political climate of Richmond. See, e.g., Douglas R. Egerton, *Gabriel's Rebellion: The Virginia Slave Conspiracies of 1800 and 1802* (Chapel Hill, 1993); Sidbury, *Ploughshares into Swords*; James Sidbury, "Saint Domingue in Virginia: Ideology, Local Meanings, and Resistance to Slavery, 1790–1800," *Journal of Southern History* 63 (1997): 531–52; Sheldon, "Black-White Relations in Richmond." The writings on TJ and this question are extensive as well. See, e.g., Tim Matthewson, "Jefferson and Haiti," *Journal of Southern History* 61 (1995): 209–48.
14. See Gary B. Nash, *Forging Freedom: The Formation of Philadelphia's Black Community, 1720–1840* (Cambridge, Mass., 1988), 14–142, discussing the political and social influences of the black arrivals from the French colony. The Pennsylvania Abolition Society helped secure freedom for many of them, and soon many "French-speaking" black people were living as free people in the city by 1793.
15. TJ to Mary Jefferson, May 15, 1797, *Papers*, 29:399.
16. Martha Randolph to TJ, Jan. 22, 1798, *Papers*, 30:43.
17. *MB*, 966, where Jefferson noted, "Arrived at Monticello between 8 & 9. aclock A.M."; *Farm Book*, 57.
18. TJ to Francis Eppes, Sept. 24, 1797, *Papers*, 29:531–32; Gordon-Reed, *TJ and SH*, 197; Brodie, "Thomas Jefferson's Unknown Grandchildren," 94–99.
19. Gordon-Reed, *TJ and SH*, 196–201.

20. Ibid.

21. *Early American Indian Documents: Treaties and Laws, 1607–1789*, vol. 5, *Virginia Treaties, 1723–1775*, ed. W. Stith Robinson (Washington, D.C., 1979), 86–87, for the Treaty of Lancaster; Warren R. Hofstra, "'The Extensions of His Majesties Dominion': The Virginia Backcountry and the Extension of Imperial Frontiers," *Journal of American History* 84 (1998): 1310; Patrice Louis-René Higonnet, "The Origins of the Seven Years' War," *Journal of Modern History* 40 (1968): 61. The LOC's American Memory site has a copy of the Fry-Jefferson map, http://memory.loc/cgi-bin/map_pl; Jefferson, *Notes*, in *Writings*, 324. See also photograph in the second insert. See also *Papers*, 4:390, referring to documents in TJ's handwriting that use the Treaty of Lancaster as a baseline for establishing rights to western lands, and ibid., 6:666, for TJ's use of the Treaty in defense of Virginia's claim to western territory; *MB*, 94, 1326 n. 36.

22. TJ to John Henry, Dec. 31, 1797, *Papers*, 29:600. Jefferson explained why he would never write to Martin directly to answer his charges by saying that his critic had forfeited the right to a one-on-one discussion by attacking him in the newspapers before writing directly to him about the problem. Luther Martin to TJ, June 24, 1797, *Papers*, 29:452. This letter was also printed in the *Porcupine Gazette*, a Federalist newspaper whose editor was the rabidly racist and anti-Jefferson William Cobbett. He continued to "write" to Jefferson throughout the rest of the year and into the next. See *Papers*, 29: 454–55, for the history of the Martin letters.

23. See, e.g., TJ to John Gibson, May 31, 1797, *Papers*, 29:408–9; TJ to Peregrine Fitzhugh, June 4, 1797, ibid., 415–18; TJ to John Gibson, Dec. 31, 1797, ibid., 599–600; TJ to John Henry, Dec. 31, 1797, ibid., 29:600–601. The last letter is particularly intriguing because, while describing his state of mind in 1774 when he took down the narrative of Logan's speech, TJ says, "I knew nothing of the Cresaps, and could not possibly have a motive to do them an injury with design." But he surely must have learned something of them after that time, or how else would he have known to write that Thomas Cresap was "infamous for many murders"?

24. *Thomas Jefferson's Library: A Catalog with the Entries in His Own Order*, ed. James Gilreath and Douglas L. Wilson (Washington, D.C., 1999), chap. 16, item 30, "Ethics. 2.Law of Nature and Nations."

25. Stith, ed., *Early American Indian Documents*, 5:87.

26. *Christopher Gist's Journals, with Historical, Geographical, and Ethnological Notes and Biographies of His Contemporaries*, ed. William M. Darlington (Pittsburgh, 1893), 202–6.

27. Anthony F. C. Wallace, *Jefferson and the Indians: The Tragic Fate of the First Americans* (Cambridge, 1999), 28–34; Coolie Verner, "The Fry and Jefferson Map," *Imago Mundi*, 21 (1967): 75–76.

28. TJ to John Gibson, May 31, 1797, *Papers*, 29:408; TJ, *An Appendix to the "Notes on Virginia" relative to the Murder of Logan's Family* (Philadelphia, 1800).

29. William Short to TJ, Feb. 27, 1798, *Papers*, 30:149–51.

30. Ibid., 150–51.

31. Hamilton, *The Making and Unmaking of a Revolutionary Family*, 42–43.

32. Short to TJ, Sept. 18 and Dec. 9, 1800, *Papers*, 32:155, 295.

33. TJ to Edward Coles, Aug. 25, 1814, *Writings*, 1345.

34. TJ to William Short, April 13, 1800, *Papers*, 501–10.

26: The Ocean of Life

1. "Old Virginia Editors," *WMQ* 7 (1898): 9–17.

2. *Richmond Recorder*, Sept. 1, 1802, cited in Brodie, *Thomas Jefferson*, 323; *New York Commercial Advertiser*, Oct. 9, 1800, cited ibid.

3. See Michael Durey, *With the Hammer of Truth*, 97–102, discussing the Reynolds affair and Callender's involvement in it; Ron Chernow, *Alexander Hamilton* (New York, 2004), 619, calling Hamilton's "intemperate indictment of John Adams . . . a form of political suicide."

4. TJ to William Evans, Feb. 22, 1801, *Papers*, 33:38.

5. TJ to Philippe de Létombe, Feb. 22, 1801, *Papers*, 33:43.

6. Francis Say to TJ, Feb. 23, 1801, *Papers*, 33:53.

7. TJ to William Evans, Feb. 22, 1801, *Papers*, 33:38.

8. Francis Say to TJ, Feb. 23, 1801, *Papers*, 33:53.

9. William Evans to TJ, Feb. 27, 1801, *Papers*, 33:91–92.

10. Stanton, *Free Some Day*, 128.

11. Thomas Jefferson Randolph, "The Last Days of Jefferson," Special Collections, ViU.

12. Carlos Martinez de Irujo to TJ, March 13, 1801, *Papers*, 33:268–69; Philippe de Létombe, March 15, 1801, ibid., 302; TJ to Philippe de Létombe, March 19, 1801, ibid., 366; Philippe de Létombe, to TJ March 26, 1801, ibid., 449; TJ to Philippe de Létombe, March 31, 1801, ibid., 506–7.

13. TJ to William Evans, March 31, 1801, *Papers*, 33:505.

14. *MB*, 1051; TJ to Philippe de Létombe, March 19, 1801, *Papers*, 33:366.

15. Gordon-Reed, *TJ and SH*, 79, 254, 195.

16. Rothman, *Notorious in the Neighborhood*, 30.

17. *MB*, 1053 n. 15.

18. TJ to William Evans, Nov. 24, 1801; Evans to TJ, Nov. 5, 1801, MHi.

19. TJ to Thomas Mann Randolph, Dec. 4, 1801, LOC, 20356.

20. *Richmond Recorder*, Sept. 1, 1802.

21. Ibid., Sept. 15, 1802.

22. Ibid., Sept. 22, 1802.

23. Ibid., Nov. 3, 1802.

24. Gordon-Reed, *TJ and SH*, 195–96.

25. *Richmond Recorder*, Sept. 15, 1802.

26. Ibid., Dec. 1, 1802.

27. Gordon-Reed, *TJ and SH*, 59–60.

28. Ibid., 60.

29. Durey, *With the Hammer of Truth*, 154–55.

27: The Public World and the Private Domain

1. Stanton, *Free Some Day*, 62, 129–30.

2. TJ to John Wayles Eppes, Aug. 7, 1804, quoted in Lucia Stanton, "'A Well-Ordered Household': Domestic Servants in Jefferson's White House," *White House History*, no. 17

(2006): 8; Cornelia Randolph to Virginia J. Trist, Aug. 22, 1831, quoted in Stanton, *Free Some Day*, 156.

3. Stanton, "'Well-Ordered Household,'" 9.

4. Ibid., 8.

5. TJ to Edward Bancroft, Jan. 26, 1789, *Papers*, 14: 492–93. TJ mistakenly date d the letter 1788.

6. TJ to Mary Jefferson Eppes, March 3, 1802, LOC, 20875.

7. Stanton, "'Well-Ordered Household,'" 8, 10–11; Stanton, *Free Some Day*, 185 n. 285.

8. Stanton, *Free Some Day*, 50.

9. *MB*, 1069. TJ noted paying expenses for Ursula's "lying in." She had come to Washington sometime after Sept. 1801. She first appears in TJ's list of servants in Nov. Her baby was born before March 22.

10. Eli Hawley Canfield to W. S. Canfield and Zaddock H. Canfield, Aug. 24, 1842, Correspondence of James Madison, 1801–1842, Accession 8005, Special Collections, ViU.

11. Stanton, *Slavery at Monticello*, 16. Reproduction of missing page from the Farm Book, "Negroes Alienated 1784–1794," *Farm Book*, 24.

12. *Farm Book*, 30.

13. George Jefferson to TJ, June 17, 1801, *Farm Book*, 425.

14. Stanton, *Free Some Day*, 131–32.

15. TJ to Joseph Dougherty, July 31, 1806, quoted in Stanton, "'Well-Ordered Household,'" 11.

16. Ibid.

17. Stanton, *Free Some Day*, 133.

18. Ibid.; Pierson, *Jefferson at Monticello*, 109.

19. Campbell, "Life of Isaac Jefferson," *WMQ*, 3d ser., 8 (1951): 579; Robert L. Self and Susan R. Stein, "The Collaboration of Thomas Jefferson and John Hemings: Furniture Attributed to the Monticello Joinery," *Winterthur Portfolio* 33, no. 4 ("Race and Ethnicity in American Material Life") (1998): 231–48.

20. TJ to Thomas Mann Randolph, May 19, 1793, *Papers*, 26:65; directions for Watson, ca. Oct. 22–25, 1793, ibid., 27:267.

21. McLaughlin, *Jefferson and Monticello*, 86–87, 311; TJ to Thomas Munro, March 14, 1815, *Farm Book*, 460.

22. James Oldham to TJ, Nov. 26, 1804, MHi.

23. Ibid.

24. Stanton, *Free Some Day*, 116.

25. Ibid.

26. James Oldham to TJ, July 16 and 23, 1805; TJ to Oldham July 20, 1805, MHi.

27. TJ to James Oldham, July 20, 1805, MHi.

28. Thomas Mann Randolph to TJ, May 30, 1803, ViU.

29. TJ to Thomas Mann Randolph, June 8, 1803, LOC, 22821.

30. James Oldham to TJ, July 30, 1805, MHi.

31. *MB*, 1315.

32. See Brodie, *Thomas Jefferson*, 544 n. 57. Brodie's biography contains the greatest number of reproductions of the satirical verse about SH and TJ, in chaps. 25 and 26. See also

"John Quincy Adams, Apostate," *Journal of the Early American Republic* 11, no. 2 (1991): 165.

33. Abigail Adams to TJ, Oct. 25, 1804, *Letters of Mrs. Adams*, 2:257; TJ to Benjamin Rush, Jan. 16, 1811, LOC, 34176.

35. Jack Shepherd, *Cannibals of the Heart: A Personal Biography of Louisa Catherine and John Quincy Adams* (New York, 1980), 114, 115.

36. Louisa Catherine Adams to John Quincy Adams, June 11, 1807, Adams Family Papers, MHi. I thank Mary T. Claffey of *The Adams Papers* for helping me find this quote after I had lost the reference.

37. *Writings of John Quincy Adams*, ed. Worthington Chauncey Ford, 7 vols. (New York, 1913–17), 3:289. I thank Professor Lynn Parsons of the State University of New York (Brockport) for calling this passage to my attention. See also Linda K. Kerber and Walter John Morris, "Politics and Literature: The Adams Family and the *Port Folio*," *WMQ*, 3d ser., 23 (1966): 450–67.

28: "Measurably Happy": The Children of Thomas Jefferson and Sally Hemings

1. Gordon-Reed, *TJ and SH*, 247.

2. Ibid., 248.

3. I thank Beverly Gray, researcher for the Getting Word Project, of the Thomas Jefferson Foundation, genealogist and expert on African American families in Ohio, for this information and insight.

4. Stanton, "Monticello to Main Street," 100.

5. TJ to Maria Jefferson Eppes, March 3, 1804, LOC, 23989.

6. Gordon-Reed, *TJ and SH*, 195–96, 247.

7. Ibid., 247; "Room in Which Martha Jefferson Died," *Thomas Jefferson Wiki*, http://www.wiki.monticello.org.; Dolley Payne Todd Madison to Ann Payne Cutts, Sept. 8, 1804, noting, "Patsy and Nelly wrote to you last week. P. goes with us tomorrow on a visit to Montecello for a week," Dolley Madison Digital Edition, http://rotunda.upress.virginia.edu. See also TJ to James Madison, Sept. 6, 1804, and James Madison to TJ, Sept. 8, 1804, Smith, *Republic of Letters*, 2:1344.

8. Malone, *Jefferson*, vol. 5, Appendix 1: "Descendants of Thomas Jefferson."

9. The literature on Jefferson and the embargo is considerable and generally negative, though there are signs that a reconsideration is under way. The most conventional treatment of the subject can be found ibid., Malone, vol. 5, chap. 25, "The Lesser Evil: The Embargo," 469–90. For the more typically negative view, see Doron S. Ben-Atar, *The Origins of Jeffersonian Commercial Policy and Diplomacy* (New York, 1993).

10. TJ to Ezra Stiles Ely, June 25, 1825, LOC, 38465.

11. TJ to John Page, June 25, 1804, LOC, 24511.

12. *Boston Repertory*, May 31, 1805.

13. The will of George Wythe, LOC, 27971. See also Julian Boyd, "The Murder of George Wythe," *WMQ*, 3d ser., 12 (1955): 513.

14. Lydia Broadnax to TJ, April 9, 1807, *Papers* (unpublished); TJ to George Jefferson, April 18, 1807, ibid. I thank Linda Monaco at the Papers of Thomas Jefferson for providing me with copies and transcriptions of these letters. *MB*, 1201.

15. TJ to William Duval, June 22, 1806, LOC, 27941; July 17, 1806, LOC, 28061; William Duval to TJ, Dec. 10, 1806, LOC, 28553; George Wythe's will, LOC, 27971–72.

16. Gordon-Reed, *TJ and SH*, 199; Ellen Randolph Coolidge to Nicholas Trist, March 28, 1823, Family Letters Project.

17. TJ to James Madison, June 22, 1817, Smith, *Republic of Letters*, 3:1786; Gordon-Reed, *TJ and SH*, 199–200; Thomas Eston Randolph to Nicholas Trist, June 30, 1826, Family Letters Project.

18. Gordon-Reed, *TJ and SH*, 247.

19. Ibid.

20. Ibid.

21. See, e.g., TJ to Joel Yancey, Sept. 16, 1816, and Oct. 14, 1820, MHi; codicil to TJ's will, MSS 5145, Special Collections, ViU. See also photograph in the second insert.

22. Pierson, *Jefferson at Monticello*, 110; *Farm Book*, 130.

23. TJ to Francis C. Gray, March 4, 1815, LOC, 36173.

24. Gordon-Reed, *TJ and SH*, 248; Pierson, *Jefferson at Monticello*, 110.

25. Susan Kern, "The Material World of the Jeffersons at Shadwell," *WMQ*, 3d ser., 62, no. 2 (2005), at http://www.historycooperative.org/journals/wm/62.2/kern.html, 24.

26. *Farm Book*, 128; TJ to Joel Yancey, Sept. 13, 1816, MHi.

27. Rhys Isaac, "Monticello Stories," in *Sally Hemings and Thomas Jefferson*, 123–24.

28. TJ to Francis C. Gray, March 4, 1815, LOC, 36173.

29. Francis Gray to TJ, March 24, LOC, 36208. In this letter Gray explained to TJ that he asked the question because he was trying to interpret the Massachusetts law on the question of the definition of a "mulatto." He answered TJ's algebra with equations of his own.

30. Peter S. Onuf, *The Mind of Thomas Jefferson* (Charlottesville, 2006), 226–31.

31. Gordon-Reed, *TJ and SH*, 247.

32. Ibid., 151–52.

33. Charles Campbell, "Life of Isaac Jefferson," 572; Pierson, *Jefferson at Monticello*, 127; from Martha Jefferson Randolph and Thomas Mann Randolph to TJ, Jan. 31, 1801, *Papers*, 32:527; Memoirs of Thomas Jefferson Randolph, 4, Special Collections, ViU.

34. *The Autobiography of T. Jefferson Coolidge, 1831–1920* (Whitefish, Mont., 2007), Mary J. Randolph to Ellen W. Randolph Coolidge postscript by Nicholas P. Trist, Nov. 26, 1826.

35. Gordon-Reed, *TJ and SH*, 14–16; Stanton, *Free Some Day*, 101.

36. Pierson, *Jefferson at Monticello*, 110; Campbell, "Life of Isaac Jefferson," 568.

37. Gordon-Reed, *TJ and SH*, 255.

29: Retirement for One, Not for All

1. Pierson, *Jefferson at Monticello*, 125.

2. Ibid.

3. See Stanton, *Free Some Day*, 131, describing comments about Fossett's cooking.

4. Anne Cary Randolph, 1805–1808, Part A: Household Accounts, LOC.

5. New York *World*, Jan. 30, 1898.

6. TJ to John Adams, Jan. 21, 1812, LOC, 34560.

7. Stanton, *Free Some Day*, 121.

8. Martha Randolph to Ellen Randolph Coolidge, Nov. 16, 1825, Family Letters Project; TJ to Ellen R. Coolidge, Nov.14, 1825, *The Family Letters of Thomas Jefferson*, ed. Edwin M. Betts and James A. Bear Jr. (1966; reprint, Columbia, Mo., 1986), 461.

9. *MB*, 1265 n. 84, 1352.

10. Cornelia Jefferson Randolph to Virginia Jefferson Randolph, Oct. 25, 1816, [Aug.?] 28, 1819, Family Letters Project; Pierson, *Jefferson at Monticello*, 109. Bacon confuses "Priscilla" Hemings's name with Ursula, another enslaved woman at Monticello.

11. Gordon-Reed, *TJ and SH*, 245.

12. Ellen Wayles Randolph Harrison, quoted in Bear, *The Hemings Family of Monticello*, 17.

13. John Hemmings to TJ, Nov. 29, 1821, MHi.

14. *The First Forty Years of Washington Society, Portrayed by the Family Letters of Mrs. Samuel Harrison Smith (Margaret Bayard)*, ed. Gaillard Hunt (New York, 1906), 71; McLaughlin, *Jefferson and Monticello*, 20; Campbell, "Life of Isaac Jefferson," 573; Pierson, *Jefferson at Monticello*, 86–87.

15. For discussion of the architecture of Jefferson's living quarters, see William L. Beiswanger, "Thomas Jefferson and Art of Living Out of Doors," *Magazine Antiques* 157 (2000): 595–605; McLaughlin, *Jefferson and Monticello*, 323–25.

16. McLaughlin, *Jefferson and Monticello*, 323–24.

17. For a general look at the lives of the enslaved people at Monticello, see Barbara J. Heath, *Hidden Lives: The Archaeology of Slave Life at Thomas Jefferson's Poplar Forest* (Charlottesville, 1999).

18. Ellen Wayles Randolph to Martha Jefferson, Aug. 18, 1817, Aug. 24, 1819, Family Letters Project.

19. TJ to John Wayles Eppes, Sept. 18, 1812. HM5841, Huntington Library, San Marino, Calif.

20. *Life, Letters, and Journal of George Ticknor*, 2 vols. (Boston, 1909), 1:34–36.

21. "Elijah Fletcher's Account of a Visit to Monticello," May 8, 1811, *The Papers of Thomas Jefferson: Retirement Series*, ed. J. Jefferson Looney et al., vol. 3 (Princeton, 2006), 610.

22. See Ellen Wayles Randolph Coolidge's memories of trips to the Poplar Forest, written in 1856 and printed in Randall, *Life*, 3:343–44. For an example of regards sent through Randolph to a member of the Hemings family, see Ellen W. Randolph to Martha Jefferson Randolph, Sept. 13, [1816?], Family Letters Project: "Aunt Priscilla begs to be remembered to the young ladies—and that they will inform John H of her well doing and constant recollection."

23. Gordon-Reed, *TJ and SH*, 245.

24. Ellen Wayles Coolidge to Joseph Coolidge, Oct. 24, 1858, Family Letters Project; Stanton, *Free Some Day*, 101.

25. TJ to Joel Yancey, Sept. 13, 1816; Nov. 10, 1818; June 25, 1819, MHi.

26. Ellen W. Randolph to Martha Jefferson Randolph, July 18, 1819; Ellen W. Randolph to Martha Randolph, Sept. 27, [1816?], Family Letters Project.

27. TJ to Francis Eppes, Feb. 17, 1825, *Family Letters of Thomas Jefferson*, 451; codicil to TJ's will, MSS 5145, Special Collections, ViU. See also photograph in the second insert.

28. Gutman, *Black Family in Slavery and Freedom*, 87–95; Morgan, *Slave Counterpoint*, 554.

29. Ellen Wayles Randolph to Martha Jefferson, Sep. 27, [1816?], Family Letters Project.

Randolph first speaks of Burwell Colbert's child who had been ill. "Critty's child is pretty much as it was, if there is any change it is for the worse, but Aunt Bet [Betty Brown] who keep it at her house and nurses it, desired me to ask you to tell Burwell, that it is just as . . . he left it."

30. Ellen Wayles Randolph to Virginia Randolph, Aug. 31, 1819, Family Letters Project.

31. Cornelia J. Randolph to Virginia J. Randolph, Oct. 25, 1815, Family Letters Project.

32. Thomas Jefferson Randolph, "The Last Days of Jefferson," Special Collections, ViU; Brodie, *Thomas Jefferson*, 352–53, quoting the *Frederick Town Herald*.

33. Ellen W. Randolph to Martha Jefferson Randolph, July 28, 1819, Family Letters Project.

34. Ibid.

35. Ibid.

36. See Stanton, *Free Some Day*, 156, discussing Colbert's height.

37. Ellen W. Randolph to Martha Jefferson Randolph, July 28, 1819, Family Letters Project.

38. TJ to Martha Jefferson Randolph, quoted in J. Jefferson Looney, "'I Never Saw Any Body More Uneasy Than Grandpapa': Thomas Jefferson as Seen by His Family" (paper presented at the 2006 annual meeting of the Society for Historians of the Early American Republic, Worcester, Mass.).

39. Malone, *Jefferson*, 6:469; Virginia Randolph Trist to Ellen Randolph Coolidge, Randall, *Life*, 540.

40. TJ to James Madison, Oct. 18, 1825, in Smith, *Republic of Letters*, 3:1942–43.

41. Virginia Randolph Trist to Ellen Randolph Coolidge, Oct. 16, 1825, Family Letters Project; Malone, *Jefferson*, 6:469–70.

30: Endings and Beginnings

1. TJ to James Madison, Sept. 24, 1814, Smith, *Republic of Letters*, 3:1745; E. Millicent Sowerby, ed., *Catalogue of the Library of Thomas Jefferson*, 5 vols. (Washington, D.C., 1952–59).

2. Steven Harold Hochman, "Thomas Jefferson: A Personal Financial Biography" (Ph.D. diss., University of Virginia, 1987), 231–32, quoted in Sloan, *Principle and Interest*, 360.

3. TJ to Madison, Sept. 6, 1789, *Papers*, 15:392. See *MB*, xviii–xix, for James A. Bear and Lucia Stanton's discussion of Jefferson's problematic approach to financial record keeping.

4. Sloan, *Principle and Interest*, 11.

5. Malone, *Jefferson*, 3:3; Catherine Allgor, *Parlor Politics: In Which the Ladies of Washington Help Build a City and a Government* (Charlottesville, 2000), 24.

6. Campbell, "Life of Isaac Jefferson," 573; TJ to John Adams, June 10, 1815, LOC, 36303.

7. Cornelia J. Randolph to Ellen Wayles Randolph, Aug. 3, 1826, Family Letters Project; Sloan, *Principle and Interest*, 221–22.

8. Sloan, *Principle and Interest*, 222.

9. Martha Jefferson to TJ, Aug. 17, 1819, *Family Letters*, 430. See also Ellen W. Randolph to Martha Jefferson, Aug. 24, 1819, Family Letters Project, describing TJ's reaction to the news about Nicholas and her own extremely ironic criticism of Nicholas's failure to be realistic about his financial situation. Wilson C. Nicholas to TJ, Aug. 5, 1819, LOC 38530; Malone, *Jefferson*, 3:314; Sloan, *Principle and Interest*, 219.

10. Morgan, "'To Get Quit of Negroes,'" 403–29.

11. See, generally, Self and Stein, "Collaboration of Thomas Jefferson and John Hemings," 231-48.

12. Stanton, *Free Some Day*, 134-35; TJ to Charles Willson Peale, Aug. 20, 1811, LOC, 34408; Sloan, *Principle and Interest*, 11.

13. Auguste Levasseur, *Lafayette in America in 1824 and 1825; or, Journal of a Voyage to the United States*, trans. John D. Godman (Philadelphia, 1829); Malone, *Jefferson*, 3:403.

14. Malone, *Jefferson*, 3:404; Peter Fossett in the New York *World*, Jan. 30, 1830, quoted in Stanton, *Free Some Day*, 97.

15. Stanton, *Free Some Day*, 101.

16. Gordon-Reed, *TJ and SH*, 27-28.

17. Ibid., 15; Stanton, *Free Some Day*, 148, "Life among the Lowly," *Pike County (Ohio) Republican*, March 13, 1873.

18. Levasseur, *Lafayette in America*, 217-20.

19. Ibid., 219.

20. McLaughlin, *Jefferson and Monticello*, 379.

21. Daniel Webster is quoted in Randall, *Life*, 3:505, as writing in 1824 that Jefferson's "general appearance indicates an extraordinary degree of health, vivacity, and spirit"; Gordon-Reed, *TJ and SH*, 247-48; Randall, *Life*, 3:538.

22. Gordon-Reed, *TJ and SH*, 245; Gordon James and James A. Bear Jr., "A Medical History of Thomas Jefferson" (unpublished manuscript), p. 119, Special Collections Research Report, Jefferson Library, Charlottesville; see also "Dunglison's Memorandum," ibid., 547. Jefferson told his final doctor that he attributed his impaired health to his trip to the springs.

23. Martha Jefferson Randolph to Ellen Randolph Coolidge, April 25, 1826, Family Letters Project.

24. Sloan, *Principle and Interest*, 222; *The Letters of Lafayette and Jefferson*, ed. Gilbert Chinard (Baltimore, 1929), 428.

25. Malone, *Jefferson*, 3:473-77.

26. Burstein, *Jefferson's Secrets*, 271-74; Randall, *Life*, 3:543.

27. Codicil to TJ's will, see photograph in the second insert.

28. See Gordon-Reed, *TJ and SH*, 26-29, discussing Harriet Hemings's departure from Monticello.

29. Randall, *Life*, 3:544.

30. Ibid., 541.

31. Ibid., 545.

32. Stanton, *Free Some Day*, 142-43. The only known account of Jefferson's funeral was provided by Andrew K. Smith, who upon seeing a notice of Thomas Jefferson Randolph's death wrote to the Washington *Republican* recounting his memories of the event. Apparently Jeff Randolph and his father were unable to curb their mutual enmity, even as the family mourned Jefferson's death. A contingent from Charlottesville was supposed to proceed up to the mountain from the courthouse, but there was a dispute about who had the right to be where in the procession. Smith and others grew exasperated and could wait no longer, so they headed to Monticello. They arrived to find that Jefferson's coffin had been taken out of the house and placed on "narrow planks" over the grave. Randolph père and fils knew that the large procession, including students from the university and

citizens from the area, was on its way, but each thought it was the other's duty to tell the minister. So they said nothing while the minister performed the ceremony for the "thirty or forty" people in attendance. Jefferson was buried, and as the assembled dispersed and started down the mountain, they ran into almost fifteen hundred would-be funeral attendees coming up. Those in the crowd were both disappointed and angry at not having been able to pay their last respects. Smith said that an explanation of the mixup was printed the next day in a Charlottesville newspaper. Family Letters Project.

Epilogue

1. Stanton, *Free Some Day*, 141.
2. Advertisement for auction at Monticello, Special Collections, ViU; Stanton, *Free Some Day*, 141.
3. Lucia Stanton, "Monticello to Main Street," 102.
4. Ibid.
5. Albemarle County Deed Book, 32:412, Deed of Emancipation, Jan. 20, 1827.
6. Gordon-Reed, *TJ and SH*, 250; Martha Jefferson Randolph's will, Family Letters Project. See Randall, *Life*, 3:562, recounting his conversation about the informal freeing of Wormley Hughes.
7. William Waller Hening, comp., *The Statutes at Large, Being a Collection of All the Laws of Virginia from the First Session of the Legislature in the Year 1619*, 13 vols. (Richmond, Va., 1809–23), 10:39; Stanton, *Free Some Day*, 156; Morris; *Southern Slavery and the Law*, 394.
8. Martha Jefferson Randolph's will, Family Letters Project.
9. Gordon-Reed, *SH and TJ*, 209; Ervin L. Jordan Jr., "A Just and True Account: Two 1833 Parish Censuses of Albemarle County Free Blacks," *Magazine of Albemarle County History* 53 (1995): 137, 136, 129.
10. Merrill Peterson, *The Jefferson Image in the American Mind* (New York, 1960), 380; Stanton, *Free Some Day*, 147–48.
11. Stanton, *Free Some Day*, 149.
12. Ibid., 158.
13. Ibid., 150–51.

Selected Bibliography

Manuscript Collections

Lancashire Record Office, Preston, United Kingdom
Library of Congress, Washington, D.C.
Library of Virginia, Richmond, Va.
Massachusetts Historical Society, Boston, Mass.
National Archives of the United Kingdom, Kew
University of Virginia Library, Charlottesville, Va.
Virginia Historical Society, Richmond, Va.

Primary Sources

Adams, Charles Francis, ed. *Letters of Mrs. Adams, the Wife of John Adams.* 2 vols. Boston: Charles C. Little and James Brown, 1848.

Baron, Robert C., ed. *The Garden and Farm Books of Thomas Jefferson.* Golden, Colo.: Fulcrum, 1987.

Bear, James A., and Lucia C. Stanton, eds. *Thomas Jefferson's Memorandum Books: Accounts, with Legal Records and Miscellany, 1767–1826.* 2 vols. Princeton: Princeton Univ. Press, 1997.

Betts, Edwin Morris. *Thomas Jefferson's Farm Book, with Commentary and Relevant Extracts from Other Writings.* Princeton: Princeton Univ. Press, 1944.

Boyd, Julian, et al., eds. *The Papers of Thomas Jefferson.* 34 vols. To date. Princeton: Princeton Univ. Press, 1950–.

Cappon, Lester J., ed. *The Adams-Jefferson Letters: The Complete Correspondence between Thomas Jefferson and Abigail and John Adams.* 2 vols. Chapel Hill: Univ. of North Carolina Press, 1959.

Hening, William Waller, comp. *The Statutes at Large: Being a Collection of All the Laws of Virginia, from the First Session of the Legislature, in the Year 1619.* 13 vols. Richmond, Va.: Pleasants, 1809–23.

Hutchinson, William T., and William M. E. Rachal, eds. *The Papers of James Madison.* 17 vols. Chicago: Univ. of Chicago Press; Charlottesville: Univ. Press of Virginia, 1959–91.

Looney, J. Jefferson, ed. Family Letters Project. The Papers of Thomas Jefferson: Retirement Series. www.monticello.org.

———, ed. *The Papers of Thomas Jefferson: Retirement Series*. 3 vols. to date. Princeton: Princeton Univ. Press, 2004–.

Peterson, Merrill D., ed. *Thomas Jefferson: Writings*. New York: Library of America, 1984.

Robinson, W. Stitt, ed. *Early American Indian Documents: Treaties and Laws, 1607–1789*. Vol. 5, *Virginia Treaties, 1723–1775*. Frederick, Md.: Univ. Publications of America, 1979.

Smith, James Morton, ed. *The Republic of Letters: The Correspondence between Thomas Jefferson and James Madison, 1776–1826*. New York: Norton, 1995.

Sowerby, E. Millicent, comp. *Catalogue of the Library of Thomas Jefferson*. 5 vols. Washington, D.C.: Library of Congress, 1952–59.

Wilson, Douglas L., ed. *Jefferson's Literary Commonplace Book*. Princeton: Princeton Univ. Press, 1989.

Newspapers

Boston Repertory
Daily Scioto Gazette
Frederick-Town Herald
Pike County (Ohio) Republican
Richmond Examiner (1802)
Richmond Enquirer (1824–26)
Virginia Gazette

Books, Articles, and Other Secondary Sources

Accomando, Christina. "'The Laws Were Laid Down to Me Anew'": Harriet Jacobs and the Reframing of Legal Fictions." *African American Review* 32 (1998): 229–45.

Adams, Henry. *History of the United States of America during the Administration of Thomas Jefferson*. 2 vols. New York: Library of America, 1986.

Adams, John Quincy. "The Character of Desdemona." *American Monthly Magazine* 1 (1836): 209–17.

Anderson, Jefferson Randolph. "Tuckahoe and the Tuckahoe Randolphs." *Register of the Kentucky State Historical Society* 35 (1937): 29–59.

Antoine, Michel. *Louis XV*. Paris: Fayard, 1989.

Arese, Francesco. *Count Francesco Arese: A Trip to the Prairies and in the Interior of North America [1837–1838]: Travel Notes*. Translated by Andrew Evans. New York: Harbor Press, 1934.

Aubert, Guillaume. "'The Blood of France': Race and Purity of Blood in the French Atlantic World." *William and Mary Quarterly*, 3d ser., 61 (2005): 439–78.

Baptist, Edward E. "'Cuffy,' 'Fancy Maids,' and 'One Eyed Men': Rape, Commodification, and the Domestic Slave Trade in the United States." *American Historical Review* 106 (2001): 1619–50.

Bardaglio, Peter. "An Outrage upon Nature: Incest and Law in the Nineteenth Century South." In *In Joy and in Sorrow: Women, Family, and Marriage in the Victorian South, 1830–1900*, edited by Carol Bleser. New York: Oxford Univ. Press, 1991.

Basch, Norma. *In the Eyes of the Law: Women, Marriage, and Property in Nineteenth-Century New York.* Ithaca: Cornell Univ. Press, 1982.

Bazin, Hervé. *The Eradication of Small Pox: Edward Jenner and the First and Only Eradication of an Infectious Disease.* Translated by Andrew and Glenise Morgan. London: Academic Press, 2000.

Bear, James A., Jr. *The Hemings Family of Monticello.* Ivy, Va.: n.p., 1980.

Bedini, Silvio. *The Life of Benjamin Banneker.* New York: Scribner, 1972.

Ben-Atar, Doron S. *The Origins of Jeffersonian Commercial Policy and Diplomacy.* New York: St. Martins Press, 1993.

Bennett, Lerone, Jr. "Thomas Jefferson's Negro Grandchildren." *Ebony*, Nov. 10, 1954, pp. 78–80.

Berlin, Ira. "American Slavery in History and Memory and the Search for Social Justice." *Journal of American History* 90 (2004): 1251–68.

———. "From Creole to Africa: Atlantic Creoles and the Origins of African-American Society in Mainland North America." *William and Mary Quarterly*, 3d ser., 53 (1996): 51–88.

———. *Generations of Captivity: A History of African American Slavery.* Cambridge: Harvard Univ. Press, 2003.

———. *Many Thousands Gone: The First Two Centuries of Slavery in North America.* Cambridge: Harvard Univ. Press, 1998.

———. "The Revolution in Black Life." In *The American Revolution*, edited by Alfred F. Young, 350–82. De Kalb, Ill.: Northern Illinois Univ. Press, 1976.

———. *Slaves without Masters: The Free Negro in the Antebellum South.* New York: Pantheon, 1974.

Berlin, Ira, and Philip D. Morgan. "Cultivation and Culture: Labor and the Shaping of Slave Life in the Americas." *Journal of the Early American Republic* 14 (1994): 264–65.

Berlin, Ira, and Ronald Hoffman, eds. *Slavery and Freedom in the Age of the American Revolution.* Charlottesville: Univ. Press of Virginia, 1983.

Billings, Warren M. "The Cases of Fernando and Elizabeth Key: A Note on the Status of Blacks in Seventeenth-Century Virginia." *William and Mary Quarterly*, 3d ser., 30 (1973): 467–74.

Bizardel, Yvon, and Howard C. Rice Jr. "Poor in Love Mr. Short." *William and Mary Quarterly*, 3d ser., 21 (1964): 516–33.

Blackburn, Robin. *The Making of New World Slavery: From the Baroque to the Modern, 1492–1800.* London: Verso, 1997.

———. *The Overthrow of Colonial Slavery, 1776–1848.* London: Verso, 1988.

Blassingame, John W. "Status and Social Structure in the Slave Community: Evidence from New Sources." In *Perspectives and Irony in American Slavery*, edited by Harry P. Owens. Jackson: Univ. Press of Mississippi, 1976.

Blight, David W. *Race and Reunion: The Civil War in American Memory.* Cambridge: Harvard Univ. Press, 2001.

Boulle, Pierre H. "Les Gens de couleur à Paris à la veille de la Révolution." In *L'Image de la Révolution française*, edited by Michel Vovelle. Vol. 1. Paris: Pergamon Press, 1989.

———. *Race et esclavage dans la France de l'Ancien Régime* (Paris: Perrin, 2007).

———. "Racial Purity or Legal Clarity: The Status of Black Residents in Eighteenth-Century France." *Journal of the Historical Society* 6 (2006): 19–46.

Boulton, Alexander O. "The American Paradox: Jeffersonian Equality and Racial Science." *American Quarterly* 47 (1995): 467–92.

Bowling, Kenneth R. "Dinner at Jefferson's: A Note on Jacob E. Cooke's 'The Compromise of 1790.'" *William and Mary Quarterly*, 3d ser., 28 (1971): 629–48.

Brands, H. W. "Founder's Chic: Our Reverence for the Founding Fathers Has Gotten out of Hand." *Atlantic Monthly*, Sept. 2003.

Breen, T. H. "'Baubles of Britain': The American and Consumer Revolutions of the Eighteenth Century." *Past and Present*, no. 119 (May 1988): 73–104.

———. "Creative Adaptations: Peoples and Cultures." In *Colonial British America: Essays in the New History of the Early Modern Era*, edited by Jack P. Greene and J. R. Pole. Baltimore: Johns Hopkins Univ. Press, 1984.

———. *The Marketplace Revolution: How Consumer Politics Shaped American Independence.* New York: Oxford Univ. Press, 2004.

Breen, T. H., and Stephen Innes. *"Myne Owne Ground": Race and Freedom on Virginia's Eastern Shore, 1640–1676.* New York: Oxford Univ. Press, 1980.

Brewer, Holly. "Beyond Education: Thomas Jefferson's 'Republican' Revision of the Laws regarding Children." In *Thomas Jefferson and the Education of a Citizen*, edited by James Gilreath. Washington, D.C.: Library of Congress, 1999.

———. *By Birth or Consent: Children, Law, and the Anglo-American Revolution in Authority.* Chapel Hill: Univ. of North Carolina Press, 2005.

Brewer, James H. "Negro Property Owners in Seventeenth-Century Virginia." *William and Mary Quarterly*, 3d ser., 12 (1955): 575–80.

Brodie, Fawn. *Thomas Jefferson: An Intimate History.* New York: Norton, 1974.

———. "Thomas Jefferson's Unknown Grandchildren: A Study in Historical Silences." *American Heritage* 27 (Oct. 1976): 23–33, 94–99.

Brown, Christopher. "The Politics of Slavery." In *The British Atlantic World, 1500–1800*, edited by David Armitage and Michael J. Braddick. New York: Palgrave Macmillian, 2002.

Brown, Kathleen M. *Good Wives, Nasty Wenches, and Anxious Patriarchs: Gender, Race, and Power in Colonial Virginia.* Chapel Hill: Univ. of North Carolina Press, 1997.

Buckley, Thomas E., and S. J. Buckley. "After Disestablishment: Thomas Jefferson's Wall of Separation in Antebellum Virginia." *Journal of Southern History* 61 (1995): 445–80.

Burg, R. R. "The Rhetoric of Miscegenation: Thomas Jefferson, Sally Hemings, and Their Historians." *Phylon* 27 (1986): 128–38.

Burrows, Edwin G., and Mike Wallace. *Gotham: A History of New York until 1898.* New York: Oxford Univ. Press, 1999.

Burstein, Andrew. *The Inner Jefferson: Portrait of a Grieving Optimist.* Charlottesville: Univ. Press of Virginia, 1996.

———. *Jefferson's Secrets: Death and Desire at Monticello.* New York: Basic Books, 2005.

Calhoun, Jeanne A. "A Virginia Gentleman on the Eve of the Revolution: Philip Ludwell Lee of Stratford." http://stratfordhall.org/pll-2.html.

Camp, Stephanie M. H. *Closer to Freedom: Enslaved Women and Everyday Resistance in the Plantation South.* Chapel Hill: Univ. of North Carolina, 2004.

———. "The Pleasures of Resistance: Enslaved Women in the Plantation South." *Journal of Southern History* 68 (2002): 533–72.

Campbell, Colin. "Life of Isaac Jefferson of Petersburg, Virginia, Blacksmith." *William and Mary Quarterly*, 3d ser., 8 (1951): 566–82.

Canville V. Earle, Carville. "Environment, Disease, and Mortality in Early Virginia." In *The Chesapeake in the Seventh Century*, edited by Thad W. Tate and David L. Ammerman. Chapel Hill: Univ. of North Carolina Press, 1979.

Carlyle, Thomas. *The French Revolution: A History*. New York: Modern Library, 2002.

Chaplin, Joyce. "Race." In *The British Atlantic World, 1500–1800*, edited by David Armitage and Michael J. Braddick. New York: Palgrave Macmillian, 2002.

Chernow, Ron. *Alexander Hamilton*. New York: Penguin, 2004.

Clinton, Catherine. *The Plantation Mistress: Woman's World in the Old South*. New York: Pantheon, 2004.

Cobb, Thomas R. R. *An Inquiry into the Law of Negro Slavery in the United States of America*. Philadelphia: T. and J. W. Johnson, 1858.

Cogliano, Francis D. *Thomas Jefferson: Reputation and Legacy*. Charlottesville: Univ. Press of Virginia, 2006.

Colley, Robert. *Slavery and Jeffersonian Virginia*. Urbana: Univ. of Illinois Press, 1973.

Cooke, Jacob E. "The Compromise of 1790." *William and Mary Quarterly*, 3d ser., 27 (1970): 523–45.

———. "Cooke's Rebuttal." *William and Mary Quarterly*, 3d ser., 28 (1971): 629–48.

Coolidge, Thomas Jefferson. *The Autobiography of T. Jefferson Coolidge, 1831–1920*, (Whitefish, Mont.: Kessinger Publishers, 2007).

Cope, Virginia. "'I Verily Believed Myself to Be a Free Woman': Harriet Jacobs's Journey into Capitalism." *African American Review* 38 (2004): 5–20.

Craven, Wesley F. *White, Red, and Black: The Seventeenth-Century Virginian*. Charlottesville: Univ. Press of Virginia, 1971.

Cresson, W. P. *James Monroe*. Chapel Hill: Univ. of North Carolina Press, 1946.

Darnton, Robert. *The Great Cat Massacre and Other Episodes in French Cultural History*. New York: Vintage, 1985.

Davis, David Brion. "American Equality and Foreign Revolutions." *Journal of American History* 76 (1989): 729–52.

———. *The Problem of Slavery in the Age of Revolution, 1770–1823*. 2d ed. New York: Oxford Univ. Press, 1999.

———. *The Problem of Slavery in Western Culture*. New York: Oxford Univ. Press, 1988.

———. *Slavery in the Colonial Chesapeake*. Williamsburg, Va.: Colonial Williamsburg Foundation, 1986.

Dawson, John P. *Gifts and Giving: Continental and American Law Compared*. New Haven: Yale Univ. Press, 1980.

Defoe, Daniel. *A Tour through the Whole Island of Great Britain*. Edited by Pat Rogers. Exeter: Webb & Bower, 1989.

Degler, Carl N. "Slavery and the Genesis of American Race Prejudice." *Comparative Studies in Society and History* 2 (1959): 49–66.

D'Elia, Donald J. "Dr. Benjamin Rush and the Negro." *Journal of the History of Ideas* 30 (1969): 413–22.

Dew, Charles B. *Ironmaker to the Confederacy: Joseph R. Anderson and the Tredegar Iron Works*. New Haven: Yale Univ. Press, 1966.

Dewey, Frank L. *Thomas Jefferson: Lawyer.* Charlottesville: Univ. Press of Virginia, 1986.

Deyle, Steven. *Carry Me Back: The Domestic Slave Trade in American Life.* New York: Oxford Univ. Press, 2005.

Dimmick, Jesse. "Green Spring." *William and Mary Quarterly,* 2d ser., 9 (1929): 129–30.

Dobson, Mary, *Contours of Death and Disease in Early Modern England.* Cambridge: Cambridge Univ. Press, 1997.

Dorigny, Marcel, and Bernard Gainot. *La Société des amis des noirs, 1788–1799: Contribution à l'histoire de l'abolition de l'esclavage.* Paris: Editions UNESCO, 1998.

Dorman, Frederick, *Ancestors and Descendants of Francis Epes.* Petersburg, Va.: Society of the Descendants of Francis Epes, 1992.

Douglass, Frederick. *The Life and Times of Frederick Douglass.* Hartford, Conn.: Park Publishing, 1882.

———. *Narrative of the Life of Frederick Douglass, An American Slave, Written by Himself.* 1845; reprint, Whitefish, Mont.: Kessinger Publishing, 2004.

Doyle, William. *Origins of the French Revolution.* New York: Oxford Univ. Press, 1980.

———. "The Parlements of France and the Breakdown of the Old Regime, 1771–1788." *French Historical Studies* 6 (1970): 415–58.

———. "Reflections on the Classic Interpretation of the French Revolution." *French Historical Studies* 16 (1990): 743–48.

Dubler, Ariela R. "Wifely Behavior: A Legal History of Acting Married." *Columbia Law Review* 100 (2000): 957–1021.

Dubois, Laurent. *A Colony of Citizens: Revolution and Slave Emancipation in the French Caribbean, 1787–1804.* Chapel Hill: Univ. of North Carolina Press, 2004.

Dumbauld, Edward. "Where Did Jefferson Live in Paris." *William and Mary Quarterly,* 2d ser., 23 (1943): 64–68.

Durey, Michael. *With the Hammer of Truth: James Thompson Callender and America's Early National Heroes.* Charlottesville: Univ. Press of Virginia. 1990.

Edwards, Laura F. "Law, Domestic Violence, and the Limits of Patriarchal Authority in the Antebellum South." *Journal of Southern History* 65 (1999): 733–70.

Egerton, Douglas R. "Black Independence Struggles and the Tale of Two Revolutions: A Review Essay." *Journal of Southern History* 64 (1998): 95–116.

———. *Gabriel's Rebellion: The Virginia Slave Conspiracies of 1800 and 1802.* Chapel Hill: Univ. of North Carolina Press, 1993.

Elder, Melinda. *The Slave Trade and the Economic Development of Eighteenth-Century Lancaster.* Halifax: Keele Univ. Press, 1992.

Ellis, Joseph J. *Founding Brothers: The Revolutionary Generation.* New York: Knopf, 2002.

Ely, Melvin Patrick. *Israel on the Appomattox: A Southern Experiment in Black Freedom from the 1790s through the Civil War.* New York: Knopf, 2005.

Evans, Emory G. "Executive Leadership in Virginia, 1776–1781: Henry, Jefferson, and Nelson." In *Sovereign States in an Age of Uncertainty,* edited by Ronald Hoffman and Peter J. Albert. Charlottesville: Univ. Press of Virginia, 1981.

Fairchilds, Cissie. *Domestic Enemies: Servants and Their Masters in Old Regime France.* Baltimore: Johns Hopkins Univ. Press, 1984.

Fenn, Elizabeth. *Pox Americana: The Great Small Pox Epidemic of 1775–1782.* New York: Hill and Wang, 2001.

Ferguson, Sally Ann H. "Christian Violence and the Slave Narrative." *American Literature* 68 (1996): 297–320.

Finkelman, Paul. "Treason against the Hope of the World." In *Jeffersonian Legacies*, edited by Peter S. Onuf. Charlottesville: Univ. Press of Virginia, 1998.

Foster, Eugene, et al. "Jefferson Fathered Slave's Last Child." *Nature* 196 (Nov. 5, 1998): 27–28.

Fox, R. Hingston. *Dr. John Fothergill and His Friends: Chapters in Eighteenth Century Life.* London: Macmillan, 1919.

Fox-Genovese, Elizabeth. *Within the Plantation Household: Black and White Women of the Old South.* Chapel Hill: Univ. of North Carolina Press, 1988.

Frey, Sylvia R. *Water from the Rock: Black Resistance in a Revolutionary Age.* Princeton: Princeton Univ. Press, 1991.

Gaines, William Harris, *Thomas Mann Randolph, Jefferson's Son-in-Law.* Baton Rouge: Louisiana State Univ. Press, 1966.

Garrioch, David. *The Formation of the Parisian Bourgeoisie, 1690–1830.* Cambridge: Harvard Univ. Press, 1996.

———. *The Making of Revolutionary Paris.* Berkeley: Univ. of California Press, 2002.

Genovese, Eugene. *The Political Economy of Slavery: Studies in the Economy and Society of the Slave South.* New York: Pantheon, 1965.

———. *Roll, Jordan, Roll: The World the Slaves Made.* New York: Pantheon, 1974.

Genovese, Eugene, and Elizabeth Fox-Genovese. *Fruits of Merchant Capital: Society and Bourgeois Property in the Rise and Expansion of Capitalism.* New York: Oxford Univ. Press, 1983.

Gist, Christopher. *Christopher Gist's Journals with Historical Geographical, and Ethnological Notes and Biographies of Contemporaries.* Edited by William M. Darlington. Pittsburgh: J. R. Weldon, 1893.

Glynn, Ian, and Jenifer Glynn. *The Life and Death of Smallpox.* Cambridge: Cambridge Univ. Press, 2004.

Godbeer, Richard. "'The Cry of Sodom': Discourse, Intercourse, and Desire in Colonial New England." *William and Mary Quarterly*, 3d ser., 52 (1995): 259–86.

Gomez, Michael. *Exchanging Our Country Marks: The Transformation of African Identities in the Colonial and Antebellum South.* Chapel Hill: Univ. of North Carolina Press, 1998.

Gordon-Reed, Annette. "Celia's Case." In *Race on Trial: Law and Justice in American History*, edited by Annette Gordon-Reed. New York: Oxford Univ. Press, 2002.

———. "Engaging Jefferson: Blacks and the Founding Father." *William and Mary Quarterly*, 3d ser., 57 (2000): 171–82.

———. "Logic and Experience: Slavery, Race and Thomas Jefferson's Life in the Law." In *Slavery and the American South: Essays and Commentaries*, edited by Winthrop D. Jordan. Jackson: Univ. Press of Mississippi, 2003.

———. *Thomas Jefferson and Sally Hemings: An American Controversy.* Charlottesville: Univ. Press of Virginia, 1997.

Govan, Thomas P. "Alexander Hamilton and Julius Caesar: A Note on the Historical Use of Evidence." *William and Mary Quarterly*, 3d ser., 32 (1975): 475–80.

Graham, Pearl N. "Thomas Jefferson and Sally Hemings." *Journal of Negro History* 44 (1961): 89–103.

Greenbaum, Louis S. "Thomas Jefferson, the Paris Hospitals, and the University of Virginia." *Eighteenth-Century Studies* 26, no. 4 (Special Issue) (Summer 1993): 607–26.

Gross, Ariela. "Beyond Black and White: Cultural Approaches to Race and Slavery." *Columbia Law Review* 101 (2001): 640–90.

Gutman, Herbert G. *The Black Family in Slavery and Freedom, 1750–1925.* New York: Vintage, 1976.

Halliday, E. M. *Understanding Thomas Jefferson.* New York: HarperCollins, 2002.

Hamilton, Philip. *The Making and Unmaking of a Revolutionary Family: The Tuckers of Virginia, 1752–1830.* Charlottesville: Univ. Press of Virginia, 2003.

Hargreaves, John D. "Assimilation in Eighteenth-Century Senegal." *Journal of African History* 6 (1965): 177–84.

Haskins, James. *The Methodists.* New York: Hippocrene, 1992.

Haulman, Kate. "Fashion and the Culture Wars of Revolutionary Philadelphia." *William and Mary Quarterly,* 3d ser., 62 (2005): 625–62.

Heath, Barbara, *Hidden Lives: The Archaeology of Slave Life at Thomas Jefferson's Poplar Forest.* Charlottesville: Univ. Press of Virginia, 1999.

Hemphill, John M., II, ed. "John Wayles Rates His Neighbors." *Virginia Magazine of History and Biography* 66 (1958): 302–6.

Herbert, Eugenia W. "Smallpox Inoculation in Africa." *Journal of African History* 16 (1975): 539–59.

Heriot, Angus. *The Castrati in Opera.* London: Secker & Warburg, 1956.

Higginbotham, A. Leon. *In the Matter of Color: Race and American Legal Process: The Colonial Period.* New York: Oxford Univ. Press, 1980.

Higginbotham, Evelyn Brooks. "African-American Women's History and the Metalanguage of Race." *Signs* 17 (1992): 251–74.

Higonnet, Patrice Louis-René. "The Origins of the Seven Years' War." *Journal of Modern History* 40 (1968): 57–90.

Hodes, Martha. *White Women, Black Men: Illicit Sex in the Nineteenth-Century South.* New Haven: Yale Univ. Press, 1997.

———, ed. *Sex, Love, Race: Crossing Boundaries in North American History.* New York: New York Univ. Press, 1999.

Hodges, Graham, ed. *Root and Branch: African Americans in New York and East Jersey, 1613–1863.* Chapel Hill: Univ. of North Carolina Press, 1999.

Hofstadter, Richard. *The American Political Tradition and the Men Who Made It.* New York: Vintage, 1989.

Hofstra, Warren R. "'The Extension of His Majesties Dominion': The Virginia Backcountry and the Reconfiguration of Imperial Frontiers." *Journal of American History* 84 (1998): 1281–312.

Holton, Woody. *Forced Founders: Indians, Debtors, Slaves, and the Making of the American Revolution in Virginia.* Chapel Hill: Univ. of North Carolina Press, 1999.

Horn, James. "Cavalier Culture? The Social Development of Colonial Virginia." *William and Mary Quarterly,* 3d ser., 48 (1991): 238–45.

Horne, Alistair. *Seven Ages of Paris.* New York: Knopf, 2002.

Huggins, Nathan I. "The Deforming Mirror of Truth: Slavery and the Master Narrative of American History." *Radical History Review* 49 (1991): 25–48.

Hughes, Sara S. "Slaves for Hire: The Allocation of Black Labor in Elizabeth City County, Virginia, 1782–1810." *William and Mary Quarterly,* 3d ser., 35 (1978): 260–86.

Hunt, Alfred N. *Haiti's Influence on Antebellum America: Slumbering Volcano in the Caribbean.* Baton Rouge: Louisiana State Univ. Press, 1998.

Hutton, Patrick H. "The Role of Memory in the Historiography of the French Revolution." *History and Theory* 30 (1991): 56–69.

Isaac, Rhys. "The First Monticello." In *Jeffersonian Legacies*, edited by Peter S. Onuf. Charlottesville: Univ. Press of Virginia, 1993.

———. "Monticello Stories Old and New." In *Sally Hemings and Thomas Jefferson: History, Memory, and Civic Culture*, edited by Jan Ellen Lewis and Peter S. Onuf. Charlottesville: Univ. Press of Virginia, 1999.

———. *The Transformation of Virginia, 1740–1790.* Chapel Hill: Univ. of North Carolina Press, 1982.

Jackson, Luther P. "Free Negroes of Petersburg, Virginia." *Journal of Negro History* 12 (1927): 365–88.

Jacobs, Harriet. *Incidents in the Life of a Slave Girl, Written by Herself.* Edited by Nell Irvin Painter. New York: Penguin, 2000.

Jacobs, Margaret C. *Living the Enlightenment: Freemasonry and Politics in Eighteenth-Century Europe.* New York: Oxford Univ. Press, 1991.

Jacques, Edna Bolling. "The Hemmings Family of Buckingham County, Virginia." http://www .buckinghamhemmings.com.

James, C. L. R. *Black Jacobins: Toussaint L'Ouverture and the San Domingo Revolution.* New York: Vintage, 1989.

Jennings, Francis. *The Ambiguous Iroquois Empire: The Covenant Chain Confederation of Indian Tribes with English Colonies, from Its Beginnings to the Lancaster Treaty of 1744.* New York: Norton, 1984.

———. *Empire of Fortune: Crowns, Colonies, and Tribes in the Seven Years War in America.* New York: Norton, 1998.

Johnson, Samuel. *The Works of Samuel Johnson.* Vol. 14. Troy, N.Y.: Pafraets, 1913.

Johnson, Walter. *Soul by Soul: Life inside the Antebellum Slave Market.* Cambridge: Harvard Univ. Press, 1999.

Jones, Bernie D. "'Righteous Fathers,' 'Vulnerable Old Men,' and 'Degraded Creatures': Southern Justices on Miscegenation in the Antebellum Will Contest." *Tulsa Law Review* 40 (2005): 699–750.

Jones, Colin. *Paris: Biography of a City.* London: Penguin, 2004.

Jordan, Winthrop D. "American Chiaroscuro: The Status and Definition of Mulattoes in the British Colonies." *William and Mary Quarterly*, 3d ser., 19 (1962): 183–200.

———. "Modern Tensions and the Origins of American Slavery." *Journal of Southern History* 28 (1962): 18–30.

———. *White over Black: American Attitudes toward the Negro, 1550–1812.* Chapel Hill: Univ. of North Carolina Press, 1968.

Kaminski, John P., ed. *Jefferson in Love: The Love Letters between Thomas Jefferson and Maria Cosway.* Madison, Wis.: Madison House, 1999.

Kaplan, Sidney, and Emma Nogrady Kaplan. *The Black Presence in the Era of the American Revolution.* Rev. ed. Amherst: Univ. of Massachusetts Press, 1989.

Kates, Don B., Jr. "Abolition, Deportation, Integration: Attitudes toward Slavery in the Early Republic." *Journal of Negro History* 53 (1968): 33–47.

Kemble, Francis. *Fanny Kemble's Journals.* Edited by Catherine Clinton. Cambridge: Harvard Univ. Press, 2000.

Kern, Susan. "The Jeffersons at Shadwell: The Social and Material World of a Virginia Plantation." Ph.D. diss., College of William and Mary, 2005.

———. "The Material World of the Jeffersons at Shadwell." *William and Mary Quarterly,* 3d ser., 62 (2005): 14–18.

Ketcham, Ralph. *James Madison: A Biography.* Charlottesville: Univ. Press of Virginia, 1990.

Kierner, Cynthia A. *Scandal at Bizarre: Rumor and Reputation in Jefferson's America.* New York: Palgrave Macmillan, 2004.

Kimball, Marie. *Jefferson: The Scene of Europe, 1784 to 1789.* New York: Coward-McCann, 1950.

Kipple, Kenneth, ed. *The Cambridge World History of Human Disease.* Cambridge: Cambridge Univ. Press, 1993.

Klepp, Susan E. "Seasoning and Society: Racial Differences in Mortality in Eighteenth-Century Philadelphia." *William and Mary Quarterly,* 3d ser., 51 (1994): 473–506.

Kolchin, Peter. "Reevaluating the Slave Community: A Comparative Perspective." *Journal of American History* 70 (1983): 579–601.

Krusen, Jessie Thompson. "Tuckahoe Plantation." *Winterthur Portfolio* 11 (1976): 103–22.

Kulikoff, Allan. "The Origins of Afro-American Society in Tidewater Maryland and Virginia, 1700–1790." *William and Mary Quarterly,* 3d ser., 35 (1978): 226–29.

———. *Tobacco and Slaves: The Development of Southern Cultures in the Chesapeake; 1680–1800.* Chapel Hill: Univ. of North Carolina Press, 1986.

Leach, Charles. "Hospital Rock." *Hog River Journal* 2, no. 2 (2004): 32.

Lefebvre, George. *The Coming of the French Revolution.* Princeton: Princeton Univ. Press, 1967.

Lehrer, Steven. *Explorers of the Body.* Garden City, N.Y.: Doubleday, 1979.

Lever, J. T. "Mulatto Influence on the Gold Coast in the Early Nineteenth Century: Jan Nieser of Elmina." *African Historical Studies* 3 (1970): 253–61.

Lewis, Jan. *The Pursuit of Happiness: Family and Values in Jefferson's Virginia.* Cambridge: Cambridge Univ. Press, 1983.

———. "The White Jeffersons." In *Sally Hemings and Thomas Jefferson History: Memory and Civic Culture,* edited by Jan Ellen Lewis and Peter S. Onuf. Charlottesville: Univ. Press of Virginia, 1999.

Looney, J. Jefferson. "Thomas Jefferson's Last Letter." *Virginia Magazine of History and Biography* 112 (2004): 179–84.

Lucas-Dubreton, J. *The Fourth Musketeer: The Life of Alexander Dumas.* New York: Coward-McCann, 1928.

Luckett, Thomas Manley. "Hunting for Spies and Whores: A Parisian Riot on the Eve of the French Revolution." *Past and Present,* no. 156 (Aug. 1997): 116–43.

Lyerly, Cynthia Lynn. *Methodism and the Southern Mind, 1770–1810.* New York: Oxford Univ. Press, 1998.

Lyons, Clare A. "Mapping an Atlantic Sexual Culture: Homoeroticism in Eighteenth-Century Philadelphia." *William and Mary Quarterly,* 3d ser., 60 (2003): 119–54.

———. *Sex among the Rabble: An Intimate History of Gender and Power in the Age of Revolution, Philadelphia, 1730–1830.* Chapel Hill: Univ. of North Carolina Press, 2006.

Malone, Dumas, *Jefferson and His Time.* 6 vols. Boston: Little, Brown, 1948–81.

Martin, Jonathan D. *Divided Mastery: Slave Hiring in the American South*. Cambridge: Harvard Univ. Press, 2004.

Matthewson, Tim. "Jefferson and Haiti." *Journal of Southern History* 61 (1995): 209–48.

Maza, Sarah C. *Servants and Masters in Eighteenth-Century France: The Uses of Loyalty*. Princeton: Princeton Univ. Press, 1984.

McCloy, Shelby T. "Further Notes on Negroes and Mulattoes in Eighteenth-Century France." *Journal of Negro History* 39 (1954): 284–97.

———. "Negroes and Mulattoes in Eighteenth-Century France." *Journal of Negro History* 30 (1945): 276–92.

McCoy, Drew R. *The Last of the Fathers: James Madison and the Republican Legacy*. New York: Cambridge Univ. Press, 1989.

McCullough, David. *John Adams*. New York: Simon & Schuster, 2002.

McIntyre, John W. R., and Stuart Houston. "Smallpox and Its Control in Canada." *Canadian Medial Association Journal* 161 (1999): 1543–47.

McLaughlin, Jack. *Jefferson and Monticello: The Biography of a Builder*. New York: Henry Holt, 1988.

McLaurin, Malcolm. *Celia, a Slave*. Athens: Univ. of Georgia Press, 1991.

Menard, Russell. "The Africanization of the Lowcountry Labor Force, 1670–1730." In *Race and Family in the Colonial South*, edited by Winthop D. Jordan and Sheila L. Skemp. Jackson: Univ. Press of Mississippi, 1987.

———. "British Migration to the Chesapeake Colonies in the Seventeenth Century." In *Colonial Chesapeake Society*, edited by Lois Green Carr, Philip D. Morgan, and Jean B. Russo. Chapel Hill: Univ. of North Carolina Press, 1988.

———. "From Servants to Slaves: The Transformation of the Chesapeake Labor System." *Southern Studies* 20 (1977): 355–90.

Miksanek, Tony. "Diagnosing a Genius: The Life and Death of Beethoven." *Journal of the American Medical Association* 297 (2007): 2643–44.

Miller, Genevieve. *The Adoption of Inoculation for Smallpox in England and France*. Philadelphia: Univ. of Pennsylvania Press, 1957.

Morgan, Edmund S. *American Slavery, American Freedom: The Ordeal of Colonial Virginia*. New York: Norton, 1975.

———. "Headrights and Head Counts: A Review Article." *Virginia Magazine of History and Biography* 30 (1972): 361–71.

Morgan, Philip D. "British Encounters with Africans and African Americans, circa 1600–1780." In *Strangers within the Realm: Cultural Margins of the First British Empire*, edited by Bernard Bailyn and Philip D. Morgan. Chapel Hill: Univ. of North Carolina Press, 1991.

———. *Slave Counterpoint: Black Culture in the Eighteenth-Century Chesapeake and Lowcountry*. Chapel Hill: Univ. of North Carolina Press, 1998.

———. "Slave Life in the Piedmont Virginia, 1720–1800." In *Colonial Chesapeake Society*, edited by Lois Green Carr, Philip D. Morgan, and Jean B. Russo. Chapel Hill: Univ. of North Carolina Press, 1988.

———. "Three Planters and Their Slaves: Perspectives on Slavery in Virginia, South Carolina, and Jamaica, 1750–1790." In *Race and Family in the Colonial South*, edited by Winthrop D. Jordan and Sheila L. Skemp. Jackson: Univ. Press of Mississippi, 1987.

Morgan, Philip D., and Michael L. Nicholls. "Slaves in Piedmont Virginia, 1720–1790." *William and Mary Quarterly*, 3d ser., 46 (1989): 211–51.

Morris, Christopher. "The Articulation of Two Worlds: The Master-Slave Relationship Reconsidered." *Journal of American History* 85 (1998): 982–1007.

Morris, Thomas D. *Southern Slavery and the Law, 1619–1860*. Chapel Hill: Univ. of North Carolina Press, 1996.

Nagel, Paul C. *The Adams Women: Abigail and Louisa, Their Sisters and Daughters*. Cambridge: Harvard Univ. Press, 1999.

———. *The Lees of Virginia: Seven Generations of an American Family*. New York: Oxford Univ. Press, 1992.

Nash, Gary B. *Forging Freedom: The Formation of Philadelphia's Black Community, 1720-1840*. Cambridge: Harvard Univ. Press, 1988.

Nash, Gary B., and Jean R. Soderlund. *Freedom by Degrees: Emancipation in Pennsylvania and Its Aftermath*. New York: Oxford Univ. Press, 1991.

Nast, Heidi J. "Mapping the 'Unconscious': Racism and the Oedipal Family." *Annals of the Association of American Geographers* 90 (2000): 215–55.

Neff, D. S. "Bitches, Mollies, and Tommies: Byron, Masculinity, and the History of Sexualities." *Journal of the History of Sexuality* 11 (2002): 395–438.

Neiman, Fraser, Leslie McFaden, and Derek Wheeler. "Archaeological Investigation of the Elizabeth Hemings Site (44AB438)." http://Monticello.org/archaeology/publications/hemings.pdf.

Nwokeji, G. Ugo. "African Conceptions of Gender and the Slave Traffic." *William and Mary Quarterly*, 3d ser., 58 (2001): 47–68.

Nymann, Ann E. "Sally's Rape: Robbie McCauley's Survival Art." *African American Review* 33 (1999): 577–87.

Oakes, James. *The Ruling Race: A History of American Slaveholders*. New York: Knopf, 1982.

———. *Slavery and Freedom: An Interpretation of the Old South*. New York: Knopf, 1990.

O' Brien, Conor Cruise. *The Long Affair: Thomas Jefferson and the French Revolution, 1785–1800*. Chicago: Univ. of Chicago Press, 1996.

Ohline, Howard A. "Republicanism and Slavery: Origins of the Three-fifths Clause in the United States Constitution." *William and Mary Quarterly*, 3d ser., 28 (1971): 563–84.

"Old Virginia Editors." *William and Mary Quarterly* 7 (1898): 9–17.

Onuf, Peter S. "Every Generation Is an 'Independent Nation': Colonization, Miscegenation, and the Fate of Jefferson's Children." *William and Mary Quarterly*, 3d ser., 57 (2000): 153–70.

———. *Jefferson's Empire: The Language of American Nationhood*. Charlottesville: Univ. Press of Virginia, 2000.

———. *The Mind of Thomas Jefferson*. Charlottesville: Univ. Press of Virginia, 2007.

Painter, Nell Irvin. *Sojourner Truth: A Life, a Symbol*. New York: Norton, 1997.

———. *Southern History across the Color Line*. Chapel Hill: Univ. of North Carolina Press, 2002.

Palmer, Paul C. "Servant into Slave: The Evolution of the Legal Status of the Negro Laborer in Colonial Virginia." *South Atlantic Quarterly* 65 (1966): 355–70.

Panton, Clifford D., Jr. *George Augustus Polgreen Bridgetower, Violin Virtuoso and Composer of Color in Late 18th Century Europe*. Lewiston, N.Y.: Edward Mellen Press, 2005.

Parent, Anthony. *Foul Means: The Formation of a Slave Society in Virginia, 1660–1740.* Chapel Hill: Univ. of North Carolina Press, 2003.

Pasley, Jeffrey L. *Tyranny of the Printers: Newspaper Politics in the Early American Republic.* Charlottesville: Univ. Press of Virginia, 2001.

Pateman, Carole. "Women and Consent." *Political Theory* 8 (1980): 149–68.

Payne, Daniel A. *History of the African Methodist Episcopal Church.* 1891; reprint, New York: Arno Press, 1969.

Peabody, Sue. *"There Are No Slaves in France": The Political Culture of Race and Slavery in the Ancien Régime.* New York: Oxford Univ. Press, 1996.

Peden, William. "A Bookseller Invades Monticello." *William and Mary Quarterly,* 3d ser., 6 (1949): 631–36.

Peebles, J. M. *Compulsory Vaccination a Curse and a Menace to Personal Liberty, Statistics Showing Its Danger and Criminality.* Los Angeles, 1913.

Pernick, Martin S. "Politics, Parties, and Pestilence: Epidemic Yellow Fever in Philadelphia and the Rise of the First Party System." *William and Mary Quarterly,* 3d ser., 29 (1972): 559–86.

Peterson, Merrill. *Thomas Jefferson and the New Nation.* New York: Oxford Univ. Press, 1970.

Phillips, Stephanie L. "Claiming Our Foremothers: The Legend of Sally Hemings and the Tasks of Black Feminist Theory." *Hastings Women's Law Journal* 8 (1997): 401–65.

Potter, Jim. "Demographic Development and Family Structure." In *Colonial British America: Essays in the New History of the Modern Era,* edited by Jack P. Greene and J. R. Pole. Baltimore: Johns Hopkins Univ. Press, 1984.

Powell, J. H. *Bring Out Your Dead: The Great Plague of Yellow Fever in Philadelphia.* Philadelphia: Univ. of Pennsylvania Press, 1949.

Price, Jacob M. "The Last Phase of the Virginia-London Consignment Trade: James Buchanan and Co., 1758–1768." *William and Mary Quarterly,* 3d ser., 43 (1986): 64–98.

Price, Virginia B. "Constructing to Command: Rivalries between Green Spring and the Governor's Palace, 1677–1722." *Virginia Magazine of History and Biography* 113 (2005): 2–45.

Pybus, Cassandra. "Jefferson's Faulty Math: The Question of Slave Defections in the American Revolution." *William and Mary Quarterly,* 3d ser., 62 (2005): 243–64.

Quinney, Valerie. "The Problem of Civil Rights for Free Men of Color in the Early French Revolution." *French Historical Studies* 7 (1972): 544–57.

Randall, Henry S. *The Life of Thomas Jefferson.* 3 vols. 1858; reprint, New York: Da Capo Press, 1972.

Randolph, Sarah N. *The Domestic Life of Thomas Jefferson.* Edited by Dumas Malone. New York: Frederick Ungar, 1958.

Ranlet, Philip. "The British, Slaves, and Smallpox in Revolutionary Virginia." *Journal of Negro History* 84 (1999): 217–26.

Remaratna, R. P., et al. "Acute Hearing Loss Due to Scrub Typhus: A Forgotten Complication of a Reemerging Disease." *Clinical Infectious Diseases* 42 (2006): e6–e8.

Reps, John W. *Tidewater Towns City Planning in Colonial Virginia and Maryland.* Williamsburg: Colonial Williamsburg Foundation, 1972.

Resnick, Daniel. "The Société des Amis des Noirs and the Abolition of Slavery." *French Historical Studies* 7 (1972): 558–69.

Rice, Howard C. *L'Hôtel de Langeac: Jefferson's Paris Residence, 1785–1789.* Paris: H. Lefebvre, 1947.

Richardson, Harry V. *Dark Salvation: The Story of Methodism as It Developed among Blacks in America.* Garden City, N. Y.: Anchor Press, 1976.

Risse, Guenter. "Medicine in the Age of Enlightenment." In *Medicine in Society: Historical Essays,* edited by Andrew Wear. Cambridge: Cambridge Univ. Press, 1992.

Roberts, Dorothy. *Killing the Black Body: Race, Reproduction, and the Meaning of Liberty.* New York: Pantheon, 1997.

Robinson, Charles F., II. *Dangerous Liaisons: Sex and Love in the Segregated South.* Fayetteville: Univ. of Arkansas Press, 2003.

Roche, Daniel. *The People of Paris: An Essay in Popular Culture in the Eighteenth Century.* Translated by Marie Evans and Gwynne Lewis. Berkeley: Univ. of California Press, 1987.

Roeber, A. G. "Authority, Law, and Custom: The Rituals of Court Day in Tidewater Virginia, 1720 to 1750." *William and Mary Quarterly,* 3d ser., 37 (1980): 29–52.

Rose, Willie Lee. *Slavery and Freedom.* Edited by William W. Freehling, New York: Oxford Univ. Press, 1982.

Rothman, Adam. *Slave Country: American Expansion and the Origins of the Deep South.* Cambridge: Harvard Univ. Press, 2005.

Rothman, Joshua D. *Notorious in the Neighborhood: Sex and Family across the Color Line in Virginia, 1787–1861.* Chapel Hill: Univ. of North Carolina Press, 2003.

Samford, Patricia. "The Archaeology of African-American Slavery and Material Culture." *William and Mary Quarterly,* 3d ser., 53 (1996): 87–114.

Schiebinger, Londa. "Anatomy of Difference: Race and Sex in Eighteenth-Century Science." *Eighteenth-Century Studies* 23 (1990): 387–405.

Schwarz, Philip J. "Emancipators, Protectors, and Anomalies: Free Black Slaveowners in Virginia." *Virginia Magazine of History and Biography* 95 (1987): 317–38.

———. *Slave Laws in Virginia.* Athens: Univ. of Georgia Press, 1996.

Self, Robert L., and Susan R. Stein. "The Collaboration of Thomas Jefferson and John Hemings: Furniture Attributed to the Monticello Joiner." *Winterthur Portfolio* 33 (1998):231–48.

Shackelford, George Green. *Jefferson's Adoptive Son: The Life of William Short, 1759–1848.* Lexington: Univ. Press of Kentucky, 1993.

Sheldon, Marianne Buroff. "Black-White Relations in Richmond, Virginia, 1782–1820." *Journal of Southern History* 45 (1979): 27–44.

Shepherd, Jack. *Cannibals of the Heart: A Personal Biography of Louisa Catherine and John Quincy Adams.* New York: McGraw-Hill, 1980.

Shepperson, Archibald Bolling. *John Paradise and Lucy Ludwell of London and Williamsburg.* Richmond, Va.: Dietz Press, 1942.

Sheriden, Richard B. "The British Credit Crisis of 1772 and the American Colonies." *Journal of Economic History* 20 (1960): 161–86.

Shyllon, F. O. *Black People in Britain, 1555–1833.* New York: Oxford Univ. Press, 1977.

———. *Black Slaves in Britain.* New York: Oxford Univ. Press, 1974.

Sidbury, James. *Ploughshares into Swords: Race, Rebellion, and Identity in Gabriel's Virginia, 1730–1810.* New York: Cambridge Univ. Press, 1997.

———. "Saint-Domingue in Virginia: Ideology, Local Meanings, and Resistance to Slavery, 1790–1800." *Journal of Southern History* 63 (1997): 531–52.

Simms, Rupe. "Controlling Images and the Gender Construction of Enslaved African Women." *Gender and Society* 15 (2001): 879–97.

Sloan, Herbert J. *Principle and Interest: Thomas Jefferson and Debt.* Charlottesville: Univ. Press of Virginia, 1995.

Smedley, Audrey. *Race in North America: Origin and Evolution of a World View.* 2d ed. Boulder, Colo.: Westview Press, 1999.

Smith, Daniel Blake. "In Search of the Family in the Colonial South." In *Race and Family in the Colonial South,* edited by Winthrop D. Jordan and Sheila L. Skemp. Jackson: Univ. Press of Mississippi, 1987.

Smith, Jean Edward. *John Marshall: Definer of a Nation.* New York: Henry Holt, 1996.

Smith, Margaret Smith. *The First Forty Years of Washington Society, Portrayed by the Family Letters of Mrs. Samuel Harrison Smith (Margaret Bayard).* New York: C. Scribner's Sons, 1906.

Sommerville, Diane Miller. "Moonlight, Magnolias, and Brigadoon; or, 'Almost like Being in Love': Master and Sexual Exploitation in Eugene D. Genovese's Plantation South." *Radical History Review* 88 (2004): 68–82.

———. *Rape and Race in the Nineteenth-Century South.* Chapel Hill: Univ. of North Carolina Press, 2003.

Stanton, Lucia. *Free Some Day: The African-American Families of Monticello.* Monticello: Thomas Jefferson Foundation, 2000.

———. "Monticello to Main Street: The Hemings Family and Charlottesville." *Magazine of Albemarle County History* 55 (1997): 94–126.

———. "The Other End of the Telescope: Jefferson through the Eyes of His Slaves." *William and Mary Quarterly,* 3d ser., 57 (2000): 139–52.

———. *Slavery at Monticello.* Charlottesville: Thomas Jefferson Memorial Foundation, 1996.

———. "'Those Who Labor for My Happiness': Thomas Jefferson and His Slaves." In *Jeffersonian Legacies,* edited by Peter S. Onuf. Charlottesville: Univ. Press of Virginia, 1999.

———. "'A Well-Ordered Household': Domestic Servants in Jefferson's White House." *White House History,* no. 17 (2006): 1–23.

Stanton, Lucia, and Dianne Swann Wright. "Bonds of Memory: Identity and the Hemings Family." In *Sally Hemings and Thomas Jefferson: History, Memory, and Civic Culture,* edited by Jan Ellen Lewis and Peter S. Onuf. Charlottesville: Univ. Press of Virginia, 1999.

Stein, Susan R. *The Worlds of Thomas Jefferson at Monticello.* New York: Harry N. Abrams, in association with the Thomas Jefferson Memorial Foundation, 1993.

Sterk, Stewart E. "Estoppel in Property Law." *Nebraska Law Review* 77 (1998): 759–69.

Stevenson, Brenda E. *Life in Black and White: Family and Community in the Slave South.* New York: Oxford Univ. Press, 1996.

Sturtz, Linda L. *Within Her Power: Propertied Women in Colonial Virginia.* New York: Routledge, 2002.

Sutton, Daniel. *The Inoculator; or, Sutton on the System of Inoculation Fully Set Forth in Plain & Familiar Language.* London, 1796.

Swem, Earl G. "The Lee Free School and the College of William and Mary." *William and Mary Quarterly,* 3d ser., 16 (1959): 207–13.

Szymński, Leszek, *Casimir Pulaski: A Hero of the American Revolution.* New York: Hippocrene Books, 1994.

Takagi, Midori. *"Rearing Wolves to Our Own Destruction": Slavery in Richmond, Virginia, 1782–1865.* Charlottesville: Univ. Press of Virginia, 1999.

Tate, Thad W. "Defining the Colonial South." In *Race and Family in the Colonial South,* edited by Winthop D. Jordan and Sheila L. Skemp. Jackson: Univ. of Mississippi Press, 1987.

Tauber, Edward S. "Effects of Castration upon the Sexuality of the Adult Male: A Review of Relevant Literature." *Psychosomatic Medicine* 2 (1940): 74–87.

Thomas, Evan. "Founder's Chic: Live from Philadelphia." *Newsweek,* July 9, 2001.

Thomas, Keith. "The Double Standard." *Journal of the History of Ideas* 20 (1959): 195–216.

Thompson, Robert Polk. "The Tobacco Export of the Upper James Naval District, 1773–75." *William and Mary Quarterly,* 3d ser., 18 (1961): 393–407.

Thornton, John. *Africa and Africans in the Atlantic World, 1400 to 1800.* Cambridge: Cambridge Univ. Press, 1998.

———. "Cannibals, Witches, and Slave Traders in the Atlantic World." *William and Mary Quarterly* 3d ser., 60 (2003): 273–94.

Trefousse, Hans L. *Andrew Johnson: A Biography.* New York: Norton, 1989.

Trumbull, John. *The Autobiography of John Trumbull, Patriot-Artist, 1756–1843, Containing a Supplement to the Works of John Trumbull.* Edited by Theodore Sizer. New Haven: Yale Univ. Press, 1953.

Tunis, Barbara. "Dr. James Latham (c. 1734–1799): Pioneer Inoculator in Canada." *Canadian Bulletin of Medical History* 1 (1984): 1–11.

Ulrich, Laurel Thatcher. *A Midwife's Tale: The Life of Martha Ballard, Based on Her Diary, 1785–1812.* New York: Random House, 1991.

Van Zwanenberg, David. "The Suttons and the Business of Inoculation." *Medical History* 22 (1978): 71–82.

Vaughan, Alden T. "Blacks in Virginia: A Note on the First Decade." *William and Mary Quarterly,* 3d ser., 29 (1972): 469–78.

———. "The Origins Debate: Slavery and Racism in Seventeenth-Century Virginia." *Virginia Magazine of History and Biography* 97 (1989): 311–54.

Verner, Coolie. "The Fry and Jefferson Map." *Imago Mundi* 21 (1967): 70–94.

Voltaire. "De la mort de Louis XV et de la fatelité (1774)." *Oeuvres complètes de Voltaire.* Vol. 29, *Melanges VIII (1773–1776).* New ed. Paris, 1879.

Von Daccke, Kirt. "Slaves without Masters?: The Butler Family of Albemarle County, 1780–1860." *Magazine of Albemarle County History* 55 (1997): 39–60.

Wade, Richard C. *Slavery in the Cities: The South, 1820–1860.* New York: Oxford Univ. Press, 1964.

Waldstreicher, David. "Founder's Chic as Culture War." *Radical History Review,* no. 84 (Fall 2002): 185–94.

———. *Runaway America: Benjamin Franklin, Slavery, and the American Revolution.* New York: Hill and Wang, 2004.

Wallace, Anthony F. C. *Jefferson and the Indians: The Tragic Fate of the First Americans.* Cambridge: Harvard Univ. Press, 1999.

Wallenstein, Peter. *Tell the Court I Love My Wife: Race, Marriage, and Law: An American Story.* New York: Palgrave Macmillan, 2002.

Waller, Ralph. *John Wesley: A Personal Portrait.* New York: Continuum, 2003.

Walsh, Lorena S. "New Findings about the Virginia Slave Trade." *Colonial Williamsburg Interpreter* 20, no. 2 (Summer 1999): 11–21.

———. "A 'Place in Time' Regained: A Fuller History of Colonial Chesapeake Slavery, through Group Biography." In *Working toward Freedom: Slave Society and Domestic Economy in the American South*, edited by Larry E. Hudson Jr. Rochester: Univ. of Rochester Press, 1994.

———. "Slave Life, Slave Society, and Tobacco Production in the Tidewater Chesapeake, 1620–1820." In *Cultivation and Culture Labor and the Shaping of Slave Life in the Americas*, edited by Ira Berlin and Philip D. Morgan. Charlottesville: Univ. Press of Virginia, 1993.

Walvin, James B. *Black and White: The Negro in English Society, 1555–1945*. London: Allen Lane, 1973.

Weber, Eugen. *My France: Politics, Culture, Myth*. Cambridge: Harvard Univ. Press, 1991.

Wells, Camille. "The Eighteenth-Century Landscape of Virginia Northern Neck." *Northern Neck of Virginia Historical Magazine* 37 (1987): 4217–55.

———. "The Planters Prospect: Houses, Outbuildings, and Rural Landscapes in Eighteenth-Century Virginia." *Winterthur Portfolio* 28 (1993): 1–31.

White, Deborah Gray. *Ar'n't I a Woman?: Female Slaves in the Plantation South*. Rev ed. New York: Norton, 1999.

White, Shane "A Question of Style: Blacks in and around New York City in the Late 18th Century." *Journal of American Folklore* 102, no. 403 (1989): 23–44.

White, Shane, and Graham White. "Slave Clothing and African-American Culture in the Eighteenth and Nineteenth Centuries." *Past and Present*, no. 148 (Aug. 1995): 149–86.

Wiecek, William M. "The Statutory Law of Slavery and Race in the Thirteen Mainland Colonies of British America." *William and Mary Quarterly*, 3d ser., 34 (1977): 258–80.

"Williamsburg—The Old Colonial Capital." *William and Mary Quarterly* 16 (1907): 1–65.

Williamson, Joel. *New People: Miscegenation and Mulattoes in the United States*. New York: Free Press, 1980.

Wilson, R. Jackson, et al. *The Pursuit of Liberty: A History of the American People*. New York: Knopf, 1984.

Winch, Julie. *A Gentleman of Color: The Life of James Forten*. New York: Oxford Univ. Press, 2002.

Wister, Mrs. O. J., and Agnes Irwin, eds. *Worthy Women of Our First Century*. Philadelphia: Lippincott, 1877.

Wood, Gordon. *The American Revolution: A History*. New York: Modern Library, 2003.

Woods, Edgar. *Albemarle County in Virginia, Giving Some Account of What It Was by Nature, of What It Was Made by Man, and of Some of the Men Who Made It*. 1901; reprint, Bridgewater, Va.: C. J. Carrier, 1964.

Wyatt, Edward A., IV. "Newmarket of the Virginia Turf." *William and Mary Quarterly*, 2d ser., 17 (1937): 481–95.

Zwelling, Shomer S. "Robert Carter's Journey: From Colonial Patriarch to New Nation Mystic." *American Quarterly* 38 (1986): 613–36.

INDEX

Page numbers in *italics* refer to illustrations.
Page numbers beginning with 673 refer to endnotes.

ABOUT THE AUTHOR

A professor of law at New York Law School and a professor of history at Rutgers University–Newark, Annette Gordon-Reed grew up in east Texas. A graduate of Dartmouth College and Harvard Law School, she began her career as a lawyer in both private and public practice. In 1997 she published her first book, *Thomas Jefferson and Sally Hemings: An American Controversy*. Gordon-Reed is also the editor of *Race on Trial: Law and Justice in American History* and coauthor with Vernon Jordan of *Vernon Can Read!: A Memoir*, for which she and Jordan received the Anisfield-Wolf Book Award. She lives in New York City with her husband, Robert Reed, and their children, Susan and Gordon.